THE Appetizer Atlas

A WORLD OF SMALL BITES

Arthur L. Meyer

Jon M. Vann

WILEY

JOHN WILEY & SONS, INC.

ISBN: 0-471-41102-7

This book is printed on acid-free paper. ♾

Published by John Wiley & Sons, Inc., Hoboken, New Jersey
Published simultaneously in Canada

For general information on our other products and services or for technical support, please contact our Customer Care Department within the United States at (800) 762-2974, outside the United States at (317) 572-3993 or fax (317) 572-4002.

Wiley also publishes its books in a variety of electronic formats. Some content that appears in print may not be available in electronic books. For more information about Wiley products, visit our Web site at www.wiley.com.

Library of Congress Cataloging-in-Publication Data:
Meyer, Arthur L.
    The appetizer atlas : a world of small bites / Arthur L. Meyer and Jon M. Vann.
        p. cm.
    Includes bibliographical references and index.
    ISBN 0-471-41102-7 (cloth : alk. paper)
        1. Appetizers.   2. Cookery, International.   I. Vann, Jon M.   II. Title.

TX740 .M42 2003
641.8'12—dc21   2002071383

Book design by Richard Oriolo
Cover and interior photography by Boyd Hagen

Printed in the United States of America

10 9 8 7 6 5 4 3 2

This book is dedicated to the memory of Helen Sadler and L. A. Vann (Dad's beaming with pride) and to Betsy Vann (the best Mom on the planet).

Contents

About This Book

THE AUDIENCE FOR which this book is written includes professional chefs, caterers, and advanced home cooks. With this in mind, several features should be noted. The ingredient list at the beginning of each recipe includes some preparation that will not be found in the instructions. For example, an entry in the ingredient list may be for "1 red bell pepper, fire roasted, seeded, peeled, and diced." Read the ingredient list carefully and keep these preparations in mind when determining how much time it will take to prepare the dish. Another entry may be for "½ cup [120 mL] carrots, finely diced." Measuring, in this case, implies that the carrots are measured *after* they have been diced. Also, it is assumed that the carrots were washed and peeled before they were diced. Another assumption is that an appropriate container or implement is selected for a particular task. You will not see the instruction "take out a bowl" or "use a wire whip" when mixing several ingredients for a marinade.

The book is divided into twenty-eight cooking region chapters, each of which begins with a general introduction containing the history of the region as it relates to the development of the area's cuisine, the geography of the region, crops and animals raised for food, cooking and flavoring techniques, and influences of other cultures on cooking in the region. Following each general introduction is a number of selected recipes for that region.

Each recipe's instructions have been organized into several sections. "Advance Preparation" is always listed first. This section lists things that can be done in advance, from several hours to several days. Advance preparation is essential in the professional setting and is quite useful to the home cook to relieve the stress associated with complex recipes requiring many stages. In addition, some things *have* to be done in advance ("marinate overnight"), so read this section carefully when preparing a dish. Next you may find several "Preparation of" sections for such things as sauces, doughs, and fillings. In the "Cooking Method" section that follows, all cooking instructions for final preparation of the dish are given. In this section it is assumed that the oven or oil has been heated to the correct temperature. For example, "Bake at 350°F [175°C] for 20 minutes" assumes that the oven has been heated first. Note also that all measured ingredients in the recipes are given in English measurements with metric measurements following in brackets. The "Service" section gives portion size, assembly method, and simple garnishing instructions.

The number of servings recommended is given at the top of the recipe. Most recipes have been written for eight servings, but occasionally twelve or sixteen servings are given. All recipes may be reduced or expanded proportionately. The home cook may halve all ingredients for four servings; in the restaurant or catering setting, recipes may be easily expanded fourfold. Many recipes can also be made into entrée-size portions by doubling the given portion size. The authors cooked both expanded and reduced quantities of each dish to ensure accuracy, authenticity, and proper flavoring. Many recipes were also cooked in a restaurant setting to ensure applicability to the commercial kitchen.

At the beginning of each recipe there is a preface containing interesting historical information about the dish as well as descriptions of unusual ingredients, personalities, and locations. Factual information on main ingredients for the dish is often provided. The title of each recipe is also given in the country of origin's language (using commonly accepted English spelling), and the regional name is often explained in the preface to the recipe. At the end of each recipe there are "Chef Notes" containing information on specialized techniques, substitutions, serving suggestions, cautions, and additional recipes.

Another feature of the book is the "Chef's Pantry." Maintaining the authenticity of numerous cooking regions of the world requires the use of specialized ingredients, some of which may be unfamiliar to the reader. The Chef's Pantry is a glossary of selected ingredients used in the book that the authors feel require further explanation. This information, along with facts gleaned from the preface to the recipe and the introduction to the chapter, allows for interesting menu descriptions and the education of waitstaff, important considerations when serving dishes that are global in nature. In the back of the book there is also an Index, which includes recipe titles and recipes listed by main ingredient.

As mentioned earlier, since all dishes were cooked, the authors can assure the reader that each recipe works—quantities and yields are accurate, seasonings are correct, and each dish is flavorful. In order to test recipes in a restaurant setting (and to defray some of the cost of ingredients), the authors created the Appetizer Atlas Dinner Club. For over a year, eight guests were invited twice a month to the home of one of the authors (which is equipped with a commercial-style kitchen). The guests were served a meal comprised of six appetizers and a dessert in a restaurant setting. Each guest was given a printed menu, all dishes were served by a professional waitperson, and dishes were prepared and cooked as they would be in a restaurant. A typical menu follows.

The Appetizer Atlas Dinner Club

SPAIN & PORTUGAL

Saturday, May 12, 2001

Lombo de Porco com Amêyoas à Alentejana **Pork with Clams Alentejo Style** · PORTUGAL

Pescado a la Naranja **Béchamel-Coated Sea Bass Morsels in Orange Sauce** · SEVILLE

Idiazábal eta Biper Opila **Basque Cheese and Chile Tart** · BASQUE REGION

Berenjenas Alpujarra **Beef and Manchego–Stuffed Eggplants** · ANDALUCIA

Pimientos del Piquillo Rellenos de Bacalao con Salsa Vizcaína **Salt Cod–Stuffed Piquillo Chiles with Biscayne Sauce** · BASQUE REGION

Paella de Cordonices y Setas **Quail and Wild Mushroom Paella** · VALENCIA

Flan **Caramel Custard** · SPAIN & PORTUGAL

Acknowledgments

We would like to thank the following for their help in making the Appetizer Atlas the book that we wanted it to be. Rosenthal USA Ltd., 355 Michelle Pl., Carlstadt, NJ 07072 (for plates and dishes for the photographs), Homer Laughlin China Co., Sixth and Harrison St., Newell, WV 26050 (for plates and dishes for photographs), Phoenicia Deli and Bakery, Austin, Texas (for advice and ingredients), It's About Thyme Nursery, Austin, Texas (for their excellent herbs), Central Market, Austin, Texas (thanks to Chris Shirley), Boyd Hagen (for his photographic insight and exceptional talent), Mary Margaret Pack (for her food styling expertise), Rita Rosenkranz (our dedicated agent), Toni Allegra, (our mentor), Debbie Dorsey and David Weber (our most devoted Dinner Club diners), and Lenore Tice (our incomparable waitperson).

For regional translations and recipes we'd like to thank Dr. Vicente Llamas—Mexico, Lenore Tice—Central America and Spain/Portugal, Annie Johnston—the Caribbean and France, Wagner de Alcantra Diniz—Brazil, Mike Quinn—Brazil and Morocco, George Carter—Oceania, Johannes and Shinta Muljadi—South Asia, Sri Owen—South Asia, Burt Jones and Maureen Shimlock—South Asia and Oceania, "Pancho" Gatchalian—the Philippines, Sachiko Kaise—Japan, Mieko Cooper—Japan, Yeong Suk Ye—Korea, Shirley and Brett Hardin—Japan and Korea, Li Zhang and Jeff Bechtold—China, Sapachai and Chatfueng Apisaksiri—Thailand, Chai and Pat Teepatiganond—Thailand, Nguyen Dzoãn Cam Vân—Vietnam, Mai Pham—Vietnam and Southeast Asia, Bahn "Ped" Phommavong—Southeast Asia, Jeffrey Alford and Naomi Duguid—Southeast Asia, Daovone Xayavong—Southeast Asia Sata Sathasivan—Indian Sub-Continent, Vajiheh "Selma" Mahdieh—Southwestern Asia, Malek and Nena Abijaoude—Middle East, Rosa Shane—Middle East, Lina Najm—Middle East, Lawrence Eguakun—Regional Africa, Csilla Somogyi—Eastern Europe, Gabor Lendvai—Eastern Europe, Karen Holcomb—Eastern European, Stefan (Steve) and Alicia Sarre—Scandinavia, Jeanette F. Fyllûm—Scandinavia, Suzana Llamas—Scandinavia, Froukje Meijer-Dreis Marek—Central Europe, Pascal Regimbeau—France, Sybil Reinhart—France, Ramona Gonzales—France and Spain/Portugal, Ed "The Singing Scotsman" Miller—United Kingdom, Jennifer Cockrall-King and Dee Hobsbawn-Smith—North America (Canada), Bill and Meg Jorn—North America (Mid-Atlantic), Peggy Dudley—North America (West Coast), Bo and Jen Rivers and Kells Rivers Faulkner—North America (the South).

Introduction

ALONG WITH DESSERTS, appetizers are the most exciting things about dining out (or in)—not enough to fill you up, just enough to stimulate the appetite. Appetizers can range from snacks and tempting starters to light meals, and they are found worldwide, in many attractive shapes and flavors. They often rely on simple, inexpensive ingredients, drawing on the techniques and flavors of regional ethnic cuisine. Appetizers also often rely on intense, concentrated flavors to wake up the palate. But what exactly is an appetizer? It depends on whom you ask. According to the great food writer M. F. K. Fisher, "[I]t is the overture to the opera. As such, its variety is infinite, dictated of course, by the seasons as well as the regions where the food is eaten." The world-renowned chef Auguste Escoffier did not include a separate section on appetizers in *The Escoffier Cookbook: A Guide to the Fine Art of Cookery* because, in his words, "I did not think it necessary to touch upon the hot kind [of appetizers and hors d'oeuvres], for they are mostly to be found either among hot Entrees or the Savories proper." Apparently, depending on the availability of ingredients, almost anything can be made into an appetizer by altering portion size.

When selecting recipes for *The Appetizer Atlas*, the ultimate goal was to provide insight into the cooking styles of the world. As such the recipes are authentic to the region addressed, adhering to regional cooking techniques and local seasonings and ingredients. Because of this, the reader will not find many substitutions for possibly difficult to obtain ingredients. With the advent of the Internet and the World Wide Web, shopping for these ingredients is not the task it might have been just a few years ago. In addition, many supermarket chains are offering more variety in produce than ever before, and some are opening upscale specialty sections as more and more cooks become interested in global cuisines and cooking in general. In the United States it is also easier to find local markets and shops specializing in regional foods as communities become more ethnically diverse. It is not uncommon to find Middle Eastern, Indian, Asian, or Hispanic markets in even the smallest communities in America.

Not all regional cuisines serve a beginning course meant to stimulate the appetite. In some regions, such as in Vietnam or Thailand, all dishes are served at once. In this case, recipes for the book were selected if they were easily adjustable to small portions and would not overwhelm the courses to follow. These may include dishes that are small packages, easy to eat by hand (such as a spring roll), but may also include a stew, salad, chop, or medallions. Recipes for "street food," popular snacks sold by vendors (usually from simple carts), are also included. Many recipes offered are versatile enough to be adapted to other courses of a meal, often by simply changing the serving size or accompaniment.

Recipes were selected to be appealing with respect to menu design and to offer ideas that would allow for improvisation in creating new dishes. Since the mid-1990s the habit of ordering several small dishes rather than one large entrée, known colloquially as "grazing," has come into being. This allows the diner to sample more flavors, have a more varied meal, and share in a more communal way of eating.

Since the countries in this book are arranged geographically as in an atlas, an understanding of the exchange of ingredients and produce, techniques, and methods can be appreciated. Burma is a fine example. Since it is bordered by India, China, and Laos, one can recognize ingredients shared with its neighbors. The Burmese are fond of such spices as turmeric, curry leaves, and cumin, an Indian influence. The use of fermented fish products, such as fish paste and fish sauce, and a fondness for lemongrass and galangal reflect the major flavoring practices of Laos. The Chinese influence is felt in ingredients made from soybeans, such as soy sauce and bean curd, as well as with noodles of all sorts.

The world's cuisines are influenced by a variety of geographical and climatic factors. Where there is sufficient energy, cooking techniques that require large amounts of fuel, such as roasting and baking, are found. North America and Europe fit into this category, while across Africa and most of Asia baking and roasting are practically unheard of as a cooking method. Where fuel is scarce, more energy-conserving techniques (slow cooking, steaming, and stir-frying) are favored methods of food preparation. Where food is scarce, diet is based on filling, starchy staples such as tubers, legumes, rice, and other grains. Small amounts of vegetables are added and, occasionally, small bits of meat or fish. Spices add needed flavor to these bland staples. Where fertile, expansive land is plentiful, herds of cattle can be raised to supply beef and dairy products. In mountainous terrain goats and sheep supply meat and milk products. In very cold and very hot climates food preservation is essential to store foodstuffs over long, harsh winters or to avoid heat-induced spoilage of a surplus harvest. Salting, curing, smoking, and drying are the most common methods of preserving meats, fish, and vegetables. Milk is preserved in cheese and fermented dairy products such as yogurt.

Exploration has contributed significantly to the cooking styles of the world. From one of the world's smallest countries (Portugal) to one of the world's largest empires (Persia), when different cultures come in contact, information on local produce, flavorings, and techniques are exchanged and spread. Portugal, almost single-handedly, changed the face of cooking around the world through the distribution of such New World produce as tomatoes, potatoes, beans, corn, and chiles. Portuguese exploration included establishing water-based trade routes to India for spice trading. Trading in spices had an enormous impact on the way the world cooks. Chinese and Indian spices were much appreciated wherever introduced. The Persians introduced these spices to the Middle East, across into Northern Africa as far as Morocco. The Arabs took these spices along with a variety of plants to Europe. Spain and Portugal, as the European center of Moorish culture, were the first to be introduced to Eastern spices, soon to become popular all across the Continent.

Colonialism was often followed by the establishment of plantations requiring cheap labor in support of large and profitable agricultural ventures. Sugarcane, for example, brought labor from India and Malaysia to the Caribbean and South America, leaving the culinary imprint of those countries on those regions. Chinese laborers brought to America's West to help build the railway infrastructure established a strong food presence all along the West Coast. Slavery was responsible for introducing important African cooking methods and ingredients to North America, especially in the American South and in Louisiana. Brazil has significant African influences in its culture and cuisine as does much of the Caribbean, also due to slavery.

Cooking styles across the world vary according to many factors, religion being an important one. As the Muslim religion spread west from the Middle East to Africa and east to South Asia, dining habits changed, since pork is not to be eaten according to that religion's tenet. Jews observe this dietary restriction as well. More beef, lamb, and goat are eaten wherever these people settle. Many Hindus are vegetarians and have developed tasty dishes with no meat. Eastern European Christians, who observe more than two hundred fast days per year when they abstain from meat, developed many creative ways to serve fish. The Crusades, a series of religion-inspired wars, were responsible for the introduction of Middle Eastern spices, produce, and cooking methods to Europe by returning Crusaders.

The Appetizer Atlas is organized as an atlas to give the reader some sense of continuity and to define relationships that can group countries into culinary families. Twenty-eight cooking regions are offered, with an attempt to keep as close to geographical lines as possible. However, a country's cooking style is the final determination when placing it in a region. The involvement of Iran (Persia) with the spice trading routes links its cooking techniques and use of spices with Afghanistan, the countries of Southwestern Asia, and other countries bordering the Caspian Sea, rather than with its more traditional geopolitical neighbors in the Middle East. Persia also has a long history influencing India's cuisine and is more aligned with countries to the east rather than to the west. The Philippines is an example of a country whose history and cooking style are so influenced by the Spanish that it is impossible to group it with the other Asian countries of the region; it is, therefore, given its own region. Whenever groups are defined, there will be some that do not fit neatly into any one category. Turkey is an example of this. Part of the country's cuisine is aligned with a Mediterranean style of cooking, while the remainder is related to Southwestern Asia.

The twenty-eight regions of the book follow a continuous path starting from North America, into Mexico, Central and South America, west toward China, across to India and the Middle East, into Africa, across the Mediterranean, into Europe, and finishing with the United Kingdom. The regions are as follows:

- North America (the continental United States, Alaska, and Canada)
- Mexico
- Caribbean
- Central America
- South America
- Brazil
- Oceania (Hawaiian Islands, Polynesia, Melanesia, Micronesia, Australia, and New Zealand)
- Philippines
- South Asia (Indonesia, Malaysia, and Singapore)
- Japan
- Korea
- China
- Vietnam
- Southeast Asia (Cambodia, Laos, and Burma)
- Thailand

- Indian Subcontinent (India, Pakistan, Bangladesh, Burma, Sri Lanka, Tibet, Bhutan, and Nepal)
- Southwestern Asia (Iran [Persia], Afghanistan, Central Asia [Turkmenistan, Tajikistan, Kazakhstan, Kyrgyzstan, and Uzbekistan], Georgia, and Azerbaijan)
- Middle East (Egypt, Syria, Lebanon, Jordan, Israel, Palestine, Iraq, and the Gulf States)
- Regional Africa
- North Africa (Morocco, Tunisia, and Algeria)
- Eastern Mediterranean
- Eastern Europe (Russia, Ukraine, Poland, Czech Republic, Slovakia, Hungary, and Romania)
- Scandinavia and the Baltic States
- Central Europe (Germany, Austria, Switzerland, Belgium, and the Netherlands)
- Italy
- Spain and Portugal
- France
- The United Kingdom (England, Scotland, Wales, and Ireland)

Whether you are enjoying *tapas* from Spain; *amuse-bouches*, *hors d'oeuvres*, and *canapés* from France; *mezze* from the Middle East, North Africa, or the Eastern Mediterranean; *empanaditas* throughout South America; dumplings from a *dim sum* cart in Hong Kong, Russian *blini*, or *matjes* herring from Scandinavia, you have the ancient Persians to thank for this special way of beginning a meal. So grab a cooking utensil, turn up the heat, and join us on a culinary tour of the world, one small bite at a time.

North America

THIS CULINARY OVERVIEW of North America covers the territories of Canada in addition to the United States. North America is divided into eight culinary regions (Hawaii is covered in the Oceania chapter): New England (including Nova Scotia and New Brunswick), the Mid-Atlantic States, the South, Louisiana, the Midwest, the Western States, the West Coast (including British Columbia), and the Southwest. Because of the size of North America, its varied but temperate climates, and its geography, it shows more variation in its regional cuisines than any other region addressed in this book. Around the world American food has been given negative marks, mostly because of the exportation of fast food. And travelers (both foreign and native) can be exposed to so much fast food when traveling America's great highway systems that the marvels of its regional cuisines are lost.

If there is one recurring theme in the development of regional cooking in America, it is the country's bounty. Fertile land is found everywhere. Forests are rich in game, berries, and nuts, and rivers, streams, lakes, and oceans teem with fish. Thanks to a temperate climate and sufficient water, almost every known crop can be grown and large numbers of animals can be raised for meat and dairy. Add to this the unique crops of the New World, passed on to European settlers by Native Americans, and the stage is set for great regional cooking.

Old World cooking styles were brought from England, continental Europe, and Africa in the earliest days of settlement. Waves of immigration in the nineteenth and twentieth centuries brought the workers who built America into the world leader it is today and added to the ethnic mix of its cuisines. The first Europeans to reach North America were the Vikings, but they did not create permanent settlements. The Spanish were the first Europeans to settle in America, in what are now the Southwest and California. By the mid-1500s they had established missions not only in the West but in Florida as well. At the same time, French explorers navigated the eastern coast of America from Newfoundland to the Carolinas. They were the first Europeans to explore the interior of the continent, setting up Catholic missions and trading posts. They left a permanent mark on the culture of Canada with the settlement of Quebec. By the beginning of the seventeenth century, the Dutch, settling in what is now the New York State area, established trading posts to trade with Native Americans seeking exports to Europe. The English established colonies in New England and Virginia by 1620. The English settlements, unlike the others, were agricultural in nature. This placed them in conflict with the Native Americans since trade was less important than land.

The regional cuisines of North America can be seen in the context of these varied European settlers combined with Native American influences and with the geography of the continent. Nowhere is this illustrated better than in New England. The ship *Mayflower* landed near Cape Cod in 1620. The settlement began in a deserted Indian village where earlier contact with Europeans had decimated the tribe with foreign disease. Initially the hope of the Pilgrims was to travel to the English settlement in Virginia or even to Dutch New Amsterdam, but the harsh winter prevented this. The Pilgrims were left in isolation in what eventually became their home. This isolation had the benefit of removing English influence from their everyday lives, allowing them to create a culture and cuisine very different from that of their homeland. English farming methods did not work in the New World, and their imported crops did not grow. By necessity these settlers were forced into adapting the three crops known to the Native Americans of the region: corn, beans, and squash. The Pilgrims discovered a method of extracting sugar from maple trees and were able to harvest the treasures of the sea. They did not have to be talented fishermen since clams could be dug from the mudflats, lobsters could be handpicked from pools created by receding tides, and fish were abundant near the shore.

Corn became a staple, and the Indians showed the Pilgrims how it was prepared and grown. First heated or parched, the corn could be pounded into meal, which in turn could be sifted to produce a fine cornmeal. Cooked as porridge, it was a new form of hasty pudding. When left over it became set and firm, and while it could not be reheated as a mush, it could be cut into squares and then fried in butter, eventually becoming the jonnycake (possibly a corruption of "journey cake," as it traveled quite well). Simmering corn in water that had been made alkaline with wood ash produced soft, puffed kernels called hominy (a Native American word). Mixing cooked corn with beans produced succotash, a New England favorite.

Beans were also a staple, easily dried to store over the harsh winters. Baked beans, associated even today with New England cuisine, satisfied both religious and economic constraints. Cooking was forbidden on the Sabbath, so dishes were developed that could be started the day before to cook slowly and be ready the next day. Cooking fuel was a precious commodity and every last bit of heat was extracted from the oven or fire. Foods that required intense heat, such as roasts, were cooked first, and as the fire cooled pots of beans could be cooked slowly, even after the fire went out, since the ovens or hearths retained some heat for many hours.

Seafood was plentiful and the Native Americans showed the settlers a new way to cook clams, oysters, and lobsters. Stones were placed in a hole dug into the ground and a fire was built on them. When the fire went out, seaweed was laid on the hot stones. Shellfish was placed on the seaweed, topped with a covering of more seaweed, and delicately steamed. The seaweed imparted a unique flavor. Today the New England clambake is the carryover of this early tradition. To survive the long, cold winters of New England, preservation of seafood and other foods was a necessity. Salting cod was found to be an excellent way to preserve the large numbers of fish caught during the fishing season.

Preserving foods in anticipation of the harsh winters led to other characteristic New England foods such as corned beef (which found its way into the New England boiled dinner) root vegetables that could be stored over the winter in a root cellar, and beans that could be dried in the attic. Fruit trees were brought from Europe and thrived in the New England climate. Apples stored quite well under chilled conditions, often lasting over the entire winter. Drying fruits was another way to preserve the fall harvest. Cattle were brought from Europe and easily adapted to the region, providing milk for dairy products. Cheese making is an excellent way to preserve milk, and New England still produces some of the finest cheese in North America. Vermont cheddar is world class.

One of the most noteworthy cooking styles of the Mid-Atlantic States is that of the Pennsylvania Dutch. In 1683 William Penn, an English Quaker, invited German families looking for religious freedom to settle in his colonial territory. They became known as Pennsylvania Dutch from the word for German in that language, *Deutsch*. These people were successful farmers in the old country and found similar land in southeastern Pennsylvania. They introduced the ideas of crop rotation and soil conservation to America. By designing a highly accurate rifle they were easily able to provide game for the dinner table. Pennsylvania Dutch cooking relies on Old World cooking techniques and flavor combinations applied to the crops of the New World. Cornmeal mixed with pork meat produced scrapple, a favorite to this day. The settlers brought their European baking traditions to America and helped to establish an authentically American baking style. The modern coffee break is an adaptation of a Pennsylvania Dutch tradition of a mid-morning pause when freshly baked breads and sweets were consumed. Sweet-and-sour flavor combinations were popularized as were dumplings. The area is known for preserving and canning, and New World crops were easily adapted to this method.

Much of the Mid-Atlantic region borders the Atlantic Ocean, and many deep-water bays dot its shoreline, providing a perfect environment for harboring fishing fleets. One of the most famous fishing industries of the region is associated with Maryland and surrounding states. Crab is king here, and there is no finer way to enjoy fresh crabmeat than in a Maryland crab cake. When it is properly made, there is only enough filler to hold the crabmeat together while cooking. Another Maryland crab dish is soft-shelled crabs, harvested precisely when the crabs have shed their old shell and are in the process of developing a larger shell (which has yet to harden) to accommodate growth. At this point the entire crab can be eaten, with a bit of trimming first. For a crab boil copious amounts of hard-shelled crabs are simmered and steamed in a large pot. Seaweed is often added for flavor and as a cover for the pot itself. Local seasoning mixes (Old Bay is a famous one) are then sprinkled on just before service.

Maryland shares a common heritage of hospitality with Virginia, the early English settlement established in Jamestown in 1607. This hospitality comes from the gracious traditions of English country life. Many families lived on large plantations and needed workers to maintain the vast landholdings. Slavery seemed the best solution. Among other things, slavery brought African cooking methods and ingredients to the region. Thomas Jefferson, the most famous resident of Virginia, was an admirer of French cuisine. He helped to introduce a sophisticated style of cooking to Virginia. One of the most famous food products of this region is the Smithfield ham, considered a delicacy around the world. Virginians were fond of the habit, found across the South, of cooking cabbage and other vegetables with beans in the water used to cook hams and often added a ham bone and bits of ham or salt pork to the bean cooking pot as well.

Many residents of North Carolina came from Virginia and Maryland, so North Carolina's cuisine is much like that of its northern neighbors. South Carolina, on the other hand, has a distinct cooking style that can be traced to rice, which grows particularly well in the coastal marshy regions of the state. African cooks combined rice with vegetables, seafood, and/or meats to produce a famous South Carolinian dish, pilau. Benne, or sesame seeds, were an African import. Added to dishes for good luck, they are a surprise element in the dishes of South Carolina.

The Deep South begins with Georgia, which borders South Carolina. Following the American Revolution people migrated from the coastal areas to the interior, bringing the foods of the coast to the interior and thus providing uniformity to this vast region's cuisine. While there is certainly British influence here, French and Spanish settlements also imparted their methods of food preparation to the South. Southern cooking is an outgrowth of Southern hospitality, which lends a certain graciousness to its cuisine. The defining ingredient must be corn, for in no other region of the United States has corn remained so central to the diet. (Many other regions adopted wheat not long after settlement of the Ohio Valley led to producing large enough quantities for commercial trade.) Corn is the most important U.S. commercial crop.

Corn comes in two forms: fresh corn (called green corn) and dried corn, which can be processed two ways. It can be ground into cornmeal or soaked in alkali solution first and thus transformed into hominy. Hominy can be dried and ground into grits. Some of the popular products made from cornmeal include "dog bread," a simple mixture of cornmeal and water, fried as crisp griddle cakes. When enriched with eggs, milk, and onions, the batter can be fried as "hushpuppies." Leave out the onion and the batter is baked as cornbread. Separate the eggs and fold in the beaten egg whites and the more elegant "spoon bread" is baked as a "soufflé."

The most recognizable regional American cuisine comes from southern Louisiana in the form of Creole and Cajun cooking. While the Creoles and Cajuns produce similar dishes, they are culturally distinct. The Creoles are descendants of upper-class French men and women encouraged to settle New France and to establish a thriving community that was quite unusual in that most people who emigrated to America were poor and/or looking for religious freedom. The Cajuns (Acadians) came from Nova Scotia when England took over Canada. Not wanting to give up Catholicism, the French language, and allegiance to France, the entire settlement was deported by the English. Many found their way to the bayou country of Louisiana. Because of these different backgrounds, Creole cooking aspires to be a grand cuisine, much like that of France, while the Acadians cook in the style of country folk, serving up hearty, assertively flavored foods.

In addition to the French influence, Africans made an important contribution to this region's cuisine as well as to that of the South. Slow cooking in large cast-iron pots is an African cooking practice that was introduced to Louisiana. Blending herbs and vegetables with stock to form a base for stews and soups is also an African technique. Okra, a native African vegetable, found its way into the stews of the region. Used as a thickener, it gave its name to the region's most recognizable dish, gumbo. Gumbo is from the Bantu word for okra, *ki-ngombo*. The Louisiana Purchase in 1803 brought refugee African slaves from Haiti and Martinique, and they carried along with them the fiery hot chile. The Choctaws, the Native Americans of the region, provided another lasting influence on the cuisine with their knowledge of native herbs and spices. Sassafras is an excellent example. When dried and powdered, sassafras added to a stew will thicken it and impart an elusive flavor to the dish. This powder was named *filé* by the Creoles, a French term that means to form threads, because after a dish is thickened by sassafras, it will form stringy threads throughout if re-boiled (for this reason sassafras is added to a finished dish and stirred in at the last moment). When gumbo is thickened by sassafras it is known as a filé gumbo, otherwise okra has been added.

Spanish influence began in 1762 when France ceded New Orleans to Spain. As with early French settlers to the region, it was the Spanish nobility who were encouraged to settle here. This allowed for the intermingling of French and Spanish upper class, the descendants of the Creole people. Spanish contributions to the regional cuisine came in the several forms. Spicy foods were part of the Spanish dining tradition as was the use of rice to accompany those dishes. Mixing meat and poultry in the same dish was another Spanish cooking tradition. Jambalaya, another easily recognizable Creole/Cajun dish, is derived from the famous rice dish of Spain, *paella*.

Certain indigenous ingredients and common techniques define Creole/Cajun cooking. Many dishes start with a roux (flour and fat cooked together to form a thickening base for stews and sauces). Unlike a French roux, the roux used in gumbos is slowly cooked for a very long period over low heat; this turns the normally light-colored mixture a deep mahogany and provides the nutty essence that is so much a part of the final flavor of the dish. Crayfish, relatively unknown to the rest of North America, are prized in Louisiana. Looking like a miniature lobster, the crayfish is found in fresh water. Familiarly called a crawfish, crawdad, or mudbug, the crayfish has a tail meat that is sweet and reminiscent of lobster. The head contains a succulent fat, and many locals eat crayfish by pinching the tail to remove the meat from its shell, then sucking the head to extract the fat and juices. Tail meat is incorporated into rich sauces (crawfish étouffé, for example), included in salads, formed into cakes, and tucked into pastry as crawfish pie. Rice farmers of the region harvest their rice in the fall and then flood the fields to harvest crayfish in the spring and summer. Rice accompanies and is part of many dishes.

As famous as Creole/Cajun cuisine is for being exciting and inventive, Midwest cuisine is considered the opposite. In many ways that reputation is not deserved. The Midwest is a true melting pot of regional American and European cuisines. Pioneers came from well-established culinary regions of America and Europe to discover and settle new lands in America's heartland. The Great Lakes provided plentiful fish, as did the many pristine rivers crisscrossing the countryside. The Shakers, members of an English sect who lived communally, left an indelible imprint on the Midwest and its cuisine. They were innovators in horticulture and designed specialized kitchen tools. They planted orchards of fruit trees, and their gardens were filled with herbs. All across America the use of herbs in cooking is strongly influenced by Shaker traditions.

Cooking in the Midwest is defined by the quality of its basic ingredients. The food is wholesome and filling, and the dishes are varied, spiced with ethnic favorites from its immigrants. Dairy farms in Wisconsin produce America's finest cheese, butter, cream, and other dairy products, while the Plains states produce its corn and wheat. Corn contributes much to Midwestern cooking. Unlike wheat, corn is native to the region, and is prepared in many creative ways. Feed corn supports raising cattle, and the bulk of America's meat processing—both beef and pork—is found in the Midwest. Game, such as deer, duck, and pheasant, is found in abundance and made it easier for pioneers to carve out a homeland in what many consider the richest, most bountiful land in the world.

The Western mountain states were settled by pioneers from the Eastern states, and they brought their cooking style with them. Wild game, such as elk, deer, and bear, and fresh fish from rivers and streams, especially trout, made their way into this region's dishes. Mushrooms are quite abundant, benefiting from two characteristics of conifer forests: a tendency to hold moisture and to promote decay of its soft woods. The chuck wagon, moving with traveling cowboys and pioneers, helped form this region's cuisine. Hearty stews and beans were cooked in cast-iron pots over open fires. Meats were grilled right over the flame. To this day outdoor dining is popular in the West as is barbecue, another vestige of the chuck wagon tradition. Breads were simple and convenient. Sour starters provided the leavening for everything from biscuits to pancakes. People who did not use starter used baking soda, the more popular type of biscuit in the West. Wild berries were there for the picking and are included in savory as well as sweet dishes.

The cuisines of the West Coast begin with the incredible richness of California. Drawn as an island on early maps of America, California shows the Spanish influence everywhere, from its architecture to the enormous variety of crops grown there. Spanish missionaries collected promising plants from around the world and adapted them to locations that suited them. That practice was certainly the beginning of the diverse offerings of California agriculture. Nowadays towns across the state often specialize in one crop, such as artichokes (which grow only in the state of California), lettuce, or garlic. Citrus is plentiful as is every type of fruit imaginable. Avocados, olives, and grapes thrive in California. The extraordinary climate permits crops to be grown throughout the year. California cuisine is known for the freshness of its ingredients and the inventiveness of its cooks in preparing dishes that allow for that freshness to shine through. In the far southern part of the state, where California borders Mexico near San Diego, Mexican influences are seen in the cooking style. Asian influences are important and have a long history in California. Chinese laborers came in the mid-nineteenth century and established their own communities within larger cities on the West Coast, such as Vancouver and San Francisco's Chinatown, for example. The twentieth century has seen an influx of Japanese, Vietnamese, Thais, Koreans, and other Asians who are leaving their imprint on the region's cuisine.

No discussion of the West Coast would be complete without mention of seafood. California is a cold water coast. Cold currents sweep down from Alaska, teeming with fish. Commercially, tuna is the most important catch, and four kinds are harvested: albacore, yellowfin, bluefin, and skipjack. Pacific salmon, rockfish, and anchovies are caught in abundance. Because of the rocky, cliff-lined coast found along much of California, few shellfish, which require shallow mudflats, are harvested. These are found in the Pacific Northwest, and the cuisines of Oregon, Washington, and the Canadian Pacific reflect this. Salmon is king in the Pacific Northwest, and it is prepared in a multitude of ways. All types of mushrooms are gathered in the Northwest where the rainy climate combines with heavily forested land to provide a perfect setting for the growth of mushrooms. Especially prized by cooks are the king bolete (related to the porcini or cèpe) and the matsutake.

Mention the Southwest and images of Texas cowboys and desert scenes with saguaro cactus come to mind. The foods of the Southwest are a tantalizing mix of chuck wagon and barbeque with strong Native American and Mexican influences. Chiles, such as the jalapeño, serrano, poblano, and New Mexico, form the basis for an exciting and spicy cuisine. While under Spanish rule, Texas became cattle country by way of the famous longhorn steer, a descendant of Spanish stock. It is no surprise that beef is important here. Cooked over coals and served in tortillas with salsa, it is the quintessential cultural hybrid Tex-Mex dish of *fajitas*. Corn is the basis for many of New Mexico's dishes. Combined with a sauce made from dried New Mexico chiles (the best are grown in Chimayo and Hatch), it produces tasty dishes such as stuffed *sopapillas* and *chiles relleños*. Blue cornmeal is unique to the region, and blue corn tortillas are made into enchiladas that are stacked rather than rolled.

To some it is surprising that Texas is not a vast desert (although there is a desert area in the southwestern region of the state). The most southern part of the state grows some of the tastiest citrus fruits in the United States. Fruits and vegetables that match the quality of those from California and Florida are grown in the Rio Grande Valley. Texas shares a long shoreline with the Gulf of Mexico. Shrimp and snapper are two of the favorite seafoods here. Pecan orchards grow on thousands of acres in Texas and New Mexico, and the piñon pine of New Mexico and Arizona produces a pine nut similar to that of Italy and the Middle East. Both pecans and pine nuts have found their way into the dishes of the Southwest.

New England

Maine, Vermont,

New Hampshire,

Massachusetts,

Connecticut, and

Nova Scotia and

New Brunswick,

Canada

Maple-Glazed Baby Back Riblets

Apple Potato Pancakes with Nova Scotia Smoked Salmon

Lobster Roll

Fried Ipswich Clams

Maple-Glazed Baby Back Riblets

serves 8 (6 riblets per serving)

Vermont is known for the quality of its maple syrup. Pure maple syrup is made by concentrating the sap to a syrup that is 67 percent sugar. Preparation for the annual harvest of the sap from the sugar maple tree occurs between late February and early March. Several factors must be considered when deciding to tap the trees. The temperature must cycle between nights that are below freezing to days that are mild, known locally as "sugaring weather." It takes forty years before a sugar maple is mature enough to harvest, with a trunk at least ten inches in diameter. During colonial times, the sap was often boiled down to a solid maple sugar, and it is sometimes found that way today. Vermonters and chefs agree that the lesser grades of maple syrup have the most flavor (grade B, dark amber, for example).

CHEF NOTES

Pan juices can be combined with remaining marinade for the final basting before grilling. Reduce any remaining marinade as a final glaze when grilling or for a sauce.

MARINADE

¼ cup [60 mL] granulated maple sugar

½ cup [120 mL] maple syrup, preferably a more flavorful lesser grade

½ cup [120 mL] chicken stock

1 tablespoon [15 mL] dry mustard

1 teaspoon [5 mL] cayenne

4 garlic cloves, minced

1 tablespoon [15 mL] pure sesame oil

3 tablespoons [45 mL] ketchup

½ teaspoon [3 mL] salt

SPARERIBS

2 racks of baby back pork spareribs, cut in half lengthwise and cut into individual ribs

ADVANCE PREPARATION

1. Combine all the marinade ingredients and mix thoroughly. Heat to dissolve the sugar, if necessary.

2. Brush the marinade over the ribs. Marinate, refrigerated, overnight. Save any leftover marinade to baste with while cooking.

COOKING METHOD

3. Bake the ribs in a tightly covered roasting pan at 425°F [220°C] for 45 minutes, basting occasionally.

4. Allow the ribs to cool in the sealed pan. Wrap the ribs in individual servings to be grilled to order.

5. Finish the ribs by brushing with marinade, then grilling over hot coals for a few minutes just before serving.

SERVICE

6. Serve about 6 riblets per person, with a bowl for bones and additional napkins.

Apple Potato Pancakes with Nova Scotia Smoked Salmon

serves 8

Atlantic salmon is caught in the St. Marys river system, including the LaHave, Medway, Margaree, and Liscomb rivers, traversing a peaceful and picturesque countryside. In order to preserve the catch over the long winter, the technique of cold smoking was developed. The process includes five steps: salt or brine curing, draining, drying, smoking, and cooling. The smoking temperature is maintained between 70° and 90°F [21° and 32°C], and the salmon is essentially raw. The removal of moisture from the fish prevents the growth of bacteria, thus preserving the fish. "Nova-style" lox can be milder in flavor and is usually less salty.

CHEF NOTES

Freshly grated horseradish, homemade applesauce, and sliced chives can be added for garnish. Salmon roe may be added as well.

1½ pounds [675 g] russet potatoes, peeled and cut in half or to fit into the feed tube of a food processor

1 large onion

2 small tart apples, peeled, cored, and quartered

1 egg

1 egg yolk

2 scallions, white parts only, finely sliced

2 tablespoons [30 mL] fresh dill, coarsely chopped

1 teaspoon [5 mL] salt

¼ to ½ cup [60 to 120 mL] all-purpose flour

Vegetable oil, for frying

8 ounces [225 g] Nova Scotia smoked salmon

1 cup [240 mL] crème fraîche

ADVANCE PREPARATION

1. All advance preparation may be found in the ingredient list.

PREPARATION OF THE BATTER

2. Coarsely grate the potatoes, onion, and apples together, using the feed tube of a food processor fitted with a grating disc. Toss together and place in the center of a piece of cheesecloth. Form a bundle and squeeze out as much liquid as possible. The more liquid removed, the crisper the pancakes will be.

3. Add the egg and the egg yolk to the drained potato mixture and stir in the scallions, dill, and salt. Add enough flour to form a smooth, thick batter.

COOKING METHOD

4. Heat some vegetable oil in a heavy skillet. Fry ¼-cup [60-mL] portions of batter in the hot oil, about 2 minutes per side, or until golden and crisp. Drain on paper towels and keep warm.

SERVICE

5. Serve 2 pancakes per person, topped with 1-ounce [30-g] rosettes of smoked salmon. Place 2 tablespoons [30 mL] of crème fraîche at the side.

Lobster Roll

serves 8

In New York one searches out the best pizza; in New England, the lobster roll. There are web sites dedicated to the quest for the ideal lobster roll. A lobster roll consists of lobster salad spread on a bun (usually a hot dog bun) that is then broiled. The bun is quite important. A commercial hot dog bun appears to be the ideal casing, being soft enough to prevent the filling from squirting out from the end opposite the bite and bland enough to allow the delicate flavor of lobster meat to shine through. In this version the lobster salad is served open faced on a hamburger bun. Seek out a local bakery to custom bake them or bake them on the premises.

CHEF NOTES

The lobster salad makes a nice summer salad on its own, served on a bed of mixed greens or in endive spears. Shrimp makes a good substitute for lobster, both in a roll and as a salad.

3 cups [720 mL] cooked lobster meat

1 cup [240 mL] mayonnaise

½ cup [120 mL] celery, strings removed, peeled, and very finely diced

1 garlic clove, finely minced

2 tablespoons [30 mL] fresh basil leaves chiffonade

1 tablespoon [15 mL] fresh parsley, finely chopped

¼ cup [60 mL] scallions, finely sliced

Tabasco to taste

Fresh lemon juice to taste

Salt and pepper to taste

4 hamburger buns, preferably homemade

Butter, for grilling

Lemon wedges, for garnish

ADVANCE PREPARATION

1. Mix the lobster meat with the mayonnaise, celery, garlic, basil, parsley, and scallions.

2. Season to taste with Tabasco, lemon juice, and salt and pepper. Allow to stand, refrigerated, for at least 4 hours or overnight.

COOKING METHOD

3. Spread the hamburger bun halves with butter and grill until toasted.

4. Spread ⅓ to ½ cup [80 to 120 mL] of lobster salad on each bun half and broil under a salamander or broiler until browned.

SERVICE

5. Serve immediately, open faced with lemon wedges.

Fried Ipswich Clams

serves 8

Soft-shell clams found off Cape Ann, Massachusetts, are considered to be the finest along the entire North Atlantic seaboard, from Maine to the Carolinas. Most agree that these clams are best when fried or steamed, prepared simply. It is said that Woodman's, in Essex, invented the fried clam in 1916. Lard is the frying fat of choice; it is said to be responsible, in part, for the ultimate flavor of the dish. Feel free to substitute oil.

CHEF NOTES

Some purists believe that steaming is the proper way to enjoy the flavor of these clams, called "steamers" when prepared in the following manner: Steam cleaned clams over high heat until open, about 10 minutes, discarding any that do not open. Reserve the steaming broth. Serve portions of broth and melted clarified butter in small cups. The steamed clam is removed from its shell by its siphon, swirled in the broth to remove sand, then dipped in the butter.

COCKTAIL SAUCE: MAKES ABOUT 1½ CUPS [360 mL]

1½ cups [360 mL] ketchup

2 tablespoons [30 mL] prepared horseradish

1 garlic clove, finely minced

½ teaspoon [3 mL] Worcestershire sauce

½ teaspoon [3 mL] fresh lemon juice

1 tablespoon [15 mL] shallots, diced fine

Salt and black pepper to taste

FRIED CLAMS

2½ cups [600 mL] corn flour

⅔ cup [160 mL] all-purpose flour

1 teaspoon [5 mL] salt

2 eggs

3 cups [720 mL] milk

2 pounds [900 g] soft-shell clams, preferably Ipswich, shucked and drained of liquor

3 pounds [1.4 kg] lard, melted and heated to 375°F [190°C], for frying

Lemon wedges, for garnish

ADVANCE PREPARATION

1. Mix all ingredients for the cocktail sauce together, stirring well to combine. Allow to stand, refrigerated, for 2 hours. (The sauce can be made several days in advance.)

PREPARATION OF THE CLAMS

2. Mix the corn flour with the flour and salt. Beat the eggs with the milk. Dip the drained clams in the egg wash, a few at a time, then toss them in the flour mixture.

COOKING METHOD

3. Fry the clams, in batches, in the hot fat at 375°F [190°C] for about 1 minute, or until golden and crisp.

SERVICE

4. Serve immediately, accompanied with lemon wedges and cocktail sauce.

Mid-Atlantic States

New York, Pennsylvania,

New Jersey, Delaware,

Maryland, Virginia,

North Carolina, and

South Carolina

Buffalo Wings

Corn Cakes with Smithfield Ham

Hudson Valley Foie Gras with Caramelized Apples

Chesapeake Bay Crab Cakes

Buffalo Wings

serves 8 (5 wing drumettes per serving)

Buffalo wings are the invention of the Anchor Bar in Buffalo, New York. The story goes something like this: At closing one day, some customers came into the Anchor Bar wanting something to eat. There was not much around, save for some chicken wings. The wings were tossed with bottled hot sauce and deep-fried. Leftover blue cheese salad dressing was sent out as a dip to accompany them. Many variations of this dish exist today. Most of them rely on preparing a sauce that is tossed with the chicken wings after they have been fried. A close to authentic version is given below and a popular sauce method can be found in the Chef Notes.

CHEF NOTES

To increase spiciness sprinkle the fried wings with additional pepper sauce before service.

An alternative method of preparing **Buffalo wings** is to toss unflavored fried wings with a sauce such as the following:

DRUMETTES

2 cups [480 mL] all-purpose flour

2 tablespoons [30 mL] cayenne, or to taste

1 cup [240 mL] white vinegar

1 cup [240 mL] Tabasco, or other Louisiana-style hot pepper sauce

40 chicken wing drumettes

Oil, for deep-frying

2 cups [480 mL] prepared blue cheese dressing (see Chef Notes)

Additional hot pepper sauce

ADVANCE PREPARATION

1. Mix the flour with the cayenne.

2. Prepare a breading station by adding the vinegar and Tabasco to (separate) shallow bowls.

COOKING METHOD

3. Dip the wings in vinegar. Add them to the flour mixture and toss to coat (can be done in a plastic or paper bag).

4. Dip the wings in the Tabasco and deep-fry at 375°F [190°C] for 8 to 10 minutes or until done.

SERVICE

5. Serve 5 wings per person, accompanied with ¼ cup [60 mL] of blue cheese dressing.

Buffalo Wings Sauce

Makes enough to coat 30 wings

6 tablespoons [90 mL] hot sauce, preferably Durkee Red Hot Sauce

2 ounces [55 g] margarine

1 tablespoon [15 mL] white vinegar

1/8 teaspoon [0.5 mL] celery seed

1/4 teaspoon [1 mL] crushed red pepper flakes

1/2 teaspoon [3 mL] cayenne, or to taste

1/4 teaspoon [1 mL] garlic powder

1/2 teaspoon [3 mL] Tabasco

1/4 teaspoon [1 mL] Worcestershire sauce

Combine all the ingredients for the sauce in a saucepan and simmer for 5 minutes, stirring occasionally. Fry the wings and toss with the prepared sauce just before serving.

An easy to prepare blue cheese dressing can be made several days in advance:

Mix 4 ounces [110 g] crumbled Maytag (or other high quality) blue cheese with 1 1/2 cups [360 mL] mayonnaise, creaming some of the cheese into the mayonnaise. Add buttermilk to thin to desired consistency. Add garlic, sliced scallions, and salt and pepper to taste. Allow to stand, refrigerated, overnight.

Corn Cakes with Smithfield Ham

serves 8 (2 cakes per person)

Corn was extremely important as a staple in Southern cooking during Colonial times. Meat preservation was accomplished by curing and smoking, which gave rise to the famous Virginia ham. The rich sweetness of corn is balanced by the saltiness of the cured ham in this first-course dish.

CHEF NOTES

The corn cakes may be topped with crème fraîche (or sour cream) and caviar instead of ham or with fresh salsa for a vegetarian version. Additional freshly grated corn can be substituted for the creamed corn, if desired, with a slight increase in liquid.

¾ cup [180 mL] yellow cornmeal, preferably stone ground

¼ cup [60 mL] all-purpose flour

½ teaspoon [3 mL] baking soda

½ teaspoon [3 mL] salt

¼ teaspoon [1 mL] sugar

½ cup [120 mL] creamed corn

½ cup [120 mL] fresh corn kernels

2 eggs

½ cup [120 mL] buttermilk, or as needed

Butter, for frying

2 tablespoons [30 mL] scallions, finely sliced

½ cup [120 mL] sour cream

4 ounces [110 g] Smithfield or other cured Virginia ham, cooked and sliced very thin

ADVANCE PREPARATION

1. Mix the dry ingredients together.

2. Mix the creamed corn with the corn kernels, the eggs, and half of the buttermilk. Stir the dry ingredients into the egg mixture, adding additional buttermilk as required to form a smooth, firm batter.

COOKING METHOD

3. Heat some butter in a large skillet. Stir the sliced scallions into the batter and drop 2-tablespoon [30-mL] portions into the pan. Do not crowd the cakes as they will spread. Cook for 2 minutes, or until golden. Flip the cakes and cook for 2 minutes more, or until golden.

4. Transfer to a warm plate lined with paper towels to drain. (The cakes should be cooked to order.)

SERVICE

5. Serve 2 corn cakes per person, topped with 1 tablespoon [15 mL] of sour cream and ½ ounce [15 g] of shaved ham. Serve immediately.

Hudson Valley Foie Gras with Caramelized Apples

serves 8

Historical evidence shows that the Egyptians practiced goose fattening (force feeding). The original intention was for a more succulent bird, with accompanying fat for cooking (considered cleaner than fat from the pig). Goose fattening spread to Greece and Rome, and it is believed that the Romans were the first to cook the enlarged liver from these fattened geese as a delicacy. Jews under Roman rule in Palestine learned these techniques and spread them throughout Europe. Eventually the French adopted the techniques and became the guardians of this special food.

The lush Hudson River valley of New York State is home to the finest American producers of foie gras, recognized for its world-class quality by top chefs. A cooperative formed among several upstate New York farms is the largest single producer of foie gras in the world.

CHEF NOTES

Separate the lobes of the liver before slicing. Slice a whole liver as close to cooking as possible for best flavor.

4 apples, preferably McIntosh or other New York variety, peeled, cored, and quartered

2 tablespoons [30 mL] unsalted butter

¼ cup [60 mL] apple cider, fresh pressed if possible

½ cup [120 mL] sugar

Pinch of ground cinnamon

¼ teaspoon [1 mL] black peppercorns, coarsely crushed

Salt to taste

1 pound [450 g] foie gras, preferably Hudson River valley, trimmed, cut into 8 slices, and scored (see Chef Notes)

ADVANCE PREPARATION

1. Cut each apple quarter in half crosswise. Melt the butter in a heavy nonstick skillet. When the foaming subsides, add the apple pieces. Sauté over high heat until the apples begin to color. Add the apple cider and simmer for 2 minutes.

2. Stir in the sugar and allow to simmer until the apples have begun to turn translucent and the liquid has thickened to a syrup. (The apples can be prepared 1 day in advance and reheated.) Stir in the cinnamon and pepper. Season to taste with salt.

COOKING METHOD

3. Heat a dry heavy skillet over high heat. Add the foie gras slices and sear 30 seconds to 1 minute, or until a brown crust has formed. Turn the foie gras and sear the other side.

SERVICE

4. Serve 1 slice of seared foie gras, accompanied with 4 caramelized apple pieces, per person.

Chesapeake Bay Crab Cakes

serves 8 (2 crab cakes per person)

The Chesapeake is the largest estuary in North America, touching on Delaware, Maryland, and Virginia. May is molting and mating season for the blue crab and the beginning of blue-crab-eating season. Soft-shelled crabs are eaten whole, steamed, sautéed, or grilled, but mature hard-shell crabs are always steamed, then often dusted with crab seasoning and dumped onto a newspaper-lined table, ready to be attacked with mallets, fingers, and picks. While fun, this can be a lot of work to get to the succulent crabmeat. The crab cake takes all of the work out of enjoying the meat of the blue crab. There are plenty of recipes around for the best crab cake, but the locals agree on one thing: mostly crab, very little filler.

CHEF NOTES

Be careful not to break up the lumps of crabmeat when folding it into the mayonnaise mixture. Do not press the crab cakes too firmly before frying. They should be loosely formed, pressed only enough to hold together when frying.

½ cup [120 mL] mayonnaise

1 egg

1 tablespoon [15 mL] Dijon mustard

¼ teaspoon [1 mL] Tabasco

1 teaspoon crab seasoning, such as Old Bay or Wye River

1 tablespoon [15 mL] Worcestershire sauce

20 saltine crackers, coarsely crushed

1½ pounds [675 g] jumbo lump crabmeat, picked over for bits of shell and cartilage

Oil, for pan frying

Additional crab seasoning

Lemon wedges, for garnish

ADVANCE PREPARATION

1. Mix the mayonnaise with the egg, mustard, Tabasco, crab seasoning, and Worcestershire sauce.

2. Sprinkle the crushed saltines over the crabmeat. Gently fold the mayonnaise mixture into the crab mixture, being careful not to break up the crabmeat. (The crabmeat mixture can be made several hours in advance.)

COOKING METHOD

3. Form the mixture into 16 crab cakes, about ¼ cup [60 mL] of mixture per cake. Dust the tops with a bit of crab seasoning.

4. Sauté in hot oil in a heavy skillet, about 2 minutes per side. Drain on paper towels and hold warm for service. (The crab cakes can also be baked at 375°F [190°C] for 8 to 10 minutes.)

SERVICE

5. Serve 2 crab cakes per person accompanied with lemon wedges.

The South

Georgia, Alabama,

Florida, Mississippi,

Arkansas, Kentucky,

Tennessee, and West

Virginia

Barbecued Pork Spareribs

Southern Fried Quail with Country Cream Gravy

Smoked Bluefish Dip

Scallion and Cheese Corn Soufflés

Barbecued Pork Spareribs

serves 8

In the South, when barbecue is mentioned, it is automatically assumed that pork is being cooked. One of the most popular of barbeque sauces found in the South is the vinegar and red pepper kind, which is also used as a dressing for pulled smoked pork shoulder meat. The fire used for cooking the spareribs should be as smoky as possible. Use green hickory or oak or soaked chips if necessary and place them at the edge of live coals. Cooking should be slow and lengthy. Although nontraditional, in this recipe a dry rub is applied before cooking for extra flavor. Baby back ribs can be used, but they will not develop the flavor of the meatier and juicier spareribs, especially over a long cooking period.

DRY RUB: MAKES ABOUT ½ CUP [120 mL]

1 tablespoon [15 mL] dry mustard

2 tablespoons [30 mL] garlic powder

2 tablespoons [30 mL] brown sugar

2 tablespoons [30 mL] paprika

2 tablespoons [30 mL] ground red chile

1 teaspoon [5 mL] cayenne

2 tablespoons [30 mL] kosher salt

1 tablespoon [15 mL] Worcestershire powder (not sauce)

½ teaspoon [3 mL] dried thyme

½ teaspoon [3 mL] dried oregano

1 rack pork spareribs, 3 to 4 pounds [1.4 to 1.8 kg]

BARBECUE SAUCE: MAKES ABOUT 2½ CUPS [600 mL]

1 cup [240 mL] sweet onion, chopped coarse

1 tablespoon [15 mL] dry mustard

6 garlic cloves, chopped

½ cup [120 mL] rich chicken or pork stock

1 cup [240 mL] cider vinegar

1 teaspoon [5 mL] salt

1 teaspoon [5 mL] black pepper

1 heaping tablespoon [20 mL] crushed red pepper

2 teaspoons [10 mL] brown sugar, or more to taste

2 bay leaves

½ teaspoon [3 mL] dried thyme

¼ cup [60 mL] peanut oil

ADVANCE PREPARATION

1. Combine all of the dry rub ingredients in a bowl and mix very well. Reserve 1 tablespoon [15 mL] of the rub for the barbecue sauce. Rub the remaining dry mixture thoroughly over the spareribs. Wrap the ribs in plastic film and allow to stand at room temperature for 2 hours.

If smoking a shoulder or butt roast, the meat is done when a thermometer inserted reads 165°F [75°C]. Allow the roast to rest at least 1 hour. Shred the meat by pulling apart with your fingers, then dress the meat with the barbecue sauce. If cooking baby back ribs, the smoking time should be about 1½ hours, with no precooking involved.

PREPARATION OF THE BARBECUE SAUCE

2. Purée the onion with the dry mustard and garlic. Combine the onion mixture with the remaining sauce ingredients in a nonreactive saucepan and bring to a boil. Reduce the heat and simmer for 5 minutes. Allow to cool. Add the reserved rub. Reserve the sauce, refrigerated. (The sauce can be made 1 day in advance.)

COOKING METHOD

3. The ribs can be precooked by steaming over barely simmering water, about 170°F [80°C], for 30 minutes. (If steaming the ribs, brush additional rub on them before smoking.)

4. Build an indirect charcoal fire with a large quantity of coals and, just before cooking, place green wood chunks at the edge of the coals nearest where the ribs will be cooking. If using dry wood, presoak it for 30 minutes in warm water.

5. Directly underneath where the ribs will be cooking, place a pan of water on the bottom of the grill to maintain moisture while smoking. Replenish the water as necessary during the cooking process.

6. Smoke the ribs for at least 2 hours over a fire whose air temperature never exceeds 225°F [110°C], maintaining the temperature by opening and closing the vents.

7. Every 30 minutes, flip the racks over and lightly baste the meat with the sauce, moving the rib racks to ensure even cooking. Near the end of the cooking process increase the frequency of basting and turning to every 10 minutes.

8. When there is at least ½ inch [1 cm] of bone showing at the end of the ribs and the meat pulls easily away from the bone, the ribs are done. Remove from the grill, cover loosely with foil and allow to rest for at least 30 minutes before serving.

SERVICE

9. Divide the rack into individual ribs and serve warm, accompanied with small ramekins of the heated sauce. Serve with plenty of napkins and provide a dish for the bones.

Southern Fried Quail with Country Cream Gravy

serves 8

Quail are hunted in the fall and raised year-round all across the South. They are especially enjoyed when pan-fried and dipped into a cream gravy made from the pan drippings. Some chefs feel that using buttermilk makes the crust too thick and prefer simply to coat the bird with seasoned flour; other chefs insist that buttermilk is essential. Both sides agree, however, that the only way to cook the quail is in a 12-inch well-seasoned heavy cast-iron skillet, and that frying in lard produces the crispest crust.

QUAIL

8 semiboneless or boneless Bobwhite quail or 4 semiboneless or boneless Pharaoh quail, halved

Salt and ground black pepper to season

1½ cups [360 mL] buttermilk

1½ cups [360 mL] all-purpose flour

1 teaspoon [5 mL] salt

½ teaspoon [3 mL] ground black pepper

½ teaspoon [3 mL] garlic powder

¼ teaspoon [1 mL] cayenne

1 cup [240 mL] lard

1½ cups [360 mL] peanut oil

GRAVY: MAKES 2 CUPS [480 mL]

3 tablespoons [30 mL] all-purpose flour

1 cup [240 mL] rich chicken stock

1½ cups [360 mL] heavy cream

½ teaspoon [3 mL] coarsely ground black pepper

ADVANCE PREPARATION

1. Season the quail halves with salt and pepper and add to the buttermilk. Marinate for 1 hour.

COOKING METHOD

2. Mix the flour, salt, pepper, garlic powder, and cayenne together and place in a shallow bowl.

3. Heat the lard and peanut oil over medium-high heat, about 365°F [170°C], in a large heavy skillet, preferably cast iron.

4. Drain the quail, discarding the buttermilk, and place in the seasoned flour. Toss gently to coat evenly. Slide the quail, in batches, into the hot oil and cook about 4 minutes per side, or until the quail are done and golden brown.

5. Remove and allow to drain on layers of newspaper or paper towels. Keep warm until service.

This method works well with dove breast, chicken pieces, strips of chicken breast, slices of ribeye steak, or pork chops. Periodically sift the breading flour to remove any lumps. For an upscale version of the gravy, consider this five-onion cream sauce.

Five-Onion Cream Sauce

Add ½ cup [120 mL] thinly sliced sweet onion, 2 minced garlic cloves, 2 thinly sliced shallots, ½ cup [120 mL] thinly sliced leeks, and ¼ cup [60 mL] sliced scallions when the stock is added to the roux (Step 7).

PREPARATION OF THE GRAVY

6. Pour off all but about 3 tablespoons [45 mL] of the frying fat, reserving any browned bits on the bottom of the pan. Whisk in the flour, stirring while the flour lightly browns.

7. Whisk in the stock and bring to a boil. Add the cream and pepper and return to a boil. Lower the heat and simmer rapidly for about 5 minutes, or until desired thickness.

SERVICE

8. Serve each guest 2 halves of Bobwhite quail or 1 half of Pharaoh quail, with ¼ cup [60 mL] of gravy on the side.

Smoked Bluefish Dip

serves 16

Smoked fish dip is one of the favorite appetizers of the Florida peninsula and is typical of coastal cuisine. Perhaps the most famous of the commercially prepared dips is Seatwang, a spread of kingfish and amberjack, made by Mrs. Peter's Food Company of Jensen Beach, Florida. Another company in Fort Pierce makes a spread called smak. There are two schools of thought with regard to mayonnaise in fish dips: one holds it essential; the other relies on cream cheese exclusively, as in this recipe. Feel free to experiment.

CHEF NOTES

Smoked whitefish, kingfish, amberjack, marlin, or mullet all work well in this dish. If fresh fish is used, brine the fish in a light saltwater mixture and then cold-smoke it. Mayonnaise can replace some or all of the cream cheese. Use 2 cups [480 mL] of mayonnaise for each pound [450 g] of cream cheese.

1 pound [450 g] smoked bluefish fillet or other rich-flavored smoked fish (see Chef Notes)

1 tablespoon [15 mL] Worcestershire sauce

Juice of 1 lemon

½ teaspoon [3 mL] cayenne

1 pound [450 g] cream cheese, cubed, at room temperature

3 garlic cloves, minced

4 ounces [110 g] scallion tops, sliced

4 ounces [110 g] sweet onion, minced

1 tablespoon [15 mL] parsley, chopped

2 tablespoons [30 mL] chile sauce

½ tablespoon [8 mL] dill, chopped (optional)

3 tablespoons [45 mL] roasted red bell pepper, peeled and finely diced (optional)

Stone-ground wheat thins or crackers, for service

Celery sticks, for service

ADVANCE PREPARATION

1. All advance preparation may be found in the ingredient list. (The entire dish may be made 1 day in advance.)

PREPARATION OF THE DIP

2. Combine the fish, Worcestershire sauce, lemon juice, and cayenne in the workbowl of a food processor. Pulse to purée. Reserve chilled.

3. Beat the cream cheese in a bowl until smooth. Add the garlic, scallions, onions, parsley, and chile sauce and mix thoroughly. Mix in the dill and red pepper, if using.

4. Stir in the reserved fish purée. Refrigerate, covered, for at least 4 hours.

SERVICE

5. Serve 2-ounce [110-g] portions per person accompanied with crackers, celery sticks, or both.

Scallion and Cheese Corn Soufflés

serves 8

Whether corn takes the form of simple Indian dog bread (crisp griddle cakes), fried hushpuppies, baked cornbread, or spoon bread (which may be its most sophisticated form), this native grain has been preferred by Southerners for their breads since the founding of Jamestown. The cornmeal used may be yellow or white, which tends to be sweeter and more flavorful, or a combination.

CHEF NOTES

This recipe is fairly forgiving. Locally stone-ground cornmeal may be used if available, but the texture of the finished soufflés will be coarser. Other cheeses or combinations of cheeses may be substituted.

1 cup [240 mL] white or yellow cornmeal or a combination

¾ cup [180 mL] water

¾ cup [180 mL] rich chicken stock

2 cups [480 mL] grated Colby longhorn or cheddar cheese

1 teaspoon [5 mL] cornstarch

1½ cups [360 mL] white or yellow corn kernels, freshly cut and cooked

¼ cup [60 mL] unsalted butter

4 garlic cloves, minced

½ teaspoon [3 mL] salt

1 cup [240 mL] whole milk

4 eggs, separated, at room temperature

4 scallion tops, minced

16 chive leaves for garnish

ADVANCE PREPARATION

1. Combine the cornmeal, water, and chicken stock. Bring to a boil, stirring constantly, then lower the heat and simmer for 1 minute, or until thickened.

2. Toss the cheese with the cornstarch to thoroughly coat, then add it to the cooking cornmeal mixture. Remove from the heat.

3. Add the corn, butter, garlic, and salt and stir well until the cheese melts and is incorporated. Mix in the milk, stirring well.

4. Beat the egg yolks until thickened and pale in color, then stir in the scallion tops. Fold this into the slightly cooled cornmeal mixture. (The batter can be made several hours in advance.)

COOKING METHOD

5. Beat the egg whites until soft peaks form. Gently fold them into the cornmeal mixture.

6. Grease 8 ovenproof soufflé cups or ramekins and dust with cornmeal. Add ½ cup [120 mL] of batter to each cup.

7. Bake at 325°F [160°C] for 25 to 30 minutes, or until the tops are lightly browned and the centers are set.

SERVICE

8. Serve 1 soufflé per person, right from the oven, garnished with 2 chive leaves inserted into the edge of the soufflé.

Louisiana

Muffuletta Pizza

Shrimp Rémoulade

Crayfish Pie

Baked Oysters Two Ways: Oysters Rockefeller and Oysters Bienville

Muffuletta Pizza

This dish is derived from the famous muffuletta sandwich, an excellent example of Italian-Sicilian influence on the cuisine of Louisiana, especially in New Orleans. Signor Lupo Salvadore created the muffuletta in 1906 at the Central Grocery on Decatur Street in the French Quarter of New Orleans. Accounts differ as to the origin of the name of the sandwich, with some suggesting that it was named after a preferred customer, others that it was named for the baker who created the bread on which it is made. The correct pronunciation of the name is "muff-foo-LET-ta." The essential ingredients for this sandwich are the bread and the olive salad. The bread is a round, ten-inch sesame-studded loaf. The original olive salad at the Central Grocery is a closely guarded secret, said to have some forty ingredients, unlike the dozen or so here, but Central Grocery now sells the salad in jars, available by mail order. The salad will keep for months in the refrigerator and is excellent as a condiment, a salad ingredient, or used in other sandwiches and dishes.

DOUGH: FOR EIGHT 6-INCH [15-CM] PIZZAS

1 tablespoon [15 mL] active dry yeast

½ teaspoon [3 mL] sugar

2 cups [480 mL] warm water (105° to 110°F [40° to 45°C])

4 to 6 cups [960 mL to 1.4 L] bread flour, as needed

⅓ cup [80 mL] olive oil, or more as needed

2 teaspoons [10 mL] salt

OLIVE SALAD: MAKES 2½ CUPS [600 mL]

2 cups [480 mL] pimiento-stuffed olives, well drained, slightly crushed, and coarsely chopped

½ cup [120 mL] pickled cauliflower, drained and thinly sliced

2 tablespoons [30 mL] capers, drained

3 peperoncini peppers, well drained and slightly crushed

¼ cup [60 mL] Greek-style black olives

3 small pickled cocktail onions

¼ stalk celery, minced

½ carrot, peeled and grated

½ teaspoon [3 mL] celery seed

½ teaspoon [3 mL] dried oregano

4 garlic cloves, peeled and minced

1 teaspoon [5 mL] minced anchovies or anchovy paste

½ teaspoon [3 mL] black pepper

¼ cup [60 mL] olive oil

½ cup [120 mL] red wine vinegar

PIZZA TOPPINGS

8 ounces [225 g] mozzarella or Emmentaler cheese, grated

8 ounces [225 g] mortadella, thinly sliced

8 ounces [225 g] cappicola ham, thinly sliced

8 ounces [225 g] salami, thinly sliced

8 ounces [225 g] provolone cheese, grated

Sesame seeds, for garnish (optional)

Olives and parsley sprigs, for garnish

If making this recipe as a large sandwich, hollow out a 10-inch [25-cm] sesame-studded loaf of bread. Some people prefer to build the sandwiches with warmed bread, which allows the cheese to melt slightly and the meats to warm. (The olive salad stays cool since it is added at the last moment.) Use rolls or small breads for small sandwiches.

ADVANCE PREPARATION

1. For the dough, stir the yeast and sugar into the warm water in the bowl of a mixer fitted with the paddle. Allow to stand 5 minutes. Stir in 2 cups [480 mL] of the flour and allow to stand 5 minutes.

2. Add ⅓ cup [80 mL] of the oil and another 2 cups [480 mL] of flour and mix to form a smooth batter. Add the salt and continue to add flour until the dough starts to stick to the paddle and the sides of the bowl. The dough will form strands that tear as the paddle rotates in the bowl.

3. Remove the paddle, install the dough hook, and start the mixer at the lowest speed; adjust the speed as necessary. Add flour, a little at a time, until the dough cleans the sides of the bowl. Continue to knead for 5 minutes.

4. Place the ball of dough in a bowl lightly coated with olive oil. Brush the surface of the dough lightly with olive oil. Cover with plastic film and place in a warm, draft-free place for 1 to 1½ hours, or until the dough has doubled in volume. (The dough may also be placed in an oiled resealable bag and allowed to rise, refrigerated, overnight.)

PREPARATION OF THE OLIVE SALAD

5. Mix all of the ingredients for the olive salad together in a large bowl. Spoon into sterilized jars and top with the remaining liquid. Allow to marinate at least 24 hours, refrigerated, turning occasionally. (The salad will keep for months refrigerated.)

ASSEMBLY OF THE PIZZAS

6. Turn out the dough on a floured surface, punch the dough down, and knead for 1 minute. Divide the dough into 8 equal portions.

7. Stretch a piece of dough to cover the bottom of a 6-inch [15-cm] pizza pan that has been brushed with olive oil. The dough may be patted, tossed in the air and spun, or rolled out with a rolling pin.

8. Top each pizza with 1 ounce [30 g] of the mozzarella cheese. Add 1-ounce [30-g] portions of mortadella, cappicola, and

salami. Spoon over ¼ cup [60 mL] olive salad and top with 1 ounce [30 g] of the provolone cheese.

9. Bake at 450°F [230°C] for 10 to 15 minutes, or until the cheese is melted and bubbling and the crust is golden. The edge of the dough may be brushed with water and sprinkled with sesame seeds, if desired, before baking.

SERVICE

10. Serves individual pizzas, quartered; garnished with olives and parsley sprigs.

Shrimp Rémoulade

The original New Orleans ré-moulade sauce is an assertive vinaigrette, meant to be served over cold, boiled shrimp on a bed of sliced romaine lettuce. Over the years, egg yolks were added to the vinaigrette, converting it to a spicy mayonnaise often paired with fried shrimp. Another version added quantities of ketchup to the vinaigrette, making it a sweet and sour tomato-based French dress-ing. The original version is still the best and it goes well with boiled or fried shrimp and crawfish or fried oysters.

CHEF NOTES

The shrimps are cooked with their shells left on to add more flavor. This sauce works well with boiled or fried crawfish tails as well as with boiled blue crabs or fried soft-shell crabs. If preparing the mayonnaise version of the sauce, add egg yolks, prepared horseradish, and Worcestershire sauce. For the French dressing version, add ketchup, prepared horseradish, shallots, and garlic.

BOILED SHRIMP

4 quarts [4 L] cold water

2 tablespoons [30 mL] liquid crab boil, such as Zatarain's or other Creole brand

I cup [240 mL] salt

2 large lemons, cut in half, juiced, and added to the pot with the squeezed lemons

I head of garlic, cut in half across the cloves

2 stalks celery, bruised with the back of a cleaver

6 drops Tabasco

2 pounds [900 g] large shrimp, deveined, shells and tails left on

RÉMOULADE SAUCE: MAKES 2½ TO 3 CUPS [600 TO 720 mL]

I bunch scallions, chopped

2 small stalks celery with greens, peeled and diced fine

2 sprigs of parsley, chopped

¼ cup [60 mL] hot Creole mustard

¼ cup [60 mL] paprika

1¼ teaspoons [6 mL] salt

½ teaspoon [3 mL] black pepper

I teaspoon [5 mL] cayenne

6 tablespoons [90 mL] red wine or tarragon vinegar

1½ tablespoons [25 mL] fresh lemon juice

I cup [240 mL] olive oil

2 shallots, finely minced

I tablespoon [15 mL] celery, minced

I tablespoon [15 mL] parsley, minced

2 cups [480 mL] shredded romaine or iceberg lettuce

ADVANCE PREPARATION

I. To the water add all of the ingredients, except the shrimp, in a heavy 8- to 10-quart [8- to 10-L] stockpot and bring to a slow boil.

2. Boil the mixture for 10 minutes, then add the shrimp. Stir well. When the pot returns to a boil, cook for 3 to 5 minutes, or until the shrimp just become opaque and pink. They will continue to cook while cooling off.

3. Pour the shrimp into a colander to drain, then quickly spread them out on a sheet pan and quickly cool to room temperature. Refrigerate, covered, to chill thoroughly. (The shrimp should be prepared several hours in advance of service.)

PREPARATION OF THE RÉMOULADE SAUCE

4. Put the scallions, celery, parsley, mustard, paprika, salt, pepper, cayenne, vinegar, and lemon juice in a food processor and pulse to purée.

5. Slowly add the olive oil while processing to emulsify the sauce. Remove the sauce from the workbowl and stir in the minced shallots, celery, and parsley. Chill for at least 3 hours. (The sauce can be made 1 day in advance.)

SERVICE

6. Remove the shells from the chilled shrimp. Place about ¼ cup [60 mL] of shredded lettuce in the center of a chilled plate. Arrange 4 to 5 chilled shrimp on the lettuce.

7. Spoon ⅓ cup [80 mL] of rémoulade sauce over the shrimp, covering completely. Serve very cold.

Crayfish Pie Crawfish Pie

This is the famous crawfish pie mentioned in the Cajun-Zydeco song "Jambalaya." In Acadian regions crayfish are known as "mudbugs," and this rich and succulent pie is loaded with the sweet, lobster-flavored tails. The recipe may be prepared either as a whole pie and served in slices or as individual potpies. If obtaining the crayfish meat from whole crayfish, save as much of the yellow fat from the back of the head as possible.

CHEF NOTES

Frozen crayfish tails can be found in the freezer section of most markets. These tails are precooked and as such need little cooking time once added to the filling. Be sure to use as much of the crayfish fat from the package as possible. Shrimp, langoustines, lobster, scallops, and monkfish may all be substituted for the crayfish.

PASTRY: MAKES ONE 9-INCH [23-CM] PIE

2½ cups [600 mL] all-purpose flour

1 teaspoon [5 mL] salt

¼ teaspoon [1 mL] garlic powder

Liberal pinch cayenne

4 ounces [110 g] unsalted butter, cut into ¼-inch [6-mm] cubes, cold

½ cup [120 mL] cold water

CRAYFISH FILLING

2 tablespoons [30 mL] unsalted butter

2 tablespoons [30 mL] all-purpose flour

6 tablespoons [90 mL] onions, diced

¼ cup [60 mL] scallions, chopped

1 tablespoon [15 mL] garlic, minced

2½ tablespoons [40 mL] green bell pepper, diced fine

2 tablespoons [30 mL] celery, minced

2 tablespoons [30 mL] parsley leaves, chopped

½ tablespoon [8 mL] tomato paste

½ teaspoon [3 mL] salt

½ teaspoon [3 mL] black pepper

¼ teaspoon [1 mL] cayenne

2 tablespoons [30 mL] heavy cream

1 tablespoon [15 mL] brandy

1 pound [450 g] crayfish tails

1 egg yolk, beaten lightly

Chopped scallions, for garnish

ADVANCE PREPARATION

1. To form the pastry, sift the flour, salt, garlic powder, and cayenne together into a large chilled bowl or into the workbowl of a food processor.

2. Add the cubes of butter and quickly cut the butter into the flour mixture with a pastry knife or in the food processor until the mixture resembles coarse meal.

3. Add the water all at once, then form into a ball, kneading the dough as little as possible. Cover with plastic film and refrigerate for 30 minutes. (The pastry can be made 1 day in advance.)

PREPARATION OF THE FILLING

4. Melt the butter in a heavy skillet and whisk in the flour, cooking while stirring, to form a light golden roux.

5. Stir in the onions, scallions, garlic, bell pepper, and celery and sauté until the vegetables are soft.

6. Add the parsley, tomato paste, salt, pepper, and cayenne, stirring well.

7. Whisk in the cream and brandy and simmer until the mixture begins to thicken slightly. Add the crayfish tails and cook for about 3 to 5 minutes, or until the tails are cooked. Allow to cool to room temperature. (The filling can be made 1 day in advance, stored refrigerated.)

ASSEMBLY OF THE PIE

8. Divide the dough into 2 balls, one slightly larger than the other. Roll the larger ball into a circle about ⅛ inch [3 mm] thick and 12 inches [30 cm] in diameter.

9. Press in the dough to line a 9-inch [23-cm] pie pan. Spoon the filling into the lined pie pan.

10. Roll out the smaller ball of dough to cover the pie. Press the edges of the dough together to form a seam. Trim and flute the seam with your fingers or a crimping tool.

11. Cut decorative slits in the top, radiating out from the center. Brush lightly with beaten egg.

COOKING METHOD

12. Bake at 375°F [190°C] for 45 minutes, or until the top crust is golden brown, the filling is heated, and the bottom crust is brown. Allow the pie to cool slightly.

SERVICE

13. Cut the pie into 8 slices. Serve 1 slice per person, spooning any sauce in the bottom of the pie plate next to the serving. Garnish with chopped scallions.

Baked Oysters Two Ways: Oysters Rockefeller and Oysters Bienville

Jules Alaciatore, the owner of Antoine's Restaurant, created the famous Oysters Rockefeller in 1899. The dish was developed as a substitute for snails, which were becoming increasingly difficult to obtain from France. Alaciatore wanted to use a shellfish that was abundant and match it with a sauce made from local greens. The resulting dish was so rich that he decided to name it after the richest man in America at that time, John D. Rockefeller. Antoine's keeps the original recipe secret and insists that it contains no spinach, but most versions today use spinach in the mix. Herbsaint, a local New Orleans liqueur developed as a substitute for absinthe, provides an anise flavor to the dish. Pharmacist J. M. Legendre developed this wormwood-free liqueur in 1934. (Pernod is an acceptable substitute.)

The dish Oysters Bienville was created by Pete Michel and Roy Alaciatore, both of Antoine's, sometime in the 1940s as a tribute to the memory of Jean Baptiste le Moyne, Sieur de Bienville, the adventurer who founded the city of New Orleans in 1718. Here the oyster topping is a simple roux-based cream sauce (Béchamel)

OYSTERS

32 large live oysters, shucked, with the deeper halves of the shells reserved, well scrubbed, or 32 large shucked oysters and 32 oyster shells, 8 large scallop shells, or 8 ramekins

Shallow baking pans lined with rock salt

ROCKEFELLER SAUCE

1½ cups [360 mL] fresh spinach, cooked in its own moisture 2 minutes and chopped

¼ cup [60 mL] watercress or sorrel leaves, chopped

6 tablespoons [90 mL] scallions, including green tops, chopped

2 garlic cloves, minced

1½ tablespoons [25 mL] celery leaves, minced

2 tablespoons [30 mL] flat-leaf parsley, chopped

1½ tablespoons [25 mL] chopped fennel greens

1 heaping tablespoon [20 mL] fresh basil, chiffonade

¼ teaspoon [1 mL] dried marjoram

1½ tablespoons [25 mL] anchovies, minced, or anchovy paste

½ teaspoon [3 mL] salt

¼ teaspoon [1 mL] white pepper

¼ teaspoon [1 mL] cayenne

1½ tablespoons [25 mL] Herbsaint or Pernod liqueur

4 ounces [110 g] unsalted butter, softened

OYSTERS BIENVILLE

4 ounces [110 g] unsalted butter

½ cup [120 mL] scallions, minced

2 garlic cloves, minced

¼ cup [60 mL] sifted all-purpose flour

½ cup [120 mL] heavy cream

6 tablespoons [90 mL] milk

2 tablespoons [30 mL] very rich chicken stock

¼ cup [60 mL] white wine

½ tablespoon [8 mL] dry sherry

½ teaspoon [3 mL] salt

flavored with bell pepper, mushrooms, white wine, and cheese. Many chefs add minced shrimp to the stuffing, which serves to enrich it even more.

CHEF NOTES

Both of these dishes may be made either from freshly shucked oysters, or oysters that are pre-shucked and then placed into oyster shells, scallop shells, or ramekins. If freshly shucking the oysters, be sure to remove the oyster to thoroughly scrub the shell before returning the oyster to the shell for preparation of the dish. The shells are broiled on a bed of rock salt, which stabilizes the oyster shells and retains the heat after removal from the oven.

To cook the shrimp for the Bienville sauce, boil the shrimp in a fairly concentrated mixture of Zatarain's shrimp and crab boil combined with beer, bay leaves, thyme, cayenne, lemon, scallions, and garlic.

¼ teaspoon [1 mL] white pepper

¼ teaspoon [1 mL] cayenne

⅓ cup [80 mL] mushrooms, chopped

⅓ cup [80 mL] grated yellow brick cheese

4 ounces [110 g] cooked shrimp, very heavily seasoned, peeled, and chopped (see Chef Notes)

2 tablespoons [30 mL] red bell peppers, roasted, peeled, and chopped

2 tablespoons [30 mL] breadcrumbs

1½ tablespoons [25 mL] grated Romano cheese

Fennel tops, for garnish

ADVANCE PREPARATION

1. For the Rockefeller sauce combine all the ingredients except the butter, in a food processor and purée very fine. Add the butter and blend until thoroughly incorporated.

2. Place the herb butter on a baking sheet lined with parchment and chill to slightly set the mixture until pliable and not hard. Form the mixture into small oval patties about 2½ × 2 inches [6 × 5 cm] and ½ inch [1 cm] thick.

3. Wrap in plastic film, refrigerate, and reserve until ready to cook. (The herb butter can be made 1 day in advance.)

4. For the Bienville sauce melt the butter in a large skillet, sauté the scallions and garlic until soft, and whisk in the flour to prevent lumps.

5. Gradually whisk in the cream, milk, stock, wine, and sherry while stirring. Continue stirring over medium heat until the sauce thickens. Season with salt, white pepper, and cayenne.

6. Add the mushrooms and cook for 3 minutes. Add the brick cheese and stir until melted. Add the shrimp and the red bell pepper and heat through. Pour the sauce into a shallow baking dish and allow it to set in the refrigerator for 1½ hours.

7. Mix the breadcrumbs and the Romano cheese together and reserve.

8. For the Oysters Rockefeller, place each oyster in a half shell and top with an herb-butter patty. Arrange the oysters, four to a prepared pan with rock salt, and bake at 500°F [260°C] for 12 to 15 minutes, or until the sauce bubbles and the edges of the oyster begin to curl. Note: If using scallop shells or ramekins, each should contain four oysters.

9. For the Oysters Bienville, place each oyster in a half shell and top with 1½ tablespoons [25 mL] of the Bienville sauce. Sprinkle the sauce lightly with the breadcrumb mixture. Arrange the oysters on a bed of rock salt and bake at 500°F [260°C] for 12 to 15 minutes, or until nicely browned on top.

SERVICE

10. Serve 4 oysters per person, all of one type or two of each, on the rock salt. Garnish the Oysters Rockefeller with fennel tops.

The Midwest

Ohio, Indiana, Illinois,

Michigan, Missouri,

Iowa, Minnesota,

Wisconsin, North

Dakota, South Dakota,

Nebraska, and Kansas

Spicy Beef and Cheddar Buns (*Runzas*)

Blue Cheese Mini Hamburgers and Mini Corndogs

Miniature Chicken and Fresh Corn Potpies

Wild Rice Griddle Cakes with Morel Mushroom Cream Sauce

Spicy Beef and Cheddar Buns (*Runzas*)

serves 10 (3 per person)

Immigrants to the Central Plains from Germany, Russia, and Luxembourg and those of Mennonite heritage all claim to have introduced the stuffed pastry known commonly as the *runza* (*bierock* to the Mennonites, *krautbrot* or *krautrunzen* to the Volga Germans from Russia). Regardless of the origin, this pie was made as a hearty, portable lunch for workers in the field. A fast food chain that originated in Lincoln, Nebraska, in 1949 registered Runza as a proprietary name in 1966, but the pie is commonly called a *runza*, whether it comes from the restaurant or not. Some variations include sauerkraut versus green cabbage and onions; no cheese; and caraway seeds in the filling or sprinkled on top of the bun before baking.

PASTRY DOUGH: MAKES THIRTY-TWO 3-INCH [8-CM] CIRCLES

½ teaspoon [3 mL] active dry yeast

I tablespoon [15 mL] warm water (110°F [45°C])

¼ cup [60 mL] sugar

¾ cup [180 mL] warm milk (120°F [50°C])

¼ cup [60 mL] unsalted butter, melted

I egg, lightly beaten

2 to 3 cups [480 to 720 mL] bread flour

½ teaspoon [3 mL] salt

¼ teaspoon [I mL] garlic powder

FILLING: MAKES ENOUGH FOR 32 PASTRIES

3 tablespoons [45 mL] lard or vegetable oil

I large onion, diced

3 garlic cloves, minced

I pound [450 g] beef chuck, handminced or ground

4 cups [960 mL] green cabbage, shredded

½ teaspoon [3 mL] coarsely ground black pepper

I½ tablespoons [25 mL] coarse-grained mustard

2 to 3 dashes of hot pepper sauce

I teaspoon [5 mL] Worcestershire sauce

Salt to taste

4 ounces [110 g] cheddar cheese, shredded

2 tablespoons [30 mL] melted butter, for brushing the tops (optional)

ADVANCE PREPARATION

1. All advance preparation may be found in the ingredient list.

PREPARATION OF THE DOUGH

2. Dissolve the yeast in the warm water with a pinch of the sugar in a large bowl and let stand for 5 minutes.

3. Add the milk, melted butter, and egg to the yeast mixture and mix well.

4. Mix the sugar, flour, salt, and garlic powder together and add to the yeast mixture. Stir to incorporate.

5. Turn the dough out onto a lightly floured surface and knead for 5 minutes, or until smooth and elastic.

6. Place the dough in a well-oiled bowl. Cover and allow to rise until doubled in volume, about 1 hour.

7. Punch the dough down and allow to rise a second time.

PREPARATION OF THE FILLING

8. Heat 2 tablespoons [30 mL] of the lard or oil in a nonstick skillet over medium heat and sauté the onion until soft. Add the garlic and sauté 30 seconds more.

9. Add the remaining 1 tablespoon of lard or oil and the beef and sauté, stirring occasionally, for about 5 minutes, or until lightly browned.

10. Add the cabbage and cook for 7 minutes more.

11. Stir in the black pepper, mustard, hot pepper sauce, and Worcestershire sauce. Adjust the seasoning with salt. Cook for 8 minutes more. Remove from the heat and allow to cool.

12. Stir in the cheese.

PREPARATION OF THE RUNZAS

13. On a lightly floured surface divide the dough into 32 balls. Roll each ball into a 3-inch [8-cm] circle.

14. Place 2 tablespoons [30 mL] of the filling in the center of each circle. Fold the edges over and seal with the tines of a fork.

15. Place the unbaked *runzas*, seam side down, on a parchment-lined baking sheet and allow to rise in a warm spot for 20 minutes.

16. Bake at 350°F [175°C] for 12 to 15 minutes, or until golden brown. Brush the tops with the 2 tablespoons of melted butter, if desired.

SERVICE

17. Serve each person 3 buns, preferably warm and right from the oven.

Blue Cheese Mini Hamburgers and Mini Corndogs

serves 12

The hamburger and the corndog are sold at every state fair throughout the Midwest, and this nostalgic pairing will please any group of diners. Iowa is home to the world-famous Maytag blue cheese, developed in conjunction with Iowa State University at the Maytag Dairy Farms of Newton, Iowa, in the 1940s. Iowa beef is known nationwide and combined in this recipe with a homemade bun and blue cheese makes a surprisingly elegant appetizer. Homemade corndogs straight from the deep-fryer and dipped in simple prepared mustard are classic Mid-American fare. High-quality frankfurters, such as an all-beef kosher frank should be used to make the corndogs.

⊙——— **CHEF NOTES**

Cocktail franks or small smoked sausages can be substituted for the frankfurter pieces.

MINI HAMBURGERS: MAKES 12

1½ pounds [675 g] premium ground beef chuck (preferably hand-ground Iowa corn-fed beef)

Garlic salt to taste

Black pepper to taste

½ tablespoon [8 mL] Worcestershire sauce

DOUGH FOR MINI BUNS: MAKES 12 BUNS

½ cup [120 mL] milk

1 tablespoon [15 mL] shortening or butter

1 tablespoon [15 mL] sugar

½ teaspoon [3 mL] salt

1 teaspoon [5 mL] dry yeast

2 tablespoons [30 mL] warm water

About 1½ cups [360 mL] all-purpose flour

Melted butter, for brushing the tops

CORNDOG BATTER

1 cup [240 mL] all-purpose flour

½ cup [120 mL] yellow cornmeal

1 teaspoon [5 mL] baking powder

1 tablespoon [15 mL] sugar

½ tablespoon [8 mL] salt

½ teaspoon [3 mL] ground black pepper

¼ teaspoon [1 mL] garlic powder

2 tablespoons [30 mL] vegetable shortening

1 egg, slightly beaten

¾ cup [180 mL] whole milk

MINI CORNDOGS: MAKES 24 CORNDOGS

8 all-beef frankfurters, cut into thirds

Wooden skewers or craft sticks, cut into 3-inch [8-cm] sections

Vegetable oil, for deep-frying

I red onion, sliced into rings, centers discarded

6 ounces [170 g] Maytag blue cheese, crumbled

Mayonnaise, preferably homemade, for service

Kosher pickle spears, for service

Yellow mustard, for service

ADVANCE PREPARATION

1. Mix the meat, garlic salt, pepper, and Worcestershire sauce together and form 12 small patties, ½ inch [1 cm] thick and about 1¾ inches [4.5 cm] in diameter (use 2 ounces [55 g] of meat mixture per patty). Reserve until ready to cook. (The patties can be made several hours in advance.)

PREPARATION OF THE BUNS

2. Combine the milk with the shortening, sugar, and salt and bring to a boil. Allow to cool to 110°F [45°C].

3. Dissolve the yeast in the warm water and add it to the cooled milk mixture.

4. Add the flour, ½ cup [120 mL] at a time, to form a smooth, elastic batter that does not stick to the bowl. Turn the dough out onto a lightly floured surface and knead for 5 minutes by machine, 10 minutes by hand.

5. Place the dough in a well-oiled bowl and rotate the dough to coat with oil. Cover with a clean towel and place in a warm, draft-free place for 1 hour, or until doubled in volume.

6. Punch down the dough and roll it out ½ inch [1 cm] thick. Cut twenty-four 2-inch [5-cm] circles. Place the circles on a sheet pan lined with parchment. Cover with plastic film and allow to rise until doubled in volume.

7. Brush the tops with melted butter and bake at 375°F [190°C] for 8 to 10 minutes, or until golden brown.

COOKING METHOD FOR HAMBURGERS

8. Grill the burger patties to the desired degree of doneness on a charcoal grill or griddle.

9. Top each patty with ½ ounce [15 g] of crumbled blue cheese while still on the grill, allowing the cheese to melt slightly.

10. For the corndog batter combine the flour, cornmeal, baking powder, sugar, salt, pepper, and garlic powder in a bowl. Using a pastry knife, cut the shortening into the dry mixture until the mixture resembles fine meal. Stir in the egg and milk and mix well to form a thick batter.

11. Insert the wooden skewers into the centers of one end of each hot dog piece. Pat the franks dry or dust lightly in flour.

12. Dip the franks into the corndog batter, twirling the frank by its skewer, to thoroughly coat.

13. Fry the battered franks in hot oil, at 365°F [185°C], cooking in batches, until golden brown. Hold the battered frank under the oil until it pushes up to float, twirling as it fries, then let go, allowing it to finish cooking. Drain on paper towels and keep warm until service.

ASSEMBLY AND SERVICE

14. Spread each side of the hamburger buns lightly with mayonnaise, then top with a beef patty. Add red onion rings and top with the other bun half. Spear with a toothpick to secure.

15. Serve each guest 1 mini hamburger accompanied with a dill pickle spear and 2 mini corndogs, accompanied with a small ramekin of mustard.

Miniature Chicken and Fresh Corn Potpies

serves 8

This recipe incorporates several Midwest pantry items: bacon, chicken, and corn in two different forms, and Iowa produces all three in copious amounts. The dish is baked in a classic American form, the potpie. These potpies can be baked in small casseroles, large ramekins, or rarebits for individual service or as a large pie for communal service.

CHEF NOTES

Turkey could easily be substituted for the chicken; leftovers are good as well. Game, such as pheasant, dove, quail, or duck, could also be substituted.

CORNMEAL-SCALLION CRUST

1½ cups [360 mL] all-purpose flour

⅔ cup [160 mL] yellow cornmeal

¼ cup [60 mL] cake flour

½ teaspoon [3 mL] salt

½ teaspoon [3 mL] black pepper

¼ teaspoon [1 mL] garlic powder

3 tablespoons [45 mL] scallion greens, minced

5 ounces [140 g] unsalted butter, cubed, chilled

½ cup [120 mL] cold water

FILLING: MAKES 6 CUPS [1.4 L]

2 tablespoons [30 mL] butter

2 ounces [55 g] meaty bacon

12 ounces [340 g] boneless chicken breasts

12 ounces [340 g] boneless chicken thighs

¼ cup [60 mL] all-purpose flour

2 carrots, diced

1 celery rib, thinly sliced

1 pound [450 g] onions, sliced

4 garlic cloves, minced

8 ounces [225 g] corn kernels, cut fresh

3¼ cups [780 mL] chicken stock

Salt and pepper to taste

Liberal pinch of cayenne

Liberal pinch of cardamom

Liberal pinch of tarragon

2 tablespoons [30 mL] parsley, chopped

1 tablespoon [15 mL] cornstarch, dissolved in 2 tablespoons [30 mL] stock or water

1 egg, beaten

2 chive leaves per casserole, for garnish

1. For the pastry combine all the dry ingredients and the scallions, and mix well. Cut the cubed butter into the dry ingredients using a pastry knife until the dough resembles coarse meal. Add only enough cold water and mix only enough to allow the dough to be gathered into a loose ball. Cover with plastic film and chill for at least 30 minutes. (The dough can be made 1 day in advance.)

PREPARATION OF THE FILLING

2. Heat the butter in a deep skillet over medium heat and cook the bacon until crisp. Remove with a slotted spoon and drain on paper towels.

3. Dust the chicken pieces with flour and brown the chicken pieces on all sides in the butter–bacon fat mixture. Remove the chicken to a platter.

4. Drain all but 3 tablespoons [45 mL] of the fat mixture from the skillet and sauté the carrots, celery, onions, garlic, and corn for 3 minutes.

5. Add the stock, salt and pepper, cayenne, cardamom, tarragon, parsley, the reserved bacon, and the chicken, and bring to a boil. Reduce the heat to a simmer, cover, and cook 20 minutes.

6. Remove the chicken pieces and rapidly reduce the liquid in the filling by one-fourth.

7. Cut the chicken into bite-size pieces and return to the filling mixture.

8. Add as much cornstarch slurry as required for desired thickness. Simmer for 2 minutes. Adjust the seasonings and allow to cool. (The filling can be made 1 day in advance and held refrigerated.)

COOKING METHOD

9. Spoon ¾ cup [180 mL] of filling into lightly greased individual 1-cup [240-mL] casseroles, ramekins, or rarebits.

10. Roll out the cornmeal pastry on a lightly floured board to a thickness of ¼ inch [6 mm]. Cut pieces of pastry just large enough to overlap the tops of the baking dishes. Pinch the

edges of the pastry against the rims of the dishes to seal, then brush the tops with beaten egg.

11. Bake at 375°F [190°C] for 20 minutes, or until the filling is hot and bubbling and the crust is evenly browned. (If the pastry is browning too quickly, cover loosely with aluminum foil.)

SERVICE

12. Serve each guest 1 casserole right from the oven. Garnish by inserting 2 chive leaves into a small hole formed into the edge of each casserole. (Lining the serving plate with a cocktail napkin before placing the casserole on it will prevent it from sliding during transport to the table.)

Wild Rice Griddle Cakes with Morel Mushroom Cream Sauce

serves 8

Not a true rice, wild rice is a cereal grain of a marsh grass (*Zizania aquatica*) native to Minnesota and Wisconsin. It has been hand-harvested from canoes by the Chippewa and Ojibway Indians for centuries. In the 1950s cultivation of the relatively expensive grain began in Minnesota and California. Wild rice has a nutty flavor and is extremely nutritious. Morel mushrooms (*Morchella esculenta*) are highly prized by the Midwest mushroom hunter. The heavily crenellated caps are unique in appearance and have a distinctly woodsy flavor. Morels are prolific all over the Midwest. They are the official state mushroom of Illinois, and Michigan claims to be the morel capital of the world.

WILD RICE

1½ cups [360 mL] water

1½ cups [360 mL] chicken stock

¾ cup [180 mL] wild rice, rinsed under cold water and drained using a fine sieve

MOREL CREAM SAUCE: MAKES ABOUT 1¾ CUPS [420 mL]

4 ounces [110 g] apple-smoked Wisconsin bacon, chopped (optional)

½ cup [120 mL] sweet onion, diced

3 garlic cloves, minced

3 ounces [85 g] fresh morel mushrooms, rinsed and sliced lengthwise

1 cup [240 mL] chicken stock

1½ cups [360 mL] heavy cream

Salt and ground white pepper to taste

GRIDDLE CAKES: MAKES ABOUT TWENTY-FOUR 2-INCH [5-CM] CAKES

1 egg

1 egg yolk

½ cup [120 mL] chopped chives

½ teaspoon [3 mL] coarsely ground black pepper

Vegetable oil, for frying the griddle cakes

Minced chives, for garnish

ADVANCE PREPARATION

1. Bring the water and stock to a boil. Stir in the rice, then reduce the heat to a simmer and cook, uncovered, for about 40 minutes, or until the grains are just tender but not opened.

2. Strain the rice through a sieve and rinse with cold water. Drain thoroughly. (The rice can be prepared 1 day in advance.) Reserve.

Other fresh wild mushrooms may be substituted for the morels. Dried morels that have been reconstituted may also be substituted. If reconstituting dried mushrooms, be sure to save the soaking liquid for the sauce (pass the liquid through a very fine sieve or coffee filter). Dry morels more than double their weight when reconstituted (reconstitute 1.2 ounces [33 g] of dried mushrooms for the recipe). The bacon may be omitted and butter added for sautéing.

PREPARATION OF THE MOREL SAUCE

3. Heat a skillet and sauté the chopped bacon, if using, over medium heat until the bacon is very lightly browned. Remove and drain on paper towels.

4. Pour off all but 2 tablespoons [30 mL] of the bacon fat and add the onion. Sauté the onion until soft, then add the garlic and mushrooms. Sauté for 3 to 4 minutes, or until the mushrooms just begin to soften.

5. Add the stock and cream and bring to a boil. Reduce the liquid by half, then season with salt and white pepper. Keep warm until service.

PREPARATION OF THE GRIDDLE CAKES

6. Beat the egg and egg yolk together and add the eggs, chives, and black pepper to the cooked wild rice, mixing well.

7. Heat a nonstick skillet or griddle over medium-high heat and add some vegetable oil. Drop heaping tablespoons of the rice mixture into the hot oil, in batches, and flatten the griddle cakes with a spatula. Cook for 1 to 2 minutes per side, or until golden brown. Drain on paper towels and keep warm until service.

SERVICE

8. Place 2 tablespoons [30 mL] of the mushroom sauce on the bottom of a plate and top with 3 wild rice griddle cakes. Finish with a drizzle of sauce, making sure that a morel mushroom slice is placed on top for visual appeal. Garnish with minced chives.

The Western States

Montana, Wyoming,
Colorado, Idaho, Utah,
and Nevada

Baked Lamb Riblets

Venison Meatballs with Spiced Wild Gooseberries

Rocky Mountain Oysters

Smoked Trout Skewers

Baked Lamb Riblets

serves 8

Colorado is becoming known for producing the finest lamb in the United States. Several producers are ethically raising their lambs hormone-free, free-range, and organically fed. Other states that contribute to the production of over 8 million sheep in the United States are Wyoming, Utah, South Dakota, and Montana. American lamb is a source of high-quality protein that is nutritionally complete, and because it possesses very little marbling, the fat can be trimmed from the outside edges. The fat that remains is relatively low in saturated fat and calories. Riblets are the featured cut of lamb in this recipe, which come from the lamb breast (similar to short ribs in beef.)

 **CHEF NOTES**

The riblets can be steamed for 10 minutes in a Chinese-style steamer before baking. Parmesan cheese can be sprinkled over the riblets 5 minutes before done.

4 pounds [1.8 kg] lamb riblets, cut into individual sections

1 cup [240 mL] red wine

3 garlic cloves, minced

1 teaspoon [5 mL] salt

1 teaspoon [5 mL] black pepper

¼ cup [60 mL] olive oil

2 tablespoons [30 mL] vegetable oil

¾ cup [180 mL] fresh breadcrumbs

3 tablespoons [45 mL] butter, melted

¼ cup [60 mL] flat-leaf parsley, chopped

2 sprigs of fresh thyme, chopped

3 garlic cloves, finely minced

½ teaspoon [3 mL] salt

Flat-leaf parsley, chopped, for garnish

ADVANCE PREPARATION

1. Combine the riblets with the wine, garlic, salt, pepper, and olive oil in a resealable plastic bag. Marinate 3 hours.

COOKING METHOD

2. Drain the riblets and pat them dry. Heat the vegetable oil in a large nonstick skillet over high heat. Brown the riblets on all sides. Transfer to an ovenproof baking dish.

3. Mix the breadcrumbs with the melted butter, parsley, thyme, garlic, and salt. Top the riblets with half of this mixture.

4. Place the riblets in a preheated 400°F [205°C] oven. Lower the heat to 325°F [165°C] and bake for 15 minutes.

5. Turn the ribs and top with the remaining breadcrumb mixture. Bake 30 minutes.

SERVICE

6. Serve 8 ounces [225 g] of riblets per person, warm, garnished with chopped parsley.

Venison Meatballs with Spiced Wild Gooseberries

serves 8 (5 meatballs per person)

Gooseberry has been the common name for the fruit of a shrub belonging to the *Ribes* family since the fifteenth century, being a favored preserve served with goose. There are two species, the American gooseberry (*Ribes hertellum*) and the European variety (*R. grossularia*). In the Middle Ages the gooseberry was called "feverberry" as it was believed to have cooling properties. The American gooseberry grows in climates that have humid summers, with temperatures not reaching above 85°F [30°C], and winters that produce deep chilling. Many cultivated gooseberries come from South America and Canada. Related to the gooseberry is the popular currant. Venison is enjoyed throughout the Western States, as deer hunting is a very popular activity. Venison is rich tasting but low in fat and cholesterol. It is quite versatile and can be prepared as a roast, as steaks, ground (as in this recipe), and dried as jerky. Venison benefits from marinating, and red wine makes an excellent base for a marinade.

SPICED GOOSEBERRIES: MAKES 3 CUPS [720 mL]

1 cup [240 mL] cider vinegar

4 cups [960 mL] light brown sugar, packed

½ tablespoon [8 mL] ground allspice

1 teaspoon [5 mL] ground cloves

½ tablespoon [8 mL] freshly grated nutmeg

½ tablespoon [8 mL] ground cinnamon

1 teaspoon [5 mL] salt

2 pounds [900 g] wild gooseberries

MEATBALLS: MAKES FORTY 1-INCH [2.5-CM] MEATBALLS

1½ pounds [675 g] ground venison

3 slices stale white bread, soaked in milk and squeezed dry

1 egg

½ medium onion, grated

2 garlic cloves, minced

1 teaspoon [5 mL] coarse salt

½ teaspoon [3 mL] freshly ground black pepper

2 tablespoons [30 mL] flat-leaf parsley, chopped fine

¼ cup [60 mL] vegetable oil, for frying

ADVANCE PREPARATION

1. Combine the vinegar, brown sugar, spices, and salt in a nonreactive saucepan. Bring to a boil and cook for 5 minutes, while stirring, to dissolve the sugar.

2. Add the gooseberries and lower the heat to a simmer. Cook for 30 minutes, or until the berries are very tender. Store in sterilized jars. (The spiced gooseberries can be made up to 1 week in advance. They will hold for several weeks, refrigerated. Warm before service.)

PREPARATION OF THE MEATBALLS

3. Mix the ground venison with the soaked bread, egg, onion, garlic, salt, pepper, and parsley, stirring in 1 direction.

Cultivated gooseberries may be substituted for wild. If unavailable, fresh currants make a good substitute. The spiced gooseberries go well with most game and poultry dishes. The venison meatballs may be served with a pan gravy instead of the gooseberries. Add 2 tablespoons [30 mL] of flour to the sauté pan after removing the cooked meatballs (add additional oil or butter if necessary). Cook for 1 minute, then stir in 1½ cups [360 mL] cream, half-and-half, or milk. Season with salt and pepper.

4. Form the mixture into forty 1-inch [2.5-cm] meatballs. (The meatballs can be made several hours in advance, covered with plastic film, refrigerated.)

COOKING METHOD

5. Heat the oil in a large nonstick skillet over medium-high heat. Add the meatballs and sauté, browning the meatballs on all sides. Lower the heat and continue to cook for about 10 minutes, or until done.

SERVICE

6. Serve 5 meatballs per person in a shallow bowl, topped with ¼ cup [60 mL] warm spiced gooseberries.

Rocky Mountain Oysters

serves 8

Popular throughout the Western States, mountain oysters are cooked testicles, usually from a calf. They can be poached, sautéed, braised, or, as in this classic preparation, deep-fried. The Western tradition of eating testicles comes from the cowboys of the 1800s, who would toss the testicles from animals that had just been castrated (done during branding time) onto a hot iron until they burst and eat them straight from the iron. Other euphemisms besides mountain oysters that may help make the dish more appealing are "cowboy caviar," "animelles" (French for testicles), and the perennial favorite from Texas, "swing steak."

CHEF NOTES

To aid in the removal of the tough outer skin of the testicles, freeze them before peeling with a sharp paring knife. A mixture of calf, bull, turkey, and sheep testicles, called "barnyard jewels," makes an interesting presentation.

2 pounds [900 g] fresh calf testicles

Salted water to cover

6 cups [1.4 L] water acidulated with 2 tablespoons [30 mL] white vinegar

Salt and pepper

1 cup [240 mL] flour

1 teaspoon [5 mL] garlic powder

¼ teaspoon [1 mL] cayenne

2 cups [480 mL] milk

1 cup [240 mL] cornmeal

Vegetable oil or lard, for deep-frying

Louisiana-style hot sauce

ADVANCE PREPARATION

1. Remove the tough outer skin from the testicles. Soak in salted water for 1 hour.

2. Remove the testicles and place them in a pot of acidulated water. Bring to a boil, reduce the heat, and simmer for 5 minutes. Drain and allow to cool. (The testicles can be prepared 1 day in advance and held refrigerated.)

3. Slice each testicle ¼ inch [6 mm] thick. Sprinkle with salt and pepper.

COOKING METHOD

4. Mix the flour with the garlic powder and cayenne. Toss the slices in the seasoned flour.

5. Dip the medallions into the milk, then into the cornmeal to coat.

6. Deep-fry in 365°F [185°C] oil that has a few dashes of hot sauce added to it (be careful, as some spattering may occur). Deep-fry the slices until golden brown, about 2 minutes. Do not overcook, as they can get quite tough.

SERVICE

7. Serve 4 ounces [110 g] of mountain oysters per person, directly from the fryer, accompanied with a bottle of hot sauce.

Smoked Trout Skewers

serves 8 (2 skewers per person)

One of the most popular sports in the United States and especially in the Western mountain states is trout fishing. Its appeal is obvious. It requires skill, especially fly-fishing. Casting and working the fly are techniques to be mastered, and there is an art to tying one's own flies. Another appeal is the surroundings; mountain streams and lakes are the favored sites.

Trout is a common name for many fish species that belong to the salmon family, and rainbow trout are the most important of the Western trout. They are prized as a game fish (they put up a good fight when caught) and are delicious when prepared in simple ways, such as pan-frying, sautéing, or grilling. Other popular trout are the mountain trout (cutthroat trout), found in the Rocky Mountains, and the steelhead.

CHEF NOTES

Other kinds of trout, such as mountain or steelhead, work nicely. Salmon prepared in this manner is excellent as well.

2 pounds [900 g] rainbow trout fillets, cut into 2-inch [5-cm] slices

Juice of 2 lemons

½ cup [120 mL] dry red wine

Zest of 1 lemon

1 garlic clove, bruised

Salt and pepper to taste

16 wooden skewers, soaked in water 30 minutes

Dry sage branches or rosemary twigs

Lemon wedges, for garnish

ADVANCE PREPARATION

1. Place the trout slices in a resealable plastic bag. Mix the lemon juice, wine, lemon zest, and garlic together and pour over the trout. Toss gently to coat. Allow to marinate, refrigerated, for 1 hour.

COOKING METHOD

2. Remove the trout fillets from the marinade, reserving the marinade for basting, and drain thoroughly. Sprinkle the trout with salt and pepper and thread 2-ounce [55-g] portions onto the skewers.

3. Grill the skewers over hot coals for 5 minutes, while basting with the marinade, turning occasionally.

4. Move the skewers to the side of the grill and add the sage branches to the fire. Cover the grill and smoke for 10 minutes.

SERVICE

5. Serve 2 skewers per person, right from the grill, garnished with lemon wedges.

The West Coast

California, Oregon,

Washington, Alaska, and

British Columbia,

Canada

Smoked Salmon Hash

Fried Abalone and Razor Clam Morsels with Olive Mayonnaise

Grilled Goat Cheese Stuffed Grape Leaves

Wild Mushroom and Hazelnut Pâté

Smoked Salmon Hash

serves 8

Coastal British Columbia was the first region of Canada to be settled, about ten thousand years ago. Images of salmon were carved into boulders that line the Gulf Islands. These people survived on, and held ceremonies to, salmon, their most important food. To this day salmon are central to British Columbia cookery. Salmon have given life to man, bear, and eagle alike. Bentwood box cookery, Canada's indigenous cooking method, has been used for centuries to prepare salmon. A cedar box is soaked in water for several days, filled with water and salmonberries; hot rocks are then added. When the water foams and boils the salmon are placed inside and covered with a woven mat. Within minutes the fish is done and ready to enjoy. The salmonberry (*Rubus spectabilis*) resembles a salmon-colored raspberry.

CHEF NOTES

Red or white new potatoes may be substituted for the Yukon gold potatoes. Any type of cured or smoked salmon may be used in this dish. Smoked lobster makes an elegant substitute for the salmon.

2 ounces [55 g] unsalted butter

1 cup [240 mL] onions, diced fine

1 pound [450 g] Yukon gold potatoes, skins on, scrubbed and very finely diced

2 cups [480 mL] rich chicken stock

¼ cup [60 mL] crème fraîche or heavy cream

8 ounces [225 g] smoked salmon, diced

¼ cup [60 mL] fresh dill leaves and stems, chopped

Pepper and salt to taste

Crème fraîche, in a squeeze bottle, for garnish

Sprigs of dill, for garnish

ADVANCE PREPARATION

1. All advance preparation may be found in the ingredient list.

COOKING METHOD

2. Melt the butter over medium-high heat in a wide nonstick skillet. Add the onions and sauté 2 minutes, stirring constantly, browning lightly.

3. Add the potatoes and sauté 2 minutes, browning the potatoes slightly. Add the stock and simmer until the potatoes are tender and the stock has been absorbed.

4. Stir in the crème fraîche and simmer until thickened.

5. Add the smoked salmon and dill and sauté 1 minute. Adjust seasonings with pepper and possibly salt.

SERVICE

6. Decorate a plate with stripes of crème fraîche from a plastic squeeze bottle. Place a 3-inch [8-cm] metal ring in the center of a plate.

7. Fill the ring with ½ to ⅔ cup [120 to 160 mL] of the hash. Gently press with the back of a spoon to mold. Carefully remove the ring. Place a dill sprig on top and serve immediately.

Fried Abalone and Razor Clam Morsels with Olive Mayonnaise

serves 8

Abalone may be the most expensive shellfish, but the delicate, sweet taste is well worth the price. The fleshy foot, which is used to anchor the abalone to a rock, is the edible part. Until recently the red abalone, the most prized species, was abundant and could be harvested by hand at low tide. By the late 1990s a ban on commercial harvesting was in effect in California, and abalone farms have sprung up to meet demand. Much of the harvest is shipped live to Japan, where it is considered a delicacy. Razor clams inhabit the beaches of Oregon, Washington, Canada, and Alaska. They are dug from the sand at low tide. The Long Beach peninsula in southwestern Washington is considered one of the prime areas for razor clams.

 CHEF NOTES

To clean razor clams, pour boiling water over the clams then rinse with cold water. Pull the clam from the shell and snip off the tough part of the neck, below the valve. Cut open the "zipper," cutting toward the end of the neck. Remove the digger and gills, then rinse.

2 abalones, shelled and soft and brown parts removed, leaving only the white muscle

2 razor clams, shelled and trimmed (see Chef Notes)

2 cups [480 mL] mayonnaise, prepared or homemade

¼ cup [60 mL] green olives, puréed

2 cups [480 mL] panko crumbs (Japanese breadcrumbs) (see page 579)

1 tablespoon [15 mL] garlic powder

1 teaspoon [5 mL] cayenne

2 eggs, beaten

Vegetable oil, for deep-frying

Roasted hot green peas, crushed, for garnish (optional)

ADVANCE PREPARATION

1. Gently pound the abalone and razor clams to relax the muscles. Cut into ½-inch [1-cm] cubes. Reserve refrigerated.

2. Mix the mayonnaise with the olive purée. Allow to stand 1 hour. (The olive mayonnaise can be made 1 day in advance.)

COOKING METHOD

3. Mix the panko crumbs with the garlic powder and cayenne.

4. Toss the abalone and razor clam morsels in the beaten egg.

5. Drain the morsels and toss them in the seasoned panko crumbs. Pat gently to remove any excess breading.

6. Deep-fry the morsels at 365°F [185°C] until golden brown and done, about 3 minutes.

SERVICE

7. Place about ⅔ cup [160 mL] of the fried morsels in the center of a plate, accompanied with a ramekin containing ¼ cup [60 mL] of olive mayonnaise. Garnish the plate with crushed roasted hot green peas, if desired.

Grilled Goat Cheese-Stuffed Grape Leaves

serves 8

Known as *chèvre* in France, fresh goat cheese is a relatively recent ingredient in American kitchens. In the early 1980s Alice Waters introduced this creamy, tangy cheese to restaurants and home kitchens through her Berkeley restaurant Chez Panisse, and goat cheese became a symbol of modern California cuisine, and has passed from a cliché to a necessary pantry item.

Originating in Italy, sun-dried tomatoes were a way to preserve the summer crop throughout the winter before modern canning methods were developed.

CHEF NOTES

To slice the cylinder of goat cheese, use fine sewing thread or dental floss, stretched tightly with both hands and pressed down to make the cuts. This will prevent crumbling, which may occur with a knife blade, although a very sharp, thin blade, dipped in warm water, also works. If using sun-dried tomatoes in dry form (not oil packed), plump them in hot water until pliable and soft and pat dry before use.

12 ounces [340 g] fresh goat cheese (in small cylinder form)

16 bottled grape leaves, rinsed and stems trimmed

16 garlic cloves, roasted until soft and peeled

16 oil-packed sun-dried tomatoes, drained

Olive oil, for grilling

Grilled baguette slices, for service

ADVANCE PREPARATION

1. Slice the goat cheese into 16 medallions, ¾ ounce [20 g] each (see Chef Notes).

ASSEMBLY OF THE GRAPE-LEAF PACKAGES

2. Spread out a grape leaf, vein side up. Place 1 piece of goat cheese in the center of the leaf. Add 1 garlic clove, followed by a sun-dried tomato.

3. Fold in the sides, over the fillings. Roll the package over, folding in the edges as you go. Shape into a round with your hands. Place, seam side down, on a sheet pan. Continue until all 16 packages are formed.

COOKING METHOD

4. Brush the packages with olive oil and grill directly over hot coals just until grill marks are formed. Rotate the packages 90 degrees and finish the grill markings.

5. Carefully turn the packages and grill 1 minute to warm the filling.

SERVICE

6. Serve 2 packages per person, grill marks up. You may want to cut 1 package open for presentation. Serve grilled baguette slices on the side.

Wild Mushroom and Hazelnut Pâté

serves 8

Oregon has the perfect climate and geography for producing wild mushrooms, which require moisture, shade, and heavily wooded areas. Decaying logs retain moisture very well, and stands of trees, especially conifers, provide the shade and a moderating effect on temperature. Most common species found in the Northwest are the American matsutake, king bolete, chanterelle, hedgehog, and truffle.

Some of the finest hazelnuts (also called filberts) in the world are grown in the Willamette River valley of Oregon, although Turkey produces the majority of the world's supply (Oregon accounts for a mere 3 percent). Oregon growers prune the hazelnut shrub into a tree for ease of harvesting, which occurs in mid-September.

6 tablespoons [90 mL] unsalted butter

2 bunches of scallions, white and light green parts only, sliced thin

4 garlic cloves, finely minced

2 pounds [900 g] assorted mushrooms, such as cèpes, matsutake, and chanterelles, finely diced

2 teaspoons [10 mL] fresh tarragon, chiffonade

½ cup [120 mL] flat-leaf parsley, chopped

2 cups [240 mL] hazelnuts, roasted, skinned, and coarsely chopped (see Chef Notes)

8 ounces [225 g] unsalted butter, cold, cut into ½-inch [1-cm] dice

⅛ teaspoon [0.5 mL] Louisiana-style hot sauce

2 tablespoons [30 mL] Pernod or other licorice-flavored liqueur

Salt and pepper to taste

Sliced mushrooms, for garnish

Assorted crackers and water biscuits, for service

ADVANCE PREPARATION

1. Melt 6 tablespoons [90 mL] of butter over medium heat in a nonstick skillet. Sauté the scallions until soft. Add the garlic and sauté 30 seconds.

2. Add the mushrooms and sauté until soft and the released liquid has evaporated. Remove from heat and add the tarragon, parsley, and hazelnuts. Allow to cool completely.

ASSEMBLY OF THE PATÉ

3. Add the cooled ingredients to the workbowl of a food processor. Add the diced butter, hot sauce, and Pernod. Pulse to form a paste that has some texture. Adjust the seasonings with salt and pepper.

4. Pack ½ cup [120 mL] of pâté into each of 8 individual ramekins. Cover with plastic film and refrigerate until firm. (The pâté can be made 1 day in advance.)

To roast and skin hazelnuts, spread raw hazelnuts in a single layer on a sheet pan and bake in a 350°F [170°C] oven until the skins darken and crack. Allow to cool. Rub the nuts between your hands, allowing the papery skins to fall to the pan below.

SERVICE

5. Allow the paté to come to room temperature before service. Top the pâté with a mushroom slice and accompany with assorted crackers.

The Southwest

Texas, New Mexico,

and Arizona

**Pastry Pockets Stuffed with Seasoned Pork
and Red Chile Sauce**
Sopapillas con Puerco y Chile Colorado

Green Corn Chicken Tamales with Tomatillo Sauce

Grilled Jalapeño-Stuffed Dove Breast Skewers with Bacon
Hunting Lease Dove Breast

Warm Cheese Dip with Chiles
Chile con Queso

Pastry Pockets Stuffed with Seasoned Pork and Red Chile Sauce Sopapillas con Puerco y Chile Colorado

serves 8 (3 *sopapillas* per person)

Sopapillas, fried puffed pastries, are New Mexican in origin. *Sopapilla* means "sofa pillow" in Spanish, and the name is descriptive of the finished shape of the pastries. They are made with a dough that is biscuit-like; in fact, they are often made using Bisquick in New Mexico restaurants. They can be eaten with butter and honey or sugar as a dessert but are more commonly served stuffed with meat and cheese then topped with the famous New Mexican red sauce made from dried red chile powder. The best dried red chile comes from the towns of Chimayo and Hatch. Care should be taken to ensure that the powder used is fresh. The heat value of the chile powder can vary widely and often the heat rating is listed on the package.

SHREDDED PORK

1¼ pounds [560 g] pork shoulder

2½ to 3 cups [600 to 720 mL] chicken stock or to cover

½ onion, chopped coarsely

4 garlic cloves, bruised

2 whole cloves

6 peppercorns

½ teaspoon [3 mL] cumin seed

1 bay leaf

Pinch of dried oregano

1 tablespoon [15 mL] New Mexico red chile powder

RED CHILE SAUCE: MAKES ABOUT 3 CUPS [720 mL]

3 tablespoons [45 mL] lard or vegetable oil

¾ cup [180 mL] onion, diced

3 garlic cloves, minced

1 teaspoon [5 mL] ground cumin

¼ teaspoon [1 mL] dried oregano

3 tablespoons [45 mL] flour

½ cup [120 mL] New Mexico red chile powder

2½ cups [600 mL] reserved pork stock or chicken stock

½ teaspoon [3 mL] salt

¼ teaspoon [1 mL] sugar

SOPAPILLA DOUGH: MAKES TWENTY-FOUR 2-INCH [5-CM] PASTRIES

2½ cups [600 mL] all-purpose flour

2½ teaspoons [12 mL] baking powder

¼ teaspoon [1 mL] salt

2 tablespoons [30 mL] lard or vegetable shortening, cold, cut into small dice

¾ cup [180 mL] cold water

Vegetable oil, for deep-frying

Sopapillas can be stuffed with a variety of fillings, including seafood, beef, or chicken. Using the tomatillo sauce found in the recipe Green Corn Chicken Tamales with Tomatillo Sauce (page 66), the *sopapillas* can be topped with half red and half green chile sauces, a common technique in New Mexico. To make the dough using Bisquick, use about ¼ cup [60 mL] water to 1¼ cups [300 mL] of the Bisquick mix.

SOPAPILLAS

2 cups [480 mL] cheddar or Monterey jack cheese, shredded

ADVANCE PREPARATION

1. Bring the pork shoulder and chicken stock to cover to a boil. Reduce the heat and simmer rapidly for 10 minutes, skimming off the foam that rises to the top.

2. Add the seasonings and return to a boil. Reduce the heat to a low simmer and cook until the meat is tender, about 45 minutes. Allow the meat to cool in the liquid, then remove and drain, reserving the strained liquid.

3. Cut the meat into large cubes. Place the cubes in a food processor with the plastic dough blade and pulse in batches, about 10 seconds per batch. The pork can also be shredded, using 2 forks to pull the meat in opposite directions. Reserve until ready to use, refrigerated. (The shredded pork can be prepared 1 day in advance.)

PREPARATION OF THE CHILE SAUCE

4. Heat the lard or oil over medium heat in a heavy saucepan and sauté the onion and garlic until soft.

5. Add the cumin, oregano, and flour and stir well to make a roux. Cook the roux, while stirring constantly, for 3 minutes, or until light brown.

6. Whisk the chile powder into the reserved stock, stirring to prevent lumps.

7. Cook at a rapid simmer, while stirring, for 15 minutes. Since red chile scorches easily, be careful when simmering. The finished sauce should be thick enough to heavily coat a spoon and should have no raw chile powder taste. Season with the salt and sugar. Taste and adjust the seasoning. Refrigerate, preferably overnight.

PREPARATION OF THE SOPAPILLA DOUGH

8. Sift the flour, baking powder, and salt together. Using a food processor or pastry knife, cut in the lard until very small flakes are formed.

9. Pour in the water all at once and mix to form a dough. Heavily flour a board and work the dough quickly, kneading for several minutes, adding flour if needed to form a smooth, elastic dough. Cover with plastic film and chill for 15 minutes.

10. Divide the dough into thirds, rolling each third into a 4 × 8-inch [10 × 20-cm] rectangle. Trim the edges and cut into eight 2-inch [5-cm] squares. Repeat for the other pieces of dough. Do not stack the squares as they will stick together. Keep them covered until needed.

COOKING METHOD

11. Heat the vegetable oil to 400°F [205°C] and fry several dough squares at a time. Do not crowd the pan. Gently lower the squares into the oil, and, using a slotted spoon, hold the squares under the oil until they begin to puff up.

12. Fry for 15 to 20 seconds, then flip the squares over and lightly brown the other side. Drain on paper towels and keep warm until service. If they don't puff at first, tap gently on the top (being mindful of the danger of hot oil).

ASSEMBLY AND SERVICE

13. Make a slit in the sides of a *sopapilla* to open. Toss the shredded pork with ¼ cup [60 mL] of the chile sauce and all but ¼ cup [60 mL] of the cheese.

14. Place about 2 tablespoons [30 mL] of filling into each *sopapilla*. Close and keep warm until service. (The *sopapillas* can be prepared in advance and warmed in the oven before service.)

15. Place 3 stuffed *sopapillas* on a plate and top with ¼ cup [60 mL] of red chile sauce. Sprinkle lightly with the remaining cheese to garnish. Serve immediately.

Green Corn Chicken Tamales with Tomatillo Sauce

serves 8

Green corn isn't really green; the expression simply means that the corn is ripe and fresh, not dried like what is used for masa and in cornmeal. The tamales can be stuffed with any filling desired, but are traditionally filled with a few strips of green chile. This version uses chicken that has been poached in a flavorful broth before shredding, then combined with cheese and scallions. The tomatillo sauce and the condiments should be served on the side, as the tamale tends to absorb sauce and crumble.

CHEF NOTES

Dried corn husks are available at Latin American markets and specialty food shops. They need to be soaked in warm water and drained before using. The tamales may be served with green or red chile sauce and with or without the pork added to the filling.

POACHED CHICKEN

One 3 to 4 pound [1.4 to 1.8 kg] whole chicken

1 onion, thickly sliced

2 garlic cloves, bruised

2 whole cloves

1 carrot, sliced

1 celery rib, sliced

1 bay leaf

2 to 3 tablespoons [30 to 45 mL] cilantro stems

TOMATILLO SAUCE: MAKES ABOUT 3 CUPS [720 mL]

1½ pounds [675 g] tomatillos, husked and rinsed

4 scallions, trimmed

3 large garlic cloves

2 to 3 serrano chiles, stems removed

½ cup [120 mL] rich chicken stock

1 tablespoon [15 mL] lime juice

½ cup [120 mL] cilantro, rinsed, chopped

Salt to taste

Pinch of sugar to taste (optional)

TAMALE MASA

3 ears fresh corn, shucked, cut into kernels

4 ounces [110 g] Monterey jack cheese, shredded

¼ cup [60 mL] masa harina

4 ounces [110 g] lard, at room temperature

2 ounces [55 g] butter, at room temperature

2 garlic cloves, very finely minced

1 tablespoon [15 mL] sugar

1 tablespoon [15 mL] cream, or more if needed

Salt to taste

24 dry corn husks, soaked in warm water 5 minutes

¾ cup [180 mL] Monterey Jack cheese, shredded

¾ cup [180 mL] scallions, thinly sliced

GARNISH

Sour cream

Black olives

Avocado slices

ADVANCE PREPARATION

1. To poach the chicken, combine all of the ingredients in a stockpot and bring to a boil. Reduce the heat and simmer until the juices run clear when the chicken is pierced at the thickest part of the thigh with the point of a knife, about 20 minutes.

2. Remove the chicken, drain, reserving the stock, and allow the chicken to cool enough to handle.

3. Remove and discard the skin. Shred the chicken meat into ½-inch [1-cm] wide pieces. Reserve until ready to assemble the tamales. (The chicken can be prepared 1 day in advance.)

PREPARATION OF THE TOMATILLO SAUCE

4. Char the tomatillos, scallions, garlic cloves, and chiles over a stove burner or under a broiler. Remove and allow to cool to room temperature.

5. Place the vegetables and any accumulated juices in a food processor and purée. Place the purée in a saucepan and add the remaining sauce ingredients. Bring just to a boil, adjust the seasonings, and keep warm until service.

PREPARATION OF THE TAMALE MASA

6. Purée the corn kernels in a food processor with 4 ounces [110 g] of the cheese. Stir in the masa harina.

7. Using an electric mixer, cream the lard and butter together until fluffy. Add the corn-cheese mixture, garlic, sugar, cream, and salt and continue to mix until the mixture is light and fluffy.

ASSEMBLY OF THE TAMALES

8. Lay out a softened corn husk. Spread 3 tablespoons [45 mL] of the corn-cheese dough down the center, approximately ¼ inch [6 mm] thick, with at least 2 inches [5 cm] of border surrounding the dough.

9. Place 1½ to 2 tablespoons [25 to 30 mL] of shredded chicken down the center of the dough and top with 1½ tablespoons [25 mL] of shredded cheese. Sprinkle ½ tablespoon [8 mL] of scallions over the top.

10. Fold in the sides of the husks, forming a cylinder to encase the filling with dough. Tie each end with kitchen twine or strips of corn husk. Continue until all the tamales are fashioned.

COOKING METHOD

11. Stack the tamales horizontally in a large steamer, being sure that steam can surround each tamale. Steam the tamales for 45 minutes.

SERVICE

12. Serve each person 3 tamales, accompanied with ½ cup [120 mL] of sauce, a dollop of sour cream, some black olives, and avocado slices. For presentation, open 1 tamale, leaving the others closed.

Grilled Jalapeño-Stuffed Dove Breast Skewers with Bacon Hunting Lease Dove Breast

serves 8

At certain times of the year, Texas skies can be filled with white wing doves. Hunting doves is a favorite pastime for Texans, and this dish, called "hunting lease dove breast," is the traditional way to prepare them. The term "hunting lease" refers to the practice of leasing the hunting rights to a parcel of land, common today as many Texans now reside in urban areas. Dove breasts are the only part of the bird used. Breasts are easiest to grill and smoke when they are secured on metal skewers, but they can be grilled and turned individually as well. Grill or smoke the breasts slowly over an indirect fire using mesquite, pecan, or oak coals.

CHEF NOTES

Chicken breasts, boneless chicken thighs, or boneless duck breast pieces may be substituted for the dove breasts. A tortilla may be placed on the plate, under the skewer for presentation.

16 boneless dove breasts

I cup [240 mL] Italian-style vinaigrette salad dressing

3 garlic cloves, finely minced, crushed with the side of a knife

3 tablespoons [45 mL] pickling juice from pickled jalapeño chiles

4 slices meaty smoked bacon, cut into fourths

16 small pickled jalapeño chiles (whole, with stem removed) or 8 large pickled jalapeño chiles, stemmed and cut in half

24 segments white parts of scallion, 2 inches [5 cm] long each

⅓ cup [80 mL] tequila

2 tablespoons [30 mL] fresh lime juice

I tablespoon [15 mL] red chile powder

½ tablespoon [8 mL] ground cumin

I teaspoon [5 mL] dried oregano

½ teaspoon [3 mL] garlic powder

Salt and pepper to taste

8 skewers, soaked in water 30 minutes if wooden

ADVANCE PREPARATION

1. Combine the dove breasts, the vinaigrette, garlic, and jalapeño pickling juice in a resealable plastic bag. Toss to coat thoroughly. Marinate at least 8 hours, or overnight, refrigerated.

2. Sauté the bacon pieces until crisp. Reserve the bacon fat.

PREPARATION OF THE SKEWERS

3. Drain the dove breasts, reserving the marinade. Place a small jalapeño chile into the center of each dove breast. Place one segment of scallion on a skewer, followed by a wrapped stuffed dove breast. Repeat with a scallion segment and a second wrapped dove breast, finishing with a scallion segment. Repeat for the remaining skewers. Refrigerate until ready to cook. (The skewers can be assembled several hours in advance.)

COOKING METHOD

4. Combine the reserved marinade, reserved bacon fat, tequila, lime juice, chile powder, cumin, oregano, garlic powder, and

salt and pepper and mix well to form a basting liquid. Bring to a boil and allow to cool.

5. Build an indirect charcoal fire of mesquite, pecan, or oak wood or briquettes on 1 side of a smoker or grill, so that it will burn slowly for an extended period, providing plenty of smoke.

6. Place the skewers as far away from the heat source as possible and cook slowly, while turning and basting frequently and lightly. The skewers are done when the dove breasts reach an internal temperature of 155°F [70°C], 8 to 10 minutes.

SERVICE

7. Serve 1 skewer per person, right from the grill, with a final basting of marinade. Top each breast with a piece of crisp bacon.

Warm Cheese Dip with Chiles Chile con Queso

serves 8 (⅔ cup [160 mL] per person)

Chile con queso is authentic Tex-Mex fare, Mexican in origin and adopted by Texans. This cheese dip is now known nationally and is available in fast food restaurants and bottled to be sold in supermarkets. Presented here is the more refined of two versions. The version most Texans grew up with uses Velveeta. This fire-roasted version utilizes chipotle chiles. Both versions are superior to manufactured cheese dips (the Velveeta version is closest to the hearts of all true Texans).

CHEF NOTES

Many mild cheeses that melt well could be substituted in this recipe. Any favorite fresh, roasted or dried chile could be substituted for the chiles used in either version. Prepared flaked crabmeat, minced grilled chicken, chopped grilled shrimp, or seasoned, cooked ground or minced beef or pork can be added as well. In the early days, Fritos were more commonly served than tostados.

1 cup [240 mL] Mexican queso blanco cheese, shredded

1 cup [240 mL] Monterrey jack cheese, shredded

1 cup [240 mL] longhorn cheese, shredded

4 teaspoons [20 mL] cornstarch

4 large Roma or Italian-style tomatoes, fire roasted and chopped

1 bunch of scallions, fire roasted and puréed

5 large garlic cloves, fire roasted, peeled, and puréed

3 to 6 canned chipotle chiles in adobo, minced, to taste

2 to 4 tablespoons [30 to 60 mL] adobo sauce from the canned chipotles to taste

½ teaspoon [3 mL] salt

2 tablespoons [30 mL] fresh cilantro, chopped

3 cups [720 mL] heavy cream, at room temperature

1 dried New Mexico or Ancho chile, toasted lightly, seeded, and cut into very fine shreds

Warm corn tortilla chips (tostados), for service

ADVANCE PREPARATION

1. All advanced preparation may be found in the ingredient list.

COOKING METHOD

2. Mix the 3 cheeses together in a bowl and toss with the cornstarch to coat.

3. Heat all ingredients, except the combined cheeses and the shredded chile, in a double boiler until thoroughly heated. Slowly sprinkle in the cheese mixture, while stirring, until well blended and the cheese has melted. (Both versions may be cooked in a microwave oven using short heating and stirring periods.)

SERVICE

4. Serve ⅔ cup [160 mL] of cheese dip in a small bowl, accompanied with a basket of warm tostados. Sprinkle minced shreds of red chile over the top as a garnish.

Mexico

Meatballs in "Burnt" Chipotle and Tomato Sauce
Albóndigas en Salsa Chipotle Quemado

Picadillo-Stuffed Poblano Chiles in Creamy Walnut Sauce
Chiles en Nogada

Braised Pork Ribs in Roasted Chile-Tomato Sauce
Costillas de Puerco con Salsa de Tuxtepec

Tortilla Stacks Layered with Shark and Black Beans
Pan de Cazón

Bacon-Wrapped Garlic Shrimp
Camarónes al Mojo de Ajo con Tocino

**Egg-Stuffed Tortillas in Pumpkin Seed and
Spicy Tomato Sauces**
Papadzules

Wild Mushroom Turnovers with Tomatillo-Mushroom Sauce
Empanadas de Hongos Silvestres con Salsa Verde

COOKING AUTHENTIC DISHES from Mexico completely changes your perception of its cuisine. It is not the Mexican cooking found throughout the southwestern United States or California, and it is certainly not that offered by fast food chains across America. Mexican cooking is as sophisticated as any of the world's renowned cooking styles. Its sauces are varied and complex. Its techniques of ingredient preparation are unique and worthy of duplication. The most modest Mexican cook understands the concept of layering flavors by the judicious use of spices and herbs as well as the concept of adding flavor and dimension to each ingredient of a dish. Robust eaters, the Mexicans' appreciation for food is seen everywhere. Street food is quite popular, and the *antojitos* (little snacks) hold you over between meals.

Mexico is the fourth largest country in the Western Hemisphere and possesses the fifteenth largest economy in the world. Its topography is extremely diverse, with tropical rain forests in the south and arid desert in the north. Two mountain ranges, both called Sierra Madre, run down the sides of the country, creating the central plateau, its most important geographical feature. Mexico is a land of volcanoes, snow-capped mountain peaks, white sand beaches, deserts, and tropical rain forests. Mexico is bordered by the United States to the north (almost 2000 miles long), the Pacific Ocean to the west, the Gulf of Mexico and the Caribbean Sea to the east, and Guatemala and Belize to the south. It has 6000 miles of coastline, two-thirds of which is on the western coast. Almost 1200 miles wide in the north, Mexico narrows to less than 150 miles across in the south.

On the basis of altitude, Mexico may be divided into regions, which parallel the distinct cuisines found throughout this vast country. These are the Central Plateau, Pacific Lowlands, Gulf Coast Plains, the Yucatán Peninsula, the Southern Highlands, the Chiapas Highlands, and the Baja Peninsula. In the north, including the Baja Peninsula across to the Gulf of Mexico, the rugged cuisine referred to as *norteño* is found. It is ranch style in nature, and the flavor of beef dominates. Tomato sauces are less spicy than in the south, with the main chile being the mild Anaheim. Unique to the *norteño* table is the *tortilla de harina* (flour tortilla), in contrast to the ubiquitous corn tortilla found throughout the rest of Mexico. The northern Pacific coast yields a staggering variety of seafood, as the Pacific joins with the Gulf of California. It is no surprise that fish and seafood are main staples of the cuisine here. Shrimp is a popular filling for tamales; tuna is served as ceviche; and swordfish is slow smoked over mesquite wood. Guadalajara, the region's famous interior city, has some of the finest food in all of Mexico. Its most famous dish is *pozole*, a stew of hominy and pork. Shredded goat meat spiced with chiles, called *birria*, is also extremely popular.

The southern coast of the Pacific, the so-called Mexican Riviera, which includes Acapulco, has more in common with the Caribbean style of cooking than with its interior highlands neighbors. Distinctly Latin in nature, the food is internationally sophisticated. Many dishes are rice based, showing the Asian influence that came when it was an important trading port in colonial times. Curry powder is an important spice in this region's cuisine.

Inland are the highland regions of Oaxaca and Chiapas. In Chiapas, more than anywhere else, the influence of native Indian cuisine has not been diluted. The chiles are among Mexico's hottest, and the natives prefer a sweet aspect to their savory dishes. A common dish is pork roast stuffed with cinnamon-scented mincemeat. Flowers are occasionally included in regional dishes, *tamales de puchulu* (corn tamales filled with orange flower petals) for example.

Oaxaca boasts some of the most original cuisine in all of Mexico, and its sauces are famous. Many consider it the heart of Mexican cooking. Moles, complex sauces that may include up to thirty ingredients, are found in seven traditional varieties (*colorado*, *amarillo*, and *negro* are the most popular). Squash, beans, and corn make up the holy trinity of this cuisine. Ground toasted seeds thicken sauces and garnish dishes; pomegranate is also quite common. Nopales, or cactus pads, are commonly served as a side dish. One favorite food of native Oaxacans that will probably not catch on with our readers is *chapulines*, toasted grasshoppers (legend has it that eating *chapulines* in Oaxaca assures the return of the visitor to that lovely state). A popular seasoning is *sal de guasano*, made from salt, chile powder, and dried *maguay* worms. Eggs are popular here, and the region is famous for its cheeses. Cacao is cultivated in Oaxaca, and chocolate makes its way into the *mole* sauces. Oaxacan cooks are known for heightening flavor by charring vegetables before incorporating them into sauces. Chiles, tomatoes, and onions are roasted in the coals while the tortillas are cooking above them on the *comal*, or griddle.

The lower states of Michoacán, Guanajuato, and Quetero show the most Spanish influence in their cuisine, with such dishes as stuffed tongue and *fiambre*, a cold meat dish. Native ingredients do appear, especially cacti of all varieties. Prickly pear cactus fruit is enjoyed in many ways, as are the cactus blossoms.

The Gulf of Mexico region is characterized by the foods found in the states of Tabasco and Veracruz. Mangoes and other tropical fruits and shellfish and seafood such as crab and shrimp are common. There is a Caribbean flavor to the cuisine, and it has distinctly Creole elements, reminiscent of Cuba, Puerto Rico, and New Orleans. The bayou region has elements of Cajun cookery as well. Mediterranean influences abound with the use of olives, capers, garlic, and limes.

The Yucatán Peninsula separates the Gulf of Mexico and the Caribbean Sea. Fiercely territorial, the local people treat the peninsula almost as a separate nation. Its people are Mayan in origin and maintain many elements of the ancient Mayan cuisine. The use of ground roasted pumpkin seeds in sauces, for example, is a holdover from this Mayan heritage. Cooking influences come from the Caribbean, especially Cuba, unlike much of the rest of Mexico. The habanero chile is grown in Mexico only in the Yucatán (habanero means Havana chile). The *xcatik* chile is also unique to the peninsula. Yucatán cuisine relies heavily on spice mixtures known as *recados*, typically comprised of allspice, oregano, cumin, chiles, and roasted garlic. Ground annatto seeds are the main ingredient of the most popular of *recados*, called achiote, which give a deep red color as well as flavor to pork and other meats cooked in a *pibil*, or pit. Game such as deer, wild turkey, and rabbit are quite common. The Gulf yields a variety of fish and shellfish. A highly favored fish is the *cazón*, a small shark, and oysters, crab, and shrimp are popular seafood. Corn, which has been cultivated for over three thousand years on the peninsula, is the staple food.

Common to all of the regional cuisines are the indigenous ingredients of corn, tomatoes, squash, and chiles. Such spices and herbs as cumin, oregano, and epazote are found everywhere. Beans are also integral to Mexican cuisine and are found in endless varieties and preparations. Brought from the Orient, rice has become a staple of the Mexican dinner table. The Spaniards introduced livestock to Mexico, and the pig proved essential to Mexican cooking. Rather than the meat, the lard rendered from the pig became significant; it is the fat most often used in cooking. Also introduced by Spain were cattle (the source of milk and cheese), citrus fruits, wheat, wine, olives, garlic, and vinegar.

Common cooking techniques include a three-stage cooking method for meats, poultry, and game. The meat is first braised or poached in a rich broth until tender, then pansautéed for color, and finally added to a sauce where it simmers for up to an hour. Ingredients meant for a sauce are first charred or roasted to heighten flavor. If fresh vegetables are puréed, they are added to a skillet and reduced before adding to stock or other liquid. The modern food processor is indispensable when making the sauces of Mexico; it takes the place of the *molcajete*, a three-legged stone mortar with pestle.

Meatballs in "Burnt" Chipotle and Tomato Sauce Albóndigas en Salsa Chipotle Quemado

CENTRAL MEXICO

serves 8 (about 4 meatballs per person)

Every world cuisine cooks meatballs, and their origin is most likely the Middle East. The meatball recipes known in Mexico were introduced by the Spanish conquerors. Regional variations have developed over the years, but this dish is enjoyed all over Mexico. This version includes the best aspects of recipes from Guadalajara, Ixtapa, and Mexico City.

 CHEF NOTES

Be sure to scrape the seeds from the chiles before using. As with all chile dishes, more or less chile may be used to reflect personal taste. A shortcut to using the dried chiles in this recipe is to use 3 canned chipotle chiles in adobo, adding a tablespoon of sauce from the can.

BEEF AND PORK MEATBALLS

3 fresh mint leaves

¼ teaspoon [1 mL] thyme

¼ teaspoon [1 mL] marjoram

½ bay leaf

½ teaspoon [3 mL] comino (ground cumin)

½ teaspoon [3 mL] black pepper

1 teaspoon [5 mL] salt

3 tablespoons [45 mL] half-and-half

1 egg yolk

2 garlic cloves, minced

½ slice stale bread

8 ounces [225 g] ground beef

4 ounces [110 g] ground pork (30% fat content)

¼ cup [60 mL] cooked rice

1 hard-boiled egg, finely chopped

CHIPOTLE AND TOMATO SAUCE

6 dried chipotle chiles

2 tablespoons [30 mL] lard or vegetable oil

1½ pounds [675 g] tomatoes, fire roasted or broiled

1 small white onion, thinly sliced

3 garlic cloves, minced

½ teaspoon [3 mL] comino

1 teaspoon [5 mL] salt, or to taste

2½ cups [600 mL] hot beef broth

6 fresh mint leaves, shredded, for garnish

16 corn tortillas

ADVANCE PREPARATION

1. To prepare the meatballs place the herbs, spices, salt, half-and-half, egg yolk, and garlic in a blender or processor and purée. Soak the bread in this mixture until soft, then com-

76 | The Appetizer Atlas

bine it with the ground beef and pork, the rice, and hard-boiled egg.

2. Blend the mixture well and form into 32 meatballs approximately 1 inch [2.5 cm] in diameter. Reserve. (The meatballs can be made several hours in advance.)

PREPARATION OF THE SAUCE

3. Lightly toast the chipotles on a griddle or over an open flame until they puff up and soften. Slit the chiles open and remove as many of the seeds as is practical.

4. Sauté the chiles in the lard or oil, flattening them as they cook with the back of a spoon, until they become very dark.

5. Drain the chiles, reserving the cooking oil, and place in a food processor with the roasted tomatoes and purée until smooth.

6. Sauté the onion in the oil used to sauté the chiles until just translucent. Add the garlic and sauté 30 seconds, then add the comino. Adjust for seasoning with salt.

7. Add the tomato-chipotle purée and sauté over medium-high heat while scraping and stirring constantly, until the sauce is reduced and thick.

COOKING METHOD

8. Add the hot beef broth to the reduced sauce. Stir well and increase the heat to a simmer. Gently lower the meatballs into the sauce. The sauce should just cover them (add a little hot water if necessary).

9. Cover the pan and simmer the meatballs for 20 minutes, turning periodically. Continue to cook, uncovered, for 20 minutes.

SERVICE

10. Serve 4 meatballs per person in a small pool of sauce. Garnish with shredded mint leaves and accompany with 2 fresh corn tortillas per person.

Picadillo-Stuffed Poblano Chiles in Creamy Walnut Sauce Chiles en Nogada

serves 8

This famous dish is said to have been developed by the residents of Puebla to honor General Don Augustín de Iturbide at a celebratory banquet held in August 1821, after the signing of the Treaty of Córdoba. All of the dishes served at the banquet featured the colors of the Mexican flag (green chiles, white sauce, and red pomegranate seeds). Still a popular dish, *chiles en nogada* is often served in August when walnuts and pomegranates come into season.

1½ cups [360 mL] walnut halves, soaked overnight (see **Advance Preparation**)

8 medium poblano chiles, roasted, peeled, and left whole

PICADILLO STUFFING

¼ cup [60 mL] butter or lard

4 garlic cloves, bruised

3 garlic cloves, minced

1 large onion, diced

1½ pounds [675 g] lean pork, ground

¼ cup [60 mL] blanched and slivered almonds

¼ cup [60 mL] raisins

3 tablespoons [45 mL] candied citron, chopped

1 pear, peeled, cored, and diced

1 peach, peeled, pitted, and diced

2 medium tomatoes, diced

1 teaspoon [5 mL] cinnamon

¼ teaspoon [1 mL] ground cloves

⅛ teaspoon [0.5 mL] grated nutmeg

2 bay leaves

1 large pinch of dried thyme

1 tablespoon [15 mL] black pepper

½ cup [120 mL] dry white wine

Salt to taste

WALNUT CREAM SAUCE

½ cup [120 mL] blanched almonds, chopped

4 ounces [110 g] cream cheese

4 ounces [110 g] goat cheese

1 cup [240 mL] half-and-half

1 cup [240 mL] heavy cream

1 tablespoon [15 mL] grated onion

1 scant teaspoon [4 mL] ground cinnamon

1 tablespoon [15 mL] dry sherry

Many cooks in Mexico hold that stuffed chiles should be dipped in an egg batter, then deep-fried. This dish, however, is already quite rich without frying, and baking provides a fresher chile taste.

The dish may be prepared without meat by substituting a cheese stuffing made of equal parts of grated farmer's white cheese, goat cheese, and cream cheese seasoned with some grated onion, parsley, reduced amounts of the fruits and more finely diced, and the spices reduced in proportion.

Chiles may be roasted over a charcoal grill, a propane chile roaster, an open flame on a stove burner, on a comal or flat griddle, under a broiler, or even in a deep-fat fryer. The purpose is to evenly blister and char the skin of the chile, causing the skin to peel off easily, and for the flesh to cook slightly during the process. Once the skin is evenly blistered, the chiles should be placed into a paper or plastic bag and sealed so that they may steam until the chiles are cool enough to handle. (This steaming process loosens the blistered skin from the flesh of the chile.) Care should be taken whenever handling chiles. Wear latex gloves to protect your hands. Do not touch your

1 teaspoon [5 mL] salt

1 teaspoon [5 mL] sugar

Seeds from 2 small or 1 large pomegranate

Cilantro or flat-leaf parsley leaves for garnish

ADVANCE PREPARATION

1. Cover the walnuts with boiling water and allow them to soak for 5 to 10 minutes, testing the nuts after 5 minutes and using the additional time if it is difficult to remove the skins. Peel the thin papery skins off the walnuts by rubbing them in a kitchen towel or with a paring knife. Cover the skinned walnuts with cold water and soak them overnight.

2. Slit the prepared poblano chiles down 1 side to remove the seeds and ribs with a spoon. This slit will be used for stuffing the chiles.

PREPARATION OF THE PICADILLO STUFFING

3. Heat the butter or lard in a nonstick skillet, add the bruised garlic, and cook for 1 or 2 minutes. Remove the garlic cloves, then add the minced garlic and onion.

4. Sauté until translucent, then add the ground pork and sauté until lightly browned.

5. Add the almonds, raisins, citron, pear, peach, and tomatoes, stirring well to combine. Cook over moderate heat for 20 to 25 minutes, or until the mixture begins to thicken slightly.

6. Add the cinnamon, cloves, nutmeg, bay leaves, thyme, pepper, and wine. Season with salt and simmer for 45 minutes, or until the mixture thickens, stirring occasionally. Remove the bay leaves and allow to cool.

PREPARATION OF THE WALNUT CREAM SAUCE

7. Place the prepared walnuts and the sauce ingredients in a blender or food processor. Blend or process to a smooth sauce. If too thin add a small piece of trimmed white bread and process. Refrigerate for at least 3 hours. The sauce should be cold for service.

eyes, nose, mouth, or any other sensitive area of the body until you have thoroughly washed your hands with soap and hot water. The charred skin may be removed under a thin stream of running water (some critics argue that doing so dilutes the flavor of the roasted chile) or by laying the chile on a work surface and, using the dull back of a knife, carefully scraping off the loosened charred and blistered skin.

COOKING METHOD

8. Gently stuff the chiles with the picadillo mixture before service. (Stuffing the chiles can be done up to 2 hours in advance.)

9. Place the stuffed chiles in a 250°F [120°C] oven for 10 minutes to warm them through.

SERVICE

10. Place a stuffed chile on a plate, slit side down. Top with the cold walnut cream sauce, leaving part of the dark green chile exposed. Sprinkle pomegranate seeds liberally over the top and garnish with cilantro or parsley leaves.

Braised Pork Ribs in Roasted Chile-Tomato Sauce Costillas de Puerco con Salsa de Tuxtepec

serves 8 (3 ribs per person)

The Tuxtepec region in the state of Oaxaca is a lush, fertile farming zone that extends through the north-central part of the state, adjacent to Veracruz. It was home to the ancient Chinantec people, and their descendants still farm the area today. The sweetness of the baby back pork ribs balances perfectly with the spicy acidity of this sauce.

CHEF NOTES

Regular racks of ribs may be used instead of baby back ribs. Cut these ribs in half lengthwise to produce riblets.

PORK RIBS

3 quarts [3 L] water

1 large onion, unpeeled, quartered

2 heads of garlic, halved

4 stalks celery with leaves

3 dried chiles de arbol or dried cayenne chiles

3 bay leaves

3 allspice berries

½ teaspoon [3 mL] black peppercorns, bruised

1 tablespoon [15 mL] salt

3 pounds [1.4 kg] baby back pork ribs, cut into individual riblets

ROASTED CHILE-TOMATO SAUCE

8 large ripe tomatoes, fire roasted

10 jalapeño chiles, fire roasted

6 scallions, fire roasted

8 garlic cloves, fire roasted

1 teaspoon [5 mL] sugar

¼ cup [60 mL] vegetable oil or lard

1 cup [240 mL] cilantro leaves

Salt and pepper to taste

16 homemade corn tortillas

ADVANCE PREPARATION

1. All advance preparation may be found in the ingredient list.

PREPARATION OF THE PORK RIBS

2. Bring 3 quarts [3 L] of water, the vegetables, herbs, spices, salt, and the pork ribs to a boil. Lower the heat and simmer for 20 to 30 minutes, or until about ¼ inch [0.5 cm] of bone shows at the end of the ribs. Skim off the foam as it rises to the top. Remove the ribs and reserve.

3. Raise the heat to a rolling boil and reduce the stock for 30 minutes, skimming the surface as it cooks.

4. Place the charred vegetables in a food processor with about 1 cup [240 mL] of the reserved rib stock and the sugar. Blend until smooth.

COOKING METHOD

5. Heat the oil in a large heavy skillet and brown the ribs. Remove the ribs and reserve.

6. Remove all but about 1 tablespoon [15 mL] of the oil. Add the chile-tomato purée and sauté while stirring constantly, for 5 minutes.

7. Add 3 cups [720 mL] of the reserved rib stock, lower the heat to a simmer, and cook the sauce for 30 minutes.

8. Return the ribs to the sauce and stir well to coat. Simmer for 10 minutes. Stir in the cilantro leaves and adjust the seasoning with salt and pepper.

SERVICE

9. Serve the ribs hot, with additional sauce in small bowls on the side. Fresh homemade corn tortillas are a perfect accompaniment. Serve 2 tortillas per person. Additional napkins will be needed.

Tortilla Stacks Layered with Shark and Black Beans Pan de Cazón

Makes 8 stacks

Pan de cazón (literally bread of small shark) is a wonderful composed stack of tortillas, shark, refried black beans, and spicy tomato sauce. In Campeche small blacktip sharks are used for this dish, and in Yucatán dogfish shark is used. Traditionally, the shark is boiled with seasonings and then shredded. Marinating and grilling the fish provides additional flavor.

CHEF NOTES

Traditionally, regular size tortillas (about 5 inches [13 cm]) are used for this dish, and it is assembled in 2 stacks, presented side by side. Then wedges are cut from each stack.

FISH

½ cup [120 mL] onion, diced

3 garlic cloves, minced

2 tablespoons [30 mL] epazote, chopped

½ teaspoon [3 mL] black pepper

I teaspoon [5 mL] salt

¼ cup [60 mL] sour orange juice (see page 116)

¼ cup [60 mL] olive oil

1½ pounds [675 g] shark fillet, sliced (mahi or other firm game fish may be substituted)

REFRIED BLACK BEANS

3 tablespoons [45 mL] lard or vegetable oil

⅓ cup [80 mL] onions, diced

3 cups [720 mL] cooked black beans, preferably cooked with epazote

I habanero chile, whole

SPICY TOMATO SAUCE

5 large tomatoes, fire roasted and diced

I onion, fire roasted and diced

2 garlic cloves, minced

⅓ cup [80 mL] sour orange juice

Salt to taste

I tablespoon [15 mL] sugar

I teaspoon [5 mL] black pepper

¼ cup [60 mL] lard or vegetable oil

¼ cup [60 mL] epazote, chopped

I habanero chile, whole

24 small (3-inch [8-cm]) fresh corn tortillas

Sprigs of epazote or cilantro, for garnish

ADVANCE PREPARATION

1. Combine the onions, garlic, epazote, pepper, salt, sour orange juice, and olive oil in a food processor and purée to form a marinade. Place the fish and the marinade in a resealable plastic bag and marinate for at least 4 hours, refrigerated.

PREPARATION OF THE REFRIED BEANS

2. Heat the lard or oil in a nonstick skillet and sauté the onion until translucent.

3. Add the beans and the whole habanero chile and sauté over medium-high heat, while stirring to prevent sticking, for 15 to 20 minutes, or until the mixture begins to thicken and can hold its shape. Remove the habanero chile and reserve the beans. (The refried beans can be made 1 day in advance, refrigerated, and reheated for service.)

PREPARATION OF THE TOMATO SAUCE

4. Combine the tomatoes, onion, garlic, sour orange juice, salt, sugar, and pepper in a food processor and pulse to form a slightly chunky sauce.

5. Heat the lard or oil in a large skillet, and sauté the sauce mixture for 5 minutes, stirring to prevent sticking.

6. Add the epazote and the habanero chile and sauté 10 minutes, or until the mixture begins to thicken. Adjust the seasoning, remove the whole habanero chile, and reserve the sauce. (The sauce may be made 1 day in advance and refrigerated until needed.)

COOKING METHOD

7. Have the tortillas, beans, and sauce hot, ready for assembly.

8. On an indirect charcoal grill over medium heat, grill the fish fillets until both sides are marked and the fish just begins to turn opaque. When it has cooled just enough to touch, shred or flake the fish and keep warm.

ASSEMBLY AND SERVICE

9. Dip a warm tortilla into the tomato sauce, place it on a work surface, and spread about 2 tablespoons [30 mL] of the refried beans over it.

10. Add about 1½ ounces [45 g] of the grilled fish, then top with 3 tablespoons [45 mL] of the sauce. Place another sauce-dipped tortilla on top of the stack and add another 1½ ounces [45 g] of fish.

11. Spread 1 ounce [30 g] of the bean mixture on a third sauce-dipped tortilla and place it on top of the stack, bean side down, and compress the stack slightly. Dress the top of the stack with about 3 tablespoons [45 mL] of sauce. Garnish with sprigs of epazote or cilantro. Serve warm.

Bacon-Wrapped Garlic Shrimp Camarónes al Mojo de Ajo con Tocino

serves 8 (2 shrimp per person)

Mojo de ajo is a classic seafood preparation found throughout Mexico; it is a specialty in Oaxacan coastal cities, such as Puerto Ángel and Ixtapa. It can be made with any type of seafood, fish fillets or shrimp being most popular. The shrimp are wrapped with bacon to prevent the garlic paste from leaking out as well as to add a smoky flavor.

CHEF NOTES

This preparation may be used with large scallops, langoustines, slipper lobsters, or lobster tails. You may also take thin fish fillets and spread one side with the garlic paste, then roll jelly-roll fashion. Secure the outside with a piece of bacon. The paste may also be placed on top of a thick fish fillet, with a little chicken stock and lime juice added to the bottom of the pan, then broiled.

16 jumbo shrimp, heads on, shells removed, tails slit lengthwise across the back for stuffing

½ teaspoon [3 mL] ground allspice

½ cup [60 mL] garlic cloves, peeled, whole

⅓ cup [80 mL] parsley leaves

1 tablespoon [15 mL] olive oil

1 tablespoon [15 mL] Worcestershire sauce

1 teaspoon [5 mL] ground black pepper

1 teaspoon [5 mL] salt

16 strips bacon, cooked until almost done, pliable but not crisp, blotted on paper towels

3 tablespoons [45 mL] vegetable oil

½ cup [120 mL] rich chicken stock

Juice of 1 lime

1 tablespoon [15 mL] chipotle chiles in adobo, drained and minced

1 tablespoon [15 mL] parsley, chopped

¼ cup [60 mL] butter, cut into ½-inch [1-cm] cubes, chilled

Parsley leaves, for garnish

ADVANCE PREPARATION

1. Combine the allspice, garlic, parsley leaves, olive oil, Worcestershire sauce, pepper, and salt in a food processor. Pulse well to form a paste. Reserve.

PREPARATION OF THE STUFFED SHRIMP

2. Place about 1 teaspoon [5 mL] of the garlic paste evenly inside the slit of each shrimp. Wrap each stuffed shrimp tightly with a strip of cooked bacon, securing each end with toothpicks. Reserve.

COOKING METHOD

3. Sauté the shrimp over medium heat in the vegetable oil for about 3 minutes per side. Remove the shrimp to a warm plate.

4. Add any remaining garlic paste to the skillet and deglaze with the stock and lime juice. Cook for 4 to 5 minutes more.

5. Remove the skillet from the heat and add the chipotle chiles, the chopped parsley, and the butter. Swirl the skillet off the heat to incorporate the butter.

SERVICE

6. Serve 2 shrimp per person on a warmed plate, topped with garlic sauce. Garnish with parsley leaves.

Egg-Stuffed Tortillas in Pumpkin Seed and Spicy Tomato Sauces Papadzules

serves 12 (one stuffed tortilla per person)

In Mayan dialect *papadzule* means "food for the lords." This attractive dish was prepared by the native Mayan people of ancient Yucatán for the arrival of the Spaniards. The use of ground pumpkin seeds is an ancient Mayan technique found across Mesoamerica. This dish should be served warm.

 **CHEF NOTES**

If the pumpkin seed sauce is lumpy after adding the remainder of the broth, whisk it vigorously or purée it in a food processor. Be careful not to burn the pumpkin seed sauce when heating.

PICKLED ONION GARNISH

1 quart [1 L] water

1 large red onion, cut into thick slices

1 large white onion, cut into thick slices

4 garlic cloves, peeled, whole

1½ cups [360 mL] cider vinegar

Salt to taste

1 tablespoon [15 mL] sugar

½ tablespoon [8 mL] ground allspice

1 tablespoon [15 mL] oregano leaves

3 bay leaves

¼ teaspoon [1 mL] dried thyme

3 güero chiles, cut into thick slices (Hungarian wax or banana peppers may be substituted)

SPICY TOMATO SAUCE (CHILTOMATE)

3 large tomatoes, roasted

1 large white onion, roasted

4 garlic cloves, roasted

2 tablespoons [30 mL] vegetable oil or lard

1 habanero chile, whole

¼ cup [60 mL] chicken stock

Salt to taste

PUMPKIN SEED SAUCE

2½ cups [600 mL] clarified chicken stock

3 sprigs of epazote

½ onion, sliced

2 garlic cloves, bruised

1 drop of Caribbean habanero hot sauce

8 ounces [225 g] unsalted pumpkin seeds, hulled

TORTILLAS

12 fresh corn tortillas, warm

5 hard-boiled eggs, coarsely chopped, salted to taste

1. Bring the water to a boil and add the red and the white onions. Simmer for 3 minutes. Drain well and place in a nonreactive bowl.

2. Combine the remaining pickling ingredients, stir well to combine, and pour over the blanched onions. Toss thoroughly, place in a resealable plastic bag, and marinate for 24 hours, refrigerated. (The pickled onions can be made several days in advance.)

PREPARATION OF THE SPICY TOMATO SAUCE

3. Purée the tomatoes, onion, and garlic in a food processor.

4. Heat the oil or lard and sauté the tomato mixture. Add the whole habanero chile and the chicken stock. Season with salt to taste.

5. Simmer for 8 to 10 minutes, or until the sauce begins to thicken. Remove and discard the habanero. Reserve the sauce.

PREPARATION OF THE PUMPKIN SEED SAUCE

6. Heat the clarified chicken stock, add the epazote, onion, garlic, and habanero hot sauce. Simmer for 15 minutes, or until the broth is strongly flavored.

7. Strain out the vegetables and return the broth to the heat. Hold the broth just below simmer.

8. Toast the pumpkin seeds very lightly in a dry skillet, stirring constantly. The seeds should turn a brighter green color (do not brown). Have a lid ready to cover, as the seeds may begin to pop "explosively." Allow the seeds to cool, then grind them as fine as possible in a food processor.

9. Transfer the ground seeds to a shallow dish and pour ¼ cup [60 mL] of the hot epazote broth over the seed paste.

10. Transfer the paste to a saucepan and add the remainder of the epazote broth, while stirring, to produce a smooth, pale green sauce. Heat the sauce, stirring constantly, over low heat until the sauce thickens slightly. Reserve off heat.

11. Dip each tortilla briefly in the pumpkin seed sauce and loosely roll the tortilla around some of the chopped egg. Top with about ¼ cup [60 mL] of pumpkin seed sauce.

12. Dress the top of the enchilada with about 2 tablespoons [30 mL] of the spicy tomato sauce. Garnish the side of the plate with the pickled onion mixture. Serve warm.

Wild Mushroom Turnovers with
Tomatillo-Mushroom Sauce Empanadas de Hongos Silvestres con Salsa Verde

QUERÉTARO

Makes 16 empanadas

Wild mushrooms grow prolifically
in the forests of the Sierra Madre
Mountains during the rainy season. One of the best ways to enjoy this bounty is in a masa turnover, with a topping of a tomatillo,
chile, and wild mushroom sauce.

⌐ CHEF NOTES

If wild mushrooms are unavailable, substitute portobello, crimini, or shiitake mushrooms with
some dried wild mushrooms
added to heighten the flavor.

TOMATILLO-MUSHROOM SAUCE

⅓ cup [80 mL] onions, diced

2 garlic cloves, minced

1½ tablespoons [25 mL] butter or lard

2 serrano chiles, seeds and ribs removed, minced

6 tomatillos, husked, rinsed, and fire roasted or broiled

1 small tomato, fire roasted or broiled

⅛ teaspoon [0.5 mL] comino (ground cumin)

¼ cup [60 mL] rich chicken or pork stock

4½ ounces [130 g] wild mushrooms, chopped

WILD MUSHROOM FILLING

1 small onion, finely diced

1½ tablespoons [25 mL] butter or lard

8 ounces [225 g] wild mushrooms, chopped

4 garlic cloves, minced

1 tablespoon [15 mL] epazote leaves, chiffonade

½ teaspoon [3 mL] black pepper

Salt to taste

EMPANADAS

3 cups [720 mL] masa harina tortilla mix or 1½ pounds [675 g]
   prepared masa dough for tortillas

1 tablespoon [15 mL] salt

½ teaspoon [3 mL] garlic powder

Melted butter, for brushing rolled pastry

8 ounces [225 g] Gouda, Edam, or Muenster cheese, shredded

ADVANCE PREPARATION

1. Sauté the onion and garlic in butter over low heat until soft.
   Add the serrano chiles and cook until softened.

2. Blend this mixture with the tomatillos, tomato, comino, and
   stock in a food processor until smooth.

91 | Mexico

3. Pour this mixture into a nonstick skillet and bring to a boil. Cook for 3 minutes, while stirring and scraping.

4. Add the mushrooms, then lower the heat to a simmer and cook for 20 minutes. Reserve. (The sauce may be made 1 day in advance and refrigerated.)

PREPARATION OF THE WILD MUSHROOM FILLING

5. Sauté the onion in butter in a nonstick skillet until translucent.

6. Add the mushrooms and garlic and sauté over low heat for 15 to 20 minutes, or until most of the liquid has evaporated, adding more butter if needed to prevent sticking.

7. Add the epazote, pepper, and salt and stir well to combine. Reserve. (The filling may be made up to 1 day in advance and refrigerated.)

PREPARATION OF THE EMPANADAS

8. To make the dough for the empanadas, combine the masa harina, salt, and garlic powder and mix well. Slowly add 2¾ cups [660 mL] of water while stirring. Knead the mixture until a soft dough is formed, about 2 minutes, adding additional masa if needed for proper rolling consistency. Allow the dough to rest, covered, for 20 minutes.

9. Divide the dough into 16 pieces. Using a pasta roller, a rolling pin, or a tortilla press, roll the dough into circles 3 inches [8 cm] in diameter and ⅛ inch [3 mm] thick.

10. Brush each circle of dough with butter, then place 1 ounce [30 g] of cheese in the center. Add 1 to 2 tablespoons [15 to 30 mL] of the mushroom filling on top of the cheese. Top with a second circle of dough. Seal the edges with your fingers or the tines of a fork. Store, covered with plastic film and refrigerated, until required.

COOKING METHOD

11. Brush the tops of the empanadas with melted butter and bake at 375°F [190°C] for 5 minutes. Turn them over and continue to bake for 3 to 5 minutes more. (They may be baked in

advance, held, and reheated to order.) They may be cooked to order in a heavy, dry skillet or pan-fried in a little vegetable oil, well drained on paper towels. Hold warm, covered, until service.

SERVICE

12. Serve 1 warm empanada per person on a pool of the tomatillo-mushroom sauce.

Caribbean

Spiced Beef Turnovers with Mango Chutney
Meat Patties

Jerk-Marinated and Smoked Pork Spareribs
Jerk Ribs

Lamb Kebabs with Pineapple, Peppers, and Long Beans
Lambchi and Boonchi

Young Goat in Curry Ragôut
Curried Goat

Rum-Marinated Fried Chicken Drumettes
Chicharrón de Pollo

Codfish Fritters
Stamp and Go

Aromatic Spice-Stuffed Fried Fish Nuggets
Baxter's Road Fried Fish

THE ISLANDS OF THE CARIBBEAN, also known as the West Indies, belong to one of three main chains: the Greater Antilles, the Lesser Antilles, and the Netherland Antilles. The Greater Antilles includes the islands of Cuba, Hispaniola, Jamaica, and Puerto Rico. The Lesser Antilles includes the Leeward and Windward Islands, Barbados, and Trinidad and Tobago. The Leewards are comprised of Antigua, Guadeloupe, Monserrat, Saint Kitts and Nevis, and the Virgin Islands (British and U.S.) to the north and Martinique, Dominica, Grenada, Saint Lucia, Saint Vincent, and the Grenadines to the south. The Netherland Antilles is divided into the Netherland Leeward Islands and the Netherland Windward Islands. Curaçao, Bonaire, and Aruba make up the Leewards, and the south half of Saint Martin, Eustacius, and Saba make up the Windwards. All islands of the Caribbean are either coral or volcanic in composition. Climate varies from desert to lush tropical.

The culinary traditions of the West Indies were formed by four main influences. The earliest settlers were the Arawaks and the Caribs (from which the name Caribbean derives). The Arawaks migrated from South America, bringing their native Indian culture, produce, and tastes with them. They grew sweet potatoes, corn, beans, papaya, guava, and cassava and developed the cooking method we know as barbecue. While South American food is not known for being a very spicy cuisine, the Arawaks incorporated fiery chiles in their traditional dishes, adapting them to the native produce at hand. The more warlike Caribs, originating from the islands of Trinidad and part of Puerto Rico, conquered the peaceful Arawaks. Their diet was biased toward meat, and their dishes, though similar to the Arawak, introduced more protein into the diet. They enjoyed spicy foods as well.

The discovery of the West Indies by the major European powers was the second influence on Caribbean cooking. English, Dutch, Spanish, Portuguese, and French influences abound, both in cooking style and in the produce and meats introduced from distant world trading centers. Bananas were brought from the Canary Islands. Sugarcane was introduced to the region by Columbus on his second voyage. Oranges, limes, mangoes, rice, oil, and vinegar and wine were brought by the Spaniards. The Dutch brought an Indonesian influence, and the French brought their heightened culinary skills and awareness of properly prepared food. The single most influential import to the Islands with respect to cuisine was the African slaves brought to work on the plantations. This third influence turned out to be long lasting and helped to provide the basis for Caribbean cuisine found throughout the approximately seven thousand islands that make up the West Indies.

Africans brought with them okra, taro root, akee, and callaloo (spinach-like greens) and their cooking methods. They cooked in cast-iron pots and casseroles and wrapped foods in banana leaves. The Africans found a climate that was familiar to them and indigenous produce that could be worked into their recipes. They, too, added a love of spicy foods to the Caribbean cuisine (often to make palatable an otherwise bland diet furnished by the slave owners). Creoles, the offspring of marriages between Africans and Europeans, have had the most lasting influence on the cuisine of the Caribbean. They stewed the tough meats available to them, and this cooking method is still quite popular today. Spices were expensive, so they sought out native herbs and other local plants.

By 1845 the emancipation of the slaves brought the final influence to Caribbean cuisine. Without African slaves to work the plantations, others were needed to work the fields. Laborers were brought over from India and China. Curries were introduced from India and were rapidly assimilated (the national dish of Jamaica is curried goat). Tropical fruit chutneys were found to be a perfect foil to spicy foods. *Roti*, a curried meat wrap of Indian origin, is a favorite street and snack food of Trinidad. The cuisine of the Caribbean is truly an international affair.

With these varied influences, scattered over thousands of islands, it is surprising that there are so many similarities in the cuisines. One should consider the cooking in the Caribbean as a single cuisine with infinite minor variations. Pepperpot, curried goat, and codfish fritters are found everywhere, as is the liberal use of the fiery Scotch bonnet chile. Chile sauces, such as *ti-malice*, *sofrito*, *pique*, *chien*, and *piquante*, are plentiful. Curries and *colombos* (named for the then capital of Ceylon, now called Sri Lanka) and other rich stews are found on all of the islands. Barbecue and grilling are common cooking techniques, and spice pastes and rubs, such as the Jamaican jerk and bajan seasoning from Barbados, are used before grilling to enhance flavor.

Fresh fish, conch, and spiny lobster are caught daily, and such meats as goat and lamb are staples of the Caribbean diet as are bananas, pineapple, papaya, citrus, coconut, corn, rice, beans, okra, and sweet potatoes. Interesting differences, often subtle to the visitor or tourist, do exist. While curried goat is made in Haiti as well as in Jamaica, for example, in Haiti butter and olive oil are used for sautéing the meat (a French influence) while coconut oil is used in Jamaica.

Spiced Beef Turnovers with Mango Chutney Meat Patties

serves 12

Meat-filled turnovers are popular throughout the West Indies. Known as patties, *pastechis*, *pasteles,* or pies, they are quite similar, with slight variations in seasonings. They are eaten out of hand from vendors in the markets or on the streets. This version from Jamaica is filled with beef, but lamb or mutton, goat, fish, and shrimp are common fillings.

CHEF NOTES

The patties can be made in muffin tins using a second dough circle to form the lid. For patties the dough may be cut into 2-inch [5-cm] circles, with about 1 heaping teaspoon [6 mL] of the filling placed inside. The patties may be prepared ahead of time and frozen, or refrigerated, then reheated for service.

MANGO CHUTNEY

4 medium unripe mangoes, about 2 pounds [900 g], peeled and cut into 1-inch [2.5-cm] dice

2 tablespoons [30 mL] salt

8 ounces [225 g] tamarind pulp

½ cup [120 mL] boiling water

2 cups [480 mL] cane vinegar or malt vinegar

3 cups [720 mL] light brown sugar

4 garlic cloves, minced

¼ cup [60 mL] onion, grated

½ cup [120 mL] ginger, julienne

½ cup [120 mL] raisins

1½ teaspoons [8 mL] ground allspice

1 tablespoon [15 mL] mustard seeds

2 Scotch bonnet or habanero chiles, minced

Salt to taste

PASTRY DOUGH

4 cups [960 mL] flour

1½ teaspoons [8 mL] curry powder

½ teaspoon [3 mL] salt

3 ounces [85 g] unsalted butter

3 ounces [85 g] lard

4 to 5 tablespoons [60 to 75 mL] cold water

FILLING

1 teaspoon [5 mL] annatto seeds

2 tablespoons [30 mL] vegetable oil

1 pound [450 g] lean ground beef

1 onion, finely diced

3 garlic cloves, minced

1 to 2 Scotch bonnet or habanero chiles, minced

1 cup [240 mL] tomatoes, seeded and chopped

Salt and pepper to taste

I teaspoon [5 mL] curry powder

½ teaspoon [3 mL] dried thyme

2 slices bread, soaked in milk and squeezed dry, chopped

I egg white, well beaten

ADVANCE PREPARATION

1. All advance preparation may be found in the ingredient list.

PREPARATION OF THE CHUTNEY

2. Mix the mango and salt together and set aside for 2 hours in a colander to drain. Discard the liquid.

3. Cover the tamarind pulp with boiling water and allow to soak for 30 minutes. Press the pulp through a sieve and reserve the liquid.

4. Combine the diced mango and the tamarind liquid with all the other chutney ingredients in a heavy saucepan. Bring to a boil, lower the heat, and simmer for 30 to 45 minutes, stirring often to prevent sticking. The mango pieces should remain intact.

5. Adjust seasonings for salt and ladle into 3 sterilized 1-pint [480-mL] jars. Seal the tops. Allow to cool to room temperature, then refrigerate. (The chutney can be stored, refrigerated, for weeks.)

PREPARATION OF THE PASTRY

6. Sift the flour, curry powder, and salt together in a chilled bowl. Using a pastry knife, cut the butter and lard into the flour mixture to resemble coarse meal.

7. Pour 4 tablespoons [60 mL] of the water into the mixture, mix lightly, and gather into a ball. If the dough crumbles, add more water by drops until the dough holds together. Dust the ball with flour, then wrap in plastic film and refrigerate at least 1 hour. (The dough can be made 1 day in advance.)

PREPARATION OF THE FILLING

8. Sauté the annatto seeds in the oil for 2 minutes, or until the seeds have colored the oil.

9. Remove and discard the seeds, then add the beef. Break up the beef as it browns. Add the onion, garlic, and chile. Cook until the onion is translucent and tender.

10. Add the tomatoes, salt and pepper, curry powder, and thyme. Cook, stirring occasionally, for about 5 minutes, or until the mixture is fairly dry.

11. Add the bread and cook 3 to 4 minutes more. Remove from the heat and allow to cool to room temperature.

ASSEMBLING THE PATTIES

12. Roll out the pastry on a floured surface to ⅛ inch [3 mm] thick. Cut the dough into thirty-six 3-inch [8-cm] circles.

13. Place about 2 tablespoons [30 mL] of the filling on one side of the pastry circle. Lightly brush the inside edge of the dough with egg white. Fold the dough over to form a half-moon shape and crimp the edges with the tines of a fork.

COOKING METHOD

14. Place the patties on a parchment-lined cookie sheet and bake at 375°F [190°C] for about 20 minutes, or until flaky and golden brown on the edges. (The patties may be prepared ahead of time and frozen or refrigerated, then reheated for service.)

SERVICE

15. Serve 3 patties per person, hot or warm, accompanied by the mango chutney.

Jerk-Marinated and Smoked Pork Spareribs Jerk Ribs

serves 16 (2 to 3 ribs per person)

It is said that the Maroons, fierce runaway slaves who fled into the Blue Mountains, developed this technique to preserve wild boar after a kill. Jerk in its many forms is Jamaica's most popular dish, and jerk pork and chicken "pits," roadside stands where jerk is sold, are everywhere. In Jamaica jerk is usually smoked over green allspice wood. In the United States pecan wood is best for producing jerk smoke, with an occasional addition of water-soaked allspice berries on the edge of the coals. Any type of meat, fish, or fowl may be jerked, and all should be tried. First a spice rub is applied, then the ribs are steamed, marinated, and then finally slow-smoked and basted to finish.

CHEF NOTES

Larger racks of ribs are preferred for this dish. Avoid baby back ribs, which have less meat and a higher cost. Use seasoned oak if pecan wood is not available, adding some green wood or soaked wood chips for smoke. Add the allspice berries periodically for extra flavor. Add a pan of water to the smoker for additional moisture.

JERK RUB: MAKES ABOUT 2 CUPS [480 mL]

3 to 4 Scotch bonnet or habanero chiles, diced

1 onion, diced

6 scallions, minced

6 garlic cloves, minced

1 teaspoon [5 mL] dried thyme

2 teaspoons [10 mL] salt

1 teaspoon [5 mL] black pepper

½ tablespoon [8 mL] ground allspice

½ teaspoon [3 mL] grated nutmeg

¼ teaspoon [1 mL] ground cinnamon

Two 4- to 5-pound [1.8- to 2.3-kg] racks of pork spareribs

JERK MARINADE: MAKES ABOUT 6 CUPS [1.4 L]

6 Scotch bonnet or habanero chiles

2 cups [480 mL] onions, diced

6 scallions, sliced fine

½ cup [120 mL] soy sauce

1½ cups [360 mL] white vinegar

1 cup [240 mL] sour orange juice (see page 116)

¼ cup [60 mL] fresh lime juice

⅓ cup [80 mL] dark rum

3 tablespoons [45 mL] ground allspice

2 tablespoons [30 mL] dried thyme

1 tablespoon [15 mL] cayenne

1 tablespoon [15 mL] black pepper

1 tablespoon [15 mL] rubbed sage

½ tablespoon [8 mL] grated nutmeg

½ teaspoon [3 mL] ground mace

1½ teaspoons [8 mL] ground cinnamon

2 tablespoons [30 mL] salt

¼ cup [60 mL] minced garlic

2 tablespoons [30 mL] sugar

3 tablespoons [45 mL] brown sugar

½ cup [120 mL] olive oil

1 cup [240 mL] allspice berries, soaked in hot water for 30 minutes

ADVANCE PREPARATION

1. Purée the chiles, onion, scallions, and garlic in a food processor, adding only enough water to free the blades. Add the remaining jerk rub ingredients and mix well.

2. Rub a generous ¼ cup [60 mL] of the mixture thoroughly over each side of the rib racks. Cover and refrigerate at least 2 hours, preferably overnight.

3. Set up a steamer and add the rib racks. Steam the ribs over barely simmering water for about 1¼ hours. Allow the ribs to cool.

4. Purée the chiles, onions, and scallions in a food processor with the soy sauce, vinegar, sour orange juice, and lime juice. Add the remaining marinade ingredients and mix well.

5. Liberally coat the rib racks with the marinade and marinate at least 4 hours, preferably overnight. Allow the ribs to come to room temperature before smoking.

SMOKING METHOD

6. Build a long-lasting indirect fire with aromatic hardwood. Periodically sprinkle water-soaked allspice berries at the very edge of the coals during the smoking process.

7. Smoke the ribs indirectly for 2 to 3 hours at a temperature of 200°F [95°C] to 225°F [110°C], or until the ends of the rib bones are exposed by about ½ inch [1 cm] and the meat begins to pull away from the bones. Baste both sides of the ribs every 30 minutes or so with the marinade.

8. Baste the ribs once after removing them from the smoker. Wrap the ribs in aluminum foil and cover with kitchen towels. Allow the ribs to rest for 30 minutes before serving.

SERVICE

9. Cut the racks into individual ribs, serving 3 or 4 ribs per order, hot or warm. Provide warm, moist towels.

Lamb Kebabs with Pineapple, Peppers, and Long Beans Lambchi and Boonchi

serves 8 (I skewer per person)

Here is another of those wonderful food names that the Caribbean is so famous for. *Lambchi* are lamb kebabs, and *boonchi* are the long beans or asparagus beans from the Orient. The sauce is a Caribbean interpretation of Indonesian satay sauces. The skewers make a striking presentation, with the long beans spiraled around the kebabs.

CHEF NOTES

Long beans should be available at Asian markets or specialty produce suppliers. If unavailable, blanched green beans or asparagus can be substituted. Use 2-inch [5-cm] sections of bean or asparagus on each end of the skewer, with pieces in the middle, next to the onion slices. Instead of wrapping the long beans around the skewer, braid 3 beans together and grill separately, brushed with butter, for a striking presentation.

MARINADE

I tablespoon [15 mL] hot paprika

I tablespoon [15 mL] Madras curry powder

I teaspoon [5 mL] salt

I teaspoon [5 mL] back pepper

3 tablespoons [45 mL] sweet onion, grated

I tablespoon [15 mL] ginger root, grated

3 garlic cloves, minced

½ cup [120 mL] fresh lemon juice

¼ cup [60 mL] light olive oil

2 pounds [900 g] lamb, cut into sixteen 2-ounce [55-g] cubes

DIPPING SAUCE

2 tablespoons [30 mL] prepared mustard

⅓ cup [80 mL] peanut butter, warmed

½ teaspoon [3 mL] turmeric

¼ cup [60 mL] mushroom soy sauce

¼ cup [60 mL] Worcestershire sauce

¼ cup [60 mL] chicken stock, hot

I teaspoon [5 mL] sugar

Caribbean hot sauce to taste

KEBABS

8 tender long beans, parboiled to be pliable and refreshed in cold water

2 large red bell peppers, cut into sixteen 1½-inch [4-cm] squares

8 slices lean bacon, cut in half, precooked to render most of the fat but not crisp

I sweet white onion, cut into 24 segments for skewering

Sixteen 1½-inch [4-cm] cubes fresh pineapple

8 skewers, soaked if wooden

ADVANCE PREPARATION

I. Combine all of the marinade ingredients and mix well. Place the lamb cubes in a resealable plastic bag and pour the marinade over. Refrigerate overnight.

PREPARATION OF THE DIPPING SAUCE

2. Combine the sauce ingredients and mix well. (The sauce can be made 1 day in advance.)

PREPARATION OF SKEWERS

3. Drain the lamb cubes, reserving the marinade for basting. Skewer the end of a long bean on the end of a skewer and allow it to hang. Wrap each piece of pepper in a piece of bacon.

4. Continue to skewer the following items in this order: onion, pineapple, bacon-wrapped pepper, lamb, onion, pineapple, bacon-wrapped pepper, lamb, onion.

5. Take the end of the long bean and spiral it around the kebab, securing the end by tucking it in between the other skewered pieces.

6. Brush the kebabs with the marinade and reserve.

COOKING METHOD

7. Broil the kebabs for 8 to 10 minutes over an indirect charcoal fire or 4 inches [10 cm] from a broiler flame until medium rare.

SERVICE

8. Serve 1 skewer, intact or removed from the skewer, with warm dipping sauce on the side.

Young Goat in Curry Ragôut Curried Goat

serves 8

The Dutch introduced curry to the Caribbean from their colonies in Indonesia. Later, workers from India reintroduced the taste of curry into the cuisine. Freed African slaves were dependent on goats for meat, and it is no surprise that goat meat would eventually merge with curry flavor. Curried goat is popular all over the Caribbean, but in Jamaica it is elevated to the national dish.

CHEF NOTES

Several island recipes call for using bone-in kid and say that the bones will soften while simmering, becoming soft and chewable. The bones will add more flavor to the dish, but whether or not you choose to use boneless meat is your decision. Bone-in meat would be more authentic. Lamb is an acceptable substitute, but goat meat is more flavorful.

2 pounds [900 g] boneless kid goat, cut into 1-inch [2.5-cm] cubes

2 large onions, diced

3 garlic cloves, minced

1 teaspoon [5 mL] ground allspice

1 or 2 Scotch bonnet or habanero chiles, minced

3 tablespoons [45 mL] Madras curry powder

1 teaspoon [5 mL] salt

1 teaspoon [5 mL] black pepper

3 tablespoons [45 mL] vegetable oil

1 bay leaf

3 scallions knotted around 2 sprigs of thyme

1 cup [240 mL] coconut milk

1 to 1½ cups [240 to 360 mL] chicken stock

1 cup [240 mL] potatoes, peeled and diced

2 teaspoons [10 mL] fresh lime juice

Minced scallion greens, for garnish

GARNISH (OPTIONAL)

Shredded and toasted coconut

Raisins

Chopped roasted cashew nuts

ADVANCE PREPARATION

1. Combine the meat with the onions, garlic, allspice, chiles, curry powder, salt, and pepper in a resealable plastic bag. Mix well and refrigerate at least 2 hours, preferably overnight.

COOKING METHOD

2. Remove the meat from the marinade, reserving the marinade. Sauté the meat in the oil until browned.

3. Add the marinade and sauté, stirring constantly, over medium heat until the onions are translucent.

4. Add the bay leaf, scallions and thyme, coconut milk, stock, and potatoes and bring to a boil. Reduce the heat, cover tightly, and simmer 1½ hours, stirring from time to time.

5. Remove the bay leaf and the thyme sprigs with scallions. Add the lime juice. Simmer, uncovered, for 5 minutes more.

SERVICE

6. Serve 4 ounces [110 g] of curry per person, garnished with minced scallions and the other garnishes, if desired. Serve hot.

Rum-Marinated Fried Chicken Drumettes Chicharrón de Pollo

serves 8

Do not confuse this *chicharrón* dish, a most delicious fried chicken, with the *chicharrónes* of Central America and Mexico, which are fried pork rinds. Very similar treatments are found in Puerto Rico and Cuba, but this version is the national dish of the Dominican Republic.

CHEF NOTES

In this recipe the chicken is pre-baked in its marinade before frying. This method provides maximum flavor and ease of production. As well, there is no worry about undercooked chicken. The chicken may be fried in the more traditional way, without baking, with increased frying time.

MARINADE

¼ cup [60 mL] dark soy sauce

¼ cup [60 mL] golden Jamaican or Dominican rum

¼ cup [60 mL] sour orange juice (see page 116)

¼ cup [60 mL] fresh lime juice

2 tablespoons [30 mL] onion, grated

2 tablespoons [30 mL] garlic, minced

1 tablespoon [15 mL] ginger, grated

24 to 36 chicken wing drumettes, depending on size

SEASONED FLOUR

1½ cups [360 mL] flour

1½ teaspoons [8 mL] baking powder

1 teaspoon [5 mL] salt

1 teaspoon [5 mL] black pepper

1 teaspoon [5 mL] hot paprika

1 teaspoon [5 mL] garlic powder

½ teaspoon [3 mL] dried oregano

2 cups [240 mL] vegetable oil, for frying

2 tablespoons [30 mL] fresh lemon juice

Thin lemon wedges, for garnish

ADVANCE PREPARATION

1. Combine the marinade ingredients in a bowl and mix well. Place the chicken drumettes in a resealable plastic bag and pour the marinade over. Marinate at least 5 hours, preferably overnight.

2. Place the chicken with the marinade in a nonreactive baking dish and bake at 375°F [190°C], basting occasionally, for 20 minutes. (The drumettes can be prepared 1 day in advance and refrigerated in the marinade.)

3. Combine the flour, baking powder, salt, pepper, paprika, garlic powder, and oregano in a paper bag.

4. Remove the chicken pieces and drain the marinade from them. Place a few pieces of chicken at a time in the bag and shake to coat with the seasoned flour.

5. Deep-fry, in small batches, in 365°F [185°C] oil for about 5 minutes, or until nicely browned. Drain on paper towels and keep warm.

SERVICE

6. Sprinkle the chicken with lemon juice and garnish with lemon wedges. Serve 3 or 4 drumettes per person.

Codfish Fritters Stamp and Go

serves 8 (3 fritters per person)

There are many interpretations of the meaning of this fanciful name, but most center on the sale of codfish cakes at bus stops. The rider would quickly hop off the bus, grab a cake or two, then return to the bus and go. With all of the islands surrounded by the Caribbean Sea, the use of fresh fish seems to make more sense than the traditional dried salt cod, but salt cod adds a flavor that fresh fish cannot match in these tasty snacks.

CHEF NOTES

Any firm white-fleshed fish will work as a substitute for the salt cod, such as fresh cod, scrod, roughy, flounder, sea bass, speckled trout, or drum. Jamaicans eat Stamp and Go at a relatively high heat level, but the Scotch bonnet chiles may be decreased if desired.

FRITTERS

8 ounces [225 g] salt cod

2 tablespoons [30 mL] annatto oil

1 cup [240 mL] onion, minced

3 garlic cloves, minced

2 cups [480 mL] flour

2 teaspoons [10 mL] double-acting baking powder

1 teaspoon [5 mL] salt

1 egg, lightly beaten

¾ cup [180 mL] milk

1 tablespoon [15 mL] butter, melted

2 Scotch bonnet or habanero chiles, minced (seeds and ribs removed for less spicy fritters)

¼ cup [60 mL] scallion greens, minced

Vegetable oil, for frying

Lime wedges, for garnish

Caribbean-style hot sauce, for garnish

ADVANCE PREPARATION

1. Rinse the pieces of salt cod under cold running water. Soak in water and refrigerate overnight, changing the water periodically. Discard the soaking liquid and rinse the cod in cold water. (The salt cod can be prepared 1 day in advance.)

2. Flake the prepared salt cod and reserve.

PREPARATION OF THE FRITTERS

3. Heat the annatto oil, sauté the onion and garlic until translucent, and reserve.

4. Sift the flour, baking powder, and salt together in a bowl. Make a well in the center and add the egg, milk, and butter. Mix together only enough to combine.

5. Add the onions and annatto oil mixture, the flaked fish, the chiles, and the scallion, combining to form a smooth batter. (The batter may be made up to 1 day in advance.)

COOKING METHOD

6. Carefully drop the fritter batter by heaping tablespoons [20 mL] into 365°F [185°C] oil and cook for about 4 minutes, or until set and golden brown, turning once during frying. Remove with a slotted spoon and drain on paper towels.

SERVICE

7. Serve 3 fritters per person, hot, warm, or at room temperature, accompanied with lime wedges and hot sauce.

Aromatic Spice-Stuffed Fried Fish Nuggets Baxter's Road Fried Fish

serves 8

These aromatic spice-stuffed fried fish nuggets have been described as the best fried fish to be found anywhere in the world. Some consider Baxter's Road risky for tourists to visit at night, but after sundown Bajans flock in droves to partake the fantastic fried fish and chicken prepared there. After dark an impromptu African street market materializes in the middle of the Bajan capital of Bridgetown, and the famous fish is flash-fried in big cauldrons of bubbling oil heated over wood fires.

CHEF NOTES

Use the freshest fish available for this dish. Use fresh herbs if at all possible because the spice mix is best as a green paste to rub into the fish. The intensity of the chile may be varied according to taste, but the spice mix should have a piquant quality. Many varieties of fish will work with this recipe, including king mackerel, sword-fish, porgy, grouper, snapper, and drum. Bajan fried chicken is almost as popular as the fish on Baxter's Road. Substitute chicken that has pockets cut to be packed with the spice paste, then follow the cooking method above.

SPICE MIX: MAKES 2 CUPS [480 mL]

3 scallions, including the tops, sliced

1 small sweet onion, diced

2 garlic cloves, minced

½ green bell pepper, seeded and finely diced

1 Scotch bonnet or habanero chile, finely diced

3 sprigs of flat-leaf parsley, chopped

2 tablespoons [30 mL] fresh thyme or 1 tablespoon [15 mL] dried thyme

2 tablespoons [30 mL] fresh marjoram or 1 tablespoon [15 mL] dried marjoram

3 allspice berries, toasted and finely crushed

Juice of 1 lime

FISH

1¼ pounds [560 g] mahi mahi fillets

2 eggs, beaten

¼ cup [60 mL] milk

1 cup [240 mL] flour

1 teaspoon [5 mL] salt

1 teaspoon [5 mL] black pepper

2 cups [480 mL] plain dry breadcrumbs

Vegetable oil, for frying

Lime wedges, for garnish

PREPARATION OF THE SPICE MIX

1. Combine all of the spice mix ingredients in a food processor and blend into a paste. Store in a covered jar, refrigerated. (The spice mix can be held under refrigeration for several weeks.)

PREPARATION OF THE FISH

2. Score the fish with crosshatch marks or cut pockets into the flesh. Press the spice mix into the cuts or pockets. Allow the fish to marinate for at least 1 hour, refrigerated.

3. Combine the beaten egg and milk in a shallow bowl.

4. Season the flour with the salt and pepper. Place the flour and the breadcrumbs in separate pans.

5. Cut the fish into nuggets and toss them in the flour to coat. Dip the fish into the egg and milk mixture and remove, using a fork. Allow the excess egg to drain off. Coat the fish with breadcrumbs.

6. Heat the oil to 365°F [185°C] and fry the breaded nuggets for 5 to 8 minutes, depending on size, or until golden brown and just flaking. Drain on paper towels and keep warm.

SERVICE

7. Serve 3-ounce [85-g] portions of fish with lime wedges for garnish.

Central America

Guatemala, Belize,
Honduras, El Salvador,
Nicaragua, Costa Rica,
and Panama

Beef and Sausage Brochettes with Red Bell Pepper Sauce
Brochetas de Carne con Salsa Chiltomas

Pork Tamalitos with Mixed Vegetable Filling
Nacatamales

Fresh Corn and Braised Pork-Layered Torte
Torta de Elote y Puerco

Turkey in Red Mole Sauce
Pepián de Chumpipe

Fried Fish Strips in Coconut Milk with Plantain
Fufu

Stuffed Tortillas
Pupusas

Angel Hair Pasta (*Fideo*) and Three-Cheese Flan
Flan Caballo de Fideo

CENTRAL AMERICA IS made up of Guatemala, Belize, Honduras, El Salvador, Nicaragua, Costa Rica, and Panama. Climate and geography vary considerably throughout the region, giving rise to different cooking styles and ingredients. Those countries with mountainous regions, such as Guatemala, experience extremes in rainfall and temperature, and those without mountains, such as Honduras and El Salvador, have little temperature variation, with seasons marked only by rainy and dry.

The cuisines of Central America are influenced by the peoples who conquered, settled, and occupied the lands. Mayan influence is greatest in Guatemala where the traditional thick soup called *pulique* is quite common, as is the use of a sauce (*yaquaste*) made from ground pumpkin seeds. The ground seeds also come in a powder form called *pepitoria*. Toasted ground corn kernels, called *pinol*, are commonly added to poultry dishes. Spanish influence is greatest in Panama and Nicaragua, where the majority of the population is mestizo, a Spanish-Indian mix. Here we find dishes such as *arroz con pollo* and Spanish-style sausages. Costa Rica, farthest from Guatemala and closest to South America, shows the least influence from native Americans and has the most eclectic offerings in its cuisine. There is a Caribbean influence among the countries with an eastern coastline, where fried plantains, tropical fruits such as papaya, and beans and rice are often served. Showing a Creole influence, coconut milk is often used in stews, sauces, and breads. The cuisine of Honduras has a Middle Eastern influence, the result of Arabic settlements. Spices such as cinnamon and coriander make their way into savory dishes here.

One finds some surprises when examining the ingredients of Central American cuisine. Unlike their Mexican neighbors to the north, Central Americans do not use chiles extensively, and the foods of Central America are not known for being spicy. Most surprising is the lack of seafood in the diet. The entire region is bordered by the Pacific Ocean on the west and the Caribbean Sea on the east, yet very little fish and shellfish find their way into the recipes of the region. One exception to this general rule is *sopa de hombre*, a seafood soup found in Honduras. Fowl and game birds are quite popular throughout Central America, especially turkey and waterfowl such as duck. This liking for waterfowl can probably be traced to the migratory routes that pass over Central America.

Cooking methods and techniques are simple. Wrapping food in banana leaves to then be steamed is common in Central America. The ubiquitous tamale is prepared this way in most countries. Stewing and steaming for extended periods is quite common, as is the technique of marinating meats before cooking. A unique marinade ingredient is the sour orange, *naranja agria*. Its taste is unique among citrus: it has a distinct orange aroma and the sour bite of a lemon. Another common technique is the dry toasting of dried chiles, spices, and seeds before incorporating them into the dish being prepared. This method releases essential oils and heightens flavor. A heavy skillet is heated without oil and the spices or seeds are slowly toasted for several minutes, until quite fragrant but not burned. Charring tomatoes, tomatillos, and dried chiles over an open flame is another popular cooking technique.

The staples of the Central American diet are those indigenous to the region. They are of Mayan origin—corn, beans, tomatoes, squash, and, to some extent, chiles (especially dried ones). Rice, introduced from Asia, is also common. Tortillas and tamales, made from cornmeal, are found everywhere. Each country prides itself on its tamale. A unique variation on this theme is the *pupusa* of El Salvador, a stuffed tortilla. Tropical ingredients find their way into many Central American dishes. Yuca, bananas, plantains, papaya, and coconut are especially prevalent in those countries with a tropical climate, bordering the Caribbean.

Beef and Sausage Brochettes
with Red Bell Pepper Sauce Brochetas de Carne con Salsa Chiltomas

serves 8 (1 brochette per person)

Central Americans, as a rule, do not eat many spicy foods. The red peppers in the sauce are sweet red bell peppers and not spicy chiles. Chile sauces, however, are used as condiments. Sour oranges, also called Seville or bitter oranges, are featured in many dishes of Central America and should be sought out for this dish. Latin American markets are a good source.

BROCHETTES

1 small onion, puréed

1 Roma or plum tomato, puréed

2 garlic cloves, minced

Juice of 1 sour orange (see Chef Notes)

1 pound [450 g] beef sirloin, cut into ¾-inch [2-cm] cubes

1 tablespoon [15 mL] salt

½ tablespoon [8 mL] black pepper

RED PEPPER SAUCE

2 tablespoons [30 mL] vegetable oil or lard

2 small red onions, minced

2 large red bell peppers, stems, seeds, and ribs removed, minced

2 Roma or plum tomatoes, finely chopped

Juice of 1 sour orange

¼ cup [60 mL] rich chicken stock

¼ cup [60 mL] red wine vinegar

1 tablespoon [15 mL] sugar

Salt and pepper to taste

6 scallions, cut into 1-inch [2.5-cm] lengths, for skewering

1 pound [450 g] small sausages, such as Spanish chorizo, cut into 1-inch [2.5-cm] lengths

8 wooden or metal skewers, soaked if wooden

ADVANCE PREPARATION

1. Combine the onion, tomato, garlic, and sour orange juice and mix well to form a marinade.

PREPARATION OF THE BROCHETTES

2. Season the beef with salt and pepper and place in a resealable plastic bag. Pour the marinade over the beef, toss the mixture well to combine, seal the bag, and refrigerate overnight.

Sour orange, bitter orange, *naranja agria, Bigarade,* and Seville orange refer to same variety of citrus. They are commonly imported into the United States from the Caribbean and Mexico and are also grown in California and Florida. They should be purchased if possible at a Latin American or specialty produce market. They have a very acidic but pleasant taste. If unavailable, there are two widely accepted substitutes. The simplest is to mix 1 part lemon juice with 2 parts orange juice. A closer alternative is to combine 1 teaspoon [5 mL] very finely grated grapefruit zest, ¼ cup [60 mL] orange juice, ¼ cup [60 mL] grapefruit juice, and 2 tablespoons [30 mL] lemon juice. The average sour orange will yield about ¼ cup [60 mL] of juice.

PREPARATION OF THE SAUCE

3. Heat the oil and sauté the red onions and bell peppers until soft. Add the tomatoes, sour orange juice, stock, vinegar, and sugar.

4. Simmer until slightly thickened, about 15 minutes. Season to taste with salt and pepper. Blend well in a processor or blender and reserve. (The sauce may be made 1 day in advance.)

COOKING METHOD

5. Remove the beef from the marinade and drain, reserving any leftover marinade for basting.

6. Skewer the beef cubes, scallion sections, and sausage sections in an alternating fashion, with 2 ounces [55 g] each of beef and sausage per skewer.

7. Grill over a medium-hot indirect charcoal fire, basting with the reserved marinade, until the beef cubes are medium rare to medium.

SERVICE

8. Serve 1 brochette per person, with or without the skewers. The reheated sauce may be applied to the plate under the brochette or piped directly on the brochettes with a squeeze bottle.

Pork Tamalitos with Mixed Vegetable Filling Nacatamales

NICARAGUA

serves 8 (2 tamales per person)

This is considered the definitive tamale of Central America. The name, a derivative of Native American and Spanish, translates literally as bad food (*nacata* from the Mayan, meaning food, and *mal* from the Spanish, meaning bad). The name is definitely a misnomer—these tamales are delicious.

CHEF NOTES

For visual appeal, if the tamalitos will be served wrapped, corn husks (instead of aluminum foil) make a better presentation. For each tamalito, soak 3 pieces of husk for 30 minutes in warm water, lay them out flat, overlapping the edges to form the wrapper. When the tamalito is stuffed and formed, secure the corn-husk wrapper with twine or a soaked strip of husk. Steam as for foil-wrapped tamales.

PORK FILLING

1 pound [450 g] pork loin, cut into ½-inch [1-cm] cubes

½ cup [120 mL] sour orange juice (see page 116)

4 teaspoons [20 mL] achiote

¼ cup [60 mL] oil

2 teaspoons [10 mL] salt

4 garlic cloves, minced

1 teaspoon [5 mL] black pepper

DOUGH

4 cups [960 mL] masa harina (corn tortilla flour)

2 cups [480 mL] half-and-half

2 tablespoons [30 mL] lard or butter

¼ cup [60 mL] sour orange juice

1 teaspoon [5 mL] salt

½ cup [120 mL] mashed potatoes

FILLINGS

16 sheets of aluminum foil, 8 × 10 inches [20 × 25 cm]

1 large new potato, cut into ⅛-inch [3-mm] slices

2 Roma or plum tomatoes, cut into ⅛-inch [3-mm] slices

1 sweet onion, French cut into ⅛-inch [3-mm] pieces

1 red bell pepper, halved and cut into ⅛-inch [3-mm] slices

½ cup [120 mL] spearmint leaves

1 cup [240 mL] raw white rice, soaked in water for 30 minutes

½ cup [120 mL] raisins

½ cup [120 mL] pimiento-stuffed olives

Mild tomato salsa, for service

ADVANCE PREPARATION

1. Combine the pork with the sour orange juice, achiote, oil, salt, garlic, and pepper and marinate in a resealable plastic bag overnight.

2. Combine all of the dough ingredients in a pot and mix well. Heat briefly over low heat stirring constantly, until the dough becomes firm and holds together. (The dough can be made several days in advance and refrigerated until ready for use.)

ASSEMBLY OF THE TAMALITOS

3. Place 3 tablespoons [45 mL] of the dough in a mound in the center of a piece of aluminum foil.

4. Drain the meat, reserving the marinade, and press 3 tablespoons [45 mL] of the meat cubes into the center of the dough and 1 slice of the potato near the bottom.

5. Top the mound with 1 slice of tomato, 1 slice of onion, and 1 slice of bell pepper. On top of this place 2 mint leaves and 1 teaspoon of the soaked rice.

6. Push the raisins and olives into the dough around the edges. Top the whole package with about ½ teaspoon [3 mL] of the marinade.

7. Fold the ends of the foil together and overlap the sides tightly to seal. Fold over the open end and tamp down slightly on the folded end to compact it. Fold over again to tightly seal. The foil package should be about 3 inches [8 cm] long and 1½ inches [4 cm] wide.

COOKING METHOD

8. Layer the packages in a large steamer over simmering water. Cover the pan and steam, covered, for 1½ hours, replenishing the water as necessary. (The cooked tamales may be prepared in advance and steamed or microwaved to order.)

SERVICE

9. Unwrap the tamalitos and serve two per person, right out of the steamer if possible, accompanied with tomato salsa.

Fresh Corn and Braised Pork-Layered Torte — Torta de Elote y Puerco

serves 12

This dish is an urban version of the traditional green corn and pork tamale, made by replacing the stuffing, wrapping, and steaming process with a baked layered casserole. A coarse purée of fresh sweet corn substitutes for the masa harina normally used to make tamales. The pork picadillo filling is made from the meat of braised thick pork ribs rather than the more traditional pork shoulder.

CHEF NOTES

Use the freshest corn possible for this dish. Use white or bicolor corn if available. Frozen corn may be substituted, but it is inferior in texture and flavor.

PICADILLO

1½ pounds [675 g] country-style pork ribs, dusted with salt and pepper to taste

3 tablespoons [45 mL] lard or oil

½ cup [120 mL] rich chicken stock

8 ounces [225 g] pork loin, minced

1 onion, diced

2 garlic cloves, minced

2 tomatoes, chopped

¼ cup [60 mL] pimiento-stuffed olives

½ cup [120 mL] raisins, soaked for 10 minutes in hot chicken stock and drained

2 tablespoons [30 mL] prepared mustard

Salt to taste

1 tablespoon [15 mL] sugar

TORTE

8 medium ears of fresh corn, kernels removed and coarsely chopped

2 tablespoons [30 mL] butter

Salt and pepper to taste

3 eggs, beaten

4 ounces [110 g] farmer's cheese, grated

1 green bell pepper, sliced into strips

1 red bell pepper, sliced into strips

Melted butter, for glazing

ADVANCE PREPARATION

1. Brown the pork ribs in 1 tablespoon [15 mL] of the lard or oil in a large skillet. Add the stock and braise the ribs, covered, until very tender, about 2 hours.

2. Drain the meat. Reserve and chill the cooking liquid, removing the layer of chilled pork fat. Cool the ribs, remove the bones, and finely chop the meat. Reserve.

3. Heat the remaining 2 tablespoons [30 mL] of the oil or lard and sauté the pork loin until lightly browned.

4. Add the onion and garlic and sauté until translucent. Add the tomatoes, olives, raisins, mustard, salt, and sugar. Simmer for 10 minutes.

5. Add the reserved chopped pork rib meat and simmer 5 minutes more. Allow to cool to room temperature and reserve. (The picadillo can be made 1 day in advance.)

PREPARATION OF THE TORTE

6. Sauté the chopped fresh corn in the butter until it begins to soften. Season with salt and pepper and allow to cool.

7. Stir in the beaten eggs and cheese and mix well.

8. Place half of the corn mixture in a greased 10-inch [25-cm] glass baking dish or 12 individual ramekins, followed by the picadillo mixture, adding some of the reserved cooking liquid from the ribs if the picadillo mixture is not moist. Top with the remainder of the corn mixture.

9. Smooth the surface with a spatula and decorate the top with the slices of green and red bell pepper.

COOKING METHOD

10. Brush the surface with melted butter and bake at 375°F [190°C] for 30 minutes, or until golden brown on top and the interior is set.

SERVICE

11. Slice the torte into 12 portions and serve hot or warm.

Turkey in Red Mole Sauce Pepián de Chumpipe

serves 8

Pepián is an ancient Mayan cooking method in which meats are cooked first in water or stock, then combined with a squash or pumpkin seed–based sauce. It is very similar to the popular central Mexican mole sauces, and to the classic *yaguaste* sauces of Guatemala, which are thickened with browned pumpkin seeds. Another Spanish name for turkey is *pavo*.

CHEF NOTES

Traditionally this dish is made with small, young turkeys of about 10 pounds [4.5 kg] dressed weight, but these are difficult to find in the United States, where turkeys are grown much larger for roasting. Many other types of poultry may be substituted for the turkey in this dish.

TURKEY

2 pounds [900 g] turkey breast

4 cups [960 mL] chicken or turkey stock

2 garlic cloves, minced

MOLE SAUCE

6 tablespoons [90 mL] sesame seeds

½ teaspoon [3 mL] black peppercorns

⅓ cup [80 mL] pumpkin or squash seeds, hulled, unsalted

I cinnamon stick, broken into pieces

Liberal pinch of ground cloves

I ripe tomato

3 tomatillos, husked and rinsed

I small onion, peeled and halved

2 garlic cloves, peeled

2 dried Guajillo or New Mexico red chiles

2 red bell peppers, chopped

I teaspoon [5 mL] achiote

I teaspoon [5 mL] sugar

Salt to taste

½ cup [120 mL] unseasoned breadcrumbs, toasted

warm tortillas

ADVANCE PREPARATION

1. Bring the turkey, stock, and minced garlic to a boil in a saucepan. Reduce the heat and simmer for 30 minutes, or until tender. Reserve warm in the stock.

PREPARATION OF THE SAUCE

2. Toast the sesame seeds, peppercorns, pumpkin seeds, and cinnamon stick together in a dry skillet over moderate heat until the seeds take on a light color. Remove from the heat and add the ground cloves. Put the toasted spice and seed mix in the workbowl of a food processor.

3. Char the tomato, tomatillos, onion, and garlic cloves under a broiler or on the grill until they are softened and lightly charred.

4. Carefully toast the dried chiles over an open flame until they puff up, being careful not to burn them. Remove the stems and some of the seeds and soak in enough of the hot turkey stock to cover for about 10 minutes.

5. Add the charred tomato mixture, soaked chiles, bell peppers, achiote, sugar, and salt to taste with the stock to the processor. Blend the contents to a smooth paste.

COOKING METHOD

6. Return the turkey breast in the stock to a simmer. Add the sauce and the breadcrumbs and cook 20 to 30 minutes. If the sauce thickens too much, add warm water or additional stock, if available, to thin it.

SERVICE

7. Remove the turkey breast and slice it. Serve 4-ounce [110-g] portions. Dress the turkey slices with the mole sauce and serve with tortillas.

Fried Fish Strips in Coconut Milk with Plantain Fufu

serves 8

This is a typical dish of Bocas del Toro, situated between the Laguna de Chiriquí and the Caribbean, on the north coast of Panama. It illustrates the popular use of coconut milk and local vegetables. Bamboo shoots, while not indigenous, are typical of ingredients used in Panama. *Fufu* is also the name of a West and Central African dish made from yam, cassava, plantain, and/or other starches, and should not be confused with this dish.

CHEF NOTES

The plantains and fish may be fried in the same oil. This dish traditionally calls for green plantains, but almost-ripe ones may be used. The fish used should not be oily fleshed. Red or black drum or snapper are ideal.

SAUCE

1 cup [240 mL] rich chicken stock

4 cups [960 mL] coconut milk

1 small can bamboo shoot strips, chopped

8 ounces [225 g] yam, finely chopped

1 pound [450 g] yuca, finely chopped

1 large jalapeño chile, minced

1 large tomato, chopped

1 onion, finely chopped

2 garlic cloves, minced

Salt and pepper to taste

PLANTAIN AND FISH

Vegetable oil or lard, for frying

1 plantain, peeled and cut into ½-inch [1-cm] slices

1 pound [450 g] firm-fleshed fish fillets, cut into ½-Inch [1-cm] strips

Flour seasoned with salt, pepper, and a little garlic powder

Cilantro leaves and chopped scallions, for garnish

ADVANCE PREPARATION

1. All advance preparation may be found in the ingredient list.

PREPARATION OF THE SAUCE

2. Heat the stock and coconut milk to a boil. Add the bamboo shoots, yam, yuca, jalapeño, tomato, onion, and garlic. Simmer over low heat until the vegetables are tender and the sauce thickens slightly. Season to taste with salt and pepper and reserve.

COOKING METHOD

3. Heat the oil to 325°F [165°C] and fry the plantains until they just start to turn golden and are tender, about 5 minutes. Remove and drain on paper towels.

4. Using the bottom of a juice glass or a *tostonera* press if you have one, gently flatten the partially fried plantains to about ¼ inch [6 mm] thick.

5. Increase the heat to about 365°F [185°C] and return the plantains to the oil. Fry until they are brown and crispy on the outside and tender inside, 1 to 2 minutes. Add the plantains (*tostones*) to the heated sauce and reserve.

6. Dust the fish slices liberally with the seasoned flour and sauté or deep-fry until golden brown and just flaky. Remove and drain on paper towels.

SERVICE

7. Ladle some of the sauce with the vegetables onto a plate, then top with 4-ounce [110-g] slices of the fried fish strips, fanned out. Garnish with cilantro leaves and chopped scallions.

Stuffed Tortillas Pupusas

serves 12 (1 *pupusa* per person)

Pupusas are a Central American appetizer that many are familiar with. They can be stuffed with many different fillings, but *chicharrones* (fried pork rinds) and bean and cheese are the most popular. *Pupusas* are commonly sold as street food at *pupuserias*, which compare closely to America's pizza parlors.

CHEF NOTES

Pork rinds, cheese, and beans are the traditional fillings found in El Salvador. Duck cracklings make a sophisticated substitute for the traditional pork rinds. Prepared masa dough or unbaked tortillas are often available through a local supplier or market. If not, buy masa harina mix (found in the flour section of a market) and follow the package directions, using a little rich chicken stock in place of some of the water for extra flavor and richness.

STUFFED TORTILLAS (*PUPUSAS*)

2 pounds [900 g] prepared corn tortilla masa (see Chef Notes)

CHICHARRONES FILLING

8 ounces [225 g] *chicharrones* (packaged pork rinds)

¼ cup [60 mL] red bell pepper, diced fine

2 cups [480 mL] ripe tomatoes, chopped

¾ cup [180 mL] onion, diced

3 garlic cloves, minced

1 teaspoon [5 mL] salt

CHEESE FILLING

¾ cup [180 mL] farmer's cheese

¼ cup [60 mL] crumbled queso blanco or feta cheese

¼ cup [60 mL] grated Parmesan cheese

3 tablespoons [45 mL] parsley, chopped

BEAN FILLING

1 tablespoon [15 mL] vegetable oil or lard

2 garlic cloves, minced

½ teaspoon [3 mL] bay leaf, ground

1¼ cups [300 mL] prepared kidney beans, puréed with their cooking liquid

1 teaspoon [5 mL] salt

½ teaspoon [3 mL] black pepper

Vinegar-based coleslaw, for service (optional)

Pickled vegetables, for service (optional)

Tomato salsa, for service (optional)

ADVANCE PREPARATION

1. All advance preparation may be found in the ingredient list.

PREPARATION OF THE TORTILLAS

2. Roll out or use a tortilla press to form 2 tablespoons [30 mL] of masa into 2½-inch [6-cm] rounds about ¼ inch [6 mm]

thick. Stack, separated with wax paper or plastic film. You should have 24 tortillas.

CHICHARROÑES FILLING

3. Combine all the *chicharroñes* filling ingredients in a food processor, process to a smooth paste, and reserve.

CHEESE FILLING

4. Combine all the cheese filling ingredients in a food processor, pulse to combine, and reserve.

BEAN FILLING

5. Heat the oil in a nonstick skillet and sauté the garlic for 30 seconds.

6. Add the ground bay leaf and sauté for 30 seconds, then add the bean purée, salt, and pepper.

7. Cook, while stirring, over moderate heat until the liquid evaporates and the purée thickens. Continue cooking until the mixture begins to come away from the skillet easily. Reserve.

COOKING METHOD

8. Place a tortilla on a flat surface and top with 1 heaping tablespoon [20 mL] of a filling or combination of fillings. Place a second tortilla on top and seal the edges with the tines of a fork.

9. Grill the *pupusas* on a hot griddle over moderate heat for about 6 minutes, or until they are nicely browned on both sides. (They may also be sautéed in a lightly greased nonstick skillet or deep-fried.) Keep warm until service.

SERVICE

10. Serve 1 *pupusa* per person accompanied with a spicy vinegar-based coleslaw, spicy pickled vegetables, or a simple tomato salsa.

Angel Hair Pasta (*Fideo*) and Three-Cheese Flan Flan Caballo de Fideo

serves 8

This substantial tart has a custard that is baked with layers of thin fideo noodles. *Fideo* is dry pasta arranged in coils. The very thin noodles, similar to fine vermicelli or capellini, are commonly sold in Latin American markets as well as American supermarkets. In Spain and Central America the noodles are first blanched to soften before using, while in Mexico they are fried first. The tart uses farmer's, Muenster, and Parmesan cheeses, which are close substitutes for the native cheeses of the area.

CHEF NOTES

The flan may be baked in ramekins instead of a cake pan for individual service. Reduce the cooking time accordingly.

TOMATO SAUCE

8 ounces [225 g] onions, minced

2 garlic cloves, minced

1 serrano chile, minced

1 tablespoon [15 mL] butter

1 small can tomato paste

Salt and pepper to taste

FLAN

8 ounces [225 g] butter

2 ounces [55 g] farmer's cheese, grated

2 ounces [55 g] Muenster cheese, grated

2 ounces [55 g] Parmesan cheese, grated

3 eggs, separated

Salt and pepper to taste

8 ounces [225 g] angel hair pasta (*fideo*), cooked al dente and rinsed in cold water

ADVANCE PREPARATION

1. Sauté the onions, garlic, and chile in the butter until the onions are translucent. Add the tomato paste, adjust seasonings, and reserve.

ASSEMBLING THE FLAN

2. Beat the butter until smooth, then add the cheeses, one at a time. Continue beating. Add the egg yolks and mix until the mixture is light and fluffy. Taste and adjust the seasoning with salt and pepper.

3. Gently stir in the pasta and mix well.

4. Beat the egg whites to form stiff peaks then fold them into the pasta mixture. Transfer to a 9-inch [23-cm] greased cake pan lined with parchment.

5. Bake the flan at 350°F [175°C] for 30 to 40 minutes, or until the top is golden brown and the interior is set. Use paper towels to blot any standing butter from the surface of the baked flan after it is removed from the oven.

SERVICE

6. Cut the flan into 8 wedges. Place 1 wedge on a plate and top with stripes of tomato sauce, applied with a squeeze bottle.

South America

Skewered Tenderloin of Beef
Anticuchos

Chile and Beef Empanadas
Empanadas a la Criolla

Spicy Meatballs
Albóndigas Picantes

Beef Pie with Apricots
Pastel de Carne y Albaricoque

Citrus-Marinated Fish
Cevíche

Potato and Cheese Pancakes
Llapingachos

Quinoa Croquettes
Frituras de Quinua

THE NAMES MAY VARY from country to country—*aperitivos* (aperitifs, appetizers), *botanas* (the stoppers on leather wine bottles), *bocaditos* (little mouthfuls), *antojitos* (little whims or fancies), *boquillas* (things to stop the mouth), *fritangas* (fried morsels or fritters), tapados (nibbles), *picadas* (on a toothpick), *entremés* (side dish), or *entradas* (dishes to be served at the table)—but one thing is certain: South Americans love their appetizers and first courses.

Our exposure to the foods of South America has been rather limited for a number of reasons. From a cultural perspective our roots are European. Because of the vast size and varied geography of South America, travel cannot expose anyone to all of its culinary regions. Few restaurants in the United States specialize in the cuisines of these countries, although this trend now seems to be changing, especially in larger cities such as New York City, San Francisco, and Chicago.

South America is comprised of thirteen countries: Argentina, Bolivia, Chile, Colombia, Ecuador, French Guiana, Guyana, Paraguay, Peru, Suriname, Uruguay, Venezuela, and Brazil, which is covered in another chapter in this book. The three major cultural influences on South America's culinary styles were the native Indians, the Europeans, and the Africans. South American cuisine owes more to the Spanish and Portuguese conquerors and settlers than it does to the indigenous population.

The cuisine of South America today is a Creole cuisine, a mix of New World foodstuffs, the ancient cuisines of the native Indian peoples, and the cuisines of Spain and Portugal (and their African slaves). In spite of the extreme diversity of land and people, a similarity in food style persists from region to region.

Economic status can be a major influence when considering the eating habits of the people of South America. Wealthier urban dwellers have a more varied diet than poorer rural inhabitants, for example. Climate plays an important role as well. Villagers of the Andean highlands and Patagonia dine on hearty, warming soups and comforting stews, while peoples of the steamy, tropical lowlands eat much lighter fare during the day, having their main meal later in the cooler evenings. Peruvians eat the spiciest food, with Bolivians not far behind. In Argentina, Uruguay, and Paraguay beef is king, due to the vast expanses of the fertile pampas region, an area rich in grain and cattle production. In Chile, where agricultural land is at a premium, the extensive coastline offers a rich diversity of seafood. The tropical lowlands of the eastern continent yield a rich harvest of tropical fruits and vegetables. In the Andean highlands of Peru and Bolivia, wide valleys are ideal for agricultural production. The civilization of the Incas was based on agriculture. They cultivated such crops as potatoes, tomatoes, corn, beans, squash, chiles, cashews, cacao, avocados, sweet potatoes, cassava, peanuts, and pineapples. The Incas were known to have developed close to two hundred varieties of potatoes and close to one hundred varieties of corn. In fact, some varieties in Peru have kernels as big as strawberries, which are skewered on toothpicks and eaten as mini brochettes.

Regardless of the country or its geography, methods of food preparation remain quite similar. Traditional, that is, ancient Indian, methods of cooking are primarily reserved for celebrations. These might include the Quecha method of burying hot stones and layered foods in an earth oven, or *panchamanca*. In Chile it might involve cooking shellfish in layers of seaweed, called *curanto*, very similar to the New England clambake.

The South American continent, fourth largest in the world, varies greatly in terms of geography, from some of the driest deserts (the driest place on earth is the Atacama Desert in Chile) to some of the wettest tropical rain forests. There are huge expanses of lowlands and a lengthy chain of the Andes Mountains rivaling the Himalayas in stature. The continent is surrounded by one of the longest coastlines in the world (providing a rich diversity in seafood), and it is bisected by one of the longest rivers on earth. A large part of the continent is tropical, being on or near the equator, yet Tierra del Fuego is very close to Antarctica.

Skewered Tenderloin of Beef Anticuchos

serves 8 (2 skewers per person)

Beef is king in South America and *anticuchos* are a classic way to enjoy it. These spicy brochettes can be charcoal-grilled, broiled, or sautéed. For an authentic version use beef hearts instead of tenderloin. The name translates from the ancient Quechua language as "Andean dish cooked on sticks."

 **CHEF NOTES**

Llama hearts are original to this dish but are probably quite difficult to obtain from your local meat purveyor. To offer an authentic version use beef hearts instead of tenderloin.

MARINADE: MAKES 1½ CUPS [360 mL]

16 garlic cloves, bruised

4 serrano chiles, minced

1½ tablespoons [25 mL] comino (ground cumin)

½ tablespoon [8 mL] dried oregano

Salt and pepper to taste

½ cup [120 mL] red wine vinegar

1 cup vegetable oil

SKEWERS

1½ pounds [675 g] beef tenderloin, cut into small cubes

4 serrano chiles, quartered, seeds and ribs removed

16 skewers, soaked in warm water for 1 hour if wooden

SAUCE

½ cup [120 mL] dried mirasol or Japanese hontaka chiles, stemmed and seeded

1 tablespoon [15 mL] ground annatto (or powder)

1 tablespoon [15 mL] vegetable oil

Salt to taste

¾ cup [180 mL] reserved marinade

ADVANCE PREPARATION

1. Mix the marinade ingredients in a bowl and then pour into a resealable plastic bag. Add the cubes of beef. Toss to coat and refrigerate for 24 hours.

PREPARATION OF THE BROCHETTES

2. Drain the beef, reserving the marinade. Thread 1½ ounces [45 g] of beef, alternating with serrano chile quarters, on each skewer. (The brochettes can be prepared several hours in advance.)

PREPARATION OF THE SAUCE

3. Soak the chiles in warm water for 30 minutes, then drain. Place the chiles, annatto, oil, salt, and about ½ cup [120 mL]

of the marinade in a blender and purée. Add more of the marinade if necessary to make a thick sauce.

4. Simmer over low heat for 5 minutes. Allow to cool. The sauce will be quite spicy.

COOKING METHOD

5. Brush the skewered beef with some of the sauce and grill over medium-hot coals or broil 3 inches [8 cm] from a broiler flame on all sides for about 4 minutes, or until cooked to medium.

SERVICE

6. Serve 2 skewers per person, brushed with the remaining sauce.

Chile and Beef Empanadas Empanadas a la Criolla

serves 8 (3 empanadas per person)

These small pastries, whose origin is probably Middle Eastern, have a delicate crust with a wonderful filling of contrasting flavors. Empanadas are very popular throughout South America as street food and are sold in bars and sandwich shops as well, filled with a variety of ingredients.

CHEF NOTES

The empanadas can be made early in the day and rewarmed before serving. They freeze well and can be made several days in advance. Other pastry recipes in this chapter work well with the filling.

PASTRY

2 cups [480 mL] flour

Dash of salt

1 cup [240 mL] vegetable shortening

¼ cup [60 mL] cold water

FILLING

8 ounces [225 g] lean ground beef

2 tablespoons [30 mL] olive oil

½ onion, finely diced

3 garlic cloves, minced

5 serrano chiles, seeded and minced

1 tablespoon [15 mL] comino (ground cumin)

Salt and pepper to taste

2 tablespoons [30 mL] parsley, chopped

2 tablespoons [30 mL] cilantro, chopped

2 plum tomatoes, fresh or canned, peeled, seeded, and finely chopped

½ cup [120 mL] raisins

12 large pimiento-stuffed olives, halved lengthwise

1 cup [240 mL] salsa, for service

ADVANCE PREPARATION

1. All advance preparation may be found in the ingredient list.

PREPARATION OF THE PASTRY

2. Combine the flour, salt, and vegetable shortening in a food processor and process until the mix resembles coarse meal. Or use a bowl and a pastry blender.

3. Add the cold water, a little at a time, until the dough reaches a smooth, slightly sticky consistency. Wrap in plastic film and refrigerate. (The dough can be made 1 day in advance.)

PREPARATION OF THE FILLING

4. Sauté the ground beef in the oil, breaking it up as it cooks. Cook until well done.

5. Add the onion, garlic, chiles, comino, and salt and pepper and continue to cook over medium heat until the onions soften.

6. Add the parsley, cilantro, tomatoes, and raisins and cook until almost no liquid remains. The mixture will be quite dry. Set aside and allow to cool. (The filling can be made 1 day in advance.)

PREPARATION OF THE EMPANADAS

7. Roll out the dough, about ⅛ inch [3 mm] thick, roughly 16 × 20 inches [40 × 50 cm], on a lightly floured surface and cut into twenty-four 3-inch [8-cm] circles.

8. Place an olive half on each round, then a teaspoonful of the filling in the center. Fold the pastry over to form a half-circle and seal the edges of the pastry with the tines of a fork.

COOKING METHOD

9. Arrange the empanadas on a parchment-lined cookie sheet and bake at 375°F [190°C] for 20 minutes, or until nicely browned.

SERVICE

10. Serve 3 empanadas per person, warm. Two tablespoons [30 mL] of salsa may be served on the side.

Spicy Meatballs Albóndigas Picantes

serves 12 (4 meatballs per person)

Meatballs are eaten throughout Latin America, and this version from Paraguay is typical of the common method of cooking them, first sautéing and then braising them in a sauce. Green jalapeños will produce a spicier version of this dish.

CHEF NOTES

For a light meal, serve the meatballs over rice or noodles. For a spicier version, do not remove the membranes and seeds from the jalapeños.

SAUCE: MAKES ABOUT 4 CUPS [960 mL]

1½ tablespoons [25 mL] olive oil

1 medium onion, minced

2 garlic cloves, minced

½ red bell pepper, seeded and minced

1 ripe red jalapeño chile, seeded and minced

1 bay leaf

½ teaspoon [3 mL] comino (ground cumin)

½ teaspoon [3 mL] dried oregano, crumbled

½ teaspoon [3 mL] sugar

Salt and pepper to taste

1 cup [240 mL] beef stock

3 cups [720 mL] tomato purée

1 teaspoon [5 mL] cayenne

MEATBALLS

1½ pounds [675 g] lean ground beef

1 teaspoon [5 mL] salt

½ teaspoon [3 mL] black pepper

4 garlic cloves, minced

1 cup [240 mL] plain breadcrumbs

½ teaspoon [3 mL] dried oregano

½ teaspoon [3 mL] comino (ground cumin)

2 eggs, beaten

Flour, for dusting

Vegetable oil, for sautéing

ADVANCE PREPARATION

1. All advance preparation may be found in the ingredient list.

PREPARATION OF THE SAUCE

2. Heat the oil in a large pot and sauté the onion, garlic, bell pepper, and jalapeño until the onion is translucent.

3. Add the bay leaf, comino, oregano, sugar, salt and pepper, stock, tomato purée, and cayenne. Simmer for 15 minutes.

4. Remove the bay leaf and purée the sauce in a food processor or blender. Keep warm.

PREPARING THE MEATBALLS

5. Combine the beef, salt, pepper, garlic, breadcrumbs, oregano, comino, and beaten eggs in a bowl and mix thoroughly. If the mixture seems too dry, add a little milk or stock to moisten.

6. Roll into 48 balls 1 inch [2.5 cm] in diameter and dust in flour.

COOKING METHOD

7. Sauté the meatballs in oil until lightly browned. Drain on paper towels. Bring the sauce to a simmer, add the meatballs, and cook 15 minutes.

SERVICE

8. Serve 4 meatballs per person, in small bowls topped with liberal amounts of sauce.

Beef Pie with Apricots Pastel de Carne y Albaricoque

serves 8

South America produces some of the tastiest apricots in the world, and they are a surprising addition to this dish. Many beef dishes from South America, especially in the south, combine the sweetness of fruit (typically raisins) with a salty or sour component. This combination of flavors has its origins in Medieval Europe and was brought over to the New World by the Spanish conquerors in the sixteenth and seventeenth centuries from their Moorish ancestors.

⊙ CHEF NOTES

Although canned apricots are called for in this recipe, plumped dried apricots or fresh apricots may be substituted (add a bit of sugar to compensate). This dish is traditionally topped with a meringue, should you feel adventurous.

PASTRY DOUGH

1½ cups [360 mL] flour

Pinch of salt

½ teaspoon [3 mL] garlic powder

2 tablespoons [30 mL] sugar

4 ounces [110 g] butter, cut into small pieces

1 egg yolk

2 to 4 tablespoons [30 to 60 mL] dry white wine, chilled

FILLING

12 ounces [340 g] beef sirloin steak, semifrozen, sliced very thin

1 tablespoon [15 mL] vegetable oil

½ onion, thinly sliced

2 garlic cloves, minced

2 tablespoons [30 mL] dry white wine

1 tablespoon [15 mL] sugar

½ teaspoon [3 mL] whole leaf oregano

½ teaspoon [3 mL] ground cinnamon

¼ teaspoon [1 mL] ground cloves

¼ teaspoon [1 mL] ground allspice

1 small bay leaf

Salt and pepper to taste

3 tablespoons [45 mL] raisins, soaked in warm water and drained

6 canned apricot halves, slivered

ADVANCE PREPARATION

1. All advance preparation may be found in the ingredient list.

PREPARATION OF THE PASTRY

2. Sift the flour, salt, garlic powder, and sugar together and place in the workbowl of a food processor. Add the butter and pulse to form a mixture that resembles coarse meal.

3. Add the egg yolk, followed by the wine, using only enough wine to form a soft dough. Divide the dough in two, wrap in plastic film, and chill 1 hour.

4. Sauté the meat quickly in hot vegetable oil to slightly brown.

5. Lower the heat and add the onion and garlic. Cook, while stirring, until the onions turn translucent.

6. Add the wine, sugar, oregano, cinnamon, cloves, allspice, bay leaf, and salt and pepper. Bring to a boil, then lower the heat and simmer, covered, for 15 minutes.

7. Remove the bay leaf and add the raisins and slivered apricots. Transfer to a bowl and allow to cool.

PREPARATION OF THE PIE

8. On a lightly floured surface roll out two-thirds of the dough and line the inside of a 9-inch [23-cm] round cake pan.

9. Add the meat filling and top with the apricot slivers, cut side down.

10. Roll out the second half of dough to fit the top of the pie. Cover the filling with the dough and seal the edges with the tines of a fork or pinch decoratively, trimming any excess dough.

COOKING METHOD

11. Bake for 30 minutes at 375°F [190°C] until the top is browned and the filling is bubbling.

SERVICE

12. Cut the pie into 8 portions. Serve 1 piece per person, warm.

Citrus-Marinated Fish Ceviche

Ceviche (also spelled seviche) originated in Polynesia. Some people are surprised that the fish in ceviche is not cooked; rather, it is marinated and served "raw." From a chemistry standpoint the fish is not raw because it has been "cooked" by the acidity of the citrus. High temperature and acidity affect the proteins of the fish in a similar way, which is why the fish appears opaque. One of the tastiest versions is found in Ecuador, where Seville (sour or bitter) oranges are used, imparting a unique flavor.

CHEF NOTES

Any firm-fleshed fish may be substituted, including shellfish, such as lobster, shrimp, or scallops, or any combination. Octopus makes an authentic version. Jalapeño chiles are known to be hottest at the end of summer. Vary the amount of chile to taste. Use fresh aji amarillo chiles for a Peruvian version. The chiles will impart a striking yellow tint to the dish, as well as the fruity flavor these chiles are known for.

1½ cups [360 mL] fresh lime juice

1½ cups [360 mL] sour orange juice, or substitute (see page 116)

4 garlic cloves, minced

2 medium red onions, finely diced

4 jalapeño chiles, minced (seeds and ribs removed to control spiciness if desired)

Salt and pepper to taste

1 cup [240 mL] vegetable oil

1½ pounds [675 g] firm white-fleshed fish fillets, cut into ½-inch [1-cm] pieces

Lettuce leaves or endive, for garnish

Cilantro leaves, for garnish

Pitted black olives, for garnish

Tortillas or tostados, for service

ADVANCE PREPARATION

1. All advance preparation may be found in the ingredient list.

PREPARATION OF THE CEVICHE

2. Combine the lime and sour orange juices with the garlic, onions, chiles, salt, pepper, and oil and mix well. Place the fish in a resealable plastic bag and pour the marinade over. Toss the fish to coat. Refrigerate for 4 to 6 hours. The fish will be done when the flesh turns white and opaque.

SERVICE

3. Using a slotted spoon, place a 4-ounce [110-g] portion of the ceviche onto a lettuce leaf. Garnish with cilantro and black olives. Serve with tortillas or tostados. For a sophisticated presentation serve the ceviche in deco-style martini glasses.

Potato and Cheese Pancakes Llapingachos

serves 8 (2 pancakes per person)

This Ecuadorian version of cheese and potato cakes is the result of the Spanish introduction of cattle and the subsequent techniques of butter and cheese making. Variations of the dish exist between highland and coastal areas, with fried plantain and a spicy peanut-sauce topping characterizing the coastal version. The highland version is accompanied by avocado, lettuce, and tomato salsa. Both versions are often cooked in oil flavored and tinted with annatto. Pan-frying these delicate cakes requires a large amount of oil (the cakes tend to fall apart when turned), so broiling offers a safer and easier cooking method.

CHEF NOTES

Traditionally the potato pancakes would be pan-fried in lard. The cakes are so delicate it is best to broil them. Brushing the cakes with melted butter before broiling adds considerable flavor.

2½ pounds [1.1 kg] baking potatoes, peeled and quartered

½ teaspoon [3 mL] garlic powder

Salt and pepper to taste

½ cup [120 mL] butter, plus 2 tablespoons

1 large onion, minced

⅔ cup [160 mL] cilantro, minced

8 ounces [225 g] Muenster cheese, cut into very small dice

Melted butter, for brushing

Avocado, for garnish

Shredded lettuce, for garnish

1 cup tomato salsa, for garnish

ADVANCE PREPARATION

1. All advance preparation may be found in the ingredient list.

PREPARATION OF THE POTATO PANCAKES

2. Boil the potatoes at a simmer until soft. Drain the potatoes and mash them with the garlic powder, salt, pepper, and butter.

3. Sauté the onion in butter until translucent. Add the onion mixture and the cilantro to the mashed potatoes and mix well. Allow to cool.

4. Stir in the cheese and shape the potato mixture into 16 balls. Flatten each ball into a patty about 1 inch [2.5 cm] thick.

5. Place the potato cakes on a greased foil-lined cookie sheet, then brush the tops with melted butter. Refrigerate for 20 to 30 minutes, or until set.

COOKING METHOD

6. Brown the cakes under a preheated broiler until the tops are deep golden brown. (Be careful when handling the cakes, as they tend to stick to the pan and can fall apart easily.)

SERVICE

7. Serve immediately, garnished with avocado slices on shredded lettuce and tomato salsa on the side.

Quinoa Croquettes Frituras de Quinua

serves 8 (3 croquettes per person)

Quinoa is called a grain, but technically it is not a grain but the seed of an annual herb. The Incas cherished it since it could grow where corn could not. Quinoa has been cultivated for thousands of years, making it one of the oldest food staples. The Inca name for quinoa is *chesiya mama,* meaning mother grain. Each year the Incan emperor would plant the first seed with a golden spade, and at the time of the solstice offerings of quinoa seeds carried in golden vessels were made to the Sun, Inti.

CHEF NOTES

Quinoa is quite versatile and may substitute for rice or other grains in dishes. The leaves are rich in vitamins and can substitute for spinach in recipes, should it be available in markets. Use Argentine Parmesan cheese for an authentic taste.

⅔ cup [160 mL] quinoa

¼ cup [60 mL] flour

½ teaspoon [3 mL] garlic powder

¼ cup [60 mL] Parmesan cheese, grated or shredded

½ tablespoon [8 mL] coarse salt

5 scallions, minced

3 tablespoons [45 mL] parsley, chopped

1 egg, beaten

1 egg yolk

¾ cup [180 mL] vegetable oil, for frying

Lime wedges, for garnish

Salsa, for service

ADVANCE PREPARATION

1. Toast the quinoa in a nonstick skillet over medium-high heat, stirring constantly while scraping the bottom of the pan, for 5 minutes.

2. Place the quinoa in a small saucepan with ½ cup [360 mL] cold water. Simmer, covered, 10 minutes, or until all the liquid has been absorbed. Allow to cool.

PREPARATION OF THE CROQUETTES

3. Combine the quinoa, flour, garlic powder, Parmesan cheese, and salt and mix well.

4. Add the scallions, parsley, beaten egg, and egg yolk and blend thoroughly.

COOKING METHOD

5. Heat the oil in a skillet over medium heat. Carefully drop 2-tablespoon [30-mL] portions of dough into the oil. Cook until the croquettes are golden brown. Drain on paper towels.

SERVICE

6. Serve 3 croquettes, warm, with lime wedges and salsa.

Brazil

**Gaucho-Style Grilled Portuguese Sausage
with Tomato Sauce**
Linguiça Churrasco a Gaucha com Môlho ao Tomates

Garlic Chicken Wings
Frango a Passarinho

Black-Eyed Pea Fritters
Acarajé

Shrimp and Fish Stew with Coconut Milk
Vatapá de camarão e peixe

Bahian-Style Mussels
Mariscos à Moda Baiana

Lobster Gratin in Pineapple Cases
Lagosta Gratinado em Abacaxi

Potato and Salt Cod Croquettes
Boliñhos de Bacalhau

Empanadas with Shrimp and Heart of Palm Filling
Empadinhas

Grilled Shrimp on Sugarcane Skewers
Cana de Açúcar com Camarão

BRAZILIAN CUISINE IS the most enticing of the cuisines of South America. Appetizers and snacks are popular in the late afternoon and early evening and are commonly served in cafés (*confeitarias*), as dinner is usually served at around ten o'clock. Street foods bought from vendors are very common. *Tiragostos* (literally, taste pullers), *salgadinhos frios* (small, cold savory things), *salgadinhos quentes* (small, hot savory things), *boliñhos* (small cakes or patties), *empadas, empadhinas,* and *pastèizinhos* (small savory turnovers and pastries), *almôndegas* (meatballs), and *fritangas* (fritters) bring excitement to Brazilian appetizers.

Brazil is the world's fifth largest nation and the largest in South America. It is bordered by Uruguay to the south, Argentina, Paraguay, Bolivia, Peru, and Colombia to the west, with Venezuela, Guyana, Suriname, and French Guiana to the north. The Atlantic Ocean borders the entire eastern coastline. The country extends from just north of the Equator to just south of the Tropic of Capricorn. It is the only country in South America with Portuguese heritage and the only one in which African slaves played a major role in its development. Brazil's lush environment provides all fruits and vegetables common to North America as well as all of the tropical fruits and vegetables of the world. Brazil's great expanse, from north to south and from jungle river basins to highlands, provides a broad temperature range, ensuring agricultural diversity. Pineapples and papaya are native to South America, and sweet potatoes have their origin in the Amazon River basin. Brazil is the world's largest producer of coffee and sugarcane and one of the largest producers of soybeans.

Brazil's large size fosters regional cooking styles. There are three distinct regional cuisines: that of Bahia on the northeast coast, that of São Paulo to the south, and *cariocan*, which is basically the food of Rio and is considered the country's style as a whole. The food of Bahia is admired across Brazil; it is the most exciting of the regional cuisines and is the most popular of the three. It is heavily influenced by the Africans and is a blend of African, Portuguese, and Indian ingredients and cooking methods. *Cariocan* cuisine is more subdued than Bahian and closer to traditional Portuguese cooking. São Paulo and Minas Gerais to the south share a regional cuisine, which is much heartier, reflecting a cooler climate. Some areas have retained dishes in their original form from centuries past. *Moquecas* and *vatapá* (seafood stews) are tasty examples. The isolation of remote areas was instrumental in preserving many of the traditional dishes while inhabitants of larger metropolitan areas were rapidly adopting new dishes from around the world.

Brazil's unique ethnic makeup directly led to the development of an original cooking style, distinguishing it from the other countries of South America. By the mid-1800s an economic recession was taking hold in Europe and Brazilian landowners brought in Swiss, German, Italian, Syrian, and Lebanese farmers to work and manage their agricultural holdings. These immigrants brought their culinary traditions with them, adding cultural diversity, although the two main influences forming Brazilian cuisine as we know it today remain the indigenous native Indian population and the Africans. Their cooking methods were adopted by the Portuguese and together the three blended to form a unique style.

The Portuguese brought sugarcane to Brazil shortly after their arrival as well as the first African slaves to work the labor-intensive crop in 1550. Peanuts (*amendoim*) are native to South America, and the Portuguese exported peanuts to West Africa, where they are now an important crop. The Africans brought their own foods, such as okra, and cooking techniques. They introduced the concept of cooking with oil, which the Indians never used. Dendê oil, extracted from the fruit or kernels of an African and South American palm, *Elaesis guineensis*, was brought to Brazil by the African slaves and is widely used in Bahian cuisine. Color and strength may vary, but dendê is a thick oil that is high in vitamin A, with an intense reddish-orange color. It is used in cooking primarily for the color it imparts, but it does also add a subtle taste and texture.

Cassava, a dry starchy root native to Brazil, comes in two forms, sweet and bitter. Sweet cassava is used as a starch, much like sweet potatoes. Manioc, or bitter cassava, is a food staple in Brazil and West Africa. It is low in protein, and since it contains cyanide, it must be processed carefully to be eaten safely. When made into flour, it is called *farinha de mandioca,* and when formed into pellets, tapioca. The toasted flour is called *farofa. Farofa* is always present on the Brazilian table, to be sprinkled over food. It is used as a condiment as frequently as salt and pepper. Among poor peoples, *farinha* is used as flour to make simple bread or a coarse porridge. *Farinha* is also made into thin cakes that are considered a delicacy. Hearts of palm, the tender young shoots of a South American palm tree, are unique to Brazilian cookery. They are used primarily in soups, stews, and salads. Coconuts are quite popular and the milk is used frequently in Bahian cuisine. The most popular chile in Brazil is the malagueta. Malaguetas are native to Brazil and were taken back to Africa during slave trade voyages. They are very small, usually less than an inch long, and extremely hot chiles. They resemble a small Tabasco chile, and are usually sold in the United States packed in vinegar, imported from Africa. The vinegar sauce may be used straight from the bottle and the chiles may be removed and chopped for use in recipes. The Bahians commonly make a paste of dried malaguetas that have been soaked in water and then mixed with garlic, salt, and spices.

Brazilians eat far less meat than their neighbors in Argentina and Uruguay, but barbecue is very popular and all types of grilled meats are served in restaurants (*churrascarias*) specializing in grilled and barbecued meats and sausages (*churrasco*). Black beans are a staple, accounting for more than 80 percent of all beans consumed. Rice is, by far, the most popular starch consumed in Brazil. The Portuguese brought many foods to Brazil, such as mangoes and bananas from India that are now major Brazilian commercial crops. Ginger-root is favored in Bahian cuisine, imported by the Portuguese via the Orient. They also introduced salt cod (*bacalhau*) and dried shrimp. Brazil has an abundant annual harvest of shrimp, and half of it is dried. Afro-Bahian recipes typically call for large amounts of dried shrimp. The salt cod is almost exclusively imported from Europe. Stewing and the use of wine in cooking were also introduced by the Portuguese.

Gaucho-Style Grilled Portuguese Sausage with Tomato Sauce
Linguiça Churrasco a Gaucha com Môlho ao Tomates

serves 8

This Brazilian version of barbecue, known as *churrasco a gaucha*, originated in the southern state of Rio Grande do Sul, bordering Argentina and Uruguay, which is prime cattle production land. When the Portuguese imported sugarcane to Brazil they also banned cattle, because they did not want the cattle eating that valuable crop. When cattle finally were introduced, all were shipped to the south, far away from the sugarcane (where, coincidentally, the best grazing land was to be found). The use of a bunch of parsley as the basting brush, called *salmora*, is an adaptation of a method used throughout the Middle East and the Iberian Peninsula. The use of seasoned brine to baste is typical of South American barbecues and the tomato sauce featured with this recipe is the traditional accompaniment for a Brazilian barbecue.

TOMATO SAUCE (MÔLHO AO TOMATE):
MAKES 4 CUPS [960 mL]

6 tablespoons [90 mL] olive oil

6 garlic cloves, minced

8 large ripe tomatoes, diced

2 tablespoons tomato paste

12 fresh basil leaves, chiffonade

½ cup [120 mL] hot water

Salt and black pepper to taste

BASTING MIXTURE

2 cups [480 mL] warm water

½ cup [120 mL] kosher, sea, or rock salt

2 small onions, puréed or grated

½ cup [120 mL] fresh parsley, chopped

8 garlic cloves, finely minced

1 bunch of parsley, washed and dried, for basting

1½ pounds [675 g] Portuguese lingüiça sausage

Sprigs of parsley or a chiffonade of basil leaves, for garnish

ADVANCE PREPARATION

1. All advance preparation may be found in the ingredient list.

PREPARATION OF THE TOMATO SAUCE

2. Heat the oil in a saucepan and add the garlic. Sauté for 30 seconds, while stirring, then add the tomatoes, tomato paste, and basil.

3. Simmer for 4 to 5 minutes, then add the hot water. Simmer the mixture over low heat, stirring occasionally, until quite thick. Season with salt and pepper.

4. Purée in a food processor. Reserve or refrigerate for later use. (The sauce can be made several days in advance.)

PREPARATION OF THE BASTING MIXTURE

5. Combine the water, salt, puréed onions, chopped parsley, and garlic in a shallow bowl. Dip the bunch of parsley into the basting mixture and baste the tops of the sausages.

COOKING METHOD

6. Sear the sausages on a charbroiler. Turn the sausages and baste again. Baste and turn frequently until the sausages are browned and cooked through. Remove from the grill and allow to stand 5 minutes before slicing.

SERVICE

7. Ladle about ¼ cup [60 mL] of the tomato sauce in a pool on a serving plate. Slice the lingüiça thin, on the diagonal, and arrange 4 ounces [110 g] attractively on the tomato sauce. Garnish with parsley sprigs or a chiffonade of basil leaves.

Garlic Chicken Wings Frango a Passarinho

serves 8 (2 to 3 pieces per person)

Baked, sautéed, and deep-fried versions of this dish can be found, but this recipe calls for baking followed by sautéing, a style of preparation that assures more control over the cooked garlic. The dish begins with a classic Brazilian marinade, known as *vinho d'alhos*, after which the chicken is cooked. The chicken wings are then tossed with the lightly fried garlic slivers for a crunchy finish.

CHEF NOTES

Be careful not to burn the garlic when frying, or it will impart a bitter taste to the dish.

32 chicken wing drumettes

Salt

6 garlic cloves, minced

Juice of 2 limes

1 tablespoon [15 mL] ground black pepper

1 cup [240 mL] dry white wine

¼ cup [60 mL] vegetable oil

16 garlic cloves, finely diced

1 tablespoon [15 mL] olive oil

ADVANCE PREPARATION

1. Rub the chicken drumettes with salt.

2. Mix the garlic, lime juice, pepper, and wine together to form a marinade (*vinha d'alhos*).

3. Place the chicken in a large bowl. Pour the marinade over and toss well. Refrigerate at least 45 minutes. (The chicken can be marinated overnight.)

COOKING METHOD

4. Place the chicken in a baking dish and bake in a preheated oven at 375°F [190°C] for 20 minutes, turning the pieces after 10 minutes.

5. Heat the vegetable oil in a large nonstick skillet and fry the chicken pieces, turning occasionally, until browned and crisp. Drain the chicken on paper towels.

6. Fry the garlic in the olive oil in a medium skillet over moderate heat, until lightly browned.

SERVICE

7. Place the chicken pieces in a bowl while still hot and toss with the fried garlic. Serve 4 drumettes per person, hot or cold.

Black-Eyed Pea Fritters Acarajé

The fritters are made locally from the *fradinho* bean, which is very similar to the black-eyed pea of the American South. African slaves brought the beans with them to the region around Bahia, where the dish originated. The dish is popular nationwide and some versions use mashed navy beans blended with dried or fresh shrimp for the batter. Normally these light fritters are split open and stuffed with one of several sauces, including *vatapá*, malagueta chile sauce, chile-okra sauce, or a sauce of dried shrimp, chiles, and ginger. For authentic color and taste, at least a portion of the oil in which the *acarajé* are fried should be dendê oil.

CHEF NOTES

Malagueta chiles can be purchased bottled, packed whole in vinegar (and occasionally in *cachaça*, Brazilian sugarcane rum). They are red, fiery hot, and resemble a short, thin Tabasco chile. They may be purchased at Latin American (and some African or Portuguese) markets and specialty stores.

3 cups [720 mL] dried black-eyed peas

1 cup [240 mL] dried shrimp, soaked in cold water 30 minutes

2 large onions, diced fine

Salt to taste, as necessary (the dried shrimp will add saltiness)

White pepper to taste

6 preserved malagueta chiles, minced

½ cup [120 mL] dendê oil

Vegetable oil heated to 355°F [180°C] in a deep fryer, for frying

ADVANCE PREPARATION

1. Soak the peas in cold water to cover for 24 hours, refrigerated. Periodically rub the peas between your hands to loosen the skins. Allow time for the skins to rise to the surface, then remove them with a slotted spoon. Drain and replenish with fresh water. When completely softened, drain the peas and reserve.

PREPARATION OF THE FRITTER BATTER

2. Place the peas and the softened dried shrimp in the workbowl of a food processor. Blend to a coarse consistency and transfer to a bowl.

3. Stir the onions, salt (if necessary), white pepper, chiles, and dendê oil into the pea mixture and blend well.

COOKING METHOD

4. Using 2 metal spoons, scoop about 1½ tablespoons [25 mL] of the mixture and shape into a small cake using the back of the second spoon.

5. Reverse the second spoon and use it to gently slide the cake into the hot oil. Turn the fritters after about 3 minutes. When golden brown, remove with a slotted spoon and drain on paper towels.

SERVICE

6. Traditionally *acarajé* are served split lengthwise, then stuffed with 2 tablespoons [30 mL] of *vatapá* (see page 151).

Shrimp and Fish Stew with Coconut Milk Vatapá de camarão e peixe

Vatapá is an African-inspired Bahian specialty that has been adopted throughout Brazil. Traditionally it is made with seafood, but it may also be made with poultry.

CHEF NOTES

Add the shrimp and fish just before serving.

3 tablespoons [45 mL] vegetable oil

1 tablespoon [15 mL] dendê oil

1 large onion, diced

3 garlic cloves, minced

1 teaspoon [5 mL] ginger, minced fine

4 tomatoes, seeded and chopped

3 preserved malagueta chiles, minced

Juice of 1 lime

2 tablespoons [30 mL] cilantro leaves

1 tablespoon [15 mL] parsley

4 cups [960 mL] coconut milk

¼ cup [60 mL] ground dried shrimp

½ cup [120 mL] ground roasted cashew nuts

¼ cup [60 mL] ground roasted almonds

¾ cup [180 mL] unsweetened coconut, grated

1-inch [2.5-cm] slice fresh ginger, minced

12 ounces [340 g] raw shrimp, peeled and deveined

1 pound [450 g] fish fillets, such as sea bass, cod, or tilapia, cut into pieces

Rice or warm *acarajé* (see page 150), for service

Sprigs of cilantro, for garnish

ADVANCE PREPARATION

1. All advance preparation may be found in the ingredient list.

COOKING METHOD

2. Heat the oils together in a heavy skillet and sauté the onion, garlic, and the 1 teaspoon of minced ginger until the onion is translucent.

3. Add the tomatoes, chiles, lime juice, cilantro, and parsley. Simmer for 5 minutes. Add the coconut milk, dried shrimp, cashews, and almonds. Simmer for 3 minutes, then add the coconut and remaining ginger. Simmer for 3 minutes more.

4. Remove from the heat and place in the workbowl of a food processor. Purée until smooth, adding a little water or chicken stock if too thick. (The sauce may be prepared up to 2 days in advance. Reheat, then add the shrimp and fish shortly before serving.)

5. Return the mixture to the pan and stir in the raw shrimp and fish. Simmer just until the seafood is cooked, 4 to 5 minutes.

SERVICE

6. Serve the *vatapá* with rice or with the warm *acarajé*, split. Fill the *acarajé* just before serving to preserve crispness of the fritters. Garnish with cilantro sprigs.

Bahian-Style Mussels Mariscos à Moda Baiana

serves 8

Mussels are harvested all along the extensive coastline of Brazil and, like oysters in the United States, are thought to be an aphrodisiac. They are also believed to lessen the effects of alcohol consumption and are commonly eaten before and after a night on the town. In Brazil, mussels are eaten raw, like oysters, as well as cooked in a number of ways. They should be served with plenty of crusty bread to soak up all of the delicious pan juices.

CHEF NOTES

To purge the mussels, soak them in salted water for 30 minutes, then in fresh cold water for 5 minutes. A nylon scrubbing pad works well to grip the beards for removal.

3 tablespoons [45 mL] olive oil

6 scallions, finely diced

3 medium onions, diced

6 garlic cloves, minced

2 malagueta chiles, minced

Juice of 1 lime

4 tomatoes, diced

½ cup [120 mL] white wine

½ cup [120 mL] coconut milk

¼ cup [60 mL] chicken stock or clam juice

1 bunch cilantro, chopped fine

Salt and black pepper to taste

8 dozen fresh mussels, all tightly closed, purged and beards removed (see Chef Notes)

Lime quarters, for garnish

Sprigs of cilantro, for garnish

Crusty bread, for service

ADVANCE PREPARATION

1. All advance preparation may be found in the ingredient list.

COOKING METHOD

2. Heat the oil in a large skillet and briefly sauté the scallions, onions, garlic, chiles, lime juice, and tomatoes.

3. Add the wine, coconut milk, and stock, and bring to a boil. Add the cilantro, salt and pepper, and the mussels. Cover the skillet. When the mussels open, they are done. Discard any mussels that do not open.

SERVICE

4. Serve 12 mussels per person. Ladle over some of the sauce. Garnish with lime wedges and sprigs of cilantro. Serve with crusty bread. (Provide a bowl for empty shells.)

Lobster Gratin in Pineapple Cases Lagosta Gratinado em Abacaxi

serves 8

Lobsters are popular seafood all along the northeast coast of Brazil, and the type caught is the clawless spiny lobster, or *lagosta*. Pineapples are native to Brazil and come in an astonishing array of varieties and sizes. The name *abacaxi* comes from the Brazilian Tupi Indian word for the fruit. The juices of the pineapple will have a tenderizing effect on the lobster meat. Mixing them together in this recipe should take place no longer than 30 minutes before baking to prevent the lobster meat from breaking down.

CHEF NOTES

While this dish is traditionally made with lobster or langoustines, rock shrimp makes an excellent substitution while keeping the taste authentic. Leave out the seafood for a vegetarian version.

2 small ripe pineapples

3 tablespoons [45 mL] butter

1½ tablespoons [25 mL] dendê oil

4 shallots, minced

4 garlic cloves, minced

1 teaspoon [5 mL] ginger, minced fine

6 ounces [180 g] mushrooms, quartered

2 chayote squash, peeled and diced

2 medium carrots, cut into ½-inch [1-cm] strips, blanched 3 minutes in boiling water and refreshed

Salt and white pepper to taste

⅓ cup [80 mL] heavy cream

⅓ cup [80 mL] thick coconut milk

¼ cup [60 mL] chopped parsley

1¼ pounds [560 g] lobster meat

¼ cup [60 mL] Parmesan cheese, shredded

⅓ cup [80 mL] *farinha* de *mandioca* (cassava meal)

Sprigs of flat-leaf parsley, for garnish

ADVANCE PREPARATION

1. Cut the top and bottom off the pineapples. Cut each into 4 "wheels." Remove the flesh from each with a corer. Chop the pulp and reserve. Place the pineapple shells on paper towels to drain.

LOBSTER FILLING

2. In a large skillet melt the butter with the dendê oil. Sauté the shallots, garlic, and ginger for 30 seconds.

3. Add the mushrooms, chayote squash, carrots, and salt and pepper. Sauté for 5 minutes, or until the squash and carrots are tender.

4. Add the cream and the coconut milk. Reduce the heat and simmer for 5 minutes.

5. Add the parsley, stirring well to combine.

6. Add the lobster meat, stirring briefly. Remove from the heat. Stir in the reserved chopped pineapple.

COOKING METHOD

7. Place the pineapple shells on a baking sheet lined with parchment paper. Stuff the pineapple shells with the prepared lobster mixture.

8. Blend the Parmesan cheese and the *farinha* together and sprinkle this mixture on top of the filling.

9. Bake in a preheated oven at 375°F [190°C] for 15 minutes, or until the topping is browned.

SERVICE

10. Serve immediately, garnished with parsley sprigs.

Potato and Salt Cod Croquettes Boliñhos de Bacalhau

Salt cod fritters are the most popular of the *salgadinhos* (small salted things). They are served with drinks at bars and are commonly found at street vendor stalls all over the country. Dried, salted codfish was imported to Brazil by the Portuguese and has been popular for more than four hundred years, although lately its high cost has discouraged some from using it. As a result, resourceful Brazilians have begun to prepare the local catch in this fashion, calling it *bacalhau brasiliero* (Brazilian salt cod), or *bacalhau do pobre* (poor man's salt cod). For the novice, these fritters are the perfect introduction to salt cod, since they have such a subtle flavor. *Boliñhos de bacalhau* are a common dish for local chefs to experiment with by adding different herbs, spices, and other flavorings. Shredded, cooked chicken meat can be substituted for the salt cod in this recipe to reduce cost. The fritters are usually served with a malagueta chile sauce on the side.

2 pounds [900 g] salt cod (dry weight)

I pound [450 g] potatoes, peeled, cubed, boiled, and mashed

⅓ cup [80 mL] parsley, chopped

⅔ cup [160 mL] onion, chopped

3 garlic cloves, minced

Salt, if necessary, and black pepper to taste

1⅓ cups [320 mL] milk

⅓ cup [80 mL] all-purpose flour

½ teaspoon [3 mL] grated nutmeg

I teaspoon [5 mL] paprika

4 eggs, beaten

Oil, for deep-frying

Peppery sauce, for side dish

Tomato sauce, for side dish

ADVANCE PREPARATION

1. Rinse the pieces of salt cod under cold running water. Soak in water, refrigerated, overnight, changing the water periodically. Discard the soaking liquid and rinse the cod in cold water. (The salt cod can be prepared 1 day in advance.)

PREPARATION OF THE CROQUETTE DOUGH

2. Simmer the reconstituted salt cod in water for 15 minutes. Drain and remove the skin. Allow to cool enough to handle, then shred the fish with your hands, feeling for and removing any bones.

3. Pulse the fish in a food processor.

4. Combine all of the ingredients and mix thoroughly. Adjust for salt, keeping in mind that some saltiness always remains in reconstituted salt cod.

5. Divide the mixture into 16 balls, flattening them slightly. Allow the croquettes to rest for 1 hour, refrigerated, covered with plastic film.

When purchasing salt cod, the belly cut, which has more meat, is preferred. When reconstituting salt cod, a portion of the total weight will be lost to removal of the salt, skin, and bones. Two pounds [900 g] of dried salt cod will yield about 1 pound [450 g] of cooked skinless and boneless salt cod.

COOKING METHOD

6. Fry the croquettes in oil heated to 355°F [180°C], turning them when slightly golden on 1 side. Remove with a slotted spoon and drain on paper towels. Keep warm until all are cooked.

SERVICE

7. Serve 2 per person, warm, with a side dish of peppery sauce with okra (*môlho de nagó*) or tomato sauce.

Empanadas with Shrimp and Heart of Palm Stuffing Empadinhas

Empadinhas can be baked as turnovers, but generally they are prepared as miniature pies in pans very similar to muffin tins that are lined with pastry and then topped with pastry circles. (The baked turnovers found in the rest of Latin America are known as empadas, or empanadas.) The stuffing is of the style found in Bahia.

CHEF NOTES

A larger version of the baked pies, called an *empadão*, can be made and served in wedges much like a quiche. For a large quantity or to make *empadinhas* on the spur of the moment, prepared egg roll wrappers, gyoza, or shau mai wrappers may be substituted for homemade pastry.

PASTRY: MAKES ENOUGH FOR TWENTY-FOUR 2½-INCH [6-CM] PIES

2½ cups [600 mL] flour

½ teaspoon [3 mL] salt

⅛ teaspoon [0.5 mL] garlic powder

2 ounces [55 g] lard, diced

2 ounces [55 g] butter, diced

2 egg yolks

4 to 5 tablespoons [60 to 75 mL] ice water

1 egg, beaten, for egg wash

SHRIMP AND HEART OF PALM STUFFING: MAKES 3 CUPS [720 mL]

2 tablespoons [30 mL] dendê oil

2 tablespoons [30 mL] olive oil

1 medium onion, minced

1 medium green bell pepper, seeded and chopped

2 preserved malagueta chiles (or fresh serranos), minced

1 pound [450 g] shrimp, peeled, deveined, and coarsely chopped

Salt to taste

⅔ cup [160 mL] canned hearts of palm, drained, chopped

2 egg yolks

½ cup [120 mL] thick coconut milk

1 tablespoon [15 mL] chopped cilantro leaves

ADVANCE PREPARATION

1. All advance preparation can be found in the ingredient list.

PREPARATION OF THE PASTRY

2. Sift the flour, salt, and garlic powder together into the workbowl of a food processor. Add the lard and butter. Pulse to form a coarse meal.

3. Add the egg yolks and just enough of the ice water to make a soft dough, pulsing to form the dough. It should not be sticky.

4. Wrap the dough in plastic film and chill at least 1 hour. (The pastry can be made 1 day in advance.)

5. Roll the dough out on a lightly floured surface to $\frac{1}{16}$ inch [1.5 mm] thick. Cut 16 circles that are 1½ inches [4 cm] larger than the diameter of a standard muffin-tin well. Cut an equal number of circles that are the same size as the tops of the wells.

PREPARATION OF THE STUFFING

6. Heat the 2 oils together in a large skillet and sauté the onion, bell pepper, and chiles until soft.

7. Add the shrimp, salt, and hearts of palm and sauté for 2 minutes.

8. Beat the egg yolks and coconut milk together and add slowly to the skillet while stirring briskly.

9. Add the cilantro and cook until the mixture thickens to the consistency of a medium white sauce. Remove the filling from the heat and allow to cool.

PREPARATION OF THE PASTRIES

10. Press the larger circles into the interior of the muffin tins, lining each cavity.

11. Spoon in the stuffing to fill three-fourths full.

12. Brush the exposed pastry with beaten egg, then place the smaller piece of dough over the top. Crimp the edges together. Brush the tops with beaten egg.

COOKING METHOD

13. Bake at 350°F [175°C] for 30 minutes, or until the tops are golden brown.

SERVICE

14. Serve 2 per person, hot from the oven, warm, or at room temperature.

Grilled Shrimp on Sugarcane Skewers Cana de Açúcar com Camarão

The occupation of Portugal by the Moors left the Portuguese with a love of sweets, which they brought to Brazil. The source of colonial wealth for the Portuguese in the 1600s was sugarcane, grown primarily in northeastern Brazil. With 4300 miles of coastline, it is no surprise that Brazilians enjoy seafood of all kinds, especially simply grilled shellfish. The pairing of sugarcane with shellfish is a natural, as this recipe illustrates.

CHEF NOTES

Any other type of shellfish, fish, or poultry can be substituted for the shrimp in this recipe. Sugarcane can be split easily lengthwise with a cleaver or kitchen knife, but it is very difficult to cut against the grain (use a wood saw). You may place pieces of split sugarcane on the edge of the coals, cut surface down, to produce smoke while cooking the skewers.

6 garlic cloves, very finely minced

¼ cup [60 mL] onion, puréed or grated

4 malagueta chiles, very finely minced

2 tablespoons cilantro root and stems, minced

2½ tablespoons [40 mL] tamarind paste

2 tablespoons [30 mL] cachaça or rum

Salt to taste

1 tablespoon [15 mL] coarsely ground black pepper

⅓ cup [80 mL] lime juice

¾ cup [180 mL] vegetable oil

24 prawns or large shrimp, shells left on, split down the back, and deveined

Sixteen 6-inch [15-cm] lengths of sugarcane skewer, ¼ inch [6 mm] wide

8 slices mango

8 small spears pineapple

Liberal pinch of cayenne, for dusting

Cilantro sprigs, for garnish

ADVANCE PREPARATION

1. Combine the garlic, onion, chiles, cilantro, tamarind, cachaça, salt, and pepper and mix well.

2. Whisk in the lime juice and oil to form a marinade. Place the shrimp in a plastic resealable bag and pour the marinade over the shrimp. Marinate, refrigerated, for at least 3 hours.

COOKING METHOD

3. Drain the shrimp and reserve the marinade for basting. Thread 3 shrimp each on 8 sugarcane skewers. Reserve.

4. Skewer 1 slice each of mango and pineapple on each of the remaining skewers. Reserve.

5. Grill the shrimp over hot coals, preferably with coconut husks or shells added when building the fire, basting frequently.

Cook each side 3 minutes or until the shrimp become opaque. Keep warm.

6. Grill and baste the fruit skewers for 3 minutes per side. Dust the fruit slices lightly with cayenne after the final turn.

SERVICE

7. Reduce any remaining marinade over high heat to a glaze.

8. Serve each guest 1 skewer each of shrimp and fruit, glazed with the reduced marinade. Garnish with sprigs of cilantro. Provide a bowl for empty shells, and plenty of napkins.

Oceania

Beef and Gravy Pot Pie
Pie and Sauce

Lamb Chop in Pastry Purse with Madeira Sauce
Jolly Jumbuck in a Tucker Bag

Chicken, Coconut, and Scallion Salad with Chile
Mannok Kelaguen

Bacon-Wrapped Duck Liver with Water Chestnut and Scallion
Rumaki

Just-Seared Tuna Salad with Ogo Seaweed
Aku Poke

Marinated Sea Bass in Lime Juice and Coconut Milk
Kokoda

Smoked Salmon–Stuffed Cherry Tomatoes
Lomi Lomi

Mussels with Spicy Black Bean and Tomato Sauce
d'Urville Mussels

OCEANIA ENCOMPASSES MANY of the islands of the Pacific Ocean, including the Hawaiian Islands, Polynesia, Melanesia, Micronesia, Australia, and New Zealand. Polynesia (Greek for "many islands") includes American and Western Samoa, the Cook Islands, French Polynesia (Tahiti is the largest), Easter Island, the Wallis and Fortuna Islands, Tonga, Tuvalu, and Tokelau. Melanesia (Greek for "dark islands," named after the dark-skinned inhabitants) includes Papua New Guinea, New Caledonia, Fiji, the Solomon Islands, and Vanuatu. Micronesia (Greek for "tiny islands") includes Guam, the Marshall Islands, Palau, Kiribati, Nauru, and the Northern Marianas.

The Hawaiian Islands were settled by people from the South Pacific. The Tahitians and Samoans brought breadfruit, yams, taro, coconuts, bananas, pigs, chickens, and dogs to this lush and fertile land. The sweet potato is a common starch of the Polynesian and Hawaiian diet and is believed by some to have been introduced by Polynesian explorers who visited South America.

Many of the Pacific Islands are barren, not particularly fertile, and often comprised of coral, with little rich soil to support agriculture. Many islands have plants with poor food quality. The volcanic soils of the Hawaiian Islands, however, are extremely fertile, and the waters surrounding Hawaii are rich in seafood and seaweed, both staples of the Hawaiian diet. With these natural resources Hawaii became one of the most advanced cultures in the Pacific Islands.

By the 1800s whaling had become a major industry around the Hawaiian Islands, bringing settlers and missionaries from distant lands and introducing their cultures, native plants, and cooking methods. During this period dried fish and meats were introduced, as was the technique of stewing. Eventually sugarcane was brought to Hawaii; migrant laborers were brought from China, Japan, Korea, and the Philippines to work in the cane fields. This influx of Asians changed forever the cooking style and ingredients commonly used in Hawaiian cooking. The Chinese laborers who came were from South China, China's richest agricultural region. They were able to grow many of the crops familiar to them in China, including rice, soybeans, and an endless array of vegetables. A taste for pork was introduced as well. The Japanese who came to work in Hawaii introduced their preference for beef, bean curd, and various other forms of soy products, such as soy sauce and fermented soy bean paste. The Koreans brought garlic and hot peppers. The last of the workers to arrive were the Filipinos, and they found many of the fruits and vegetables from home already growing in Hawaii. They added Spanish and Malay influences to this "melting pot" cuisine. Pastry and spicy sausages were introduced by the Portuguese from the Azores and Madeira Islands.

Cooking methods among the people of the Pacific Islands are fairly simple. Without metal pots for cooking, most food was prepared by wrapping in leaves and then steaming. Ti leaves require little preparation and impart a special flavor to meats and fish. Too strong in flavor for fruits, ti leaves are replaced by banana leaves as the wrapper when cooking them. Leaf-packaged foods could be tossed directly into a wood fire to be cooked. The ceremonial Hawaiian dinner known as the luau derives its name from the ti leaf itself, called *lu'au* in Polynesian. In Tahiti the leaves are known as *fafa* and the feast is called *tamaaraa*. Another cooking method for the wrapped food was the *imu*, a hole-in-the-ground oven covered with banana leaves. A pig meant for a ceremonial dinner would be stuffed with hot stones before being buried in the *imu*, and it would come out "falling off the bone" tender, with little fat.

In addition to the famous luau, *pupu* is an eating style made popular in Hawaii. The original meaning of *pupu* is shell or any morsel of fish, chicken, or banana. Modern *pupu* is finger food, perfect for appetizers or hors d'oeuvres. *Poke* is one popular *pupu*, consisting of sashimi-style fish, seaweed, chile, and roasted kukui nut paste. The appetizer *lomi lomi* contains salted salmon with onion and tomato, and *laulau* contains pork and taro leaves steamed in ti-leaf bundles. Wrapped bundles are a popular street food throughout the islands, and fresh seafood, caught that morning, finds its way into leaf packages bought by Samoans on the go for lunch or brought home for an easy-to-prepare dinner.

Australia is an island continent whose people are mainly of English and Irish descent (95 percent of the total population). It is the most sparsely populated of the continents (excluding Antarctica) with fewer than twenty million inhabitants, most of whom live in urban settings. The native Aborigines settled the continent about 40,000 years ago and today make up less than 2 percent of the population, while Asians and Middle Easterners account for about 5 percent. Recently there has been an influx of Southeast Asians. The cuisine of Australia can be understood in the context of its people and its geography. Surrounded by water, Australians enjoy an abundance of fish and shellfish in their diet. Very little of the continent is dedicated to crop production, and what is farmed is usually under irrigation due to the arid climate. The most fertile region is in the south, on the coastal fringe of Queensland. Wheat, oats, and barley are the common grains. Australia produces a variety of fruits including apples, pears, peaches, and citrus. Dairy and beef cattle are raised in Victoria and Tasmania, and irrigation is relied on to produce fodder for the cattle. Sheep are raised as well, both for wool and as a source of meat.

In stark contrast to the flat plains of Australia, New Zealand is quite mountainous, with most of the two islands (North Island and South Island) well above sea level with more than 200 mountains over 7,000 ft in height. The land is perfect for farming and for raising sheep and cattle. Rivers and lakes abound with fish and shellfish, including freshwater cray-fish, trout, and salmon. The ocean produces snapper, flounder, squid, cod, and shellfish such as oysters, lobsters, and the famous green lip mussel. As in Australia, most of the population is of British heritage, with the remainder native Maori (who came from the Pacific Islands in the ninth century), Polynesian, and Asian. Most people live in urban areas, with half of the population occupying four cities.

The cuisines of Australia and New Zealand are very British in nature. It is difficult to find a true style that could be called Australian or New Zealand cooking. It is through local ingredients that the cooking style emerges as unique, especially when it comes to seafood. Yabbies (freshwater crayfish), mud crabs, Moreton Bay bugs (similar to slipper lobster), pearl perch, red emperor fish, trevally, barramundi, coral trout, blue grenadier, King George whiting, and giant deep-sea crabs are unique to these lands. New Zealand produces excellent farm-raised salmon. Lamb and beef are common on the Australian and New Zealand table, and meats such as kangaroo, crocodile, and emu are becoming popular fare as today's chefs explore the heritage of their countries. Australia and New Zealand's Asian connection has brought those flavors and cooking techniques. There is a strong Mediterranean influence, mainly Greek, which has recently come on the food scene. Olives are an important crop in Australia now, and olive oil is influencing the flavors of its cuisine.

Beef and Gravy Pot Pie Pie and Sauce

serves 12

The Cornish pastie is the likely origin of this famous Australian pie. It is available as take-out food all over Australia, and numerous variations and fillings exist. In Australia the pies would be served with plenty of what Australians call "tomato sauce" (ketchup to Americans). The pies are quite tasty without the sauce, as offered in this recipe, but feel free to put a bottle of ketchup on the table.

CHEF NOTES

These pastries are often topped with puff pastry for a more formal look. The addition of 1 small chopped beef kidney to the meat mixture will yield a steak and kidney pie version. The pies may be baked in advance and warmed for service, to order. Standard muffin tins (2-ounce [55-g] capacity pan) will make 12 pies. Small muffin tins (1-ounce [30-g] capacity) will yield 24 small pies (serve two per order).

PASTRY

3 cups [720 mL] flour

1 teaspoon [5 mL] baking soda

1 teaspoon [5 mL] baking powder

½ teaspoon [3 mL] salt

½ teaspoon [3 mL] garlic powder

4 ounces [110 g] butter, chilled, cut into small cubes

4 ounces [110 g] solid vegetable shortening

⅓ cup [80 mL] ice water

FILLING

12 ounces [340 g] ground chuck

1 tablespoon [15 mL] flour

1 tablespoon [15 mL] butter

2 garlic cloves, minced

¼ cup [60 mL] leeks, sliced fine

2 tablespoons [30 mL] celery, diced fine

¼ cup [60 mL] carrots, diced fine

¼ cup [60 mL] mushrooms, sliced thin

1 tablespoon [15 mL] parsley, chopped

½ teaspoon [3 mL] dried thyme

1 tablespoon [15 mL] red wine

1 cup [240 mL] rich beef stock

¼ cup [60 mL] demi-glace

Salt and pepper to taste

ADVANCE PREPARATION

1. To prepare the pastry, sift the flour, baking soda, baking powder, salt, and garlic powder together. Cut in the butter and shortening until the mixture resembles coarse meal.

2. Mix in enough ice water to form a firm dough into a ball. Turn out onto a floured work surface and knead slightly. Wrap in plastic film and refrigerate until needed. (The pastry can be made 1 day in advance.)

3. Dust the ground meat with the flour and sauté in the butter with the garlic, leeks, celery, carrots, mushrooms, parsley, and thyme until the meat is browned and the vegetables are soft.

4. Add the wine, beef stock, and demi-glace. Simmer briefly. Adjust the seasonings and reserve. (The filling can be made 1 day in advance.)

PREPARATION OF THE PIES

5. Roll out the dough as thin as possible and cut circles 2 inches [5 cm] larger than the diameter of a muffin-tin well. Line the interior of greased muffin tins with the dough.

6. Fill each muffin tin with the filling mixture and cap with a circle of dough to cover.

COOKING METHOD

7. Bake in a preheated 425°F [220°C] oven for 10 to 15 minutes, or until the tops are golden brown.

SERVICE

8. Serve the pastries hot, right from the oven. They may also be served warm.

Lamb Chop in Pastry Purse with Madeira Sauce Jolly Jumbuck in a Tucker Bag

AUSTRALIA

serves 8

This dish is named after the refrain from a famous Australian song, and some explanation for non-Australians may be in order. A "jolly jumbuck" is a sheep, or in this case, a lamb. "Tucker" refers to food. Therefore a "tucker bag" would be a sack for carrying food in the bush. In spite of its unusual name, this dish is actually quite elegant.

CHEF NOTES

In one variation of this dish, 1¼ pounds [560 g] of lamb loin are minced together with the other ingredients and a beaten egg. This mixture is formed into patties, placed in the puff pastry, and a lamb chop bone is then inserted into the meat, forming a faux chop.

MADEIRA SAUCE

2 shallots, minced

1 garlic clove, minced

1 tablespoon [15 mL] butter

¼ cup [60 mL] Madeira wine

½ cup [120 mL] demi-glace

1 cup [240 mL] chicken stock

LAMB

8 mint leaves

2 sprigs of parsley

2 sprigs of fresh marjoram

½ onion, minced

2 garlic cloves, minced

Salt and pepper to taste

1 rack of lamb with bones Frenched, cut into individual chops

2 sheets prepared puff pastry

8 strands parboiled fettuccine, cooked al dente and tossed in oil to prevent sticking

Egg wash

2 tablespoons [30 mL] cold butter, cut into ½-inch [1-cm] cubes

Mint leaves, for garnish

ADVANCE PREPARATION

1. Sauté the shallots and garlic in butter until transparent. Deglaze the pan with the Madeira. Add the demi-glace and chicken stock and reduce by two-thirds. Remove the pan from heat and hold for service. (The sauce can be made 1 day in advance.)

PREPARATION OF THE LAMB

2. Chop the mint, parsley, marjoram, onion, and garlic together to form a paste by hand or in a small processor.

3. Salt and pepper the lamb chops. Rub liberally on both sides with the herb-garlic paste.

4. Roll out the puff pastry and cut into 6-inch [15-cm] squares. Place each chop in the center of a pastry square and gather up the sides of the pastry around the chop with the bone sticking out, to form a purse.

5. Tie the strand of pasta around the gathered puff pastry to form a knot or bow.

COOKING METHOD

6. Brush the puff pastry with egg wash, wrap the bones with foil to prevent browning, and bake on a parchment-lined baking sheet at 425°F [220°C] for 15 minutes, or until the lamb is medium rare and the puff pastry is a golden brown.

7. Place the cubes of butter in the warm Madeira sauce and rapidly swirl to incorporate and emulsify the sauce.

SERVICE

8. Ladle a portion of the sauce on 1 side of a plate, placing the bone of the chop over the sauce. Garnish with mint leaves and serve immediately.

Chicken, Coconut, and Scallion Salad with Chile Mannok Kelaguen

serves 8

While there are several stages to preparing this dish, none are lengthy and preparation time is short. The result is a wonderfully refreshing salad for a warm, tropical evening (or any time of the year). This recipe may be the tastiest chicken salad ever devised. *Finidini* is a table condiment used in home kitchens in Guam that is also an excellent marinade.

CHEF NOTES

The marinade makes an excellent basting sauce for most grilled items. Try duck meat or pheasant for an interesting variation. The grilled marinated thighs make an excellent dish on their own.

MARINADE (*FINIDINI*)

I cup [240 mL] soy sauce

I cup [240 mL] lemon juice

I onion, grated

½ cup [120 mL] hot red chiles, minced

1½ pounds [675 g] boneless chicken thighs

SALAD

⅔ cup [160 mL] coconut milk

⅔ cup [160 mL] lemon juice

4 scallions, minced

½ cup [120 mL] coconut meat, grated or shredded

6 Thai chiles, roasted and very finely minced

Salt and pepper to taste

Pita bread or flour tortillas, for service

Mixed salad greens, for service

ADVANCE PREPARATION

1. Combine the soy sauce, lemon juice, onion, and chiles and mix well to form a marinade. Place the chicken in a resealable plastic bag and pour the marinade over the chicken. Refrigerate overnight.

PREPARATION OF THE CHICKEN

2. Char-grill the chicken while basting frequently with the marinade, until the chicken is just done. Cool the chicken and shred the chicken meat. Reserve in the refrigerator.

ASSEMBLY AND SERVICE

3. Combine the coconut milk, lemon juice, scallions, coconut, and roasted chiles in a nonreactive bowl. Season to taste with salt and pepper and refrigerate.

4. Mix the reserved chicken meat with the chilled coconut milk mixture. Stir well to combine.

5. Serve with pita bread or flour tortillas on a bed of salad greens.

Bacon-Wrapped Duck Liver with Water Chestnut and Scallion Rumaki

serves 8

Rumaki is a Hawaiian classic with a strong Japanese influence. It is a mainstay of the famous Hawaiian *pupu* platter. *Rumaki* can be done as individual portions on toothpicks for party food or threaded onto wooden skewers for sit-down dinners. Traditionally rumakis are made with chicken livers, but the use of duck liver adds a sophisticated twist.

CHEF NOTES

Foie gras may be substituted for a more elegant presentation, or 12 chicken livers, halved, may be used for the traditional version. The skewers may be char-grilled or broiled. Prunes may be substituted for the liver to create Devils on Horseback (the prunes may be stuffed with smoked almonds before wrapping with the bacon). If making Devils on Horseback, increase the cayenne to ½ teaspoon [3 mL]. Round skewers tend not to split the water chestnuts, and a twisting motion of the skewer helps to avoid splitting them as well. Toothpicks may be used instead of skewers, to make individual *rumaki*.

LIVERS

1½ pounds [675 g] duck liver, cut into 1-ounce [30-g] pieces and soaked in milk for 10 minutes

12 slices smoked bacon, cut in half and cooked half done

12 whole water chestnuts (fresh, if available), cut in half

24 scallions, white parts only, cut into 1½-inch [4-cm] segments

8 wooden skewers, soaked in water for 30 minutes if char grilling

MARINADE

½ cup [120 mL] soy sauce

2 tablespoons [30 mL] brown sugar

2 garlic cloves, minced

½ teaspoon [3 mL] grated ginger

½ teaspoon [3 mL] Madras curry powder

¼ teaspoon [1 mL] cayenne (optional)

½ teaspoon [3 mL] dark sesame oil

1 scallion, minced

¼ cup [60 mL] minced scallion greens, for garnish

ADVANCE PREPARATION

1. Place a piece of duck liver on top of a section of bacon. Top with half a water chestnut. Wrap the bundle tightly with the bacon and place on a skewer.

2. Skewer a scallion portion and repeat until 3 bundles are in place. Repeat to make 8 skewers, each with 3 rumaki bundles. Place the skewers in a resealable plastic bag.

PREPARATION OF THE MARINADE

3. Combine the soy sauce, brown sugar, garlic, ginger, curry powder, cayenne, if using, sesame oil, and scallion and mix well to blend. Pour the marinade over the skewers in the bag and marinate at least 4 hours, refrigerated.

COOKING METHOD

4. Drain and reserve the marinade. Place the skewers on a parchment-lined baking sheet.

5. Bake at 375°F [190°C] for 12 to 15 minutes, turning halfway through the cooking process, or until done. The bacon should be crisp and the liver cooked medium.

6. While the skewers are baking, heat the marinade to a boil and reduce the volume by half. Reserve.

SERVICE

7. Garnish with the minced scallion greens and serve the skewers hot, 1 skewer per person, brushed with the reduced marinade.

Just-Seared Tuna Salad with *Ogo* Seaweed Aku Poke

serves 8

Poke (pronounced PO-kay) means to cut into pieces in Hawaiian. It is a dish that resembles ceviche, in that it is usually composed of raw or rare fish that is marinated. But *poke* is so much more. It is also an amalgam of traditional Hawaiian and Asian influences from the Chinese and Japanese immigrants who settled in Hawaii, illustrating how Hawaiian food has become a true melting pot of the Orient and the South Pacific.

CHEF NOTES

Seaweed may be ordered directly from Hawaiian Marine Enterprises (808-293-1230) or Royal Hawaiian Sea Farms (808-329-5468). *Ogo* is the Japanese term for *Graciliaria* seaweed. *Ahi* is the Hawaiian term for yellow-fin and big-eye or albacore tuna, the fresher the better (sashimi or sushi grade preferred). Many recipes for *poke* call for merely combining the ingredients, with no searing. The seared versions are superior, both in taste and appearance. The tuna should be just seared on the outside and raw in the center. Consider using a kitchen torch (as used for crème brûlée) to sear the outside of the tuna cubes.

1 pound [450 g] *ahi* tuna, preferably sashimi grade, cut into ¾-inch [2-cm] cubes

4 teaspoons [20 mL] sesame oil

4 teaspoons [20 mL] soy sauce

2 garlic cloves, minced

1 cup [240 mL] sweet onions, such as Vidalia, Maui, or Walla Walla diced

¼ cup [60 mL] scallions, chopped

1 cup [240 mL] chopped *limu ogo* seaweed, rinsed and drained

1 hot red chile, very finely minced

3 tablespoons [45 mL] vegetable oil

1 teaspoon [5 mL] fresh lemon juice

Mixed greens combined with seaweed for lining plates

Furikake (a mixture of toasted sesame seeds and crushed, toasted *nori* seaweed), for garnish

ADVANCE PREPARATION

1. Combine the tuna with the sesame oil, soy sauce, garlic, onion, scallions, *limu ogo*, and chile and mix well. Marinate for 1 hour.

COOKING METHOD

2. Preheat a wok until very hot. Add the vegetable oil, then the tuna mixture. Stir-fry for 1 or 2 minutes only (the tuna should be extremely rare). Immediately remove from the heat and allow to cool.

3. Drizzle lemon juice over the mixture and toss gently.

SERVICE

4. Line a plate with mixed greens combined with seaweed. The *poke* may be served immediately from the wok or it may be chilled very quickly and served cold. Garnish with *furikake*.

Marinated Sea Bass in Lime Juice and Coconut Milk Kokoda

serves 8

This is the Fijian version of ceviche, in which the fish is cooked chemically by the acidic lime juice. Variations of this dish are popular all over the South Pacific. Some scholars feel that the ancient Polynesians carried this recipe to South America, while others feel the opposite is true.

 **CHEF NOTES**

Do not make the entire dish in advance. Refrigeration of the mixture too long after the coconut milk has been added will solidify it, making an unpleasant presentation. For thick coconut milk, allow the can of coconut milk to sit, undisturbed. Carefully open the can and a top layer of thick coconut "cream" can be poured off.

1½ pounds [675 g] sea bass fillet (freshest possible), cut into bite-size cubes

Juice of 3 large limes

1 tablespoon [15 mL] kosher salt

1 cup [240 mL] thick coconut milk

1 large sweet onion, minced

3 garlic cloves

8 Thai green chiles, roasted and minced

2 cups [480 mL] green papaya, diced, salted, allowed to drain 10 minutes, and rinsed

Salt to taste

Lettuce or greens, for serving (optional)

8 half coconut shells, for serving (optional)

Diced green papaya, for garnish

ADVANCE PREPARATION

1. Combine the fish, lime juice, and salt in a nonreactive bowl and refrigerate for 3 hours.

ASSEMBLY AND SERVICE

2. Stir in the coconut milk, onion, garlic, chiles, and papaya. Allow the flavors to combine for 30 minutes, refrigerated. Adjust the seasonings.

3. Serve on a bed of lettuce or greens, in a large bowl, or in half coconut shells. Garnish with green papaya.

Smoked Salmon-Stuffed Cherry Tomatoes Lomi Lomi

serves 8

Lomi (or *lomi lomi*) in Hawaiian means to knead, rub, squeeze, or massage with the fingertips. This is the action traditionally used to mash the salmon. Originally this dish was made with salted salmon, which is much like salt cod. Smoked salmon is a more flavorful and refined substitute, is easier to obtain, and has a clean, fresh taste.

CHEF NOTES

If possible use yellow pear-style cherry tomatoes for half of the tomatoes, lending visual appeal, and use red Belgian endive for half of the endive leaves, if available. Nova-style smoked salmon or gravad lax will do nicely in this dish. You may use salted salmon if it can be obtained, but it should be soaked in milk for 30 minutes before using.

32 cherry tomatoes

6 ounces [180 g] smoked salmon, preferably Nova style, finely chopped

¼ cup [60 mL] sweet onion, minced

¼ cup [60 mL] scallions, minced

1 garlic clove, minced

1 teaspoon [5 mL] fresh cilantro, chopped

½ teaspoon [3 mL] fresh lemon juice

¼ teaspoon [1 mL] crushed red pepper

Salt and pepper to taste

Cilantro leaves or scallion curls, for garnish

16 Belgian endive leaves, for service

ADVANCE PREPARATION

1. Cut off and discard the tops of the tomatoes. Slice off a small section from the bottoms (to aid in standing upright). Using a small melon scoop or demitasse spoon, scoop out the seeds and pulp of the tomatoes, reserving the pulp. Place the tomatoes upside down on a paper towel in the refrigerator.

PREPARATION OF THE STUFFING

2. Combine the tomato pulp, smoked salmon, onion, scallions, garlic, cilantro, lemon juice, and red pepper and blend the ingredients very well. Adjust the seasonings and cover with plastic film. Chill until very cold.

ASSEMBLY AND SERVICE

3. Using a pastry bag or demitasse spoon, stuff the chilled tomatoes with the cold salmon filling. Serve immediately by placing 2 stuffed tomatoes on each of 2 leaves.

Mussels with Spicy Black Bean and Tomato Sauce d'Urville Mussels

serves 8

Jules-Sébastian-César Dumont d'Urville was a French explorer who visited both Australia and New Zealand. D'Urville Island is at the north end of New Zealand's South Island, on Tasman Bay, and is a prime site for New Zealand's famous green lip mussels, which are exported all over the world. This dish captures the essence of the Australian culinary melting pot, using New Zealand mussels, Oriental black bean sauce, and New World tomatoes.

CHEF NOTES

If fresh mussels are unavailable in your area, New Zealand green lip mussels are usually available frozen and the quality is acceptable. Warm water mussels may be slightly open when live. Tap the shells and they should close. Discard any with an off smell.

2 heaping tablespoons [35 mL] Oriental black bean sauce with garlic

¼ cup [60 mL] tomato paste

6 garlic cloves, minced

4 large tomatoes, chopped

2 medium onions, diced

4 Thai chiles, minced, or 1 to 2 teaspoons [5 to 10 mL] *sambal oelek*, to taste

3 to 4 cups [720 to 960 mL] dry white wine

4 pounds [1.8 kg] fresh mussels, preferably green lip, scrubbed and beards removed

Peasant-style bread, for serving

ADVANCE PREPARATION

1. All advance preparation may be found in the ingredient list.

COOKING METHOD

2. Combine the bean sauce, tomato paste, garlic, tomatoes, onions, and chiles in a saucepan large enough to hold the mussels. Heat, while stirring to combine. Add enough wine to form a sauce of medium consistency, then heat to a rolling boil.

3. Add the mussels and toss thoroughly to coat. Cover the saucepan with a tight-fitting lid and steam the mussels for 5 minutes. Check to see if the mussels have opened. If not, steam until all the shells have opened, discarding any that remain closed.

SERVICE

4. Serve 8 ounces [225 g] of mussels in a wide shallow bowl with ample sauce spooned over the top. Provide a bowl for empty shells. Serve with crusty, peasant-style bread.

**Sweet-and-Sour Eggplant Curry
with Pineapple in Lacy Pancakes**
Terong Balado Kari Roti Jala
(page 208)

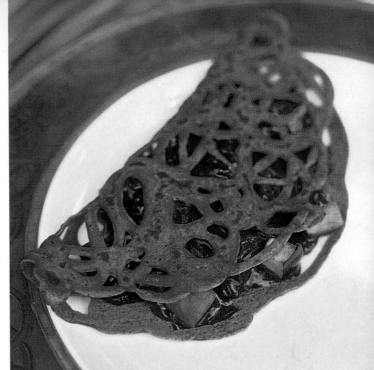

**Shrimp Paté on Sugarcane and
Lemongrass** *Chao Tom*
(page 270)

Three-Cheese Flan
Flan Caballo de Fideo
(page 127)

Twice-Cooked Bean Curd
Tubu Choerim
(page 239)

Lamb, Pomegranate, and Mint "Pizza"
Lahem bil Ajeen

(page 357)

Rice-Stuffed Dates Wrapped in Sole with Sweet-and Sour Sauce
Samak Mehshi bi tamr

(page 406)

Filipino Tamales *Tamales*
(page 187)

Beef Pie with Apricots
Pastel de Carne y Albaricoque
(page 138)

Lobster Gratin in Pineapple Cases
Lagosta Gratinado em Abacaxi
(page 154)

**Jerk-Marinated and Smoked
Pork Spareribs** *Jerk Ribs*
(page 100)

**Sweet Rice-Crusted
Pork Meatballs**
Jun Jiu Kau
(page 251)

**Spinach and Cheese
Dumplings with Chile
Sauce** *Tse tang Churo
Momo* with *Sonam
Penzom Sibeh*

(page 326)

**Chicken Breast and Sour Plum
Roll with Ponzu Sauce**
Torinuku no Bainiku Age
(page 217)

**Smoked Trout and Green
Mango Salad**
Yoam Makah Trey Ang
(page 290)

Stuffed Boneless Chicken Wings in Red Curry Sauce *Peek Gai Yad Sai Pha-naeng*

(page 301)

Grilled Eggplant and Roasted Red Pepper Terrine with Prosciutto *Terrina di Melanzane con Peperoni e Prosciutto*

(page 492)

Philippines

Grilled Pork Tenderloin Cubes with Papaya Relish
Inihaw na Baboy na Achara

Miniature Pork and Papaya Pies
Panara

Fresh Spring Rolls with Hearts of Palm
Lumpia Ubod

Filipino Tamales
Tamales

Marinated Fish in Lime Juice with Coconut Milk
Kilawing Tanguigue

Shrimp, Bean Sprout, and Sweet Potato Fritters
Ukoy con Sausawang Suka

Bacon-Wrapped Stuffed Shrimp with Sweet-and-Sour Sauce
Rellenong Hipon con Agre Dulce

THE PHILIPPINES, named after King Philip (II) of Spain, have had many cultural influences to shape its cuisine. The indigenous people of the islands are related to the Malay and Polynesians and can be traced back over 10,000 years. Chinese traders exchanged their cooking techniques, and Muslim missionaries passed along their strict dietary laws. The Spanish conquered the islands in 1521 and stayed until 1898, when the United States began its influence. Spanish rule seems to have had the most significant and lasting effect on the country's cooking style. With these diverse cultures influencing the Filipino people, it is no wonder that Philippine cuisine is known for the blending of so many flavors.

The Spanish influence is so great that even dishes that originated in the islands by the Malays have Spanish names. Olive oil, garlic, and tomatoes were brought from Spain and the techniques of sautéing garlic slowly in olive oil and simmering foods over long periods form the basis of most of the savory dishes of the Philippines. *Adobo,* which may be considered the national dish, has its roots in Mexico. (Since Spain had to sail west to reach the Philippines, Mexico became the administration center for the Spanish government.) So characteristic of the melding of cultural influences, *adobo* in the Philippines is a stew consisting of pork and chicken, seasoned with soy sauce, vinegar, garlic, and peppercorns. Chinese influences are pervasive as well, with noodle dishes found throughout the country. Known as *pansit,* these dishes have little in common except for the main ingredient of noodles. Egg rolls (*lumpia*) are a popular appetizer, as are dumplings (*siomai*). Some of the exotic regional specialties that call for coconut and coconut milk are probably Malay in origin. *Pinakbet*, field greens mixed with pork and fermented fish in coconut milk, is one such example. Whole roasted pig may be another. American influence is limited to the introduction of canned foods just after World War II, when fresh produce was scarce. Filipino cooks cleverly disguised them and assimilated them into their cooking methods.

Philippine cuisine is a blend of the familiar with the exotic. In particular, the combination of sour, salty, and peppery is a most desirable facet of their dishes. The mainstays of their diet are rice and fish. More than twenty varieties of rice are presently grown in the Philippines, including short- and long-grain rice, glutinous rice, fragrant rice, and blue and brown varieties. It should come as no surprise that fish dominate the diet, with over 2,000 species from which to choose. What may be surprising is that Filipinos developed aquaculture over a thousand years ago, raising shellfish and fish under controlled conditions in freshwater ponds. In some of the island regions people prefer their fish dried, a practical method of food preservation, while others prefer a fresh preparation of marinated raw fish (*kilawin*) quite similar to the Mexican or South American ceviche. The fish sauce, known as *patis*, is similar to *nam pla* in Thailaind and *nuoc mam* in Vietnam.

Filipino cooking is quite tasty without being overbearing. It is well seasoned but not overly spicy. It is based on contrasts in texture and taste, with meals served not in courses but all at once. A meal is planned around textures—crispy, smooth, crunchy, and chewy—and flavors—sour, spicy, bitter, and salty. For example, fried *lumpias* (egg rolls) provide the crisp and crunch when noodle dishes are also served.

Filipinos enjoy eating throughout the day and the *merienda*, enjoyed between lunch and dinner, can be a whole meal of snacks or appetizers. Rice cakes (*puto*), *lumpia*, noodles topped with oysters, pastries made of mango and banana (*panyo-panyo*), and fruit pies with a guava-like fruit called *guapple* can all be found.

With so many islands comprising the Philippines, regional cooking styles have inevitably developed. On the island of Luzon, rice is the staple. On Cebu, Leyte, and Samar, the Visayans rely on corn. On Mindanao root vegetables such as cassava, yams, and sweet potatoes, which would be considered pauper food on the other islands, are the staple. Hot chiles are found throughout the islands (the hottest and most popular are called *sili labuyo*) but are most prevalent in dishes from Bicol in southern Luzon as well as among the Muslims of western Mindanao. Coconut is used extensively in the regional cuisine of Bicol and Tagal. Dry, salted fish is used among the Visayans, as are fermented fish and shrimp paste (*guinamos*), and the regional cuisine is known for being quite salty. Fish is prepared simply, either grilled over charcoal or simmered in seasoned vinegar.

The most popular meat in the Philippines is pork, although in Mindanao, which has strong Islam influence, the meat tends to be beef. Mindanao cooking has borrowed extensively from Indonesia and Malaysia with their fondness for hot chiles, curries, and spicy foods. While not culturally acceptable in the West, dog meat is quite popular among the people of northern Luzon.

Grilled Pork Tenderloin Cubes with Papaya Relish Inihaw na Baboy na Achara

Inihaw is a traditional way of grilling meat, fish, or poultry over live coals. Pork is the most popular meat consumed in the Philippines and the *achara* relish is the perfect foil to the rich taste of the grilled pork. Before the days of refrigeration, pickling was a common method of preservation in the tropics and spicy relishes were used to mask the flavor of foods that were past their prime. This strongly Indian-influenced relish is a favorite condiment for any grilled or fried meat or fish.

CHEF NOTES

The *achara* relish is excellent as a condiment to accompany a variety of grilled meats. It will keep refrigerated for a week. Substitute mango for papaya as an interesting variation. The grilled meat is best cooked indirectly over live coals. "Lite" soy sauce is preferable for marinades, since it goes through a distillation process that reduces salt and intensifies flavor.

ACHARA RELISH: MAKES 3 CUPS [720 mL]

½ cup [120 mL] palm, rice, or apple cider vinegar

⅓ cup [80 mL] sugar

1 teaspoon [5 mL] salt

1 cup [240 mL] green papaya, julienne

3 garlic cloves, minced

¼ cup [60 mL] carrots, grated

1 small red bell pepper, cored, seeded, julienne

2 serrano chiles, minced

1½-inch [4-cm] piece ginger, cut into very thin julienne

¼ cup [60 mL] onions, minced

1 cup [240 mL] bamboo shoot strips

⅓ cup [80 mL] raisins

2 tablespoons [30 mL] fish sauce

INIHAW

½ cup [120 mL] rice or palm vinegar

2 tablespoons [30 mL] garlic, minced

2 teaspoons [10 mL] chile paste, such as *sambal oelek* or similar Asian chile paste

2 tablespoons [30 mL] sugar

1 tablespoon [15 mL] salt

¼ cup [60 mL] "lite" soy sauce

1½ pounds [675 g] pork tenderloin, cut into small cubes

16 wooden skewers for grilling, soaked for at least 30 minutes in tepid water

ADVANCE PREPARATION

1. Bring the vinegar, sugar, and salt to the boil in a medium nonreactive saucepan. Add all the remaining *achara* ingredients and stir well to combine.

2. Turn off the heat, leaving the pan on the burner. Cover immediately. Stir occasionally while the mixture cools.

PREPARATION OF THE *INIHAW*

3. Combine the vinegar, garlic, chile paste, sugar, salt, and soy sauce in a bowl. Mix well then add the pork cubes. Marinate overnight, refrigerated.

COOKING METHOD

4. Thread 1½ ounces [45 g] of pork cubes onto each skewer.

5. Grill the skewers over a medium charcoal fire for about 5 minutes on each side. Use any leftover marinade to baste after the first turning. If broiling in the oven, preheat to 425°F [220°C] and cook for 5 to 7 minutes per side.

SERVICE

6. Serve 2 skewers per person with *achara* relish on the side.

Miniature Pork and Papaya Pies Panara

These little pies are similar to the Latin American empanada but have ingredients in the filling that make them uniquely Filipino. The blending of pork and shrimp with the hot red pepper and green papaya, with just a hint of anise, gives these pies their Filipino character. *Panara* are sold by street vendors and are popular as *merienda* fare. (The *merienda* is a light meal eaten at mid-morning or mid-afternoon.)

CHEF NOTES

To prepare the annatto water soak 1 tablespoon [15 mL] crushed annatto seeds in ¼ cup [60 mL] warm water. Allow to stand 30 minutes. Strain and discard the seeds. If available, use rice flour made from glutinous rice or grind your own in a blender or coffee grinder. This is known as sweet rice flour.

FILLING

2 cups [480 mL] green papaya, grated or shredded

3 tablespoons [45 mL] salt

2 tablespoons [30 mL] vegetable oil

3 garlic cloves, minced

1 small onion, diced

8 ounces [225 g] ground pork

½ cup [120 mL] rich chicken stock

1 tablespoon [15 mL] shrimp paste (*bagoong alamang*)

½ teaspoon [3 mL] crushed red pepper

8 ounces [225 g] shrimp, peeled, deveined, and chopped

PASTRY

2 cups [480 mL] rice flour

2 cups [480 mL] water

2 eggs, beaten

1 teaspoon [5 mL] anise extract

1 teaspoon [5 mL] salt

3 tablespoons [45 mL] annatto water (see Chef Notes)

½ cup [120 mL] vegetable oil

1 to 2 cups [240 to 480 mL] all-purpose flour, as needed

2 cups [480 mL] vegetable oil, for frying pies

ADVANCE PREPARATION

1. All advance preparation may be found in the ingredient list.

PREPARATION OF THE FILLING

2. Sprinkle the papaya with the salt and toss well. Allow to stand 5 minutes. Rinse with water and squeeze out any moisture.

3. Heat the 2 tablespoons [30 mL] of oil in a large skillet over medium-high heat and sauté the garlic 30 seconds. Add the onion and sauté until translucent.

4. Add the pork and sauté for 3 minutes.

5. Add the chicken stock, shrimp paste, and red pepper and simmer for 2 minutes. Stir in the papaya and cook until it is tender and the filling is quite dry.

6. Stir in the shrimp, remove from heat, and allow to cool.

PREPARATION OF THE PASTRY

7. Combine the rice flour, water, eggs, anise extract, salt, annatto water, and oil in a saucepan and mix well. Cook the mixture over medium heat, stirring constantly, until it is thick enough to form into balls. Remove from the heat and allow to cool.

8. Knead in about 1 cup [240 mL] all-purpose flour. Add flour as necessary to produce a workable dough.

9. Pinch off 1-inch [2.5-cm] balls and flatten them into rounds with your hands. Using a rolling pin or a pasta roller, roll each round into a thin circle 3 inches [8 cm] in diameter. Stack with plastic film between each. Refrigerate until ready to use.

PREPARATION OF THE PIES

10. Place a liberal tablespoon [15 to 20 mL] of filling into the center of each round. Brush the edges with water and fold over, as for a turnover.

11. Press the edges together to seal tightly, using a fork to crimp the edges. Arrange so the pies do not touch, then cover with plastic film until ready to fry.

COOKING METHOD

12. Heat the vegetable oil to 355°F [180°C] in a large skillet. Fry a few pies at a time for 4 to 5 minutes per side, or until golden brown. Drain on paper towels. Keep warm until all are cooked.

SERVICE

13. Serve 3 or 4 pies per person. (*Achara* relish goes nicely with this dish; see the recipe on page 180).

Fresh Spring Rolls with Hearts of Palm Lumpia Ubod

Every Asian cuisine has its version of an egg roll or spring roll. The Philippines has the elegant *lumpia*, which may be prepared fresh or fried. The unique quality of *lumpia* is the wrapper itself, which is much closer to a delicate crêpe than an egg roll or wonton wrapper. Premade *lumpia* wrappers are available, but they pale in comparison to the freshly made, which are not difficult to make. The rolls are always dipped into a sauce of one kind or another, and Filipinos are slowly adopting the Vietnamese method of wrapping *lumpia* in lettuce leaves before dipping.

FRESH *LUMPIA* WRAPPERS: MAKES 16

5 eggs, beaten

3 cups [720 mL] water

3⅓ cups [800 mL] cornstarch

½ teaspoon [3 mL] garlic powder

Vegetable oil for cooking

BROTH

2 cups [480 mL] chicken stock

2 whole garlic cloves, bruised, left intact

1 scallion, tied in a knot

8 ounces [225 g] chicken breast, diced

8 ounces [225 g] pork loin, diced

8 ounces [225 g] shrimp, peeled, deveined, and diced

SWEET *LUMPIA* SAUCE: MAKES ABOUT ¾ CUP [180 mL]

1 cup [240 mL] broth, reserved from preparing the meat and shrimp

⅓ cup [80 mL] light brown sugar

4 garlic cloves, minced

1 tablespoon [15 mL] cornstarch, dissolved in 3 tablespoons [45 mL] soy sauce

1 teaspoon [5 mL] *sriracha* sauce (see page 586)

FILLING

1 tablespoon [15 mL] vegetable oil

2 tablespoons [30 mL] garlic, minced

1 small onion, diced

1 cup [240 mL] boiling potatoes, diced

⅔ cup [160 mL] hearts of palm, shredded

¼ cup [60 mL] cabbage, thinly shredded

1 tablespoon [15 mL] fish sauce

½ teaspoon [3 mL] black pepper

Salt and pepper to taste

16 Boston lettuce leaves, washed and thoroughly dried

Do not make the *lumpia* wrappers too thin, as they will crack when rolled. Several fillings may be substituted for the one given here. While the hearts of palm filling was considered the food of royalty, items such as jicama, French-cut, blanched green beans, roasted and chopped peanuts, diced ham or Spanish sausage, chick peas or lima beans, diced green papaya, or diced tofu are just a few of the many possible combinations. *Lumpia* may also be fried. To fry, both ends of the *lumpia* must be folded in during rolling and the seams well sealed with beaten egg.

ADVANCE PREPARATION

1. Combine the eggs, water, cornstarch, and garlic powder and mix very well to form a smooth batter. Allow to stand 15 minutes.

2. Lightly oil an 8-inch [20-cm] nonstick skillet or crêpe pan over medium heat. Ladle ¼ cup [60 mL] of the batter into the pan and quickly tilt and swirl so that the batter completely covers the bottom. Cook about 1 minute, or until the edges begin to curl up.

3. Gently lift the edge, turn over, and cook for 30 seconds on the other side. Do not brown. Turn out onto a plate, and continue cooking until all are done.

PREPARATION OF THE MEAT AND BROTH

4. Heat the chicken stock, garlic, and scallion to a boil in a small saucepan. Add the chicken and pork and stir to separate. Cook until the meat begins to turn opaque, 1 to 2 minutes.

5. Add the shrimp, stirring to separate, and cook another minute. Remove the meats and shrimp with a slotted spoon and reserve. Save the broth, discarding the garlic and the knotted scallion.

PREPARATION OF THE SAUCE

6. Combine the reserved broth, brown sugar, and garlic in a small saucepan and bring to a boil. Reduce the volume by one-third, stirring to dissolve the sugar.

7. Stir in the dissolved cornstarch mixture and cook until the sauce becomes thick and glossy.

8. Stir in the *sriracha* sauce.

PREPARATION OF THE FILLING

9. Heat the oil in a wok or saucepan, over medium-high heat. Add the garlic and sauté for 30 seconds.

10. Add the onion and potatoes and sauté until the potatoes soften.

11. Add the hearts of palm, cabbage, fish sauce, and black pepper and toss well to combine. Cook 2 minutes, then add the reserved meats, stirring well to combine and heat through. Adjust seasoning and allow to cool to room temperature.

12. To prepare the rolls lay a wrapper on a work surface, then place a lettuce leaf on top. Spoon about 2 tablespoons [30 mL] of filling onto the lettuce leaf and spread evenly, staying about ¾ inch [2 cm] from the side edges.

13. Drizzle a little of the sauce over the filling and begin to roll the *lumpia* into a cylinder. One-third of the way through rolling, fold about 1 inch [2.5 cm] of 1 end of the *lumpia* wrapper toward the center and continue rolling until the cylinder is complete. Store seam side down to help seal the roll. (The rolls may be stuffed and wrapped individually in plastic film a few hours before service.)

SERVICE

14. Serve 2 *lumpias* per person with some of the remaining sauce on the side or drizzled over the rolls.

Filipino Tamales Tamales

This tamale recipe is an adaptation of the Latin American tamale, using white and red seasoned rice mixtures in place of cornmeal. The ingredients are native and the method of wrapping is borrowed from the Chinese practice of wrapping food in lotus leaves. In the Philippines the tamales are enclosed in banana leaves, which should certainly be used in place of foil.

CHEF NOTES

Banana leaves will add subtle flavor and be more authentic than the foil wrappers, but they are more difficult to work with and to obtain. Blanch them first in boiling water for 5 minutes, then refresh in cold water before cutting.

2 cups [480 mL] raw peanuts, in shell

3½ cups [840 mL] uncooked rice

7 cups [1.7 L] coconut milk

1 cup [240 mL] light brown sugar

2 teaspoons [10 mL] salt

1 teaspoon [5 mL] white pepper

1 cup [240 mL] unsalted roasted peanuts, coarsely crushed

¼ cup [60 mL] annatto water (see page 182)

2 garlic cloves, whole

1 scallion, tied in a knot

1 pound [450 g] pork loin

2 boneless and skinless chicken breast halves

1 pound [450 g] shrimp, shelled and deveined

8 ounces [225 g] cooked ham, cut into strips, ½ inch [1 cm] wide and ¼ inch [6 mm] thick

3 hard-boiled eggs, sliced

16 pieces of aluminum foil, 10 × 12 inches [25 × 30 cm], or banana leaves, blanched in hot water

Sriracha sauce, to garnish (see page 586)

ADVANCE PREPARATION

1. Boil the raw peanuts in water to cover for 45 to 60 minutes, or until soft. Drain and allow to cool. Shell the peanuts and reserve.

PREPARATION OF THE FILLINGS

2. Combine the rice, coconut milk, brown sugar, salt, and pepper in a deep saucepan. Cook over low heat for 25 minutes, stirring often to prevent sticking or scorching.

3. Add the crushed roasted peanuts and cook for 5 minutes more.

4. Divide the rice mixture, placing half in a bowl, and reserve. Add the annatto water to the remaining half in the saucepan and mix well. Cook for 5 minutes more. Allow the red rice mixture to cool.

5. Bring a medium saucepan of water to a boil. Add the whole garlic and knotted scallion. Lower the heat, add the pork, and simmer until cooked through.

6. Remove the pork, reserving the water. Allow the pork to cool, then slice it into ½ × ¼-inch [1 × ½-cm] pieces.

7. Add the chicken to the water and simmer until cooked through. Remove the chicken. Allow it to cool, then cut it into ½ × ¼-inch [1 × ½-cm] pieces.

8. Add the shrimp to the water and simmer for 2 to 3 minutes. Remove the shrimp and allow to cool, then coarsely chop. Have the pork, chicken, shrimp, ham, and egg slices ready for assembly.

ASSEMBLING THE TAMALES

9. Lay the foil sheets on a flat work surface. Place ¼ cup [60 mL] of the white rice mixture in the center of each piece of foil, shaping it into a 3-inch [8-cm] square.

10. Arrange pieces of pork, chicken, shrimp, ham, egg, and boiled peanuts on top of the white rice. Place ¼ cup [60 mL] of the red rice mixture on top and shape into a 3-inch [8-cm] square.

11. Fold the edges of the foil around the tamale to seal. Place the foil packets, seam side down, in a large steamer. Continue until all are done.

COOKING METHOD

12. Steam the tamales in the steamer, covered, for 30 minutes. Check periodically to make sure there is enough water remaining to prevent scorching.

SERVICE

13. Serve 2 tamales per person, hot or cold, garnished with stripes of *sriracha* sauce. If banana wrappers are used, allow the guests to unfold their tamales at the table or cut them in half for presentation.

Marinated Fish in Lime Juice with Coconut Milk Kilawing Tanguigue

Kilawing (or *kilawin*) is the Filipino equivalent of ceviche of Latin America, and was most likely introduced by the Spaniards. It is a common dish throughout the Pacific Islands and is especially popular in Tahiti (known there as *e'ia ota*). The fish is not raw but chemically cooked by the acid in the lime juice. Coconut milk adds depth and richness.

CHEF NOTES

Use the freshest seafood possible for this dish. Substitute shrimp or scallops or a combination of shellfish and fish.

1½ pounds [675 g] firm fish fillets, cut into ½-inch [1-cm] cubes

½ cup [120 mL] lime juice

1 teaspoon [5 mL] salt

3 garlic cloves, minced

1 tablespoon [15 mL] ginger, cut into very thin julienne

1 medium onion, thinly sliced

¼ teaspoon [1 mL] ground turmeric

½ teaspoon [3 mL] black pepper

1 cup [240 mL] thick coconut milk

1 bell pepper, seeded and diced

4 scallions, minced

⅔ cup [160 mL] ripe papaya, diced

3 firm red tomatoes, diced

Salt to taste

8 leaves leaf lettuce

Cilantro leaves, for garnish

ADVANCE PREPARATION

1. Place the fish in a resealable plastic bag. Pour in the lime juice, salt, half of the garlic and ginger, and the onion. Toss to coat the pieces of fish. Refrigerate at least 8 hours.

COOKING METHOD

2. Lightly toast the turmeric and black pepper in a small dry skillet over low heat until fragrant.

3. Add the coconut milk and the remaining garlic and ginger and heat through. Remove from the heat and refrigerate until very cold.

ASSEMBLY AND SERVICE

4. Strain the fish. Add the bell pepper, scallions, papaya, and tomatoes and toss well. Add the coconut milk mixture and toss well. Adjust seasoning for salt.

5. Line a plate with a lettuce leaf. Add a 3-ounce [85-g] portion of fish salad and garnish with cilantro leaves.

Shrimp, Bean Sprout, and Sweet Potato Fritters Ukoy con Sausawang Suka

In the Philippines the shrimp commonly used for this dish are very tiny. The only preparation they receive is to have their horns and whiskers removed. Larger, peeled shrimp have been substituted in this recipe. *Sausawang suka* is a staple dipping sauce on the Filipino table. *Ukoy,* commonly sold by street vendors and in bars and cafes, are a snack for *merienda* (a light meal eaten at mid-morning or mid-afternoon) and to go with drinks.

CHEF NOTES

To prepare roasted rice powder, toast jasmine rice in a dry skillet, broiler, or the oven until light tan. Allow to cool, then grind as fine as possible in an electric spice mill. (Roasted rice powder can be found in Asian markets.) Acceptable substitutes for shrimp would be lobster medallions or langoustines, bay scallops, or crayfish tails.

DIPPING SAUCE (*SAUSAWANG SUKA*)

¼ cup [60 mL] soy sauce

⅓ cup [80 mL] rice vinegar

3 garlic cloves, minced

I teaspoon [5 mL] sugar

Dash of hot red pepper sauce or chile sauce

FRITTERS (*UKOY*)

1½ cups [360 mL] all-purpose flour

½ cup [120 mL] roasted rice powder (see Chef Notes)

¼ cup [60 mL] corn flour (masa harina)

2 eggs, beaten

¾ cup [180 mL] water

¼ cup [60 mL] annatto water (see page 182)

½ tablespoon [8 mL] fish sauce

½ teaspoon [3 mL] black pepper

I cup [240 mL] raw sweet potato, shredded

I cup [240 mL] mung bean sprouts, blanched 10 seconds in boiling water and rinsed in cold water

4 scallions, minced

Oil, for pan-frying

24 medium shrimp, peeled and deveined

Minced scallions, for garnish

ADVANCE PREPARATION

1. Combine all of the ingredients for the dipping sauce and mix well. Reserve. (The sauce can be made 1 day in advance.)

PREPARATION OF THE BATTER

2. Mix the flour, roasted rice powder, and corn flour together, combining well. Add the eggs, water, annatto water, fish sauce, and pepper. Mix until a slightly lumpy batter is formed. Add the sweet potato, bean sprouts, and half of the scallions and mix well.

3. Heat the oil in a large skillet to about 350°F [175°C]. Add heaping tablespoons [20 mL] of the batter to the hot oil without crowding the pan.

4. Top each fritter with 1 shrimp and a light sprinkling of the remaining scallions. Spoon oil over the fritters as they cook. When the bottoms of the fritters are golden brown, flip the fritters and cook the other side. When both sides are golden brown and crisp, remove with a slotted spoon, drain on paper towels, and keep warm in an oven until all are prepared.

SERVICE

5. Serve 3 fritters per person, garnished with minced scallion. Serve a ramekin of dipping sauce on the side.

Bacon-Wrapped Stuffed Shrimp
with Sweet-and-Sour Sauce Rellenong Hipon con Agre Dulce

The stuffing of this dish illustrates the Chinese culinary influence on the islands, but the final product is uniquely Filipino. The crispness of the bacon, the sweetness of the shrimp, and the intense flavor from the pork stuffing combine to produce a surprisingly complex blend of flavors and texture. In fried versions of this dish the stuffed shrimp are enclosed in wonton wrappers or are dipped in a simple flour batter, with the tip of the tail exposed (the bacon wrap is omitted).

CHEF NOTES

Prepare sole fillet rolls as in this recipe for a variation. The stuffing is quite versatile and can be used with crab or lobster.

SWEET-AND-SOUR SAUCE: MAKES ABOUT 3 CUPS [720 mL]

1 cup [240 mL] chicken stock

½ cup [120 mL] water

¾ cup [180 mL] ketchup

⅓ cup [80 mL] sugar

1 teaspoon [5 mL] fish sauce

1 teaspoon [5 mL] hoisin sauce

1 garlic clove, minced

½ teaspoon [3 mL] serrano chile, minced (optional)

2 tablespoons [30 mL] cornstarch dissolved in ¼ cup [60 mL] water

STUFFED SHRIMP

24 large shrimp (16 to 20 count), peeled and deveined

1½ cups [360 mL] ground pork

4 scallions, minced

4 garlic cloves, minced

1½ cups [360 mL] carrots, grated

½ cup [120 mL] water chestnuts, diced

½ cup [120 mL] mushrooms, chopped

2 egg yolks, beaten

¼ cup [60 mL] cornstarch

1 teaspoon [5 mL] salt

12 slices bacon, cut in half, partially cooked

Vegetable oil, for frying

ADVANCE PREPARATION

1. Combine all of the sauce ingredients and bring to a boil. Reduce the heat and simmer for 5 minutes, or until thickened. Cool and reserve.

PREPARATION OF THE STUFFED SHRIMP

2. Make a slit down the back of each shrimp, being careful not to cut through, leaving the tail intact.

3. Combine the pork, scallions, garlic, carrots, water chestnuts, and mushrooms and blend well.

4. Mix the egg yolks, cornstarch, and salt together, then add the mixture to the pork mixture. Mix thoroughly.

5. Divide the filling into 24 equal portions and stuff each shrimp by mounding the filling into the slit. Wrap each stuffed shrimp with a piece of bacon and secure with a toothpick.

COOKING METHOD

6. Heat oil in a saucepan or deep-fryer to 355°F [180°C]. Fry the stuffed shrimp until the filling is set and the shrimp are opaque. Drain on paper towels.

SERVICE

7. Remove the toothpicks and serve 2 shrimp per person, with the sweet and sour sauce on the side.

South Asia

Indonesia, Malaysia,

and Singapore

Pineapple Flavor Lamb Satay with Chile Lime Sauce
Umtuk Satay Kambing Sambal Kecap

Spicy Pork Rolls in Bean Curd Sheets
Lo Bak

Sweet Chicken Satay with Peanut Sauce
Satay Ayam Manis Bumbu Satay

Javanese Fried Chicken Drumettes
Ayam Goreng Jawa

**Miniature Beef Meatballs with Baby Shrimp
in Coconut Milk**
Sambal Goreng Printil

Tofu Pouches Stuffed with Shrimp Sambal
Tahu Isi Sambal Udang

**Sweet-and-Sour Eggplant Curry with Pineapple
in Lacy Pancakes**
Terong Bacado Kari Roti Jala

SOUTH ASIA IS comprised of Indonesia, Malaysia, and Singapore. The main islands of Indonesia are Sumatra, Java, and Sulawesi (formerly Celebes). Indonesia shares the island of Borneo with Malaysia; it is called Kalimantan by the Indonesians. Indonesia also shares New Guinea with Papua New Guinea; it is called Irian Jaya by the Indonesians. The lesser islands include Bali and the Moluccas (formerly known as the Spice Islands).

Indonesia has rich volcanic soil, but much of it cannot be cultivated because of swampy conditions, eroded soil, and steep slopes. About half of the population of Indonesia lives in Java. Almost all of Indonesia is Muslim, and those religious beliefs and traditions influence the types of foods that are consumed (Muslims do not eat pork, for example). Rice is the staple of most Indonesian diets. Besides rice, major crops include corn, sweet potatoes, sugarcane, soybeans, and peanuts.

Malaysia is separated into West Malaysia and East Malaysia. West Malaysia, also known as peninsular Malaysia, shares a border with Thailand. East Malaysia shares the island of Borneo and some nearby islands with Indonesia. Almost all of the population lives in West Malaysia, half in cities. Ethnic Malays make up a little more than half of the population; they are Muslims. The remainder of the population is mostly Chinese and Indians. Rice is a major food staple, along with cassava and bananas. Malaysia is the world's leading exporter of palm oil. Important cash crops include cacao, sugarcane, pepper, coconuts, and pineapples.

Singapore, an independent city-state, lies off the southern tip of Malaysia. Over 75 percent of the population is Chinese, with significant Malay and Indian populations. Agriculture and fishing contribute less than 1 percent to Singapore's economy, and most food is imported. Singapore is the financial center of South Asia and provides its most important seaport.

While rice is the staple of Indonesian cooking, cassava and sago palm can be important in regions unsuitable for rice production. In addition, sweet potato is sometimes grated into rice to add flavor and texture. Although the Dutch settled in Indonesia from the early seventeenth century through the twentieth century, the main influence on Indonesian cuisine is from the Chinese. Stir-frying is a most common cooking technique, and meats are cut into small pieces before cooking. Noodles, soy sauce (modified with sugar and called *kecap manis*), bean curd, mung beans (for bean sprouts), and soybeans are all Chinese imports to Indonesian cuisine. Indonesians learned to ferment the soybeans to make *tempeh*, a nutritious addition to the diet. A unique cooking technique is "bamboo cooking." Meats and seasonings are packed into a section of green bamboo, with the ends sealed with leaves. This package is then tossed into a fire to cook (green bamboo does not burn and the moisture helps to steam the contents).

Spices are added before and during cooking. Much of Indonesian food is quite spicy, but often that spiciness can be controlled since the hot pepper is commonly served separately in chile *sambals*. Spices are added to dishes as spice mixtures called *bumbus*, or combinations of chiles, shallots, garlic, ginger, galangal, and other spices and herbs ground to a paste with a mortar and pestle. In addition to locally grown spices, such as cloves and nutmeg, Middle Eastern spices, such as cardamom and cinnamon, are grown and used in Indonesia. Cumin, peppercorns, and coriander are popular as well.

Vegetables are not common in the Indonesian diet, with cooked star fruit, papaya, tapioca (cassava), and sweet potatoes taking that role. Water spinach, eggplant, and squash are included in prepared dishes, as are the potato and cabbage introduced by the Dutch. The addition of coconut milk is common in many of Indonesia's tasty dishes.

There are some important differences among the islands' cuisines, however. In Sumatra, hearty food is common, with large quantities of meat included in the dishes. Some of Indonesia's most famous (and finest) cuisine is from the Padang region of Sumatra, known for being fiery hot. In Java, where the daily pace is less hectic than in Sumatra, the foods are less substantial and there is a fondness for sweet flavors in their savory dishes. Taken from the Arabic influence, skewers of meats, called satays, are extremely popular. Sweet potatoes are an important staple in the Sulawesi diet, with the greens cooked as a vegetable. Leaves too tough to eat are fed to pigs, giving a rich, sweet flavor to the pork produced there. Fish is an important ingredient and charcoal grilling is a favorite method of preparation.

The Balinese eat small portions of meat in their dishes and pork is favored. Surprisingly, little fish is included in the diet in spite of Bali being surrounded by water. Greens are usually harvested from the wild, and mature coconut is almost always included in Balinese dishes. Whether pork or duck, grilling over charcoal is a frequent preparation method. Balinese cuisine favors unusual ingredients as well; bats, frogs, crickets, and dragonflies can be found in many local dishes. The most surprising thing about the cuisine of the Moluccas (Spice Islands) is the absence of spices. Although the islands are famous for growing nutmegs and cloves, only small amounts of grated nutmeg can be found in their rich soups. Moluccans regard spices as medicinal.

Malaysian cuisine features the best of Indonesian, Chinese, and Indian influences. Traditional spices join with those from the Middle East and India to produce some of the tastiest dishes in Asia. Malay curries incorporate cumin and coriander as well as peppercorns, star anise, and cardamom. Spices, both fresh and dried, are usually ground into a paste and cooked in oil before adding them to a developing dish. Chile-based *sambals* accompany dishes on the table; this practice allows guests to control spiciness to taste.

The peninsular region of Malaysia shares some of the best cuisine that Thailand has to offer. Seafood is very popular, with a wide array of fish, shrimp, crab, lobster, and dried fish. In the temperate climates of Malaysia, asparagus and mushrooms are grown. While the staple is rice, noodles can be eaten at every meal. The northern states show a distinct Thai influence, with an appreciation of the tartness of lime and tamarind and the heat of fiery chiles. Thai basil and makroot leaves are also Thai-influenced ingredients found in northern cuisine. In the south a Javanese influence appears.

The isolated province of Pahang is known for its love of fish and its simple approach to cooking. Nanyang cooking highlights the best of Chinese cuisine with the addition of copious amounts of spices and hot chiles. The Indian influence is greatest in the south where coconut, Indian spices, *roti canari* (flat bread), and *dhal* (lentils) are ubiquitous. Malaysian Borneo's inhabitants enjoy a more rustic cuisine of wild boar, pig, deer, and other wild game. Many of the greens are gathered from the wild as well. Coastal regions base their diet on fish, and the non-rice-growing regions rely on sago.

Bamboo cooking is most popular in Borneo. Meats, fish, rice, and vegetables are packed into green bamboo cylinders and are placed near an open fire to steam. Singapore's cuisine is comprised of traditional dishes that are found in the neighboring countries of China, Indonesia, Southeast Asia, and the Philippines. Many of these dishes are quite assertive in flavor and piquancy, Chile Crab being one example (and one dish most associated with Singapore cuisine).

Pineapple Flavor Lamb Satay with Chile Lime Sauce Umtuk Satay Kambing Sambal Kecap

serves 8

This satay from Jakarta is considered to be ceremonial fare, usually reserved for special guests. The pineapple pairs nicely with the lamb, and the accompanying sauce has just the right balance of sweet, sour, and spice.

CHEF NOTES

Other meats may be used in this satay. Goat is commonly used throughout Indonesia. Pork is used only in non-Muslim regions.

CHILE LIME SAUCE: MAKES ½ CUP [120 mL]

5 shallots, grated

¼ cup [60 mL] *kecap manis* (see page 575)

4 hot green chiles, seeded and minced

1 teaspoon [5 mL] grated lime zest

1 tablespoon [15 mL] lime juice

SATAY

1 cup [240 mL] puréed fresh pineapple

¼ cup [60 mL] *kecap manis*

1 teaspoon [5 mL] *sambal oelek* (chile paste)

2 tablespoons [30 mL] vegetable oil

½ teaspoon [3 mL] salt

5 shallots, diced

1 slice galangal, minced

1½ pounds [675 g] boneless lamb, cut into ¾-inch [2-cm] cubes

16 skewers, soaked 30 minutes in warm water if wood

ADVANCE PREPARATION

1. Combine all the ingredients for the chile lime sauce. (The sauce can be made 1 day in advance and refrigerated.)

PREPARATION OF THE SATAY

2. Combine the pineapple purée, *kecap manis*, *sambal oelek*, oil, salt, shallots, and galangal. Add the lamb cubes and allow to marinate for at least 30 minutes.

3. Thread 1½-ounce [45-g] portions of lamb on each of 16 skewers. Reserve any leftover marinade for basting.

COOKING METHOD

4. Grill the skewers over an indirect charcoal fire for 5 to 6 minutes, basting and turning frequently.

SERVICE

5. Serve 2 skewers per person, warm, with 1 tablespoon [15 mL] of chile lime sauce on the side.

Spicy Pork Rolls in Bean Curd Sheets Lo Bak

serves 12

Bean curd sheets (*pucuk*) are made from the crusty thin skin that rises to the surface when tofu is made. They are sold in Asian markets. The sheets are often brittle when purchased, but they soften and become pliable when a damp towel is placed on them. Other fillings may be substituted for this pork filling. Experiment with bean curd sheets as an attractive and nutritious wrapper in other recipes.

CHEF NOTES

Shrimp mixed with pork makes a tasty variation, as do scallops or shrimp alone. Handle the bean curd sheets carefully, as they tear easily. Small tears will be covered since the rolls are produced with many layers.

DIPPING SAUCE: MAKES ½ CUP [120 mL]

3 red chiles, minced

3 garlic cloves, minced

3 tablespoons [45 mL] sweet chile garlic sauce

2 tablespoons [30 mL] *kecap manis* (see page 575)

I tablespoon [15 mL] rice wine

PORK ROLLS

I pound [450 g] lean ground pork

4 shallots, diced

6 freshwater chestnuts, coarsely chopped (use jicama if unavailable)

½ teaspoon [3 mL] black pepper

1½ tablespoons [25 mL] sugar

2 teaspoons [10 mL] *sambal oelek* (chile paste)

I tablespoon [15 mL] *kecap asin* (dark soy sauce)

I teaspoon [5 mL] hoisin sauce (*kecap tauco*)

½ cup [120 mL] glutinous rice flour

Bean curd sheets, softened, cut into six 10 × 15-inch [25 × 38-cm] pieces

About 2 cups [480 mL] vegetable oil

2 cucumbers, peeled, seeded, and chopped, for garnish

One 6-ounce [180-g] block firm tofu, drained (under pressure), cut into ½-inch [1-cm] dice, tossed in rice flour and then fried, for garnish

ADVANCE PREPARATION

1. For the dipping sauce combine all of the sauce ingredients and mix well. Reserve at room temperature or refrigerate for later use. (The dipping sauce can be made 1 day in advance.)

PREPARATION OF THE PORK ROLLS

2. Combine the pork, shallots, water chestnuts, pepper, sugar, *sambal oelek*, *kecap asin*, hoisin sauce, and rice flour. Mix thoroughly. Roll this mixture into six 8-inch [20-cm] cylinders about ¾ inch [2 cm] thick.

3. Soften the bean curd sheets by placing them between 2 damp towels for 10 minutes. When softened place a sheet on top of another damp towel.

4. Place one of the pork rolls on top of a softened bean curd sheet and roll up inside the sheet. If it breaks, just continue rolling, as there will be several layers of sheet enclosing the pork. Fold over the ends and press firmly to seal with a few dabs of water.

COOKING METHOD

5. Place the rolls in a wide Chinese-style duck steamer and steam 10 minutes. (The rolls may be made in advance to this stage, wrapped in plastic film, and stored, refrigerated, overnight.)

6. Heat the vegetable oil in a large wok or wide skillet and fry the rolls at 365°F [185°C] until golden brown. Drain on paper towels.

SERVICE

7. Slice each roll diagonally into 12 pieces. Serve 6 pieces per person. Drizzle some sauce over the rolls and top with the diced cucumber and fried tofu garnish.

Sweet Chicken Satay with Peanut Sauce Satay Ayam Manis Bumbu Satay

serves 10

The satays of Thailand are most familiar to the general public, but Indonesian satays offer more depth of flavor and character. The traditional Balinese satay is made with pork and has no accompanying sauce, but the intensity of *bumbu manis* (the seasoning paste) to marinate and baste skewered chicken combined with a peanut sauce produces an exceptional dish. Satays may be broiled in an oven or under a salamander, but grilling over a low charcoal fire will produce the best results.

SATAY SKEWERS: MAKES 10 SKEWERS

8 macadamia nuts or candlenuts if available

4 shallots, sliced

4 garlic cloves, sliced

4 hot red chiles, seeded if milder flavor is desired, and sliced

1 teaspoon [5 mL] salt

½ teaspoon [3 mL] black pepper

1 teaspoon [5 mL] ground turmeric

2 teaspoons [10 mL] ground coriander

½ teaspoon [3 mL] *trassi* (concentrated, fermented shrimp paste; see Chef Notes)

1 teaspoon [5 mL] tamarind paste, dissolved in 2 tablespoons water and strained

2 tablespoons [10 mL] vegetable oil

2 slices galangal (*laos*)

1½ stalks lemongrass, cut into 3-inch [8-cm] pieces, bruised

¼ cup [60 mL] brown sugar or palm sugar

1¼ pounds [560 g] boneless chicken, cut into ¾-inch [2-cm] cubes

PEANUT SAUCE: MAKES ABOUT 3 CUPS [720 mL]

6 hot red chiles, seeded if milder flavor is desired, and sliced

2 garlic cloves, minced

6 shallots, sliced

1 tablespoon [15 mL] brown sugar or palm sugar

½ teaspoon [3 mL] salt

¼ cup [60 mL] fresh lemon juice

1 cup [240 mL] chunky peanut butter, at room temperature

About 2 cups [480 mL] hot water, as needed

10 wooden skewers, soaked 30 minutes in warm water if wood

2 tablespoons [30 mL] crispy fried shallots (see Chef Notes), for garnish

Pork may be substituted for the chicken in this recipe. Use 1 to 1¼ pounds [450 to 560 g] boneless pork loin. Simmer for about 30 minutes in enough stock to cover, then cut into ¾- to 1-inch [2- to 2.5-cm] cubes.

Trassi, a concentrated paste of fermented shrimp or a mix of shrimp and fish with a thick consistency, is used in small quantities much like shrimp or fish sauce is used in Southeast Asia. *Trassi* can be purchased in small bottles in Asian markets and should be refrigerated after opening.

Crispy fried shallots can be purchased in an Asian market. If not available, they can be made by frying ¼ cup [60 mL] sliced shallots in vegetable oil, then draining them. The chiles called for in this recipe are not extremely hot. Ripe, red serrano, or finger hot chiles will do nicely.

If cooking in full view of guests, an impressive way to cook the satays is to insert the ends of the skewers into the rib of a 9-inch [23-cm] section of banana stalk, as they do in Indonesia. This will allow the satays to be turned simultaneously.

ADVANCE PREPARATION

1. Chop the macadamia nuts in a food processor. Add the shallots, garlic, chiles, salt, pepper, turmeric, coriander, *trassi*, and tamarind. Pulse to form a paste.

2. Heat the oil in a skillet and stir-fry the processed paste, galangal slices, lemongrass pieces, and sugar over low heat for 10 minutes. Allow to cool.

3. Marinate the chicken pieces in this paste for 1 to 2 hours or in the refrigerator overnight.

PREPARATION OF THE PEANUT SAUCE

4. Combine the chiles, garlic, shallots, sugar, salt, and lemon juice in a food processor and blend into a paste (called a *bumbu* in Indonesia). Mix the paste with the peanut butter and enough hot water to form a thick but pourable sauce and reserve. (The peanut sauce can be held overnight, refrigerated.)

COOKING METHOD

5. Drain the marinated chicken, reserving the marinade. Skewer the chicken pieces, dividing equally among the wooden skewers.

6. Grill the skewers over a low charcoal fire (or broil), turning and basting often with the reserved marinade, for 5 to 6 minutes, or until done.

SERVICE

7. Serve 1 skewer per person, accompanied with a side dish of the peanut sauce and garnished with the crispy fried shallots.

Javanese Fried Chicken Drumettes Ayam Goreng Jawa

serves 8

Indonesians love fried and broiled chicken, and each region has its own way of cooking and seasoning it. Common to all regional variations is the practice of first simmering the chicken in herbs and spices with coconut milk, tamarind, or soy to flavor the meat and keep it moist. The chicken is then fried, broiled, or grilled to make it crisp. It is quite possible that the Javanese make the tastiest fried chicken in the world.

CHEF NOTES

A cut-up whole chicken, boned quail, or dove breasts are excellent when prepared in this manner.

24 to 36 chicken wing drumettes (depending on size)

I tablespoon [15 mL] salt

Juice of I small lemon

½ onion, sliced

3 garlic cloves, minced

6 macadamia nuts, chopped

2 fresh hot chiles, diced

2 teaspoons [10 mL] ground coriander

¼ teaspoon [1 mL] ground turmeric

½ cup [120 mL] chicken stock

3 tablespoons [45 mL] tamarind liquid

2 slices galangal

I stalk lemongrass, cut into 2-inch [5-cm] pieces, diced

½ cup [120 mL] vegetable oil, for frying

ADVANCE PREPARATION

1. Rub the chicken drumettes with 1 teaspoon [5 mL] of the salt and the lemon juice and allow to marinate for 10 minutes. Rinse briefly under cold water, drain, and pat dry.

2. Blend or process the remaining salt, the onion, garlic, macadamia nuts, chiles, coriander, turmeric, and chicken stock.

3. Pour this mixture over the chicken pieces in a saucepan, then add the tamarind liquid, galangal, and lemongrass. Cook over medium heat for 20 minutes, turning periodically, or until most of the liquid has evaporated. Remove the chicken and drain, reserving the cooked spice mix.

COOKING METHOD

4. Fry the chicken drumettes in 360°F [180°C] oil for about 5 minutes, or until crisp and golden brown. Drain on paper towels.

SERVICE

5. Dab the chicken drumettes with reserved spice mix and serve 3 or 4 drumettes per person, warm or at room temperature.

Miniature Beef Meatballs with Baby Shrimp in Coconut Milk Sambal Goreng Printil

serves 8

The mixture of spices in this dish represents the full Javanese palette. The combination of beef with shrimp is an adaptation of a Chinese method, unusual, but not uncommon, for pure Indonesian cuisine. Fiddlehead fern shoots, which are harvested throughout the heavily forested islands, are quite an authentic addition, but optional due to availability.

CHEF NOTES

Snow peas or snow pea leaves may be used in place of the fiddlehead ferns for color balance. Add snow peas to the cooking meatballs; add snow pea leaves to the cooking shrimp.

CHILE PASTE

4 shallots, diced

2 garlic cloves, minced

3 fresh hot chiles, chopped

I cup [240 mL] coconut milk

MEATBALLS

I½ pounds [675 g] ground beef

2 egg yolks, beaten

2 teaspoons [10 mL] salt

2 tablespoons [30 mL] vegetable oil

2 small ripe tomatoes, chopped

2 medium-hot red chiles, seeded and sliced thin on the diagonal

2 *daun salam* leaves or bay leaves

2 slices galangal

¼ teaspoon [1 mL] shrimp paste, (*trassi*) (see page 202)

½ tablespoon [8 mL] light brown sugar

I teaspoon [5 mL] salt

½ cup [120 mL] fiddlehead fern shoots, rinsed well and trimmed (optional)

12 ounces [340 g] small shrimp, peeled and deveined

Sliced scallion, for garnish

Shrimp chips, for service (see page 585)

ADVANCE PREPARATION

1. Blend the shallots, garlic, and hot chiles with ¼ cup [60 mL] of the coconut milk and reserve. (The chile paste can be made 1 day in advance.)

PREPARATION OF THE MEATBALLS

2. Mix the beef, egg yolks, and salt together and form small meatballs, ½ inch [1 cm] in diameter.

3. Steam the meatballs for 10 minutes. (Steaming ensures that the meatballs will hold their shape when simmered.)

4. Heat the oil in a skillet and fry the reserved chile paste until fragrant, about 2 minutes.

5. Add the tomatoes, medium-hot chiles, *daun salam* leaves, galangal, *trassi*, brown sugar, and salt. Stir-fry for 5 minutes.

6. Add the remaining coconut milk and bring to a boil. Add the meatballs and cook for 5 minutes, basting frequently.

7. Add the fiddlehead fern shoots, if using, and small shrimp to the mixture. Cook for 2 to 3 minutes more.

SERVICE

8. Serve 4-ounce [110-g] portions, warm or at room temperature, with shrimp chips for scooping the stew.

Tofu Pouches Stuffed with Shrimp Sambal _Tahu Isi Sambal Udang_

serves 8

Sambal is a generic Indonesian-Malaysian term that can refer to a range of items, usually hot and spicy. A _sambal_ can be a side dish, main dish, sauce, stew, or condiment. It refers to a spicy shrimp stew in this context.

Stuffed tofu cake shows a decidedly Chinese influence. The stuffing selected for this recipe is a Balinese shrimp _sambal_ instead of a traditional egg roll filling. The stuffed cakes can be steamed or briefly fried, as they are prepared in Sumatra. The steamed version, which is soft and moist, is offered here.

CHEF NOTES

Tofu pouches can be found in Asian markets. The stuffed pouches may be fried instead of steamed. Dredge the pouches in flour, dip in egg wash, and deep-fry until golden. Small shrimp are specified for stuffing into the tofu pouches, but use large shrimp if serving the _sambal_ with lacy pancakes (see page 208).

SPICE PASTE FOR SEAFOOD (_BASE BE PASIH_): MAKES ¾ CUP [180 mL].

2 large red chiles, chopped

2 garlic cloves, sliced

3 shallots, sliced

1-inch [2.5-cm] piece ginger, thinly sliced across the grain

1 teaspoon [5 mL] ground turmeric

4 cherry tomatoes

1 tablespoon [15 mL] coriander seeds

3 macadamia nuts or candlenuts if available

¼ teaspoon [1 mL] dried shrimp paste

1 tablespoon [15 mL] oil

1 tablespoon [15 mL] tamarind pulp

1 _daun salam_ leaf or bay leaf

1 stalk lemongrass, cut into thirds, bruised

½ cup [120 mL] water

SHRIMP _SAMBAL_

1½ pounds [675 g] small shrimp, peeled, deveined, and coarsely chopped

1 teaspoon [5 mL] salt

½ teaspoon [3 mL] black pepper

2 tablespoons [30 mL] fresh lime juice

½ cup [120 mL] vegetable oil

1 cup [240 mL] coconut milk

Pinch of sugar

2 packages (16 each) tofu pouches (found in Asian markets)

ADVANCE PREPARATION

1. Place the chiles, garlic, shallots, ginger, turmeric, tomatoes, coriander, macadamia nuts, and shrimp paste in a food processor and process until coarsely ground.

2. Heat the oil and add the ground spices, tamarind, _daun salam_ leaf, lemongrass, and water. Stir-fry over medium-high heat

for 5 minutes, or until golden. Allow to cool, then reserve. (The spice paste can be made 1 day in advance and stored refrigerated.)

PREPARATION OF THE SHRIMP SAMBAL

3. Toss the shrimp with the salt, pepper, lime juice, and reserved spice paste. Heat the oil and stir-fry the shrimp mixture for 2 minutes.

4. Add half of the coconut milk, bring to a boil, and reduce the heat to a simmer. Add sugar to taste and cook for 2 minutes. Immediately remove from the heat, place in a large metal bowl to cool, and reserve.

COOKING METHOD

5. Hollow out the tofu pouches with a paring knife. Using half of the *sambal* (reserve the other half to top the steamed packages), firmly stuff the shrimp mixture into the cavities of the tofu pouches and reserve, open side up.

6. Steam for 5 minutes in a large Chinese-style steamer lined with parchment paper.

7. While steaming, add the remaining coconut milk to the reserved *sambal* and keep it warm.

SERVICE

8. Serve 2 hot tofu pouches per guest, topped with the *sambal*–coconut milk mixture.

Sweet-and-Sour Eggplant Curry with Pineapple in Lacy Pancakes
Terong Balado Kari Roti Jala

serves 8

These delicate, lacy crêpes make an ideal wrapper for the intensely flavorful eggplant and pineapple combination. Traditionally these pancakes are served with any dry, spicy curry, especially shrimp curry (*sambal udang*). Eggplant and pineapple pairs well with the crêpe, offering a vegetarian alternative. The visual effect of the dark curry showing through the holes in the lacy crêpe is quite appealing. In Indonesia cooks use a special funnel with concentric holes (called a *roti jala*) to form it, but you may utilize a short coffee can with holes punched through the bottom, a squeeze bottle with a wide-cut spout, or a pastry bag for the same effect.

CHEF NOTES

This dish may also be served at room temperature or cold. The curry will develop more flavor if made in advance and reheated. Japanese long eggplant may be substituted. Reduce the covered cooking period to 15 minutes.

PANCAKES: MAKES 8 CRÊPES

2 cups [480 mL] all-purpose flour

½ teaspoon [3 mL] salt

¼ teaspoon [1 mL] ground turmeric

1 cup [240 mL] coconut milk

2 eggs

1 cup [240 mL] water

1 tablespoon [15 mL] vegetable oil

EGGPLANT

2 teaspoons [10 mL] cumin seeds

2 teaspoons [10 mL] ground coriander

5 dried hot red chiles, or to taste

4 whole cloves

2-inch [5-cm] piece cinnamon stick

¼ cup [60 mL] vegetable oil

2 large onions, thinly sliced

2 garlic cloves, minced

1-inch [2.5-cm] piece fresh ginger, shredded

¾ cup [180 mL] chicken stock

¾ cup [180 mL] coconut milk

1 tablespoon [15 mL] paprika

¼ cup [60 mL] tamarind paste

2 tablespoons [30 mL] dark brown sugar

2 teaspoons [10 mL] salt

1 large globe eggplant, unpeeled, cut into 1-inch [2.5-cm] cubes

½ cup [120 mL] cubed fresh pineapple

Minced chives, for garnish

ADVANCE PREPARATION

1. Sift the flour, salt, and turmeric together into a large bowl.

2. Beat the coconut milk, eggs, and water together, then add the flour mixture and stir to form a smooth batter.

3. Pass the batter through a sieve. Stir the oil into the batter and reserve. (The batter may be made several hours in advance and refrigerated until needed.)

PREPARATION OF THE LACY PANCAKES

4. Heat an 8-inch [20-cm] nonstick skillet to medium-high and brush lightly with oil.

5. Fill a squeeze bottle with batter and quickly make overlapping, concentric circles around the skillet to form a crêpe with a lacy pattern. Cook until the edges begin to curl, about 2 minutes, then flip over to cook briefly on the other side.

6. Stack the pancakes with layers of parchment between them. Continue until you use all of the batter. Reserve. (The pancakes may be made several hours in advance and wrapped in plastic film until needed or they may be frozen for future use.)

PREPARATION OF THE EGGPLANT

7. Grind the cumin seeds, coriander, chiles, cloves, and cinnamon together in an electric spice mill or with a mortar and pestle.

8. Heat the oil to medium-high heat and stir-fry the onions, garlic, and ginger for about 4 minutes, or until the onions are translucent and soft. Add the ground spice mixture and cook 1 minute.

9. Add the stock, coconut milk, paprika, tamarind, brown sugar, and salt. Stir well to dissolve the tamarind and sugar, then add the eggplant. Reduce the heat to a simmer and cook, covered, for 30 minutes, stirring occasionally.

10. Remove the lid and add the pineapple. Reduce the liquid until almost all has evaporated, leaving a thick sauce clinging to the eggplant. Keep warm until service. (The filling may be made 1 day in advance, refrigerated, and reheated for service.)

SERVICE

11. Place a lacy pancake on a plate and spoon about ½ cup [120 mL] of the warm eggplant curry onto half of the pancake. Fold the pancake over to form a semicircle. Garnish with minced chives.

Japan

OF THE WORLD'S CUISINES none can compare to that of Japan with respect to its approach to food. Japanese cooking has been evolving for more than two thousand years, and that is reflected in its restraint and elegance. Food is prepared simply, within its season of harvest. The natural texture, colors, and shapes of ingredients are as important as flavor. Using the freshest possible ingredients allows the prepared food to be in harmony with nature, and a dish is decorated with appropriate seasonal garnishes. It has been said that the skills of the Japanese chef are secondary to the quality of the ingredients, and this point is well illustrated by the most famous of Japanese appetizers, sushi. Using the most perfectly fresh fish and shellfish, the chef has no reason to cook it. When fresh raw seafood is sliced and arranged in an artistic manner, it is known as sashimi. When placed on top of delicately vinegared rice it is called *nigirizushi*; when rolled into a cylinder with rice and seaweed it is called *makizushi*.

The four main islands of Japan are surrounded by cold waters that teem with fish. It is no surprise that fish and seafood are the main staples of the Japanese diet, along with rice. The Japanese fishing fleet and annual catch are the second largest in the world. The waters surrounding the islands also contribute seaweed and kelp to the diet, which are rich in nutrients and minerals. More than 40 percent of the land available to agriculture (less than 20 percent of total land area is arable) is devoted to rice production, and nowhere else on earth is rice so revered. The Japanese word for rice is *gohan*, which means honorable food. More than with any other food, the Japanese cook is measured by his or her ability to cook rice properly. It must be tender and moist and sticky enough to cling to chopsticks. Rice is served at every meal and can be considered to be the national delicacy.

Hokkaido, the northernmost island, produces superior dairy products and is home to cattle production and thoroughbred horse ranches. Hokkaido is sparsely populated and the original indigenous people of Japan, the Ainu, reside there. The main island, Honshu, is home to Tokyo (considered to be the modern embodiment of Japanese cuisine), Kyoto, and Osaka. Kyoto was the ancient capital of Japan, and this is reflected in a cuisine that is traditional in its elegance and refinement. The southernmost island is Kyushu. It is here that foreign contact and influence on the cuisine of Japan are greatest. Pork is very popular, a result of Chinese influence, and the technique of deep-frying was introduced to the Japanese people by European traders. Korea is closest to Japan at Kyushu, and Korean food is quite popular as well. The Chinese influence is so strong in the small, southern islands of the Ryukus and Okinawa that a unique style of cooking (a hybrid of Japanese and Chinese cooking) called *shippoku ryori* has developed.

The Chinese have had a profound influence on the development of Japanese cuisine as a whole. It is believed that rice cultivation originally came to Japan from China over 2,000 years ago. Soy products, such as tofu and soy sauce, are Chinese influences as well. By the sixteenth century the Dutch had introduced squash, corn, and potatoes to the Japanese diet. The Portuguese are credited with introducing the technique of deep-frying, and tempura, a popular Japanese dish, is the result.

Japanese ingredients follow the seasons. Bamboo sprouts, fiddlehead ferns, and bracken come on the menu in the spring, as does the first catch of bonito. Eel is popular in the summer as are octopus and abalone. Summer brings a bounty of fresh fruits and vegetables. The famous matsutake mushroom is the harbinger of fall. Fall is the time of the new buckwheat harvest and soba noodles, made with this grain, appear. Chestnuts and persimmons arrive in the markets in the fall. Late fall signals the time for pickling, an important technique of preserving (and cooking) in Japan. Winter brings the mandarin orange and the precarious delicacy of *fugu* sashimi (blowfish), lethal if prepared incorrectly by the careless chef. (Japanese chefs must be licensed to prepare this fish because of its toxic liver and ovaries.)

Japanese food is characterized by its style and method of preparation, not by the ingredients of the dish. Grilled or pan-fried (*yakimono*), steamed (*mushimono*), fried (*agemono*), vinegared (*sunomono*), and simmered (*nimono*) are the categories of preparation. Selection of individual dishes is based on these categories rather on the main ingredient as in the Western approach to planning a meal. A typical meal will start with a soup, followed by three courses of differing preparation. Noodle dishes, quite popular in Japanese cuisine, are also served. Styles of cuisine are numerous. *Cha kaiseki* is the ceremonial cuisine of Japan, reserved for the tea ceremony. Haute cuisine is known as *kappo ryori*; it is served in Japan's most exclusive restaurants.

Beef-Wrapped Green Beans, Scallions, and Asparagus Bundles with Two Dressings Gyuniku no Hiya Mori, Sukiyaki Niku Itame-Ni, Asupara Maki

serves 8

This recipe offers three different beef-wrapped bundles, one served cold and two warm or at room temperature, with two dressings, *goma aye*, a light sesame-soy mixture, and *goma miso aye*, a more substantial, dark, creamy sesame-miso mixture. The Japanese would traditionally grind the sesame seeds in a *suribachi*, a kind of mortar and pestle. These rolls may be sliced into bite-size pieces for hors d'oeuvres.

SUKIYAKI MARINADE

3 tablespoons [45 mL] Japanese soy sauce (*shoyu*)

2 tablespoons [30 mL] mirin

1 tablespoon [15 mL] sugar

SESAME-SOY DRESSING (*GOMA AYE*): MAKES ¾ CUP [180 mL]

2½ tablespoons [40 mL] hulled sesame seeds, dry toasted until fragrant and golden brown

1½ tablespoons [25 mL] Japanese soy sauce (*shoyu*)

1 tablespoon [15 mL] mirin

1 tablespoon [15 mL] dashi stock (see Chef Notes)

SESAME-MISO SAUCE (*GOMA MISO AYE*): MAKES ¾ CUP [180 mL]

3 tablespoons [45 mL] sesame seeds, dry toasted until fragrant and golden brown

2 tablespoons [30 mL] sugar

¼ cup [60 mL] red miso paste (*aka* or *Sendai miso*)

2 tablespoons [30 mL] mirin

GREEN BEAN ROLLS

24 green beans, trimmed to 4 inches [10 cm]

2 teaspoons [10 mL] wasabi paste

8 slices rare roast beef, 4-inch [10-cm] square

⅛ teaspoon [0.5 mL] sansho powder (see page 584)

black pepper

SCALLION BUNDLES

5 ounces [140 g] beef ribeye steak, sliced very thin against the grain

2 teaspoons [10 mL] wasabi paste

1 sheet *nori*, cut into 8 strips, 1¾ × 4 inches [5 × 10 cm] each

8 scallions, white and green parts, cut into 4-inch [10-cm] slivers

½ cup [120 mL] cornstarch, for dredging

ASPARAGUS ROLLS

5 ounces [140 g] lean beef sirloin, sliced thin against the grain

8 fresh medium asparagus spears, trimmed to 4-inch [10-cm] lengths

3½ tablespoons [50 mL] vegetable oil

½ cup [120 mL] plus 1 tablespoon [15 mL] dashi stock

5 tablespoons [75 mL] Japanese soy sauce (*shoyu*)

3½ tablespoons [50 mL] sugar

2 tablespoons [30 mL] mirin

1½ tablespoons [25 mL] vegetable oil

1 teaspoon [5 mL] sake

1½ tablespoons [25 mL] sugar

3 tablespoons [45 mL] Japanese soy sauce (*shoyu*)

1 tablespoon [15 mL] dashi stock

2 teaspoons [10 mL] black sesame seeds (*kuro gama*), toasted briefly and lightly crushed

Red chiles cut into flower shapes or red bell peppers cut into stars or triangles, for garnish

ADVANCE PREPARATION

1. Combine the soy sauce, mirin, and sugar and mix well. Reserve. (The sukiyaki marinade may be made 1 day in advance.)

PREPARATION OF THE SESAME-SOY DRESSING

2. Reserve ½ tablespoon [8 mL] of the toasted seeds for garnish. Finely grind the remaining 2 tablespoons [30 mL] of seeds in a spice or coffee grinder until they just start to form a paste. Mix well with the soy sauce, mirin, and the dashi stock to combine. Reserve.

PREPARATION OF THE SESAME-MISO SAUCE

3. Combine the sesame seeds and the sugar in a spice or coffee grinder and process until the mixture forms a paste. Mix in the miso paste and mirin. Reserve.

PREPARATION OF THE GREEN BEAN ROLLS

4. Blanch the trimmed beans in lightly salted boiling water for 2 to 4 minutes, then refresh in cold water. Drain and pat dry.

For a lighter and less salty version of the *goma miso aye*, substitute *shiro* or white miso for the *aka* or red miso. Both of these dressings pair well with fresh vegetable crudités. The green beans should be parboiled to taste; they should retain a bright color and some crunchiness. Since the dominant color of this dish is green, an excellent edible garnish is organic yellow chrysanthemum flowers, perched on a red shiso leaf, prepared in the following manner. Blanch the flowers in a mixture of 1 quart [1 L] boiling water with 1 teaspoon [5 mL] salt for 10 seconds, then plunge immediately into cold water. When sufficiently cooled, gently squeeze out the water, and dress with "flavor vinegar" (*sanbai-zu*), made by combining 3 tablespoons [45 mL] rice wine vinegar, 2 teaspoons [10 mL] "lite" soy sauce, 2 tablespoons [30 mL] dashi stock, ½ teaspoon [3 mL] salt, and 2 teaspoons [10 mL] sugar. To prepare dashi stock, a recipe follows:

5. Spread a thin layer of wasabi paste across the surface of the beef slices and sprinkle lightly with sansho powder and black pepper. Fold the edges of the beef slices under to create straight edges on both sides.

6. Wrap each slice around 3 blanched green beans and place them, seam side down, on a sheet pan. Reserve, refrigerated. The rolls may be made in advance, individually wrapped in plastic film.

PREPARATION OF THE SCALLION BUNDLES

7. Toss the sukiyaki marinade with the beef slices. Marinate for 10 minutes, then drain, reserving the marinade.

8. Lay the beef slices flat and evenly spread about ¼ teaspoon [1 mL] of the wasabi paste across the surface of each. Top with a strip of nori.

9. Place one-eighth of the scallion slivers on the end of a beef slice and roll it up to encase the scallion. Secure with a toothpick (skewer the rolls lengthwise to facilitate turning). Repeat for all the slices of beef.

10. Toss the beef rolls in the cornstarch to coat evenly, patting to remove excess cornstarch.

PREPARATION OF THE ASPARAGUS ROLLS

11. Wrap a slice of beef snugly around an asparagus spear. Secure with a toothpick. Repeat for all the slices of beef.

COOKING METHOD

12. Sauté the scallion bundles on all sides in 2 tablespoons [30 mL] of the vegetable oil in a nonstick skillet over high heat for 3 minutes. Reduce the heat to low and add the reserved marinade, ½ cup [120 mL] of the dashi stock, 2 tablespoons [30 mL] of the soy sauce, 2 tablespoons [30 mL] of the sugar, and the mirin. Simmer the rolls for 8 to 10 minutes, or until the sauce becomes a glaze. Cut the rolls in half, and keep warm until service.

13. Heat the remaining 1½ tablespoons [25 mL] oil in a nonstick skillet and sauté the asparagus rolls, starting seam side down to seal, for 2 minutes. Add the sake, the remaining 1½ table-

Dashi Stock
(Katsuo Dashi)
Makes 6 cups [1.4 L]

2 × 3-inch [5 × 8-cm] piece of dried kelp (konbu)

1½ ounces [45 g] dried bonito flakes

7 [1.7 L] cups water

1. To prepare the dashi stock, wipe the kelp with a damp towel and place it in a saucepan with the cold water. Heat and, just before boiling, remove the kelp and discard.

2. Sprinkle in the bonito flakes and remove from the heat. When the bonito flakes begin to sink to the bottom, strain the stock and discard the bonito flakes (may be kept refrigerated for up to 3 days).

spoons [25 mL] sugar, the remaining 3 tablespoons [45 mL] soy sauce, and the remaining 1 tablespoon [15 mL] dashi stock and simmer, covered, for 3 minutes.

14. Take the rolls out and remove the toothpicks. Reduce the liquid in the pan to a glaze. Put the rolls back into the pan and cook over high heat while shaking the skillet, to glaze the rolls. (The rolls may be prepared up to 1 hour in advance and kept at room temperature.)

SERVICE

15. Arrange 1 roll of each kind on a large plate, with the cold green bean roll in the center. Place small dishes containing the 2 sauces, to one side.

16. Sprinkle the green bean roll with the toasted black sesame seeds. Garnish the plate with the chiles or red peppers or the edible garnish given in the Chef Notes.

Chicken Breast and Sour Plum Roll with Ponzu Sauce Torinuku no Bainiku Age

Pickled sour plums (*umeboshi*) are one of the most popular condiments in Japan and are commonly eaten with rice for breakfast. Their flavor is refreshingly sour and salty yet fruity. They are thought to be a remedy for an upset stomach.

CHEF NOTES

Another method of preparation is to cut slits into small cubes of chicken and insert pieces of sour plum, wrap with *shisho* and *nori*, seal the ends with a slurry of cornstarch, and cook as in Step 4. This dish may also be made using the jelly-roll method with pounded-out pork loin instead of chicken. Ponzu sauce may be purchased at Asian markets.

PONZU SAUCE

One 3 × 2½-inch [8 × 6-cm] piece of dried *konbu* kelp

1¾ cups [420 mL] musk lime juice (or kalamansi lime), or 1 cup [240 mL] lime juice with ¾ cup [180 mL] orange juice and 1 tablespoon [15 mL] grapefruit juice

1¾ cups [420 mL] dark soy sauce

⅓ cup [80 mL] mirin

¼ cup [60 mL] tamari soy sauce

1½ ounces [45 g] dried bonito flakes (about 4 cups [960 mL])

CHICKEN ROLLS

4 boneless and skinless chicken breast halves (about 1½ pounds [675 g]), pounded flat

4 to 6 sour plums (*umeboshi*), chopped, or 1 to 2 tablespoons [15 to 30 mL] sour plum paste

1 teaspoon [5 mL] salt, or less to taste

16 *shiso* leaves

4 sheets of nori seaweed, about 6 × 8 inches [15 × 20 cm], toasted

3 tablespoons [45 mL] cornstarch blended with a little water to make a paste

Cornstarch, for dusting

Oil, for frying

Citrus wedges, for service

Sansho powder (see page 584), for sprinkling (optional)

ADVANCE PREPARATION

1. For the ponzu sauce, toast the kelp over a flame or under a broiler. Place the toasted kelp in a bowl with all the other sauce ingredients. Store, refrigerated and covered, for 3 days.

2. Strain through a sieve and reserve, refrigerated. (The sauce will keep for 1 year refrigerated.)

PREPARATION OF THE CHICKEN ROLLS

3. Spread the pounded chicken breasts with the chopped sour plums or sour plum paste. Sprinkle with salt. Roll up jelly-

roll fashion, then wrap each roll with 4 shiso leaves, then nori. Seal the nori seam with the cornstarch paste.

COOKING METHOD

4. Dust the rolls with cornstarch and fry in batches at 325°F [160°C] until golden brown, 8 to 10 minutes. Do not allow the *nori* wrapper to burn, or it will get bitter. Drain the rolls on paper towels and keep warm.

SERVICE

5. Slice each roll in half. Serve a half roll, sliced into medallions, per person, with ponzu sauce at room temperature and wedges of citrus fruit. Sprinkle the rolls with sansho powder just before service, if desired.

Bamboo-Skewered Chicken Pâté Tori no Matsukaze

serves 8

This dish is poetically known as wind in the pines, perhaps because the poppy seeds resemble sand on a windswept, pine-lined beach. The mixture of chicken and miso is flavorful and easy to prepare. The rectangles of chicken are placed between sections of split bamboo, which serve as a handle to make a unique presentation.

CHEF NOTES

Use wooden craft sticks inserted into the base of each chicken section, in place of bamboo (the whimsical name "chicken popsicles" comes to mind). For tray service at parties the loaf may be cut into bite-size portions.

MUSTARD SAUCE

1 tablespoon [15 mL] dry Chinese mustard powder

½ tablespoon [8 mL] dashi stock (see page 216)

½ tablespoon [8 mL] mirin

¼ teaspoon [1 mL] salt

CHICKEN LOAF

1 pound [450 g] ground chicken

2 eggs, lightly beaten

1-inch [2.5-cm] section of ginger, finely minced

3 tablespoons [45 mL] red miso (aka miso)

2 teaspoons [10 mL] sake

2 teaspoons [10 mL] dark soy sauce

2 tablespoons [30 mL] sugar

1 tablespoon [15 mL] all-purpose flour

1 tablespoon [15 mL] blanched carrots, finely diced

1 tablespoon [15 mL] scallion greens, finely sliced on the diagonal

1 tablespoon [15 mL] shiitake mushroom caps, cut into slivers

1 tablespoon [15 mL] white poppy seeds

8 bamboo strips, 4 inches [10 cm] long

¾ cup [180 mL] goma aye (see page 213), for service

ADVANCE PREPARATION

1. Combine all the sauce ingredients and allow to stand 1 hour.

PREPARATION OF THE CHICKEN LOAF

2. Combine the ground chicken with the eggs, ginger, miso, sake, soy sauce, sugar, flour, carrots, scallions, and mushrooms in the workbowl of a food processor. Process to form a smooth, uniform paste.

3. Press the chicken mixture into a lightly oiled 8-inch [20-cm] square baking pan lined with parchment. (The chicken loaf can be prepared several hours in advance.)

4. Sprinkle the poppy seeds evenly over the top of the chicken and place the filled baking pan in a water bath. Bake at 350°F [175°C] for 30 minutes, or until a knife point inserted into the center comes out clean. Allow to cool.

SERVICE

5. Remove the baked chicken loaf from the pan and remove the parchment. Slice the chicken loaf into 8 rectangular portions. Take pieces of bamboo, ½ inch [1 cm] wide, and carefully split lengthwise down the middle but not all the way through to form a V when spread open. Spread the V apart and insert a rectangle of the baked chicken loaf, using the tension of the bamboo to secure it. Serve with mustard sauce and *goma aye*.

Matsutake-Stuffed Duck Dumplings in Rich Broth Kamo Tsumire

In terms of desirability, the matsutake mushroom comes close to the truffle, and in Japan, there is no equal. Matsutakes are harvested in pine forests in the fall and can be quite expensive. If matsutake mushrooms are not available, substitute cèpes (porcini) in these mushroom-stuffed quenelles.

— CHEF NOTES

A less glamorous version can be made with ground chicken and crimini or shiitake mushrooms. Game hens make an excellent substitute for the duck meat. Pheasant would be delicious as well.

STOCK

6 cups [1.4 L] dashi stock (see page 216)

1 teaspoon [5 mL] salt

4 teaspoons [20 mL] "lite" soy sauce

1 tablespoon [15 mL] sake

DUMPLINGS

8 ounces [225 g] ground duck meat (about 1 cup [240 mL])

1 tablespoon [15 mL] red miso (aka miso)

½ teaspoon [3 mL] ginger, grated

2 eggs, lightly beaten

1 teaspoon [5 mL] mirin

8 matsutake mushroom caps, cut into 1-inch [2.5-cm] pieces, blanched briefly in dashi stock, and cooled

½ tablespoon [8 mL] cornstarch

1 block silken tofu, cut into ½-inch [1-cm] rectangles or decorative shapes

3 scallions, green parts only, very finely sliced diagonally, for garnish

ADVANCE PREPARATION

1. Combine the dashi stock, salt, soy sauce, and sake and bring to a boil. Reserve, simmering. (The stock can be made several days in advance and reheated for use.)

PREPARATION OF THE DUMPLINGS

2. Mix the ingredients for the dumplings together, except for the mushrooms and cornstarch. (The dumpling filling can be prepared 1 day in advance.)

COOKING METHOD

3. Scoop some of the duck mixture onto a kitchen spoon.

4. Dust the mushroom pieces in cornstarch, press a piece of mushroom into the center of the duck mixture, and add a bit more duck mixture to encase the mushroom.

5. Using a second kitchen spoon, scrape the dumpling off into the simmering stock, as in preparing quenelles. Repeat until all of the dumplings are formed and are poaching in the simmering stock.

6. Simmer the dumplings for 5 minutes, or until firm enough to hold their shape.

7. Remove the dumplings and add the tofu to the simmering stock and continue to cook for 2 to 3 minutes more.

SERVICE

8. Slice the dumplings in half, trimming the bottom of each half so they will stand up in the bowl. Place 2 halves in each bowl and add some tofu and broth. Garnish with sliced scallion. Serve immediately.

Layered Tuna Sushi Cake Maguro Oshi Zushi

Oshi-style sushi is most often made using a wooden rectangular form; a more convenient way to mold the cake is offered in this recipe. The style is said to have originated in the Osaka-Kyoto region of Japan, using cooked or salt-preserved seafood. Due to the distance from the Sea of Japan, fresh seafood was difficult to obtain in that region in the days before refrigeration. *Maguro* means tuna, but feel free to substitute any type of seafood, fresh or smoked, layered between the seasoned sushi rice.

CHEF NOTES

Any type of seafood, fresh or smoked, may be substituted for the tuna. A layer of thin-sliced cucumber, salted and drained, may be used to cover the *furikake* before adding the second layer of rice. The molds may be done in individual ramekins instead of baking pans. The traditional Japanese wooden molds may also be used. *Furikake* is a blend of toasted sesame seeds and chopped *nori* seaweed. It is available in Asian markets.

RICE

1½ cups [360 mL] short-grain Japanese rice, rinsed gently under cold water until water runs clear

1¾ cups [420 mL] cold water

One 4-inch [10-cm] square of dried kelp (*konbu*)

¼ cup [60 mL] rice vinegar

2 tablespoons [30 mL] sugar

1 teaspoon [5 mL] salt

SUSHI CAKE

6 ounces [180 g] very fresh sashimi-grade tuna, very thinly sliced

1 teaspoon [5 mL] wasabi powder, blended with 1 teaspoon [5 mL] dashi stock (see page 216)

2 cups [480 mL] seasoned sushi rice

1 teaspoon [5 mL] *ao nori furikake* (see Chef Notes)

2 teaspoons [10 mL] black sesame seeds (*kuro gama*), toasted 30 seconds

Japanese soy sauce (*shoyu*), for dipping

Wasabi paste, for dipping

Pickled ginger slices, for garnish

ADVANCE PREPARATION

1. Allow the rinsed rice to drain in a colander for 1 hour. Place the drained rice in a saucepan with the cold water and kelp and bring to a boil over high heat.

2. When the water boils, remove and discard the kelp, cover the saucepan, reduce the heat to medium, and simmer for about 15 minutes, or until the rice is cooked and the water is absorbed.

3. Remove the lid, place a dishtowel over the top of the pan to absorb condensation, and replace the lid. Allow the rice to stand for 20 minutes.

4. Mix the vinegar, sugar, and salt together and stir to dissolve. Reserve.

5. Empty the cooked rice into a large bowl. Stir the rice gently in a circular motion with a wide wooden spoon while sprinkling seasoned vinegar over the rice, a little at a time. It is best to have a fan blowing on the rice while stirring or use a piece of cardboard to fan the rice.

6. After the rice has been seasoned and is cool, cover the bowl with a damp towel. Use within 4 hours. Do not refrigerate.

PREPARATION OF THE SUSHI CAKE

7. Line the bottom and sides of a 9-inch [23-cm] baking pan with plastic film, leaving enough to cover the top.

8. Line the bottom of the prepared pan with thin slices of tuna. Brush the top of the tuna slices with wasabi paste.

9. Dampen your hands and place half of the rice on top of the wasabi-seasoned tuna, molding to cover evenly. Gently compress the rice into the pan with the moistened bottom of another similar-size baking pan, compressing the volume by half.

10. Sprinkle on the *furikake* evenly to form a layer. Add the remaining half of the rice and compress as before.

11. Cover the sushi cake with the plastic film. Place the bottom of the other baking pan on top, and place about 5 pounds [2.3 kg] of weight, evenly distributed, in the top pan. Allow the sushi to rest at room temperature for 30 minutes.

SERVICE

12. Remove the top pan, unfold the plastic film to expose the rice, and place a clean cutting board over the top.

13. Invert. Lift off the baking pan and remove the plastic film. Press the toasted black sesame seeds evenly around the sides of the molded sushi cake.

14. With a thin, sharp knife, cut the cake into 8 to 12 slices, wiping the knife blade with a damp towel between cuts to prevent sticking. Serve a slice of sushi cake with soy sauce, wasabi paste, and pickled ginger slices.

Mixed Tempura of Misty-Fried Shrimp, Scallop-Stuffed Shiitake Mushrooms, Eggplant, and Spicy Leaves Ebi no Kakiagi Hotategai, Mamenasu, Yakumi

serves 6

The Portuguese first introduced the technique of batter-frying to Japan in the seventeenth century. The Japanese have perfected the batter over the years to produce a very light coating that seals the food while cooking, leaving the interior juicy and perfectly cooked. Tempura should be served as soon as possible after frying.

CHEF NOTES

Traditionally the flour used in tempura batter is *tempura-ko*, a low-gluten wheat flour ground for this purpose. If not available, cake flour may be substituted. This battering and frying method will work with almost any vegetable or seafood, so the chef is limited only by imagination. The key to success is for the batter to be very lightly combined and very cold when items are dipped into it.

DIPPING SAUCE: MAKES ABOUT 3 CUPS [720 mL]

½ cup [120 mL] mirin

2 cups [480 mL] dashi stock (see page 216)

¾ cup [120 mL] "lite" soy sauce

I teaspoon [5 mL] sansho powder (see page 584)

TEMPURA BATTER: MAKES ABOUT 2¼ CUPS [540 mL]

I cup [240 mL] tempura flour (*tempura-ko*) or cake flour

¼ cup [60 mL] cornstarch

½ teaspoon [3 mL] baking powder

½ teaspoon [3 mL] salt

I large egg white

About 1¼ cups [300 mL] ice-cold sparkling water or seltzer

MISTY-FRIED SHRIMP

I ounce [30 g] dried *harusame* (spring rain) noodles

I tablespoon [15 mL] sake

I tablespoon [15 mL] mirin

I teaspoon [5 mL] ginger, grated

I teaspoon [5 mL] scallions, sliced fine

½ teaspoon [3 mL] sansho powder

6 large shrimp, peeled with tails attached

¼ cup [60 mL] all-purpose flour

½ teaspoon [3 mL] salt

¼ teaspoon [1 mL] sansho powder

SCALLOP-STUFFED SHIITAKE MUSHROOMS

8 ounces [225 g] scallops, coarsely puréed

½ teaspoon [3 mL] dashi stock

¼ teaspoon [1 mL] Japanese soy sauce (*shoyu*)

¼ teaspoon [1 mL] mirin

¼ teaspoon [1 mL] sake

½ teaspoon [3 mL] arrowroot

12 fresh shiitake mushrooms, stems removed, brushed clean, star-shape cuts on the caps

1 egg white, lightly beaten with ¼ teaspoon [1 mL] dashi stock

Vegetable oil, for deep-frying

6 to 12 small Japanese eggplants, depending on size

6 bunches of young red giant Chinese mustard or 12 sprigs of watercress

ADVANCE PREPARATION

1. For the dipping sauce, heat the mirin until it ignites. Cook until the alcohol has burned off, then add the dashi stock, soy sauce, and sansho powder. Keep warm until service or reheat just before service. (The dipping sauce can be made 1 day in advance.)

PREPARATION OF THE TEMPURA BATTER

2. Mix the dry ingredients together in a bowl.

3. In a separate bowl, combine the egg white and the sparkling water. Add this liquid to the dry mixture, stirring only enough to incorporate the liquid. The batter should be lumpy and undermixed.

4. Place the bowl containing the batter in an ice bath to keep it very cold. Ideally, the batter should be made just before serving. If the batter gets too smooth, sprinkle in more flour and stir lightly. If you like a thinner coating, add a bit more seltzer.

PREPARATION OF THE SHRIMP

5. Trim the noodles to lengths of ½ inch [1 cm]. The easiest way to do this is to pound the noodles in a heavy plastic bag, using a kitchen mallet, until the desired length is attained.

6. Mix the sake, mirin, ginger, scallions, and sansho powder together.

7. Make 3 small diagonal slits on the underside of the shrimp tails to prevent curling while frying. Marinate the shrimp for 30 minutes in the sake mixture.

8. Mix the flour, salt, and sansho powder together and reserve.

9. Mix the scallop purée, dashi stock, soy sauce, mirin, sake, and arrowroot together well. Stuff this mixture into the mushroom caps. Cover with plastic film until needed.

COOKING METHOD

10. For the misty-fried shrimp, roll the shrimp in the dry flour mixture, then dip into the egg white mixture. Drain briefly, then roll the shrimp in the broken noodles to coat completely. (The shrimp can be prepared up to 2 hours in advance, covered with paper towels, and refrigerated.)

11. Fry at 360°F [180°C] for 1½ to 2 minutes, turning halfway through cooking. Drain on paper towels and keep warm.

12. For the stuffed mushrooms, dust lightly in flour and dip into the tempura batter. Gently lower into the oil, stuffed side up. Fry for 4 to 5 minutes, or until the mushrooms float and are crisp and lightly golden. Drain on paper towels and keep warm.

13. For the eggplant, make several slices along the length of the eggplant, from the stem end all the way down to the bottom, so that the eggplant slices may be fanned out. Dust lightly with flour and dip into the tempura batter. Hold the eggplant by the stem end for a few seconds as it drains, to maintain a fan shape. Fry 2 to 3 minutes, or until crisp and lightly golden. Drain on paper towels and keep warm.

14. For the mustard greens, dust lightly with flour and dip into the tempura batter. Dip the leaf part into the hot oil first (to set the shape), then lower the entire green into the oil to submerge. Fry for 1½ to 2 minutes. Drain on paper towels and keep warm.

SERVICE

15. Serve 1 shrimp, 2 stuffed mushrooms, 1 eggplant fan, and 1 mustard bunch per person, with a scant ½ cup [120 mL] of the warmed dipping sauce in a small bowl.

Deep-Fried Ginger Oysters with Tonkatsu Sauce Kaki no Shoga Age Tonkatsu Sōsu

These fried oysters are very popular on the floating oyster boat restaurants of Hiroshima. The panko crumbs makes a crispy golden coating that contrasts perfectly with the succulent sake and ginger-marinated oysters within.

CHEF NOTES

This breading and sauce combination works well with fresh clams and shrimp as well as with oysters. A combination platter of all three would make an excellent appetizer.

TONKATSU SAUCE

½ teaspoon [3 mL] dry Chinese mustard powder

I tablespoon [15 mL] hot water

¼ cup [60 mL] ketchup

½ teaspoon [3 mL] ginger, minced

I garlic clove, minced

I tablespoon [15 mL] sake

4 teaspoons [20 mL] Japanese soy sauce (*shoyu*)

4 teaspoons [20 mL] Worcestershire sauce

4 teaspoons [20 mL] sugar

4 teaspoons [20 mL] white vinegar

½ teaspoon [3 mL] ground allspice

Pinch of ground cloves

OYSTERS

2 teaspoons [10 mL] fresh ginger, grated

I tablespoon [15 mL] sake

32 fresh oysters

½ cup [120 mL] cornstarch or rice flour

½ teaspoon [3 mL] sansho powder (see page 584)

I teaspoon [5 mL] salt

2 eggs, beaten

⅓ cup [80 mL] milk

2 cups [480 mL] panko breadcrumbs (see page 579)

Vegetable or peanut oil, for frying

Leaves of red giant Chinese mustard, for plate liners

Lemon wedges, for garnish

Sprigs of mitsuba or parsley, for garnish

ADVANCE PREPARATION

1. Mix the mustard with the hot water then combine with all the other sauce ingredients and reserve (can be made 1 day in advance.)

2. Mix the ginger and sake together and marinate the oysters in this mixture for 15 minutes.

3. Assemble a frying station with the cornstarch or rice flour, sansho powder, and salt mixed together in a bowl or pan. Combine the eggs and milk in another bowl, and the panko breadcrumbs in a third.

COOKING METHOD

4. Drain the oysters from their liquor and toss them in the cornstarch mixture to coat. Dip into the egg mixture. Drain and coat liberally with panko breadcrumbs.

5. Deep-fry the oysters at 365°F [185°C], in batches, for 3 to 4 minutes, or until crisp and golden brown. Drain on paper towels and keep warm until all are done.

SERVICE

6. Line a plate with red mustard leaves and top with 4 fried oysters. Garnish with lemon wedges and mitsuba sprigs. Serve warm accompanied with tonkatsu sauce.

Korea

Tartare of Beef Fillet with Asian Pears and Pine Nuts
Yukhoe

Beef and Scallion Brochettes
Yuk Sanjook

Charbroiled Pork Spareribs
Taegi Kalbi Gui

Mung Bean Pancakes with Pork and *Kimchee*
Pindaettok

Pork and Bean Curd Meatballs in Rich Broth
Wanja Kuk

Korean-Style Crab Cakes
Keh Sulchon

Twice-Cooked Bean Curd
Tubu Choerim

THE KOREAN PEOPLE are descendants of the nomadic tribes of Mongolia and Manchuria and also perhaps of the Caucasian tribes of western Asia. Historically and culturally Korea is quite different from neighboring China and Japan. Several influences on Korean culture, including those from China and Japan, have led to its particular style of cuisine. The earliest Korean state was conquered by China in 108 B.C., forever cementing their cultures. By the fourth century A.D. the Korean peninsula and the Japanese islands were divided among several fiefdoms. By the tenth century Korea was united under a single leader. A stable central government, modeled after the Chinese government, was in place by the twelfth century. Buddhism was the main religion and philosophy at the time. The French sent Catholic missionaries in the latter part of the nineteenth century, but their influence was short-lived. The United States intervened in Korean affairs, also in the late nineteenth century, to establish trade. At about that time Korea was annexed by Japan, from which it was liberated at the end of World War II. The thirty-eighth Parallel, which began as a surrender line at the end of World War II, turned into a dividing line, splitting Korea into the communist state of North Korea and South Korea. The Korean conflict of the early 1950s involved the United States and helped to introduce Korean cuisine to America.

Since Korea is a peninsula, it has a long coastline, teeming with sea life. Korea is bordered on the west by the shallow, warm waters of the Yellow Sea, which produces many kinds of shellfish and edible seaweed. The East Sea is much deeper, and the cold waters yield a vast array of deepwater fish as well as cuttlefish and squid. Red snapper, herring, mackerel, tuna, sea bass, and halibut are favorites in Korea, as are oysters, clams, sea cucumbers, whelks, abalone, and mussels. The mountains are an important source of wild vegetables, herbs, roots, and fungi. The southern lowlands and plains are ideal for producing cultivated vegetables and grains. Most of the rainfall occurs in the spring and summer, which is ideal for rice production. Not a native plant, rice was brought to Korea by a Chinese nobleman in the twelfth century B.C. Millet is native to all of Korea. The lack of good crop production areas in the north limits food production capabilities (and increases political tension).

The farther south you travel, the spicier, hotter, and saltier the food. This trend is common around the world. Spiciness may mask off-flavors of foods caused by spoilage. The chile, a New World spice, was brought to Korea by Portuguese Catholic priests who accompanied Japanese troops during a war in 1592. Before that time, a peppercorn (*tang chu*) similar to the Szechwan peppercorn provided piquancy to Korean dishes.

It is surprising that beef is the most popular meat in Korea. Most of the country is mountainous, normally not conducive to cattle production. It may be the nomadic heritage of the Korean people that dictates their love of beef. Beef is more popular in the south, while pork dishes find their way into the northern regions. Koreans prefer to grill their food, but they also cook in clay stewing pots called *tukbagge*, as well as in woks. Beef lends itself well to these methods of preparation. Typical flavorings that accompany these cooking methods are sesame oil and sesame seeds, garlic, scallions, mustard, and soy.

Korean cuisine places great emphasis on fresh greens, grains, and small portions of meat. Since winters in Korea are harsh, much emphasis is placed on preserving and pickling, especially dried and pickled seafood and *kimchee*, a spicy form of pickled vegetables. Preserved in more than two hundred different combinations, some with seafood, herbs, and fruits, *kimchee* is unique to Korea and is about 2,000 years old. There are two main types of *kimchee*, seasonal and winter. Examples of the former include young cabbage *kimchee*, cucumber *kimchee*, and sliced radish *kimchee*. Winter *kimchee* could be whole cabbage, whole radish, and "pony tail." *Jahng dak*, the black earthenware pots in which *kimchee* is made, line rooftops and patios, are tucked away in corners, and are buried in the garden to ferment. The flavor components of *kimchee* are the hot taste of chile, salt, sweet, sour, bitter, and astringent. Ingredients for intensifying flavor, such as MSG, seaweed, and sesame seeds are often added. Pickled octopus, preserved oysters, salted pollock roe, and dried shrimp all have an important place in Korea's cuisine, along with the preserved vegetables.

Usually well seasoned and assertive, Korean food is much spicier than that of Japan, yet milder than the food of Thailand. Appetizers are separated into two categories, *anjou* (literally, party or drinking snacks) and *ganshik* (little dishes). The former are much like the Spanish *tapas* and are similarly paired with drinks. The little dishes are not served before a main course, as with most appetizers, but are served together as the main meal. Eating Korean-style consists of "grazing" on many small dishes; the success of a meal is often gauged by the quality and quantity of small dishes presented, with little emphasis placed on one main dish. A sumptuous array of side dishes, relishes, and sauces, called *panchan*, accompany the Korean meal, along with the ubiquitous *kimchee*. Balance is the key to a Korean meal and contrast is an important aspect of this, much akin to Japanese traditions of food combinations. Spiciness is countered by rice, raw fish is balanced by barbecued beef, and no one flavor dominates the meal.

Tartare of Beef Fillet with Asian Pears and Pine Nuts Yukhoe

This dish may be one of the world's tastiest tartare recipes. Marinating the beef masks any raw taste and compliments the flavor of the beef. The sweet crunch of Asian pears provides contrast to the smooth richness of the beef, as do the pine nuts. These bundles can be served prerolled, or they may be assembled at the table.

CHEF NOTES

Use the highest quality beef available for this dish. Have the beef in a semifrozen state for ease in uniform slicing.

¼ cup [60 mL] soy sauce

2 tablespoons [30 mL] sugar

4 scallions, very thinly sliced

6 garlic cloves, finely minced

3 tablespoons [45 mL] sesame oil

2 tablespoons [30 mL] sesame seeds, toasted and crushed

1¼ pounds [560 g] beef fillet, semifrozen, cut into very thin matchsticks

2 crisp Asian pears

2 tablespoons [30 mL] sugar, dissolved in ½ cup [120 mL] water

8 leaves soft lettuce, such as Boston or Bibb, stems removed, rinsed, and patted dry

2 egg yolks, beaten (optional)

¼ cup [60 mL] pine nuts, toasted lightly and very finely minced

Scallions or leek greens, blanched (optional)

ADVANCE PREPARATION

1. Prepare a marinade by combining the soy sauce, sugar, scallions, garlic, sesame oil, and sesame seeds. Mix well to dissolve the sugar.

2. Place the meat in a resealable plastic bag. Add the marinade and toss to coat. Cover and refrigerate for 1 hour.

PREPARATION OF THE PEARS

3. Peel, core, and cut the pears into matchsticks and immediately place them in the sugar-water to cover. Refrigerate until ready to assemble.

ASSEMBLY AND SERVICE

4. Place a 3-ounce [85-g] portion of the marinated beef in the center of a lettuce leaf. Make a well in the center and drizzle in some egg yolk, if using.

5. Place several matchsticks of Asian pear across and top with pine nuts. These lettuce cups may be served as is or tied into a purse or roll with a blanched scallion or leek green. This dish may be assembled tableside.

Beef and Scallion Brochettes Yuk Sanjook

In Korea the name for beef is *yuk* and for skewer, *sanjook*. The sesame and scallion flavors go well with beef, and the sugar in the marinade caramelizes to form a mahogany glaze. The heat in this dish comes from black pepper rather than the ubiquitous chile of which Koreans are so fond.

CHEF NOTES

The brochettes may be char-grilled, using 2 skewers per brochette to aid in turning. Baste with additional sesame oil when grilling. Presoaking the wooden skewers keeps them from burning.

1 tablespoon [15 mL] sugar

⅓ cup [80 mL] soy sauce

2 tablespoons [30 mL] sesame seeds, toasted

2 tablespoons [30 mL] garlic, minced

2 tablespoons [30 mL] scallion greens, chopped

¼ cup [60 mL] pure sesame oil

½ tablespoon [8 mL] freshly ground black pepper

1½ pounds [675 g] beef sirloin, trimmed and sliced into 3½ × ¼-inch [9-cm × 6-mm] pieces

10 scallions, white and very firm green parts only, cut into 1-inch [2.5-cm] lengths

8 wooden skewers, soaked in warm water for 30 minutes

Toasted sesame seeds

ADVANCE PREPARATION

1. Combine the sugar, soy sauce, sesame seeds, garlic, chopped scallions, 2 tablespoons [30 mL] of the sesame oil, and black pepper. Mix well to dissolve the sugar.

2. Place the sirloin into a resealable plastic bag. Add the marinade and toss to coat. Refrigerate 1 hour.

PREPARATION OF THE BROCHETTES

3. Alternate beef strips (a total of 3 ounces [85 g]) and scallion segments on a skewer, centering them, beginning and ending with beef.

COOKING METHOD

4. Add the remaining sesame oil to a large skillet and sauté the skewers, a few at a time, over medium-low heat, 5 minutes per side.

SERVICE

5. Serve hot or warm, sprinkled with toasted sesame seeds.

Charbroiled Pork Spareribs Taegi Kalbi Gui

Korean-style ribs are cut in half lengthwise to allow for more of the marinade to make contact with the meat (and also to facilitate eating ribs with chopsticks). The method of steaming meat before grilling is an age-old Asian method of meat preparation, especially for pork and duck. In Korea ribs are always served with *kimchee* to help cut the fat and richness of the meat. *Kochu jang*, called for in this recipe, is an essential flavoring in Korean cooking. It is prepared each year on March 3rd and allowed to ferment for a minimum of three months. It is made from glutinous rice, fermented soybean cake, hot chiles, and malt syrup. It has a jam-like consistency and its major flavor component is derived from the chiles.

CHEF NOTES

To make *kochu jang* paste, combine equal amounts of hot chile paste, soy sauce, and bean paste (miso). Four teaspoons [20 mL] of each will make the correct amount for this recipe. While dark miso would be most appropriate, its saltiness can be controlled by using *shiro miso* (light miso).

2 tablespoons [30 mL] sugar

¼ cup [60 mL] soy sauce

¼ cup [60 mL] *kochu jang* chile paste (see Chef Notes)

1 tablespoon [15 mL] ginger juice (about ¼ cup [60 mL] grated ginger, squeezed through cheesecloth)

4 garlic cloves, minced

1 tablespoon [15 mL] toasted sesame seeds, crushed

1 tablespoon [15 mL] pure sesame oil

3 tablespoons [45 mL] ketchup

3 pounds [1.4 kg] pork baby back sparerib racks, cut in half lengthwise, then cut into individual ribs

Kimchee, for serving

ADVANCE PREPARATION

1. Combine all ingredients, except for the ribs, and mix well. Coat the ribs with this mixture, using any remaining to baste the ribs while cooking. Marinate, refrigerated, overnight.

COOKING METHOD

2. Bake the ribs in a tightly covered roasting pan at 450°F [230°C] for 30 to 40 minutes. Allow the ribs to cool in the sealed pan. Finish the ribs by grilling them over hot coals for a few minutes just before serving.

SERVICE

3. Serve about 6 ounces [180 g] of ribs per person. Garnish with *kimchee* and a bowl for the bones.

Mung Bean Pancakes with Pork and Kimchee Pindaettok

serves 8

This is a flourless pancake batter, made from a blend of puréed mung beans and rice. The mung beans give nuttiness to the pancake as well as some structure to the batter, while the rice binds the ingredients together. *Kimchee* contributes a spicy note while the pork adds richness.

CHEF NOTES

These pancakes work well with seafood and shellfish and would make an excellent vegetarian offering.

Yank Nyum Jang Dipping Sauce

4 garlic cloves, minced

4 scallions, sliced very thin

1 cup [240 mL] soy sauce

½ cup [120 mL] rice vinegar

¼ cup [60 mL] pure sesame oil

1½ tablespoons [18 g] sugar

1½ tablespoons [25 mL] sesame seeds, roasted, crushed

1 teaspoon [5 mL] ground cayenne pepper

Mix all ingredients, stirring well (can be made one day in advance).

1½ cups [360 mL] dried, split, and shelled mung beans, soaked in warm water for 3 hours

½ cup [120 mL] uncooked rice, soaked in warm water for 3 hours

½ cup [120 mL] chicken stock

8 ounces [225 g] lean pork loin, cut into matchsticks

2 teaspoons [10 mL] soy sauce

1 tablespoon [15 mL] pure sesame oil

3 garlic cloves, minced

½ cup [120 mL] *kimchee*, squeezed to extract any liquid

3 scallions, minced

6 dried red chiles, seeded and cut into very thin threads (see page 239)

Vegetable oil, for pan-frying

Yank Nyum Jang dipping sauce (see Chef Notes)

ADVANCE PREPARATION

1. Purée the soaked mung beans, rice, and the chicken stock in a blender, forming a batter. (The batter can be made 1 day in advance.)

2. Marinate the pork in the soy sauce, 1 teaspoon [5 mL] of the sesame oil, and the garlic for 1 hour.

3. Cut the *kimchee* into thin shreds and marinate in the remaining sesame oil for 1 hour.

COOKING METHOD

4. Heat a lightly oiled large nonstick skillet over medium heat. Ladle in about 2 tablespoons of batter [30 mL].

5. Top each pancake with a portion of the pork, *kimchee*, scallions and chile threads. Cook until golden brown, about 3 to 4 minutes.

6. Flip the pancakes over and cook for 4 to 5 minutes more. Remove the pancakes and drain on paper towels.

SERVICE

7. Serve 2 hot or warm pancakes per person with a dipping sauce on the side (see page 238).

Pork and Bean Curd Meatballs in Rich Broth Wanja Kuk

serves 8

This dish is more like meatballs in a background of rich broth, rather than a soup. The sieved bean curd provides an airy texture to the pork, making the meatballs incredibly light. The watercress, scallions, and chile threads provide color and texture.

CHEF NOTES

Sliced shiitake mushrooms make an excellent addition to this dish. Place the mushrooms on top of the meatballs before pouring over the hot broth. The traditional garnish for this dish is watercress leaves and chile threads.

12 ounces [340 g] bean curd

4 garlic cloves, minced fine

4 scallions, very thinly sliced

1 pound [450 g] lean ground pork

2 tablespoons [30 mL] soy sauce

1½ tablespoons [25 mL] pure sesame oil

1½ tablespoons [25 mL] sesame seeds, toasted and crushed

¼ teaspoon [1 mL] cayenne

2 quarts [2 L] rich chicken stock

2-inch [5-cm] piece of ginger, cut into thin slices

4 scallions, cut into 2-inch [5-cm] sections

Salt to taste

1 cup [240 mL] flour

2 eggs, beaten

2 scallions, chopped, for garnish

ADVANCE PREPARATION

1. All advance preparation may be found in the ingredient list.

PREPARATION OF THE MEATBALLS

2. Place the bean curd in a piece of cheesecloth and squeeze to extract as much moisture as possible. Pass it through a sieve.

3. Combine the sieved bean curd, garlic, sliced scallions, pork, soy sauce, sesame oil, sesame seeds, cayenne, and mix well.

4. Lightly oil your hands and form about 40 small meatballs, using a small-portion scoop if available.

COOKING METHOD

5. Heat the stock, ginger, the scallion pieces, and salt to a boil. Reduce the heat and simmer for 10 minutes.

6. Roll the meatballs in the flour and then dip them in the beaten eggs. Drop the meatballs into the simmering stock and cook about 8 minutes.

SERVICE

7. Serve 5 meatballs per person in shallow bowls. Top with some of the cooking broth. Garnish with chopped scallions.

Korean-Style Crab Cakes Keh Sulchon

These crab cakes are a typical form of *anjou*, or drinking snack (very similar in concept to the Spanish *tapa*). Cooked rice, rather than the more traditional bread-crumbs, holds the delicate cakes together and allows the taste of the crabmeat to shine through. The cakes are traditionally served with a dipping sauce of soy sauce, sesame oil and seeds, scallions, and red pepper.

CHEF NOTES

Be careful not to break up the crabmeat when combining it with the rice purée. Use a full-flavored, nutty rice, such as jasmine or basmati, to add an extra dimension to the dish.

DIPPING SAUCE

I cup [240 mL] soy sauce

I tablespoon [15 mL] pure sesame oil

1½ tablespoons [25 mL] sesame seeds, toasted and crushed

4 scallions, minced

1½ tablespoons [25 mL] crushed red pepper

CRAB CAKES

2 cups [480 mL] cooked rice

12 ounces [360 g] lump crabmeat, picked over for bits of shell

I small onion, finely minced

2 garlic cloves, finely minced

I carrot, peeled and grated

½ tablespoon [8 mL] freshly ground black pepper

Vegetable oil, for frying

ADVANCE PREPARATION

1. Combine the sauce ingredients, mixing well. (The sauce can be made several days in advance.)

PREPARATION OF THE CRAB CAKES

2. Purée the rice in a food processor, pulsing to form a smooth paste. Mix the rice purée with the crabmeat, onion, garlic, carrot, and pepper.

3. Form into 16 small cakes, about ½ inch [1 cm] thick. (The crab cakes can be made several hours in advance, refrigerated.)

COOKING METHOD

4. Heat some oil in a nonstick skillet over medium heat. Saute for 3 minutes per side. Drain on paper towels.

SERVICE

5. Serve 2 crab cakes per person, warm or at room temperature, with dipping sauce on the side.

Twice-Cooked Bean Curd Tubu Choerim

serves 8

This is an excellent vegetarian appetizer that will appeal to all. It is meant to be quite spicy, and the cooking process gives the normally soft, relatively bland bean curd a slightly chewy texture with complex flavors. The tofu picks up a nice reddish-brown color from the sauce as it reduces. To this day Korean vendors still deliver blocks of fresh tofu door-to-door every day, reminiscent of milk delivery in the United States several decades ago.

◯ CHEF NOTES

To make dry chile threads, presoak seeded dried chiles in warm water for about 10 minutes. Using a sharp knife, slice into very thin threads and allow to dry, separated. Cayenne may be replaced with African bird pepper, Thai, or Japanese hontaka chile powders.

4 soft bean curd cakes, quartered

Salt

¼ cup [60 mL] vegetable oil

¼ cup [60 mL] soy sauce

¼ cup [60 mL] water

1 tablespoon [15 mL] hot red chile powder, such as cayenne or bird chile

½ tablespoon [8 mL] sesame salt

6 garlic cloves, finely minced

3 scallions, cut into 2-inch [5-cm] pieces

About 20 dried chile threads (see Chef Notes)

ADVANCE PREPARATION

1. Pat the bean curd pieces with paper towels. Sprinkle lightly on one side with salt. Allow to stand for 10 minutes.

2. Heat the oil in a large skillet over medium-high heat and sauté the bean curd until browned, about 3 minutes per side. Drain them on paper towels.

COOKING METHOD

3. Mix the soy sauce, water, chile powder, sesame salt, garlic, and a few of the scallions in a bowl. Add ¼ cup [60 mL] of this sauce and a few of the scallions to a large skillet.

4. Add a layer of bean curd. Add sauce, scallions, and a few chile threads. Build up layers, until all the bean curd, sauce, scallions, and chile threads have been used.

5. Simmer, partially covered, for 15 minutes, allowing most of the liquid to evaporate.

SERVICE

6. Serve 2 pieces of bean curd per person. Garnish with additional chile threads.

China

Cantonese Roast Pork in Pancakes with Shredded Scallion
Ca Sao Rou Mu Shu

Garlic-Braised Spareribs with Preserved Black Beans
Douchi Paigu

Pan-Fried Potsticker Dumplings
Jiaozi (Guotie)

Sweet Rice–Crusted Pork Meatballs
Jun Jiu Kau

Soup Dumplings and Soup Buns
*Siu Long Bau **he** Gun Tong Gau*

Chilled Pepper Clams
Liang La Geli

Shrimp and Scallion Dumplings (Phoenix Eyes)
Fung Ngan Gau

CHINESE CUISINE IS the oldest of the world's cuisines. There is evidence of rice cultivation in China as far back as ten thousand years ago. Food steamers from an archeological site in northern China have been dated to 3000 B.C. Cooking in China has developed as no other cuisine could, setting out specific rules that must be followed. There are four elements that must be addressed in every Chinese dish: flavor, shape, fragrance, and color. Flavor is divided into five tastes: sweet, salty, sour, bitter, and pungent; and shapes are broken down into eleven categories (slices, strips, slivers, dice, and so on). There are sixteen ways to cut food with a Chinese cleaver and four levels of heating (weak, low, medium, and intense). There are thirteen cooking techniques, including stir-frying (*chao*), deep-frying (*ja*), steaming (*jing*), stewing (*men*), and roasting (*kao*). It is said that when stirring ingredients, they must be stirred in one direction only (to prevent separation and crumbling).

Chinese cuisine can be looked at in the context of five broad geographical regions. Within each region a variety of cooking styles can be found. However, there are common themes that tie all regions together. Meat is served in small portions, with vegetables dominating the diet. There is an almost complete absence of dairy products in the diet of the Chinese people. All ingredients are precut to bite-size pieces, the philosophy being that the chef, not the diner, cuts the food. The same holds true for seasoning. The diner does not season food, the chef does. Each dish should come out of the kitchen properly seasoned. Contrasts play an important part in planning a Chinese meal. Texture contrasts such as crunchy versus smooth work well with dishes that are hot versus cold. Heavily sauced dishes should be paired with those that are "dry."

The name of a dish adds significantly to the experience of eating in China. Sounds that are pleasing, such as "jade," or whimsical names, such as "ants crawling up a tree," are often used. Occasionally the translation of Chinese characters into English produces a confusing name, however, such as "strange flavor chicken" or "fish flavor pork." Strange here refers to a combination of sweet, sour, salty, and bitter flavors used together to season a dish. "Fish flavor" has nothing to do with fish; it is a mixture of seasonings, apparently from a geographical region where the confluence of two major rivers occurs and yields a bounty of fish and seafood.

Regional cooking is more a matter of how a dish is cooked rather than the particular ingredients comprising a dish. Differentiating culinary regions can be a matter of observing, for example, the type of soy sauce used rather than whether or not soy sauce is used. The type of ginger, onion, or garlic used, rather than unique indigenous ingredients, separates one culinary region from another. The cuisine of northern China, commonly referred to as Peking cuisine, is a cuisine of an area with short growing seasons. Unlike most of China, rice is not the staple in the north. Wheat is more adaptable to cold winters, and wheat flour is the starch of the diet. Fruits, such as apples and pears, all types of onions, and soybeans are found in northern cuisine. Mongol dishes are interlaced with those of Chinese origin. Carp and lamb are popular, and Shanxi Province is known for its ample use of vinegar.

Eastern China is famous for its so-called "red-cooked dishes," and braising is a common cooking technique. Seafood is quite popular and the tastiest and most prized crab in China, the freshwater hairy crab, is found there. Known for its spicy dishes and use of hot chiles, Sichuan is located in the third culinary region, central China. Sichuan cooking is one of the most vibrant of regional cuisines. Hunan, also in central China, possesses a cuisine that is both spicy and sophisticated.

Fujian and Taiwan comprise the fourth cooking region, featuring soups, local seafood, and a small, thin pancake called *amoy popia*. Canton is in southern China, the fifth cooking region. Many consider it the most sophisticated of the Chinese cuisines. A Chinese saying is "to eat, go to Canton." The dishes are extremely well prepared, natural in appearance, and often contain many ingredients, but usually prepared with only one or two spices. There are hundreds of dishes to choose from, and the Cantonese chef is not afraid to incorporate the ingredients and techniques of other cultures into Cantonese cuisine.

China is roughly the size of the United States and is at about the same latitude, yet its climate, less affected by oceans' influences, has more extremes than the United States. Mountain ranges, rain forests, deserts, and subarctic regions support an incredible diversity of plants and animals. Since only 10 percent of China's land is arable and China has the world's largest population, it is no surprise that all of the arable land is under cultivation. Northern China produces wheat, oats, millet, and soybeans. Root vegetables and cabbage also grow well there. Fruits and nuts are well adapted to the northern climate, as are peanuts. The more temperate climate of central China produces rice (20 percent of all cultivatable land is dedicated to rice production), squash, bamboo (for shoots), lotus, and water chestnuts. The more exotic fruits and vegetables are grown in southern China. Citrus, bananas, olives, and tropical fruits, such as papaya and pineapples, thrive in this tropical climate. Bitter and fuzzy melons, Chinese broccoli, and snow peas are produced in the south. Corn, potatoes, and peas are harvested throughout China, as are many types of fungi and mushrooms.

Abundant fish and shellfish from the southeastern coast and inland waters are caught, including flounder, tuna, cod, salmon, cuttlefish, sea crabs, shrimp, carp, and sturgeon. Aquaculture is important on many of China's inland waterways. Aquatic plants, such as seaweeds, are harvested as well. Eels, turtles, and conch are fished in the China Sea. Lamb and kid goat are popular in the north, and game such as deer, rabbit, ducks, and quail are eaten throughout China. Camel's hump and bear paws are considered quite a delicacy in some regions. With cattle too important to agriculture as beasts of burden and demanding large amounts of land for grazing, the Chinese turned to pigs and chickens for meat. Both can be raised in the yard, requiring little grazing land. This economy of land use is critical when feeding such a large population. Since firewood is scarce for so many people, cooking techniques such as stir-frying and steaming are used since they are fast and require less fuel.

Cantonese Roast Pork in Pancakes with Shredded Scallion Ca Sao Rou Mu Shu

Anyone who has strolled past a Chinese deli has seen the roast pork hanging next to the ducks and chickens in the windows. This is, perhaps, the most versatile of Chinese pork products since it is eaten by itself as an appetizer, snack, or main course and is used as an ingredient in stir-fries, rice and noodle dishes, and dim sum. Traditionally the meat is roasted hanging from meat hooks in tall ovens, but we propose a simpler method, using a common range oven. We love the roast pork wrapped in Mandarin pancakes with shredded scallion, "*mu-shu* style," but it is also wonderful served alone. No matter how much you prepare it, it will never be enough.

CHEF NOTES

In China saltpeter is added to the marinade to obtain the red color of the roasted pork. Red food color is a reasonable alternative but a natural roasting avoids added chemicals. Premade Mandarin pancakes are available at Asian markets, either refrigerated or frozen. Homemade pancakes may be made ahead of time, wrapped in foil and refrigerated or frozen, and then re-

MANDARIN PANCAKES: MAKES 16 PANCAKES

¾ cup [180 mL] boiling water

2 cups [480 mL] unbleached flour

Peanut or sesame oil, or a blend of the two

MARINADE

6 scallions, cut into 2-inch [5-cm] lengths

10 garlic cloves, bruised

3 tablespoons [45 mL] "lite" soy sauce

3 tablespoons [45 mL] rice wine or dry sherry

3 tablespoons [45 mL] sugar

2½ tablespoons [40 mL] hoisin sauce

2 tablespoons [30 mL] brown bean paste

2 tablespoons [30 mL] chicken stock

1 teaspoon [5 mL] sesame oil

Several drops red food coloring (optional)

ROAST PORK (*CHAR SIU*): MAKES ABOUT 2 POUNDS [900 g]

3 pounds [1.4 kg] boneless pork butt roast, sliced into strips, 2 × 8 inches [5 × 20 cm], ¾ inch [2 cm] thick

GLAZE

¼ cup [60 mL] honey

3 tablespoons [45 mL] sesame oil

MU SHU

6 scallions, thinly sliced lengthwise

Reserved meat juices

Plum sauce (optional)

Chile paste (optional)

Chile oil (optional)

ADVANCE PREPARATION

1. Gradually add the boiling water to the flour while blending with a chopstick or fork. Turn onto a floured board, knead for 4 to 5 minutes, and form into a ball. Cover with a damp towel

heated by steaming for 10 minutes. For frozen pancakes, add an additional 10 minutes to the steaming time.

Traditional Method for Roasting Pork

1. Using S-shaped meat hooks, skewer one end of each piece of meat, about 1 inch [2.5 cm] from the end. Remove all but the uppermost rack from your oven and place a pan with 1 inch [2.5 cm] of boiling water on the bottom. Hang the hooks from the rack so that the pork strips are suspended over the water pan and are not touching each other.

2. Roast at 350°F [175°C] for 45 minutes. Turn the oven to 450°F [230°C] and remove the roasting pork. Brush each piece with the honey and sesame glaze then rehang the strips.

3. Roast an additional 10 minutes. Pour the drippings from the water pan into a saucepan and reduce to thicken. Chill the drippings and remove any congealed fat from the surface.

and allow the dough to rest for 30 minutes. The dough should be soft but not sticky.

2. Knead again for 1 minute and roll with your hands into a rope 1½ inches [4 cm] thick. Cut the rope into 16 equal pieces and flatten each into a round ½ inch [1 cm] thick.

3. Brush a little of the oil onto the top of each round. Place 1 oiled round on top of another, oiled sides touching, and roll into a 5- to 7-inch [13- to 18-cm] circle.

4. Heat a nonstick skillet and cook the rounds 30 seconds per side, or until small golden spots appear on the surface underneath. Immediately remove from the heat, separate the 2 rounds and stack on top of each other, and cover with a towel or foil. Repeat until all are cooked. (The pancakes can be made 1 day in advance, wrapped, and frozen.)

5. Mix the marinade ingredients together and stir to dissolve the sugar.

6. Place the meat strips in a large resealable plastic bag, pour in the marinade, and toss vigorously to completely coat the meat. Allow the meat to marinate 24 to 36 hours, refrigerated.

COOKING METHOD

7. Allow the meat to come to room temperature. Drain and discard the marinade. Place the meat on a wire mesh rack placed over a large baking pan filled with 1 inch [2.5 cm] of boiling water. The water will keep drippings from smoking while keeping the meat moist.

8. Roast the pork at 350°F [175°C] for 45 minutes. Increase the heat to 450°F [230°C] and remove the pan and the rack with the meat. Drain off the water, line the pan with aluminum foil, and place the rack back on the pan.

9. Brush the meat strips with honey, then with sesame oil, and roast the pork for 10 minutes more. About 3 minutes before removing the roast pork, glaze the meat again with the honey and sesame oil. The roast pork should be deep golden brown and juicy when done.

10. Save any pan juices and reserve. Allow the meat to rest at least 20 minutes before slicing.

11. Slice the meat against the grain approximately ⅛ inch [3 mm] thick. Spread out a pancake and stack about 2 ounces [55 g] of the shredded roast pork into the center. Top with scallions and spoon over some of the reserved pan juices. Roll the pancake into a cylinder. Serve, seam side down, accompanied with plum sauce, chile paste, and/or chile oil, as desired.

Garlic-Braised Spareribs with Preserved Black Beans Douchi Paigu

This recipe epitomizes Chinese "comfort food." The riblets are slow-cooked in a rich, spicy black bean sauce until falling-off-the-bone tender. This dish is simple to assemble and does not need attention while cooking. Obtain the meatiest ribs that you can and saw the rack in half, lengthwise (a butcher or purveyor will do this for you).

CHEF NOTES

This dish will keep several days refrigerated (it may be cooked several days in advance of service) and should be reheated with the sauce. Baby back ribs are more uniform in size, but a full rack will be meatier.

2 racks baby back pork spareribs, about 3 pounds [1.4 kg], cut in half lengthwise

2 tablespoons [30 mL] garlic, minced

¼ cup [60 mL] packaged Chinese salted black beans (do not rinse), coarsely chopped

2 tablespoons [30 mL] "lite" soy sauce

1 tablespoon [15 mL] sugar

3 cups [720 mL] pork or chicken stock, heated

2 tablespoons [30 mL] vegetable oil

1 teaspoon [5 mL] crushed red pepper

¼ cup [60 mL] scallions, sliced

ADVANCE PREPARATION

1. Trim any excessive fat and connective tissue from the ribs and slice between the bones, to produce riblets.

2. Combine the garlic, black beans, soy sauce, sugar, and stock. Reserve.

COOKING METHOD

3. Heat a wok or a deep heavy skillet very hot. Add the oil to coat the bottom and sides of the pan. Add the red pepper and scallions and sauté until fragrant, about 15 seconds.

4. Add the riblets and sauté for 5 minutes. Add the reserved stock mixture and bring to a boil, stirring to coat the riblets.

5. Reduce the heat to a low simmer, cover the pot, and simmer for 45 minutes to 1 hour, or until the riblets are very tender and the meat is falling off the bones. Stir from time to time to coat the ribs with the sauce. Add additional stock as required.

6. Remove the riblets from the heat and strain off the sauce. Skim as much fat as possible from the sauce. Add the sauce back to the riblets, adjust the seasonings, and reserve, warm.

SERVICE

7. Serve 6 to 8 riblets per person, topping with any remaining sauce. Provide an empty bowl for the bones.

Pan-Fried Potsticker Dumplings Jiaozi (Guotie)

These dumplings are very popular wherever they are sold. Once the method of pleating the dumplings is mastered, they are quite easy to produce. The classic potsticker is first pan-fried then braised until the liquid from the stock is reduced to a glaze. The dumplings may also be boiled, steamed, or deep-fried. According to legend, one of an emperor's chefs got distracted and deeply caramelized the bottom of a pan of dumplings. Fearing the loss of his head, he told the emperor that they were a new type of dumpling, and the emperor loved them.

FILLING

1 cup [240 mL] Napa cabbage or bok choy, chopped

3 cups [720 mL] boiling water

½ teaspoon [3 mL] salt

½ teaspoon [3 mL] baking soda

1 pound [450 g] coarsely ground pork

½ cup [120 mL] scallions, sliced

½ teaspoon [3 mL] salt

2 teaspoons [10 mL] sugar

½ tablespoon [8 mL] ginger, minced

½ tablespoon [8 mL] garlic, minced

½ cup [120 mL] water chestnuts, finely chopped

½ tablespoon [8 mL] rice wine

1 teaspoon [5 mL] "lite" soy sauce

1 tablespoon [15 mL] oyster sauce

2 teaspoons [10 mL] sesame oil

1 egg, beaten

2 tablespoons [30 mL] cornstarch

DIPPING SAUCE

⅓ cup [80 mL] "lite" soy sauce

¾ cup [180 mL] rice vinegar

1½ teaspoons [8 mL] ginger, minced

1½ teaspoons [8 mL] garlic, minced

2 teaspoons [10 mL] sesame oil

2 teaspoons [10 mL] chile oil

½ teaspoon sugar [3 mL], or to taste

1 scallion, minced

1 package gyoza wrappers or wonton wrappers

Peanut oil, for sautéing the dumplings

1 to 1½ cups [240 to 360 mL] chicken stock

Chile sauce with garlic, for serving

Chile oil, for serving

Minced scallion, for garnish

To make fresh dumpling skins use the following recipe:

Fresh Dumpling Skins

2 cups [480 mL] unbleached flour

½ teaspoon [3 mL] salt

Approximately ¾ cup [180 mL] hot water

1. Combine the flour and salt. Gradually add the hot water while stirring with chopsticks or a fork to form a smooth dough.

2. Turn the dough onto a floured board and knead 5 minutes. Cover with damp towel and allow to rest 20 minutes.

3. Knead again for 5 minutes and roll into ropes 1 inch [2.5 cm] in diameter. Cut the ropes into forty 1-inch [2.5-cm] portions, rolling each portion into a 3-inch [8-cm] round.

ADVANCE PREPARATION

1. Briefly blanch the cabbage in the water with the salt and baking soda (used to retain color). Drain and refresh in ice water, then squeeze dry in a dishtowel.

2. Place the cabbage in a bowl and add the ground pork, scallions, salt, sugar, ginger, garlic, water chestnuts, rice wine, soy sauce, oyster sauce, sesame oil, and egg. Mix the ingredients thoroughly to combine, stirring in one direction only.

3. Sprinkle the cornstarch evenly over the top, and stir again to incorporate. Cover and store refrigerated, about 4 hours.

PREPARATION OF THE DIPPING SAUCE

4. Blend all the sauce ingredients together and stir to dissolve sugar. Allow to stand at least 10 minutes. (The dipping sauce can be made 1 day in advance.)

PREPARATION OF THE DUMPLINGS

5. To fold the dumplings, form a circle with your thumb and index finger. Lay a gyoza wrapper on this circle and scrape 1 tablespoon of filling against the thumb side of the wrapper.

6. Lightly moisten the edges of the wrapper, using the moistened index finger of your other hand. Begin pleating the outside edge of the wrapper against the edge facing you, using the index finger of the other hand. The side closest to you will have no pleats while the outer side will develop a curved pleat. Lightly press the pleats as you form them.

7. Place the finished dumpling on a baking sheet lined with parchment paper and push down gently to flatten the bottom. (The dumplings can be held, refrigerated, for 1 day, tightly covered. The dumplings may be frozen, after first dusting them liberally with cornstarch and then wrapping them in plastic or a resealable plastic bag. Allow the dumplings to defrost completely before cooking.)

COOKING METHOD

8. Heat a skillet until very hot. Swirl in 1 to 2 tablespoons [15 to 30 mL] peanut oil to cover the bottom. Lay the dumplings flat bottom down, arranging them so that they do not touch each other.

9. Cook until the bottoms become dark golden brown, then add ⅓ cup [80 mL] of chicken stock. Reduce the heat to medium and cover the pan, allowing the dumplings to steam. After about 5 minutes the tops of the dumplings will turn translucent and very little liquid will be left in the pan.

10. When the liquid has completely evaporated, remove from the heat. Using a flexible metal spatula, carefully remove the dumplings, being careful to not tear the skins.

SERVICE

11. Serve 4 to 6 dumplings, placed on their side exposing the browned bottoms, per person. Accompany with dipping sauce, a small bowl of chile sauce with garlic, and a small bowl of chile oil. Garnish with minced scallion.

Sweet Rice-Crusted Pork Meatballs Jun Jiu Kau

These are known in Chinese slang as "porcupine balls," but they resemble meatballs studded with seed pearls as much as they do porcupines. These meatballs are light pork dumplings rolled in sweet glutinous rice, then steamed for an extended period to cook the rice. Use fresh water chestnuts in this dish for best results. If fresh water chestnuts are not available, do not use canned water chestnuts. Substitute jicama instead. As with all Chinese dumpling fillings, stir the filling mixture in one direction only; apparently this technique ensures cohesion of the mixture.

CHEF NOTES

The meatballs are best made with ground pork, but they can be made with veal or a blend of pork and veal. To prepare fresh water chestnuts, first rinse them thoroughly in cold water to remove any dirt. Slice off the top and bottom, then pare. If preparing in advance, the peeled water chestnuts may be stored in cold water for several hours.

GARLIC-PEPPER SAUCE

2 tablespoons [30 mL] "lite" soy sauce

2 tablespoons [30 mL] dark soy sauce

1 teaspoon [5 mL] crushed red pepper, toasted

1 teaspoon [5 mL] sesame oil

1 tablespoon [15 mL] white vinegar

2 teaspoons [10 mL] rice wine

1 tablespoon [15 mL] sugar

1 tablespoon [15 mL] garlic, minced

2 tablespoons [30 mL] scallion, minced

½ teaspoon [3 mL] pepper

Pinch of salt

PORK BALLS

1 pound [450 g] lean ground pork

4 fresh water chestnuts or equivalent amount of jicama, peeled and cut into ⅛-inch [3-mm] dice

2 scallions, white parts only, minced

1 large egg, beaten

1½ tablespoons [25 mL] cornstarch, mixed with 2 tablespoons [30 mL] chicken stock

1 tablespoon [15 mL] salt

1 tablespoon [15 mL] sugar

1 teaspoon [5 mL] sesame oil

2 teaspoons [10 mL] "lite" soy sauce

2 teaspoons [10 mL] rice wine

Pinch of white pepper

1 cup [240 mL] glutinous sweet rice, soaked in cold water 1 hour, drained, and rinsed until water runs clear

Chile oil, for lining steamer

ADVANCE PREPARATION

1. For the garlic-pepper sauce mix all of the sauce ingredients together, stirring to dissolve the sugar. Reserve at room

temperature or refrigerate for later use. (The sauce can be made 1 day in advance.)

PREPARATION OF THE PORK BALLS

2. Mix all the pork ball ingredients, except the rice, together, stirring in only one direction. Refrigerate, covered, for 2 hours.

3. Line 2 trays with parchment paper. Spread the slightly damp rice evenly over one pan. Moisten your hands with oil and form 1-inch [2.5-cm] meatballs (a scoop works well for this) and place them on the empty tray. Repeat until all the meat mixture is formed into balls.

4. Roll each ball in the rice, coating evenly. The rice-coated meatballs may be loosely covered with plastic film and refrigerated for up to 4 hours. Allow the meatballs to come to room temperature before cooking.

COOKING METHOD

5. Line a steamer with parchment that has been oiled with chile oil. Pierce holes in the paper and add the meatballs, being careful to leave at least 1 inch [2.5 cm] between them to allow for expansion while cooking.

6. Steam the meatballs for 20 minutes, or until the rice is translucent and puffed and the pork is cooked. Serve immediately.

SERVICE

7. Serve 3 meatballs per person with garlic-pepper sauce.

Soup Dumplings and Soup Buns Siu Long Bau he Gun Tong Gau

serves 16

The term "soup dumplings" refers to soup contained within dumplings, rather than dumplings in a bowl of soup; eating each dumpling produces an explosion of rich broth. These are a favorite dim sum of Shanghai. Traditionally the congealed broth used in the filling was made by boiling down pigskin in water for two days until it became gelatinous. Today, with the advent of prepared gelatin, the process is much simpler. In the few restaurants where these dumplings can be found outside of China, they are often served cradled in a Chinese soupspoon, so as to catch all of the luscious broth.

STOCK: MAKES 1 TO 2 CUPS [240 TO 480 mL]

2 slices fresh ginger, bruised

2 garlic cloves, bruised

4 scallions, knotted

1 onion, quartered

3 quarts [3 L] cold water

5 pounds [2.3 kg] chicken bones, necks, and feet if available

Salt to taste

1 package (1 tablespoon [15 mL]) gelatin, softened in 2 tablespoons [30 mL] cold water

FILLING

1 pound [450 g] ground pork

8 ounces [225 g] shrimp, peeled, deveined, and chopped

1 teaspoon [5 mL] salt

2 slices ginger, minced

1½ teaspoons [8 mL] sesame oil

1 teaspoon [5 mL] soy sauce

1 teaspoon [5 mL] rice wine

1 egg, lightly beaten

3 tablespoons [45 mL] cornstarch

¼ teaspoon [1 mL] white pepper

DOUGH

2½ cups [600 mL] flour

1 teaspoon [5 mL] baking powder

1 teaspoon [5 mL] salt

4 eggs

½ cup [120 mL] flour mixed with ½ cup [120 mL] boiling water

Cornstarch, for dusting

Cabbage leaves, for lining steamer (optional)

Dipping sauce (see page 248) (see potsticker recipe)

3 scallions, finely minced, for garnish

If you prefer to use pork stock in place of chicken, substitute pork neck bones and pig's feet for the chicken bones and feet. These dumplings should be cooked as soon as possible after being formed, or they will dry out and begin to leak; refrigeration can help to hold them for a few hours. They should not be frozen. Pre-made gyoza wrappers or wonton wrappers work well as a substitute for the homemade wrappers; they do offer a bit less texture than homemade. Ideally, make the stock and filling one day, then make the dough and the dumplings the next day.

ADVANCE PREPARATION

1. Bring the seasonings, the water, and the chicken parts to a boil. Skim the surface as the stock simmers and cook the stock for 4 to 5 hours (there should be 1 to 2 cups [240 to 480 mL] of very rich chicken stock when done). Adjust the seasoning for salt.

2. Bring 1 cup [240 mL] of the stock to a boil in a saucepan, remove from the heat, and add the softened gelatin, while stirring. Allow the mixture to cool to room temperature, then pour the gelatin stock into a small square baking pan (about 4 to 6 inch [10 to 15 cm]) to chill. (The solidified gelatin will be cut into ¼-inch [6-mm] cubes.)

PREPARATION OF THE FILLING

3. Combine all of the filling ingredients and mix well, stirring in only one direction. Refrigerate at least 2 hours, preferably overnight.

PREPARATION OF THE DOUGH

4. Mix the flour, baking powder, and salt together. Stir in the eggs, one at a time. Make a well in the center, add the flour mixed with boiling water, and stir well to combine.

5. Knead the sticky dough into a smooth, elastic mass, dusting the work surface with flour as needed. Once the dough has become smooth, continue kneading for 10 minutes. Cover the dough with plastic film and allow it to rest for 1 to 2 hours, refrigerated.

PREPARATION OF THE DUMPLINGS AND BUNS

6. Cut the gelatinized chicken stock into ¼-inch [6-mm] cubes. Stir the filling mixture and gently mix in the chicken stock cubes, quickly to prevent the gelatinized chicken stock from liquefying.

7. Divide the dough into 4 equal pieces. Roll each into a 10-inch [25-cm] cylinder, then divide each cylinder into 16 equal portions. Using a rolling pin, roll each of the 16 pieces into a 3-inch [8-cm] circle. If the dough starts to stick, dust the work surface with cornstarch as the dough is worked. Cover the circles as they are formed.

8. To form soup buns, fill the circles by placing 1½ tablespoons [25 mL] of the filling into the center of each round. Pleat the edges in a circular fashion and gather all the edges in the center, forming a purse. Leave a small hole in the center of the crimped pleats to allow steam to escape while cooking. Continue until all are filled, always keeping the dough and the finished dumplings covered with plastic film.

9. To make soup dumplings, place 1½ tablespoons [25 mL] of filling on one half of the circle. Wet the edges and fold the dough over the filling, forming a semicircle. Begin to pinch the seam, starting at the ends, working your way to the top of the dumpling. Leave a small space unsealed at the top.

10. Pinch the dough around the opening, forming a pleat perpendicular to the seam. Continue to pinch the pleat all the way across the dumpling. When done, there should be 2 seams, perpendicular to each other, with a small steam hole on top. Continue until all are filled, always keeping the dough and the finished dumplings covered with plastic film.

COOKING METHOD

11. Line a Chinese steamer with cabbage leaves or oiled parchment paper, place the buns or the dumplings in it, and steam for 12 minutes.

SERVICE

12. Serve 4 dumplings per person, directly from the steamer, in small bowls. Top with minced scallion. (A dipping sauce should not be needed, but if one is preferred, use the dipping sauce recipe from Pan-Fried Potsticker Dumplings.) Alternatively, 1 tablespoon [15 mL] of chicken stock may be ladled over the dumplings.

Chilled Pepper Clams Liang La Geli

This dish from Beijing has a robust flavor to accent the subtle, briny taste of the clams. Prepared in advance, the clams are served cold, making it the perfect dish for a summer evening. Mussels may be substituted for the clams in this dish, and it may also be served warm over a bed of pan-fried Chinese egg noodles. If served cold, this dish is excellent accompanied with warm crusty bread to soak up the spicy broth.

 **CHEF NOTES**

To clean clams of sand and grit, prepare a solution of salted water, using 1 teaspoon [5 mL] salt for every 1 cup [240 mL] of water and soak the clams for 2 hours. To test clams to see if they are alive and fresh, simply touch the inner lip with a pointed object or finger and the shell should close. Many feel that the smallest clams have the best flavor, so seek those out if possible. This dish may be served with pan-fried noodles as an accompaniment.

2 tablespoons [30 mL] peanut oil

4 garlic cloves, minced

½ teaspoon [3 mL] ginger, grated

3 tablespoons [45 mL] scallion, minced

1 teaspoon [5 mL] crushed red pepper

¼ cup [60 mL] "lite" soy sauce

2 tablespoons [30 mL] rice vinegar

2 teaspoons [10 mL] sugar

3 tablespoons [45 mL] rice wine or dry sherry

1 tablespoon [15 mL] sesame oil

48 small clams (about 3 pounds [1.4 kg]), purged (see **Chef Notes**) and scrubbed

Cilantro leaves, for garnish

ADVANCE PREPARATION

1. All advance preparation may be found in the ingredient list.

COOKING METHOD

2. Heat a wok or skillet very hot, then swirl in the oil. Add the garlic, ginger, and scallions and briefly stir-fry for 15 seconds. Add the red pepper and stir to combine.

3. Add the soy sauce, vinegar, sugar, rice wine, and sesame oil. Reduce the heat to a brisk simmer. Add the clams and toss to coat well with the sauce.

4. Immediately cover the wok or skillet and cook for 4 to 5 minutes, or until the all of the shells have opened (discard any that remain closed). Toss the clams periodically in the sauce to ensure that all have been coated with sauce.

5. Pour the clams and sauce into a wide shallow bowl to cool. Transfer to a resealable plastic bag. Refrigerate immediately. Allow at least 4 hours for chilling in the sauce, mixing periodically.

SERVICE

6. Serve 6 clams per person, topped with some of the sauce. Garnish with cilantro leaves. Serve with crusty bread on the side and a bowl for empty shells.

Shrimp and Scallion Dumplings (Phoenix Eyes) Fung Ngan Gau

serves 8

These steamed dumplings are similar to the traditional *shau mai* dumplings but are folded into a shape that resembles the eyes of the Phoenix. In China, the Phoenix is the traditional symbol of the bride or a woman of nobility.

CHEF NOTES

The filling may be made with shrimp, scallops, lobster, or langoustines, or with any combination. Substitute sautéed leeks for the scallions in this recipe. Use the filling for potstickers (see page 248) for an interesting variation.

FILLING: MAKES ENOUGH FOR 40 DUMPLINGS

12 ounces [340 g] shrimp, peeled, deveined, and chopped fine

½ teaspoon [3 mL] salt

1 large egg white, beaten

2½ tablespoons [40 mL] tapioca flour

1½ teaspoons [8 mL] sugar

1 teaspoon [5 mL] sesame oil

1 tablespoon [15 mL] oyster sauce

Pinch of white pepper

¼ cup [60 mL] scallions, white portions only, minced

½ teaspoon [3 mL] garlic, minced

2 teaspoons [10 mL] rice wine

DUMPLINGS: MAKES 40 DUMPLINGS

1 package dumpling or gyoza wrappers

2 to 3 dried Chinese black mushrooms, soaked and cut into eye shapes

1 tablespoon [15 mL] chile oil

Dipping sauce (see page 248)

Hot Chinese mustard (optional)

ADVANCE PREPARATION

1. Mix all filling ingredients together and stir the mixture for 5 minutes in 1 direction. Store refrigerated, covered, overnight.

2. A dipping sauce of your choice may be made one day in advance.

PREPARATION OF THE DUMPLINGS

3. Place 1 tablespoon [15 mL] of the filling mixture in the center of a dumpling wrapper and fold over into a semicircle. Crimp the edge only at the top of the dumpling (do not seal the entire seam).

4. Pinch a seam down the center of the dumpling, from the curved to the straight end, dividing it into two quarter-circles. Push the sides in toward the pinched seam, forming an

H-shape. Crimp the inside of the pointed ends together, closing the H at top and bottom, to form the classic phoenix-eye shape.

5. Top the 2 sections of the exposed filling of each dumpling with 2 pieces of soaked mushroom, to form the eyes. (The formed dumplings may be frozen or refrigerated, carefully wrapped and sealed.)

COOKING METHOD

6. Line a steamer with parchment that has been oiled with chile oil. Pierce holes in the paper and add the dumplings, being careful to leave space between them. Steam for 7 minutes. Serve immediately.

SERVICE

7. Serve 5 dumplings per order accompanied by a dipping sauce or Chinese mustard.

Vietnam

Barbecued Beef Wrapped in Rice Paper
Bahn Uot Thit Nuong

Pork and Shrimp–Filled Crêpes ("Sound" Pancakes)
Bahn Xeo

Pork and Mushroom–Stuffed Squid
Muc Nhoi Thit

Steamed Pork and Shrimp Bundles
Bahn La

Shrimp and Pork Dumplings
Bahn Bot Loc

Shrimp Pâté on Sugarcane and Lemongrass
Chao Tom

Crab Spring Rolls
Cha Gio

VIETNAM BORDERS ON Laos and Cambodia to the west, the South China Sea and Gulf of Thailand to the east and south, and China to the north. China has exerted great influence on Vietnam through ten centuries of rule. China introduced Confucianism, its architecture, and its method of governmental administration. Its culinary impact can be seen in such cooking methods as stir-frying and wok cookery, such foods as noodles, bean curd, and soy products, and the use of chopsticks for eating. Buddhism, another Chinese influence, introduced vegetarianism to Vietnam. In seeming opposition, Mongol invaders of the thirteenth century introduced beef to the cuisine of the region. This influence is seen mainly in northern dishes.

Influences in the southern regions can be seen in the curries and Indian spices from Vietnam's Southeast Asian neighbors. New World products such as chiles and tomatoes were brought into the country by sixteenth-century European explorers. Considered one of the most sophisticated cuisines of the entire region, Vietnam owes much of its culinary skills to the French, who occupied Vietnam from 1859 to 1954. To this day skillet sautéing is preferred to wok cooking in the south. French baking methods were adopted, and butter, milk, and other dairy products make a surprising appearance in Vietnamese dishes.

In spite of foreign influence throughout its history, Vietnam's cooking style has kept a unique character. Many ingredients and techniques were adapted from the Thai and the Chinese, but Vietnamese cuisine is much less intense than Thai food and much more subtle than Chinese. It is generally light in nature and uses very little fat, even to stir-fry. Braising, steaming, and grilling are the most popular cooking methods. Unlike many Chinese sauces, sauces in Vietnam are rarely thickened. Meals are almost always accompanied by a salad of lettuce or greens, fresh bean sprouts, raw cucumber slices, fresh chile slices, lime wedges, and such fresh herbs as mint, cilantro, and basil. With more than sixteen hundred miles of coastline, it is no surprise that fish and seafood are the mainstays of the diet.

Essential to the Vietnamese style of flavoring is the use of *nuoc mam*, or fish sauce, which is made from fermented anchovy-like fish. Tasted alone, it can be quite strong, very fishy and salty. When added to foods as a seasoning, though, it adds a subtle saltiness and depth of flavor. *Nuoc mam* is made by layering the tiny fish with salt in wooden casks fitted with spigots, then setting them aside for three to six months to ferment. The first pressing, intended for table use, is the highest quality (denoted by the words *nhi* or *thuong hang* on the label) and is dark amber in color and very flavorful. Water is then added to the pressed fish and allowed to ferment for three months more, producing lesser quality grades, which are used in cooking. *Nuoc cham*, a ubiquitous dipping sauce, graces every table in Vietnam. It is made by combining *nuoc mam* with water, lime juice, sugar, garlic, and chiles. Occasionally vinegar, grated carrots, daikon radish, and/or peanuts are added.

Vietnam is a country that is about 70 percent of the area of California. It is divided into three regions, north, central, and south. The Red River to the north and the Mekong River to the south form two large river deltas that are connected by a highland mountain range. The deltas are the primary regions for rice production. The tropical climate of Vietnam, governed by the ebb and flow of the monsoon flow off the Indian Ocean, produces dry winters and wet summers, ideal for rice production. Vietnam is the third largest exporter of rice in the world, with more than 60 percent of its arable land dedicated to rice production. Almost 80 percent of the population depends on rice for their livelihood.

Regionally, the north shows the most Chinese influence. With a cooler and drier climate than the south, more stews and stir-fries are found. The food tends to be milder because there are fewer chiles and spices available. Some of the favorite delicacies of China are also favored in the north, such as chicken feet and dog meat. *Pho*, a rich beef broth with noodles, is a dish from the northern region. The central region tends to be more sophisticated, more stylistic, and more visually oriented. It uses Western-style vegetables such as potatoes, asparagus, artichokes, and cauliflower, and more chiles than in the North. The central region is famed for its sausages and pâtés. The south, with the hottest climate, has the simplest and spiciest food, calling on the widest assortment of fruits and vegetables, many of which are used uncooked. Less cooking time is preferred in a hotter climate, and brief stir-frying or pan sautéing is favored. The grilling and barbecuing of meats is popular as well. Lettuce leaves are often used as wrappers for foods, which are then dipped into chile and peanut sauces. Curries are more prevalent in the south as well. Dinner is the central meal of the day all over Vietnam. All food is presented communally, with no formal order to the dishes. Appetizers are served along with soups and noodles.

Barbecued Beef Wrapped in Rice Paper Bahn Uot Thit Nuong

These morsels of marinated beef, studded with sesame seeds and wrapped with herbs in soft rice paper, are extremely popular. The flavors are typically Vietnamese, with the mint and cilantro providing a fresh, herbal finish. The beef is best cooked over coals but can be broiled as well. If you live near a community with Vietnamese markets, you may be able to find fresh rice papers, which are traditionally served with this dish.

CHEF NOTES

Lemongrass powder, if available, may be substituted for the fresh stalks in the marinade. Store fresh lemongrass in a vase with some water in contact with the roots. The stalks will last for at least a week and may begin to form roots.

MARINADE

4 garlic cloves, minced

1 tablespoon [15 mL] sugar

3 shallots, minced

1 tablespoon [15 mL] fish sauce (nuoc mam)

1 tablespoon [15 mL] sesame seeds

¼ teaspoon [1 mL] freshly ground pepper

1 tablespoon [15 mL] sesame oil

2 stalks lemongrass, sliced very thin and minced very fine

BEEF

1½ pounds [675 g] ribeye steak, cut into ¼-inch [6-mm] slices

16 small (6½ inches [16 cm] in diameter) dried rice papers

Fresh mint and cilantro leaves

ADVANCE PREPARATION

1. Combine the garlic, sugar, and shallots in a food processor and pulse to form a paste. Add the fish sauce, sesame seeds, pepper, sesame oil, and lemongrass and pulse briefly to combine.

2. Pour the marinade over the beef slices in a resealable plastic bag and marinate for 1 hour.

COOKING METHOD

3. Thread the beef strips onto metal skewers or use a fine-mesh grid to grill the beef slices over medium-hot coals or under a broiler, 2 minutes per side. Allow to cool to room temperature.

SERVICE

4. Soften the rice papers by dipping them in warm water or by swirling wetted fingers over the surface of the paper.

5. When softened, place 1½ ounces [45 g] of the beef on a rice paper along with several leaves of mint and cilantro. Roll into a cylinder and trim the ends for a neat appearance. Serve 2 rolls per person with the *nuoc leo* sauce on the side.

Pork and Shrimp-Filled Crêpes ("Sound" Pancakes) Bahn Xeo

serves 8

Bahn xeo means "sound pancake," and it has two meanings. The first is "soft," as opposed to the crunchy traditional Happy Pancake of Hue, in the central region. The second meaning refers to the sizzling sound produced when you pour the batter into the pan. Adding coconut milk to the batter is typical of recipes from the south region. It is a good dish to prepare up to three hours in advance for parties, since it may be served at room temperature or reheated without loss in flavor. Traditionally pieces of the pancake are broken or cut off, wrapped in lettuce with vegetables and herbs, then dipped into *nuoc cham* sauce.

CHEF NOTES

Traditionally this dish is made in a wok, but using a nonstick skillet is more practical. The pancakes can be prepared several hours in advance, then served at room temperature or reheated. Be sure to stir the batter well before cooking each pancake.

NUOC CHAM SAUCE: MAKES I CUP [240 mL]

3 small garlic cloves, minced

2 fresh chile peppers, seeded and minced

¼ cup [60 mL] sugar

¼ cup [60 mL] fresh lime juice

½ teaspoon [3 mL] rice wine vinegar

¼ cup [60 mL] fish sauce (*nuoc mam*)

⅓ cup [80 mL] water

PANCAKE BATTER: MAKES 4 PANCAKES

⅔ cup [160 mL] cornstarch

⅓ cup [80 mL] cake flour

1⅓ cups [320 mL] rice flour

1⅓ cups [320 mL] water

1⅔ cups [400 mL] coconut milk, fresh or canned

½ teaspoon [3 mL] turmeric

FILLINGS

10 ounces [300 g] lean pork, semifrozen, sliced very thin

5 garlic cloves, minced

1 tablespoon [15 mL] fish sauce (*nuoc mam*)

4 scallions, white parts minced, green parts sliced thin for garnish

Freshly ground black pepper

10 ounces [300 g] shrimp, shelled, deveined, and halved lengthwise

2½ cups [600 mL] thinly sliced mushrooms

10 ounces [300 g] bean sprouts, rinsed

1 medium onion, sliced very thin

4 eggs, beaten

1½ tablespoons [25 mL] vegetable oil for each pancake

VEGETABLE PLATTER

16 leaf lettuce leaves

1⅓ cups [320 mL] mint leaves

1⅓ cups [320 mL] cilantro leaves

1½ cups [320 mL] cucumber, decoratively peeled, halved
lengthwise, seeded, and sliced

4 jalapeño chiles, sliced

ADVANCE PREPARATION

1. Combine all of the sauce ingredients in a blender or processor and pulse until it is well blended and the sugar is dissolved. (The sauce can be made 1 day in advance.)

2. Combine the cornstarch, cake flour, rice flour, water, coconut milk, and turmeric in a blender. Strain through a sieve and refrigerate. Stir the batter well before use. (The batter can be made 1 day in advance.)

PREPARATION OF THE FILLINGS

3. Marinate the pork for 30 minutes in half of the garlic, 1 teaspoon [5 mL] of the fish sauce, half of the scallions, and a sprinkling of pepper.

4. Marinate the shrimp for 30 minutes in the remaining garlic, fish sauce, and scallions. Add a sprinkling of black pepper.

COOKING METHOD

5. Heat a nonstick skillet over medium heat. Add one-fourth of the pork, shrimp, and mushrooms and stir until cooked.

6. Reduce the heat to medium and add ¼ cup [60 mL] of the batter and one-fourth of the sprouts and onion. Cover and cook for 2 minutes.

7. Sprinkle 3 tablespoons [45 mL] of the beaten egg over the top of the pancake. Cover and cook for 2 minutes more. Fold in half, like an omelet. Place on a sheet pan lined with paper towels and keep warm. Repeat for all 4 pancakes.

SERVICE

8. Cut each pancake into 4 wedges. Place wedges of the pancake inside lettuce leaves filled with mint, cilantro, cucumber, and jalapeños. Serve 2 bundles per person with *nuoc cham* sauce on the side. The pancakes may be served warm or at room temperature. Guests may also assemble their own wraps by providing a salad plate and some softened rice wrappers with the pancake wedges.

Pork and Mushroom-Stuffed Squid Muc Nhoi Thit

serves 8

Pork-stuffed squid is a dish that originated in the central region of Vietnam. Baby squid make bite-size servings to pop right into the mouth, or larger squid can be used, served sliced on the diagonal. The Vietnamese people appreciate the textural contrast between the soft filling and the chewy squid casing. The squid may be steamed for a healthier version, but the browning process of pan-frying greatly enhances the flavor.

CHEF NOTES

Use prepared squid tubes (already cleaned and dressed) to speed up production. Chop additional tubes for the filling, as there will be no tentacles to use.

8 small squid, heads and tentacles removed, cleaned, cuttle bone removed, and patted dry

6 large dried Chinese mushrooms, soaked in warm water to soften, stems removed, and caps chopped

1 ounce [30 g] bean thread cellophane noodles, soaked in warm water 30 minutes, drained, and chopped

1 pound [450 g] ground pork

6 shallots, diced

4 garlic cloves, minced

1 tablespoon [15 mL] fish sauce (*nuoc mam*)

½ teaspoon [3 mL] sugar

½ teaspoon [3 mL] salt

Freshly ground black pepper

½ cup [120 mL] vegetable oil

1 cup [240 mL] *nuoc cham* sauce (see page 263), for dipping

ADVANCE PREPARATION

1. All advance preparation may be found in the ingredient list.

2. Mince the squid tentacles. Combine the tentacles, mushrooms, noodles, ground pork, shallots, garlic, fish sauce, sugar, salt, and pepper. Mix well.

3. Stuff the mixture into the cavity of the squid bodies, filling them three-fourths full with a pastry bag fitted with a large plain tip. Secure the ends with toothpicks.

COOKING METHOD

4. Heat the oil in a large skillet over medium heat. Add the stuffed squid and cook for 5 to 7 minutes, turning to brown all sides.

5. Using a long-handled fork or skewer, carefully pierce each squid (watch for spattering) to release any liquid trapped inside. Continue cooking for 10 minutes, turning occasionally.

SERVICE

6. Place the squid on a cutting board and remove the toothpicks. Slice each squid on the diagonal and arrange slices on a plate. Serve with *nuoc cham* sauce on the side.

Steamed Pork and Shrimp Bundles Bahn La

Bahn la are as close to a Vietnamese tamale as possible, and they hold together much better. The dough, made from rice flour and tapioca, turns translucent when properly steamed. The soft texture contrasts nicely when paired with crisp and crunchy appetizers, such as fried spring rolls. The bundles can be cooked in aluminum foil but banana leaves, although more difficult to work with, add to the presentation and flavor.

CHEF NOTES

Banana leaves may be used to replace the foil wrappers, allowing your guests to unwrap them at the table (have one unfolded to reveal the contents). Serve lettuce leaves on the side. Blanch the banana leaves in boiling water for 5 minutes, then refresh in cold water before cutting to size.

FILLING

4 ounces [110 g] shrimp, shelled, deveined, and diced

8 ounces [225 g] pork, coarsely ground

2 scallions, green parts only, diced

1 tablespoon [15 mL] fish sauce (*nuoc mam*)

¼ teaspoon [1 mL] freshly ground black pepper

2 teaspoons [10 mL] vegetable oil

3 garlic cloves, minced

2 scallions, greens separated from the white bulbs, white bulbs diced

BATTER

2 cups [480 mL] rice flour

1 quart [1 L] water

¼ teaspoon [1 mL] salt

¼ cup [60 mL] tapioca flour

Twenty-four 6 × 10-inch [15 × 25-cm] aluminum foil rectangles

24 Boston lettuce leaves

1 cup [240 mL] *nuoc cham* sauce (see page 263), for dipping

ADVANCE PREPARATION

1. All advance preparation may be found in the ingredient list.

2. Toss the shrimp and pork with the scallion greens, fish sauce, and pepper. Allow to stand for 10 minutes.

3. Heat the oil over high heat and sauté the garlic and scallion bulbs briefly.

4. Add the shrimp and pork mixture. Stir-fry until the pork is no longer pink. Set aside.

PREPARATION OF THE BATTER

5. Combine the rice flour, water, salt, and tapioca flour in a saucepan over high heat, stirring constantly, until the batter thickens to the consistency of cooked cereal, about 5 min-

utes. Remove from the heat and continue to stir for 2 minutes more, forming a smooth batter.

6. Spread 2 tablespoons [30 mL] of the batter over the center of a piece of foil, using an offset spatula, to form a rectangle about 3 × 5 inches [8 × 12 cm].

7. Spread 1 tablespoon [15 mL] of the filling mixture over the batter, pressing gently into the surface. Fold the foil in half, lengthwise, across the filling, to encase it in the batter. Roll the foil down to form a cylinder and fold the 2 ends toward the center. Repeat until all of the bundles are formed.

COOKING METHOD

8. Place the packets on the rack of a steamer (a multi-tiered Chinese-style steamer works best) and steam, covered, over simmering water for 30 minutes. Test a packet to make sure all of the batter has turned transparent (if opaque, cook longer). Allow the packets to cool before serving.

SERVICE

9. Unwrap the packages and serve 3 bundles, wrapped in lettuce leaves, per person, with *nuoc cham* dipping sauce on the side.

Shrimp and Pork Dumplings Bahn Bot Loc

These dumplings originated in the central region. The addition of tapioca to the dough is common in Vietnam. It adds a chewy texture and a degree of translucency to the wrapper, both loved by the Vietnamese. The dumplings are first boiled, then quickly dipped in cold water, which turns the wrapper translucent. The unique warm scallion oil bath reheats the dumplings, adds flavor, and prevents the dumplings from sticking together.

CHEF NOTES

If time is short, substitute gyoza or potsticker wrappers for the homemade (the texture of homemade dumpling wrappers, however, is superior). The scallion oil bath is easily adapted to a variety of steamed dumplings and noodle dishes.

SCALLION OIL

½ cup [120 mL] peanut oil

¼ cup [60 mL] sesame oil

3 scallions, finely diced

FILLING

4 ounces [110 g] ground pork

4 ounces [110 g] shrimp, peeled, deveined, and chopped

1 teaspoon [5 mL] chile paste

4 garlic cloves, minced

1½ tablespoons [25 mL] fish sauce (*nuoc mam*)

⅛ teaspoon [0.5 mL] sugar

Freshly ground black pepper

2 tablespoons [30 mL] vegetable oil

3 shallots, diced

1 teaspoon [5 mL] tomato paste

2 large dried Chinese mushrooms, soaked in warm water to soften, stems removed and caps chopped

½ tablespoon [8 mL] dried wood ear mushrooms, soaked in warm water to soften and chopped

¼ cup [60 mL] bamboo shoot strips, diced fine

DUMPLINGS

½ cup [120 mL] tapioca flour

½ cup [120 mL] cornstarch

½ cup [120 mL] all-purpose flour

¼ teaspoon [1 mL] salt

About 1 cup [240 mL] water

32 fresh cilantro leaves

1 cup [240 mL] *nuoc cham* sauce (see page 263)

ADVANCE PREPARATION

1. Heat the peanut and sesame oils in a skillet to about 300°F [150°C]. Remove from the heat and add the scallions. Allow the scallions to steep in the oil until the oil has completely cooled.

PREPARATION OF THE FILLING

2. Combine the pork, shrimp, chile paste, garlic, fish sauce, sugar, and pepper and mix well. Cover and refrigerate.

3. Heat 1 tablespoon [15 mL] of the vegetable oil in a skillet, add the shallots, and stir-fry for 30 seconds.

4. Add the tomato paste and stir-fry for 1 minute.

5. Add the pork mixture and stir-fry for 3 minutes.

6. Add the mushrooms and bamboo shoots and cook until heated through. Set aside to cool. Cover and refrigerate.

PREPARATION OF THE DUMPLING WRAPPERS

7. Mix the tapioca flour, cornstarch, flour, and salt in a mixing bowl. Add the water, a little at a time, to form a soft dough that is not sticky. Knead the dough until smooth.

8. Roll out portions of the dough and cut 3-inch [8-cm] rounds. Cover with plastic film to avoid drying out.

PREPARATION OF THE DUMPLINGS

9. Brush a wrapper with water. Place 1 tablespoon [15 mL] of the chilled filling in the center, top with a cilantro leaf, and fold over to form a half-moon shape. Seal by pinching. Place the dumplings on an oiled cookie sheet and cover with plastic film. Continue until all the dumplings are formed.

COOKING METHOD

10. Bring a large pot of water to a boil over medium heat. Have a bowl of cold water and a slotted spoon nearby. Working in batches of 6 to 8, drop the dumplings into the boiling water and cook for 2 to 2½ minutes.

11. Transfer the dumplings into the cold water with the slotted spoon and allow them to stand for a minute or so, until the wrappers turn transparent.

SERVICE

12. Heat the scallion oil, and warm the dumplings in the oil. Cut the dumplings in half and serve 4 dumplings per person, with *nuoc cham* sauce on the side.

Shrimp Pâté on Sugarcane and Lemongrass Chao Tom

Chao tom is classically Vietnamese in style, with the soft shrimp pâté contrasting with crispy, sweet sugarcane. The cane is not eaten, but chewed on to release its sugary essence after the shrimp has been eaten. The lemongrass will add a tart, citrus quality that contrasts nicely with the sugarcane. This dish tastes best if grilled over charcoal, but may be prepared in the oven. The *nuoc leo* sauce, the traditional dipping sauce of the central region, makes the ideal accompaniment to the dish.

CHEF NOTES

Sugarcane is readily available in most major supermarkets, as well as in Latin American and Caribbean specialty markets. In cities with large Asian communities, shrimp paste may be available already prepared in Asian markets, though homemade will be superior.

NUOC LEO SAUCE: MAKES 2 CUPS [480 mL]

1½ tablespoons [25 mL] tamarind paste

1 cup [240 mL] chicken stock

1½ tablespoons [25 mL] vegetable oil

3 garlic cloves, minced

½ cup [120 mL] Vietnamese soybean sauce (*tuong*) or yellow bean paste mixed with water

1 tablespoon [15 mL] fish sauce (*nuoc mam*)

½ tablespoon [8 mL] chile paste

½ tablespoon [8 mL] sugar

1 teaspoon [5 mL] black pepper

2½ tablespoons [40 mL] peanut butter

2½ tablespoons [40 mL] roasted peanuts

PÂTÉ ON SUGARCANE

1⅓ pounds [600 g] shrimp, shelled, deveined, and dried thoroughly

5 garlic cloves, finely minced

5 shallots, minced

½ tablespoon [8 mL] sugar

3 egg whites, beaten until slightly frothy

1½ tablespoons [25 mL] roasted rice powder

¼ teaspoon [1 mL] ground black pepper

2½ tablespoons [40 mL] salt pork, boiled in water 10 minutes and very finely minced

One 8-inch [20-cm] section sugarcane, peeled, cut crosswise in half and quartered lengthwise

8 stalks lemongrass, trimmed to 4 inches [10 cm] in length

⅓ cup [80 mL] vegetable oil

2½ cups [600 mL] leaf lettuce

1⅓ cups [320 mL] fresh mint leaves

1⅓ cups [320 mL] fresh cilantro leaves

1⅓ cups [320 mL] cucumber, decoratively peeled, halved lengthwise, seeded, and sliced horizontally

4 jalapeño chiles, sliced

16 dried rice papers (*bahn trang*)

1. Soak the tamarind paste in 3 tablespoons [45 mL] of the stock for 30 minutes.

2. Heat the oil and briefly sauté the garlic. Add the tamarind liquid, discarding the pulp and seeds.

3. Add the soybean sauce, fish sauce, the remaining ¾ cup [180 mL] of stock, the chile paste, sugar, black pepper, and peanut butter. Mix well and simmer for 2 minutes, stirring constantly. Add the peanuts just before service.

PREPARATION OF THE PÂTÉ

4. Pulse the shrimp in a food processor until it just forms a paste. Add the garlic, shallots, sugar, and egg whites. Pulse until well blended. Add the rice powder, pepper, and salt pork and pulse until just blended.

5. Oil your hands and mold about 2 tablespoons [30 mL] of the shrimp paste around the upper half of the sugarcane and the lemongrass, leaving the lower half to serve as a handle. Repeat for all the sugarcane and lemongrass segments. Wrap them individually in plastic film and refrigerate for 1 hour.

COOKING METHOD

6. Grill the shrimp pâtés over medium coals for 8 minutes, turning frequently, until golden brown.

SERVICE

7. Moisten the surface of 2 rice papers, allowing them to become soft and pliable. On each rice paper place some lettuce, mint, cilantro, cucumber, and sliced chilies. Top with one wrapped stalk of sugarcane and one stalk of lemongrass. Serve *nuoc leo* dipping sauce on the side. Instruct the diner to remove the pâté from the stalks and wrap in the rice papers. (Note that chewing on the sugarcane stalk is accepted practice.)

Crab Spring Rolls Cha Gio

These tasty little packets, also called *nem*, are considered the national dish of Vietnam. They are usually made at home for special occasions, but are commonly available as street food from vendors. Since production can be time consuming, it is best to assemble the rolls the day before they are cooked. They can also be fried in advance and then frozen for later use. Wrapping the crab rolls in lettuce leaves with aromatic herbs is a unique way to serve them, making these rolls distinctly different from other egg rolls found across Asia.

CHEF NOTES

The sugar added to the water used to moisten the rice papers gives the spring rolls a golden brown color and additional crispness when fried.

FILLING

4 ounces [110 g] thin rice vermicelli (*bun*), boiled 5 minutes, refreshed under cold water, and drained

6 large dried Chinese mushrooms, soaked 30 minutes in warm water, stems discarded, and chopped

1 tablespoon [15 ml] dried wood ear mushrooms, soaked 30 minutes in warm water and chopped

1 small can sliced water chestnuts, chopped

4 ounces [110 g] fresh crabmeat, picked over

8 ounces [225 g] shrimp, shelled, deveined, and chopped

12 ounces [340 g] ground pork shoulder

1 medium onion, minced

5 shallots, minced

5 garlic cloves, minced

2 tablespoons [30 mL] fish sauce (*nuoc mam*)

1 teaspoon [5 mL] freshly ground black pepper

3 eggs, beaten

CRAB ROLLS

½ cup [120 mL] sugar

4 cups [960 mL] warm water

80 small rice paper rounds (*bahn trang*), about 6½ inches [16 cm] in diameter

Peanut oil, for frying

4 cups [960 mL] *nuoc cham* sauce (see page 263) with 1 large peeled and shredded carrot added

Basic vegetable platter, including lettuce leaves, mint, cilantro, cucumbers, and jalapeño chiles

ADVANCE PREPARATION

1. All advance preparation may be found in the ingredient list.

PREPARATION OF THE FILLING

2. Combine the filling ingredients together in a large bowl and mix well. Reserve. (The filling can be made 1 day in advance.)

3. Stir the sugar into the warm water to dissolve. Have a damp towel to cover the rice paper wrappers, a dry towel for the rice paper skins to drain on, and two cookie sheets lined with parchment to hold the assembled spring rolls.

4. Working with 4 rice papers at a time and keeping the remaining sheets covered with a damp towel to prevent curling, dip each rice paper into the warm sugar water. (The dried rice paper wrappers are very brittle and must be handled with care.) Lay them on the dry towel to drain. They will begin to soften almost immediately. (Avoid having the sheets touch each other, or they will stick together.)

5. Fold over the bottom third of a rice paper and place 1 teaspoon [5 mL] of the filling in the center of the folded portion.

6. Shape the filling into a small rectangle, then fold the left side of the wrapper over the filling, followed by the right side. Roll from the bottom to the top to completely enclose the filling. Place the rolls, seam side down, on the cookie sheet. Do not allow the rolls to touch each other. Repeat for all the rolls.

COOKING METHOD

7. Heat 1½ inches [4 cm] of oil in a pan to 325°F [160°C]. Fry in batches, being careful to not crowd the skillet. Fry 10 to 12 minutes, turning often. Drain the crab rolls on paper towels, then transfer to a slow oven to keep warm.

SERVICE

8. Place some mint, cilantro, cucumbers, and jalapeño chiles on a lettuce leaf. Wrap around a crab roll and serve 5 rolls per person, with *nuoc cham* sauce on the side.

Southeast Asia

Cambodia, Laos,

and Burma

Lettuce-Wrapped Venison Packages with Two Sauces
Phan Sin Fahn

Spicy Pork Bundles Wrapped in Lettuce
Saik Chrouk Chralouark

Chiles Stuffed with Pork and Glutinous Rice
Mawk Mak Phet Jaew Issaan

Velvet Chicken Cubes with Shrimp
Kyehtar Tobu

Caramelized Chicken Morsels with Chiles and Cilantro
Kyethar Ahcho Kyaw

Grilled Fish and Eggplant Dip with Crudités
Pon Pla

Smoked Trout and Green Mango Salad
Yoam Makah Trey Ang

Crab Cakes with Fire-Roasted Chile Sauce
Poo Ja Jaew Bong

SOUTHEAST ASIA INCLUDES Cambodia, Laos, and Burma as well as Thailand and Vietnam, which are treated in their own chapters. Because of its geographical location (between China and India), Southeast Asia is at a crossroad, and it has seen many cultures pass through. Many conquerors have stayed on and left their imprint on the developing cuisine of the area. India was first to exert its influence on the region, and it provided much of the underlying culture found there. By the fifteenth century, Europe, seeking spices from the East, became the main influence, and the result was widespread colonialism, which lasted through the twentieth century. The British settled Burma while the French controlled Cambodia and Laos as well as Vietnam. The Europeans introduced many new foods and cooking techniques. Chiles, tomatoes, corn, and peanuts were introduced by the Spanish explorers. Cabbage, broccoli, and green beans were brought by Dutch traders by way of Indonesia, and the French introduced baking and their particular cooking talents and sophisticated techniques. Surprisingly, Chinese influence did not come to this region until the latter part of the nineteenth century, and then only in the form of restaurants as part of the dining scene.

Common ingredients tie the region together. Coconut milk, lemongrass, chiles, and cilantro can be found in dishes throughout Southeast Asia. Cooking techniques are the same and the diet is similar across boundaries. Rice is the staple for all countries in the region, although Laos has a particular fondness for glutinous rice (sweet or sticky rice) in savory dishes (in other countries, it is reserved for desserts). The coconut palm provides cooking oil, coconut milk, and the coconut itself. Fish and shellfish, both fresh and dried, provide the main protein source. With a sweltering climate and little refrigeration, drying and other means of preserving are essential to storing these foods. With an abundance of inland rivers, the people of this region are particularly fond of freshwater fish and shellfish. Laos, the only landlocked country in the region, is particularly dependent on freshwater fish. Each country has its own version of fish sauce, a salty condiment found on every table.

Stews and curries, popular throughout Southeast Asia, are favorites of the Cambodian people. They learned the art of mixing spices from the Indians and include such spices as cardamom, star anise, and tamarind in their dishes. Cambodian cuisine relies on salty and sour components to which textural aspects are added. The crunch of fried shallots often tops a smooth curry or fresh bean sprouts are added to a bowl of soft noodles. Cambodian cuisine does not differentiate between fruits and vegetables, and they are enjoyed in combination. Cambodian cuisine is more subtle than Vietnamese cuisine and does not rely so heavily on sweet components, as does Thai cuisine (it is also a bit less spicy). As one travels close to the border with Thailand, the use of coconut milk, sweeteners, and fiery chiles increases. Unique to Cambodian cuisine is the use of *prahok*, a fermented fish paste. Very strong in flavor, its presence signals a Cambodian dish. Cambodians are fond of pickled foods, such as pickled cucumbers and papaya, certainly an Indian influence. Grilling is an extremely popular method of food preparation. The Laotian taste for glutinous rice in savory dishes is unique. The rice is used to soak up sauces and move food around the plate. Laotians often eat with their hands and do not use chopsticks, so the sticky rice is kneaded into a small ball and picked up along with the food. The practice of wrapping food in leaves is another popular way of eating with the hands. Lao ginger, an important flavoring throughout Southeast Asia, is more commonly called galangal. It is a rhizome, like ginger, but it has a medicinal-lemony component to its flavor. Ginger is a major flavoring ingredient in Laotian cuisine.

In addition to the ubiquitous fish sauce found throughout the region, Laotians use *padek*, a fish sauce with chunks of preserved fish included, along with rice powder and husks. Fish are plentiful in Laos, and the giant catfish, one of the largest freshwater fish in the world, is a particular delicacy here. Noodles are enjoyed throughout Southeast Asia and, in Laos rice vermicelli (*khao poo*) is the favored form. Game is enjoyed in Laos and deer is extremely popular as a treat, especially the liver, which is cooked with ground fried chiles and roasted glutinous rice powder.

With China, Thailand, and India surrounding Burma, Burmese cuisine has been influenced by all three countries. British influence in the region is found exclusively in Burma, which also heightens the Indian influence to Burmese cuisine (due to the dominating presence of the British in India). Chick peas and lentils appear as unique ingredients to Burmese cuisine. Chick peas are used to make a product similar to bean curd, and beans sprouts may be made from chick peas as well. A traditional Burmese meal is quite structured, having one chile condiment, a raw salad, one soup, several curries, a pickle, and the Burmese favorite, *balachaung*, fried dried shrimp with chile. Burmese cuisine can be either quite different from that of its neighbors or remarkably similar. Soybean flour is often used to thicken soups of northern Burma, unusual for Southeast Asia. However, fish sauce and shrimp paste, both essentials of Thai cuisine, are also found in Burmese dishes. Tamarind is used to provide the sour component in Burmese cuisine, in contrast to others in the region, which rely on lime juice or vinegar. The Burmese cook appreciates textural contrasts, and popular garnishes include crispy fried garlic and onions. More beef is eaten by northern Burmese than in other places in Southeast Asia, and this region of Burma is known for its love of pork.

Lettuce-Wrapped Venison Packages with Two Sauces _Phan Sin Fahn_

serves 8

One of the favored game animals in Laos is known as barking deer (*fahn*), a small forest deer of the species *Muntiakus muntjak*. Laotians also hunt a larger type of deer known as *kuoang* and a small (2- to 5-pound [900-g to 2.3-kg]) mouse deer called a *kaiy*. You won't find these at your local market, but you should be able to obtain New Zealand stag or axis venison year-round. Venison packages, a common method of using edible wrappers, can be prerolled for table service, or the ingredients may be arranged on a platter for guests to assemble to their own liking.

⌒ **CHEF NOTES**

You may substitute beef for the venison in this dish, following the same procedure. If substituted, the dish is known as *phan sin ngoua*.

VENISON

1½ pounds [675 g] venison loin or tenderloin, cut into slices 3 inches [8 cm] long by ½ inch [1 cm] thick, pounded to tenderize

Salt and pepper to taste

5 garlic cloves, minced

DIPPING SAUCE: MAKES I CUP [240 mL]

7 shallots, minced

I heaping tablespoon [20 mL] garlic, minced

I tablespoon [15 mL] toasted sesame seeds, finely ground

I tablespoon [15 mL] toasted peanuts, finely ground

3 dried shrimp, pounded with mortar and pestle until fluffy

12 small dried red chiles, seeded and soaked in water to soften

I tablespoon [15 mL] sugar

Pinch of salt

I tablespoon [15 mL] fish sauce

Chicken stock or water, as needed

TOMATO SAUCE

I tablespoon [15 mL] butter

I small onion, minced

I garlic clove, minced

2 tablespoons [30 mL] tomato paste

2 tablespoons [30 mL] venison or beef broth

SALAD

2 heads butter lettuce, large outer leaves reserved

4 ounces [110 g] rice vermicelli, soaked in warm water 15 minutes, then briefly boiled, drained, and rinsed

½ cup [120 mL] watercress leaves

½ cup [120 mL] mint leaves

4 scallions, cut in half lengthwise and julienned

¼ cup [60 mL] Asian pickled garlic cloves

2 star fruit, very thinly sliced

2 medium tomatoes, seeded and chopped

I cucumber, peeled, seeded, and thinly sliced

I semiripe banana, cut in half crosswise and thinly sliced lengthwise

Scallion greens or Chinese leek, blanched and softened, for tying bundles

Dry-roasted peanuts, chopped, for garnish

Cilantro leaves, chopped, for garnish

ADVANCE PREPARATION

1. Combine the venison and salt and pepper and the minced garlic and mix well. Place in a resealable plastic bag and marinate overnight.

PREPARATION OF THE DIPPING SAUCE

2. Combine all of the sauce ingredients, except the chicken stock or water, in the workbowl of a food processor and blend to form a smooth paste. Add chicken stock or water to make the sauce thick but pourable. Reserve. (The dipping sauce can be made 1 day in advance.)

PREPARATION OF THE TOMATO SAUCE

3. Heat the butter and sauté the onion until translucent. Add the garlic and sauté for 2 minutes. Add the tomato paste and the broth and bring to a boil while stirring. Reserve. (The tomato sauce can be made 1 day in advance.)

PREPARATION OF THE SALAD

4. Arrange all of the salad ingredients in small piles on a tray or cookie sheet. Cover with plastic film or a damp towel and refrigerate. (The salad can be prepared several hours in advance.)

COOKING METHOD

5. Place a tightly woven wire rack over a wood fire or charbroiler. Quickly grill the slices of venison, slightly charring the exterior while keeping the interior rare to medium rare.

6. Allow the meat to rest for 5 minutes. Slice into bite-size pieces, pour the tomato sauce over the meat, and reserve for assembly.

7. Top a lettuce leaf with small strips of rice vermicelli. Add 1½-ounce [40-g] portions of the venison in tomato sauce.

8. Add some watercress, mint, scallions, pickled garlic, star fruit, tomato, cucumber, and banana. Roll up to form a bundle and place seam side down.

9. Using lengths of blanched scallion or Chinese leek, tie the bundle to secure. Serve 2 bundles per person accompanied by the dipping sauce.

10. Just before service, sprinkle the bundles lightly with the chopped peanuts and garnish the dipping sauce with cilantro leaves.

Spicy Pork Bundles Wrapped in Lettuce Saik Chrouk Chralouark

serves 8

You may want your guests to make their own bundles by supplying the components on a serving platter (for a unique presentation), or they may be bundled just before service and tied with strips of blanched scallion or Chinese leek. Regardless of the presentation method, diners will love the combination of the rich pork with the fresh herbs combined with the zesty dipping sauce.

⸺ CHEF NOTES

Pork tenderloin may be substituted for the loin. Pork belly or fresh ham is traditionally used in Cambodia for this dish and could be substituted.

PORK LOIN

3 slices galangal

3 garlic cloves, bruised

3 dried red chiles

1½ pounds [675 g] pork loin, cut into slices 1 inch [2.5 cm] thick

DIPPING SAUCE: MAKES 1 SCANT CUP [240 mL]

3 slices galangal, flame grilled until lightly browned

3 large garlic cloves, minced

1 large shallot, minced

½ cup [120 mL] dry-roasted peanuts, coarsely ground

6 tablespoons [90 mL] fish sauce

3 tablespoons [45 mL] sugar

2 tablespoons [30 mL] white vinegar

4 fresh bird or Thai chiles, very thinly sliced, for garnish

BUNDLES

1 large head butter or leaf lettuce, leaves separated

1 cup [240 mL] (loosely packed) mint leaves

1 cup [240 mL] (loosely packed) basil leaves

8 ounces [225 g] mung bean sprouts

1 small cucumber, cut in half lengthwise and thinly sliced

Chinese leek or scallion greens, blanched in hot water to soften

Chopped peanuts for garnish

Sliced bird chiles for garnish

ADVANCE PREPARATION

1. Combine the galangal, garlic, and chiles in a food processor and process into a paste. Spread the spice paste over the sliced pork, place in a resealable plastic bag, and marinate overnight.

PREPARATION OF THE PORK LOIN

2. Charbroil the pork over medium coals until medium. (The pork may be prepared 1 day in advance.)

PREPARATION OF THE DIPPING SAUCE

3. Combine the grilled galangal, garlic, shallot, and 2 table-spoons [30 mL] of the peanuts together in a mini-processor or blender and blend into a paste.

4. Add the fish sauce, sugar, vinegar, and chiles, stirring well to dissolve the sugar. Reserve at room temperature. (The dipping sauce can be made 1 day in advance and refrigerated.)

ASSEMBLY METHOD

5. Slice the grilled pork against the grain into ⅛-inch [3-mm] strips. Divide the bundle ingredients and the pork into 8 portions.

6. Lay the lettuce leaves on a flat surface and top with the sliced pork, mint, basil, bean sprouts, and cucumber. Roll each bundle into a cylinder.

7. Tie securely with blanched leek or scallion greens. Or serve the ingredients on platters and allow diners to assemble their own bundles.

SERVICE

8. Serve one lettuce roll per person accompanied by dipping sauce topped with some chopped peanuts and sliced bird chiles.

Chiles Stuffed with Pork and Glutinous Rice Mawk Mak Phet Jaew Issaan

serves 8

Laotians prefer sticky rice to jasmine rice for savory dishes. In this dish spicy chiles are stuffed with a blend of sticky rice paste, minced pork, and seasonings and then steamed. The chiles are served with an anchovy sauce from northern Laos, a superb combination.

CHEF NOTES

Any hot chile approximately 4 inches [10 cm] in length will work for this dish. Be careful that you do not split the chiles open down the side or at the top when stuffing them. *Bong* sauce (page 292) works nicely with these chiles, as does the anchovy sauce here.

DIPPING SAUCE: MAKES ABOUT I CUP [240 mL]

4 large garlic cloves, fire roasted and peeled

3 shallots, fire roasted, diced

2 slices galangal, fire roasted, diced

Pinch of salt

½ stalk lemongrass, very finely minced

2 dried Thai chiles, toasted lightly, chopped

4 large cherry tomatoes, briefly fire roasted, chopped

2 tablespoons [30 mL] anchovy fillets, chopped fine

2 tablespoons [30 mL] lime juice

½ tablespoon [8 mL] sugar

I large makroot leaf, central rib removed, finely shredded, as garnish

CHILES

24 large fresh jalapeño peppers

8 ounces [225 g] ground pork

2 garlic cloves, minced

7 small shallots, minced

½ cup [120 mL] cooked glutinous rice, pounded or processed into a paste

I makroot leaf, central rib removed, finely shredded

½ teaspoon [3 mL] salt

I teaspoon [5 mL] black pepper

2 teaspoons [10 mL] fish sauce

Strips of banana leaves, for wrapping the chiles

Dried chiles, seeded and finely julienned, for garnish

ADVANCE PREPARATION

1. Combine the garlic, shallots, galangal, salt, and lemongrass in a food processor and process to a smooth paste. Add the chiles, tomatoes, and anchovy and process to blend.

2. Stir the lime juice and sugar together to dissolve the sugar, then add this mixture to the processor and pulse to combine.

Transfer to a small bowl, top with the makroot leaf, and reserve. (The dipping sauce can be made 1 day in advance.)

PREPARATION OF THE STUFFED CHILES

3. Cut off a small slice down the length of each jalapeño pepper. Hollow out the peppers, removing the ribs and seeds.

4. Combine the pork, garlic, shallots, rice, makroot leaf, salt, pepper, and fish sauce and mix thoroughly to form the stuffing.

5. Stuff each chile with 1 tablespoon [15 mL] of filling, mounding the filling on top of the chile.

6. Wrap the stuffed chiles in strips of banana leaves and reserve. (The stuffed chiles can be made 1 day in advance and refrigerated.)

COOKING METHOD

7. Place the chiles on a piece of parchment or foil with holes punched in the parchment or foil to allow for steam to penetrate the food in a Chinese-style steamer. Steam the chiles for 10 minutes, or until the pork is done.

SERVICE

8. Unwrap the chiles and serve 3 chiles per order, accompanied with a small ramekin of dipping sauce. Serve hot. Or for presentation serve 1 chile unwrapped and the remaining chiles in their banana leaf wrappers. Garnish with julienne dried chiles.

Velvet Chicken Cubes with Shrimp Kyehtar Tobu

serves 8

These silken cubes of chicken with egg and tidbits of shrimp melt in the mouth. They are made from a firm egg custard, dusted with cornstarch, and deep-fried. In Burma, they are eaten simply with plain granulated sugar or chile sauce, or both.

CHEF NOTES

For a more elegant presentation, substitute lobster or scallops for the shrimp. Handle the custard cubes carefully both before and after cooking, as they are quite delicate.

ROASTED CHILE SAUCE: MAKES ABOUT 1½ CUPS [360 mL]

4 ounces [110 g] hot banana chiles

4 ounces [110 g] shallots, halved

6 garlic cloves, peeled

8 ounces [225 g] cherry tomatoes

3 tablespoons [45 mL] cilantro leaves

1 teaspoon [5 mL] salt, or to taste

2 tablespoons [30 mL] lime juice

CUSTARD: MAKES 25 SQUARES

4 cups [960 mL] clear rich chicken stock

4 ounces [110 g] shrimp, peeled, deveined, and finely diced

4 ounces [110 g] chicken breast, minced

3 scallions, minced

1 teaspoon [5 mL] black pepper

1¼ cups [300 mL] cornstarch, dissolved in 2 cups [480 mL] water

6 eggs, beaten

Salt to taste

Cornstarch, for dredging

Vegetable oil, for frying

Sugar, for dusting (optional)

ADVANCE PREPARATION

1. Roast the chiles, shallots, garlic, and tomatoes over an open flame until completely charred. Remove the stems of the chiles (and the seeds and ribs if a less piquant sauce is desired) and finely chop all of the roasted vegetables.

2. Place in a bowl with the cilantro, salt, and lime juice and stir well to combine. Allow the flavors to develop for at least 30 minutes before serving. (The sauce will keep, refrigerated, for 5 days. Serve at room temperature.)

3. Bring the stock to a boil in a large saucepan. Reduce the heat to low and add the shrimp, chicken breast, scallions, and black pepper. Simmer for 3 minutes.

4. Stir the cornstarch slurry to recombine, then beat in the eggs. Slowly add the cornstarch slurry to the shrimp and chicken mixture, stirring constantly, until thick but pourable. Salt to taste.

5. Pour this mixture into a 10×12-inch [25×28-cm] baking pan lined with parchment and allow to cool. When cooled, cover the pan with plastic film and refrigerate. (The custard may be prepared 1 day in advance.)

COOKING METHOD

6. Slice the chilled, set custard into 2-inch [5-cm] squares.

7. Place the cornstarch in a shallow pan for dredging. Preheat a skillet containing 1 inch [2.5 cm] of oil at 365°F [185°C]. Dust the squares with cornstarch and gently slip them into the hot oil.

8. Cook 1 side for 3 to 5 minutes, or until golden brown. Turn over and cook for 3 to 5 minutes more. Cook in batches to avoid crowding the squares while cooking. Remove from the oil and drain on paper towels. Keep warm until all are fried.

SERVICE

9. Serve 3 to 4 cubes per person accompanied with the chile sauce or a light dusting of granulated sugar, if desired.

Caramelized Chicken Morsels with Chiles and Cilantro Kyethar Ahcho Kyaw

serves 8

In this dish the caramelized garlic with chile and cilantro makes a tasty, crunchy garnish. The original recipe calls for a cut-up whole chicken, but that is rather messy to eat in a formal dining setting. Boneless thighs, which are more flavorful than breast meat, are substituted here for ease of eating and portion control, but you can substitute a whole chicken as directed in the Chef Notes.

 CHEF NOTES

To cut up a whole chicken for this recipe first remove the skin and cut off the wings, removing and discarding the wing tips. Separate the wings at the joints. Remove the legs, separate the thighs at the joints, and cut each portion in half. Cut away the backbone, remove the breast, divide it into halves, and cut each into 4 segments, for a total of 20 pieces. This recipe works well with halves of boneless quail, for a more upscale presentation. Shrimp may be prepared this way as well.

1 teaspoon [5 mL] ground turmeric

1 teaspoon [5 mL] salt

2 tablespoons [30 mL] garlic, minced

1 teaspoon [5 mL] ginger, minced

1 tablespoon [15 mL] "lite" soy sauce

1 tablespoon [15 mL] fish sauce

2 egg yolks

8 boneless chicken thighs, quartered

1 cup [240 mL] flour

1½ cups [360 mL] vegetable oil

6 tablespoons [90 mL] sugar

1 tablespoon [15 mL] crushed red pepper

¼ cup [60 mL] cilantro, chopped

2 tablespoons [30 mL] white vinegar

Cilantro leaves, for garnish

ADVANCE PREPARATION

1. Combine the turmeric, salt, 1 tablespoon [15 mL] of the garlic, the ginger, soy sauce, fish sauce and egg yolks and mix well. Pour this mixture over the quartered chicken thighs and toss to thoroughly coat the chicken pieces. Cover and refrigerate for 1 hour.

2. Add the flour and stir well to coat all the pieces. Cover and marinate for 3 hours more. (The chicken can be prepared the night before.)

COOKING METHOD

3. Heat the oil in a large skillet over medium-high heat. Add the marinated chicken and cook about 10 minutes, turning often, or until golden brown. Drain the chicken pieces on paper towels and hold warm.

4. Drain off all but 2 tablespoons [30 mL] of the oil in the skillet, then reduce the heat to medium-low. Add the sugar and

the remaining 1 tablespoon [15 mL] of the garlic and stir constantly until the sugar dissolves and slowly caramelizes.

5. Add the red pepper and stir for 30 seconds. Add the reserved chicken, the cilantro, and the vinegar and stir gently but thoroughly, to coat completely. Serve at once.

SERVICE

6. Serve 4 pieces of chicken per serving, sprinkled with fresh cilantro leaves.

Grilled Fish and Eggplant Dip with Crudités Pon Pla

serves 8

This traditional dish is loved by all Lao peoples. Catfish (or other freshwater fish), eggplant, and aromatics are first grilled and then the ingredients are pounded with a mortar and pestle to form a smooth paste. The spicy, smoky, and subtly herbed spread can be served with fresh vegetables or crispy glutinous rice cakes.

CHEF NOTES

Tilapia or any other mild tasting freshwater fish may be used in place of the catfish.

CATFISH

I teaspoon [5 mL] lemongrass, minced very fine

2 garlic cloves, minced

2 teaspoons [10 mL] makroot leaf, minced

2 tablespoons [30 mL] vegetable oil

I pound [450 g] catfish fillets or other freshwater fish fillets

DIP

10 Thai chiles, fire roasted

4 small shallots, fire roasted

4 garlic cloves, fire roasted

6 sweet round Lao or Thai eggplant, fire roasted (or I Japanese eggplant, fire roasted)

I teaspoon [5 mL] shrimp paste

I scallion, minced

2 sprigs of cilantro, chopped fine

3 makroot leaves, central rib removed, finely minced

I to 2 cups [240 to 480 mL] chicken stock

I tablespoon [15 mL] fish sauce

I½ tablespoons [25 mL] fresh lemon juice

I tablespoon [15 mL] palm sugar or brown sugar

½ teaspoon [3 mL] salt

Vegetables for dipping, such as cucumber slices, carrot slices, Belgian endive leaves, baby romaine lettuce leaves, and/or radicchio leaves

Cilantro leaves, for garnish

Finely shredded makroot leaves, for garnish

ADVANCE PREPARATION

1. Combine the lemongrass, garlic, makroot leaf, and oil and mix well. Place the fish fillets in a resealable plastic bag and pour in the marinade to cover. Marinate at least 2 hours or overnight, refrigerated.

PREPARATION OF THE FISH

2. Grill the marinated fish over a charcoal fire until cooked and flaking. Chop the cooked fish and reserve. (The fish can be prepared 1 day in advance.)

PREPARATION OF THE DIP

3. Combine the fish, chiles, shallots, garlic, eggplants, shrimp paste, scallion, cilantro, and makroot leaves in a food processor and blend into a smooth paste.

4. With the processor running, add just enough stock to achieve a spreadable consistency.

5. Stir the fish sauce, lemon juice, sugar, and salt together to dissolve. Add this to the fish and eggplant purée. Adjust the seasonings and reserve. (The dip can be made 1 day in advance, stored refrigerated.)

SERVICE

6. Place a portion of the dip in the center of a plate ringed with the cut vegetables. Garnish with cilantro and shredded makroot leaf. This dip may be served warm or cold.

Smoked Trout and Green Mango Salad Yoam Makah Trey Ang

serves 8

This spicy, tart salad of smoked fish and shredded green mango makes an excellent first course. Preserving fish by smoking is quite common throughout Southeast Asia. The area around Angkor Wat, near the northern end of Tonle Sap Lake, is widely known for its excellent smoked fish. Any smoked freshwater fish will work in this recipe. (We prefer using smoked trout.) Sautéing the smoked fish is optional, but the crisp textural contrast adds interest.

CHEF NOTES

Remove the skin of the smoked fish if you prefer not to sauté it. Smoked farm-raised catfish, if available, makes an excellent substitute for the trout, or you may choose to smoke your own. Smoked mudfish may be found in Asian markets and this would be the most traditional option.

DRESSING: MAKES ¼ CUP [60 mL]

4 to 5 small Thai chiles, minced

I teaspoon [5 mL] garlic, minced

I tablespoon [15 mL] shallots, minced

I tablespoon [15 mL] galangal, minced

I tablespoon [15 mL] cilantro stems, minced

2 tablespoons [30 mL] rice vinegar

I tablespoon [15 mL] fish sauce

I tablespoon [15 mL] sugar

SALAD

2 tablespoons [30 mL] butter, for pan-frying

I medium smoked trout, boned

2 green mangoes, peeled, pitted, julienne

I large carrot, peeled, julienne

⅓ cup [80 mL] red onion, thinly sliced

¼ cup [60 mL] loosely packed cilantro leaves

¼ cup [60 mL] loosely packed mint leaves

Butter lettuce leaves, for plate liners

Minced scallion, for garnish

ADVANCE PREPARATION

1. Combine all of the dressing ingredients in a nonreactive bowl and stir well to dissolve the sugar. Reserve at room temperature. (The dressing can be made 1 day in advance.)

COOKING METHOD

2. Heat the butter in a skillet and quickly fry the smoked trout fillets. Remove and drain on paper towels.

PREPARATION OF THE SALAD

3. Combine the mangoes, carrot, red onion, cilantro, and mint in a nonreactive bowl and toss well. Dress the salad with 5 to 6 tablespoons [75 to 90 mL] of the dressing. Toss to coat lightly.

4. Line a plate with lettuce leaves. Top with some of the dressed salad. Just before serving drizzle the fish fillets with 2 to 3 tablespoons [30 to 45 mL] of dressing to coat.

5. Slice the fillets into sections and arrange pieces of the smoked fish on the salad. Garnish with minced scallion.

Crab Cakes with Fire-Roasted Chile Sauce Poo Ja Jaew Bong

serves 8

Crab cakes are a colonial French introduction to Laos and have been well received. *Bong* means pickled in Laotian, and, although this sauce is not pickled, it will keep for extended periods if refrigerated. Traditionally Laotians would use strips of grilled, dried water buffalo skin (*nang kuai haeng*) in the sauce, but we use fried pork rind due to availability.

⊙ **CHEF NOTES**

The crab cakes may be broiled instead of sautéed for a lighter presentation.

BONG SAUCE: MAKES ¾ CUP [180 mL]

10 dried red chile peppers, lightly fire roasted but not charred

5 shallots, fire roasted, diced

1 small head garlic, fire roasted, peeled, and chopped

2 slices galangal, fire roasted, diced

1 tablespoon [15 mL] cilantro leaves and stems, chopped fine

1 tablespoon [15 mL] sugar

1 tablespoon [15 mL] fish sauce

3 to 4 tablespoons [45 to 60 mL] warm water

CRAB CAKES: MAKES EIGHT 3-OUNCE [85-g] CAKES

1 pound [450 g] cooked lump crabmeat, picked over for bits of shell and cartilage

2 eggs, beaten

1 cup [240 mL] breadcrumbs

2 tablespoons [30 mL] celery, minced

3 tablespoons [45 mL] green mango, diced

1 teaspoon [5 mL] salt

3 makroot leaves, central rib removed, minced fine

1 tablespoon [15 mL] red curry paste

1 teaspoon [5 mL] sugar

Vegetable oil, for frying

Shredded lettuce and sliced cucumber and carrot, for garnish

3 pieces fried pork rind, diced

ADVANCE PREPARATION

1. Combine all of the sauce ingredients, except the pork rind, in the workbowl of a food processor and process into a smooth sauce. Reserve at room temperature. (The sauce can be made 1 day in advance and refrigerated.)

PREPARATION OF THE CRAB CAKES

2. Combine the crabmeat, eggs, half of the breadcrumbs, the celery, mango, salt, makroot leaves, curry paste, and sugar. Mix well, being careful not to break up the crabmeat.

3. Shape into 8 cakes and reserve. (The crab cakes can be pre-pared several hours in advance, covered with plastic film, and refrigerated.)

COOKING METHOD

4. Heat the oil in a skillet. Coat the cakes with the remaining ½ cup [120 mL] of breadcrumbs and sauté. Cook until golden brown on both sides. Drain on paper towels.

SERVICE

5. Serve 1 crab cake per person, on top of a bed of shredded lettuce and garnished with cucumber and carrot. Serve the sauce on the side, topped with the pork rind.

Thailand

Beef Meatballs in Hot Peanut Sauce
Panaeng Neua

Grilled Skewered Pork with Roasted Chile Sauce
Jin Ping Nam Prik Pao

Stuffed Boneless Chicken Wings in Red Curry Sauce
Peek Gai Yad Sai Pha-naeng

Minced Roast Duck Salad with Spicy Herb Dressing
Laab Ped Yang

**Crispy Rice Noodles with Mixed Meats in Spicy
Sweet-and-Sour Sauce**
Mee Krob

Fish Cakes with Cucumber-Peanut Chile Relish
Tod Mun Pla

Scallops in Roasted Chile Sauce with Holy Basil
Pla Hoi Prik

THAILAND OCCUPIES A central position on the Indochina peninsula, with its south-ern region occupying the Malay Peninsula. It holds a unique position in Southeast Asia as the only country never to be a dependent of other countries. It has been influenced by its neighbors, but through its independence, Thailand has developed a unique cuisine. Its na-tional identity spans 800 years, dating back to the thirteenth century. Unlike other coun-tries in the region, Thai women play an important role in business, economics, and the arts (including the culinary arts). A full 75 percent of the population is Thai, with Chinese, Malay, and refugee Laotians and Cambodians making up the difference.

Thailand can be separated into three distinct regions. The central region is known as Issan. To the south and west is Pak Thai, and the northern region is called Lana Thai. To-gether they make up one of the most unique of the world's cuisines. The north is known for its assertive use of chiles, wild game such as deer, and the absence of the otherwise per-vasive coconut milk and other coconut products. In southern Thailand Arab and Malay in-gredients are common, and there is a stronger Indian influence than elsewhere. Central Thailand includes Bangkok, the city most identified with Thai cuisine.

Thai cuisine is based on five flavors: bitter, salt, sweet, sour, and hot (spicy). The art of Thai cuisine is in the balance of these elements. Thai dishes and flavors are based on such ingredients as lemongrass, fish sauce, cilantro, galangal (similar to ginger but with a more medicinal flavor), fiery hot chiles, sweet basil, and coconut milk. Thai cooking is about flavor and method, not ritual. It is the ingredients that most define Thai cuisine. The Thai cook is open to experimentation and outside influence. The same dish prepared in differ-ent homes or restaurants may have different flavor elements, the result of an enthusiastic cook's willingness to add a new spice or to try a new method. Above all, cooking is a gift to others, an act of love.

Of all the ingredients used and grown in Thailand, one of the most important is the coconut. Every part of the plant is used. Coconut shells are made into utensils or are burned as fuel for the cooking fire. The flesh of the coconut is made into coconut milk, one of the dominant ingredients in Thai cuisine. In addition to contributing flavor, it balances the fire produced by hot chiles. Coconut oil is made by pressing the dried flesh of mature coconuts. The remainder of the coconut palm is used for making rope, mats, roofing materials, and for other construction purposes.

Central to the diet and economy of Thailand is rice. It is at the foundation of Thai culture. It was the Mon (the original inhabitants of the country) who learned to cultivate rice and passed this gift on to the world. Thailand is still one of the major exporters of rice, which is at the center of a self-sustaining economy. It has shaped the culture, social struc-ture, and religion. In many rural regions rice cultivation is a way of life, passed down for many generations. Thailand is known for producing a fragrant variety known as jasmine or aromatic rice.

Thai cooking methods are simple and straightforward. Dry roasting (*pow*), steaming (*neung*), stir-frying (*padd*), and stewing or braising (*keang*) are the practical methods of cooking when cooking fuel is limited. Of the techniques used to prepare ingredients, none is more important than pounding herbs, spices, and chiles together with a mortar and pestle. The process of pounding (*tumm*) releases essential oils in a way that cannot be duplicated by the modern food processor. A strict order to the addition of ingredients is followed. First garlic is pounded with salt into a paste. Chiles are added next, followed by roasted spice powder, lemongrass, makroot leaf, and then juicy aromatics such as shallots. Finally all is bound together with shrimp or bean paste. Spices are often dry roasted to release essential oils and are then ground to a fine powder, a second important technique. The combination of these techniques produces one of the most important preparations in Thai cooking, *nam prik*, a quite pungent sauce made from pounded shrimp, chiles, fish sauce, and a variety of regional spices and herbs.

Outside influences on Thai cooking begin with the Chinese. Many of Thai cooking methods are Chinese in origin. Noodles, a favorite snack food, are of Chinese origin. Interestingly, noodles are the only food that Thais eat with chopsticks; they prefer the fork and spoon for most dishes. Spice traders from India and the Middle East brought new spices such as coriander, cardamom, and cumin, the Indian stews known as curries, and the Middle Eastern love for grilled strips of marinated meat, which became a Thai snack favorite, satay. The Portuguese may have had the most lasting influence with their introduction of the chile. One cannot imagine Thai food without the taste of the fiery chile.

Beef Meatballs in Hot Peanut Sauce Panaeng Neua

This popular dish, often sold by street vendors, is also served with drinks or as a side dish in a Thai dinner. The rich curry-peanut sauce complements the mild taste of the beef meatballs. Although nontraditional, Belgian endive leaves or shrimp crackers make an attractive and practical scoop with which to eat the meatballs and sauce.

CHEF NOTES

The meatballs may be made with beef, pork, veal, or in any combination. The meatballs may be steamed in advance and sautéed briefly for service. Red curry paste may be purchased at Asian markets, or prepared in the following manner:

Red Curry Paste

1 cup [240 mL] dried red Thai chiles, stems and seeds removed, soaked ½ hour in warm water

1½ tablespoons [25 mL] coriander seeds, dry toasted

1 teaspoon [5 mL] cumin seeds, dry toasted

¼ teaspoon [1 mL] black peppercorns, dry toasted

2 stalks lemongrass, finely minced, ground into a paste in a spice grinder

MEATBALLS: MAKES ABOUT 32 MEATBALLS

1¼ pounds [560 g] lean ground beef

1 tablespoon [15 mL] minced garlic

1 teaspoon [5 mL] black pepper

1 teaspoon [5 mL] salt

¼ cup [60 mL] rice flour

SAUCE

3 tablespoons [45 mL] peanut oil

4 garlic cloves, coarsely chopped

2 tablespoons [30 mL] red curry paste (*krung gaeng deng*) (see Chef Notes)

2 cups [480 mL] thick coconut cream from top of unshaken cans of coconut milk

2 tablespoons [30 mL] chunky peanut butter

2 tablespoons [30 mL] Thai fish sauce (*nam pla*)

1½ tablespoons [25 mL] palm or light brown sugar

Belgian endive leaves or prepared shrimp crackers, for scooping

1 tablespoon [15 mL] mint leaves, for garnish

2 tablespoons [30 mL] dry roasted peanuts, finely chopped, for garnish

ADVANCE PREPARATION

1. Combine the ground beef, garlic, pepper, and salt and mix well. Shape into thirty-two 1-inch [2.5-cm] balls and roll them in the rice flour, dusting off any excess. (The meatballs can be made several hours in advance and stored, refrigerated, covered with plastic film.)

COOKING METHOD

2. Heat a skillet to medium-high and add 2 tablespoons [30 mL] of the oil. Sauté the garlic for 1 minute, then add the meatballs. Cook the meatballs, turning them occasionally, until browned on all sides. Remove the meatballs and drain on paper towels. Reserve and keep warm. (The meatballs can be cooked 1 day in advance and stored, refrigerated.)

1 tablespoon [15 mL] cilantro stems, chopped

¼ cup [60 mL] galangal, diced

1 teaspoon [5 mL] minced wild lime zest, or 1 teaspoon lime zest combined with 2 makroot leaves, very finely minced

¼ cup [60 mL] peeled garlic cloves, diced fine

¼ cup [60 mL] shallots, diced fine

1 teaspoon [5 mL] salt

½ tablespoon [8 mL] shrimp paste

1. Place the toasted coriander, cumin, and black pepper in an electric spice grinder and grind very fine.

2. Drain the chiles and reserve the soaking water. Place the cilantro, galangal, garlic, and shallots in the bowl of a processor and blend into a paste.

3. Add the reserved ground spices, lemongrass, lime zest, salt, and shrimp paste and blend again.

4. Add the drained chiles and process, adding some of the reserved chile soaking water to process to a smooth paste. Store in a sealed glass jar, refrigerated, for up to 2 months.

PREPARATION OF THE SAUCE

3. Pour the remaining 1 tablespoon [15 mL] of oil and the red curry paste in a nonstick skillet over medium-high heat.

4. Stir-fry for 2 minutes, then add the coconut cream and the peanut butter. Stir to incorporate. Simmer, while stirring, until a smooth consistency is obtained.

5. Add the fish sauce and sugar, then the reserved meatballs. Simmer over low heat, while stirring, for 5 minutes.

SERVICE

6. Serve 4 meatballs per person, on plates or in small bowls. Top with any remaining sauce.

7. Place endive leaves or prepared shrimp crackers on the side. Garnish with mint leaves and chopped peanuts. Serve immediately.

Grilled Skewered Pork with Roasted Chile Sauce Jin Ping Nam Prik Pao

This is the northern version of pork satay, a favorite snack of central Thailand (Issan). It shows a Chinese influence with the use of soy in the marinade. Authentic Issan marinades would employ simply cilantro root, chiles, and garlic, but soy adds a depth of flavor. The accompanying sauce has countless regional variations and bottled sauce can be purchased in Asian groceries, but this homemade version is much better. Many versions of this sauce call for frying the chiles and aromatics instead of roasting them, but slow roasting over a charcoal fire will enhance the flavor considerably.

ROASTED CHILE SAUCE (*NAM PRIK PAO*)

½ cup [120 mL] dried Thai chiles, fire roasted

½ cup [120 mL] shallots, unpeeled, fire roasted

½ cup [120 mL] garlic cloves, unpeeled, fire roasted

1 tablespoon [15 mL] dried shrimp, rinsed and soaked in water to soften

3 tablespoons [45 mL] tamarind liquid

2 tablespoons [30 mL] palm sugar or light brown sugar

¼ cup [60 mL] peanut oil

1½ tablespoons [25 mL] Thai fish sauce (*nam pla*)

PORK

3 tablespoons [45 mL] garlic, minced

¼ cup [60 mL] cilantro stems, minced

1 tablespoon [15 mL] coarsely ground black pepper

1 teaspoon [5 mL] dark soy sauce

1 tablespoon [15 mL] soy sauce

1½ pounds [675 g] pork loin or tenderloin, cut into 2-inch [5-cm] strips, thinly sliced

16 metal skewers or wooden skewers soaked in water 30 minutes

16 balls of sticky rice, 1½ inches [4 cm] in diameter, for garnish (see Chef Notes)

ADVANCE PREPARATION

1. Cut off and discard the stems and most of the seeds of the chiles and place the chiles in the workbowl of a food processor.

2. Peel the roasted shallots and garlic and add them to the chiles. Add the shrimp, tamarind, and sugar and blend to a smooth paste. Add a small amount of water or stock, if necessary, to ensure thorough processing.

3. Add the oil to a skillet over medium heat and sauté the chile paste, stirring constantly, for 5 minutes, or until the paste becomes fragrant and the color deepens.

CHEF NOTES

Chicken, beef, or shrimp may be substituted for the pork skewers. Two variations for the sauce include substituting grilled shrimp or chicken for the dried shrimp in the sauce recipe or shrimp paste that has been wrapped in banana leaf and grilled.

To prepare sticky rice use the following method. Traditionally individual portions are steamed in banana-leaf packages or hollowed-out bamboo segments.

Cover the rice with water and rub the kernels between your palms. Drain the milky water and repeat until the water is clear. Soak the rice in hot water for 3 hours. Drain and place in a parchment or cheese-cloth lined steamer and steam for 30 minutes.

4. Remove from heat and stir in the fish sauce. Adjust the flavorings. Allow to cool, then place in a sealed glass jar. (This sauce will hold for 3 to 4 months, refrigerated in sterilized jars.)

PREPARATION OF THE PORK

5. For the pork combine the garlic, cilantro, pepper, and both soy sauces and mix well. Place the strips of pork in a resealable plastic bag. Add the marinade, toss thoroughly, and marinate at least 2 hours, or overnight, refrigerated.

COOKING METHOD

6. Drain the marinade and reserve for basting. Prepare 16 skewers using 1½ ounces [45 g] of pork per skewer.

7. Grill over a charcoal fire, basting occasionally, until lightly seared and cooked medium Do not overcook. The skewers may also be cooked under a broiler.

SERVICE

8. Serve 2 skewers per person, accompanied by a small dish of dipping sauce and garnish with 2 balls of sticky rice. Serve immediately.

Stuffed Boneless Chicken Wings in Red Curry Sauce Peek Gai Yad Sai Pha-naeng

These boneless chicken wings, served in a shallow pool of red curry sauce, are a Bangkok favorite. The task of boning the wings can be frustrating at first, but the effort is well worth it. If you prefer not to serve the wings with the red curry sauce, a traditional accompaniment is bottled *sriracha* sauce or a spicy sweet-and-sour sauce topped with chopped peanuts. For restaurant production, steaming the wings prior to deep-frying simplifies and speeds up final cooking.

FILLING

1 tablespoon [15 mL] cilantro stems, chopped fine

4 garlic cloves, minced

1 tablespoon [15 mL] Thai fish sauce (*nam pla*)

1 tablespoon [15 mL] black pepper

½ teaspoon [3 mL] salt

1 teaspoon [5 mL] dried shrimp, ground (or prepared shrimp powder)

2 tablespoons [30 mL] scallion tops, sliced thin

2 tablespoons [30 mL] carrot, grated

¾ cup [180 mL] bean thread noodles, cut into 1-inch [2.5-cm] lengths and soaked in water

12 ounces [340 g] minced pork

4 ounces [110 g] shrimp, shelled, deveined, and finely diced

8 boned chicken wings (see Chef Notes)

SAUCE

3 cups [720 mL] coconut milk, unshaken (allowing the thicker cream to rise to the top)

3 tablespoons [45 mL] red curry paste (see page 297)

1 to 2 tablespoons [15 to 30 mL] Thai fish sauce (*nam pla*), or to taste

½ teaspoon [3 mL] tamarind liquid

1½ tablespoons [25 mL] palm or light brown sugar (optional)

1 tablespoon [15 mL] makroot leaf minced very fine (half reserved for garnish)

2 cups [480 mL] rice flour

1 cup [240 mL] milk

1 egg, beaten

1 cup [240 mL] panko breadcrumbs (Japanese-style breadcrumbs)

Vegetable oil, for deep-frying

⅓ cup [80 mL] basil leaves, for garnish

1 tablespoon [15 mL] dried red chile, sliced lengthwise very fine, for garnish

It is easier to use chicken wings that you have cut from the carcass yourself, as you can leave extra skin for the end flaps. To bone the chicken wings, first bend the two joints backward to loosen the cartilage and tendons. Using the tip of a sharp, flexible, thin-bladed knife, carefully cut a ring around the top of the shoulder bone. Scrape and cut the meat from the bone while working your way down to the first joint, turning the skin and attached meat inside-out, sliding it down toward the wing tip as you progress. When the first joint is completely exposed, break off the first bone, and slide a fingertip between the skin and the meat of the next section, being careful not to pierce the skin. Continue working your way down toward the wing tip using the knife to scrape the meat away from the bone, turning the skin and attached meat inside-out. When the next pair of bones is exposed, cut out the smaller bone first, then remove the larger bone. Roll the skin and attached meat skin side out (back into its original shape prior to boning). The wing tip, with its bone, should still be attached.

ADVANCE PREPARATION

1. For the filling combine the cilantro, garlic, fish sauce, pepper, salt, and ground dried shrimp in a small processor and process into a smooth paste.

2. Remove the paste to a bowl, stir in the scallions, carrot, noodles, pork, and diced shrimp, and combine well. (The filling can be made 1 day in advance.)

3. Stuff this mixture into the boned chicken wings, being careful not to overstuff them, as the filling will expand while cooking. A pastry bag fitted with a large plain tip is helpful. Close the skin around the open end and seal with a toothpick. (The stuffed chicken wings can be prepared 1 day in advance, wrapped individually in plastic film, and stored, refrigerated.)

4. Steam the stuffed wings for 15 to 20 minutes, or until the filling is cooked and set. Remove the toothpicks. The chicken wings may be used immediately or stored, refrigerated, overnight.

PREPARATION OF THE SAUCE

5. Heat a skillet over medium-high heat and add 1 cup [240 mL] of the thick coconut cream. Simmer until some of the oil separates. Add the red curry paste and stir well to combine. When fragrant, add the fish sauce, tamarind, sugar, and half the makroot leaf, then add the remaining coconut milk while stirring. Cook until the sauce has reduced by half, and reserve warm.

COOKING METHOD

6. Place 1 cup [240 mL] of the rice flour in a bowl or bag for dredging.

7. Combine the milk and egg together for an egg wash.

8. Combine the remaining rice flour with the panko breadcrumbs.

9. Dust the wings lightly in the rice flour by shaking briefly in the bag. Dip the wings in the egg wash, allowing the excess to drain off. Coat the wings in the panko breadcrumb mixture.

10. Deep-fry the wings at 365°F [185°C], in small batches, for about 5 minutes, or until they rise to the surface and are golden brown.

11. Add the fried wings to the warm red curry sauce and stir to coat the wings completely.

SERVICE

12. Ladle 3 tablespoons [45 mL] of sauce onto a plate and top with a stuffed chicken wing. The stuffed wing may also be sliced into medallions for presentation, with the wing tip standing. Garnish with the reserved makroot leaf, basil leaves, and red chile strips.

Minced Roast Duck Salad with Spicy Herb Dressing Laab Ped Yang

Known as *laab* in Thailand, *larb* in Cambodia, and *lap* in Laos, this dish originated in a region that is now part of northeastern Thailand and Laos. The flavors should be intense to be authentic. This version, from central Thailand, utilizes succulent roast duck for the meat of the salad, and is tossed with the fiery, tart dressing.

DRESSING: MAKES ½ CUP [120 mL]

¼ teaspoon [1 mL] salt

2 tablespoons [30 mL] Thai fish sauce (*nam pla*)

2 tablespoons [30 mL] sugar

¼ cup [60 mL] lime juice

4 garlic cloves, minced

4 Thai chiles or 6 serrano chiles, minced

SALAD

1 pound [450 g] roasted duck meat, minced (see Chef Notes)

1 tablespoon [15 mL] galangal, minced

Juice of 2 limes

1½ tablespoons [25 mL] roasted rice powder

1 to 2 tablespoons [15 to 30 mL] ground bird pepper, to taste

3 shallots, minced

2 scallions, sliced

½ cup [120 mL] watercress leaves, chiffonade

¼ cup [60 mL] cilantro leaves, minced

¼ cup [60 mL] mint leaves, roughly torn

2 large makroot leaves, central rib removed, finely shredded

GARNISH

8 leaves Napa cabbage, chiffonade

16 cherry tomatoes, halved

8 long beans, cut into 2-inch [5-cm] lengths, or 40 thin green beans, trimmed and lightly blanched

Cilantro and mint leaves

ADVANCE PREPARATION

1. Combine all the dressing ingredients in a nonreactive bowl and stir well to dissolve the sugar. Reserve. (The dressing can be made 1 day in advance.)

PREPARATION OF THE SALAD

2. Combine the duck with the galangal and half of the lime juice in a large bowl and toss gently.

Laab is made with a variety of minced meats (raw and cooked), including pork, water buffalo, beef, and fish. It is also commonly made with minced poached chicken or turkey, a popular heart-healthy alternative. You may purchase roasted ducks from a Chinese market or roast your own. To roast your own duckling for this dish, rub it liberally with a mixture of dry-roasted and ground coriander and white peppercorns, minced garlic, and cilantro stems. Allow the duck to marinate overnight, then steam for 45 minutes. Allow the duck skin to cool to room temperature, then place in a 375°F [190°C] oven for 45 minutes. Broil at 500°F [260°C] for 10 to 15 minutes, or until the skin is browned and crispy.

The method of mincing meats for this dish utilizes a syncopated chopping technique with 2 sharp cleavers. The goal is to obtain minced meat that is not uniform in texture. Processing in a food processor does not produce the irregular texture that is important for this dish.

For an authentic version, the skin of the duck is chopped with the meat. We recommend that the duck skin be crisped in a very hot oven, then chopped and folded into the duck meat just before service.

3. Pour the dressing over the duck and taste for tartness (it should be quite tart). Allow this mixture to stand 10 minutes before assembling the salad.

ASSEMBLY METHOD

4. Immediately before service, add the roasted rice powder and the ground bird pepper and toss gently to incorporate.

5. Add the shallots, scallions, watercress, cilantro, mint, and the shredded makroot leaves. Toss well. Taste the salad for a balance of spice, sour, and salt and adjust if necessary (it should be very spicy).

SERVICE

6. Place 2 ounces [55 g] of the duck mixture on a bed of shredded cabbage. Arrange the cherry tomatoes and beans on the side and garnish with cilantro and mint leaves.

Crispy Rice Noodles with Mixed Meats in Spicy Sweet-and-Sour Sauce Mee Krob

Fried noodles are Chinese in origin. Thai cooks have transformed this dish by using a combination of seafood, meat, and poultry in a spicy sweet-and-sour sauce. The sauce should taste sweet, sour, and then salty, in that order. Care should be taken when frying the noodles to ensure that they puff up properly. They should be mixed with the sauce very gently to prevent the noodles from breaking up. Since the noodles begin to lose their crispness as soon as they are combined with the sauce, restaurants usually precook the noodles and hold them in a very low oven, then toss the noodles with the prepared sauce just before service. This dish provides balance to spicy curries, and the two are often served together during Thai meals.

NOODLES, TOFU, AND EGG THREADS

8 ounces [225 g] thin rice vermicelli noodles (*sen mee*)

3 cups [720 mL] vegetable oil

8 ounces [225 g] firm tofu, pressed to remove excess water and sliced into thin strips

Rice flour, for dusting

3 eggs, beaten with ½ teaspoon [3 mL] salt

SAUCE

2 tablespoons [30 mL] soy sauce

1½ tablespoons [25 mL] tamarind liquid

Juice of 1 lime

2 tablespoons [30 mL] rice wine vinegar or cider vinegar

½ cup [120 mL] palm or light brown sugar, or to taste

3 tablespoons [45 mL] Thai fish sauce (*nam pla*)

ACCOMPANIMENTS

5 garlic cloves, diced

4 shallots, diced

8 ounces [225 g] pork loin, cut into 1-inch [2.5-cm] slices

8 ounces [225 g] chicken breast, cut into 1-inch [2.5-cm] slices

6 dried shiitake mushrooms, soaked to soften and thinly sliced

4 fresh Thai chiles, thinly sliced

⅓ cup [80 mL] fresh shrimp, shelled, deveined, and diced

¾ cup [180 mL] mung bean sprouts

GARNISH

4 scallions, sliced

½ cup [120 mL] cilantro leaves

¼ cup [60 mL] sliced pickled garlic or cocktail onions

4 hot red chiles, seeded and thinly sliced lengthwise

ADVANCE PREPARATION

1. Separate the noodles in a large paper bag (this will keep the brittle noodles from scattering all across the kitchen).

2. Preheat the oven to 200°F [95°C].

3. Heat the oil to 365°F [185°C], reserving 5 tablespoons [75 mL] of the oil for later use.

4. Line 2 half-sheet pans with paper towels.

5. Slip the noodles into the hot oil in small batches. They will immediately puff up and expand. Cook for 2 seconds on 1 side, flip them over, and cook for 2 seconds more.

6. Remove the noodles from the oil, allowing the excess oil to drain off, then place on the paper towels. Repeat until all noodles are cooked, then place in the warm oven to hold until needed. (The noodles can be made several hours in advance.)

PREPARATION OF THE TOFU

7. Dust the strips of tofu lightly in rice flour and deep-fry in some of the reserved oil, stirring to separate the tofu strips, until crisp and golden brown. Drain on paper towels and hold in the warm oven. (The tofu strips can be made several hours in advance.)

PREPARATION OF THE EGG THREADS

8. Place the beaten egg mixture in a plastic squeeze bottle. Heat 1 tablespoon [15 mL] of the reserved oil in a nonstick skillet and drizzle the eggs to form an overlapping lacy pattern.

9. Cook 2 minutes, or until set, then flip the "omelet" and cook 2 minutes. Drain on paper towels. When cool, coarsely chop the omelet and reserve. (The egg threads can be made several hours in advance.)

PREPARATION OF THE SAUCE

10. Heat all of the sauce ingredients in a small skillet and swirl to dissolve the sugar. Heat to a low boil and cook the sauce until it caramelizes and reduces slightly in volume. Reserve and keep warm. (The sauce can be made several hours in advance.)

COOKING METHOD

11. Heat a wok or skillet to medium-high heat and swirl in the remaining ¼ cup [60 mL] of reserved oil. Add the garlic and stir-fry until lightly golden. Add the shallots and sauté 30 seconds. Add the sliced pork and chicken and sauté 3 minutes. Add the mushrooms, chiles, and shrimp. Stir-fry until the shrimp just begin to turn opaque.

12. Add about ¼ cup [60 mL] of the reserved sauce and toss well with the meat mixture to coat. Turn off the heat and add the sprouts, tossing just to soften slightly and coat with sauce. Reserve.

ASSEMBLY AND SERVICE

13. Put enough noodles for the number of servings to be prepared at one time in a large bowl. Up to 4 servings (half a recipe) can be safely tossed without breaking up the noodles).

14. Add a proportionate amount of sauce, tofu, egg, and meat mixture. Using 2 forks or oiled hands, toss gently to combine, being careful to not break the noodles. Serve immediately, garnished with scallions, cilantro, pickled garlic, and slivered red chiles.

Fish Cakes with Cucumber-Peanut Chile Relish Tod Mun Pla

Tod mun is commonly served along Thailand's Gulf coast and in larger cities with reliable transportation that can import fresh fish. *Tod* means fried, but broiling produces fish cakes with a lighter taste. The dipping sauce is a sweet, sour, and spicy cucumber- and peanut-based mixture that blends perfectly with the fish cakes. Thai cooks in the United States prefer king mackerel for these cakes, but the less oily taste of mahi seems best. Any firm-fleshed ocean fish will do.

CHEF NOTES

Shrimp may be substituted for, or used in combination with, the fish for these cakes. If using shrimp, leave the shrimp in pieces large enough to give texture to the finished cakes.

FISH CAKES

1½ pounds [675 g] mahi fillet, dark vein removed, diced

2 shallots, finely minced

1½ tablespoons [25 mL] red curry paste (see page 297)

1 large egg, beaten

½ cup [120 mL] yard-long beans or thin green beans, cut into ⅛-inch [3-mm] diagonal slices

⅓ cup [80 mL] (loosely packed) makroot leaves, central rib removed, shredded very thin

1 teaspoon [5 mL] salt

2 teaspoons [10 mL] granulated sugar

DIPPING SAUCE

1 cup [240 mL] white vinegar

½ cup [120 mL] granulated sugar, or to taste

¼ cup [60 mL] (loosely packed) brown sugar

1 teaspoon [5 mL] salt

2 large shallots, minced fine

1 large cucumber, peeled, seeded, and diced

6 Thai green chiles, minced, or more to taste

½ cup [120 mL] unsalted roasted peanuts, coarsely chopped

4 to 6 sprigs of cilantro, chopped

Cilantro leaves, for garnish

ADVANCE PREPARATION

1. Pulse the fish in a processor until it just begins to form a ball. Combine the puréed fish with all the other fish cake ingredients in a bowl and mix well.

2. Form the mixture into 16 patties, ½ inch [1 cm] thick, and place them on a parchment-lined baking sheet. Cover with plastic film and reserve, refrigerated. (The fish cakes can be made several hours in advance.)

PREPARATION OF THE SAUCE

3. Heat the vinegar, granulated sugar, brown sugar, and salt together until the sugar has completely dissolved. Cool this mixture to room temperature. (The mixture can be made 1 day in advance.) Just before service, add the remaining sauce ingredients and stir well.

COOKING METHOD

4. Broil the fish cakes under a broiler or salamander for 3 to 4 minutes, or until golden brown. It is not necessary to turn the cakes during cooking.

SERVICE

5. Arrange the sauce in ramekins on small platters. Serve each person 2 patties, garnished with cilantro leaves. The fish cakes may be served hot or at room temperature.

Scallops in Roasted Chile Sauce with Holy Basil Pla Hoi Prik

This dish, enjoyed throughout the Gulf region of Thailand, is simple and takes very little time to prepare. It utilizes the roasted chile sauce recipe (*nam prik pao*) from Grilled Skewered Pork with Roasted Chile Sauce, may be purchased to save time (but will be inferior to freshly made). Holy basil (*Ocimum sanctum*) called *bai graprow* in Thailand, adds a sweet basil and herbal essence, which complements the taste of the scallops nicely.

CHEF NOTES

Asian basil or sweet basil may be substituted for holy basil. Squid, shrimp, langoustines, or lobster may be substituted for the scallops.

⅓ cup [80 mL] peanut or vegetable oil

¼ cup [60 mL] garlic cloves, peeled and thinly sliced

1¼ pounds [560 g] bay scallops

2 tablespoons [30 mL] roasted chile sauce (see page 299)

2 tablespoons [30 mL] cilantro leaves, sliced fine

2 tablespoons [30 mL] scallions, tops only, sliced fine

1 tablespoon [15 mL] Thai fish sauce (*nam pla*)

3 tablespoons [45 mL] holy basil leaves

8 small timbales of cooked jasmine rice

Holy basil florets or stem tips, for garnish

ADVANCE PREPARATION

1. All advance preparation may be found in the ingredient list.

COOKING METHOD

2. Add the oil to a very hot wok and swirl to coat. Add the garlic and sauté until light golden. Immediately add the scallops and stir-fry 1 minute.

3. Add the chile sauce and sauté quickly until fragrant.

4. Reduce the heat and add the cilantro, scallions, and fish sauce. Cook for 1 minute, then remove from the heat. Just before service, add the holy basil leaves and stir to incorporate.

SERVICE

5. Serve about 4 ounces [110 g] of the scallop mixture with the timbales of rice. Garnish with holy basil florets.

Indian Subcontinent

India, Pakistan,
Bangladesh, Burma,
Sri Lanka, Tibet,
Bhutan, and Nepal

Lamb Meatballs with Cashews
Keema Kofta

Moghul Chicken with Almonds
Shah Jahani Murghi

Fish Fillets Stuffed with Caramelized Onions
Masala Meen Bajji

Sole Fillets in Fragrant Mustard Sauce
Sorso Bhatte Maach

Curried Shrimp with Tomato and Tamarind
Jhinga Varathiathu

Spinach and Cheese Dumplings with Chile Sauce
Tse tang Churo Momo, Sonam Penzom Sibeh

Puffed Flat Bread Stuffed with Potatoes, Chickpeas, and Tamarind Broth
Gol Gappa ya Paani Poori

THE INDIAN SUBCONTINENT, including India, Pakistan, Bangladesh, Burma, Sri Lanka, Tibet, Bhutan, and Nepal, offers some of the most diverse geography in the world. With the Himalayan mountain range in the north, the Gangetic plains, the Rajasthan deserts, the forests, the rivers of Punjab, and the lush tropics of Kerala, India, this region possesses most of the world's geographical features. This startling diversity is reflected in the varied cuisine known as Indian food. Adding to these physical influences on India's cooking are the dominant religions that markedly affect what the people can and will eat. One important religious influence results in a largely vegetarian diet, since more than 80 percent of the population of this region is Hindu.

In spite of this diversity, it is possible to find recurring themes among India's varied cuisines. The use of spices and the specialized techniques of incorporating them into dishes tie together the region's cooking styles and methods. Cumin, cloves, coriander, turmeric, ginger, cinnamon, cardamom, chiles, mustard seeds, fennel seeds, poppy seeds, peppercorns, and ginger form the palette that Indian cooks rely upon to add character and variety to vegetables and meats alike. Most remarkable is how the method of a spice preparation can give entirely different aspects to the same vegetable dish. A spice may be used whole, ground, dry roasted and then ground, or fried in oil or *ghee* (clarified butter) to impart different tastes and aspects. Spices are used to impart aroma as well as flavor. Regardless of the region, spice mixes, known as *masalas*, form the foundation of a dish; only the types of spices vary according to region. One of the most famous and ubiquitous spice combinations is *garam masala*, usually made from cinnamon, cardamom, cumin seed, peppercorns, cloves, and coriander seed. Some of the most popular types of dishes are known as curries, which take advantage of the endless combinations of spices. Curry powder is a British invention, concocted to bring the essence of Indian cooking to the United Kingdom.

A vast majority of Indians are Hindu, which imparts a distinct vegetarian cast to its cuisine. Indians have learned to combine lentils and legumes (*pulses*) with grain (rice, wheat, or corn, depending upon the region) and dairy to their diet. Hindus believe the cow is a sacred animal and so do not eat beef (although they do use milk, which does not involve killing the animal). Others do not eat any animal products. Stricter vegetarians avoid cheese as it is produced by the action of rennet, a meat by-product. Some Hindus, especially Jains, avoid eating even root vegetables, because of the possibility of killing insects when the vegetables are uprooted. Yogurt, introduced by the Moghuls of Persia, is a common ingredient that adds milk proteins to the diet. It is either whipped or hung to remove some of the moisture and to form a thick, cheese-like product. In regions where there is a bounty of fish, as in Bengal and the Malabar Coast, a certain relaxation of dietary rules allows for the consumption of fish. In the sweltering climates to the south, including Sri Lanka, it is much easier to abstain from meat, and here the more dedicated vegetarians are found.

In the northern provinces, the Muslim influence is considerable, and Muslims have contributed much to India's cuisine. Heartier meals, including such meats as lamb and goat, are served. Rice dishes, known by Westerners as pilafs (*pilaus* in India), are popular as well. Food quality is high in the north and fewer chiles and spices are used. *Ghee* is the preferred cooking oil and wheat is the grain of choice. Flat breads, in the form of griddle-baked *chapatis* and *rotis,* and fried breads, known as *parathas,* are served plain or as an accompaniment to a meal or are stuffed with meats and vegetables. These culinary elements are found in the northern countries of Nepal and Bhutan as well. Homemade cheese (*panir*) is popular as a rough curd it is called *chenna*, when compressed and cut into cubes it is called *panir*. (Lamb is often cooked as kebabs in the north.) Another Muslim influence is a cooking style known as *tandoori*, roasting at very high temperatures in a clay oven called a *tandoor*. Very popular with Westerners, *tandoori* food is found only in the northern parts of India (in spite of the fact that it is found in almost all Indian restaurants in the United States).

To the east is Bengal, and Bengali food usually features fish, often wrapped in pumpkin or squash leaves. Flowers and unusual fruits are featured in Bengali dishes. In southern India and Sri Lanka coconut is found, in some form, in almost every dish. Coconut oil is the preferred cooking oil, and curries include coconut milk and the cream that rises to its surface. Fresh coconut is added to the mostly vegetarian dishes, and the coconut water (*neera*) forms the basis of refreshing drinks. Rice is the staple in this area.

For centuries, Kerala, on the southwestern coast, has been influenced by foreign traders, travelers, and immigrants. Jewish settlers arrived almost two thousand years ago, bringing along their dietary laws and a love of meat and fish. Syrian Christians also settled Kerala at the same time and established a cuisine based on beef. Wild duck is popular in this region as well.

In addition to the British, the Portuguese established a colony on the subcontinent, in Goa, and remained there until the 1960s. Goan food is unique in its use of vinegar and features copious amounts of fiery chiles. *Vindaloo* is the famous vinegar curry dish of Goa. Goans enjoy a sour component to their dishes, using a fruit (*kokum*) rarely used in other regions to provide the sour flavor (in most regions tamarind, lime, or mango powder is used for this purpose).

The Moghuls, originally from Persia, have left an indelible mark on Indian cuisine. Their cuisine is lush, often enriched with ground nuts, cream, and butter sauces. The Parsees, practitioners of Zoroastrianism, who fled Persia for religious freedom and settled in Gujarat, brought with them a taste for meat and egg dishes.

Condiments play an important supporting role in meals throughout the subcontinent, adding contrast to dishes. Pickles, relishes, and chutneys are popular accompaniments. Some are quite simple and fresh, chopped tomatoes and onions for example. Others are more elaborate, such as pickles and chutneys, which can take several weeks or months to mature. *Pulses* are another dish served at most Indian meals. Lentils, split peas, and other dried beans (together refered to as *dahls*) provide needed protein in a diet mostly based on vegetables. This type of protein is lacking in certain essential amino acids and must be supplemented with grains and dairy.

Lamb Meatballs with Cashews Keema Kofta

These assertively spiced meatballs are from the Uttar Pradesh region of India. The sauce is rich in cashews and almonds and fragrant with spice; it is not particularly piquant. These meatballs are excellent party or cocktail fare and match well with *chapati,* griddle-baked bread. This recipe uses *ghee,* or clarified butter (see Chef Notes).

LAMB MEATBALLS: MAKES THIRTY-TWO 1-INCH [2.5-CM] MEATBALLS

1½ pounds [675 g] lean lamb, ground

4 hot green chiles, minced

½-inch [1-cm] piece ginger, minced

¼ teaspoon [1 mL] ground cloves

¼ teaspoon [1 mL] ground mace

Pinch of *garam masala* (see Chef Notes)

½ teaspoon [3 mL] salt

1 tablespoon [15 mL] *ghee* or clarified butter

SAUCE

3 tablespoons [45 mL] raw cashews, soaked in hot water for 10 minutes and drained

3 tablespoons [45 mL] blanched almonds, soaked in hot water for 10 minutes and drained

1 to 2 tablespoons [15 to 30 mL] yogurt, if necessary

1½ tablespoons [25 mL] *ghee* or clarified butter

3 onions, minced

1 teaspoon [5 mL] minced garlic

1 teaspoon [5 mL] minced ginger

¼ teaspoon [1 mL] ground turmeric

½ teaspoon [3 mL] cayenne

3 tomatoes, finely diced

¼ cup [60 mL] yogurt, beaten until smooth and creamy

½ cup [120 mL] water

1 tablespoon [15 mL] mint leaves, chiffonade

2 teaspoons [10 mL] salt

Pinch of *garam masala*

8 *chapati* breads

Sprigs of mint and cilantro, for garnish

ADVANCE PREPARATION

1. Combine the ground lamb with the chiles, ginger, cloves, mace, *garam masala,* and salt and mix well.

Ghee is clarified butter; it has a slightly nutty taste and a higher smoking point than plain butter. It can be held without refrigeration for 1 month or refrigerated for 6 months. The process involves slowly simmering the butter so that the water evaporates, the milk solids collect at the bottom and brown slightly, and the foam is skimmed from the surface. *Garam masala* is a spice mixture that varies from region to region and uses "hot" spices—those that are believed to warm the body. It is normally added at the end of the cooking process. It can be purchased in Indian markets or made fresh using this typical recipe.

Garam Masala

Makes about 3 tablespoons [45 mL]

I tablespoon [15 mL] cardamom pods

One 2-inch [5-cm] cinnamon stick

I teaspoon [5 mL] black cumin seeds

I teaspoon [5 mL] whole cloves

¼ whole nutmeg, freshly grated

Pinch of fennel seeds

I teaspoon black peppercorns

Place all the spices in a dry skillet over low heat and heat gradually until fragrant. Allow to cool. Grind the roasted spices in an electric spice grinder. Seal in an airtight glass container and store in a cool, dark place.

2. Shape the mixture into meatballs 1 inch [2.5 cm] in diameter and sauté in the *ghee* until firm and lightly browned. Reserve warm. (The meatballs can be made 1 day in advance, held refrigerated.)

PREPARATION OF THE SAUCE

3. Process the cashews and almonds into a paste, adding 1 to 2 tablespoons [15 to 30 mL] of yogurt to help process if necessary, and reserve.

4. Heat the *ghee* in a sauté pan over medium heat and sauté the onions until lightly golden. Add the garlic, ginger, turmeric, and cayenne and sauté until fragrant.

5. Add the tomatoes and cook for 5 minutes. Add the yogurt and the reserved nut paste and simmer over low heat until the oil separates.

6. Stir in the water and add the reserved meatballs. Cover the pan and simmer for 5 to 10 minutes, allowing the meatballs to absorb the flavorings of the sauce. Add the mint, salt, and pinch of *garam masala* and stir to combine.

SERVICE

7. Serve 4 meatballs per person, topped with some of the sauce and a quarter-folded *chapati* bread on the side. Garnish with the sprigs of mint and cilantro.

Moghul Chicken with Almonds Shah Jahani Murghi

serves 8

This dish is a Muslim royal court dish from the north of India. Shah Jahan was the Moghul emperor who built the Taj Mahal and was quite fond of all-white banquets. On nights with a full moon, the palace was decorated with all white trappings, the guests wore all white, and all the banquet food white as well. This light-colored dish fit perfectly into that color scheme. It was later refined by the Nawabi culture during the eighteenth century to become what it is today. Most prefer to use chicken breasts, but boneless thighs will provide a tastier version.

CHEF NOTES

Originally this dish was made only with almonds, but modern cooks seem to prefer a mixture of almonds and cashews. The traditional recipe also includes 1 ounce [30 g] of *chaar magnaz*, which is a blend of melon, squash, and pumpkin seeds. Either may be used if desired.

1-inch [2.5-cm] piece of ginger, sliced thin against the grain

9 garlic cloves, minced

⅓ cup [80 mL] slivered almonds, dry-toasted until golden

¼ cup [60 mL] chicken stock

½ cup [120 mL] *ghee* or vegetable oil

1½ pounds [675 g] boneless chicken breasts, tenders, or thighs, cut into small pieces

10 whole cardamom pods

1-inch [2.5-cm] piece of cinnamon stick

2 bay leaves

5 whole cloves

2 onions, minced

2 teaspoons [10 mL] ground cumin

½ teaspoon [3 mL] cayenne

½ cup [120 mL] plain yogurt, whipped until smooth and light

1 cup [240 mL] heavy cream

1½ teaspoons [8 mL] salt

2 tablespoons [30 mL] sultana raisins

½ teaspoon [3 mL] saffron, dissolved in 1 tablespoon [15 mL] warm chicken stock

½ teaspoon [3 mL] *garam masala* (see page 317)

½ teaspoon [3 mL] rose water or 1 teaspoon [5 mL] powdered rose petals

8 timbales of rice pilaf seasoned with onion, garlic, green chile, and *garam masala*

Organic fresh rose petals, for garnish

ADVANCE PREPARATION

1. Place the ginger, garlic, ¼ cup [60 mL] of the almonds (reserving the remainder for garnish), and the chicken stock in a food processor and blend into a smooth paste. (The paste can be made 1 day in advance.)

2. Heat the *ghee* in a large nonstick skillet and brown the chicken pieces. Remove the chicken pieces to a bowl, reserving any oil in the skillet.

3. Add the cardamom, cinnamon, bay leaves, and cloves to the skillet and sauté briefly until fragrant. Add the onions and sauté 4 to 5 minutes, or until lightly browned.

4. Add the reserved spice-almond paste, cumin, and cayenne. Sauté, while stirring, for 3 minutes, or until the oil begins to separate and the spices are very lightly browned.

5. Slowly add the yogurt, stirring to incorporate. Add the cream, salt, and reserved chicken pieces with any accumulated juices to the skillet. Simmer 20 minutes.

6. Add the raisins and the dissolved saffron. Stir and simmer 10 minutes more, or until the chicken is tender.

7. Sprinkle the *garam masala* and rose water over the top and stir to incorporate.

SERVICE

8. Serve 4-ounce [110-g] portions of the chicken, topped with sauce and accompanied with a timbale of seasoned rice. Take care to remove any whole spices in the sauce, as they are not to be eaten. Garnish with the reserved toasted almonds and rose petals.

Fish Fillets Stuffed with Caramelized Onions Masala Meen Bajji

serves 8

This is a Muslim dish from northern Kerala, known for its preference for fish dishes. Thin, flat fish fillets are spread with a thick, spicy onion curry, then rolled "jelly-roll fashion." The fish normally used for this dish in India is pomfret (*Stromateidae* family), but sole, flounder, pompano, or sand dabs may be substituted.

CHEF NOTES

An alternative method of preparation is to use a whole fish with the bones removed. Stuff the interior cavity of the fish with some of the caramelized onions and cook about 10 minutes per side in the remaining onion mixture. Carefully remove the fish, cut into thin steaks, and then top with the remaining caramelized onions. Garnish with cashews and raisins.

MARINADE

1 teaspoon [5 mL] cayenne

1 teaspoon [5 mL] turmeric

2 teaspoons [10 mL] salt

Eight 3- to 4-ounce [85- to 110-g] fillets of sole or other delicate white-fleshed fish

GARNISH

1 tablespoon [15 mL] *ghee* or clarified butter

3 tablespoons [45 mL] cashews, chopped

3 tablespoons [45 mL] golden sultana raisins

MASALA

4 teaspoons [20 mL] coriander seeds, ground

1 teaspoon [5 mL] ground cumin

½ teaspoon [3 mL] cayenne

½ teaspoon [3 mL] turmeric

FILLING: MAKES 1¾ CUPS [420 mL]

⅓ cup [80 mL] *ghee* or vegetable oil

4 cups [960 mL] sliced onions

1 tablespoon [15 mL] garlic, minced

1 tablespoon [15 mL] ginger, minced

3 hot green chiles, minced

¼ cup [60 mL] cilantro sprigs, chopped

¼ cup [60 mL] mint leaves, chiffonade

½ teaspoon *garam masala* (see page 317)

1 cup [240 mL] tomatoes, diced fine

1 teaspoon [5 mL] fresh lime juice

1 teaspoon [5 mL] salt

1 teaspoon [5 mL] sugar

ADVANCE PREPARATION

1. Combine the marinade ingredients and mix well. Rub the fish fillets with the spice marinade. Cover and marinate 15 minutes or up to 1 hour.

2. Heat the *ghee* and sauté the cashews until golden. Remove them and add the raisins to the same skillet. Sauté the raisins until they plump and are slightly browned. Combine with the cashews and reserve.

PREPARATION OF THE MASALA

3. Mix the *masala* ingredients together and reserve.

PREPARATION OF THE FISH ROLLS

4. Heat a nonstick skillet and swirl in the *ghee*. Add the onions and sauté slowly until they begin to caramelize. Add the garlic, ginger, green chiles, cilantro, and mint. Sauté for 1 minute.

5. Add the reserved *masala* mixture, the *garam masala*, tomatoes, lime juice, salt, and sugar. Sauté the mixture until the onions are nicely browned and the mixture thickens. Remove from the heat and allow to cool slightly.

6. Spread 1 tablespoon [15 mL] of the onion mixture on top of each fish fillet. Roll the fillets jelly-roll fashion and secure the rolls with toothpicks.

COOKING METHOD

7. Heat the remaining onion mixture to a low simmer and place the fish rolls in the onions to cook, adding some water if the onion mixture is too thick. Cook for 3 minutes, then turn the rolls and cook 3 minutes more, or until the fish firms slightly and just begins to flake.

SERVICE

8. Serve 1 roll per person, topped with some of the caramelized onions from the pan. Garnish with the reserved sautéed cashews and raisins.

Sole Fillets in Fragrant Mustard Sauce Sorso Bhatte Maach

serves 8

Bengali cuisine favors the use of mustard oil to cook with, and mustard seeds are often included in Bengali dishes. Fish and seafood are widely enjoyed in Bengal, which is situated on the Bay of Bengal, penetrated by many tributaries of the Ganges River. This assertive curry, strongly flavored with mustard, is tempered slightly with tomato and lime. Serve the fillets with a small timbale of basmati rice, seasoned, if you wish, with a touch of lime juice.

CHEF NOTES

Fragrant mustard oil is pressed from mustard seeds. It has a mustard-like aroma and a slightly bitter taste, and it has been used as a liniment for arthritis and rheumatism for centuries. Bengali women also use it as a hair tonic. It is the preferred cooking oil in Bengal, and it should be available at health food and Indian markets. A reasonable substitute would be to sauté some crushed mustard seeds in vegetable oil (and strain before use).

Eight 3-ounce [85-g] sole fillets or other delicate white-fleshed fish, such as flounder

Salt and black pepper to taste

2 tablespoons [30 mL] poppy seeds

2 tablespoons [30 mL] brown mustard seeds

1 teaspoon [5 mL] turmeric

2 ounces [55 g] fresh coconut, diced, or desiccated, unsweetened coconut

¾-inch [2-cm] piece of ginger, minced

6 garlic cloves, minced

2 serrano chiles, stemmed and diced

1 onion, diced

2 teaspoons [10 mL] ground coriander

2 teaspoons [10 mL] ground cumin

1½ teaspoons [8 mL] cayenne

1¼ teaspoons [6 mL] salt

3 to 4 tablespoons [45 to 60 mL] mustard oil (see Chef Notes)

3 Roma or plum tomatoes, diced fine

Juice of ½ lime

8 timbales of cooked basmati rice

2 tablespoons [30 mL] cilantro leaves, for garnish

ADVANCE PREPARATION

1. Lightly season the fish fillets with the salt and pepper.

PREPARATION OF THE SPICE PASTE

2. Toast the poppy seeds in a dry skillet and finely grind in an electric spice grinder. Combine the ground poppy seeds with the mustard seeds, turmeric, coconut, ginger, garlic, chiles, onion, coriander, cumin, cayenne, salt, and ½ cup [120 mL] water in a food processor. Finely process to make a smooth paste. (The spice paste can be made 1 day in advance and stored tightly sealed.)

3. Heat the mustard oil over medium heat and sauté the spice paste for 5 to 6 minutes, stirring constantly. It may be necessary to add up to ½ cup [120 mL] water if the mixture gets too dry.

4. Add the tomatoes and cook for 3 minutes more. Add 2 cups [480 mL] water and the lime juice and simmer for 5 minutes. Season to taste.

5. Add the fish fillets and simmer in the sauce until just done and beginning to flake.

SERVICE

6. Place a timbale of rice at the edge of a small plate. Arrange a fillet of fish next to the rice and top with sauce. Garnish with cilantro leaves.

Curried Shrimp with Tomato and Tamarind Jhinga Varathiathu

serves 8

This dish reflects the Keralans' love of locally available seafood and their fondness for tamarind and curry leaves as flavorings. The thick sauce is reddish in color, tangy with the slightly sour and fruity essence of tamarind, and is piquant from the addition of chiles and cayenne. It needs no accompaniment but can be eaten with soft Indian flatbreads such as *naan*.

CHEF NOTES

Scallops, lobster, or in combination with shrimp may be substituted in this dish.

MASALA

1 tablespoon [15 mL] ground coriander

¾ teaspoon [4 mL] cayenne

½ teaspoon [3 mL] ground cumin

SHRIMP

¼ teaspoon [1 mL] cayenne

¼ teaspoon [1 mL] turmeric

1¼ teaspoons [6 mL] salt

1½ pounds [675 g] medium shrimp, peeled and deveined

¼ cup [60 mL] *ghee* or vegetable oil

¾ teaspoon [4 mL] brown mustard seeds

⅛ teaspoon [0.5 mL] fenugreek seeds

10 fresh curry leaves

2 onions, sliced

2 teaspoons [10 mL] garlic, minced

2 teaspoons [10 mL] ginger, minced

2 teaspoons [10 mL] serrano chiles, minced

¼ cup [60 mL] tamarind liquid

¾ cup [180 mL] tomato, chopped

Cilantro leaves, for garnish

ADVANCE PREPARATION

1. Combine the *masala* spices and stir well. Reserve.

PREPARATION OF THE SHRIMP

2. Combine the cayenne, turmeric, and ¼ teaspoon [1 mL] of the salt and mix well. Rub the shrimp with this mixture and allow to marinate for 20 minutes or up to 2 hours.

COOKING METHOD

3. Heat 2 tablespoons [30 mL] of the *ghee* and sauté the marinated shrimp until they just begin to turn opaque. Immediately turn out onto a plate and separate the shrimp to cool quickly.

4. Heat the remaining *ghee* over medium-high heat and add the mustard seeds, covering immediately (the seeds will pop). Shake gently until spattering declines, remove the cover, add the fenugreek seeds and curry leaves and sauté briefly.

5. Add the onions and stir-fry until they begin to brown. Add the garlic, ginger, and serrano chiles. Continue cooking until the onions are thoroughly browned, then add the tamarind, tomato, and remaining 1 teaspoon [5 mL] of salt.

6. Cook, while stirring, for 10 minutes, or until the tomatoes soften into the sauce. Add the shrimp to the sauce and cook just to heat through. Sprinkle the *masala* over the dish and serve immediately.

SERVICE

7. Serve 3 to 4 shrimp per person and garnish with the cilantro leaves.

Spinach and Cheese Dumplings with Chile Sauce Tse tang Churo Momo, Sonam Penzom Sibeh

serves 12 (4 dumplings per person)

Momos are the definitive Tibetan appetizer. The true *momo* aficionado knows that the proper way to eat them is to first bite a small hole in one end and sip the juices out. The hole also serves to allow the interior to be filled with hot sauce before popping the *momo* in your mouth. The one rule for eating these dumplings is that they can never be eaten on the first day of the New Year, because, it is believed, a filling sealed inside a dough wrapper represents a sealing off of good luck. *Momos* can be stuffed with a variety of fillings; this recipe offers a delectable vegetarian version with spinach and cheese. The traditional cheese for this dish is *chusip* (see the Chef Notes for a recipe to make your own *chusip*), but you may substitute feta or ricotta with a little Parmesan blended in with it. A recipe is also given for the dumpling skins, but you may choose to use frozen gyoza skins instead.

CHILE SAUCE

1 bunch cilantro, chopped

5 Thai chiles or 3 serrano chiles, minced

½ cup [120 mL] dried hot red chiles, crushed

1 large tomato, chopped (1 cup [240 mL] yogurt may be substituted for a variation)

5 garlic cloves, minced

1½ teaspoons [8 mL] salt

½ teaspoon [3 mL] sugar

½ cup [120 mL] water

DUMPLING WRAPPERS

2½ cups [600 mL] flour

¾ cup [180 mL] water

SPINACH AND CHEESE FILLING:
MAKES ENOUGH FILLING FOR 48 DUMPLINGS

¼ cup [60 mL] *ghee* or vegetable oil (yak butter is authentic, but difficult to obtain)

1½ cups [360 mL] diced onions

4 garlic cloves, minced

2-inch [5-cm] piece ginger, sliced thin against the grain, minced

¾ teaspoon [6 mL] *emma* (Sichuan peppercorns), toasted and ground

6 scallions, diced

1 pound [450 g] spinach or Swiss chard leaves, washed and drained, chiffonade

1 pound [450 g] sheep's milk feta cheese, crumbled

ADVANCE PREPARATION

1. Combine all of the chile sauce ingredients in a food processor and pulse until slightly chunky. (The sauce will keep, refrigerated, for several days.) For a variation omit the tomato and blend the remaining ingredients with yogurt.

CHEF NOTES

The dumplings can be filled with beef, chicken, or a variety of vegetables. Use the same spices as called for above, adding celery and some stock to the beef or chicken versions. Consider dividing the sauce into 2 parts, adding tomato to one and yogurt to the other, and serving both as accompaniment.

Chusip

To make your own *chusip* use:

2 teaspoons [10 mL] sugar

4 cups [960 mL] natural, plain yogurt

1. Mix the sugar into the yogurt and bring to a boil over medium heat. Continue at a low boil until the curds begin to separate from the clear, watery whey.

2. Pour the mixture through several layers of cheesecloth lining a sieve and allow to drain for several hours.

3. Compress the cheese mixture after draining to form small balls. Place these on a tray and allow to dry, uncovered, in the refrigerator for several days. The cheese may be stored in an airtight container and kept for a week.

2. Combine the flour and water to form a smooth, elastic dough, kneading well. Cover the dough and allow it to rest for 1 hour.

3. Knead the dough until it becomes elastic again, about 3 minutes. (The dough can be made several days in advance, wrapped tightly in plastic film, and refrigerated.)

PREPARATION OF THE DUMPLINGS

4. Keeping the dough well floured, roll the dough into a cylinder 1 inch [2.5 cm] in diameter. Cut off 1-inch [2.5-cm] segments of dough. Roll out each segment into a circle, stacking them with a little flour between layers.

PREPARATION OF THE FILLING

5. Heat the *ghee* and sauté the onions until transparent. Add the garlic, ginger, and *emma*, and sauté briefly.

6. Add the scallions and spinach and stir well to combine. Remove from the heat, add the cheese, and stir just to combine. Reserve.

7. To fold the dumplings, form a circle with your thumb and index finger. Lay a dough circle on this circle, and scrape 1 tablespoon [15 mL] of filling against the thumb side of the wrapper.

8. Lightly moisten the edges of the wrapper, using the moistened index finger of your other hand. Begin pleating the outside edge of the wrapper against the edge facing you, using the index finger of your other hand. The side closest to you will have no pleats while the outer side will develop a curved pleat. Lightly press the pleats as you form them. Place on a tray until all are finished. Keep covered until ready to cook. (The dumplings may be frozen at this point.)

COOKING METHOD

9. To cook the dumplings, place them on a round of lightly oiled parchment fitted inside a steamer. Steam the dumplings for 4 minutes. Hold warm until service.

SERVICE

10. Serve 4 dumplings per person with a small ramekin of chile sauce.

Puffed Flat Bread Stuffed with Potatoes, Chickpeas, and Tamarind Broth Gol Gappa ya Paani Poori

serves 8

These miniature stuffed breads are the Indian equivalent of a Chinese broth-filled soup dumpling. The hollow breads are filled with a potato and chickpea filling with a small amount of hot-and-sour tamarind broth ladled into them. This appetizer is assembled at the table, making it an "interactive" dish. *Gol gappa* means "bloated rounds" and are commonly sold by street vendors, assembled to order.

CHEF NOTES

Use only the *pooris* that puff up well for this dish (you should expect to make about 4 dozen perfect *pooris* from the recipe given). A variety of fillings may be used instead of the potatoes and chickpeas. You may want to offer several different fillings (some with meat) arranged on a platter.

MINIATURE *POORI* BREADS: MAKES ABOUT 5 DOZEN

¾ cup [180 mL] all-purpose flour, plus additional flour for dusting

¾ cup [180 mL] very fine whole wheat flour (*chapati* flour or *atta*)

1 tablespoon [15 mL] instant cream of wheat

½ cup [120 mL] warm water

Vegetable oil, for frying

HOT-AND-SOUR TAMARIND BROTH (*IMLI PAANI*): MAKES ABOUT 7 CUPS [1.7 L]

6 cups [1.4 L] tamarind liquid

2 tablespoons [30 mL] unsulphured molasses

1 tablespoon cumin seeds, toasted and ground

3 tablespoons [45 mL] fresh lemon juice

2 teaspoons [10 mL] cayenne

½ cup [120 mL] mint leaves, minced

2 teaspoons [10 mL] ginger, minced

2 teaspoons [10 mL] salt

FILLING

2½ cups [600 mL] cooked chickpeas

1½ cups [360 mL] cooked potatoes, cut into ¼-inch [6-mm] dice

Salt to taste

Crushed red pepper, for garnish

2 tablespoons [30 mL] hot green chiles, minced

¼ cup [60 mL] chopped cilantro, for garnish

36 well-puffed *pooris*

4 cups [960 mL] hot-and-sour tamarind broth

ADVANCE PREPARATION

1. Combine the all-purpose and whole wheat flours and the cream of wheat in a food processor. With the motor running add the water in a steady stream and process until the mixture forms into a ball.

2. Knead the dough by processing for 30 seconds total time, pulsing for 5- to 10-second intervals.

3. Turn the dough out onto a floured board and divide the dough into 4 equal portions. Roll 1 piece of dough, covering the remaining pieces of dough, into an 8-inch [20-cm] circle, dusting with flour as necessary to prevent sticking. Cut 2-inch [5-cm] circles with a cookie cutter. Repeat until all the dough is rolled and cut, keeping the cut circles covered at all times.

4. Heat the oil to 375°F [190°C] and fry the *pooris,* in batches to avoid crowding. When they pop up to the surface, allow them to cook for 20 seconds then flip them over to cook for about 30 seconds more, or until they puff up and are lightly browned.

5. Drain on paper towels and allow to cool. The *pooris* will soften as they cool.

6. Place the *pooris* in a 375°F [190°C] oven for 5 minutes to crisp. (If kept dry and tightly sealed, the *pooris* can be stored for 1 week.)

PREPARATION OF THE BROTH

7. Stir the broth ingredients together. Bring the mixture to a boil. Remove from the heat and reserve warm. (The broth can be stored for 1 week, refrigerated.)

SERVICE

8. Arrange the cooked chickpeas and potatoes on a platter. Sprinkle with salt, red pepper, green chiles, and cilantro.

9. Supply each person with ½ cup [120 mL] of warm tamarind broth and a small soup spoon for a ladle. Tap the *pooris* gently on the side to open them so that they can be filled. Insert a few chickpeas and some potatoes into the hollow center, then ladle in hot broth to fill the cavity. Pop the filled breads into the mouth. Allow 6 *pooris* per person.

Southwestern Asia

THREE SUBREGIONS COMPRISE the broader region of Southwestern Asia—Iran (Persia) and Afghanistan, Central Asia, and Georgia and Azerbaijan. Central Asia covers the five republics Turkmenistan, Tajikistan, Kazakhstan, Kyrgyzstan, and Uzbekistan, all formerly part of the Soviet Union. This area is bordered by the Caspian Sea to the west and China to the east. Iran is bordered on the north by the Caspian Sea and Central Asia, on the east by Afghanistan, and on the west by Iraq and Turkey. Pakistan borders Afghanistan on the south. Southwestern Asia has been influenced by the Silk Route and by spice traders for centuries. Afghanistan, in particular, has felt the influence of invaders, traders, and marauders, being located at the intersection of four major cultures: China, the Middle East, Central Asia, and the Indian Subcontinent. Mostly mountainous, Afghanistan's mountain passes allowed many invading armies to cross between Europe and Asia, forever leaving their influence on Afghanistan's cuisine (and the cuisines of the entire region.)

Iran possesses one of the world's most ancient cuisines, its people settling the Iranian plateau by 1000 B.C. It was the Europeans that called these people Persians; most likely derived from the name Pars, homeland to the first Persian Empire. Iran derives from the name of the Indo-Aryan people. Persians have been known since the time of Herodotus for being excellent cooks, often experimenting and developing new dishes. Their ancient cuisine was formed by absorbing the cultures of Mesopotamia, Egypt, and Greece. Although records are sketchy, agriculture thrived through irrigation as early as the fifth century B.C., bringing new plants and seeds from afar. Caravan trade from Mesopotamia to China brought new foods to and from Persia by the second century B.C. Wild fowl from India became the domesticated chicken of Persia. Persia introduced the world to the grape, walnut, pistachio, sesame, pomegranate, cucumber, and pea, as well as coriander and basil, and passed on to Europe the peach and apricot from China. Persian cuisine has had a profound influence on the cuisines of the world. In addition to shaping the foods of India and the surrounding countries of Western Asia, the Persian style of eating included the concept of starting a meal with a broad range of appetizers. This concept eventually became the *tapas* of Spain, *mezedes* of Greece, the *mezze* of the Middle East, and the *meze* of Turkey.

If there is one unifying theme to this region's cuisines, it is hospitality. Hospitality is central to Persian life, and food is an essential way to express this hospitality. Persian cooking relies on fresh ingredients, and what is in season becomes the center of the dish to be cooked. Fragrance is as important as taste, and the importance of presentation has encouraged an artistic style of garnishing. Balance is another feature of Persian cooking; Persians separate foods into "cold" and "hot" categories (based on energy content rather than temperature). Fish, dairy, and fresh fruits are considered to be cold, while animal fat, nuts, wheat, and dried fruits are hot. This has led to a characteristic cooking style that, among other things, combines meats and vegetables with fruits and nuts. *Dolmehs* (stuffed vegetables) are a uniquely Persian dish that embodies this style of preparation (and have become popular throughout the Middle East and the Mediterranean). Persian cooking also relies on a sweet-and-sour component to flavoring. Tart cherries and pomegranates are often augmented with lime juice or verjuice to ensure a strong measure of tartness. Richness is often provided by walnuts, almonds, and pistachios. Sweetness comes from the addition of honey, date syrup, and sweet fruit juices.

Staples such as bread and rice are found throughout Southwestern Asia. It is Persia that influenced bread baking across the entire region. The popular flat breads of India are Persian in origin, as is the tandoor oven in which it is baked (called a *tanoor* in Persia). Uzbekistan calls their clay oven a *tandir* and the region is known for its excellent breads. Georgians also bake their bread as the Persians and Indians, and their clay oven is known as a *toné*. Rice is certainly the staple to the diet of the region and the Persians are masters of rice cookery. What Westerners call pilaf and Indians and Afghanis call *palau* (or *pilau*) are Persian in origin (called *polou* in Persian). Meats, vegetables, fruits, herbs, and spices are added to some of the finest rice grown in the world (*sadri* and *dom siyah* are two of the best varieties). Basmati rice from India and Pakistan is used throughout Southwestern Asia, and it makes an excellent substitute for Persian rice in the United States. Wheat and corn are significant in Georgia, unlike the rest of the region.

Fruits and vegetable abound in this area of the world, although soil conditions in some places, particularly Afghanistan, have deteriorated because of war and neglect, making it difficult to raise cash crops. Consequently, Afghanis eat only foods that are in season, obtained mostly from backyard gardens. Because of Afghanistan's unique geographical position along the trade routes, Afghani cuisine has been influenced in the past by traders from Europe, China, and the East. Pasta dishes make a surprising appearance in this country, with filled and layered noodles quite reminiscent of ravioli and lasagna from Italy. Other noodle dishes can be traced to the Mongol invasion, centuries ago. A popular seasoning known as four spices (*char marsala*) is quite similar to the *garam masala* of India, and the Indian-Pakistani influence is quite formidable in Afghanistan's cuisine. Poppy seeds are common here, a fortunate benefit of an otherwise seedy side to Afghanistan's economy, opium production. (Afghanistan is one of the world's largest producers of opium.) Afghanis prefer an oily component to their dishes, using large amounts of lamb fat and *ghee* in their cooking. As in Iran, sauces are thickened with purées of split peas, and a surprising addition is mung beans, a Chinese influence. Slow cooking is a favored method of food preparation in Afghanistan and is quite popular among its neighboring countries (curries from India and khoreshes from Iran are two examples).

Spices unite the flavors of the entire region. Turmeric, cinnamon, saffron, cloves, cardamom, and cumin are found in abundance in dishes from Iran, Afghanistan, and Central Asia. Spice mixes, as seen in India as *masalas*, are used in a similar fashion in Iran and Afghanistan. Georgia has its own spice mix known as *khmeli-suneli*, a mixture of fenugreek, chiles, coriander, garlic, and black pepper. Spicier foods are found in western Georgia, while in the east, a cooler, fresher taste is appreciated. The use of nuts is seen in many of Southwestern Asia's favorite dishes, but walnuts are unique to the cuisine of Georgia. Georgians have learned that adding a sour component will cut the overbearing richness of nuts. Vinegar, yogurt, immature wine, and fruit juices lend balance to walnut-enriched sauces and fillings. More than any other country in the region, Georgians are fond of greens. Wild greens, such as nettles, ramp, purslane, and savory, are enjoyed freshly harvested. Summer savory, field mint, and fenugreek combine to form the definitive taste of Georgia. Georgian cuisine has other unique ingredients not normally included in the rest of Southwestern Asia's cuisines. Kidney beans, rather than lentils and chickpeas, are a favorite legume. Dried marigold takes the place of the saffron, found in so many dishes of Iran, Afghanistan, and Central Asia.

Grilling is a favorite method of cooking in Georgia, and it is said that Georgians would rather cook over an open flame than by any other method. Grilling is essential to the preparation of Southwestern Asia's most famous meat dish, the *kabob*. There are many different versions, some featuring bone-in meats skewered on broad metal skewers. Seasoned ground meats are also formed around these broad metal skewers. When ground meat mixtures are pan-sautéed rather than skewered, they are known as *kotlets*. *Kabobs* are eaten in combination with rice to yield the "national dish" of Iran, *chelo kabob*. Afghanis enjoy their *kabobs* from street vendors and are served wrapped in flat bread (the bread is used to slide the meat from the skewer). The Turkmenians of Central Asia enjoy their *kabobs* made from mountain goat, camel, and horsemeat. Primarily a nomadic people, Turkmenians (as well as others from Central Asia) enjoy a diet primarily comprised of meat and dairy products. Yogurt is used in sauces and marinades and as a fermented beverage throughout this country, Central Asia, and across Southwestern Asia.

Chinese influence is strong in Central Asia. Fried noodles, steamed buns, and dumplings appear, as do mung beans and a taste for chiles. (Korean inhabitants of Kazakhstan also contributed their taste for chiles.) Steaming, a Chinese cooking preference, is a favored method of food preparation in Tadzhikistan and Uzbekistan, two Central Asian countries known for their refined cuisines. Persian, Afghani, and Indian influences abound here, adding to the spectrum of ingredients, spices, and cooking techniques. Apples, peaches, plums, cherries, melons, figs, pomegranates, quince, and grapes are found both fresh and dried. Kazikistan is known for its luscious apples, some as large as soccer balls, while Turkmenia is renowned for its grapes, some the size of plums. Uzbekistan produces almost 1,000 varieties of melons, and almost every fruit and spice that is grown in the world may be found in Central Asian markets. Truly a melting pot, Central Asia (and to a lesser extent all of Southwestern Asia) is one of the most ethnically diverse regions of the world. In addition to the Iranians, Turks, Mongols, and Huns, the Chinese, Koreans, Arabs, Jews, and Indians have passed through and settled in this area, leaving their indelible mark on the cuisines of the entire region.

Tart Cherry-Stuffed Beef Meatballs Koftah Aloo Bokhara

serves 8

Versions of this dish can be found in Iran and in Azerbaijan as well as in Afghanistan, with the meatballs stuffed with sour plums or cherries, in a vegetable broth, or with slightly different spices added. The dried cherry filling offers a tart, fruity contrast to the richness of sirloin. The broth used in this recipes shows a Pakistani and northern Indian influence.

CHEF NOTES

The meatballs may be made with ground lamb or a mixture of beef and lamb. Dried sour plums may be substituted for the tart cherries if desired.

MEATBALLS

1½ pounds [675 g] beef sirloin, twice-ground

3 garlic cloves, minced

1½ tablespoons [25 mL] ground cinnamon

½ teaspoon [3 mL] ground cloves

1 teaspoon [5 mL] salt

1 teaspoon [5 mL] ground black pepper

4 ounces [110 g] pitted dried tart cherries, soaked in water for 30 minutes if very dry and drained

¼ cup [60 mL] vegetable oil

SAUCE

1 quart [1 L] chicken stock

4½ ounces [125 g] dried yellow split peas

2 small onions, minced

3 garlic cloves, minced

½ cup [120 mL] tomato paste

2 small tomatoes, seeded and chopped

⅛ teaspoon [0.5 mL] ground cinnamon

⅛ teaspoon [0.5 mL] ground cloves

⅛ teaspoon [0.5 mL] cayenne

Salt and ground black pepper to taste

Parsley leaves, for garnish

ADVANCE PREPARATION

1. Combine the beef, garlic, cinnamon, cloves, salt, and pepper in the bowl of an electric mixer and mix well for 2 to 3 minutes.

2. Form the meat mixture into 32 walnut-size balls, push 4 dried cherries into the center of each, and reform the meatball to enclose the cherry. Reserve, covered and refrigerated. (The meatballs can be made several hours in advance.)

PREPARATION OF THE SAUCE

3. Add half of the chicken stock to the split peas and bring to a boil in a small saucepan. Reduce to a low simmer and cook

the split peas for 25 minutes, or until softened. If you have to add more liquid, add only as much water as necessary. (The split peas can be prepared 1 day in advance and stored, refrigerated.)

COOKING METHOD

4. Sauté the reserved meatballs in 2 tablespoons [30 mL] of vegetable oil over medium heat until browned. Remove the meatballs to paper towels, drain, and keep warm.

5. Add the remaining vegetable oil to the pan used to cook the meatballs and sauté the onions until transparent. Add the garlic and sauté an additional 30 seconds.

6. Add the remaining chicken stock, tomato paste, and the chopped tomatoes. Bring to a boil and reduce the liquid by half. Add the split peas and the meatballs, reducing the heat to a simmer.

7. Add the cinnamon, cloves, and cayenne and simmer 5 minutes. Adjust seasonings with salt and pepper.

SERVICE

8. Serve each guest 4 meatballs on a pool of sauce. Garnish with parsley.

**Picadillo-Stuffed Poblano
Chiles in Creamy Walnut Sauce**
Chiles en Nogada
(page 78)

**Lamb Chop in Pastry Purse
with Madeira Sauce**
Jolly Jumbuck in a Tucker Bag
(page 168)

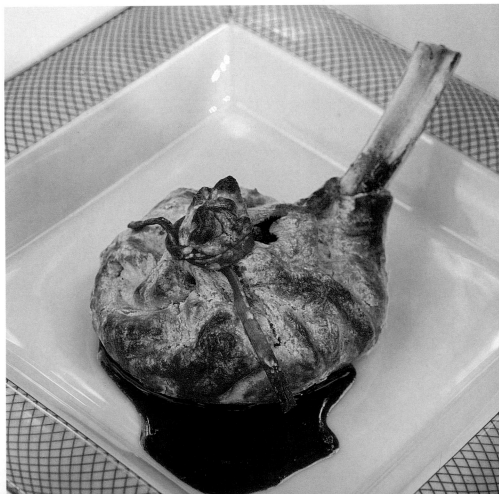

Grilled Veal Kebabs with Apricot-Curry Glaze *Sosaties*

(page 377)

Lamb and Split Pea Forcemeat-Encased Stuffed Chicken Breast
Kufteh-ye Tabrizi

(page 343)

Cheese Soufflés in a Tomato Shell *Tomates Soufflées Jurassiennes*
(page 481)

Layered Crêpe, Mushroom, and Cheese Torte *Blinchaty Pirog s Gribami*
(page 439)

**Lemon-Garlic Glazed
Chicken Wing
Drumettes** *Ailerons de
Poulet en Gigots au
Citron et à l'Ail*
(page 531)

**Braised Octopus with
Fennel, Green
Peppercorns, and Olives**
*Htapothi me Maratho
kai Prasines Elies*

**Glass Blower's Trout
(Spicy Pickled Trout)**
Lasimestarin Silli

(page 460)

**Salt Cod-Stuffed Piquillo
Peppers with Bayonne Ham
and Chile Sauce** *Pimientos del
Piquillo Rellenos de Bacalao
con Salsa Vizcaína*

(page 513)

**Pheasant and Leek Pies
with Port Cream Sauce**
Phesand Pye
(page 555)

**Crab-Stuffed Portabella
Mushroom**

**Wild Rice Griddle Cakes
with Morel Mushroom
Cream Sauce**

(page 48)

**Southern Fried Quail with
Country Cream Gravy**

(page 23)

**Pastry Pockets Stuffed with
Seasoned Pork and Red Chile Sauce**
*Sopapillas con Puerco y Chile
Colorado*
(page 63)

**Grilled Goat Cheese-Stuffed
Grape Leaves**

(page 59)

Steamed Lamb Dumplings with Yogurt-Garlic Sauce Manti Sikhdorov Madzoon

serves 8

These delicious dumplings are one of the most popular foods in Uzbekistan. Every household has a special, multilevel steamer used to cook them. In Uzbekistan the lamb in the filling is minced finely by hand, providing a texture not possible by grinding. To mince by hand, chill the meat to a semi-frozen state and mince with a sharp cleaver (use 2 cleavers to be authentic).

 CHEF NOTES

Thicker styles of frozen gyoza or potsticker wrappers may be substituted for the dough should you choose not to make your own. For a vegetarian version, omit the lamb and add pine nuts and additional rice. The amounts and types of herbs may be varied to taste.

SAUCE: MAKES ABOUT 1½ CUPS [360 mL]

1 cup [240 mL] plain natural yogurt, whipped

2 teaspoons [10 mL] garlic, minced

Salt to taste

1½ tablespoons [25 mL] cilantro, chopped

1½ tablespoons [25 mL] mint leaves, chiffonade

FILLING

1 medium onion, diced fine

1 teaspoon [5 mL] garlic, minced

1 tablespoon [15 mL] vegetable oil or *ghee*

12 ounces [340 g] boneless shoulder or leg of lamb, minced by hand

3 tablespoons [45 mL] lamb or chicken stock

2 tablespoons [30 mL] cilantro, chopped

2 tablespoons [30 mL] mint leaves, chiffonade

1 teaspoon [5 mL] coarsely ground black pepper

Salt to taste

DOUGH

3 cups [720 mL] all-purpose flour

1 teaspoon [5 mL] salt

3 large egg yolks

1½ tablespoons [25 mL] vegetable oil

About ¾ cup [180 mL] water

2 ounces [55 g] unsalted butter, cut into 40 pieces, chilled

Cilantro and mint sprigs, for garnish

ADVANCE PREPARATION

1. For the sauce, combine all the sauce ingredients and mix well. Store, covered and refrigerated, overnight.

PREPARATION OF THE FILLING

2. Sauté the onion and garlic in the oil until the onion is translucent. Combine all the remaining filling ingredients and mix well. (The filling can be made one day in advance.)

PREPARATION OF THE DOUGH

3. Combine the flour and salt in the workbowl of a food processor. With the motor running, add the egg yolks and the oil in a steady stream. Slowly add enough water until the dough forms into a ball.

4. Place the dough on a floured work surface and knead for 2 minutes. Cover the dough and allow to rest 30 minutes. (The dough can be made 1 day in advance.)

PREPARATION OF THE DUMPLINGS

5. Divide the dough in two, keeping 1 half covered while working with the other. Roll 1 half of the dough out very thin on a floured surface. Cut the dough into 3-inch [8-cm] circles. Repeat with the second half of the dough, keeping the cut circles covered as they are formed.

6. To fill and form the dumplings, have a small dish of water handy. Place approximately ½ tablespoon [8 mL] of filling in the center of each dough circle and top with a piece of chilled butter. Gather the edges of the dough around the filling, moisten the inside edge, pinch, and twist to seal the top.

7. Place the formed dumplings on parchment paper, without letting them touch, and cover with plastic film until ready to steam. (The dumplings may be made several hours in advance.)

COOKING METHOD

8. Place the dumplings into racks of a Chinese steamer that has been lined with oiled, perforated parchment paper, arranging them so that they do not touch.

9. Heat several inches of water in the bottom of the steamer until simmering. Place the racks over the simmering water and cover to steam. If multiple racks are used, switch the top and bottom racks after 10 minutes to allow the dumplings to cook evenly. Cook for 10 minutes more.

SERVICE

10. Serve the dumplings hot, 5 dumplings per serving, accompanied with the chilled yogurt-garlic sauce. Garnish with sprigs of cilantro and mint.

Grape Leaves Stuffed with Lamb, Rice, and Herbs Dolmeh-ye Barg-e Mo

Dolmeh in Persian means "stuffed" and *barg* means "leaves." This dish is enjoyed in the Caucasus, Armenia, Turkey, Greece, and throughout the Middle East as well as in Iran. Tracing the heritage of this dish proves difficult, as it was documented in early Persian manuscripts, in medieval Arabian cookery manuals, and in the vine-growing regions of the Caucasus. Stuffed grape leaves may be served cold, but when served hot, the flavors are more pronounced. Long-grain rice is essential to the success of this dish; short- and medium-grain rice will become sticky and absorb too much of the juices. For a vegetarian version omit the meat and substitute ⅓ cup [80 mL] of pine nuts. Prepared this way, the dish is known as *dolmeh-ye barg-e mo ba senobar*.

One 16-ounce [450-g] jar grape leaves or 60 fresh tender organic grape leaves

FILLING

⅔ cup [160 mL] basmati rice

¼ cup [60 g] yellow split peas

1 teaspoon [5 mL] salt

1½ cups [360 mL] chicken stock

1½ cups [360 mL] water

½ cup [120 mL] clarified butter or vegetable oil

1 onion, thinly sliced

2 garlic cloves, minced

8 ounces [225 g] lean ground lamb

1 cup [240 mL] scallions or Chinese leeks, chopped

¼ cup [60 mL] fresh summer savory, chopped

½ cup [120 mL] fresh dill, chopped

¼ cup [60 mL] fresh tarragon, chopped

¼ cup [60 mL] fresh mint, chopped

3½ cups [840 mL] fresh parsley, chopped

½ cup [120 mL] dried barberries (see page 563) or dried cranberries, plumped and drained

1 teaspoon [5 mL] black pepper

1 teaspoon [5 mL] finely ground cinnamon

½ teaspoon [3 mL] salt

1 cup [240 mL] lamb or beef broth

⅔ cup [160 mL] sugar

⅓ cup [80 mL] red wine vinegar

⅓ cup [80 mL] fresh lime juice

Lavash bread, for service

Natural yogurt, whipped, for service

ADVANCE PREPARATION

1. If using fresh grape leaves, blanch, rinse, and drain them. If using bottled, rinse under running water and drain. Reserve.

For a vegetarian version, omit the lamb and add pine nuts and additional rice. The amounts and types of herbs may be varied to taste. Barberries have a wonderful tartness and should be sought out in Middle Eastern markets. Dried cranberries make a reasonable substitute.

PREPARATION OF THE FILLING

2. Combine the rice, split peas, salt, chicken stock, and water in a saucepan. Bring to a boil, reduce the heat to medium, and simmer 15 minutes. Drain and reserve the rice and split peas.

3. Heat 3 tablespoons [45 mL] of the clarified butter in a large skillet over medium heat and sauté the onion, garlic, and lamb for 15 minutes, or until the meat has browned and the onion has softened. Add the reserved rice mixture, scallions, herbs, barberries, pepper, cinnamon, and salt. Mix thoroughly and adjust the seasonings. Reserve. (The filling can be made one day in advance.)

PREPARATION OF THE GRAPE-LEAF ROLLS

4. Line the bottom of a baking pan with parchment paper. Trim the stems from the leaves. Place 1 tablespoon [15 mL] of the filling mixture in the center of each leaf, vein side up, and roll the leaf up, egg-roll fashion, folding in the edges as they are being rolled to seal.

5. Place, seam side down, in the baking pan. Continue until all are prepared. (The leaves may be prepared and held overnight, covered and refrigerated.)

COOKING METHOD

6. Pour in enough of the broth to come halfway up the sides of the grape leaves. Add the remaining clarified butter, distributing it evenly over the top of the rolls. Cover and bake at 400°F [205°C] for 30 minutes.

7. Mix the sugar, vinegar, and lime juice together. Remove the casserole from the oven, uncover the pan, and baste with the sugar mixture.

8. Cover again and bake for 30 minutes more. Test for tenderness and adjust seasonings. The sauce should be quite reduced.

SERVICE

9. Serve 5 stuffed grape leaves per person. Spoon the remaining sauce over the rolls. Serve with lavash bread and side dishes of whipped yogurt.

Ground Beef and Lamb Kabobs Kabab-e Kubideh

serves 12

Kabobs are a favorite Persian food, commonly sold by vendors at the bazaar. These kabobs may be made with ground beef, veal, or lamb, or a combination of any two, as here, normally molded around broad, sword-like skewers. If the specialized skewers are not available, the kabobs may be formed onto metal skewers and grilled suspended over glowing coals, that is, never coming in contact with the grill surface, or on a perforated piece of aluminum foil. Kabobs made from red meat are normally garnished with ground sumac, which adds a sour accent.

CHEF NOTES

Sumac, a powder ground from the red berries of the sumac bush (*Rhus corioria*), is popular as a souring spice throughout the Middle East. Other members of this plant family (with white berries) are poisonous; do not collect and dry your own. Sumac is placed on the table as a condiment. It is also prized as a digestive.

MEAT MIXTURE

1 large onion, diced

2 garlic cloves, bruised

1 pound [450 g] twice-ground beef sirloin, at room temperature

1 pound [450 g] twice-ground lamb shoulder, at room temperature

2 teaspoons [10 mL] salt

1 teaspoon [5 mL] ground black pepper

¼ teaspoon [1 mL] ground cinnamon

1 tablespoon [15 mL] fresh lime juice

BASTING MIXTURE

3 tablespoons [45 mL] melted butter

1 teaspoon [5 mL] fresh lime juice

½ teaspoon [3 mL] salt

¼ teaspoon [1 mL] ground black pepper

GARNISH

Lavash flat bread

½ cup [120 mL] ground sumac (see Chef Notes) or lime wedges

6 scallions, minced

1 cup [240 mL] (loosely packed) basil leaves, torn

Plain natural yogurt, whipped

ADVANCE PREPARATION

1. Combine the onion and garlic in the workbowl of a food processor and purée very fine.

2. Add the onion-garlic purée to the remaining ingredients of the meat mixture in the bowl of an electric mixer. Beat the meat mixture for several minutes, using the paddle attachment, until the mixture develops elasticity. Or stir vigorously in one direction by hand, with a wooden spoon.

3. Divide the meat mixture into 24 balls. Roll each ball into an oblong shape about 5 inches [13 cm] long, and form around a broad skewer, pressing the meat firmly to the metal. Cover

and chill until ready to cook. (The skewers can be prepared several hours in advance.)

PREPARATION OF THE BASTING MIXTURE

4. Combine the butter, lime juice, salt, and pepper and stir well. Reserve warm until needed.

COOKING METHOD

5. Heat a charcoal grill until the coals are evenly glowing and covered with ash. Suspend the skewers 3 inches [8 cm] over the coals by placing firebricks at a proper distance for the skewers to be suspended over the coals. Handle the skewers gently so the meat does not fall off, and cook the first side until the meat browns.

6. Carefully turn the skewers over and cook until the meat browns, sealing the meat to the skewers. Continue to grill the meat for 5 minutes more, turning occasionally. When done, the meat should be seared on the outside and pink, juicy, and cooked medium on the inside. Baste liberally on the last turn of grilling the skewers.

SERVICE

7. Place a piece of lavash flat bread on a plate. Carefully loosen the meat from the skewer with a knife and grasp the meat with another piece of lavash bread. Remove the meat to the plate, on top of the bread, and sprinkle with the ground sumac.

8. Cover the seasoned kabob with the bread used to remove it from the skewer. Garnish with scallion and basil. Accompany with a ramekin of yogurt. Serve 2 kabobs per person.

Lamb and Split Pea Forcemeat-Encased Stuffed Chicken Breast Kufteh-ye Tabrizi

PERSIA

serves 8

This unique dish comes from the Tabriz region of northwestern Iran, near Azerbaijan. Originally the dish was made with an egg, fruit, and nut stuffed game hen encased in a meat and pea mixture. It was then sautéed, like a large meatball. The method offered here, using a pounded chicken breast, is much easier to prepare and allows for better portion control and presentation. A pounded chicken breast is stuffed and then encased in a forcemeat mixture. This parcel is then baked and served with a pan juice–enriched tomato sauce.

CHEF NOTES

Ground beef may be substituted for the ground lamb. Different fillings may be made by varying (or omiting) the fruits and nuts listed above.

GROUND SPICE MIX (*ADVIYEH-YE MAKHLUT*):
MAKES ¼ CUP [60 mL]

2 tablespoons [30 mL] dried rose petals, ground

I tablespoon [15 mL] finely ground cinnamon

½ teaspoon [3 mL] finely ground cardamom

½ teaspoon [3 mL] coarsely ground black pepper

½ tablespoon [8 mL] finely ground dried marjoram

½ teaspoon [3 mL] grated nutmeg

¼ teaspoon [1mL] finely ground caraway

LAMB AND PEA CASING

I tablespoon [15 mL] basmati rice

½ cup [120 mL] chicken stock

½ teaspoon [3 mL] turmeric

3 ounces [85 g] dried yellow split peas, simmered 25 minutes in ½ cup [120 mL] chicken stock and puréed

8 ounces [225 g] ground lamb

½ onion, grated or puréed

1½ tablespoons [25 mL] tomato paste

I tablespoon [15 mL] chicken stock

2½ tablespoons [40 mL] leeks, minced

2 tablespoons [30 mL] fennel tops, chopped

I egg yolk, beaten

I tablespoon [15 mL] ground spice mix (see recipe above)

I teaspoon [5 mL] salt

FRUIT STUFFING

I onion, thinly sliced

2 tablespoons [30 mL] olive oil or butter

2 garlic cloves, minced

2 pitted prunes, finely chopped

3 pitted dates, finely chopped

2 dried apricots, chopped

3 tablespoons [45 mL] dried barberries (see page 563) or dried cranberries

2 tablespoons [30 mL] walnuts, chopped fine

⅛ teaspoon [0.5 mL] ground saffron, dissolved in 1 tablespoon
  [15 mL] hot chicken stock

1 egg, hard-boiled, cut into 4 slices

4 boneless chicken breast halves, pounded thin

½ cup [120 mL] chicken stock for deglazing roasting pan

2 cups [480 mL] canned or freshly made tomato sauce

1 teaspoon [5 mL] ground spice mix (see recipe above)

2 tomatoes, quartered, for garnish

Sprigs of fennel tops, for garnish

ADVANCE PREPARATION

1. Combine the spices for the ground spice mix and mix well. Store in an airtight container and reserve. (The spice mix can be made several days in advance, but it is most aromatic if used immediately.)

PREPARATION OF THE FORCEMEAT

2. Simmer the rice in the chicken stock with the turmeric for 10 minutes. Drain and reserve the rice. (The rice can be prepared one day in advance.)

3. Combine the puréed split peas, lamb, onion, tomato paste, and chicken stock in the bowl of a mixer and knead for 5 minutes.

4. Add the leeks, fennel tops, beaten egg yolk, spice mix, and salt to the meat mixture and stir well to combine. Reserve. (The forcemeat can be made one day in advance.)

PREPARATION OF THE STUFFING

5. Sauté the onion in the oil until transparent. Add the garlic and sauté an additional minute. Add the prunes, dates, apricots, barberries, walnuts, and the saffron-stock mixture. Gently simmer until the liquid has been absorbed. Reserve. (The stuffing can be made one day in advance.)

PREPARATION OF THE BUNDLES

6. Place a slice of cooked egg in the center of each pounded chicken breast half and top with a portion of stuffing. Fold the chicken breast around the stuffing to seal and arrange in

a greased roasting pan just large enough to hold all of the stuffed breasts, seam side down.

7. Carefully mold a portion of the lamb mixture around each stuffed chicken breast. (The stuffed breasts may be prepared one day in advance, wrapped tightly in plastic film, and refrigerated.)

COOKING METHOD

8. Roast the bundles at 375°F [190°C], uncovered, for 30 minutes, or until browned and the filling is hot (test with a metal skewer or thermometer). Carefully remove the breasts and keep warm.

9. Deglaze the roasting pan over a stove burner with the chicken stock, scraping to remove any solids. Add the tomato sauce and the ground spice mixture and stir well.

SERVICE

10. Ladle 2 ounces [55 g] of spiced tomato sauce onto a plate. Carefully slice a chicken bundle in half and serve one half on top of the sauce. Garnish with tomato quarters and sprigs of fennel tops.

Char-broiled Saffron Chicken Skewers Jujeh Kebab

serves 8

Kebabs are Persian in origin. In ancient times, the kebab was the food of the soldier, the herdsman, the hunter, and the nomad. Originally cooked over an open fire, the skewered meat is now marinated first for flavor and tenderness. When combined with saffron-steamed rice, it becomes Persia's national dish, *chelow kebab*. Kebabs may be paired with lavash bread (a large, thin flat bread), especially when prepared by street vendors (the bread is used to grip the meat to pull it from the skewer or is laid over the meat to keep it warm). In Iran chicken kebabs are normally made with bone-in chicken, but boneless chicken will make the dish much easier for guests to eat. Traditionally yogurt is not used in the marinade, but inclusion of a small amount will tenderize the meat and create a glaze when broiled (yogurt is a very common ingredient in Persian cooking).

MARINADE: MAKES ABOUT 2¾ CUPS [660 mL]

1 teaspoon [5 mL] ground saffron, dissolved in 2 tablespoons [30 mL] hot water

½ cup [120 mL] fresh lime juice

2 tablespoons [30 mL] olive oil

2 medium onions, grated or puréed

2 teaspoons [10 mL] salt

½ cup [120 mL] natural yogurt, whipped (optional)

1½ pounds [675 g] boneless and skinless chicken breasts, cut into 1-inch [2.5-cm] strips

32 small cherry tomatoes

16 skewers soaked in warm water 30 minutes if wooden

BASTING LIQUID

Juice of 1 lime

2 tablespoons [30 mL] melted butter

⅛ teaspoon [0.5 mL] ground saffron, dissolved in 1 tablespoon [15 mL] hot water

1 teaspoon [5 mL] ground black pepper

Lavash bread, heated and cut into serving size pieces

1 cup [240 mL] plain yogurt mixed with 1 teaspoon [5 mL] minced garlic and 1 teaspoon [5 mL] chopped cilantro

Lime wedges, for garnish

Parsley leaves, for garnish

ADVANCE PREPARATION

1. Combine the dissolved saffron, lime juice, olive oil, onions, salt, and yogurt, if using, and mix well.

2. Place the chicken pieces in a large resealable plastic bag and pour the marinade over the chicken pieces. Toss thoroughly to ensure all pieces of chicken are coated.

3. Allow to marinate for at least 8 hours, or up to 2 days, refrigerated. (If using yogurt in the marinade, allow the chicken

to marinate no more than 8 hours as marinating too long in a yogurt mixture can overtenderize the meat.)

4. Drain and reserve the marinade. Skewer the chicken onto 8 skewers. Cherry tomatoes may be placed at each end of a skewer, but it will be more practical to cook a separate skewer of tomatoes, allowing them to cook at their own rate.

PREPARATION OF THE BASTING LIQUID

5. Bring the reserved marinade to a boil for 2 minutes. Remove from the heat, add the lime juice, melted butter, dissolved saffron, and black pepper, and stir well to combine.

COOKING METHOD

6. Grill the chicken skewers over an indirect charcoal fire, turning the skewers and basting frequently, until the chicken pieces are just cooked through.

7. If cooking the tomatoes separately, add them to the grill near the end of the cooking time for the chicken. Cook the tomatoes until slightly charred and just softened. Serve immediately.

SERVICE

8. Using a piece of lavash bread, remove the meat from the skewers. Serve 2 skewers per person with 2 tablespoons [30 mL] of yogurt sauce, and garnish with lime wedges and parsley leaves.

Leek-Filled Dumplings with Lamb and Yogurt Sauces Ashak

serves 8

Ashak is a special-occasion dish in Afghanistan; it originated in the northern provinces of the country. The traditional filling in Afghanistan uses Chinese leeks (*gandana* in Afghani), but we prefer the milder and sweeter common leek. This dish also employs a drained yogurt "cheese" called *chaka*, which is made by draining plain, natural yogurt through cheesecloth for an hour, to eliminate the whey and some of the bitterness of the yogurt. Drained yogurt is usually available from Greek or Middle Eastern grocers, should you not wish to make *chaka*.

DOUGH

4 cups [960 mL] all-purpose flour

I egg

I tablespoon [15 mL] salt

2 tablespoons [30 mL] vegetable oil

About ½ cup [120 mL] water

FILLING

I pound [450 g] leeks, tender parts only, washed thoroughly, and minced

½ teaspoon [3 mL] cayenne

I teaspoon [5 mL] salt

I tablespoon [15 mL] garlic, minced

2 tablespoons [30 mL] vegetable oil

YOGURT SAUCE

3 garlic cloves, minced

I teaspoon [5 mL] salt

2 cups [480 mL] natural yogurt, drained I hour through cheesecloth

LAMB SAUCE

I large onion, finely diced

6 tablespoons [90 mL] vegetable oil

2 garlic cloves, minced

I pound [450 g] ground lamb

I tablespoon [15 mL] finely ground coriander

½ teaspoon [3 mL] ground ginger

½ teaspoon [3 mL] salt

½ teaspoon [3 mL] black pepper

I large tomato, seeded and diced

½ cup [120 mL] tomato sauce

I cup [240 mL] lamb stock

Lean ground beef sirloin or a mixture of beef and lamb may be used for the meat sauce. The meat sauce may be omitted and replaced with a tomato-eggplant sauce for a vegetarian version. Whipped, plain, natural yogurt may be used in place of the drained yogurt, but it will be less authentic. Chinese leeks can be used as a substitute for leeks and wonton or gyoza wrappers may be substituted for the home-made dough. In Afghanistan the oily layer on the meat sauce is appreciated as a necessary part of the dish, but you may remove it, as in Step 9.

7 cups [1.7 L] water

1 teaspoon [5 mL] cider vinegar

1 teaspoon [5 mL] salt

2 tablespoons [30 mL] mint, chiffonade

Fresh mint leaves, for garnish

PREPARATION

1. Put the flour in the workbowl of a food processor. Add the egg, 1 teaspoon [5 mL] of the salt, and the oil while the processor is running. Add the water slowly until a dough forms.

2. Remove the dough to a floured surface and knead until smooth, about 2 minutes. Allow the dough to rest for 1 hour. (The dough can be made one day in advance, wrapped in plastic film, and stored, refrigerated.)

PREPARATION OF THE FILLING

3. Sauté the leeks with the cayenne, salt, and garlic in the oil over medium heat until the leeks soften. Reserve. (The filling can be made one day in advance.)

PREPARATION OF THE DUMPLINGS

4. Roll out half of the dough on a lightly floured surface until very thin, keeping the remaining dough covered with plastic film. Cut the dough into 3-inch [8-cm] rounds.

5. Place 1 tablespoon of the leek filling onto a dough round, lightly brush the edge with water, and fold over into a half-moon shape. Seal the dumpling seam carefully, crimping with the back of a fork. Repeat until all dough rounds are filled.

6. Place the formed dumplings on a parchment-lined sheet pan (do not allow the dumplings to touch, or they may stick together). Repeat the process, using the second half of the dough. Cover and refrigerate until needed. (The dumplings may be made several hours in advance.)

PREPARATION OF THE SAUCES

7. Stir the minced garlic and salt into the drained yogurt. Mix well and reserve at room temperature until service.

8. For the lamb sauce, sauté the onion in vegetable oil until lightly browned. Add the garlic and ground lamb and cook

until the lamb is browned. Stir in the coriander, ginger, salt, pepper, tomato, tomato sauce, and lamb stock.

9. Bring to a boil, reduce the heat, and simmer for 30 to 40 minutes, or until thickened. An oily layer may separate to the top of the sauce. The oil may be spooned off or the sauce may be chilled and the layer removed. Reserve the sauce until service.

COOKING METHOD

10. Bring the water, vinegar, and salt to a slow boil. Lower the dumplings into the water and simmer for 10 minutes, periodically turning them to cook evenly. Gently remove the dumplings with a slotted spoon and keep warm for service.

SERVICE

11. Spread some of the yogurt sauce onto a plate. Add 4 dumplings and top with additional yogurt sauce.

12. Sprinkle with mint and ladle some of the meat sauce over. Garnish with fresh mint leaves. Serve immediately.

Middle East

Egypt, Syria,

Lebanon, Jordan,

Israel, Palestine;

Iraq, and the

Gulf States

Lebanese Steak Tartare
Habrah Nayeh (Lahm Ba'ar Nayeh)

Lamb, Pomegranate, and Mint Pizza
Lahem bil Ajeen

Lamb and Feta Cheese Filled Pastries
Sambusak bil-Areesh

Pork Brochettes with Sour Plum Sauce
Lahm Meshwi ma' Salat Khoukh

Aromatic Sweetbread Morsels
Halaweyaat

Stuffed Shrimp Balls in Tamarind Sauce
Chebeh Rubyan

Fish Balls Stuffed with Apricots and Dates
Kibbeh Samak

ALTHOUGH SOME CULINARY differences can be found in the Middle East, which is steeped in a common history, there is a certain homogeneity to the cuisine. The boundaries of the individual countries are more political than geographical. The countries have been grouped into five distinct regions: Egypt; Syria, Lebanon, and Jordan; Israel and Palestine; Iraq; and the Gulf States. Historically, Syria, Lebanon, Jordan, Israel, and parts of Iraq and Turkey were designated the Fertile Crescent.

The ancient Egyptians developed agriculture in the Nile River valley. They developed a strain of wheat that could be thrashed without heating, thus preserving the unique properties so important to the proper texture of bread. They captured wild yeast and used its fermentation properties to leaven breads and brew beer.

Areas of northern Mesopotamia and parts of Greater Syria are known to have supported crop cultivation and animal husbandry. Mesopotamia, the land between the Tigris and Euphrates rivers, the site of present-day Iraq, had a sophisticated cuisine—one based not on sustenance but on complex flavors and artistry.

The Sumerians of southern Mesopotamia used cuneiform, an early form of writing, and ancient tablets to document recipes for stuffing intestinal casings with meat (sausages), preparing shellfish and fish, and using staple grains, barley, millet, and wheat. The use of herbs and spices, such as mint, cumin, and coriander, was documented as well; these are still at the core of modern Middle Eastern flavorings. Olive and sesame oils were mentioned in the texts as cooking oils; they are still modern Middle Eastern cooking methods. Butter was clarified to preserve it, and milk was soured to produce cheese. Preservation methods documented in the ancient texts include drying, smoking, and salting. The Mesopotamians had a fondness for grilling and roasting over coals, as well as for slow cooking or stewing. Both of these cooking methods are typical of the modern cooking methods of the entire region, including Iran, India, and Central Asia. The baking of unleavened bread is Mesopotamian in origin, and the name of the oven, *tinuru*, became the *tanoor* of Persia, the *tandoor* of India, and the *tandir* of Central Asia.

The Fertile Crescent had a mostly vegetarian cuisine. Its staple was bread, sometimes made from wheat, although barley was more often the grain of the poor. In a diet augmented by legumes, flavoring came from the use of coriander, mint, mustard, anise, cumin, and capers. Onions, radishes, leeks, and cucumbers were common vegetables. One of the important staples (in addition to wheat and wine) was olives, which provided dishes with richness and flavor, and which were made into cooking oil. Fruits, such as grapes, dates, pomegranates, and figs, and nuts were eaten in quantity. The cuisine was influenced by the many conquerors who came and went, including the Egyptians, Babylonians, Greeks, Persians, Romans, Arabs, and the Crusaders.

The Arabs have had a most profound influence on the cuisine of the Middle East and that of the entire Mediterranean region, northern Africa, and Spain. Following the death of the prophet Mohammed, the Arabs moved across this whole area, and the Islamic empire became centered in what is now Iraq. A vast crossroads, it was home to the exchange of foods between the Middle East, China, and the Mediterranean. As such, it contributed to a European cooking revolution. Chinese cooking techniques were brought to the Middle East, and various fruits and vegetables were introduced predominantly into Spain and then filtered into Europe. Meanwhile, the Crusades brought the influence of European cookery to the Middle East.

The Ottoman Turks eventually conquered most of the Middle East and influenced the region for centuries. It was the defeat of Turkey at the end of World War I that led to the breakup of the Ottoman Empire and the formation of Syria, Lebanon, Trans-Jordan, and Palestine.

Occupied by France until 1946, Lebanon became an independent country in 1941. French influence on Lebanese cooking methods was significant, and Lebanese cuisine is considered the most refined in the Middle East, mostly due to the brief period of French domination. Because of the varied geography of Lebanon and, to a lesser extent, Syria and Jordan, there are significant variations in temperature, rainfall, and soil that allow for vast amounts of crops to be grown. Apples and pears are cultivated at high altitudes. Below that are found orchards of other fruit trees, including cherries, apricots, plums, and peaches, and of nut trees, such as walnuts and hazelnuts. At a slightly lower altitude grow almonds, grapes, olives, and figs. Along the coastal plains vegetables, dates, citrus, bananas, and sugarcane flourish. The Bekaa valley, considered the nation's breadbasket, has one of the world's most fertile soils. Lebanese cuisine is different from most of the neighboring countries because Lebanon has no desert and, therefore, no nomadic population. Secondly, there is a strong Christian influence in Lebanon, with different eating traditions. Pork, for example, is eaten in Lebanon by the fairly significant non-Muslim population.

The Lebanese engage in the tradition of serving *mezze*, as do many of the countries of this region. Specialties include savory pastries (*al-muajjanat*) filled with cheese, spinach, or minced meats and *kibbeh*, that is, highly seasoned mixtures of minced lamb, bulgur, and onion. Fresh mint and basil are often added for fragrance. *Tabbouleh*, a parsley and bulgur salad known in the United States and around the world, is found in Syria and Jordan, as well as in Lebanon. The region is also known for using fresh mint and parsley, cinnamon and allspice, *tahini* (sesame seed paste), bulgur rice, yogurt, fruity olive oils, and eggplant. A popular spice blend that is quite versatile is called *zaatar* (*za'tar, za'atar*). While the spice blend varies from region to region, it usually includes sumac and thyme. Sesame seeds are often added and when this spice mix is blended with olive oil, it is spread before baking or used as a dip with freshly baked bread. *Zaatar* is a name that also refers to the wild thyme itself or the bread baked with the spice mix. Orange and rose waters are common flavorings. Syrians have a particular fondness for chicken and prepare it as kebabs, simply roasted, and as a stuffing for *kibbeh*. The Syrians make cheese from dried and salted yogurt.

Iraqi cuisine is strongly influenced by Persian cooking. After Damascus, Baghdad became the center of Arabic culture and trade, bringing the Spice Route through Iraq. The Ottoman Turks followed the Mongols and occupied the region, further changing its eating habits. Unlike the Syrians and Jordanians, Iraqis love potatoes, including them in dishes whenever they are in season. Rice dishes (basmati rice from Pakistan is favored) are much like those found in Persia, with a bit of spice from the Gulf region added for an Iraqi "twist." Iraqis are not particularly fond of soups. They combine allspice with hot chile and paprika in a favorite spice mix, and they use dried lime as do those in the Gulf States (called *loomi* in the Gulf). Iraqis call dried lime *noomi Basra*, for the Gulf port that ships the dried limes to Iraq. Lamb, chicken, and beef are favorite meats, and watercress and flat-leaf parsley are essential greens.

The Gulf States include the United Arab Emirates, Kuwait, Saudi Arabia, Bahrain, Oman, and Qatar. Boiled meat served over spiced rice is classic Bedouin fare, but is not so common in the cities. Gulf Arabs are fond of skewered meats, both ground and cubed. Rice is highly seasoned with cardamom, cumin, nutmeg, clove, cinnamon, and ginger, and the spice mix known as *baharat* is used to flavor soups, fish, meat, and rice dishes. Gulf fish and shellfish are available year round and find their way into Gulf cuisine more than in any other region of the Middle East, often cooked over coals. *Loomi*, ground or used whole, imparts a unique flavor to Gulf States dishes. Gulf cucumbers are loved by all in this region. Onions are used in most Gulf dishes and tamarind is still relied on for tartness, although the tomato is slowly making inroads as a replacement for tamarind.

Egyptian cuisine is the most ancient of the region. Bread is the most important element in the Egyptian diet, and rightly so since the Egyptians discovered bread making and the use of yeast as leavening. The ancient Greek name for Egyptians translates as "bread eaters." The grains of ancient Egypt are still the staples of their diet today—barley, millet, and wheat. Fava beans are a popular legume of this region and are made into a favorite purée called *ful Medamis*. The cuisine of Israel and Palestine is well documented. Archeological digs at Jericho indicate villages supported by wheat crops and the cultivation of barley on riverbanks. Records show that King Solomon served roast partridge, fattened goose liver, and stews enriched with marrow and onions and spiced with coriander and garlic. Until the rise of Islam, the cuisine of the region was that of the Middle East as a whole. Then religious influences on the cuisine became entrenched. Both Jews and Muslims refrain from eating pork. Lamb and goat become the meats of choice. Foods unique to Israel developed as strict dietary laws evolved. Since dairy products and meat may not be eaten together, for example, many vegetable dishes that incorporate dairy products can be found in Israel. Stews are popular, since honoring the Sabbath forbids the act of lighting a stove or working, and cooking is work. Slow cooking allows for a stew to be placed on the fire before Sabbath on Friday sundown and simmered slowly until the end of the next day. Modern Israeli cuisine is predominantly Mediterranean, with Arabic influences. Olives, dates, figs, barley, wheat, pomegranates, and grapes form the basis of many of its dishes. Immigration to Israel and the establishment of the nation of Israel in 1948 brought the cuisines of Eastern and Central Europe to the Middle East.

Lebanese Steak Tartare Habrah Nayeh (Lahm Ba'ar Nayeh)

serves 8

The tradition of eating raw meat is an ancient one in the Middle East. Raw lamb mixed with bulgur wheat, or *kibbeh nayeh*, is as popular as the cooked version (*kibbeh rass*). This beef dish is considered a luxury, as meat, especially beef, is seldom eaten. Historically, cattle and oxen were too valuable as beasts of burden to be slaughtered for food. Grazing land is at a premium in this part of the world as well, but modern transportation methods are providing urban areas with excellent beef, and it is becoming increasingly popular throughout the Middle East.

CHEF NOTES

This dish may also be made with very finely trimmed leg of lamb. The Arabic word *habrah* refers to "well-trimmed raw meat, with no fat." *Lahm ba'ar* refers specifically to beef. If mincing by hand, the beef tenderloin will benefit by chilling to a point just short of freezing.

I large red onion, diced

2 garlic cloves, minced fine

I ½ pounds [675 g] beef tenderloin, finely minced

I tablespoon [15 mL] ground cinnamon

I tablespoon [15 mL] ground allspice

I teaspoon [5 mL] coarsely ground black pepper

Salt to taste

3 tablespoons [90 mL] very finely minced mint leaves

I ½ tablespoons [25 mL] extra virgin olive oil

I ½ tablespoons [25 mL] pine nuts

3 scallions, minced

Sprigs of mint, for garnish

Crusty country bread or pita bread, for serving

ADVANCE PREPARATION

1. All advance preparation may be found in the ingredient list.

PREPARATION OF THE TARTARE

2. Process the onion and garlic in a small food processor until very finely minced. Add the beef, cinnamon, allspice, pepper, and salt. Process until the mixture is very smooth.

3. Seal tightly in plastic film and chill until very cold.

SERVICE

4. Stir in the mint just prior to service, or the mint will discolor, and portion the meat into 3-ounce [85-g] servings. Flatten each portion of the meat into a thin cake.

5. Using a fingertip or the back of a small spoon, make several small indentations on the surface of the tartare. Drizzle a bit of olive oil into the depressions, then scatter the pine nuts over.

6. Garnish with scallions and mint sprigs. Serve with crusty bread or pita bread.

Lamb, Pomegranate, and Mint Pizza Lahem bil Ajeen

Makes 8 individual pizzas

These pies are enjoyed throughout the Middle East and are considered by most culinary scholars to be the original pizza. Probably originating in Syria or Lebanon, some believe that the Armenians developed the dish. Armenian bakers dominated the bakery trade in Syria for hundreds of years, and it is likely they adopted the dish from their host country and carried it back to Turkey and Armenia. Middle Eastern Jews emigrating to the south of Rome could have been responsible for the migration of this dish to Italy. (Anatolians emigrating to Naples after the fall of Byzantium is another possibility.) Regardless, we have this region of the world to thank for the luscious pizza enjoyed by all.

TOPPING

3 onions, minced

2 tablespoons [30 mL] olive oil

1½ pounds [675 g] ground lamb

2 large tomatoes, seeded, chopped, and drained

3 tablespoons [45 mL] tomato paste

⅓ cup [80 mL] parsley, minced

2 tablespoons [30 mL] mint leaves, chiffonade

¼ cup [60 mL] pine nuts, toasted

1 tablespoon [15 mL] pomegranate molasses or plain molasses

1 tablespoon [15 mL] fresh lemon juice

½ tablespoon [8 mL] Lebanese spice mix (see Chef Notes)

Salt and black pepper to taste

½ teaspoon [3 mL] cayenne (optional)

Whipped yogurt, for garnish

DOUGH

2 cups [480 mL] warm water

½ teaspoon [3 mL] sugar

1 tablespoon [15 mL] active dry yeast

6 to 8 cups [1.4 to 1.9 L] bread flour, plus more for kneading

1 teaspoon [5 mL] salt

¼ cup [60 mL] olive oil

ADVANCE PREPARATION

1. Sauté the onions in the oil until just translucent. Drain off excess oil and allow to cool.

2. Mix the ground lamb, tomatoes, and tomato paste together. Add the onions and all the other topping ingredients and stir well to combine. Adjust seasonings and reserve. (The topping can be made 1 day in advance and stored refrigerated.)

These pizzas may be made with beef or veal instead of lamb. *Labneh* cheese, made by draining plain natural yogurt through suspended cheesecloth overnight, may be substituted for the tomatoes and tomato paste. (Use I quart [I L] yogurt for this recipe.) Sheep's milk feta or Greek-style kasseri cheese may be used for an additional topping. Lebanese spice mix varies from kitchen to kitchen; it is really a matter of personal taste. Here is a common mixture from which to start. Other spices to consider adding are allspice, coriander, and cumin.

Lebanese Spice Mix

Makes approximately 2 tablespoons [30 mL]

I tablespoon [15 mL] ground cinnamon

I teaspoon [5 mL] grated nutmeg

I teaspoon [5 mL] ground cardamom

½ teaspoon [3 mL] ground cloves

½ teaspoon [3 mL] ground black pepper

¼ teaspoon [1 mL] cayenne (optional)

Thoroughly mix together all the ingredients and store in a sealed glass jar in a cool, dry place.

PREPARATION OF THE DOUGH

3. Add the warm water to a warmed bowl. Dissolve the sugar in the warm water and sprinkle the yeast over the surface. Do not stir. Allow to stand 10 minutes, then stir to dissolve the yeast. Stir in about 1 cup [240 mL] of the flour and allow to stand for 10 minutes.

4. Add the salt and oil and stir in the remaining flour to form a smooth dough. Turn out onto a floured surface and knead 10 minutes, or until smooth and elastic, sprinkling with additional flour to prevent sticking as the dough is worked.

5. Place the dough in an oiled resealable plastic bag, rotating the dough to lightly oil all surfaces. Place in a warm, draft-free spot until doubled in volume, about 1 to 1½ hours, depending on temperature and location. The dough may be refrigerated overnight, instead of leaving it out to rise. Remove it about 1 hour and allow it to come to room temperature before proceeding.

6. Punch the dough down and divide into eight 5-ounce [140-g] portions, forming each into a ball. Cover the balls and allow to rest 15 minutes.

7. Roll out the dough portions into rounds about 5 to 6 inches [13 to 15 cm] in diameter. Place the rolled rounds on parchment-lined baking sheets and reserve, covered.

COOKING METHOD

8. Top each round with some of the topping mixture, spreading it to the edge of the dough with a spatula. Bake at 450°F [230°C] for 10 minutes or until the crust is lightly browned.

SERVICE

9. Cut each pizza into quarters and using a squeeze bottle, garnish with stripes of whipped yogurt. Serve immediately.

Lamb and Feta Cheese Filled Pastries Sambusak bil-Areesh

serves 12

Sambusak are enjoyed throughout the Middle East, and are found on the table as appetizers (*mezze*) and sold by street vendors. The three traditional fillings are a mixture of meat and pine nuts, cheese, and greens with pine nuts. When formed into a triangular shape, they are called *fatayer*. *Sambusak* may be baked or fried. The method for preparing *sambusak* is thought to be the origin of Cornish pasties and English meat pies, brought back to Britain after the Crusades.

PASTRY: MAKES ABOUT SIXTY 3-INCH [8-CM] CIRCLES

½ cup [120 mL] butter, melted

½ cup [120 mL] olive oil

½ cup [120 mL] warm water

¼ teaspoon [1 mL] salt

⅛ teaspoon [0.5 mL] garlic powder

3½ cups [840 mL] flour

CHEESE FILLING: MAKES ENOUGH TO FILL 24 TO 30 PASTRIES

1 large egg, beaten slightly

1 tablespoon [15 mL] butter

7 ounces [200 g] small curd cottage cheese, drained of as much liquid as possible

5 ounces [140 g] feta cheese, grated

2 tablespoons [30 mL] parsley, chopped

2 tablespoons [30 mL] mint leaves, chiffonade

2 scallions, very finely minced

¼ teaspoon [1 mL] ground cinnamon

1 teaspoon [5 mL] ground allspice

½ teaspoon [3 mL] black pepper

Pinch of cayenne

Salt to taste

MEAT FILLING: MAKES ENOUGH TO FILL 24 TO 30 PASTRIES

1 tablespoon [15 mL] olive oil

1 onion, minced

2 garlic cloves, minced

12 ounces [340 g] ground lamb

1 ripe tomato, skinned, seeded, and chopped

3 tablespoons [45 mL] pine nuts, toasted and coarsely chopped

Salt and black pepper to taste

1 tablespoon [15 mL] Lebanese spice mix (see page 358)

1 tablespoon [15 mL] chopped parsley

2 tablespoons [30 mL] chopped mint

Any type of pie crust pastry dough will work for this dish, but the traditional dough offers the most authentic flavor and provides an excellent texture. To make the version with greens, sauté I minced small onion and 2 minced garlic cloves in 2 tablespoons [30 mL] olive oil. Add a chiffonade of 8 ounces [225 g] spinach or chard leaves. Stir until just wilted. Remove from the heat and add salt and pepper to taste, I tablespoon [15 mL] ground sumac, I tablespoon [15 mL] toasted pine nuts, and the juice of ½ lemon. To fold these pastries bring three sides of a dough circle over the filling to form a triangle. Pinch the seams to seal in the filling, forming a Y-shape seam. The finished pastry will resemble a tricornered hat. Bake as for the other pastries. When made in this shape, they are called *fatayer*.

I teaspoon [5 mL] sugar

I tablespoon [15 mL] fresh lemon juice

I egg, lightly beaten

Sesame seeds (optional)

ADVANCE PREPARATION

1. Combine the butter and oil, then stir in the water.

2. Sift the salt, garlic powder, and flour together, and slowly add the flour mixture to the liquid, mixing by hand (a bit more or less of the flour mixture may be required). Mix the dough only enough to form a soft, rather oily dough. Allow to rest at room temperature for 30 minutes. (The pastry can be made 1 day in advance, wrapped in plastic film, and stored in the refrigerator.)

PREPARATION OF THE FILLINGS

3. For the cheese filling, soft-scramble the egg in the butter and place in a large bowl, add the remaining cheese filling ingredients, and stir well. Adjust seasonings and chill the mixture until ready to use.

4. For the meat filling, heat the oil in a skillet over medium heat. Sauté the onion and garlic to soften. Add the ground lamb and sauté to break up the meat and brown evenly.

5. Stir in the tomato, pine nuts, salt and pepper, spice mix, parsley, mint, and sugar. Cook for 3 minutes more. Remove from the heat and stir in the lemon juice. Cool and reserve.

PREPARATION OF THE FILLED PASTRIES

6. On a lightly floured surface, roll the dough out ⅛ inch [3 mm] thick. Cut the dough into 3-inch [8-cm] circles.

7. To fill and fold the pastries, place a heaping teaspoon [6 mL] of a filling in the center of a dough circle. Moisten the edge lightly with beaten egg and fold the dough over to form a half-moon shape. Continue until all the pastries are filled.

8. Seal the edges with the tines of a fork and place on a baking sheet lined with parchment paper. Brush the top of the pastries with beaten egg. Sprinkle the top with sesame seeds, if desired.

9. Bake the filled pastries at 350°F [175°C] for 20 minutes, or until golden brown. (The baked pastries may be frozen or refrigerated and reheated for service.)

SERVICE

10. Serve 4 pastries per person, warm or at room temperature.

Pork Brochettes with Sour Plum Sauce Lahm Meshwi ma' Salat Khoukh

serves 8

Sour plums are merely plums that have not completely ripened. Pork is forbidden by Islamic and Jewish dietary laws but is relished by Christians in the Middle East. Plums are grown throughout the region and this recipe is based on ancient culinary texts. The sour plums are cooked with rose water, ginger, and spices to make a flavorful, exotic sauce.

CHEF NOTES

This preparation works well with poultry and veal. When using veal, cook until medium rare.

PLUM SAUCE: MAKES ABOUT 1½ CUPS [360 mL]

1½ pounds [675 g] fresh sour plums, pitted and chopped

½ cup [120 mL] chicken stock

1 tablespoon [15 mL] pomegranate molasses

5 tablespoons [75 mL] sugar

½ teaspoon [3 mL] grated ginger

½ teaspoon [3 mL] rose water

Pinch of ground cardamom

Pinch of ground allspice

2 tablespoons [30 mL] chopped toasted almonds

Salt and ground black pepper to taste

PORK

1½ pounds [675 g] boneless pork loin or shoulder, cut into ½-inch [1-cm] cubes

Light sprinkling of Lebanese spice mix (see page 358)

Salt and ground black pepper to taste

8 metal skewers

2 scallions, minced, for garnish

Mint leaves, for garnish

Chopped toasted almonds, for garnish

ADVANCE PREPARATION

1. Place the plums, stock, and pomegranate molasses in a nonreactive pan and bring to a boil. Reduce to a simmer and cook about 15 minutes, or until the plums are tender.

2. Pit the plums, remove them to the workbowl of a food processor, and pulse to purée. Pass the purée through a sieve and return it to the saucepan.

3. Add the sugar, ginger, rose water, cardamom, and allspice and simmer 10 minutes more, or until thickened. Stir in the almonds, adjust seasonings, and reserve. (The plum sauce can be made 1 day in advance.)

PREPARATION OF THE PORK

4. Toss the pork cubes with the spice mix and salt and pepper. Allow to marinate 1 hour.

COOKING METHOD

5. Skewer the pork and cook 3 to 4 inches [8 to 10 cm] above an indirect charcoal grill, turning frequently, until well browned and cooked through.

SERVICE

6. Remove the meat from the skewers onto plates and drizzle some of the plum sauce over the cubes of pork. Sprinkle lightly with scallions, mint leaves, and almonds.

Aromatic Sweetbread Morsels Halaweyaat

serves 8

Sweetbreads, unlike most organ meats, are surprisingly popular as a restaurant menu item. Sweetbreads are thymus glands from calves or lambs, with lamb sweetbreads being preferred in the Middle East (they may be more difficult to obtain in the United States). This recipe uses veal sweetbreads, easily obtainable from a meat purveyor.

CHEF NOTES

Lamb sweetbreads may be available fresh during the spring and early summer, while veal sweetbreads may be available fresh in late winter through spring. Both should be available frozen year round.

1½ pounds [675 g] veal sweetbreads or lamb sweetbreads if available

2 teaspoons [10 mL] salt, dissolved in 4 cups [960 mL] cold water

½ teaspoon [3 mL] ground cinnamon

½ teaspoon [3 mL] sweet paprika

¼ teaspoon [1 mL] ground cardamom

¼ teaspoon [1 mL] ground allspice

¼ teaspoon [1 mL] cayenne

1½ tablespoons [25 mL] unsalted butter

1½ tablespoons [25 mL] olive oil

2 cups [480 mL] flour seasoned with ½ teaspoon [3 mL] garlic powder

Salt and ground white pepper to taste

Mixed field greens, for service

Juice of 2 lemons

Minced parsley, for garnish

Lemon wedges, for garnish

ADVANCE PREPARATION

1. Place the sweetbreads in the salted cold water and refrigerate for 1½ hours. Drain and discard the water. Bring enough lightly salted water to cover the sweetbreads to a boil and add the sweetbreads. Lower the heat and simmer for 5 minutes.

2. Drain the sweetbreads and cool under cold running water. Pat dry. Remove any tough outer membranes or vessels. (The sweetbreads may be prepared to this point 1 day in advance and stored in the refrigerator.)

3. Mix the cinnamon, paprika, cardamom, allspice, and cayenne together.

COOKING METHOD

4. Melt the butter with the olive oil in a skillet over medium heat. Dust the sweetbreads lightly in the seasoned flour and add to the skillet.

5. Season the sweetbreads with the salt and white pepper and the spice mixture. Cook 3 minutes and turn the sweetbreads.

Repeat seasoning and cook 3 minutes more, or until they are firm and are lightly browned. Reserve.

6. Line a plate with field greens. Top with 3 ounces [85 g] sautéed sweetbreads.

7. Deglaze the sauté pan with the lemon juice and scrape the pan to loosen the browned bits. Spoon a small amount of the pan juices over the top of the sweetbreads and sprinkle with parsley. Serve with lemon wedges.

Stuffed Shrimp Balls in Tamarind Sauce Chebeh Rubyan

serves 8

The Gulf States are one region of the Middle East that has plentiful access to shrimp and seafood. The people of this region are quite fond of this dish of shrimp balls stuffed with onion and spices and simmered in tamarind broth. It is normally served with *muhammar*, a sweetened, saffron-scented rice, which balances perfectly with the rich, slightly sour sauce. A unique ingredient used is *loomi* (dried lime). *Loomi* can be found in Middle Eastern markets, but if unavailable, it can be made (see Chef Notes), or substitute the grated zest of ½ lemon for ½ teaspoon [3 mL] of ground *loomi*.

SHRIMP BALLS: MAKES THIRTY-TWO 1-OUNCE [30-g] BALLS

2 pounds [900 g] shrimp, shelled and deveined

¼ cup [60 mL] cilantro leaves and stems, chopped

½ teaspoon [3 mL] turmeric

½ teaspoon [3 mL] ground dried lime (*loomi*) or grated zest of ½ lemon or lime

¾ cup [180 mL] raw basmati rice, ground

1 teaspoon [5 mL] salt

STUFFING

1 large onion, diced fine

2 tablespoons [30 mL] *ghee* or olive oil

1 teaspoon [5 mL] baharat spice mix (see Chef Notes)

½ teaspoon [3 mL] ground dried lime (*loomi*) or grated zest of ½ lemon or sour lime

SAUCE

¼ cup [60 mL] tamarind pulp

1 cup [240 mL] hot water

1 cup [240 mL] rich chicken stock, hot

1 small onion, minced

1 tablespoon [15 mL] *ghee* or olive oil

1 cup [240 mL] tomatoes, peeled, seeded, and chopped

1 teaspoon [5 mL] baharat spice mix

½ teaspoon [3 mL] hot chile pepper or more to taste, minced

2 teaspoons [10 mL] sugar

Salt to taste

POACHING

2 cups [480 mL] rich chicken stock

GARNISH

Small timbales of sweetened saffron rice (*muhammar* rice) (see Chef Notes)

Sprigs of cilantro

Lime zest

1. Combine all of the ingredients for the shrimp balls in the workbowl of a food processor and process to a smooth paste. Reserve chilled. (The shrimp ball paste can be made one day in advance and stored in the refrigerator.)

PREPARATION OF THE STUFFING

2. Gently sauté the onion in *ghee* or olive oil until transparent. Stir in the baharat and dried lime. Reserve. (The stuffing can be made one day in advance.)

PREPARATION OF THE SAUCE

3. Dissolve the tamarind pulp in a mixture of the water and stock and allow to soak 10 minutes. Sieve this mixture, reserving the tamarind stock.

4. Sauté the onion in *ghee* in a large skillet until transparent. Add the tomato, baharat, spice mix chile, sugar, and salt and bring to a boil.

5. Reduce the heat to a simmer, cover, and gently cook the sauce for 20 minutes. (The sauce can be made one day in advance.)

PREPARATION OF THE STUFFED SHRIMP BALLS

6. Moisten your hands and place 1 tablespoon [15 mL] of the shrimp paste in the palm. Place 1 teaspoon [5 mL] of the onion stuffing in the center of the shrimp paste and mold the paste around the stuffing. Repeat until all the balls are formed.

COOKING METHOD

7. Heat the chicken stock to a simmer. Gently slip the stuffed shrimp balls into the simmering liquid and cook gently for 5 minutes, turning once.

8. Heat the sauce to a simmer and add the poached shrimp balls. Cook over low heat for 5 minutes.

SERVICE

9. Serve 4 shrimp balls per person, topped with the sauce and accompanied by a timbale of sweetened saffron rice. Garnish with cilantro sprigs and lime zest.

Loomi

Place whole, small limes in water to cover and add 1 tablespoon [15 mL] salt. Boil rapidly for 5 minutes. Drain and dry in a warm oven for 3 to 4 days, or until completely dry. Grind in a spice mill or food processor.

Baharat Spice Mix

Makes ½ cup [120 mL]

Combine the following and dry-toast in a skillet:

2 tablespoons [30 mL] black peppercorns

1 tablespoon [15 mL] coriander seeds

1 tablespoon [15 mL] cassia bark or stick cinnamon

1 tablespoon [15 mL] cloves

4 teaspoons [60 mL] cumin seeds

½ teaspoon [3 mL] cardamom seeds

1 whole nutmeg, freshly grated

2 tablespoons [30 mL] paprika

Combine the peppercorns, coriander, cassia, cloves, cumin, and cardamom and toast them in a dry skillet. Allow to cool. Grind the spices together. Add the nutmeg and paprika and mix well. Store in a glass jar in a cool, dark place.

Sweetened Saffron Rice (*Muhammar* Rice)

Makes 6 cups [1.4 L]

¼ teaspoon [1 mL] saffron threads

3 cardamom pods, cracked

2 tablespoons [30 mL] rose water, hot

2 cups [480 g] basmati rice

6 cups [1.4 L] water

1 tablespoon [15 mL] salt

½ cup [120 mL] sugar or honey

¼ cup [60 mL] ghee

Steep the saffron threads and cardamom pods in the rose water for at least 15 minutes. Cook the rice in the water with the salt for 8 minutes. Drain and reserve the rice. Pour the sugar or honey over the hot rice and heat the *ghee* in a pan. Add the sweetened rice, pour the rose-water mixture over the top, and poke 3 holes in the rice with the end of a wooden spoon. Cook, tightly covered, over low heat for 25 minutes or until tender.

Fish Balls Stuffed with Apricots and Dates Kibbeh Samak

LEBANON

serves 8

This dish is a specialty of the southern Lebanese fishing port towns of Sidon and Tyre. It is quite popular, prepared at home or in restaurants as part of an array of appetizers (*mezze*) and is sold on the street by vendors. Although a non-traditional pairing, fish balls go well with a tangy, piquant Saudi Arabian hot sauce (*dugus*).

CHEF NOTES

Once fried, the fish balls may be stored frozen or refrigerated until needed. The uncooked fish balls may be refrigerated, covered, for several hours before cooking. Be sure to use fine bulgur when making this recipe.

HOT SAUCE: MAKES 2 CUPS [480 mL]

Juice of 2 lemons

2 large, ripe tomatoes, diced

3 garlic cloves, minced

½ teaspoon [3 mL] salt

2 teaspoons [10 mL] cider vinegar

2 large jalapeño chiles, minced (seeds and ribs removed for less piquancy)

2 tablespoons [30 mL] flat-leaf parsley, chopped

BULGUR MIXTURE: (*KIBBEH*)

12 ounces [340 g] white fish fillets, coarsely chopped

2 tablespoons [30 mL] cilantro leaves and stems, chopped

Grated zest of ½ orange

¼ teaspoon [1 mL] ground cinnamon

1 tablespoon [15 mL] lemon juice

½ onion, peeled and quartered

8 ounces [225 g] fine bulgur, rinsed thoroughly under cold water and squeezed of as much water as possible

1 egg

1 egg yolk

Salt and black pepper to taste

FILLING

1 tablespoon [15 mL] butter or olive oil

1 large onion, minced

3 tablespoons [45 mL] cilantro leaves and stems, minced

⅓ cup [80 mL] dried apricots, diced fine

2 tablespoons [30 mL] pitted dried dates, diced fine

¼ teaspoon [1 mL] white pepper

Vegetable oil, for deep-frying

Sprigs of cilantro, for garnish

369 | Middle East

1. Combine all of the hot sauce ingredients in a nonreactive bowl and mix well. Refrigerate at least 2 hours before serving to allow flavors to meld. (The sauce can be made one day in advance.)

PREPARATION OF THE BULGUR MIXTURE

2. Pulse the fish carefully in a food processor. Do not purée the fish. Remove the fish.

3. Add the cilantro, orange zest, cinnamon, lemon juice, and onion to the food processor and purée. Add the bulgur, egg, egg yolk, and salt and pepper to taste, and pulse to incorporate.

4. Combine this mixture with the reserved fish, stirring in one direction. Cover and chill thoroughly.

PREPARATION OF THE FILLING

5. Heat the butter or oil in a skillet over medium heat and sauté the onion until transparent but not browned. Stir in the cilantro, apricots, dates, and white pepper and mix well. Allow to cool to room temperature. Reserve. (The filling can be made one day in advance.)

ASSEMBLING THE FISH BALLS

6. Divide the filling into 24 portions. Moisten your hands with cold water and form the bulgur mixture into 24 small balls.

7. Using a moistened finger, form a cavity in each fish ball. Stuff each ball with filling and reshape the balls to enclose the filling. Reserve, chilled and covered, until ready to fry.

COOKING METHOD

8. Heat the oil to 365°F [185°C] and deep-fry the balls, in batches, until golden brown. Remove and drain on paper towels. Serve warm or at room temperature.

SERVICE

9. Serve each guest 3 fish balls, accompanied with a small ramekin of hot sauce. Garnish with cilantro sprigs.

Regional Africa

Rare Cooked Beef Tartare
Kitfo Leb Leb

Grilled Veal Kebabs with Apricot-Curry Glaze
Sosaties

Sweet Potato Pastry Turnovers with Grilled Tuna and Chile
Pastel com Diabo Dentro

Yam and Fish Cakes with Red Chile Sauce
Iyan Ehan Akara Ata

Grilled Prawns with Chile-Lemon Glaze
Camarão Grelhado Piri Piri

Fried Oysters with Chile, Smoked Shrimp, and Peanut Sauce
Huitres Azi Dessi

Pumpkin Fritters with Sweet-Hot Sauce
Pampoenkoedes Blatjang

Plantain and Banana Griddle Cakes with Fried Pepper Sauce
Kyekyire Krakro Atadindin

TOO OFTEN WE think of Africa as one large country, when in fact it is the second largest continent, home to 12 percent of the world's population living in fifty-four nations. Within these nations there are almost a thousand different cultural and linguistic groups. The countries of Morocco, Algeria, Tunisia, and Libya are included in a separate chapter entitled North Africa. (Egypt is in the Middle East chapter.)

Africa claims the longest human history on Earth, at least 4 million years. Over 20,000 years ago villages were settled by the water's edge and fish and tubers were harvested. Millet, sorghum, rice and t'eff are some of the earliest grains to be harvested by man, creating cuisines based on a staple diet. The concept of crop cultivation seems to have come to Africa by way of Southwestern Asia 6,000 years ago, allowing for the great Egyptian civilization to evolve some 2,500 years later.

European colonialism, which began in the fifteenth century, had a lasting effect on the cuisines of Africa. This influence started with the Portuguese exploration of the coasts of Africa in search of a route to India. By 1499 Vasco da Gama reached India and coastal trading stations soon followed. The Dutch, French, and English explorations of the interior of Africa during the eighteenth and nineteenth centuries added to the mystique of the so-called Dark Continent. The French colonized much of western Africa, while the sphere of influence of the British was in eastern and southern Africa. Portugal settled along both the west and east coasts of southern Africa, as did the Dutch. The Spanish had possessions on the northern coast, as did the Italians and Germans; the Belgians occupied the Congo and by 1912 all of Africa (except Ethiopia and Liberia) was under the control of Europeans.

Little is known of the cuisines of Africa before European colonization, but the indigenous foods, such as pumpkins, squashes, okra, peanuts (groundnuts), and black-eyed peas, give us insight into the diet. Grains, varying by the type of grain, determined by climactic conditions, formed the staple of the diet. Often cooked as a porridge or fritter, the grain was supplemented by a vegetable stew, occasionally with meat added. Dishes of this type are still the most common meal eaten across Africa. Indigenous vegetables and legumes play an important dietary role, supplying essential protein for a diet based primarily on grains and vegetables.

World exposure to Africa's cuisines has been sparse, due, in part, to so few Africans emigrating (voluntarily). Many of the foods of Western Africa are familiar to people in the United States, commonly known as "soul food." Slavery played an important part in spreading the food culture and crops of western Africa to the New World. Because of large slave populations in the West Indies and Brazil, a Creole cooking style developed in the Western Hemisphere. The chile and tomato quickly crossed the Atlantic Ocean to Africa and became extremely popular in the African pantry. West African food can be extremely spicy from the copious use of hot chiles. Tomatoes, chiles, and onion form the basis of most dishes, and this trio is referred to as simply "the ingredients" in West African recipes.

The Sahara Desert is a formidable physical and cultural barrier in Africa, and few of the exciting spices from North Africa made their way across it. True yams and cassava are favorite starches and are complemented by the peanut, okra, and dried peas and beans. Vegetable soups and stews are favorite dishes, with meat saved for festive occasions. When there is meat, it is usually beef or mutton; except in South Africa, pork is rarely consumed. Frying and sautéing often feature *dendê* oil (palm oil), which adds both color and flavor to foods prepared with it. West Africa has had such a strong French influence that many believe the best meals on the continent can still be found in the former French colonies.

As one gets nearer the center of the continent, food becomes more limited, both in availability and variety. The soil is poor, parasite-carrying tsetse flies cause sickness in cattle and it is difficult to raise cattle here. The staple is corn; it is dried in kernels and ground as cornmeal for porridge (accented by a stew of greens, dried fish, and/or a modest portion of meat). Many of the foodstuffs must be imported, and the cost of living can be high. East Africa, the land of Mount Kilimanjaro, safaris, and Hemingway adventure stories, shows a strong British colonial heritage, and its cuisine is less than adventurous. But this region also has a large Indian population, going back to when Indian laborers were brought in to build the railroads. The local cuisine is spiced up by an Indian cuisine. Depending on soil conditions, either corn or rice is the staple crop. Coconut milk is used when cooking stews. Ethiopia, Somalia, and the Sudan form a distinct cooking region. Their cultures were heavily influenced by Arabic, Christian, and Hebrew traditions and yet this region has never been colonized. Ethiopia has a long history and a cuisine that can trace its roots for 2,000 years or more. Ethiopia was known in those days as Abyssinia and was the home to the Queen of Sheba. Having little contact with its neighbors allowed Ethiopian culture and cuisine to mature on its own. The climate is temperate, with a considerable amount of rainfall common in most years. Ethiopia is an African watershed; the runoff can swell and flood the Nile thousands of miles away. Many crops grow year round, t'eff being one of the most important. Ground to a flour, t'eff is made into *injera*, a flat, soft, fermented bread that serves as the plate on which other food is served. Pieces of the *injera* are torn off and used to scoop up the food.

Other common foodstuffs found in Ethiopia are peas, lentils, onions (especially favored in Ethiopian cuisine), peppers, garlic, and a wide variety of fruits and vegetables. Ethiopians love meat and often eat it raw (finely chopped as in a *tatare*), yet the Orthodox Christians abstain from meat for two hundred days of the year, which exerts a strong vegetarian influence on the cuisine. A spicy chicken stew (*doro we't*) can be considered the national dish of

Ethiopia. The cuisine treats peppers as a vegetable as well as a condiment. Many varieties are grown, from the mild red bell pepper to fiery hot chiles. Ethiopian cuisine is the spiciest to be found in Africa, due in part to their chile and garlic spice mix called *berbere*. It may be one of the better-known cuisines of Africa.

South Africa is the most technologically advanced and richest country in Africa. The Dutch established settlements in Cape Town, on the southern tip of the continent, by 1652. The purpose of these settlements was to provide food and water to ships sailing around the continent, from Holland to the East Indies. Malay slaves were brought to the Cape to work the fields where crops were grown to support the spice trade. They carried their spices and condiments with them, introducing an Indonesian influence to the developing cuisine. By the 1860s Indians were brought to South Africa to work the cane fields, and they added another interesting culture's cuisine to this region. Today the so-called "mixed blood" descendents of native blacks, Malays, and Indians form one of the most exciting cuisines of South Africa, known as Cape Malay cooking. This style of cooking has been described as primarily Dutch food with the spices of native African, Indian, and Malaysian workers and slaves.

As South Africa grew, the original Dutch settlers became known as Afrikaners; they lived in the rural areas as farmers. The British established a strong presence in South Africa, but they settled mainly in the cities. Afrikaner cooking is country-style cooking and Afrikaners prefer a home-cooked meal to dining out in restaurants. This habit makes it difficult to be exposed to true Afrikaner cuisine, which has certain characteristics of European and Far Eastern cooking. Barbecue is a popular cooking method, and the meats cooked in this way are of very high quality. It is said that vegetable dishes and breads illustrate its European heritage, while meat and fish preparation has a Far Eastern component. In the more urban areas, such as Capetown, the sweet-and-sour contrasts of Southeast Asia and North Africa are appreciated. Indian food abounds and curries are extremely popular. For native Africans, most of whom speak the Bantu languages, meals are primarily a cooked starch accompanied by small amounts of stew, occasionally containing a modest amount of meat. Few seasonings beyond salt are added to these stews. The staple for this region is corn, which is quite expensive to buy in its common forms: mealie (cornmeal) and maize (samp or dried kernels).

Rare Cooked Beef Tartare Kitfo Leb Leb

serves 8

Ethiopians are very fond of beef and what better way to eat it than uncooked. *Kitfo* is Ethiopia's version of beef tartare. It is considered the national dish of Ethiopia. *Kitfo leb leb* is the slightly cooked, medium-rare version. When making this dish choose the very highest grade of beef possible and use sound, hygienic methods. Hand-mincing will produce a more authentic texture, but the meat may be ground instead.

1½ pounds [675 g] beef tenderloin, semifrozen, minced finely by hand or ground

1½ teaspoons [8 mL] serrano chile, minced

¼ teaspoon [1 mL] ground cardamom

Pinch of ground cloves

Pinch of ground fenugreek

Pinch of ground cinnamon

¼ teaspoon [1 mL] black pepper

Salt to taste

½ cup [120 mL] red onion, minced

1 garlic clove, minced

⅛ teaspoon [0.5 mL] ginger, minced

6 ounces [180 g] unsalted butter

Injera bread, for service (see Chef Notes)

Crumbled soft goat cheese, for service

ADVANCE PREPARATION

1. At least 30 minutes before cooking, mix together the meat, chile, spices, salt, onion, garlic, and ginger and stir well to combine. Form into 8 thick round patties. Reserve, refrigerated. (The patties can be made several hours in advance.)

COOKING METHOD

2. Heat a heavy nonstick skillet over high heat. Add the patties and sear one side until a dark crust forms. Turn and sear the other side. When properly cooked, the patties should be raw throughout with the center warm. Serve immediately.

SERVICE

3. Arrange a piece of *injera* bread so that it just overhangs the rim of a plate. Place one patty, cut in half for presentation, in the center of the *injera*. Place a small mound of goat cheese next to the patty.

CHEF NOTES

Lamb may be substituted for the beef in this recipe. It may be more difficult to obtain highest quality lamb, but it would be worth the special effort. It is a must if the meat is served raw. The recipe for *injera* bread follows on the next page.

Injera

Makes eight 12-inch [30-cm] rounds

4 cups [960 mL] self-rising flour (or 4 cups [960 mL] flour plus 2 teaspoons [10 mL] baking soda)

1 cup [240 mL] buckwheat flour

1 teaspoon [5 mL] baking powder

2 cups [480 mL] club soda (sparkling water is preferred)

3½ to 4 cups [840 to 960 mL] water

1. Combine the flours with the baking soda and mix well in a large bowl. Stir in the club soda and the water, mixing well to form a smooth, crêpe-like batter (the consistency of heavy cream). For an authentic flavor, the batter should be allowed to ferment and sour before use. An alternative to fermentation is to add ¼ teaspoon [1 mL] of white vinegar to the batter.

2. Heat a nonstick skillet slightly larger than the serving plate fairly hot. (A drop of water should bounce across the surface of the pan before evaporating.)

3. Quickly pour in enough batter off heat to cover the surface of the pan, swirling to coat evenly. Return to the heat and cook one side only (do not allow the *injera* to brown or get crisp in any way). The *injera* bread is done when the moisture has evaporated and small holes are visible on the surface of the bread.

4. Stack the *injera*. They can be made several hours in advance.

Grilled Veal Kebabs with Apricot-Curry Glaze _Sosaties_

serves 8

The name of this dish, _sosaties_, comes from the combination of two Malay words: _saté_, meaning spiced sauce, and _sésatie_, meaning skewered meat. Malaysian curry powder is the dominant flavoring in this dish. _Sosaties_ are the favored fare at the _braai_, or backyard barbecue cookout. Traditionally they are made with cubes of lamb, but _sosaties_ are just as delicious made with pork or veal (and are enjoyed with chicken and seafood as well). Whatever the meat, marinate it for at least twelve hours, or up to three days. The preferred method of cooking is on the outdoor grill, but the skewers may also be broiled.

CHEF NOTES

For a truly authentic flavor substitute lamb or mutton tail fat (if available), sliced into cubes, for the bacon. Shrimp or prawns, scallops, langoustines, or lobster meat may be substituted with reduced marinating and cooking time.

½ cup [120 mL] apricot jam

2 tablespoons [30 mL] light brown sugar

6 garlic cloves, minced

2 teaspoons [10 mL] corn flour

3 bay leaves or lemon leaves

2 tablespoons [30 mL] curry powder

1 tablespoon [15 mL] ground coriander

1 teaspoon [5 mL] ground cumin

½ teaspoon [3 mL] ground African bird pepper or cayenne

½ cup [120 mL] fresh lemon juice

½ cup [120 mL] rich chicken stock

2 teaspoons [10 mL] salt

1 teaspoon [5 mL] black pepper

2 medium onions, quartered

1½ pounds [675 g] boneless veal loin, cut into ½-inch [1-cm] cubes

16 skewers, soaked in water for 30 minutes if wooden

16 dried apricots, plumped in a blend of warm dry sherry and chicken stock, halved

6 slices smoked fatty bacon, cut into thirty-two 1-inch [2.5-cm] pieces

ADVANCE PREPARATION

1. Combine the apricot jam, brown sugar, garlic, corn flour, bay leaves, curry, coriander, cumin, bird pepper, lemon juice, chicken stock, salt, and pepper in a skillet and bring to a boil. Reduce the heat to a simmer, then add the onion quarters.

2. Cook, covered, until the onions begin to soften and the marinade begins to thicken, about 5 minutes. Remove and reserve the onions, separating some of the layers for skewering. Allow the marinade to cool.

3. Combine the sauce with the veal cubes in a resealable plastic bag. Marinate the veal cubes for at least 12 hours or up to several days, refrigerated.

4. Drain the veal cubes from the marinade, reserving the marinade for basting and service. Skewer the veal cubes, alternating with the reserved onions, plumped apricot halves and bacon pieces. Each skewer should be comprised of 3 cubes of veal, 2 onion segments, 2 apricot halves, and 2 pieces of bacon.

5. Bring the marinade to a boil, lower the heat, and simmer for 3 minutes. Reserve warm.

COOKING METHOD

6. Slowly cook the skewers over an indirect charcoal fire until cooked medium rare to medium. Baste the skewers periodically with the warm reserved marinade.

SERVICE

7. Serve 2 skewers per person, accompanied by a portion of the warm marinade.

Sweet Potato Pastry Turnovers with Grilled Tuna and Chile Pastel com Diabo Dentro

CAPE VERDE

serves 8

The Portuguese claimed the island of Cape Verde, and the Portuguese name of this dish means "pastry with the devil inside." The filling may be as "devilish" as you like; just vary the amount of chiles added to the filling. Fresh tuna grilled over a charcoal fire will give the best results, but you may use high-quality canned tuna in a pinch. The pastry is a blend of cooked and puréed sweet potato, mixed with fine corn flour. Mayonnaise is found all across the African continent; this spicy version is enhanced with pineapple.

⌒ CHEF NOTES

Other tropical fruits, especially mango, may be substituted for the pineapple. Be sure to balance the sweetness with acidity. The sweet potatoes may be boiled or microwaved, then mashed, processed, or riced to purée them.

MAYONNAISE: MAKES 1½ CUPS [360 mL]

2 large egg yolks

½ teaspoon [3 mL] dry mustard

½ teaspoon [3 mL] salt

½ teaspoon [3 mL] cayenne, or to taste

2 teaspoons [10 mL] fresh lemon juice

1 teaspoon [5 mL] palm (dendê) oil

1½ cups [360 mL] olive oil

1 tablespoon [15 mL] fresh pineapple juice

1 teaspoon [5 mL] hot water

¼ cup [60 mL] minced fresh pineapple

PASTRY: MAKES SIXTEEN 3-INCH [8-CM] CIRCLES

1 large sweet potato, unpeeled, cooked until very tender, and puréed to a smooth paste

1 egg yolk, lightly beaten

1 tablespoon [15 mL] melted butter

2 to 3 cups [480 to 720 mL] fine corn flour, as needed to form a dough

FILLING: MAKES ENOUGH FOR 16 PASTRIES

1 tablespoon [15 mL] olive or palm (dendê) oil

1 onion, minced

3 garlic cloves, minced

4 hot chile peppers, minced, or to taste

1 pound [450 g] fresh tuna fillet or steak, grilled over charcoal to medium rare and cooled and sliced

2 plum tomatoes, finely diced

1 teaspoon [5 mL] salt

Vegetable oil with a few drops of palm (dendê) oil added for color, for deep-frying

Minced chives, for garnish

379 | Regional Africa

1. Place the egg yolks, mustard, salt, cayenne, and lemon juice in the work bowl of a food processor. Process the mixture to blend.

2. With the processor running, add the palm oil, then slowly add half of the olive oil. With the processor still running, add the pineapple juice and hot water, then slowly add the remaining olive oil and stir in the minced pineapple. Chill and reserve. (The mayonnaise can be made one day in advance.)

PREPARATION OF THE PASTRY

3. Mix the sweet potato purée in a large bowl with the egg yolks and melted butter. Mix in enough corn flour to form a stiff dough. Add a few spoonfuls of the cooking water from the sweet potatoes if necessary.

4. Form the dough into a ball and chill for one hour.

PREPARATION OF THE FILLING

5. Heat the olive or palm oil over medium heat and sauté the onion until transparent. Add the garlic and sauté 30 seconds, then add the chiles and cook 2 minutes.

6. Toss with the tuna, tomatoes, and salt. Allow the mixture to cool and reserve.

ASSEMBLY METHOD

7. On a lightly floured surface roll the dough out ⅛ inch [3 mm] thick. Cut the dough into sixteen 3-inch [8-cm] circles.

8. Place 2 teaspoons [10 mL] of the filling slightly off center of each circle and fold over to enclose the filling. Press the edges firmly to seal. Reserve, covered and refrigerated. (The turnovers can be made several hours in advance.)

COOKING METHOD

9. Heat the vegetable oil to 365°F [185°C] and fry the turnovers, in batches, 3 minutes per side, or until golden brown. Drain on paper towels, and keep warm until service.

SERVICE

10. Serve each person 2 turnovers, cut in half, accompanied with the pineapple mayonnaise, garnished with minced chives.

Yam and Fish Cakes with Red Chile Sauce Iyan Ehan Akara Ata

The yams used here are true yams, not sweet potatoes, which are called yams in most American markets. The yam is a tropical, white-fleshed tuber, similar to a potato. The fish cakes are a perfect use for leftover cooked fish. The chile sauce, called *ata,* which means "hot," is used on almost every dish in Nigeria; it pairs nicely with these cakes.

CHEF NOTES

Chopped cooked or smoked shrimp works well in this recipe, as does smoked fish (bluefish and whitefish are particularly good).

RED CHILE SAUCE (ATA): MAKES ABOUT 4 CUPS [960 mL]

2 large ripe tomatoes, chopped

1½ tablespoons [25 mL] tomato paste

5 red bell peppers, roasted, peeled, seeded, and chopped

1 large onion, chopped

4 garlic cloves, chopped

5 hot red chile peppers or 2 to 3 tablespoons [30 to 45 mL] crushed red pepper

¼ teaspoon [1 mL] dried thyme

2 teaspoons [10 mL] fresh lemon juice

½ teaspoon [3 mL] sugar

Pinch of hot Madras curry powder

2 tablespoons [30 mL] peanut oil

2 tablespoons [30 mL] palm (*dendê*) oil

Salt to taste

1 teaspoon [5 mL] ground dried shrimp (optional)

YAM AND FISH CAKES: MAKES 16 CAKES

2 cups [480 mL] cooked fish, boned and flaked

2 cups [480 mL] cooked yams, riced, mashed, or puréed

2 tablespoons [30 mL] onion, grated

1 teaspoon [5 mL] minced garlic

3 tablespoons [45 mL] peanut oil

1 tablespoon [15 mL] butter, melted

½ teaspoon [3 mL] cayenne

1 egg, beaten

Salt and black pepper to taste

ADVANCE PREPARATION

1. For the chile sauce, combine the tomatoes with the tomato paste, bell peppers, onion, garlic, chiles, thyme, lemon juice, sugar, and curry powder in the work bowl of a food processor. Purée until smooth.

2. Heat the peanut and palm oils in a nonstick skillet over medium heat. Add the puréed chile mixture and sauté for 10 minutes, or until the bell peppers are cooked and the sauce is slightly reduced. Salt to taste and add dried shrimp, if using. (The sauce may be made several days in advance or frozen for later use.)

PREPARATION OF THE FISH CAKES

3. Combine the cooked fish, yams, onion, garlic, 1 tablespoon [15 mL] of the peanut oil, the butter, cayenne, egg, and salt and pepper and mix well to combine.

4. Form the mixture into 16 balls and flatten them into oval cakes. Keep refrigerated, covered, until ready to cook. (The fish cakes can be made one day in advance and stored in bulk. Form the cakes just before cooking.)

COOKING METHOD

5. Heat the remaining peanut oil in a nonstick skillet and sauté the fish cakes, in batches, until golden brown on both sides. Remove from the pan and drain on paper towels, keeping the cakes warm until service.

SERVICE

6. Serve 2 fish cakes per person, accompanied by the red chile sauce at room temperature.

Fried Oysters with Chile, Smoked Shrimp, and Peanut Sauce   Huitres Azi Dessi

serves 8

Oysters are popular all along the vast shoreline of Africa, where they are harvested for export. In this dish from Togo, a former French colony, plump spicy fried oysters pair perfectly with the uniquely African (and unusual) sauce of hot chiles, tomatoes, onions, smoked shrimp, and ground peanuts. West Africans use dried smoked shrimp for the sauce, but fresh smoked shrimp adds greatly to the flavor.

CHEF NOTES

For a most authentic flavor to the sauce, roast raw peanuts, then grind them to a paste just before service. Clams, mussels, shrimp, langoustines, or South African rock lobster nuggets prepared in this manner go well with the sauce.

SAUCE *AZI DESSI:* MAKES 2½ CUPS [540 mL]

3 tablespoons [45 mL] palm (*dendê*) oil

1¼ pounds [560 g] tomatoes, peeled, seeded, and puréed

2 medium onions, minced

3 garlic cloves, minced

¼ to ½ teaspoon [1 to 3 mL] minced habanero chile

1 teaspoon [5 mL] fresh ginger, minced

3 tablespoons [45 mL] chunky peanut butter or freshly ground peanuts, processed to a paste

⅔ cup [160 mL] smoked shrimp, very finely minced

OYSTERS

1 quart [1 L] plump oysters, shucked

1 cup [240 mL] fresh lemon juice

1 teaspoon [5 mL] garlic powder

1½ cups [360 mL] flour

2 teaspoons [10 mL] cayenne

1 teaspoon [5 mL] salt

½ teaspoon [3 mL] black pepper

Peanut oil or vegetable oil, for deep-frying

Lemon wedges, for garnish

ADVANCE PREPARATION

1. For the sauce, heat the palm oil in a nonstick skillet over low heat. Add the tomato purée and sauté for about 10 minutes, or until the purée thickens slightly.

2. Add the onions, garlic, chile, and ginger and cook for 5 minutes more. Remove the pan from the heat and allow to cool 10 minutes. (The sauce can be made to this point one day in advance.) Stir in the peanut butter. Just before service, add the smoked shrimp and stir well to combine.

PREPARATION OF THE OYSTERS

3. Place the oysters in a resealable plastic bag. Mix the lemon juice with the garlic powder and add this mixture to the oys-

ters. Toss to coat. Allow to marinate for 15 minutes. Drain and reserve the oysters.

4. Combine the flour, cayenne, salt, and pepper in a paper bag or bowl and shake well to mix.

COOKING METHOD

5. Just before cooking, toss the oysters, in batches, into the bag and shake to ensure complete coating with the flour mixture.

6. Deep-fry the oysters in oil at 365°F [185°C], in batches, for 3 to 4 minutes, or until they rise to the surface and are golden brown and crisp. Drain on paper towels, keeping the oysters warm until service.

SERVICE

7. Serve 4 oysters per person, accompanied by a small ramekin of the chile sauce and a lemon wedge.

Pumpkin Fritters with Sweet-and-Hot Sauce Pampoenkoedes Blatjang

Serves 8

Savory and sweet fritters, made with a wide variety of vegetables and fruits, are popular throughout Africa. The Dutch brought pumpkins to Africa, and in South Africa the white-skinned Boer pumpkin is a favorite for these fritters. They may be made from pumpkin, calabaza, acorn squash, Blue Hubbard, or any type of orange-fleshed squash. *Blatjang* is a Cape Malay spicy chutney-like condiment, a Creole favorite.

CHEF NOTES

The cooked pumpkin for this recipe may be boiled in lightly salted water, baked, broiled, or microwaved. Sweet potato or white-fleshed yam can be substituted for the pumpkin. The high sugar content of some squashes and tubers may overly darken the fritters when frying. Lower the heat and turn frequently.

SWEET-AND-HOT SAUCE (BLATJANG):
MAKES ABOUT 2 CUPS [480 mL]

2 medium onions, peeled and blanched in simmering water for 5 minutes or microwaved for 3 minutes

3 to 4 fresh hot red chiles, diced (seeds and ribs removed for less piquancy)

1½ tablespoons [25 mL] fresh lemon juice

1 tablespoon [15 mL] cider vinegar

2 tablespoons [30 mL] almond paste

1 tablespoon [15 mL] apricot jam or preserves

2 tablespoons [30 mL] dried apricots, minced

3 garlic cloves, minced

2 teaspoons [10 mL] fresh ginger, minced

½ teaspoon [3 mL] salt, or to taste

¾ cup [180 mL] rich chicken stock

2 bay leaves

FRITTERS: MAKES 24 FRITTERS

5 cups [1.2 L] cooked pumpkin, puréed

2 cups [480 mL] grated raw pumpkin, blanched briefly in boiling salted water, refreshed, and drained

1 teaspoon [5 mL] baking powder

½ cup [120 mL] flour

Pinch of ground cinnamon

Pinch of cayenne

½ teaspoon [3 mL] salt

1 egg, beaten

Spicy cinnamon sugar (2 parts sugar, 1 part cinnamon, a pinch of cayenne), for dusting

ADVANCE PREPARATION

1. Quarter the blanched onions and place in the workbowl of a food processor. Pulse the onions to a paste. Add all other sauce ingredients and process thoroughly, forming a smooth paste. Reserve, covered and refrigerated. (The sauce can be made one day in advance.)

PREPARATION OF THE FRITTERS

2. Mix the puréed pumpkin and grated blanched pumpkin with all the other fritter ingredients and beat the mixture until smooth. Reserve, covered and refrigerated. (The fritter batter can be made several hours in advance.)

COOKING METHOD

3. Drop tablespoons of fritter batter into 365°F [185°C] oil, in batches. Cook until golden brown, turning once during the frying process. Drain on paper towels and keep warm. Continue until all the batter has been used.

SERVICE

4. Serve 3 fritters per person, dusted with the cinnamon sugar, accompanied with the sauce.

Plantain and Banana Griddle Cakes with Fried Pepper Sauce Kyekyire Krakro Atadindin

serves 8

These savory cakes with a fiery sauce are a good example of West African "small chop," which refers to snacks, finger food, and street food eaten throughout the day before the large, main meal at night.

CHEF NOTES

Adding ¼ cup [60 mL] of creamed corn to the batter will bring out the corn flavor a bit more (adjust the consistency of the batter with water after first adding the creamed corn). Cayenne may be used in place of the serrano chiles.

FRIED PEPPER SAUCE: MAKES ABOUT 2 CUPS [480 mL]

2 large red bell peppers, roasted, peeled, and chopped

4 hot red chiles, diced

1 tablespoon [15 mL] small hot red dried chiles, crushed

1 medium onion, diced

2 garlic cloves, minced

4 ripe cherry tomatoes

¼ cup [60 mL] peanut oil

1 teaspoon [5 mL] salt

GRIDDLE CAKES: MAKES SIXTEEN 3-INCH [8-CM] CAKES

1 cup [240 mL] white cornmeal

Warm water

½ cup [120 mL] all-purpose flour

1 teaspoon [5 mL] baking powder

½ teaspoon [3 mL] salt

½ teaspoon [3 mL] ground ginger

2 tablespoons [30 mL] peanut oil

½ cup [120 mL] mashed ripe plantain

½ cup [120 mL] mashed ripe banana

1 small onion, diced

2 serrano chiles, minced

Water, as needed

Peanut oil, for pan-frying

Minced chives or scallions, for garnish

ADVANCE PREPARATION

1. Combine all of the sauce ingredients, except the oil and salt, in the workbowl of a food processor and purée.

2. Heat the oil in a skillet and sauté the purée over medium heat, stirring constantly, until the chiles and peppers are soft. Add the salt and stir. (This sauce may be made several days in advance or frozen until needed.)

PREPARATION OF THE GRIDDLE CAKES

3. Mix the cornmeal with enough water to form a slurry.

4. Combine the flour with the baking powder, salt, and ginger. Mix these dry ingredients with the cornmeal slurry, oil, plantain, banana, onion, chiles, and enough water to make a slightly thick, smooth pancake batter. Allow the mixture to rest for 1 to 2 hours, covered.

COOKING METHOD

5. Brush a small amount of peanut oil onto a nonstick griddle or skillet over medium heat. Drop 3 to 4 tablespoons [45 to 60 mL] of batter, in batches, onto the griddle. When brown, flip the cakes over and brown the other side. Stack the cakes, covered with a clean towel, until all are cooked.

SERVICE

6. Serve each guest 2 griddle cakes with a generous portion of the sauce. Garnish with minced chives or scallions.

North Africa

Morocco, Tunisia,

and Algeria

Olives Stuffed with Ground Beef in a Spicy Ragout
Marquit Zeitoun

Lamb Kebabs, Marrakech Style, with Spicy Chile Paste
Al Kotban Mrakchiya

Baked Fennel Bulbs Stuffed with Lamb
Bisbas Michchi

Phyllo Rolls with Two Fillings (Fatima's Little Fingers)
Maasems (Doigts de Fatma)

Phyllo Triangles with Quail, Eggs, Onions, and Spices
Briouat el B'stila (Braewat el Bisteeya)

Grilled Tuna Kebabs with Herb-Lemon Marinade
Thon bì Chermoula (Tchermila)

**Rice-Stuffed Dates Wrapped in Sole with
Sweet and Sour Sauce**
Samak Mehshi bi Tamr

THE COUNTRIES OF MOROCCO, Tunisia, and Algeria, because of their indigenous people, history, and unique geographical position, have a culinary tradition quite different from the rest of the African continent. These three countries are known as the Maghreb from the Arabic for "the land farthest west." Two thousand years ago the three countries were one. Cooking in the Maghreb has been influenced by the Persians, Phoenicians, Greeks, Romans, Vandals, Arabs, Ottoman Turks, Spanish, British, and French. Spices from the Far East and Middle East passed across this region, and there was an exchange of produce between Europe and North Africa. The Romans made this region the "breadbasket" of its empire, and the Maghreb supplied the empire with more than 60 percent of the wheat and other grains it needed to feed its people and its armies. The Moors brought citrus and olives back to North Africa from Spain, forever leaving a Mediterranean imprint on the cuisines of Morocco, Tunisia, and Algeria.

Dried sausages were introduced to the northern Coast of Africa by the Phoenicians (this drying technique was used to preserve meats for long sea journeys). The Carthaginians are thought to have introduced durum wheat in the form of semolina, which became the staple of the region, couscous. It is believed that the North Africans developed a way to dry pasta made from semolina, a precursor of the dried pasta so appreciated in Italy. When the Romans expelled the Carthaginians, they named the region Mauretania Tingitana (it is from this name that the term "Moors" about). The most lasting effect on the region came in the year 683, when Morocco was invaded by the Arabs. The Arabs brought their religion and the culture of the Middle East to a people known as the Berbers, an indigenous Caucasian tribe, possibly of Nordic descent. While they did adopt the Muslim religion, they formed a specialized branch that mainstream Muslims considered heresy, a split that keeps the two cultures in conflict to this day.

The Arabs were the world's spice merchants for many centuries and they introduced cinnamon, saffron, ginger, cloves, and nutmeg to North Africa. The Arabs went on to conquer Spain in 711. Known as the Moors, they kept North Africa connected to Spain for centuries. This helped to fuse the ingredients of the Mediterranean with those of the Maghreb. When the Spanish Moors and Sephardic Jews were expelled from Spain in 1492, many chose to settle in Morocco, and they brought their cuisines with them. The Ottoman Turks were repelled from ever crossing into Moroccan territory, and so the Ottoman Empire did not have as much influence on the cuisine of Morocco as it did elsewhere. Portuguese and Spanish influence in the fifteenth and sixteenth centuries introduced the region to the New World. Chiles and tomatoes had a powerful impact on the tastes of the Maghreb. Tunisian cuisine became the spiciest of the three countries (harissa is the fiery chile condiment for which

Tunisia has become famous). France had annexed Algeria in 1834, and at the beginning of the twentieth century Britain struck a deal with France: the French could keep control over Morocco in exchange for British control in Egypt. The French influence in the region was greatest in Algeria, but it provided an elegance in presentation of food in all of the countries in North Africa.

There is a Maghrebi proverb to the effect that Algeria is the man, Tunisia is the woman, and Morocco is the lion. The food of Morocco certainly lives up to this analogy. Moroccan cuisine is assertive and aggressive, with liberal use of a multitude of spices. Only India can compare in its copious use of multiple-spice combinations. It is spice that characterizes Moroccan food. Brought to Morocco from India and elsewhere were ginger, turmeric, saffron, black peppercorns, coriander, cumin, cinnamon, paprika, and garlic. A surprising spice to be found in the region is caraway, normally associated with foods of northern Europe. Moroccan cuisine is a Mediterranean cuisine, with reliance on lemons, olives, olive oil, and garlic. Persian influence can be seen in Morocco's taste for meats combined with fruits and the use of "sweet" spices in savory dishes. Flaky pastries (*b'stilla*), filled with meat and spices are often dusted with powdered sugar and cinnamon. Sweet dates and raisins are combined with lamb and chicken.

The staple in Morocco (and across the region) is couscous, a unique pasta made from durum wheat. It may be flavored with butter, spices, vegetables, and meats. It can be served alone or accompanied by a rich tagine. *Tagines* are wonderfully flavorful stews, slowly cooked in a special ceramic cooking vessel. Couscous is often steamed by placing it over a simmering *tagine*, with the flavors of the stew infused into the small pasta kernels. Favorite meats include lamb, beef, and poultry, with a fondness for pigeon or squab. With a coastline on the Mediterranean Sea and the Atlantic Ocean, fish is quite popular. Sardines are especially enjoyed throughout the Maghreb.

Algeria is one of the largest countries in Africa, yet 90 percent of the land lies in the Sahara Desert. At the same time, 90 percent of the population lives along the Mediterranean, in what is known as the Tell region. These northern regions have suffered from deforestation, overgrazing, and erosion. Farming accounts for little more than 10 percent of the gross national product of Algeria. France annexed Algeria in the early 1800s. Because of its long association with France, modern Algerian cuisine is most like the French in its care of presentation and preparation. Algerian cuisine can be seen as the intermediary between the highly aromatic and fruit-filled dishes of Morocco and the use of fiery chiles (as *harisa*) in Tunisia. Algerians have a fondness for salads that surpasses the other countries of the Maghreb. Unusual vegetables such as artichokes, fennel, and cardoons are eaten along with the more common carrots, tomatoes, and potatoes. Flat-leaf parsley is added to most dishes and caraway is a surprise note in the spice spectrum of the region. Lamb is the most common meat, since sheep can thrive in semiarid conditions. Poultry and fish are enjoyed as well.

Tunisia was an important wheat-growing region from the time of the Roman Empire. Because of this early history, dishes based on couscous are extremely popular, and Tunisian bakeries produce wonderful breads. Unlike Algeria, Tunisia's northern regions are quite fertile and have plant life similar to that of southern Europe. Grape vines flourish in this Mediterranean climate. Mediterranean crops such as oranges, lemons, figs, grapes, and pomegranates also flourish in the rich soil and balmy climate of the northern lands. The history of Tunisia is similar to that of the rest of the region, with one exception. The Phoenicians established Carthage in an area now known as Tunis. The Carthaginian Empire ruled the Iberian Peninsula and parts of Sicily and Sardinia intermittently until the Punic Wars (149 to 146 B.C.). This interaction cemented the influence of the Mediterranean on the cooking style and crops grown in modern Tunisia. In addition to this strong Mediterranean influence, Tunisians embraced the New World crops of chiles, tomatoes, potatoes, and squash. Tunisian cuisine is the spiciest of the countries of North Africa. A symbol of this love of chiles comes in the form of its famous chile condiment, *harissa*. Cumin, black peppercorns, and caraway are the spices most often encountered, and olive oils produced in Tunisia are world class (as are their table olives). Eggs are used in abundance, and lamb, beef, and poultry are popular meats. Fish from the Mediterranean provides needed protein and a varied diet, and it is also reasonably priced.

Olives Stuffed with Ground Beef in a Spicy Ragout Marquit Zeitoun

TUNISIA

Serves 8

This dish is a specialty of the city of Tunis, the capital of Tunisia. The olives are pitted in a spiral fashion, and a spicy ground beef filling is inserted into the center. The stuffed olives are then braised in a piquant beef-and-tomato sauce laced with *harissa*, the hot chile paste, and *tabil*, the basic spice mix of Tunisia. Here the dish is topped with roasted green chiles, but in Tunisia they would be fried in olive oil.

CHEF NOTES

Lamb or veal may be substituted for the beef in this dish. Care should be taken at all steps to ensure that the ragout does not dry out and scorch.

RAGOUT

1 pound [450 g] lean beef, cut into ¼-inch [6-mm] cubes

½ teaspoon [3 mL] black pepper

1 tablespoon [15 mL] *tabil* (see page 399)

1 tablespoon [15 mL] olive oil

½ cup [120 mL] onion, diced

1 tablespoon [15 mL] tomato paste

1 cup [240 mL] tomatoes, diced

1 tablespoon [15 mL] fresh lemon juice

1 teaspoon [5 mL] *harissa* (see page 396), diluted in 1 tablespoon chicken stock

1 teaspoon [5 mL] paprika

2½ cups [600 mL] chicken stock, plus more if needed

STUFFING

12 ounces [360 mL] lean beef, minced or coarsely ground

⅓ cup [80 mL] parsley, chopped

¼ cup [60 mL] Parmesan cheese, grated

1 egg

1 egg yolk

3 tablespoons [45 mL] onion, diced very fine

2 garlic cloves, minced

½ tablespoon [8 mL] *tabil* spice mix

1 teaspoon [5 mL] *harissa*, diluted in 2 tablespoons cold water

32 large Sicilian olives, pitted in a spiral fashion, leaving corkscrew-shaped strips, soaked in several changes of water to remove excess saltiness, and well drained

¾ teaspoon [4 mL] fennel seeds, lightly toasted until fragrant, cooled, and ground

GARNISH

Freshly ground black pepper

8 Anaheim or New Mexico medium-hot green chiles, roasted, peeled, and cut into thin strips

Crusty country bread, for service

393 | North Africa

1. Place the beef in a resealable plastic bag. Add the black pepper and *tabil* spice mix, tossing to fully coat the meat with the spices. Marinate at least 4 hours, preferably overnight.

PREPARATION OF THE RAGOUT

2. Heat the olive oil in a large nonstick skillet to medium-high heat and sauté the beef cubes until lightly browned. Add the onion and sauté until soft.

3. Add the tomato paste, tomatoes, lemon juice, *harissa*, paprika, and chicken stock. Simmer for 1 hour, covered, or until the meat is very tender. Reserve. (The ragout can be made one day in advance.)

PREPARATION OF THE STUFFED OLIVES

4. Combine all of the stuffing ingredients in the workbowl of a food processor and blend to a uniform mixture. Form the stuffing into 32 marble-size ovals.

5. Place a piece of stuffing into the center of each olive strip. Using wet hands, wrap and press the olive strips firmly around the stuffing, reforming an olive shape, and reserve. (The stuffed olives can be made one day in advance and stored wrapped and refrigerated.)

COOKING METHOD

6. Gently place the stuffed olives in the simmering ragout, tightly cover the skillet, and cook for 45 minutes. Gently turn the olives after 20 minutes, adding more stock or water only if necessary.

7. Using a slotted spoon, remove the olives to an ovenproof dish. Reduce the sauce to 1¾ cups [420 mL] and skim off any fat.

8. Just before service, place the olives under a broiler to heat and glaze them. Heat the chile strips and reserve. Stir the fennel seeds into the ragout and adjust seasonings.

9. Place 4 stuffed olives on a plate and top generously with the ragout. Add a twist of freshly ground black pepper and garnish with chile strips arranged attractively. Serve with bread on the side.

Lamb Kebabs, Marrakech Style, with Spicy Chile Paste (*Harissa*) Al Kotban Mrakchiya

serves 8

Harissa, the fiery Tunisian spice paste, is widely used as a condiment at the table in Morocco. It can be made as mild or as hot as desired by varying the kind of dried chiles used. For a milder sauce, use guajillo or ancho chiles. For a more piquant version use dried chipotle, habanero, or Thai chiles.

CHEF NOTES

Other meats or poultry appropriate for grilling may be substituted for the lamb. The kebabs may be broiled or grilled on a gas grill, but the best flavor will come from grilling over a wood fire. You can buy *harissa* or make your own. Prepared chile paste (*sambal oelek*) may be substituted for the chiles.

SPICY CHILE PASTE (*HARISSA*): MAKES ABOUT 1 CUP [240 mL]

12 dried chiles (6 guajillo, 4 pasilla, 2 chipotle recommended, soaked in warm chicken stock)

4 garlic cloves, chopped

½ cup [120 mL] extra virgin olive oil

1 tablespoon [15 mL] fresh lemon juice

1 teaspoon [5 mL] salt, or to taste

1 teaspoon [5 mL] ground cumin

MARINADE

6 tablespoons [90 mL] olive oil

¼ cup [60 mL] cilantro, chopped

¼ cup [60 mL] parsley, chopped

1 small onion, quartered

3 garlic cloves, chopped

½ tablespoon [8 mL] ground cumin

1½ tablespoons [25 mL] sweet paprika

6 tablespoons [90 mL] fresh lemon juice

½ tablespoon [8 mL] black pepper

KEBABS

1½ pounds [675 g] leg of lamb, well trimmed, cut into 1-inch [2.5-cm] cubes

16 skewers, soaked in water 30 minutes if wooden

Salad greens and mint leaves, to line plates

Harissa, for service

Salt mixed with ground cumin, for service

Pita bread

ADVANCE PREPARATION

1. To prepare the spice paste, lightly char the chiles over a burner flame until they begin to expand. Split the chiles open and remove the seeds and stems.

2. Chop the chiles coarsely and soak in a bowl of warm water until they soften, about 25 to 30 minutes. Drain the chiles and squeeze as much moisture as possible from them.

3. Place the chiles in a blender or food processor with all remaining spice paste ingredients and process to a smooth paste. Top with a layer of olive oil and store in the refrigerator. The *harissa* should be made at least a day in advance for the flavors to blend.

PREPARATION OF THE MARINADE

4. Combine all the marinade ingredients in a food processor and pulse to a smooth paste. Place the marinade and lamb cubes in a resealable plastic bag and marinate, refrigerated, for at least 4 hours, preferably overnight.

PREPARATION OF THE KEBABS

5. Drain the meat and place 1½ ounces [45 g] of lamb on each skewer.

COOKING METHOD

6. Grill the kebabs for 6 to 8 minutes over a medium-hot indirect wood or charcoal fire for medium rare, turning occasionally. Do not char the meat.

SERVICE

7. Line a plate with greens and mint leaves. Serve 2 warm kebabs per person with small dishes of *harissa* and salt mixed with a little cumin. Serve with pita bread.

Baked Fennel Bulbs Stuffed with Lamb Bisbas Michchi

serves 8

Fennel is popular during the winter and spring in Tunisia and Algeria, and the technique of baking stuffed vegetables is found throughout the Middle East, the Maghreb, and the Mediterranean. Tunisians would add some *harissa* to spice up the tomato sauce for this dish.

4 large fennel bulbs

FILLING

1 pound [450 g] ground lamb

2 garlic cloves, minced

¼ cup [60 mL] parsley, minced

½ tablespoon [8 mL] *tabil* spice mix (see Chef Notes)

½ tablespoon [8 mL] ground black pepper

3 tablespoons [45 mL] olive oil

2 eggs, lightly beaten

¼ cup [60 mL] grated Parmesan cheese

1 cup [60 mL] spicy tomato sauce, homemade or prepared

Parmesan cheese, for garnish

Minced fennel leaves, for garnish

ADVANCE PREPARATION

1. Trim the hard base off each fennel bulb and remove the tops. Reserve some of the fennel leaves for garnish. Blanch the bulbs in simmering salted water for 15 minutes, or until just tender. Drain, cool, cut in half lengthwise, and reserve. (The fennel bulbs can be prepared one day in advance.)

PREPARATION OF THE LAMB

2. Combine the lamb, garlic, parsley, *tabil* spice mix, and pepper in a bowl and mix well. Sauté this mixture in the olive oil until browned. Allow to cool.

3. Mix in the eggs and Parmesan cheese. (The lamb mixture can be made 1 day in advance and stored refrigerated.) The bulbs may be stuffed and wrapped in plastic film, then cooked to order.

COOKING METHOD

4. Place the fennel bulbs in an oiled shallow baking dish, cut side up. Top with the lamb mixture. Cover with tomato sauce

Tabil is a classic Tunisian spice mixture that can be purchased premixed in Middle Eastern groceries, or you can make your own.

Tabil Spice Mix

Makes about 3 tablespoons [45 mL]

> 2 tablespoons [30 mL] coriander seeds
>
> 2 teaspoons [10 mL] caraway seeds
>
> ½ teaspoon [3 mL] cayenne
>
> ¼ teaspoon [1 mL] fennel seeds
>
> ¼ teaspoon [1 mL] aniseed
>
> ¼ teaspoon [1 mL] ground cumin
>
> ¼ teaspoon [1 mL] turmeric
>
> 1 teaspoon [5 mL] black pepper

1. Lightly toast the spice mixture in a nonstick skillet over medium heat until aromatic.
2. Allow to cool, then finely grind in a blender or spice grinder. Store in a glass jar in a dark, cool place.

and bake at 400°F [205°C] for 15 to 20 minutes, or until nicely browned and set.

5. Serve 1 fennel bulb half per person. garnish with Parmesan cheese and minced fennel leaves.

Phyllo Rolls with Two Fillings (Fatima's Little Fingers) Maasems (Doigts de Fatma)

TUNISIA

serves 8 (4 rolls per person)

These delicate phyllo rolls can be filled with cheese and hard-boiled egg or with chicken, cheese, and egg. Traditionally they are encased in a thin, chewy pastry called a *malsouka*, which is very similar to the Moroccan *warka* leaves used to make *bisteeya* (see page 402). These traditional wrappers are difficult to make, so many chefs use phyllo, thin spring roll wrappers, or even egg roll wrappers as a substitute. These appetizers are sometimes called *doights de Fatima*, after the daughter of Mohammed, because it is said (with great respect) that they resemble her thin, delicate fingers.

CHEESE FILLING: MAKES ENOUGH FOR 20 ROLLS

¾ cup [180 mL] ricotta cheese

¾ cup [180 mL] Gruyère cheese, grated

¼ cup [60 mL] Parmesan cheese, grated

1 teaspoon [5 mL] black pepper

Pinch of cayenne, or more to taste

¾ teaspoon [4 mL] salt

1 egg plus 1 yolk, beaten

CHICKEN FILLING: MAKES ENOUGH FOR 20 ROLLS

1 tablespoon [15 mL] *tabil* spice mix (see page 393)

1 teaspoon [5 mL] *harissa* (see page 396)

1 tablespoon [15 mL] tomato paste

1½ cups [360 mL] rich chicken stock

2 boneless chicken thighs, both sides scored with a sharp knife

2 hard-boiled eggs, peeled and chopped

½ cup [120 mL] parsley, chopped

1 egg, beaten

3 tablespoons [45 mL] Parmesan cheese, grated

½ teaspoon [3 mL] salt, or more to taste

½ teaspoon [3 mL] black pepper

Pinch of cayenne

WRAPPERS

8 phyllo leaves or 32 spring roll or egg roll wrappers

2 eggs, hard-boiled and peeled, each cut into 8 pieces

2 egg whites, beaten slightly

Olive oil

Olive or vegetable oil, for frying

Lemon wedges, for garnish

ADVANCE PREPARATION

1. Combine the ricotta, Gruyère, and Parmesan cheese, pepper, cayenne, salt, egg, and egg yolk and mix well. Reserve, re-

These rolls are quite versatile and may be filled with minced lamb seasoned with onions, *tabil* spice mix, *harissa*, and tomato paste. If a Tunisian or Moroccan market is nearby, genuine *malsouka* or *warka* pastry may be available. The rolls may be baked rather than fried. Brush the stuffed pastries with olive oil and bake at 400°F [205°C] until crisp and browned.

frigerated and covered. (The cheese filling can be made 1 day in advance.)

PREPARATION OF THE CHICKEN FILLING

2. Bring the *tabil* spice mix, *harissa*, tomato paste, and stock to a boil in a small skillet, then reduce the heat to a simmer.

3. Simmer the chicken thighs in the seasoned stock until cooked through. Allow the chicken thighs to remain in the poaching liquid to cool.

4. Remove the chicken thighs and finely dice them. Combine the diced chicken with the remaining chicken filling ingredients and mix well. Reserve, refrigerated and covered. (The chicken filling can be made one day in advance.)

ASSEMBLY METHOD

5. Unroll one sheet of phyllo, keeping the rest covered to prevent drying out, and cut it into quarters. Fold each quarter in half and place 1 to 2 tablespoons [15 to 30 mL] of the cheese filling near the bottom of each folded phyllo quarter. Leave ½ inch [1 cm] borders filling-free. Place a section of hard-boiled egg on top of the cheese filling. Do the same with the chicken filling. Repeat, using half of the phyllo sheets.

6. Lightly brush the edges of the phyllo with egg white and roll up the phyllo to form cylinders. Place them seam side down on a tray.

7. Brush the tops lightly with olive oil. Pinch the ends to seal them securely. (If using spring roll or egg roll wrappers, trim them into 5-inch [13-cm] squares and proceed as with the phyllo sheets.) Keep tightly covered until ready to cook.

COOKING METHOD

8. Fill a large skillet to a depth of 1 inch [2.5 cm] with olive or vegetable oil and heat it to 360°F [180°C]. Fry the rolls in batches, turning halfway through the cooking process, until golden brown on both sides. Remove and drain on paper towels. Keep warm until service.

SERVICE

9. Serve 4 rolls per person (two of each kind) with a lemon wedge.

Phyllo Triangles with Quail, Eggs, Onions, and Spices Briouat el B'stila (Braewat el Bisteeya)

serves 8

B'stila (*bisteeya*) is traditionally made with very thin sheets of pastry called *warka*. It takes a true master to produce these sheets of pastry and in Morocco they are made by *dadas*, women descended from Sudanese slaves. Modern Moroccan housewives no longer make their own pastry sheets, preferring to purchase them at the market from the *dadas*. Phyllo dough makes an excellent substitute for *warka*. *B'stila* (*bisteeya*) is normally made in the shape of a large, flattened pie, but this version, known as a *briouat*, is made into small triangles for individual service.

The spice mix in this recipe, *ras el hanout*, is a complex blend that may contain more than twenty spices. Most recipes in Morocco include an aphrodisiac such as Spanish fly, but this ingredient is not present in the recipe given in the Chef Notes. The literal translation of *ras el hanout* is "top of the shop."

3 tablespoons [45 mL] blanched almonds, coarsely chopped

3 tablespoons [25 mL] unsalted butter

½ tablespoon [8 mL] confectioner's sugar

¾ teaspoon [4 mL] ground cinnamon

QUAIL

2 quail

1 small onion, minced

2 garlic cloves

½ teaspoon [3 mL] ground ginger

¼ teaspoon [1 mL] *ras el hanout* (see **Chef Notes**)

⅛ teaspoon [0.5 mL] dried hot chile

4 threads saffron, toasted and crushed

¾ cup [180 mL] chicken stock

1½ tablespoons [25 mL] parsley, minced

1 tablespoon [15 mL] cilantro, minced

2 eggs, lightly beaten

Salt to taste

PHYLLO TRIANGLES

8 sheets phyllo pastry, thawed and covered with a damp cloth

Clarified butter, melted, to brush on triangles

Confectioner's sugar, to dust triangles

Ground cinnamon, to dust triangles

ADVANCE PREPARATION

1. Sauté the almonds in butter until golden brown and aromatic. Add the confectioner's sugar and ¼ teaspoon [1 mL] of the cinnamon, and stir to coat. Reserve.

PREPARATION OF THE QUAIL

2. Heat the butter and brown the quail over medium-high heat. Remove and reserve the quail.

Chicken, squab, or partridge may be substituted for the quail. *Ras el hanout* can be purchased at some Middle Eastern groceries or you can make your own.

Ras el Hanout

Makes about ¼ cup [60 mL]

> 2½ tablespoons [40 mL] allspice berries
>
> ¼ cup [60 mL] black peppercorns
>
> 2 tablespoons [30 mL] dried galangal
>
> 1½ tablespoons [25 mL] mace blades
>
> 1½ whole nutmegs, cracked
>
> 10 cardamom pods
>
> 20 threads saffron
>
> ¾ cup [180 mL] ground ginger
>
> ¼ cup [60 mL] ground cinnamon
>
> 2 tablespoons [30 mL] turmeric
>
> 1 clove
>
> 3 dried rosebuds or 2 tablespoons [30 mL] dried rose petals

1. Place all the ingredients in a dry nonstick skillet over medium-high heat and toast, stirring constantly, until the mixture becomes fragrant, about 3 minutes.

2. Grind the mixture in a blender or spice grinder until very fine. Pass through a very fine sieve. Store in a cool, dark place.

3. Add the onion and garlic. Sauté until the onion is translucent. Add the remaining ½ teaspoon [3 mL] of cinnamon, the ginger, *ras el hanout*, hot chile, and saffron. Briefly sauté until aromatic. Immediately add the chicken stock, the reserved quail, and any accumulated juices and bring to a boil.

4. Reduce the heat and simmer until the quail are cooked, about 15 minutes. Remove the quail to cool and reduce the liquid until most has evaporated.

5. While the liquid is reducing, bone the quail, reserving the meat and any accumulated juices. Add the parsley and cilantro to the reduced liquid.

6. Stir the beaten egg into the reduction and scramble the mixture until the eggs are cooked and fluffy. Season to taste with salt. Add the quail meat and any juices and mix well. Reserve and allow to cool. (This filling may be prepared 1 day in advance and refrigerated.)

PREPARATION OF THE PHYLLO TRIANGLES

7. Remove 1 phyllo sheet and brush it with melted clarified butter. Immediately cover the remaining phyllo sheets with the cloth. Fold the sheet in half lengthwise and brush the surface with more clarified butter.

8. To form triangles, place 1 to 2 tablespoons [15 to 30 mL] of filling at the bottom of the folded sheet, about ¼ inch [6 mm] from the edge. Top with some of the reserved almond mixture.

9. Bring 1 corner of the pastry over the filling and fold to form a triangle. Brush with clarified butter and fold over again. Continue brushing with butter and folding (as you would fold a flag) until the opposite end of the pastry is reached. Fold any excess phyllo under the triangle to maintain the shape.

10. Place on a parchment-lined sheet pan and cover with plastic film. Continue until all the triangles are formed in this way. (The phyllo triangles may be made several hours in advance and stored covered and refrigerated.)

COOKING METHOD

11. Place the folded phyllo pastries on a parchment-lined sheet pan. Brush the tops of the triangles with clarified butter and bake at 400°F [205°C] for 10 to 15 minutes, or until golden brown.

SERVICE

12. Dust the tops of the triangles with confectioner's sugar. Create an interesting pattern (lattice or geometric is traditional) with cinnamon sprinkled over the confectioner's sugar.

Grilled Tuna Kebabs with Herb-Lemon Marinade Thon bì Chermoula (Tchermila)

serves 8 (2 kebabs per person)

Chermoula is a marinade that can be used on most meats, poultry, and seafood; it is especially good with tuna or swordfish steaks. Prepared in this manner, the marinated food can be char-grilled, broiled, sautéed, or baked. Cooking over live coals provides the most flavorful dish. In this recipe the fish is first marinated with a portion of the *chermoula*, then dressed with the rest after grilling. The *chermoula* may also be used to baste the fish as it cooks.

CHEF NOTES

This method works very well with most shellfish, is excellent with poultry, and is often used with lamb. The fish may be cut into medallions and grilled rather than skewered as a kebab. Preserved lemons can be purchased in Middle Eastern markets.

CHERMOULA MARINADE: MAKES ABOUT I CUP [240 mL]

I preserved lemon, rinsed and minced fine

3 tablespoons [45 mL] parsley, chopped

3 tablespoons [45 mL] cilantro, chopped

⅛ teaspoon [0.5 mL] crushed saffron, lightly toasted

½ teaspoon [3 mL] paprika

¼ teaspoon [I mL] cayenne, or more to taste

½ teaspoon [3 mL] ground cumin

I teaspoon [5 mL] salt

2 tablespoons [30 mL] fresh lemon juice

¼ cup [60 mL] olive oil

1½ pounds [675 g] tuna or swordfish steaks, cut into ¾-inch [2-cm] cubes

16 skewers, soaked for 30 minutes in water prior to use if wooden

I preserved lemon, rinsed, pulp removed, and cut into thin strips

Sprigs of cilantro or parsley, for garnish

ADVANCE PREPARATION

1. Combine all of the *chermoula* ingredients in the workbowl of a food processor and process to a coarse purée.

2. Place the fish in a resealable plastic bag and pour in half of the marinade. Toss to coat. Allow to marinate at least 4 hours, preferably overnight, refrigerated.

COOKING METHOD

3. Make the kebabs, using 1½ ounces [45 g] of fish (about 3 cubes) per skewer. Grill the skewers slowly over indirect heat of a live coal fire. The fish should be cooked to medium rare and not be charred.

SERVICE

4. Serve 2 skewers per person, topped with the reserved *chermoula*. Garnish with the thin strips of preserved lemon and sprigs of cilantro or parsley.

Rice-Stuffed Dates Wrapped in Sole with Sweet and Sour Sauce Samak Mehshi bi Tamr

serves 8

In this surprising dish, a small strip of sole fillet is wrapped around a date that has been stuffed with a mixture of cooked ground rice, almonds, ginger, and onion, then broiled. The rolls are paired with a sweet and sour sauce of onions and raisins, infused with saffron. In Morocco, a whole fish stuffed with filled dates is a popular way to enjoy this dish.

CHEF NOTES

Many types of white-fleshed fish work in this dish, especially flounder, cod, halibut, sea bass, or tilapia. Split large shrimp may also be wrapped around the stuffed dates with the same effect.

SAUCE

3 tablespoons [45 mL] olive oil

1½ pounds [675 g] onions, thinly sliced

5 ounces [140 g] white raisins

⅛ teaspoon [0.5 mL] saffron threads, crushed

1 teaspoon [5 mL] ground cinnamon

½ teaspoon [3 mL] black pepper

¼ cup [60 mL] sugar

¼ cup [60 mL] white wine vinegar

2 tablespoons [30 mL] orange flower water

FISH ROLLS

16 strips fillet of sole or other delicate-flavored fish, 2 inches [5 cm] by 3 to 4 inches [8 to 10 cm]

Salt and pepper

3 fluid ounces [85 mL] water

Pinch of salt

1½ tablespoons [25 mL] cream of rice

2½ ounces [75 g] ground almonds, lightly toasted until fragrant but not browned

¼ teaspoon [1 mL] ground ginger

1 teaspoon [5 mL] sugar

¼ teaspoon [2 mL] ground black pepper

2 tablespoons [30 mL] melted unsalted butter

16 large Medjool dates, pitted with skins left intact

2 tablespoons [30 mL] grated onion

½ cup [120 mL] water or fish fumet

Ground ginger, for dusting

Ground cinnamon, for dusting

Toasted almonds, for garnish

ADVANCE PREPARATION

1. Heat the olive oil in a nonstick skillet over medium-low heat. Add the onions and raisins. Sauté until the onions are golden.

2. Add the saffron, cinnamon, pepper, sugar, and vinegar. Simmer, stirring occasionally, until the mixture begins to reduce and thickens. (The sauce can be made 1 day in advance.) Just before service, stir in the orange flower water and reserve, warm.

PREPARATION OF THE FISH ROLLS

3. Lightly season the fish fillet strips with salt and pepper and reserve.

4. Bring 3 fluid ounces of water to boil, season with a pinch of salt, and quickly stir in the cream of rice. Boil, stirring constantly, for 30 seconds. Remove from the heat. Allow the cream of rice to cool.

5. Add all but 2 tablespoons [30 mL] of the ground almonds, all of the ginger, the sugar, black pepper, and 1 tablespoon [15 mL] of the melted butter. Mix well and stuff each date with about ½ teaspoon [3 mL] of the mixture.

6. Place each stuffed date at 1 end of a strip of fish and roll up to enclose the date, securing each roll with a toothpick. Lightly tap the rolls on a hard surface so they stand upright. Place the rolls in a buttered baking dish, leaving a small amount of space between the rolls.

7. Mix the grated onion with ½ cup [120 mL] of water or fish fumet and pour it into the dish. Avoid pouring the liquid directly on top of the fish rolls. Top each roll with the remaining melted butter, and dust the tops of the rolls with ginger, the remaining almonds, and cinnamon.

COOKING METHOD

8. Bake the fish rolls for 15 minutes at 375°F [190°C], or until the tops begin to turn golden brown and the fish is opaque but moist.

9. Remove the rolls and reserve warm. Pour the pan juices into a small skillet and reduce over high heat.

SERVICE

10. For each serving, place 2 fish rolls on a pool of warm sauce. Spoon the reduced pan juices over each roll. Garnish with toasted almonds and dust with cinnamon.

Eastern Mediterranean

Greece, Turkey,

Armenia

Pork Riblets with Spiced Quince
Sergevilov Dubgvadz Khozi Miss

Lamb and Rice Meatballs in Lemon-Egg Sauce
Yuverlakia

Lamb Kebabs with Onion-Sumac Relish
Güneydogu Andalou Usulü Sis Kebabi

Grilled Swordfish Kebabs with Lemon-Herb Glaze
Xifias Souvlaki

Mussels Stuffed with Aromatic Rice
Midia Dolma (Tsgnaganchi Litzk)

Grape Leaves Stuffed with Rice, Lemon, and Herbs
Dolmades Yinlandzi

Phyllo Pie with Feta, Wild Greens, and Leeks
Hortopita me Avga

MUCH HAS BEEN made of the Mediterranean diet, known for being a healthy way of eating. Olive oil, citrus, simply prepared vegetables, and lean meats form the basis of the cuisines of the Mediterranean.

The foods of Greece reflect an open-air style of dining and food preparation. The climate—with long, hot dry summers and short, mild winters—and geography have much to do with this style. Few rivers exist on the mainland, and the climate is arid. Soils are poor and irrigation is not practical, since the rivers that do run soon dry up during the summer months. Greece is mountainous, with few flat plains to promote large-scale agriculture. In spite of this, Greece is primarily an agricultural country and is self-sufficient in feeding its people. Exports include wheat, citrus, olives and olive oil, and grapes. With little grazing land, cattle are scarce. Sheep and goats, able to graze on the sparse grasses of the hilly land, are the common source of meats and cheeses. Bordered by the Mediterranean, Ionian, and Aegean seas, Greece enjoys a thriving fishing industry. Greece encompasses many out islands as well, and fish is quite popular throughout the country; octopus is enjoyed across the region.

Turkey may be divided into two broad regions: European Turkey, which borders Greece and the Aegean and the Black seas, and Asian Turkey, which is separated from Europe by the Bosporus and Dardanelles straits and the Sea of Marmara. Turkey borders the Mediterranean and Aegean seas as well as Iran, Iraq, Syria, and the former Soviet Union. European Turkey is known as Eastern Thrace, and Asian Turkey is generally known as Anatolia. Climate varies greatly in this vast country, from a typical Mediterranean climate to a cooler, mountainous climate (the average elevation of Turkey is over 3,500 feet). Since Turkey is located at the intersection of five tectonic plates, it is one of the world's most geologically unstable countries. (Turkey is one of the most earthquake-prone regions of the world.) Only one-third of the land is under cultivation, and the soil is not very productive. Cereal grains are the principal crop. Cattle have caused a severe overgrazing of the land, and sheep, goats, and chickens provide the meat in the Turkish diet. Root vegetables, such as potatoes and sugar beets, are grown. Turkish cuisine is influenced by its unique position in the world, located at the crossroads of Europe and Asia. Turkish cuisine has striking similarities to that of Greece, with Middle Eastern and Southwestern Asia accents. It is believed that the technique of cooking skewered meats (kebab) is of Turkish origin and was rapidly assimilated into the cuisines of Iran, the Middle East, North Africa and Southwestern Asia (and has become a most popular snack and appetizer worldwide).

Armenia borders Turkey on the west, Azerbaijan on the east, and Georgia on the north. It has a pleasant, healthy climate with cold, dry winters and dusty, hot summers. The average elevation is almost 6,000 feet. The numerous river valleys have soils that are quite rich, and agriculture is important economically (over one-third of its people are employed in agriculture). Wheat, barley, root vegetables such as potatoes and beets, grapes, and citrus are the major crops. The high plateaus are primarily pastoral.

The countries of this region, and thus their cuisines, are closely tied through a common history. Anatolia emerged as a major center of the world's agricultural development by cave dwellers of the Neolithic period. It is one of the oldest, continually inhabited regions of the world. By 2000 B.C. trading centers were established by the Assyrians, initializing the food connection between this part of the world and the Middle East.

In spite of being under the political control of the Byzantine and Ottoman empires for over a thousand years, Greek cooking, being passed on from generation to generation within the family unit, maintained its individual character. Professional chefs of the Byzantine courts relied on ancient Greek cuisine to form a basis for their cooking style and incorporated spices and foods from around the world. Ottoman cooks, studying in Europe, brought back techniques and knowledge to invent new dishes. Many traditional Greek dishes have Turkish names, but a nationalistic movement in the 1920s motivated Greeks to rename their old recipes. Many so-called "foreign" ingredients were purged from Greek recipes as well, in the hope of returning to a purer and more authentic Greek cuisine.

Many Greek dishes are connected to religious festivals. The eating patterns of modern Greeks mirror those of the ancients. The diet is (and always was) based on little meat. Vegetarianism as a way of life was introduced into Greek culture by Pythagoras. Modern Greeks also rely heavily on vegetables, often not by choice but by necessity. With poor soils, wild greens were, and still are, a common source of vegetables in the diet.

The staple of the Greek diet is wheat bread, and when there is little else to eat, bread dipped in olive oil could be the entire meal. Olive oil is the cooking fat used, and may be one reason for the healthy aspect of the Mediterranean diet. Greece consumes more olive oil per capita than any other country. The olive oils produced are richer tasting than those in most other countries producing olive oil, since olive trees are not irrigated in Greece. Cheese, made from goat's milk and ewe's milk, is enjoyed throughout the country, although milk itself is rarely consumed. Citrus thrives in the region and is included in many savory dishes. Appetizers (*mezze*), such as stuffed vine leaves (*dolmades*) and small meatballs, are quite popular.

Diversity is the key to describing Turkish cuisine. The southern coast of Turkey has a Mediterranean component to its cuisine. Turkey has coasts on the Mediterranean and Black seas. Seafood is popular, and olive oil is the cooking fat of choice. The classic Mediterranean flavors of olives, citrus, and grapes are common. To the east, Southwestern Asian influences abound, especially where Turkey borders Georgia and Iran. This is the region of the spiciest of Turkish dishes, and clarified butter and the fat from sheep's tails becomes the cooking fat of choice. Nuts, such as pistachios and walnuts, are often included in savory dishes. Middle Eastern flavors are found near the borders with Iraq and Syria, and spices such as cinnamon and coriander can be found in Turkish recipes from this region.

One of the most popular dishes is the kebab. Although a Persian word, the kebab appears to be a Turkish invention, which spread across most of the Western world. *Sis kebop* (shish kebab) is the classic skewered meat cubes (most popular is lamb) and *doner kebop* uses stacked slices of boned leg of lamb, rotating near a vertical broiler. Meat is sliced from the cooked exterior, onto flat bread, exposing the uncooked interior. Most Turkish households have a charcoal grill, the preferred method of cooking meats.

Early in Turkey's history, China had a strong influence on its cuisine. Today, filled dumplings are widely enjoyed, as are stuffed vegetables and sausages. Were it not for Turkey's conversion to Islam, there would have been a much greater influence on its cuisine by eastern Asia. Islam kept the cultures separate, maintaining a strong national identity for the Turks. Another indication of the separation of the Chinese influence from Turkish cuisine is found in Turkey's fondness for dairy products, which the Chinese generally do not eat. Yogurt, a Turkish word, is extremely popular as an addition to sauces, as a condiment, and as a beverage. Cheeses, especially those made from ewe's milk and goat's milk, are enjoyed everywhere in Turkey.

Armenia has been the battleground of many wars throughout its long history, as it is at the crossroads of the East and West. Many have come and influenced its cuisine, yet Armenians are passionate about their heritage. They have maintained an identity, in part, due to their religious preference. Armenia was the first country to convert to Christianity (and thus provided another reason for wars to be fought on its land). Unlike their Muslim neighbors, pork is enjoyed as well as lamb (Muslims, like Jews, do not eat pork). Because of the rich soil, grazing cattle can be raised, and beef is eaten more than in the surrounding lands. As in Turkey, charcoal grilling is the most popular cooking method for meats. Domestic fowl are also featured in its cuisine. Grains such as millet, wheat, barley, and rye are all cultivated, and rice and bulghur are the cereals of choice. Armenian cuisine relies heavily on olive oil as its cooking fat, and butter is popular since the dairy industry is one of the most important in Armenia. Armenian cheese is prized throughout the region, especially in Russia and the Balkans. Eggplant is a favorite vegetable and fruits and nuts are often found in Armenian appetizers. Many Armenian dishes have Turkish names, as this land has been under Turkish control for many years.

Pork Riblets with Spiced Quince Sergevilov Dubgvadz Khozi Miss

ARMENIA

serves 8

This dish features tender, bite-sized pork ribs that are stewed with quince and spices. Quince is very popular throughout the area. Care should be taken when preparing the dense fruit, as quince can be quite tough to cut. Quince and pork pair well together and both are compli-mented by the flavors of clove and cinnamon. Ask your butcher or meat supplier to cut the rib rack in half, lengthwise. The ribs may then be cut into individual riblets.

CHEF NOTES

Apples may be substituted for the quince (but will lack the unique aroma and flavor of the quince). If using apples, add ¼ cup [60 mL] quince paste (found in most Latin American markets as *membrillo*). Baby back ribs provide more uniform portion control, but a regular rack is meatier.

I rack lean pork ribs, chine bone removed, cut in half lengthwise, separated into individual riblets, pounded slightly to tenderize

Salt and ground black pepper to taste

¼ cup [60 mL] clarified butter

1½ cups [360 mL] red onions, sliced

4 garlic cloves, minced

2 pounds [900 g] unpeeled quince, cored and cut lengthwise into thick slices

6 whole cloves

I teaspoon [5 mL] cinnamon, or to taste

I tablespoon [15 mL] sugar, or to taste

2 tablespoons [30 mL] parsley, minced

I tablespoon [15 mL] mint, chiffonade

¾ cup [180 mL] rich beef or pork stock

I teaspoon [5 mL] lemon juice

Lavash or pita bread, for service

Mint and parsley sprigs, for garnish

ADVANCE PREPARATION

1. All advance preparation may be found in the ingredient list.

PREPARATION OF THE RIBLETS

2. Season the riblets with salt and pepper. Heat 2 tablespoons [30 mL] of the clarified butter in a heavy casserole or skillet over medium heat. Sauté the riblets, browning them evenly. Remove and reserve the riblets.

3. Add the remaining butter and sauté the onion until soft. Add the garlic and sauté an additional minute. Add the quince slices and sauté until golden. Add the cloves, cinnamon, sugar, parsley, mint, stock, lemon juice, and the reserved riblets. Stir the mixture and cover.

COOKING METHOD

4. Bake the covered casserole at 375°F [190°C] for 1½ hours, or until the riblets are tender. (The casserole can be made one day in advance and held refrigerated overnight.)

5. Prior to service, remove the ribs from the quince sauce. Place them on a parchment-lined sheet pan and roast in a 450°F [235°C] oven for 10 to 15 minutes, or until crisp and warmed. Return the ribs to the warm quince sauce.

SERVICE

6. Serve 4 to 5 riblets per person, accompanied by warm sauce and wedges of Middle Eastern flat bread. Garnish with sprigs of parsley and mint. (Include an extra plate for the bones.)

Lamb and Rice Meatballs in Lemon-Egg Sauce Yuverlakia

serves 8 (4 meatballs per person)

This extremely popular dish is served all across Greece. The name translates as "little spheres." If the amount of liquid is increased, it is served as a soup or stew; it is then called *yuverlakia soupa avgolemono. Avgolemono* is, perhaps, the best known of Greek sauces. The key to making it correctly is to beat the egg mixture until frothy, then add the simmering liquid by ladleful while whisking constantly, making sure that the eggs do not curdle. Once the liquid has been added, be careful that the mixture does not boil. (This sauce is similar to a hollandaise sauce in its method of preparation.)

CHEF NOTES

The meatballs may be made from beef, veal, or lamb (lamb is traditional). Poultry or seafood may be used as long as sufficient egg yolks are added to bind the mixture.

MEATBALLS: MAKES 32 MEATBALLS

1 pound [450 g] ground lamb

1 onion, grated

3 garlic cloves, minced

⅓ cup [80 mL] long-grain white rice

⅓ cup [80 mL] parsley, minced

2 tablespoons [30 mL] dill, minced

1 tablespoon [15 mL] mint, minced

1 teaspoon [5 mL] dried oregano

⅛ teaspoon [0.5 mL] grated orange zest

2 egg yolks

Salt and black pepper to taste

Flour, for dredging

2 tablespoons [30 mL] olive oil

LEMON-EGG SAUCE: MAKES ½ CUP [120 mL] SAUCE

3 to 4 cups [720 to 960 mL] chicken stock, simmering, as needed

1 medium onion, minced

2 garlic cloves, minced

1 stalk celery, minced

1 carrot, finely diced

3 eggs, at room temperature

¼ cup [60 mL] lemon juice or to taste

Parsley, for garnish

8 lemon wedges, for garnish

ADVANCE PREPARATION

1. Combine the lamb, onion, garlic, rice, parsley, dill, mint, oregano, orange zest, egg yolks, and salt and pepper and mix well.

2. Sauté a small piece of this mixture and taste for correct seasoning. Adjust for seasoning. Form the mixture into meatballs, 1 inch [2.5 cm] in diameter. Reserve, tightly covered, refrigerated.

COOKING METHOD

3. Dredge the meatballs in flour and sauté in the olive oil over medium heat. Brown the meatballs.

PREPARATION OF THE SAUCE

4. Add enough chicken stock to just cover the meatballs. Bring the liquid to a boil. Add the onion, garlic, celery, and carrot.

5. Reduce the heat to a simmer and cook the meatballs for 25 minutes, adding more stock if necessary.

6. Place the eggs in a blender and blend until frothy. Add the lemon juice. Using a strainer, remove about 2 cups [480 mL] of the liquid from the meatballs. Return the strained vegetables to the skillet.

7. With the blender running slowly, add 1½ to 2 cups [360 to 480 mL] of the strained hot broth. Cook this mixture over simmering water in a double boiler until thickened to the desired consistency. Stir the thickened sauce into the meatballs and hold over a very low heat for service. Do not allow the sauce to boil, or it will curdle.

SERVICE

8. Serve 4 meatballs per person, with about 3 tablespoons [45 mL] sauce ladled over the top. Garnish with sprigs of parsley and a lemon wedge on the side.

Lamb Kebabs with Onion-Sumac Relish Güneydogu Andalu Usulü Sis Kebabi

serves 8

Food scholars have argued for years as to the origin of the kebab. Many insisted that the dish came about by Ottoman soldiers skewering meat on their swords and then cooking over the campfire. References for the *shish kebab* have been found in cooking texts written as early as the eleventh century, and there is mention of the kebab in very early Persian texts that predate the rise of the Ottoman empire (the word "skewer" appears in these texts as well, indicating that swords were not the first device used for meats cooked in this fashion). Scholars now agree that the dish probably developed in Turkey and spread to the Middle East and Persia. Kebab stands are found throughout Turkey, featuring regional variations on the basic theme of skewered marinated meat grilled over live coals. Kebabs from the southeast of Turkey are among the spiciest. Kebabs are normally served wrapped in a piece of flat bread to absorb the juices from the meat.

RELISH: MAKES ¾ CUP [180 mL]

2 medium-size sweet onions, sliced paper thin

1 teaspoon [5 mL] salt

2 tablespoons [30 mL] sumac

½ teaspoon [3 mL] thyme leaves

Pinch sugar

MARINADE: MAKES 1½ CUPS [360 mL]

1 onion, grated or puréed

½ cup [120 mL] olive oil

2 tablespoons [30 mL] garlic, minced

1 tablespoon [15 mL] paprika

½ tablespoon [8 mL] cayenne

½ teaspoon [3 mL] crushed red pepper

1 tablespoon [15 mL] ground cumin

1 tablespoon [15 mL] fresh thyme leaves, minced

½ cup [120 mL] parsley leaves and stems, chopped

½ cup [120 mL] mint leaves, chiffonade

1 teaspoon [5 mL] salt

½ teaspoon [3 mL] black pepper

SKEWERS

1½ pounds [675 g] boneless lamb, cut into ½-inch [1-cm] cubes

16 skewers, soaked in warm water for 30 minutes if wooden

16 small cherry tomatoes

2 red onions, quartered and separated into segments

2 red bell peppers, seeds and ribs removed, cut into 1-inch [2.5-cm] squares

4 jalapeño or other similar chiles, quartered

Flat bread for service

ADVANCE PREPARATION

1. Combine the onions, salt, sumac, thyme leaves, and sugar and allow to stand for 30 minutes before serving. (The relish can be made several hours in advance.)

PREPARATION OF THE MARINADE

2. Combine all of the marinade ingredients in a bowl and mix well. Place the meat cubes in a resealable plastic bag and add the marinade. Toss the lamb with the marinade to coat. Allow the lamb to marinate for at least 4 hours, refrigerated, or preferably overnight.

ASSEMBLY OF THE SKEWERS

3. Drain and reserve the marinade from the meat. Skewer the meat cubes, alternating with cherry tomatoes, onion segments, bell pepper squares, and the jalapeño quarters. Reserve, refrigerated. (The skewers may be prepared 1 day in advance and refrigerated until needed.)

COOKING METHOD

4. Grill the skewers over an indirect charcoal fire until the meat cubes are cooked medium rare. The skewers should be lightly charred but care should be taken that they don't cook too quickly.

SERVICE

5. Wrap a piece of flat bread around a skewer. Twist, while pulling the meat and vegetables from the skewer. Place the wrap on a plate containing a small mound of the onion relish on the side. Serve immediately.

Grilled Swordfish Kebabs with Lemon-Herb Glaze Xifias Souvlaki

serves 8 (2 skewers per person)

Swordfish kebabs are enjoyed all across Greece. At the fish market (*psaragora*) fish that is more than a half-day old is rejected as not being fresh. The Greek approach to cooking fish is minimal preparation and simple cooking methods. The method of cooking the swordfish in this recipe is remarkably similar to the Turkish version of the dish, known as *kilic sis kebap*. Unlike long-line-caught swordfish found in the United States, most swordfish caught in Greece is landed on small boats, using baited lines. Deepwater trenches and shallow seamounts adjacent to Greece's coastline are the ideal environment to find swordfish, and Greek fishermen have fished for them in this way for centuries.

MARINADE

½ cup [120 mL] olive oil

2 tablespoons [30 mL] fresh lemon juice

½ tablespoon [8 mL] dried oregano

½ tablespoon [8 mL] dried thyme

2 garlic cloves, minced

Salt and pepper to taste

1½ pounds [675 g] swordfish steaks or fillets

SKEWERS

16 skewers, soaked in warm water for 30 minutes if wooden

1 large onion, quartered and separated into segments

8 fresh bay leaves, cut in half lengthwise

16 cherry tomatoes, halved

1 red bell pepper, seeds and ribs removed, cut into 1-inch [2.5-cm] squares

Lemon wedges, for garnish

Sprigs of oregano, for garnish

Sprigs of thyme, for garnish

ADVANCE PREPARATION

1. Mix the olive oil, lemon juice, oregano, thyme, garlic, and salt and pepper together and whisk to combine. (The marinade may be made one day in advance.)

2. Combine the swordfish cubes with the marinade in a resealable plastic bag and allow the fish to marinate for 1 to 2 hours, refrigerated.

ASSEMBLY OF THE SKEWERS

3. Drain the marinade from the fish and reserve for basting. Prepare the skewers by adding the ingredients in the following order: onion segment, fish, bay leaf, ½ cherry tomato, bell pepper square, fish. Repeat, ending with onion.

In Greece, where traditional methods are still used to harvest the swordfish, stocks are much less depleted than with methods employed elsewhere. If possible, try to purchase line-caught swordfish; it will be fresher and will have less environmental impact. Any white, firm-fleshed fish or shellfish may be substituted. Mahi mahi makes an excellent alternative to regionally endangered swordfish.

COOKING METHOD

4. Cook the fish skewers over an indirect medium-hot charcoal fire for 10 to 15 minutes, or until the fish flakes easily and the vegetables are done. Turn the skewers occasionally during cooking and baste frequently with the reserved marinade.

SERVICE

5. Serve 2 skewers per person, accompanied with lemon wedges or sprigs of fresh oregano or thyme.

Mussels Stuffed with Aromatic Rice Midia Dolma (Tsgnaganchi Litzk)

ARMENIA

This ancient dish, developed by the Armenians during the Byzantine era, is also prepared in Turkey, known there as *midye dolmasi*. The mussels are served cold, with some of the pan juices. Traditionally, the stuffing is held in place with a piece of string tied around the mussel. The mussel shells are brushed with a bit of olive oil, making them glisten attractively for service.

 CHEF NOTES

The mussels may be served at room temperature or chilled. This recipe makes a unique dish for a picnic (leave the rubber bands on the mussels during transport) or for finger food at parties.

MUSSELS

48 large mussels, well scrubbed

½ cup [120 mL] olive oil

4 cups [960 mL] onions, diced

4 garlic cloves, minced

¼ cup [60 mL] pine nuts

½ cup [120 mL] long-grain white rice, rinsed

1 ripe tomato, peeled, seeded, and diced

¼ cup [60 mL] barberries or currants

½ teaspoon [3 mL] allspice, ground

¼ teaspoon [1 mL] cinnamon

¼ teaspoon [1 mL] cayenne

Pinch of grated nutmeg

Salt and ground black pepper to taste

1 teaspoon [5 mL] sugar

Water or stock as needed

48 thick, small rubber bands

2 tablespoons [30 mL] fresh lemon juice

2 tablespoons [30 mL] olive oil

Lemon wedges, for garnish

ADVANCE PREPARATION

1. Place the mussels in a bowl of warm, salted water for 5 minutes to open and purge them. Remove any beards and waste matter, and rinse under cold running water.

2. Over a clean bowl, insert a thin knife to sever the mussel from the shell, allowing the liquids collect in the bowl. Strain the liquids through a fine sieve and reserve. Add enough water or stock to the reserved liquids to make 1½ cups [360 mL]. Refrigerate until needed.

PREPARATION OF THE STUFFED MUSSELS

3. For the stuffing, heat the olive oil in a skillet over medium heat. Sauté the onions, garlic, and pine nuts until the nuts are golden and the onions have softened.

4. Add the rice and sauté for 5 minutes, while stirring. Add the tomato, barberries, allspice, cinnamon, cayenne, nutmeg, salt, pepper, sugar, and lemon juice. Stir well to incorporate.

5. Add ¾ cup [180 mL] of the reserved mussel liquor and simmer until the liquid is absorbed. Set aside and allow to cool. (The stuffing can be made 1 day in advance.)

6. Place 1 tablespoon [15 mL] of filling inside each mussel and secure with a rubber band. Arrange the mussels, in one layer, in a large skillet.

COOKING METHOD

7. Add the remaining reserved mussel liquor and lemon juice to the pan and bring the liquid to a boil (add stock if additional liquid is required). Reduce the heat to a simmer. Cover and cook the mussels for 5 to 10 minutes. Remove the cover and allow the mussels to cool in the pan.

SERVICE

8. Add the olive oil to the pan and swirl to coat the mussels. Remove the rubber bands (be careful, as the mussels will "pop" open). Strain the pan juices and reserve. Place 6 mussels on each plate and top with a small amount of the pan juices. Garnish with lemon wedges.

Grape Leaves Stuffed with Rice, Lemon, and Herbs Dolmades Yinlandzi

serves 8 (4 stuffed rolls per person)

There is evidence that stuffed grape leaves originated in Greece and spread across the Mediterranean into Southwestern Asia. This dish is very popular throughout Greece, both as a Lenten dish and as everyday fare, and it is a favorite at parties and taverns. The tangy rice stuffing contains dill and parsley as well as lemon pulp. These stuffed leaves are perfect with drinks on a hot summer day or evening. They can be served cold, warm, or hot and, once cooked, they will keep for a week in the refrigerator.

I cup [240 mL] long-grain rice

¾ cup [180 mL] olive oil

2 cups [480 mL] onions, minced

4 garlic cloves, minced

I teaspoon [5 mL] salt

3 cups [720 mL] chopped scallions, green parts included

6 tablespoons [90 mL] fresh lemon juice

¼ cup [60 mL] lemon pulp, seeds removed

2 to 3 cups [480 to 720 mL] rich chicken stock

½ cup [120 mL] parsley leaves, chopped (stems reserved for lining cooking pot)

½ cup [120 mL] fresh dill, chopped (stems reserved for lining cooking pot)

Salt and black pepper to taste

32 grape leaves, rinsed, carefully separated, stems trimmed

I cup [240 mL] chicken stock or water, simmering, or more as needed

Parsley sprigs, for garnish

Lemon wedges, for garnish

ADVANCE PREPARATION

1. Sauté the rice in a large skillet over medium heat in ½ cup [120 mL] of the olive oil, until opaque. Add the onions, garlic, salt, and sauté for 5 minutes, or until softened.

2. Add the scallions, 1½ tablespoons [25 mL] of the lemon juice, and the lemon pulp. Sauté for 2 minutes.

3. Add 2 cups [480 mL] of the stock and simmer for 10 minutes, or until the rice is cooked al dente, adding more stock if necessary. Stir in the chopped parsley, chopped dill, and salt and pepper. Taste and adjust the seasoning, allow to cool, and reserve. (The rice filling can be prepared one day in advance.)

ASSEMBLY

4. Place 1 heaping tablespoon [20 mL] of the filling near the lower end of the underside of a grape leaf. Fold the bottom

If using fresh grape leaves, blanch them first in boiling water, for 5 minutes, or until tender. In Macedonia and Thrace, a few tablespoons of pine nuts and raisins are added to the rice mixture before stuffing. Lean ground beef with a pinch of cinnamon may be substituted for half of the rice in the stuffing and half the amount of lemon juice to make *dolmades me avgolemono* (grape leaves stuffed with meat and rice with egg-lemon sauce). To make the sauce, see the recipe for Lamb and Rice Meatballs in Lemon-Egg Sauce (page 414), using 1 cup [240 mL] of the cooking liquid from this recipe.

of the leaf over the filling, fold the sides in, and roll the leaf toward the point of the leaf. Place the rolls, seam-side down, on a tray until ready to cook. Repeat until all of the leaves are stuffed.

COOKING METHOD

5. Line the bottom of a roasting pan with the parsley and the dill stems. Arrange the stuffed leaves in one layer, seam side down. (If necessary, use several pans.)

6. Add the remaining ¼ cup [60 mL] of the olive oil and another 1½ tablespoons [25 mL] of the lemon juice over the top of the leaves. Add enough simmering stock or water to come halfway up the sides of the rolls.

7. Bake, covered, at 350°F [175°C] for 45 minutes, or until the leaves are tender. Sprinkle the remaining lemon juice over the leaves and allow to cool completely in the liquid. Drain, reserving some of the liquid before service.

SERVICE

8. Serve each person 4 stuffed grape leaves, topped with a drizzle of the cooking liquid and garnished with sprigs of parsley and lemon wedges.

Phyllo Pie with Feta, Wild Greens, and Leeks Hortopita me Avga

GREECE

serves 8 to 12

Made with eggs as well as greens and cheese, this pie is an upscale version of the well-known *spanakopita*. Traditionally the village women would gather wild greens to use for this pie, but chefs may substitute a combination of spinach and dandelion greens, or endive. This dish may be made as individual pies or as one large pie, as in this version.

CHEF NOTES

Any combination of greens may be used for this dish. Aromatic and bitter greens, arugula for example, pair well with less flavorful greens.

2 pounds [900 g] fresh greens (spinach, chard, endive, dandelions, etc.), washed, trimmed

Juice of 1 lemon

1 cup [240 mL] parsley, loosely packed, chopped

1 cup [240 mL] dill, loosely packed, chopped

¼ cup [60 mL] fresh chervil, chopped

¼ cup [60 mL] clarified butter

3 leeks, including green parts, thoroughly washed and chopped

½ teaspoon [3 mL] ground allspice

½ teaspoon [3 mL] ground cinnamon

½ teaspoon [3 mL] grated nutmeg

1 teaspoon [5 mL] black pepper

Salt to taste

2 teaspoons [10 mL] sugar

5 eggs, beaten

1 cup [240 mL] crumbled feta cheese, preferably sheep's milk

⅔ cup [160 mL] heavy cream

12 sheets prepared phyllo dough, covered to prevent drying out

Melted butter, for brushing the layers

Beaten egg, for brushing the top of the pastry

Sprigs of parsley and/or dill, for garnish

ADVANCE PREPARATION

1. All advance preparation may be found in the ingredient list.

PREPARATION OF THE FILLING

2. Place the greens in a nonstick skillet over medium-low heat and sauté until they begin to release their juices. Sprinkle the lemon juice over the greens and mix well. Cook the greens in their own moisture until wilted.

3. Place the parsley, dill, and chervil in the bottom of a colander set over a bowl. Add the heated greens and allow to stand for 10 minutes. Press down on the greens to remove all moisture.

424 | The Appetizer Atlas

4. Heat the clarified butter in the skillet used to wilt the greens over medium heat and sauté the leeks until transparent. Add the drained greens and herbs, the allspice, cinnamon, nutmeg, pepper, salt, and sugar and mix thoroughly.

5. Partially cover the pan and cook for 20 minutes, or until the liquid has been absorbed. Place the mixture in a large bowl and allow to cool. Stir in the eggs, feta, and cream and reserve.

ASSEMBLY METHOD

6. Butter the bottom and sides of an 8 × 10 × 2-inch [20 × 25 × 5-cm] baking dish. Brush 1 sheet of phyllo with melted butter. Place another sheet of phyllo on top of it and repeat, stacking a total of 6 layers of phyllo dough. Press the stacked sheets into the pan, draping the excess over the sides of the pan.

7. Add the filling and level with an offset spatula. Prepare another stack of 6 phyllo sheets as in Step 6. Top the pie with these phyllo sheets, folding over the edges to seal the top to the sides.

8. Brush the top of the pie lightly with beaten egg and bake for 45 minutes at 350°F [175°C], or until the top is golden brown and the filling has set. Allow the pie to cool slightly before service.

SERVICE

9. Cut the pie into 8 to 12 pieces. Serve one piece, garnished with sprigs of parsley or dill, to each person.

Eastern Europe

Russia, Ukraine,

Poland, Czech Republic,

Slovakia, Hungary,

Romania

Cabbage Rolls Stuffed with Beef and Rice with Sweet-and-Sour Sauce
Gwumpky (Holipches)/Golubtsy

Meatballs with Cranberry-Leek Sauce
Bitki s Klyukvoy i Lukom Poreyem

Grilled Trout Fillet with Dried Cherry–Rose Petal Vinegar and Mayonnaise
Rózsaszirmos Meggyecete Hallal

Leek and Cod Croquettes in Aromatic Horseradish Sauce
Rybnyye Kotlety s Goryachim Sousom iz Khrena

Layered Crêpe, Mushroom, and Cheese Torte
Blinchaty Pirog s Gribami

Mushrooms Stewed in Sour Cream au Gratin
Griby Tushonyye v Smetane

Pan-Fried Potato-Filled Dumplings
Pirozhki s Kartofelnoy Nachinkoy

EASTERN EUROPE HAS undergone considerable upheaval in the twentieth century. The end of World War I saw the arbitrary creation of countries with no regard for the ethnic makeup of the peoples to be included, a policy that led to serious political problems later. In 1991 the U.S.S.R. was dismantled, and the Balkan states underwent dramatic changes in their borders and names. Regardless of political borders, the region is united by common ethnic bonds. Many of its people and its languages are Slavic in origin, although the Hungarian people—their origin, their language (of the Finno-Ugric language group), and their cuisine—are not. Christianity is the principal religion (within this broad designation there are Catholics, Orthodox Russians, and Lutherans), and many Jews can trace their roots to this area of the world.

The recipes to be considered in this chapter are from the classic cuisines of Russia, Ukraine, Poland, Hungary, and Romania. Many of the now independent countries of the former Soviet Union are included in other chapters in this book (see Southwestern Asia for Azerbaijan, Georgia, Kazakhstan, Uzbekistan, Turkmenistan, and Tajikistan; and refer to Scandinavia for Latvia, Lithuania, and Estonia).

In spite of climactic variations and differences in customs, there is a commonality to the cuisines of Russia, Ukraine, and Poland. Staple vegetables, such as cabbage, potatoes, and beets are seen in all the cuisines of the region. Sweet and sour combinations are popular, as are sour cream (and dairy products in general) and dumplings. Within the Austro-Hungarian Empire, wealthy Polish families traveled across Europe, returning with dishes from those countries visited. Invited guests introduced their cusines to the region as well. There is a strong French influence, dating back to the eighteenth century when Catherine the Great imported French chefs to Russia and continuing in the nineteenth century when Alexander I invited the great French chef Antonin Carême to St. Petersburg. There are Dutch, German, and Swedish influences, brought by chefs of those countries to cook for Peter the Great, earlier in the seventeenth and eighteenth centuries. A fine example is the adaptation of the smörgasbord to Russia, known there as *zakuski* (literally, small bites). Smoked fish savory pastries and sometimes caviar are present in this first course, and the largesse exhibited by the formidable spread reflects the generous character of the Slav people.

One of the earliest influences on Russia's developing cuisine came from the Scandinavians. Pre-Christian rulers of Russia were Scandinavian, and with them came the taste for herring and preserved foods. Long known by the Vikings were the techniques of pickling and smoking to preserve foods, quite practical for long (conquering) journeys. Harsh winters dictate the necessity for preserving foods and Russians easily adopted the techniques of pickling and smoking. To this day pickled vegetables, fish, and meats are found on the Russian table. Smoked fish is also extremely popular. Dumplings and noodles are a mainstay of the Russian diet, as well as fermented dairy products, soups, and stuffed vegetables. Fruit preserves are universally served with tea. The Byzantine influence can be seen in Russia's love for buckwheat (*kasha*) and rice.

One of the more important influences on Russian cuisine is religion. Russians still observe more than one hundred religious festival days a year, when meat and animal fats are not eaten. This has led to a remarkable number of vegetable dishes. The Volga River and the Caspian Sea are great sources of fresh fish such as carp, perch, whitefish, and pike. The true star of this array must be the sturgeon, its roe known as caviar. Caviar is a true Russian gift to the world's cuisines, which first became popular toward the end of the nineteenth century. Iran borders the Caspian Sea and became a major producer of caviar soon after the Russian introduction. The major varieties are Sevruga, Ossetra and Beluga (in order of increasing quality and price).

Modern Russian cuisine has several common components, derived from its earliest form. Meat is served in large pieces (much of the Eastern world cuts meat into bite-size pieces). There is an extensive array of pickled and smoked foods as well as an abundance of filled pies and dumplings. There are an inordinately large number of fish and vegetable dishes, and the vegetables are of the cold weather variety—cabbages, root vegetables, and onions. Dairy is quite popular, especially sour cream and buttermilk. Cheeses are popular, as are mushrooms, and are often found in combination.

Poland borders the Baltic Sea and Russia to the north, Lithuania and the Ukraine to the east, Germany to the west, and the Czech Republic to the south. Poland was the major force in Eastern Europe from the fourteenth to the seventeenth centuries, when it was divided and ceased to be an independent country until the end of World War I. Religious tolerance and diversity in Poland led to a cuisine that had an influence from the large Jewish community that was allowed autonomy in the fourteenth century. Poland has a continental climate and rich soils. Grains such as barley, oats, rye, and wheat thrive. Poland is one of the world leaders in potato and beet production and both are favorites in its dishes. Pork is the traditional meat of Poland, except for the Jews, whose dietary laws forbid its consumption. Pork products such as ham, sausages, and cracklins are favorites. Wild boar and venison are enjoyed throughout Poland, a country of hearty meat eaters. Although Poland has access to the sea, agriculture is its primary source of food. As with much of the region, there is a fondness for dairy, and fermented dairy products, such as buttermilk and sour cream, are widely used in its cuisine. The Ashkenazi Jews of Eastern Europe brought their own style to Polish cooking, with a fondness for sweet and sour combinations, parsley and dill, horseradish for spice, chicken or goose fat for cooking, and a reliance on egg noodles for starch in the diet. New World potatoes were welcomed and were easily assimilated into their style of cooking.

Hungary is landlocked, bordered by Slovakia to the north, the Ukraine to the northeast, Serbia and Croatia to the south, Romania to the east, and Austria to the west. Its principal waterway is the Danube River, and the primeval river deposited rich soils on the Great Plains, the heartland of Hungarian agriculture. The climate is moderate and over two-thirds of the land is under cultivation. The main crops are potatoes, cereal grains of all kinds, corn, beets and other root vegetables, peppers, and grapes. Over 95 percent of the people are ethnic Magyars, who migrated from the area around the Urals and the Black Sea around the ninth century. Conquered by the Mongols and then the Turks, most of Hungary became part of the Ottoman Empire. Transylvania, a semi-autonomous region within the Ottoman Empire, where the Magyar spirit and culture were preserved, is the home of a true ethnic cuisine of Hungary. The use of such spices as ginger and saffron and such herbs as wild thyme characterizes this cuisine as distinct from classic Hungarian cuisine. Fruit soups and sauces are very popular and Hungary is known for growing fruit of the highest caliber. New World crops such as corn and eggplant are used more frequently in Transylvanian cooking.

Hungarian cuisine offers several well-known dishes to the world. Goulash, from the Magyar word *gulyás*, or herdsman, is a true Hungarian specialty. This slow-cooked dish reflects the influence of the Asian Magyars, who brought the technique of kettle cooking to this country. No gulash would be complete without the famous spice of Hungary, paprika. Introduced into Hungary in the seventeenth century, the pepper that, when dried and ground, produces paprika was considered a poor man's spice, as it replaced the expensive black pepper from India. Paprika is available in different grades in Hungary, based primarily on pungency and not on the cultivar of pepper used. *Különleges* is made from the finest and ripest of peppers, *csemege* or common grade has a more pronounced flavor with little piquancy, *èdesnemes* or noble paprika is subtly piquant, *rózsa* or rose paprika, is most pungent. Paprikash (*paprikás*), a very popular stew, highlights the favored combination of cooking fat, onions, and paprika. Sour cream is stirred in to finish a paprikash. Without sour cream it is known as *pörkölt*. A Transylvanian version, called *tokány* is rarely made with paprika. Marjoram and black pepper substitute for paprika, and the meat tends to be richer in flavor, such as venison and mutton.

Romanian cuisine can be linked to Transylvania, as Transylvania included parts of Romania as well as Hungary. The other two regions of Romania are the Eastern Carpathians (surrounding Transylvania) and the Southern Carpathians. Romania borders the Black Sea on the east, the Ukraine to the north, Hungary to the west, and Bulgaria to the south. Romania became a country independent from Turkey in 1862. Its name is derived from its early Roman heritage of the second and third centuries (when it was the province of Dacia). Foreign influences on Romania's cuisine came from Russian, German, and Turkish invaders, as well as from more peaceful avenues. By the mid-nineteenth century, upper-class Romanians sent their children to France to be educated. France became the language of the aristocracy, and French cuisine was introduced into Romania. French culture was so strong that Bucharest became known as "little Paris."

Romania's soils are fertile and there are many lakes and tributaries of the major waterway, the Danube River. Principal crops include corn, wheat, rye, root vegetables such as potatoes and sugar beets, and a variety of fruits. Dairy and viniculture are important as well. Romanian cuisine is linked to that of Hungary, with some regional variations. For example, while Hungarians and Romanians both enjoy soups made with root vegetables, Hungarians will thicken the soup with a roux and Romanians will not. Romanians use seed oils to cook with and Hungarians use animal fats. Romanians are extremely fond of corn porridges (*mamaliga*), a similar preparation to the polenta of their Roman "cousins." Horseradish provides a piquancy to their dishes, and sweetness is added in the form of honey. Fruits such as quince, plums, and apples are featured in many savory dishes (to provide both sweet and sour components), and dill, basil, marjoram, and tarragon are popular herbs. Favorite meats include castrated male sheep (*wether*), lamb, and piglet.

Cabbage Rolls Stuffed with Beef and Rice with Sweet-and-Sour Sauce Gwumpky (Holipches)/Golubtsy

serves 8 (2 rolls per person)

Stuffed cabbage rolls are popular throughout Eastern Europe. In Hungary they are called *töltött káposzta* and are stuffed with rice and meat sausage, pork chops, and/or sauerkraut. They are usually served with a sauce of paprika and tomato with sour cream. In Ukraine they are called *holubtsi* and are stuffed with beef, pork, and rice, topped with a béchamel and cheese sauce. A Russian version has a filling of dried wild mushrooms mixed with barley, buckwheat, or rice. In Russia these rolls are known as *golubtsy* (which means "pigeons") and are served with a tomato sauce with sour cream on the side. This Polish version, quite similar to the Russian style, has beef and rice filling, simmered with a sweet-and-sour tomato sauce.

CABBAGE ROLLS: MAKES 16 ROLLS

1 large head green cabbage, about 2 to 2¼ pounds [900 g to 1.1 kg]

2 pounds [900 g] ground beef

2 garlic cloves, minced

2 teaspoons [10 mL] salt

1 teaspoon [5 mL] black pepper

½ cup [120 mL] raw long-grain white rice

SAUCE

2 tablespoons [30 mL] butter

1 medium onion, sliced thin

One 46-fluid ounce [1.4 L] can tomato juice

½ cup [120 mL] fresh lemon juice

1 cup [240 mL] sugar

Salt and pepper to taste

½ cup [120 mL] raisins (optional)

Chopped parsley, for garnish

ADVANCE PREPARATION

1. Core the cabbage. Carefully separate the leaves. Blanch 16 large leaves in boiling water for about 1 minute, or until bright green and just softened. Immediately refresh the blanched leaves in ice water. Drain and reserve.

2. Chop some of the remaining leaves to make 4 cups [960 mL] of chopped cabbage and reserve.

PREPARATION OF THE CABBAGE ROLLS

3. Mix the ground beef with the garlic, salt, pepper, and rice. Divide this mixture into sixteen 2-ounce [55-g] balls. Using moistened hands, form the balls into cylinders.

4. Place a cylinder of filling near the bottom of a cabbage leaf. Begin to roll it up, fold in the sides, and complete rolling to

If citric acid is not available (check the canning section of a supermarket), increase the amount of fresh lemon juice to ½ cup [120 mL]. Cooked rice may be added to the meat mixture instead of raw rice. Reduce the cooking time to 1 hour (total time). For a meatless version, use raw rice alone as the filling. Ground pork or veal may be used alone or in combination with ground beef.

enclose the filling. Continue, filling all the cabbage leaves. Place them, seam side down, on a tray. Reserve, covered and refrigerated.

PREPARATION OF THE SAUCE

5. Melt the butter in a heavy, nonreactive saucepan large enough to hold the sauce and cabbage rolls. Sauté the onion until soft and golden. Add the reserved chopped cabbage and sauté briefly.

6. Add the tomato juice, lemon juice, sugar, salt and pepper to taste, and stir to combine. Increase the heat and simmer the sauce for 5 minutes.

COOKING METHOD

7. Add the reserved cabbage rolls to the sauce, lower the heat to a very low simmer, and cover, leaving a small gap for steam to escape. Cook 1½ hours.

8. Remove the lid, add the raisins, if desired, and simmer 30 minutes more, or until the filling is tender and the rice is cooked. This dish is more flavorful if made one day in advance and held refrigerated.

SERVICE

9. Serve 2 cabbage rolls per person, topped with ample sauce. Garnish with chopped parsley.

Meatballs with Cranberry-Leek Sauce Bitki s Klyukvoy i Lukom Poreyem

serves 8 (4 meatballs per person)

This dish originates from western Russia. The sauce is traditionally made with lingonberries and certainly use them if available. The forcemeat is formed into thick patties or meatballs, and for informal service they may be served simply, with a dish of cranberry or lingonberry preserves on the side, but the cranberry-leek sauce adds considerably to this dish. Sour cream is often stirred into the pan after cooking the meatballs to heat it through, but it is much more attractive to heat the sour cream in a squeeze bottle and use it to garnish the plate.

CHEF NOTES

Homemade cranberry vinegar would be preferable to raspberry vinegar when making the sauce. Raspberry or lingonberry jam or jelly may be used in place of the cranberry jelly.

CRANBERRY-LEEK SAUCE

1¼ cups [300 mL] fresh or frozen cranberries

1 cup [240 mL] rich chicken stock

½ cup [120 mL] demi-glace or very rich beef stock

3 tablespoons [45 mL] unsalted butter

2 cups [480 mL] leeks, washed and sliced, white and pale green parts only

3 tablespoons [45 mL] cranberry jelly

1 tablespoon [15 mL] raspberry or other fruity vinegar

MEATBALLS: MAKES THIRTY-TWO 1-INCH [2.5-CM] MEATBALLS

2 tablespoons [30 mL] unsalted butter

½ medium onion, minced

2 garlic cloves, minced

12 ounces [340 g] lean ground beef

6 ounces [180 g] lean ground veal

2 ounces [55 g] minced pork fat

1 egg, beaten

½ teaspoon [3 mL] salt

½ teaspoon [3 mL] black pepper

1½ cup [360 mL] unseasoned dry breadcrumbs

⅓ cup [80 mL] duck fat, chicken fat, or vegetable oil

⅔ cup [160 mL] sour cream (optional)

ADVANCE PREPARATION

1. Combine the cranberries, chicken stock, and the demi-glace in a nonreactive saucepan and bring to a boil. Reduce the heat to a simmer and cook until all of the cranberries have popped and are tender.

2. While the cranberries are cooking, heat the butter in a small skillet over medium heat and sauté the leeks until softened. Reserve.

3. Combine the cranberries and their simmering liquid, the leeks, cranberry jelly, and vinegar in the workbowl of a food processor and purée. Return the purée to the saucepan and adjust flavoring for a balance between sweet and sour. Reserve. (The sauce can be made one day in advance.)

PREPARATION OF THE MEATBALLS

4. Heat the butter in a large skillet over medium heat and sauté the onion until lightly browned and soft. Add the garlic and sauté 1 minute. Add the onion to the beef, veal, pork fat, egg, salt, pepper, and ½ cup [120 mL] of the breadcrumbs in a bowl and mix well.

5. Break off a small piece of the mixture, sauté until browned, and taste for seasonings. Adjust if necessary.

6. Using a small scoop, form the meatballs, place them on a parchment-lined sheet pan, and cover until ready to cook. (The meatballs can be made several hours in advance.)

COOKING METHOD

7. Heat the fat in the skillet over medium heat. Place the remaining 1 cup of breadcrumbs in a bowl and roll the meatballs in the crumbs to coat.

8. Sauté the meatballs evenly until golden brown and cooked to an internal temperature of 160°F [70°C]. Drain on paper towels and reserve warm.

SERVICE

9. Serve 4 meatballs per person. Top with cranberry-leek sauce. If using sour cream, heat it in a squeeze bottle to warm, using a microwave oven. Pipe a design with the warmed sour cream over the sauce and serve immediately.

Grilled Trout Fillet with Dried Cherry-Rose Petal Vinegar and Mayonnaise Rózsaszirmos Meggyecetes Hal

serves 8

This recipe is based on an old, very involved Transylvanian recipe for vinegar made with fresh sour cherries and rose petals. It uses difficult to locate ingredients (such as sprigs of young cherry trees) and requires weeks of fermentation. This shortened method captures the essence of the dish but involves a much simpler procedure. The original recipe calls for the use of thick, oily, red rose petals, which might be difficult to locate, but Near Eastern markets and herb shops sell dried rose petals that work nicely. (Check with organic rose growers in your area for a source of fresh petals.) Regardless of the source, be sure that the petals have been organically grown, are free of pesticides, and are very fragrant.

CHERRY–ROSE PETAL VINEGAR:
MAKES ABOUT 2 CUPS [480 mL]

4 cups [960 mL] champagne or white wine vinegar

2 cups [480 mL] fresh organic red rose petals, crushed, or 1 cup [240 mL] dried rose petals

½ teaspoon [3 mL] rose water

1 cup [240 mL] dried sour cherries, pitted, finely chopped in a processor

1 teaspoon [5 mL] grated lemon zest

Pinch of ground cloves

MARINADE

1 cup [240 mL] sweet onion, grated

2 garlic cloves, minced

½ cup [120 mL] cherry–rose petal vinegar (see above recipe)

¼ cup [60 mL] walnut oil

½ teaspoon [3 mL] salt

¼ teaspoon [1 mL] black pepper

Pinch of sweet paprika

FISH

8 boneless trout fillets, skin on

MAYONNAISE: MAKES ABOUT 1½ CUPS [360 mL]

1 large egg, at room temperature

1 egg yolk

½ teaspoon [3 mL] Dijon-style mustard

¼ cup [60 mL] cherry–rose petal vinegar, or to taste

¼ teaspoon [1 mL] rose water

½ teaspoon [3 mL] salt

Ground white pepper to taste

1 cup [240 mL] vegetable oil

⅛ teaspoon [0.5 mL] sugar, or to taste

¼ cup [60 mL] puréed fresh sour cherries or dried sour cherries, plumped in hot water and drained

If cooking the fish by the charcoal method, cooking over a fire fla- vored with fruitwood (cherry wood is recommended) would be preferable. If broiling, an alterna- tive method of preparation is to coat the fillet with the mayon- naise prior to broiling to create a browned glaze. This method works well with shrimp, lobster or langoustines, scallops, skate wings, monkfish, or any poultry.

2 tablespoons [30 mL] organic fresh red rose petals, minced, or
  1 tablespoon dried rose petals

Fresh red rose petals, for garnish

Fresh sour cherries on stem, clustered, for garnish

ADVANCE PREPARATION

1. Heat the champagne vinegar to about 110°F [45°C], add all of the remaining vinegar ingredients, and mix well in a nonreactive bowl. Pour the mixture into a sterile glass jar, cover to seal, and place in a warm spot to infuse for at least 24 hours. The longer the ingredients infuse before straining and use, the more intense the flavor will be.

2. Strain the vinegar by pouring through a fine mesh strainer. Using the back of a wooden spoon, press to extract as much liquid as possible from the solids. Store in a sterile, sealed glass container. (The vinegar can be made several days in advance.)

PREPARATION OF THE MARINADE

3. Combine all of the marinade ingredients in a nonreactive bowl and mix well. Place the fish in a resealable plastic bag and add the marinade. Toss the fish with the marinade to coat. Marinate at least 4 hours, refrigerated.

PREPARATION OF THE MAYONNAISE

4. Place the egg, egg yolk, mustard, vinegar, rose water, salt, and pepper in the bowl of a small processor and pulse to blend. With the processor running, add the oil in a thin, steady stream to emulsify.

5. Transfer the mayonnaise to a nonreactive bowl and stir in the sugar, cherries, and minced rose petals, mixing well. Reserve chilled. (The mayonnaise can be made one day in advance.)

COOKING METHOD

6. Drain the fish from the marinade and grill indirectly over a charcoal fire (or cook under a broiler or in the oven) until firm, juicy, and just beginning to flake. Serve immediately.

SERVICE

7. Serve 1 fillet per person, accompanied with 2 tablespoons [30 mL] of the mayonnaise on the side. Garnish with rose petals and sour cherry clusters.

Leek and Cod Croquettes in Aromatic Horseradish Sauce

Rybnyye Kotlety s Goryachim Sousom iz Khrena

Serves 8 (2 croquettes per person)

Leeks are an excellent cold weather vegetable and more complex in flavor than onions. Cod is plentiful near the coasts of Russia and is easily frozen for transport to the interior regions. These croquettes of fish and leek seasoned with dill can be shaped as balls or made into small ovals. First covered with the robust horseradish sauce, the dish is quickly browned in a hot oven; it is served as individual casseroles.

CHEF NOTES

Any type of white, firm-fleshed fish can be substituted for the cod. Shrimp, scallops, or monkfish are excellent when prepared in this manner. The croquettes may be deep-fried rather than pan-sautéed.

CROQUETTES: MAKES 16 CROQUETTES

¼ cup [60 mL] unsalted butter

2 cups [480 mL] leeks, finely chopped

½ cup [120 mL] half-and-half

3 slices white bread, crusts removed, torn into pieces

1¼ pounds [560 g] cod fillet, coarsely chopped

I large egg, slightly beaten

2 tablespoons [30 mL] fresh dill, chopped

2 tablespoons [30 mL] fresh lemon juice

½ teaspoon [3 mL] salt

½ teaspoon [3 mL] white pepper

2 tablespoons [30 mL] vegetable oil

Unseasoned dry breadcrumbs, for frying

HORSERADISH SAUCE: MAKES ABOUT 3½ CUPS [840 mL]

3 tablespoons [45 mL] unsalted butter

3 tablespoons [45 mL] flour

2 cups [480 mL] warm chicken or seafood broth

2 cups [480 mL] sour cream

½ cup [120 mL] grated horseradish

¼ teaspoon [I mL] sugar

I teaspoon [5 mL] white vinegar

Salt to taste

Sprigs of dill, for garnish

ADVANCE PREPARATION

1. All advance preparation may be found in the ingredient list.

PREPARATION OF THE CROQUETTES

2. Heat 3 tablespoons [45 mL] of the butter in a skillet over medium heat and sauté 1 cup [240 mL] of the chopped leeks until golden. Reserve.

3. Combine the half-and-half and bread and soak for 5 minutes. Pulse the fish with the remaining chopped leeks in a food processor to form a coarse paste. Squeeze the bread of excess liquid and break it into small pieces. Add the bread to the reserved sautéed leeks.

4. Combine the fish mixture, egg, dill, lemon juice, salt, and white pepper with the leek and bread mixture and stir well to combine. Cover the bowl and refrigerate 1 hour. Form into 16 croquettes and reserve.

5. Heat the remaining 1 tablespoon [15 mL] of butter with the oil in a large skillet over medium-high heat. Toss the croquettes in the breadcrumbs to coat and sauté until golden. Reserve warm.

PREPARATION OF THE SAUCE

6. Heat the butter in a skillet over medium heat. Whisk in the flour to make a light roux. Whisk in the broth, beating constantly to prevent lumps. Stir in the sour cream, horseradish, sugar, vinegar, and salt and heat through. Adjust for seasonings and reserve.

COOKING METHOD

7. Place the croquettes in a single layer in a lightly buttered baking dish and top with the sauce. Bake at 425°F [220°C] for 10 minutes, or until the sauce begins to bubble and brown.

SERVICE

8. Serve 2 croquettes per person, topped with sauce and garnished with sprigs of dill.

Layered Crêpe, Mushroom, and Cheese Torte Blinchaty Pirog s Gribami

RUSSIA

serves 8

Russian crêpes, (*blinchiki*), called *naliesnski* in Poland and Ukraine, are unleavened "relatives" of the Russian *bliny*. This torte is normally made with leftover *bliny*, and it is especially popular during *Maslenitsa*, or the Butter Festival (the Russian equivalent of Mardi Gras). This dish can be made as a large stacked torte and then sliced, or with smaller crêpes, formed in straight-sided muffin tins for individual service. Russian caviar makes an excellent accompaniment to the torte.

⎯ **CHEF NOTES**

A muffin tin with straight sides can be used for individual tortes. Make the crêpes to fit the muffin tin and proceed with the recipe. Smoked black cod (sablefish) or smoked salmon may also be used to accompany the torte, in place of the caviar.

CRÊPES: MAKES EIGHT TO TEN 8-INCH [20-CM] CRÊPES

2 large eggs, lightly beaten

I large egg yolk, lightly beaten

I cup [240 mL] milk, at room temperature

½ teaspoon [3 mL] sugar

¼ teaspoon [I mL] salt

1⅓ cups [320 mL] unbleached flour

½ cup [120 mL] seltzer or sparkling water

About ¼ cup [60 mL] melted clarified butter

FILLING

I ounce [30 g] dried mixed wild mushrooms or porcini

I cup [240 mL] warm chicken stock

3 tablespoons [45 mL] unsalted butter

⅔ cup [160 mL] minced onion

2 garlic cloves, minced

I pound [450 g] fresh crimini mushrooms, sliced

2 tablespoons [30 mL] dry vermouth

Salt and ground black pepper to taste

¼ cup [60 mL] heavy cream

I tablespoon [15 mL] sour cream or crème fraîche

¾ cup [180 mL] grated Gruyère cheese

½ cup [120 mL] béchamel sauce, made with I tablespoon [15 mL] butter, I tablespoon [15 mL] flour, and ½ cup [120 mL] milk

2 tablespoons [30 mL] chopped fresh dill

¼ cup [60 mL] unseasoned dry breadcrumbs

2 tablespoons [30 mL] butter

Minced scallions, for garnish

I ounce [30 g] Russian caviar (optional)

439 | Eastern Europe

1. Combine the eggs, egg yolk, milk, sugar, and salt in the work-bowl of a food processor. With the machine running, gradually add the flour through the feed tube and process until a smooth batter is formed. Allow to rest at room temperature for 30 minutes and then stir in the seltzer.

2. Heat an 8-inch nonstick skillet over medium heat and brush with about ½ teaspoon [3 mL] of the melted clarified butter. Remove the pan from the heat and ladle in 3 tablespoons [45 mL] of the batter, swirling to evenly coat the bottom. Cook 1 minute until golden, and then flip the crêpe over to cook the opposite side for 10 seconds. Stack the crêpes and cook in batches until all the batter is used. Reserve, covered, until needed. (The crêpes can be made one day in advance and held refrigerated.)

PREPARATION OF THE FILLING

3. Soak the dried mushrooms in the chicken stock for 30 minutes. Strain the soaking liquid through a very fine sieve or coffee filter and reserve the liquid and the soaked mushrooms. Chop the mushrooms.

4. Melt the butter in a nonstick skillet over medium heat and sauté the onion, garlic, and dried mushrooms together until the onions are soft. Add the fresh mushrooms and sauté until they begin to release their juices.

5. Increase the heat to medium-high, add the reserved mushroom soaking liquid, and sauté about 5 minutes, or until the liquid is absorbed. Add the vermouth and cook 2 minutes.

6. Season the mixture with salt and black pepper and stir in the cream, sour cream, and half of the cheese. Reduce the heat to medium and cook 5 minutes more, or until the sauce begins to thicken. Remove from the heat and reserve.

PREPARATION OF THE TORTE

7. Place a circle of parchment on the bottom of a greased 8-inch [20-cm] round cake pan. Place a crêpe on the bottom and spread ¼ cup [60 mL] of filling evenly over it. Repeat, alternating crêpes and filling until all are used, finishing with a crêpe.

8. Mix the béchamel sauce with the remaining cheese and dill. Spread this mixture over the top crêpe. Sprinkle with the breadcrumbs and dot with butter.

COOKING METHOD

9. Bake at 400°F [205°C] for 15 minutes, or until the top has browned and is bubbling. Allow to cool for 15 minutes before serving.

SERVICE

10. Cut the torte into 8 slices and serve 1 slice per person. Garnish with minced scallions and a small mound of Russian caviar, if desired.

Mushrooms Stewed in Sour Cream au Gratin Griby Tushonyye v Smetane

serves 8

This dish is prepared in the style of the port city of Odessa, on the Black Sea. Mushrooms stewed in sour cream are popular all over Russia, in the Ukraine, Belorussia, and Moldavia. This version of the dish adds an extra dimension by topping the dish with grated cheese and then broiling it to brown. In Russia gathering wild mushrooms is a favorite pastime and this dish would most likely be prepared with them. The dish can be made as a large gratin as well as individual portions.

CHEF NOTES

This dish would use either wild mushrooms, especially morels, or brown cultivated mushrooms. A mixture is an excellent choice, as would thick slices of portobello mushrooms (though not Russian). In Odessa the cheese used would more than likely be a *syr orbryndza*, but a dry, salty type of feta or an aged Monterey jack would both work as substitutes.

MUSHROOMS

⅓ cup [80 mL] unsalted butter, softened

4 scallions, chopped

3 garlic cloves, minced

1¼ pounds [560 g] small to medium crimini or wild mushrooms, sliced

1 tablespoon [15 mL] flour

Salt to taste

½ teaspoon [3 mL] black pepper

½ cup [120 mL] sour cream

⅓ cup [80 mL] plus 1 tablespoon [15 mL] heavy cream

4 ounces [110 g] dry feta or aged Monterey jack cheese, grated

Minced scallion, for garnish

ADVANCE PREPARATION

1. All advance preparation may be found in the ingredient list.

PREPARATION OF THE MUSHROOM CASSEROLES

2. Melt ¼ cup [60 mL] of the butter in a skillet over medium heat and sauté the scallions and garlic for 2 minutes. Add the mushrooms and cook 5 minutes, or until the mushrooms are lightly browned and beginning to soften.

3. Knead 1 tablespoon [15 mL] of the butter with the flour, mixing well. Add this to the mushrooms and cook for 2 minutes, while stirring. Season the mushrooms with salt and pepper and stir in the sour cream and cream.

4. Place the mushroom mixture in 8 lightly buttered individual gratin dishes, top with the grated cheese, and dot with the remaining butter.

COOKING METHOD

5. Bake at 350°F [175°C] for 20 to 25 minutes, or until the top is browned and the sauce is bubbling.

SERVICE

6. Serve at once, garnished with the minced scallion.

Pan-Fried Potato-Filled Dumplings Pirozhki s Kartofelnoy Nachinkoy

POLAND

Savory pies and filled dumplings are found all across Eastern Europe, and they can be stuffed with vegetables, cheese, meat, poultry, or fish, or in many combinations. A variety of dessert fillings can be added to this versatile dough. Russian in origin, these dumplings are known as *piroshki* (or *pirozhki*) as the smaller pies, and they are called *pirog* when made as larger versions. The dumplings may be boiled, then pan-fried or baked (and are certainly enjoyed straight from the boiling pot as well). This version is from Poland and the dumplings are filled with seasoned potatoes. They are boiled to cook the dough and heat the filling, then pan-fried in butter to finish them. A unique feature to this Polish version is the dark fried onions, known as *griebens* by Jewish Poles, usually fried in chicken fat.

CHEF NOTES

Other fillings to consider include potatoes mixed with sharp cheese (such as cheddar), sauerkraut, or sauerkraut mixed with potatoes and cheese. Fresh fruit, such as peaches, apples, or strawberries, make a delicious filling for a dessert dumpling. Sauté the fruit in butter and add sugar or honey and cinnamon, cloves, or any complementary spices.

DOUGH: MAKES ENOUGH FOR 40 DUMPLINGS

3 cups [720 mL] flour

I teaspoon [5 mL] salt

I egg, lightly beaten

I cup [240 mL] water, more or less, to form a smooth dough

FILLING: MAKES ENOUGH FILLING FOR 40 DUMPLINGS

I small onion, diced

I cup [240 mL] chicken fat or vegetable oil

2 pounds [900 g] russet potatoes, peeled, diced, boiled, and cooled

⅓ cup [80 mL] pot cheese or dry curd cottage cheese

½ tablespoon [8 mL] salt

Butter

GARNISH

2 large onions, sliced

2 tablespoons [30 mL] butter

Sour cream

PREPARATION OF THE DOUGH

1. Place the flour and salt in the workbowl of a food processor. While processing, add the egg in a steady stream. Add water until a ball is formed. Remove the dough and knead by hand for 2 minutes. Cover with plastic film and allow to rest for 30 minutes. (The dough can be made several hours in advance.)

PREPARATION OF THE FILLING

2. Fry the diced onion in the chicken fat or oil over medium-high heat, stirring constantly, until the onions are very dark brown, but not burned. Drain on paper towels and allow to cool. (The onions can be prepared one day in advance and stored in an airtight container.)

3. Mash the potatoes and stir in the pot cheese, salt, and ¼ cup [60 mL] of the fried onions.

PREPARATION OF THE DUMPLINGS

4. Roll out the dough and cut forty 3-inch [8-cm] circles. Place 1 tablespoon [15 mL] of the filling near the center of a dough circle. Moisten the edge with water, fold over to form a half-moon-shaped dumpling, and pinch to seal. Repeat until all are formed. Place the formed dumplings on a sheet pan until ready to cook, taking care that the dumplings do not touch.

COOKING METHOD

5. Drop the dumplings, a few at a time, into rapidly boiling water. Cook 5 minutes, or until the edges are cooked and tender. Do not overcook. Place the dumplings in a bowl with some butter added to prevent sticking. Swirl the cooked dumplings in the bowl to coat with butter. Repeat until all the dumplings are cooked. (The boiled dumplings may be held, refrigerated, for two days.)

PREPARATION OF THE GARNISH

6. Sauté the sliced onions in butter until they are golden and beginning to caramelize. Reserve. (The onions can be prepared one day in advance.)

SERVICE

7. Heat a nonstick skillet over medium-high heat. Add 2 teaspoons [10 mL] of butter and pan-fry 5 dumplings per person until both sides are golden brown. Serve immediately, accompanied with the sautéed onions and a dollop of sour cream.

Scandinavia and the Baltic States

Beef, Potato, Beet, and Caper Sausage (Lindström's Beef)
Lindströmin Pihvit

Browned Cabbage in Broth with Veal Dumplings
Vitkålsoppa med Frikadeller

Potato Dumplings Stuffed with Ham and Onion
Kroppkakor

Beef, Veal, and Pork Meatballs
Små Köttbullar

Pickled Cooked Goose Breast
Gus Prigotovlyenny v Marinadye

Glass Blower's Trout (Spicy Pickled Trout)
Lasimestarin Silli

Cured Salmon with Dill and Mustard Sauce
Gravad Lax (Gravlax, Gravlaks)

SCANDINAVIA IS USUALLY defined as the countries of Sweden, Norway, and Denmark. They have similar languages as well as common history. Finland, while in the geographic area, is linguistically unrelated but certainly shares the cuisine. Iceland is often included, since its language is related to the other Scandinavian countries' languages. The term Nordic is probably the best term to describe these countries. With respect to cuisine, the defining influence on the entire region is the unique geographical location and climate. Isolation is key, as there is very little influence on Scandinavia's cuisines by other cultures. In addition, the extremely short growing season requires storage of food over the long, dark winters. Preservation is essential and Scandinavians are experts in the various techniques of storing meat, fish, and vegetables. Salting, brining, curing, and smoking are all basic to the palette of Scandinavian food. Among fresh produce, root vegetables store well, and dill and parsley thrive in the cool, short growing season.

Because of the unique seasons of this area, "feast or famine" could easily describe the eating patterns of Scandinavians. Cows, at the brink of starvation by the end of winter, are literally carried to pasture in the spring. They soon calve, and milk flows, offering the basics for the dairy products so enjoyed by all Scandinavians. Salmon begin to run as the surface ice of streams and lakes starts to melt with the appearance of the sun. Herring clogs the waters in late summer, and granaries swell by late autumn, brimming with barley, rye, and oats. The first sign of winter brings fresh meat in the form of game and game birds. Scandinavians enjoy all forms of organ meats, with no parts of the animal wasted—including the blood.)

Nordic food is certainly fish. The icy waters of the North Atlantic and the Baltic Sea teem with fish, as do inland lakes and streams. Preparations are very simple, allowing the flavor of the sea to speak through the dish. Since fish is often eaten within hours of the catch, minimal seasonings and sauces are in order. Poaching in court bouillon spiked with vinegar and pan-frying in butter after stuffing the fish with fresh dill and other herbs are the principal methods of preparation. Herring is extremely popular and abundant and is fished from the Baltic Sea as well as the North Sea. Herring has been so important to the survival of the Scandinavian people that this humble fish has been given divine attributes. Some years herring fills the waters, and at other times there is almost no fish to be caught, adding to the herring's mystique.

Dairy products are a dominant ingredient in Scandinavian cooking. Butter is the fat of choice when sautéing or frying. Fermented and ripened dairy products are important as a way to store the bountiful milk of the spring season through the long winter. Cheeses are an excellent way to preserve milk, and Scandinavians are great consumers of cheese. Denmark produces world-class cheeses such as *havarti*, Danish blue, and *samsö*, while Norway produces an excellent brown goat cheese, *gjetöst*, and the cow's milk *gammelost*. Caraway-infused cheeses from Sweden are familiar to many cheese lovers. The whey from cheese making is used as well. When boiled down, it produces a cheese-like product, and this is the method of producing the brown Norwegian goat cheese mentioned earlier.

Enjoyed straight from the pantry, cheese is rarely incorporated into cooked dishes. Fermented dairy products such as sour cream and buttermilk are common ways to store fresh milk, and curdled milk has been enjoyed for centuries. Known as *skyr*, curdled milk can last for months, continuously ripening and souring in the process. Today the term *skyr* is used only in Iceland, where *skyr* is eaten as a fresh yogurt-like product. *Tette* milk is produced in Norway; the leaves of the *tette* plant are added to boiled milk and the mixture is allowed to stand and thicken. The leaves seem to have a preserving power, since spring milk can last through winter when treated in this manner.

Food preservation is essential in a climate with long, harsh, and dark winters and the techniques have been passed down from those great explorers the Vikings. Extensive sea journeys required foods that could be stored over long periods of time, and the Vikings learned early of the benefits of drying, salting, and smoking fish and meat. Salting, in particular, became a most important method of preservation, and to this day Scandinavians have a very strong taste for salty food. Salt was rare in early times and quite expensive. Because of the weak sun in these northern climes, it was not practical to produce salt from the saline waters of the North Sea. Often a shortage of salt would threaten the herring catch, which without salt would spoil well before winter set in. Today many Scandinavian dishes rely on salting. *Gravad lax*, or cured salmon, one of the most famous and tasty delicacies of the region, is prepared by coating salmon fillets with a mixture of salt and sugar (saltpeter is sometimes added to preserve color), covering it with fresh dill and allowing it to stand with heavy weights on top. Salting is still the common method of storing and preparing herring. Brining is another common preservation technique. Game and game birds are often prepared this way. The raw meat is submerged in brine for a period of time, then simmered in water (or salted or acidulated water) to cook. Because of these preserving techniques, Scandinavians, as a whole, enjoy very salty foods, whether or not the food has been preserved in salt.

The countries of Scandinavia share much in the way of a common history. In addition to common Viking ancestry, throughout the years various alliances were forged between countries, allowing for the transfer of culture and cooking style. Norway was formed by the Vikings in the ninth century and for the next 1,000 years was under the rule of either Sweden or Denmark. It wasn't until the Napoleonic Wars that Norway was allowed to emerge as an independent country (first separating from Denmark, then disavowing the treaty that gave the country to Sweden).

With its very cold climate, the Norwegian approach to food was one of fuel to get through the day. Being a poor country until the twentieth century, Norwegian food is one with no frills. The rocky terrain of Norway precludes a large agricultural sector, and much of its grain requirement must be imported. But what ingredients it does have, especially fish, are remarkably fresh. Meat is scarce, but game, such as elk, waterfowl, and hare supplement the diet for winter. Salting is the method for preserving and fermentation produces a locally appreciated dish called *rakørret*, fermented trout (described as having the aroma of raw petroleum with a taste of strong cheese).

Sweden is a vast country spreading almost 1,000 miles across with remarkably contrasting climates. Forests cover 50 percent of the land, and Sweden is dotted with many lakes, which are among the largest in Europe. Sweden is rich in natural resources, wildlife, and quality of life. Its dairy products are some of the finest in the world, and the Swedish people enjoy a bounty of such game as elk and deer. With the arrival of autumn, wild mushrooms and berries laden the dinner table. Fish, especially herring, is featured on the world-famous *smörgåsbord*. In no other Scandinavian country is herring so appreciated. It is served marinated, pickled, baked, stewed, jellied, and fried and in every conceivable shape and form. *Smörgåsbord* (literally, bread-and-butter table) is a carefully arranged feast of cold and hot dishes, displayed as attractively as possible. It is a buffet table that may have as its origin "pot luck" suppers in rural communities. It is carefully orchestrated, with cold dishes followed by hot, and guests are expected to sample the dishes in the order in which they are presented.

Not to be confused with the Swedish *smörgåsbord* is *smørrebrød*, the famous "open-face" sandwich of Denmark. Danes love good food and do not need encouragement to partake of a snack between meals. The unique geographical location of Denmark forms a link between Europe and Scandinavia, and Danish cuisine (compared to the other countries of Scandinavia) is most influenced by its European neighbors, especially France. Denmark had been an ally of France until the defeat of Napoleon in 1814. Throughout the nineteenth century French chefs went to Denmark to demonstrate their culinary skills. For this reason, Denmark has the most sophisticated cuisine of Scandinavia, relying more heavily on cream sauces and complex preparations than elsewhere.

More meat is consumed in Denmark than in the other countries of the region. Although fish is extremely fresh and available, the Danish eating pattern is more of a "meat and potatoes" diet. Danes consume more meat per capita than other Scandinavians, with pork the preferred meat. Danish pork products are held in high regard around the world, and pork is one of Denmark's chief exports (there are almost 3 pigs to every Dane in this small country). With little arable land, Denmark welcomed the cheap grains being exported from the United States at a time when other countries were adding tariffs to protect their grain industries. In this way Denmark could focus its agricultural efforts on raising crops for human consumption. Danes are fanatical about the quality of their ingredients and the government sees to it that only the finest dairy, eggs, and meats are sold. Copious amounts of butter and cream are used in the preparation of Danish dishes, and the raw materials come from immaculate government-inspected facilities. Some of the finest cheeses in Scandinavia are produced in Denmark.

Finland is unique among the Scandinavian countries because of its language (Finno-Ugric) and history. Unlike the Danes, Swedes, and Norwegians, Finns are descendants of a tribe from Central Asia and their language is not related to the Scandinavian dialects. Russia and Sweden have fought over Finland for centuries, and Finish culture and cuisine reflect this. Flat breads, common in Sweden, are served alongside sour rye bread, common in Russia. Finland serves its version of *smörgåsbord*, while offering borscht and meat kebabs. Only 8 percent of the land is under cultivation, and the major crops are oats, wheat, sugar beets, and potatoes. Freshwater fish such as trout, pike, and salmon are harvested, and wild goose and bear are game commonly found on the Finnish table. Stews, gratins, and porridges are common dishes.

The Baltic states of Estonia, Latvia, and Lithuania may be included in this region. Estonia is closely related, by language and history, to Finland. Fishing is an essential part of the economy of Estonia, since there is little land suitable for cultivation. The cuisine is simple, comprised mostly of fish, dairy products, and grains. Spices are rarely used, but the ingredients are remarkably fresh and need little accompaniment. Until recently the Baltic states were under the domination of the Soviet Union, with significant impact on their cuisines. Much of the fish caught were channeled to Russia to feed its troops, so much so that the heritage of eating fresh and smoked fish is almost lost in Latvia. Like the Scandinavians, Latvians enjoy fermented dairy products such as sour milk and sour cream. Lithuania is more aligned than Latvia or Estonia with Russia in its cuisine, but with independence a resurgence of traditional cooking has occurred.

Beef, Potato, Beet, and Caper Sausage (Lindström's Beef) Lindströmin Pihvit

serves 8

Lindström's beef resembles the common hamburger in shape only. A piquant mix of beef seasoned with mashed potato, pickled beets, capers, and onions produces a complex range of flavors. This dish is very popular all across Sweden. The forcemeat can be stuffed into natural casings to produce attractive link sausages, or they can be fried as patties. Prepared in either fashion, the mixture is excellent paired with onion gravy or eaten with a simple garnish of chopped parsley.

CHEF NOTES

If cooking the forcemeat as sausage links, cook them on a greased grate indirectly over a charcoal fire until browned and cooked to an internal temperature of 160°F [70°C].

SAUSAGES: MAKES EIGHT 3-OUNCE [85-g] PATTIES

1 pound [450 g] ground lean beef

1 medium potato, boiled and mashed

1½ tablespoons [25 mL] beet pickling liquid (from the pickled beets below)

1 egg

1 egg yolk

½ cup [120 mL] pickled beets, diced

2 tablespoons [30 mL] onions, diced

1½ tablespoons [25 mL] capers, drained

1 teaspoon [5 mL] salt

¼ teaspoon [1 mL] white pepper

¼ teaspoon [1 mL] paprika

3 tablespoons [45 mL] unsalted butter

ONION SAUCE

1 onion, sliced

⅔ cup [160 mL] rich beef or chicken broth

Thin-cut fried potatoes, for service

Chopped parsley, for garnish

ADVANCE PREPARATION

1. Mix the beef and mashed potato together in a bowl. Gradually stir in the pickling liquid, the egg, and the egg yolk and mix well.

2. Fold in the beets, diced onions, capers, salt, pepper, and paprika and mix gently. Shape into 8 patties ½ inch [1 cm] thick. Reserve, covered and refrigerated, until ready to cook. The forcemeat may be stuffed into sausage casings and twisted into 4-inch [10-cm] links if desired.

COOKING METHOD

3. Heat the butter in a large nonstick skillet over medium heat. Cook the patties for 3 to 4 minutes per side, or until nicely

browned and cooked medium. Drain the patties on paper towels and keep warm for service.

PREPARATION OF THE SAUCE

4. Add the sliced onion to the pan and sauté until lightly browned and soft. Add the broth and heat to a boil, scraping the bottom of the pan to remove all browned bits. Reduce the sauce slightly to thicken. Reserve warm.

SERVICE

5. Serve 1 patty per person, topped with 2 tablespoons [30 mL] of the onion sauce. Serve a small mound of thin fried potatoes on the side and garnish with chopped parsley.

Browned Cabbage in Broth with Veal Dumplings Vitkålsoppa med Frikadeller

SWEDEN

Browned cabbage is a traditional Christmas dish in Sweden and is often paired with veal dumplings at times other than the holidays. The cabbage is first sautéed, then slightly caramelized with molasses or brown sugar before stock is added. The dumplings may be cooked in the broth or cooked separately, then added to the cabbage broth.

CHEF NOTES

The dumplings may be poached separately in a meat broth or in boiling salted water. Once cooked, the dumplings may be refrigerated or frozen and reheated for service. Homemade rye bread with caraway would be an excellent accompaniment.

BROWNED CABBAGE IN BROTH

¼ cup [60 mL] pork fat, bacon drippings, or butter

1½ pounds [675 g] green cabbage, cut into 1-inch [2.5-cm] squares, core sections discarded

2 small leeks, white and light green parts only, sliced thin

1 tablespoon [15 mL] molasses, dark brown sugar, or dark corn syrup

5 cups [1.2 L] veal, beef, or pork stock

6 whole allspice berries

9 whole white peppercorns

Salt to taste

VEAL DUMPLINGS: MAKES 32 SMALL DUMPLINGS

1 pound [450 g] ground veal

6 ounces [180 g] lean ground pork

⅓ cup [80 mL] dry breadcrumbs

2 teaspoons [10 mL] salt

1 teaspoon [5 mL] white pepper

3 tablespoons [45 mL] onion, grated

⅔ cup [160 mL] heavy cream

½ cup [120 mL] water

Chopped parsley, for garnish

ADVANCE PREPARATION

1. Melt the fat in a saucepan and sauté the cabbage and leeks over medium-high heat until lightly browned. Add the molasses and sauté while stirring constantly. Continue to cook for 5 minutes more.

2. Add the stock, allspice berries, peppercorns, and salt to taste and bring to a boil. Simmer for 30 minutes. (The browned cabbage in broth can be prepared 1 day in advance and reheated.)

452 | The Appetizer Atlas

3. Combine the veal, pork, breadcrumbs, salt, and pepper. Gradually add the onion, cream, and water, stirring in 1 direction only.

4. Form a small portion of the forcemeat into a ½-inch [1-cm] ball. Simmer it in the cabbage broth for 3 to 5 minutes, or until cooked, and test for flavor and texture. If the dumplings are tough, mix in a bit more water to the forcemeat mixture. Refrigerate. (The dumplings can be made several hours in advance.)

COOKING METHOD

5. Bring the cabbage and broth to a simmer in a large skillet. Drop thirty-two ½-tablespoon [8-mL] portions of the forcemeat into the simmering liquid. Cook the dumplings for 3 to 5 minutes, or until thoroughly cooked.

SERVICE

6. Ladle ¾ cup [180 mL] of the browned cabbage and broth into a wide shallow bowl and top with 4 dumplings. Garnish with chopped parsley.

Potato Dumplings Stuffed with Ham and Onion Kroppkakor

serves 8 (3 dumplings per person)

These dumplings are very popular on the *smörgåsbord* table and can be made with a variety of fillings. The dough can be made with instant potatoes, but dry mashed potatoes make the best dough. This recipe has a cheese sauce to finish the dish, and any type of Scandinavian cheese can be used (Danish blue and *havarti* are both recommended), or the dumplings may be served simply with melted butter or sour cream.

CHEF NOTES

Three ounces [85 g] each of pork belly and smoked bacon in equal proportions may be substituted for the bacon and ham in this recipe.

FILLING: MAKES ENOUGH FOR 24 DUMPLINGS

2 ounces [55 g] bacon, diced

I medium onion, chopped

4 ounces [110 g] Danish ham, diced

½ teaspoon [3 mL] black pepper

I tablespoon [15 mL] chopped parsley

SAUCE: MAKES ABOUT 1½ CUPS [360 mL]

I tablespoon [15 mL] butter

I tablespoon [15 mL] flour

¼ cup [60 mL] chicken stock

¾ cup [180 mL] heavy cream

I cup [240 mL] Danish blue or *havarti* cheese, crumbled or grated or a combination

DUMPLINGS: MAKES 24 DUMPLINGS

I pound [450 g] russet potatoes, cooked, mashed or riced, and cooled

I egg, beaten

I egg yolk

I cup [240 mL] flour

¼ teaspoon [1 mL] garlic powder

I teaspoon [5 mL] salt

½ teaspoon [3 mL] white pepper

10 cups [2.4 L] lightly salted water, simmering rapidly

Parsley sprigs, for garnish

ADVANCE PREPARATION

1. Heat a skillet over medium heat and sauté the bacon until lightly browned.

2. Add the onion and sauté until soft and lightly browned.

3. Add the ham, black pepper, and parsley and cook 3 to 4 minutes. Reserve. (The filling can be made one day in advance.)

PREPARATION OF THE SAUCE

4. Melt the butter in a small skillet over medium heat. Whisk in the flour to make a roux and cook over low heat for 2 minutes.

5. Whisk in the stock and cream and cook until the sauce thickens. Stir in the crumbled cheese. Reserve warm. (The sauce can be made several hours in advance.)

PREPARATION OF THE DUMPLINGS

6. Mix the mashed potatoes with the egg, egg yolk, flour, garlic powder, salt, and pepper to form a stiff dough. More or less flour may be required. The dough should not be allowed to rest or it will become sticky and more flour will be required to make it workable.

7. Knead the dough on a floured surface until smooth. Roll out the dough ¼ inch [6 mm] thick and cut twenty-four 3-inch [8-cm] circles.

8. Place about ½ tablespoon [8 mL] of filling in the center of a dough circle. Close the dough around the filling, shape the dumpling into a bun, and twist the top to seal. Repeat for the remaining dumplings and place them on a floured surface.

COOKING METHOD

9. Gently lower the dumplings, in batches, into the simmering water and cook for 5 to 7 minutes, or until they float to the top and the dough has cooked. Remove the cooked dumplings with a slotted spoon to a lightly buttered dish and continue until all are cooked.

SERVICE

10. Serve each guest 3 dumplings, topped with 3 tablespoons [45 mL] of cheese sauce. Garnish with parsley sprigs.

Beef, Veal, and Pork Meatballs Små Köttbullar

serves 8 (5 to 6 meatballs per person)

These delicate meatballs have no resemblance to those found coated in sweet-and-sour ketchup sauce on American buffet tables. They are a favorite item on the Swedish *smörgåsbord* and are usually eaten without sauce. The meatballs are excellent dipped into mustard or lingonberry preserves or a mixture of the two blended together.

CHEF NOTES

The meatballs may be cooked in advance and frozen, then reheated for service. The meatballs may also be lightly dusted in flour and cooked in a deep-fryer.

MEATBALLS: MAKES ABOUT 50 MEATBALLS

1 tablespoon [15 mL] butter

¼ cup [60 mL] onion, minced

1 cup [240 mL] cooked potatoes, whipped

¼ cup [60 mL] dry breadcrumbs

1 pound [450 g] lean ground beef

4 ounces [110 g] ground veal

4 ounces [110 g] lean ground pork

⅓ cup [80 mL] heavy cream

1 teaspoon [5 mL] salt

½ teaspoon [3 mL] white pepper

Pinch of ground allspice

1 egg, beaten

1 tablespoon [15 mL] parsley, chopped

¼ cup [60 mL] clarified butter

GRAVY (OPTIONAL)

1 tablespoon [15 mL] flour

¾ cup [180 mL] chicken stock

¾ cup [180 mL] cream

Mustard

Lingonberry preserves

ADVANCE PREPARATION

1. Melt the butter in a skillet over medium heat. Sauté the onion until soft.

2. Combine the sautéed onions, whipped potatoes, breadcrumbs, beef, veal, pork, cream, salt, pepper, allspice, egg, and parsley in a bowl. Stir vigorously, in one direction only to thoroughly mix.

3. Form the forcemeat into about fifty 1-inch [2.5-cm] balls. Cover and reserve, refrigerated, until ready to cook. (The meatballs can be made several hours in advance.)

COOKING METHOD

4. Heat the clarified butter in a large nonstick skillet over medium heat. Sauté the meatballs in batches until evenly browned and cooked to an internal temperature of 160°F [70°C]. Keep warm until service.

PREPARATION OF THE GRAVY

5. If making gravy, pour out all but about 2 tablespoons [30 mL] of the clarified butter. Whisk in the flour and cook over low heat for 2 minutes.

6. Slowly whisk in the stock. Increase the heat to a boil and add the cream. Simmer the cream sauce until reduced by one-third.

7. If serving with the gravy, the meatballs should be added to the gravy and simmered for 5 to 7 minutes prior to service.

SERVICE

8. Serve each guest 5 to 6 meatballs, topped with some of the gravy, if using. If serving with the mustard or lingonberry preserves or both, serve in small ramekins on the side.

Pickled Cooked Goose Breast Gus Prigotovlyenny v Marinadye

serves 8

Eastern Scandinavians and those who live in the Baltic states are very fond of goose and duck, and people enjoy hunting them. Domestic geese and ducks are popular because they are tolerant of the cold climate and need relatively little care. Pickled goose can be stored throughout the cold winter, then cooked when needed. This Estonian dish is an adaptation of an ancient Swedish recipe, *sprängd gås.*

CHEF NOTES

This dish may be made with wild or domestic goose or duck. If using hunted wild birds, check carefully for shot before cooking and serving.

PICKLING MIXTURE

Juice of ½ lemon

½ cup [120 mL] salt

1 teaspoon [5 mL] saltpeter

1½ pounds [675 g] goose or duck breast

BRINE AND POACHING BROTH

3 tablespoons [45 mL] salt and 1 tablespoon [15 mL] sugar to every 2½ cups [600 mL] water

Water, as needed

Chicken stock, as needed

1 onion, unpeeled and quartered

3 garlic cloves, unpeeled and bruised

1 large carrot, split lengthwise

6 whole black peppercorns

4 whole white peppercorns

3 bay leaves

½ bunch parsley, tied

8 ounces [225 g] crushed lingonberries or cranberries, for service

ADVANCE PREPARATION

1. To pickle the goose breast, mix the lemon juice, salt, and saltpeter together to combine. Rub all parts of the goose or duck breast with this mixture and place in a resealable plastic bag. Marinate, refrigerated, for 24 hours, turning several times.

2. To brine the goose breast, place it in a saucepan and add water to cover by 1½ inches [4 cm]. Remove the breast and measure the water. Apply the formula for salt and sugar to determine how much of each to use. Stir until the sugar and salt have dissolved.

3. Place the breast in a resealable plastic bag and pour the brine over the breast. Place in the refrigerator and allow to marinate for 3 days, turning occasionally.

COOKING METHOD

4. Drain the goose breast and place in a saucepan. Cover with chicken stock and add the onion, garlic, carrot, black and white peppercorns, bay leaves, and parsley.

5. Bring to a boil, reduce the heat, and simmer the goose breast for 1 hour, or until fork tender. Drain the breast and slice thin. The goose may be served warm or cool.

SERVICE

6. Fan out the slices of breast on a small plate, about 3 ounces [85 g] per person. Serve crushed berries on the side.

Glass Blower's Trout (Spicy Pickled Trout) Lasimestarin Silli

serves 8

The name of this dish refers to its being served in the glass jar in which the fish marinates. Pickled fish is made all across Scandinavia using salted herring, but fresh trout makes an excellent substitute. In Denmark the dish is called *glarmestersild*, in Norway it is known as *glassmestersild*, and in Sweden by the name *glasmästarsill*. Easy to assemble, the fish must marinate in the refrigerator for two to three days before service.

CHEF NOTES

If using salted herring, soak the herring for 12 hours in the refrigerator, submerged in water or milk. Drain and thoroughly rinse the herring before trimming into 1-inch [2.5-cm] pieces. Individual servings may be assembled, using small Mason-type jars or glasses (about ½-cup [120-mL] capacity).

I cup [240 mL] distilled white vinegar

½ cup [120 mL] water

¾ cup [180 mL] sugar

4 fresh trout, filleted with pin bones removed, fillets cut crosswise into 1-inch [2.5-cm] pieces

1½-inch [4-cm] piece fresh horseradish, thinly sliced

½-inch [1-cm] piece fresh gingerroot, thinly sliced

2 teaspoons [10 mL] whole allspice berries

2 teaspoons [10 mL] whole yellow mustard seeds

3 bay leaves

6 cloves, whole

I carrot, sliced

¾ cup [180 mL] red onion, sliced

Toasted light rye bread, for service

Softened butter, for service

ADVANCE PREPARATION

1. Combine the vinegar, water, and sugar and bring to a boil in a nonreactive saucepan, stirring to dissolve the sugar. Reserve and allow to cool completely.

2. In a 1-quart [1-L] glass Mason-style jar with a tight-fitting lid, build repeating layers of fish, spices, and vegetables in an attractive fashion.

3. Pour the cooled vinegar solution over the layers, being sure to remove air bubbles and to completely cover the contents. Cover tightly and place in the refrigerator to marinate for 2 to 3 days.

SERVICE

4. Serve the fish and vegetables directly from the jar, or arrange them on individual plates, 4 to 5 pieces of fish with assorted vegetables. Garnish with slices of toasted light rye bread and butter, as well as cocktail forks or toothpicks to skewer the fish and vegetables.

Cured Salmon with Dill and Mustard Sauce Gravad Lax (Gravlax, Gravlaks)

serves 8

Gravad lax, or cured salmon, with dill is an ancient Swedish dish that has been adopted by the entire region. This dish symbolizes the essence of Scandinavia, with spawning salmon representing the confluence of fresh and salt water, the dill being reminiscent of the rich green growth of an abbreviated summer, with the white salt and sugar mixture representing ice and snow. This dish is made primarily in the spring, to coincide with the abundance of fresh fish and dill. Some Norwegian versions use a mixture of pine needles with the dill for a more aromatic flavor. Many versions call for a pinch of saltpeter to help retain the reddish color of the flesh.

SALMON

I large bunch of fresh dill, bruised to release flavor

3 tablespoons [45 mL] kosher salt

¼ cup [60 mL] sugar

1½ tablespoons [25 mL] white peppercorns, crushed

Pinch of saltpeter (optional)

1½ pounds [675 g] center-cut salmon fillet, scaled, pin bones removed, divided into 2 portions

SAUCE

¼ cup [60 mL] mild prepared mustard (not coarse grained)

2 to 3 tablespoons [30 to 45 mL] sugar, to taste

I egg yolk

¼ cup [60 mL] malt vinegar

¾ cup [180 mL] vegetable oil

¼ cup [60 mL] fresh dill, chopped

Salt to taste

Ground white pepper to taste

Dill sprigs, for garnish

Freshly ground white pepper, for garnish

ADVANCE PREPARATION

1. Sprinkle a thin layer of dill on the bottom of a glass baking dish.

2. Mix the salt, sugar, white peppercorns, and saltpeter, (if using) together. Liberally rub all surfaces of the fish with this cure mixture to thoroughly coat.

3. Place 1 fillet, skin side down, on the dill and place most of the remaining dill over the surface of the fillet. Arrange the other fillet on top of the bottom piece of fish so that the thick end of the top fillet is over the thin end of the bottom fillet. Top with any remaining cure mixture and dill.

This method works well with sea-run trout and all types of salmon. The curing may be done in a re-sealable plastic bag if the bag is periodically turned so that the marinade reaches all portions of the fish. The bag should be placed on a flat object and weighted from the top. The skin may be cut into thin strips and fried in butter until golden brown, making an excellent garnish. Slices of cured salmon are also delicious when very briefly sautéed in a nonstick skillet with a light brushing of butter. Ideally this dish should be made with the middle cut from a 6- to 8-pound [2.7- to 3.6-kg] fresh salmon, and old timers insist that the fish be frozen for 24 hours before curing to kill any possible parasites and break down the flesh slightly to enable a more flavorful curing. The ideal curing temperature is 45° to 50°F [7° to 10°C], but the refrigerator will work over 2 to 3 days. *Gravad lax* is always served with a mustard-dill sauce.

4. Loosely cover with plastic film and top the fish with a flat board, such as a small cutting board. Place canned goods or a pot on top of the board to compress the fish.

5. Marinate the fish in the refrigerator for 2 to 3 days, basting every 12 hours with the accumulated juices. When basting, separate the fillets to make sure the center has adequate cure mixture and dill.

PREPARATION OF THE SAUCE

6. Combine the mustard, sugar, egg yolk, and vinegar in the workbowl of a small processor or blender. Slowly drizzle in the oil in a thin stream while processing or blending, to emulsify the sauce.

7. Stir in the chopped dill and add salt and pepper to taste. Reserve at room temperature.

SERVICE

8. Remove the salmon and scrape the seasonings and dill from the flesh and skin. With a flexible, thin-bladed knife, cut paper-thin slices diagonally from the fillet, being sure to exclude the skin.

9. Arrange 2 to 3 ounces [55 to 85 g] of the sliced salmon on a plate in an overlapping fashion. Drizzle the sauce across the center of the slices, adding a small pool of sauce near the edge of the plate.

10. Garnish with dill sprigs and a few twists of white pepper over the top.

Central Europe

Germany, Austria,

Switzerland, Belgium,

and the Netherlands

Braised Stuffed Beef Roll
Rouladen (Rindsrouladen)

Leek, Bacon, and Emmentaler Tart
Basler Lauchwähe

Venison Medallions with Gin and Juniper Berries
Côtelettes de Chevreuil au Genièvre (Reebokkoteletten met Genever)

Twice-Fried Potatoes
Pommes Frites (Frietjes)

Rabbit and Veal Terrine
Hazen Konijnenpastei

Mussels Stuffed with Bacon, Garlic, and Herbs (Mock Snails)
Moules à l'Escargot (Mossels met Lookboter)

Cheese and Wild Mushroom Croquettes
Verwildered Paddestoel Kaascroquetten/ Fondue Bruxelleoise aux Champignons

Cheese Soufflés in a Tomato Shell
Tomates Soufflées Jurassiennes

CENTRAL EUROPE INCLUDES the countries of Germany, Austria, Switzerland, Belgium, and the Netherlands For centuries this region has been a patchwork of many small states and kingdoms and their cuisines are quite similar, relying on common ingredients and flavor combinations. The cuisine of Germany is representative of Central Europe. In spite of its small size, German geography falls into three distinct zones. In the north, the low plains extend from the Netherlands to Russia. This cold and damp climate necessitates hearty fare, and rich, thick soups are prevalent. The cold northern waters offer up a bounty of such seafood as lobster, crab, and shrimp, as well as flounder and herring. Cold weather vegetables such as cabbage and potatoes are popular and the flavoring combination of sweet and sour reflects the culinary traditions of Germany's neighbors Russia and Poland.

In the central region, covered with forests, hills, and fertile valleys, vineyards produce grapes for Germany's famous wines. The Rhine and Mosel river valleys are home to many world-class white wines. Orchards are found everywhere, and pastureland supports the herds of cattle and sheep. Pork is the favorite meat of this region and of Germany as a whole Westphalian ham is world famous. The pigs are fed acorns from the numerous stands of oak found in the forests. The south is the granary of Germany. Wheat for bread and barley and hops for beer brewing are grown on the plateaus of this hilly land. Potatoes are a staple and are often combined with apples, another important crop. Dishes based on deer, game birds, and wild boar are found everywhere.

Because of its central location within Europe, German cuisine has been influenced strongly by its neighbors. Upper-class Germans would bring workers, including chefs, from neighboring countries to work within Germany's borders. Being in a strange land, these transplanted chefs would, by necessity, have to adapt their methods to the ingredients at hand, forever modifying the local cuisine. By the mid-1700s France had exerted a strong influence on German cooking. Food became more sophisticated, and recipes were beginning to be recorded. When Napoleon invaded Prussia in 1806, and for the next seven years when Prussia was part of the French Empire, French influence was at its peak. German cooks were used as helpers in the French kitchens, and after the defeat of Napoleon and the subsequent removal of the French chefs, the German cooks remained, with their education in the art of French cooking.

As a whole, German foods are very familiar to Americans, and appetizers play an important role in the dining patterns of Germans. Called *vorspeisen*, these small dishes are popular with Germans, who like to eat many little meals and snacks throughout the day. Overall, German cuisine can be considered a "meat and potatoes" diet. In particular, Germans and Austrians are fond of cutlets, which are dressed in a variety of ways or left without accompaniment. Pork is often the meat of choice and it is eaten both fresh and preserved, usually smoked. Veal is considered elegant and is favored when ground meat is required for a dish. Ragouts and stews are popular, and liver is treated with the greatest of respect, often served with sautéed apples and onions. Liver pastes and pâtés and organ meats and other offal round out the meat dishes. In spite of tasty chicken dishes, the German palate for poultry leans toward goose and duck, the latter being meatier and much leaner than that found in America. Fish from the North Sea is prepared simply, and freshwater salmon and trout are prepared with the fresh taste of fish in mind. Rainbow trout, introduced to Germany from the United States, was an instant hit. Herring is prepared in a multitude of ways.

For Germans, ingredients must be fresh and unadulterated. Germans demand foods that are free of pesticides, preservatives, and chemical additives. Pickles, mustards, and sauerkraut, associated most often with German cuisine, are quite popular, as are fresh dairy and cheese. Sauerkraut is associated most often with German cuisine, and it has an interesting history. Introduced by the ancient Romans (who, in turn, acquired it from the Orient), the technique of fermenting cabbage was lost during the first millennium. By the thirteenth century Tatars reintroduced this delicacy from China to Austria, which named it "sour plant" (*sauerkraut*). Vegetables are assigned a status; cabbage is a most humble vegetable, while asparagus and wild mushrooms are elevated to a noble position in this vegetable hierarchy.

When one thinks of Austrian cuisine, Vienna and its magnificent pastries immediately come to mind. The style of cooking may be characterized as rich and satisfying. Stews are hearty and sauces that accompany roasts are cream based. Austrians have a fondness for dumplings, and the most famous Austrian dish must be *wiener schnitzel*. Unlike the German variation, a true *wiener schnitzel* is not napped in a brown gravy. It is delicately battered and fried, usually accompanied with potatoes. The escallopes of veal may be stuffed with mushrooms and the dish is then called *wiener schnitzel mit schwammerlfülle*.

Like German cooking, Swiss cooking is based on a strict reliance on quality ingredients. Many of those ingredients must be imported, since only 60 percent of Switzerland's food requirements can be produced at home. This gives the Swiss a particularly good insight into foreign foods and exposes them to different cuisines. The Swiss have a direct, matter-of-fact approach to cooking, with few frills. Recipes, many quite old, are specialties from individual towns and cantons. When the Swiss refer to a dish, the name always includes its place of origin. Not just a fondue, it is *fondue Neuchâtel*, for example. In many ways the people have strong local loyalties, whether to Bern, Geneva, or Lausanne. Some dishes are so laden with cream and butter that they require adaptation to modern dietary awareness.

Meats are secondary in the Swiss diet. Soups, potatoes, and cheese make up most average Swiss meals. When meat is served, pork is preferred, usually smoked, taking the form of sausages and head cheeses. Chicken can be expensive. Fish and game are prized in Switzerland and are usually reserved for special occasions. Cheese has been popular for centuries, and Swiss cheeses store and travel well. Pastry dough, especially puff pastry, is formed into shells and filled with mushrooms, sweetbreads, fish, and chicken. Pastry encases beef filets or game or goose liver pie.

Belgian cuisine is the most sophisticated in the region. Belgium is divided into two ethnic groups, the Flemings, who speak Flemish, and the Walloons, who speak French. Belgian cuisine takes advantage of these two diverse cultures. It was the Congress of Vienna in 1815 that united Belgium and the Netherlands under a Dutch king. A subsequent uprising divided the two for the last time, leaving an influential Dutch presence in Belgium. Belgian cuisine also reflects a deeply rooted foundation in the Middle Ages in its use of such spices as nutmeg, ginger, cinnamon, and bay. A culinary benefit of colonialism is the Belgian appreciation for spicy foods, which can be traced to its involvement in Africa with the Congo. *Piri piri* peppers were brought back by travelers to the region. A Mediterranean influence can be seen in the use of saffron and other spices of that region.

Belgium is a small country with no natural borders. Almost half of the land is under cultivation or is used to raise livestock. Enough food is grown to make Belgium an exporter. Bell peppers of all colors appear on world market shelves. On the southern edge of the region known as Kempen, rich river bottom soils dredged up from the Dyle River are added to the already rich soils, producing world-famous vegetables, such as Belgian carrots, baby peas and string beans, tiny onions, huge cauliflowers, and tender lettuces. Endive and asparagus are also Belgian specialties. Belgium has a love affair with the humble potato, cooking it in every manner. The Belgians claim to have invented so-called French fries (*pommes frites*), which are served as part of the national dish of steak and fried potatoes. Fried potatoes are often eaten alone as a snack, and even mussels, a Belgian passion, are served with *frites*. Hazelnuts are added to mashed potatoes, elevating this simple vegetable to regal status.

Whether dining on meat, fish, or fowl, Belgians have a love affair with food. In addition to rich sauces using ample amounts of butter, quantity is an important measure of Belgian dining habits. Whether Flemish or Walloon, the approach to cooking is quite similar. Differences are as subtle as cooking with wine versus beer (and drinking one or the other during meals), the Walloons preferring wine. Seafood is appreciated all across Belgium. The entire mussel harvest of the Netherlands is exported to Belgium. Tiny shrimp, oysters, eels, and a variety of freshwater fish, including trout, are simply prepared. The famous *waterzooi*, a soup-stew of fish or chicken with vegetables, is said to have started as a Flemish version of the French *bouillabaisse* and became chicken based in the interior regions. Fat little chickens are usually roasted and finished with melted butter. In the Ardennes game birds, such as pheasant, quail, and partridge, are hunted, as is wild boar and deer. The famous Ardennes ham is from this region. Its unique flavor and quality come from letting the pigs feed on native heather and smoking the hams over juniper wood.

Since the sixteenth century the Dutch have left their mark on the world as traders, and colonialism brought a unique Eastern influence to its cuisine. Occupation of the East Indies and the spice trade that resulted left an indelible mark on the cuisine of the Netherlands. In addition to the *rijsttafel* (literally, rice table), a main dish of rice surrounded by many small dishes of fish and vegetables, the Dutch enjoy the flavor of ginger in many savory and sweet dishes, and classic Indonesian dishes have been transformed into Dutch specialties. The Dutch colonization of the West Indies brought a Caribbean component to Dutch cuisine as well. The Dutch have a special love affair with butter. Rich dairy products are found in many dishes, and a meal is not a meal without cheese. With its Calvinist heritage and gloomy weather, the cuisine of the Netherlands is a bland one, with few spices and herbs except when cooking Indonesian style. Potatoes, accompanied with a modest portion of meat, constitute a usual meal, and the plate is commonly bathed in gravy. Hot pot is a familiar Dutch dish, combining the potatoes with meat and vegetables in a one-pot meal.

Braised Stuffed Beef Roll Rouladen (Rindsrouladen)

serves 8

Rouladen are enjoyed throughout Central Europe and can be found made with a variety of fillings and sauces. Traditionally they are stuffed with bacon, dill pickles, anchovy, and onion, then braised in a vegetable-enriched beef broth. In Austria, where they are known as *rindsrouladen*, the broth almost always contains red wine, while in Germany cream may be introduced in the final stages of cooking.

CHEF NOTES

Veal, pork, or turkey breast cutlets work well in this dish. After reduction of the sauce, ½ cup [120 mL] of heavy cream may be added. In some versions of the dish 8 ounces [225 g] of ground veal is added to the filling.

BEEF

16 thin scallops of beef top round, about 1½ ounces [45 g] each, pounded and trimmed to 3 × 2-inch [8 × 5-cm] rectangles

Salt and black pepper

Sweet paprika

3 tablespoons [45 mL] Düsseldorf-style hot prepared mustard

FILLING

4 slices lean smoked bacon, cut into quarters

8 anchovies, separated into 16 fillets

4 small dill pickles, quartered

½ cup [120 mL] thinly sliced onions

4 garlic cloves, minced

BROTH

¼ cup [60 mL] vegetable oil

¼ cup [60 mL] dry red wine

2½ cups [600 mL] rich beef stock

⅓ cup [80 mL] leeks, white and light green parts only, minced

¼ cup [60 mL] parsnips, diced fine

¼ cup [60 mL] celeriac, diced fine

¼ cup [60 mL] carrots, diced fine

2 tablespoons [30 mL] parsley, chopped

½ teaspoon [3 mL] black pepper

Parsley sprigs, for garnish

ADVANCE PREPARATION

1. Season one side of each beef scallop with salt and pepper and paprika. Turn each scallop over and spread about 1 teaspoon of mustard across the surface, leaving a ½-inch [1-cm] border with no mustard.

PREPARATION OF THE FILLING

2. Arrange one quarter piece of bacon across the scallop, near the bottom. Top the bacon with an anchovy fillet and a quar-

ter pickle slice. Add several slices of onion and some of the minced garlic.

3. Roll up each beef scallop jelly-roll fashion and secure with toothpicks, being sure to press the filling into the ends of the rolls. Trim if necessary and reserve. (The rolls can be prepared to this point several hours in advance, wrapped in plastic film, and refrigerated.)

COOKING METHOD

4. Heat the oil to medium in a nonstick skillet. Evenly brown the beef rolls.

5. Deglaze the pan with red wine. Add the beef stock, leeks, parsnips, celeriac, carrot, parsley, and pepper and bring to a boil. Reduce the heat to a low simmer, cover the skillet, and cook for 1½ hours, or until the rolls are very tender, adding stock as necessary. Remove the rolls to a platter and keep warm.

6. Strain the solids from the broth and purée them in a food processor. Bring the strained broth to a boil and reduce the volume by one-third. Lower the heat to a simmer and add the puréed vegetables, stirring gently to incorporate. Add the beef rolls and simmer for 5 minutes.

SERVICE

7. Remove the toothpicks and serve each person 2 beef rolls, sliced diagonally and topped with sauce. Garnish with parsley sprigs.

Leek, Bacon, and Emmentaler Tart Basler Lauchwähe

serves 12

Variations on the onion-and-leek-tart theme are found throughout Central Europe. In Belgium it is called *flamiche*, in the Netherlands *porei taart,* and in Germany it is called *lauchkuchen* (and can be made with puff pastry instead of a pie dough). This version comes from the Basel region of Switzerland and is especially popular during Carnival season. For a meatless version the bacon can be omitted. The tart is usually made with onions, but leeks add additional flavor.

CHEF NOTES

Canadian bacon, prosciutto, or ham may be substituted for the bacon. Onions may be used instead of leeks. This recipe can be made as individual tarts, cutting 3-inch [8-cm] circles of dough, and using a muffin pan to bake them in.

DOUGH

2 cups [480 mL] all-purpose flour

½ teaspoon [3 mL] salt

½ teaspoon [3 mL] garlic powder

4 ounces [110 g] butter

About ¼ cup [60 mL] ice water

FILLING

1½ tablespoons [25 mL] unsalted butter

6 large leeks, white and pale green parts only, well washed and thinly sliced

½ teaspoon [3 mL] salt

⅓ cup [80 mL] diced bacon

3 tablespoons [45 mL] all-purpose flour

2 eggs, beaten

1 cup [240 mL] milk

1 cup [240 mL] half-and-half

Several gratings of fresh nutmeg

½ teaspoon [3 mL] salt

2 cups [480 mL] grated Emmentaler or other Swiss cheese

Chive leaves, for garnish

ADVANCE PREPARATION

1. Sift the flour, salt, and garlic powder together. Using a pastry knife, cut in the butter until the pieces are pea size. Add the ice water, a little at a time, until a stiff dough is formed (more or less water may be required). Allow the dough to rest for 20 minutes.

2. Roll out the dough and line a 9-inch [23-cm] pie pan, fluting the edge.

3. Stipple the bottom of the dough and prebake for 10 minutes at 350°F [175°C]. Pie weights, rice, dry beans, or foil may be used to hold the shape of the crust while baking blind. (The

dough can be made one day in advance. The pie shell may be baked several hours in advance.)

4. Melt the butter in a skillet and sauté the leeks over medium heat. Add the salt and bacon and cook until the leeks are golden and the bacon is crisp. Slowly whisk in the flour.

5. Whisk the eggs into the milk and half-and-half. Add the nutmeg and salt. Place the leek and bacon mixture into the pie shell. Add the grated cheese and pour in the egg mixture.

6. Bake at 350°F [175°C] for 40 minutes, or until the custard is just set. (The tart can be made one day in advance to this point.) Increase the heat to 400°F [205°C] and bake for 5 to 7 minutes more, or until the top is nicely browned. Remove the tart just before the center is set, as it will continue to cook when removed from the oven.

SERVICE

7. Cut the tart into 12 pieces. Serve 1 warm slice, garnished with chive leaves, per person.

Venison Medallions with Gin and Juniper Berries
Côtelettes de Chevreuil au Genièvre (Reebokkoteletten met Genever)

serves 8

Venison is raised domestically in Belgium, and hunters bring in their fair share. In the United States, inspected venison is available from meat suppliers or specialty meat markets. The sauce for this dish is popular all across Belgium and Holland. Traditional accompaniments include a tart applesauce paired with puréed roasted chestnuts, a baked apple stuffed with fresh berries matched with a purée of celery root, or classic French-fried potatoes (*pomme frites* or *frietjes*).

CHEF NOTES

This dish can be prepared with buffalo, beef, veal, pork, or lamb tenderloin.

VENISON

8 venison tenderloin medallions, about 3 ounces [85 g] each

Salt and black pepper

I teaspoon [5 mL] dried thyme

SAUCE: MAKES ¾ CUP [180 mL]

¼ cup [60 mL] unsalted butter

¼ cup [60 mL] gin

I cup [240 mL] demi-glace, *glace de viande*, or rich venison stock

½ cup [120 mL] heavy cream

10 juniper berries, crushed

I tablespoon [15 mL] green peppercorns, crushed (optional)

Salt to taste

I to 1½ teaspoons [5 to 8 mL] lemon juice, to taste

8 small slices brioche, buttered and grilled service

Thin *pommes frites*, for service (see page 474)

ADVANCE PREPARATION

1. Rub the venison medallions with salt, pepper, and thyme. Allow to marinate 30 minutes.

COOKING METHOD

2. Heat the butter in a nonstick skillet over medium-high heat. Briefly sear both sides of the medallions to brown lightly. Reduce the heat and cook 2 to 4 minutes per side, or until cooked rare. The meat will continue to cook to medium rare while holding. Reserve and keep warm until service.

3. Deglaze the pan with the gin, remove the pan from the burner, and ignite the gin. When the flames subside, add the demi-glace and cream. Bring to a boil and reduce the heat to medium.

4. Add the juniper berries, green peppercorns, if using, and salt. Reduce the sauce by one-third. Add the lemon juice to taste and remove from the heat.

SERVICE

5. Place a slice of grilled brioche on a plate and top with a venison medallion. Coat with 1 to 1½ tablespoons [15 to 25 mL] of sauce and serve with *pommes frites* on the side.

Twice-Fried Potatoes Pommes Frites (Frietjes)

serves 8

The method that produces the finest fried potatoes is to blanch them first by frying in low-temperature oil, then fry them briefly at a high temperature to brown and crisp the potatoes. It is best to avoid freshly harvested potatoes when making this dish.

3 to 4 cups [720 to 960 mL] vegetable oil, for frying

2 pounds [900 g] Idaho or russet potatoes, cut into thin julienne 3 to 4 inches [8 to 10 cm] long

Salt to taste

Mayonnaise, for serving

ADVANCE PREPARATION

1. Preheat the oil to 325°F [160°C]. Dry the potato sticks thoroughly to prevent spattering. Fry the potatoes, in batches, for 3 to 4 minutes, or until they just begin to color but do not brown. Remove and drain the potatoes. (This step can be done several hours in advance.)

COOKING METHOD

2. Heat the oil to 365° to 375°F [185° to 195°C] for the final frying. Fry the blanched potatoes for 1 to 2 minutes, or until golden brown and crisp. Drain on paper towels and salt to taste.

SERVICE

3. Serve immediately, accompanied by a ramekin of mayonnaise.

Rabbit and Veal Terrine Hazen Konijnenpastei

serves 12

The Dutch, Flemish, and Germans are particularly fond of rabbit and hare and enjoy it baked, roasted, braised ("jugged"), stewed, and as in this recipe, as a terrine. In Europe hare is fairly accessible and domesticated rabbit is plentiful. Hare tends to be larger, tougher, and stronger in taste, while domesticated rabbit is tender and light in flavor. Fall and winter are the seasons that hare and rabbit are most popular in Europe, but rabbit is available in the United States year-round, either frozen or fresh.

CHEF NOTES

If using wild hare, soak the meat in Cognac or wine prior to cooking, to remove some of the gaminess. Hare will need to cook appreciably longer than domestic rabbit. Hollandaise sauce makes an excellent accompaniment.

RABBIT

2 ounces [55 g] butter

1 large rabbit (about 3 pounds [1.4 kg]), cut into 10 pieces

Salt and black pepper

4 slices bacon

1 cup [240 mL] rabbit, chicken, or beef stock

1 cup [240 mL] sour cream

TERRINE

8 ounces [225 g] lean ground veal

8 ounces [225 g] ground lean pork

4 egg yolks

¼ teaspoon [1 mL] dried thyme

¼ teaspoon [1 mL] black pepper

½ teaspoon [3 mL] salt

⅛ teaspoon [0.5 mL] grated nutmeg

1 tablespoon [15 mL] Cognac

12 slices lean smoked bacon

8 ounces [225 g] cured ham, such as Smithfield or Virginia, cut into wide strips

2 bay leaves

Buttered toast points, for service

Cornichons or gherkin pickles, for service

Mustard, for service

ADVANCE PREPARATION

1. Melt the butter in a skillet over medium heat. Season the rabbit with salt and pepper and sauté the rabbit to brown evenly. Line the bottom of a heavy casserole with the bacon slices and top with the browned rabbit, stock, and pan juices.

2. Add the sour cream, cover the casserole, and bake at 325°F [160°C] for 2 hours.

3. Allow the rabbit to cool enough to handle. Remove the meat from the bones, leaving the larger pieces whole. Coarsely chop the smaller pieces of rabbit meat and the bacon from the bottom of the pan by pulsing in a food processor. Reserve the meat and ¾ cup [180 mL] of the sauce from the casserole. (The rabbit can be prepared one day in advance.)

PREPARATION OF THE TERRINE

4. Combine the chopped rabbit meat, the reserved ¾ cup [180 mL] of sauce, the veal, pork, egg yolks, thyme, pepper, salt, nutmeg, and Cognac and mix well.

5. Cover the sides and bottom of a terrine mold with the bacon slices. Let the slices hang over the sides of the terrine mold to fold over when the mold is filled.

6. Place a layer of the chopped rabbit mixture on the bottom of the mold. Add a few larger pieces of rabbit meat and a few strips of the ham. Top with the chopped rabbit mixture. Repeat the layering sequence until all of the components are used, finishing with the meat mixture. Place the bay leaves on top and fold the bacon slices over. Cover with aluminum foil and reserve.

COOKING METHOD

7. Place the terrine in a baking pan and pour boiling water into the pan to come halfway up the sides of the terrine. Bake at 350°F [175°C] for 1 hour.

8. Remove the foil and bake for 20 minutes more, or until the terrine is set and the top has browned. Pour off any accumulated fat. Allow the terrine to cool in the mold, cover with plastic film, and chill thoroughly before service. (The terrine can be made several days in advance.)

SERVICE

9. Serve slices of the terrine on small plates accompanied with buttered toast, *cornichons*, and mustard.

Mussels Stuffed with Bacon, Garlic, and Herbs (Mock Snails)
Moules à l'Escargot (Mossels met Lookboter)

serves 8

The reference to snails in the French recipe title is ascribed to the escargot-like taste of the mussels, as well as to the method of preparation. Compared to the rest of Europe, Belgians consume a large amount of seafood per capita. They enjoy a modest 40-mile ocean coast from which all kinds of seafood are caught. Belgians are particularly fond of mussels. This dish is said to have originated at a culinary competition held in Brussels. It is now considered a Belgian classic.

MUSSELS

4 slices smoked bacon

6 garlic cloves, bruised

½ cup [120 mL] rich court bouillon or chicken stock

½ cup [120 mL] dry, fruity white wine

40 large mussels, purged, scrubbed, beards removed

FILLING

4 ounces [110 g] unsalted butter, at room temperature

2 tablespoons [30 mL] shallots, diced

4 garlic cloves, minced

1 slice smoked bacon

2 tablespoons [30 mL] fresh parsley, chopped

½ teaspoon [3 mL] dried chervil

Pinch of dried tarragon

½ teaspoon [3 mL] lemon juice

½ teaspoon [3 mL] salt

¼ teaspoon [1 mL] black pepper

2 cups [480 mL] rock salt, to line broiling pan

¼ cup [60 mL] dry breadcrumbs

Crusty bread, for service

Lemon wedges, for garnish

Parsley sprigs, for garnish

ADVANCE PREPARATION

1. Place the bacon slices on the bottom of a pot that is large enough to hold the mussels. Scatter the garlic cloves evenly on top of the bacon and pour over the court bouillon and wine. Add the mussels, cover the pot with a lid, and bring the liquid to a simmer.

2. Cook the mussels until they have opened, discarding any that remain closed, and allow to cool. Reserve, refrigerated, until ready to use. (The mussels can be steamed one day in advance.)

PREPARATION OF THE FILLING

3. Cream the butter in a food processor until light and fluffy. Add the shallots, garlic, bacon, parsley, chervil, tarragon, lemon juice, salt, and pepper and process to mix thoroughly. Reserve until ready to cook. (The filling can be made one day in advance.)

COOKING METHOD

4. Line a shallow sheet pan with rock salt, to level and stabilize the mussels and retain heat. Discard the upper shell of each mussel and set the mussels onto the salt. Top each mussel with 1 teaspoon [5 mL] of the reserved butter filling, spread across the shell with a metal spatula. (The mussels can be filled and stored, covered and refrigerated, until ready to cook.) Sprinkle on a small amount of the breadcrumbs just before cooking.

5. Broil the stuffed mussels under a very hot broiler for 2 to 3 minutes, or until the butter is melted and the breadcrumbs are evenly browned.

SERVICE

6. Serve each guest 4 to 5 mussels, accompanied with warm, crusty bread. Garnish with lemon wedges and parsley sprigs.

Cheese and Wild Mushroom Croquettes

Verwildered Paddestoel Kaascroquetten/Fondue Bruxelleoise aux Champignons

serves 8 (3 croquettes per person)

These golden fried cheese croquettes with their soft, fluid centers are extremely popular with
the Belgians and the Dutch. The
size of the finished croquette may
be altered to fit the dining situa-
tion, and the blend of cheeses used
can be varied. Flash-fried parsley
or other greens or herbs makes
an excellent accompaniment.

CHEF NOTES

**Larger or smaller croquettes
may be fashioned and may be
shaped as desired. Many combinations of cheeses may be used
as long as the cheeses are not too
strongly flavored. Diced lobster,
shrimp, or scallops make an excellent addition.**

CROQUETTES

3 tablespoons [45 mL] unsalted butter

½ cup [120 mL] flour

½ cup [120 mL] half-and-half

⅓ cup [80 mL] heavy cream

½ cup [120 mL] shredded Parmesan or Asiago cheese

½ cup [120 mL] grated Emmentaler cheese

1¼ cups [300 mL] grated Gruyère cheese

2 egg yolks

½ teaspoon [3 mL] prepared mustard

½ teaspoon [3 mL] salt

½ teaspoon [3 mL] white pepper

⅛ teaspoon [0.5 mL] grated nutmeg

⅛ teaspoon [0.5 mL] cayenne

**¼ cup [60 mL] wild mushrooms (morels, cèpes), diced fine, sautéed
  briefly in butter**

COATING

3 large egg whites

½ teaspoon [3 mL] salt

1 tablespoon [15 mL] vegetable oil

½ cup [120 mL] flour

1½ tablespoons [25 mL] finely grated Parmesan cheese

½ cup [120 mL] dry breadcrumbs

Pinch of grated nutmeg

Pinch of cayenne

Vegetable oil for frying

3 cups [720 mL] parsley leaves, washed and thoroughly dried

Vegetable oil, for frying

ADVANCE PREPARATION

I. Melt the butter in a skillet over medium-low heat, being care-
    ful not to let it brown. Whisk in the flour to form a light roux.

2. Cook 2 minutes and slowly add the half-and-half while whisking constantly. Whisk in the cream and then the three cheeses. Cook, while stirring, until the cheeses have been incorporated and the paste is smooth and thick.

3. Remove from the heat and allow to cool 5 minutes Beat in the egg yolks followed by the mustard, salt, white pepper, nutmeg, and cayenne. Gently fold in the sautéed mushrooms.

4. Press this mixture into an 8-inch [20-cm] square cake pan lined with plastic film. Smooth the surface with a spatula and cover with plastic film to prevent a skin from forming. Refrigerate for at least 30 minutes. (The paste can be made one day in advance.)

PREPARATION OF THE CROQUETTES

5. Combine the egg whites, salt, and vegetable oil in a bowl, beat until slightly thickened and frothy, and reserve. Place the flour in a shallow bowl next to the egg white mixture and reserve.

6. Combine the Parmesan, breadcrumbs, nutmeg, and cayenne in a shallow bowl and mix well.

7. Turn out the chilled cheese mixture onto a lightly floured board, remove the plastic film, and cut into 24 rectangles. In batches, dust the croquettes in the reserved flour, dip into the reserved egg white mixture, and then into the seasoned breadcrumbs to coat completely.

COOKING METHOD

8. Heat the oil to 375°F [190°C] and fry, in batches, for 3 to 4 minutes, or until golden brown. Remove with a slotted spoon to drain on paper towels, holding the croquettes warm until all are cooked.

9. Fry the parsley leaves in oil for about 15 to 20 seconds, or until crisp but not brown. Drain on paper towels and hold until service.

SERVICE

10. Serve each guest 3 cheese croquettes, accompanied with about 2 tablespoons [30 mL] of fried parsley.

Cheese Soufflés in a Tomato Shell — Tomates Soufflées Jurassiennes

serves 12

Cheese soufflés are favorite fare in Switzerland, Germany, and Belgium. The idea of encasing a soufflé in a hollowed tomato is decidedly Swiss. It makes a colorful and unique presentation and the tomato contributes to the flavor of the soufflé.

CHEF NOTES

Other cheeses that would go well in the soufflés would be Edam, Gouda, or Emmentaler. Several other vegetables could be used in place of the tomatoes, such as artichokes, sweet yellow onions, or small round squash.

TOMATOES

12 firm large tomatoes, tops removed and hollowed out, with pulp reserved for another use

Salt and pepper

4 tablespoons [60 mL] chives, minced

SOUFFLÉS

3 tablespoons [45 mL] unsalted butter

2 tablespoons [30 mL] flour

1 teaspoon [5 mL] cornstarch

⅛ teaspoon [0.5 mL] dry mustard

⅛ teaspoon [0.5 mL] garlic powder

Pinch of cayenne

½ teaspoon [3 mL] salt

¼ teaspoon [1 mL] white pepper

½ cup [120 mL] half-and-half

6 eggs, separated, whites beaten until stiff but not dry

1¾ cups [420 mL] grated Gruyère cheese

Chives, for garnish

ADVANCE PREPARATION

1. Sprinkle the hollowed-out interior of the tomatoes with salt and pepper. Place 1 teaspoon [5 mL] of the minced chives in the bottom of each tomato and reserve until needed. (The tomatoes can be prepared several hours in advance.)

PREPARATION OF THE SOUFFLÉS

2. Melt the butter over medium-low heat, then whisk in the flour to form a light roux. Gradually whisk in the cornstarch, mustard, garlic powder, cayenne, salt, white pepper, half-and-half, and three of the egg yolks. Cook over low heat, without boiling, until the mixture has thickened, stirring constantly.

3. Remove from the heat and stir in the cheese and the remaining 3 egg yolks. Allow the mixture to cool before fold-

ing in the beaten egg whites. Spoon the mixture into the tomatoes, filling them three-fourths full.

COOKING METHOD

4. Arrange the filled tomatoes in a parchment-lined baking pan and bake at 350°F [175°C] for 15 to 20 minutes, or until the soufflés have risen and are golden brown. Serve immediately.

SERVICE

5. Serve each guest one tomato, garnished with chive leaves inserted into the soufflé at its edge.

Italy

Pumpkin-Filled Tortellini with Rabbit Sauce
Tortellini di Zucca con Ragù alla Coniglio

Tuna Carpaccio with Herb Sauce
Carpaccio di Tonno alla Salsa Verde

Grilled Eggplant and Roasted Red Pepper Terrine with Prosciutto
Terrina di Melanzane con Peperoni e Prosciutto

Three-Cheese Tart with Soppressata
Torta Rustica con Soppressata

Pizza Two Ways: Tomato, Basil, and Mozzarella and Onion, Olive, and Anchovy
Pizza alla Margherita e Pizzadalina

Grilled Toasts with Cannellini Purée and Wilted Greens
Capriata

Grilled Polenta with Wild Mushroom Sauté
Crostini di Polenta con Peverada di Funghi

ITALY POSSESSES ONE of the most sophisticated and influential of the world cuisines. It is surprising that a country only seven hundred miles long could possess so many regional variations. The topography of Italy has much to do with this regionality. Many natural boundaries (mountains, rivers, and valleys) tend to isolate one region from another. History plays an important role as well. Most sections of Italy were parts of other countries until the twentieth century, and much of Italy was under the influence of various conquerors at one time or another throughout its long history, including the Greeks, Etruscans, Arabs, Normans, and Lombards.

The earliest of the people we think of today as "Italians" settled the Tiber River valley. This settlement became the city of Rome, which ultimately gave birth to the Roman Empire. The ancient Romans were simple farmers and shepherds, with a diet based on wheat porridge (called *puls* or *pulmentum*), leafy vegetables, and legumes. What little meat was consumed came in the form of game such as donkey and deer, as well as from domesticated animals (especially pork and beef). One curious animal consumed was the dormouse. These small rodents were kept in the kitchen and were fed very well to fatten them (dormouse cooked in honey is a recipe found in the earliest cookbook, about 200 A.D.) As Rome became more settled, vegetables began to be cultivated.

During the height of the Roman Empire, North Africa became the "breadbasket" of the empire, growing most of the wheat that fed Rome's people. *Pulmentum* was the form in which grains were prepared, as the technology of the day was not sophisticated enough to grind wheat fine enough to bake bread. When flour was finally made from the grain, breads came into their own. Millet and spelt were replaced by barley, then by *far* (a tastier grain to the Roman palate). As bread making moved from the home to the market, the first professional cooks were bakers. By the time of the Crusades, buckwheat had been introduced by the Saracens. Pasta, an indispensable grain product of Italy, can be documented from books of the late thirteenth century, dispelling the myth that Marco Polo brought pasta to Italy from China. Scholars believe that the North Africans developed dried pasta, which they brought to Italy.

Marco Polo did, however, influence the developing cuisine of Italy in a very different way. By opening a trade route to the East, the Arabs could be bypassed as middlemen in the lucrative spice trade of Europe. Salt, used as a preservative, had a profound influence on the cuisines of Italy. Seawater was evaporated, and salt was to become the basis of the commerce centers of Italy. The development of regional cuisines is due, in part, to the growing upper middle class in the north. A more sophisticated cuisine could develop, leaving the south with a more rustic, peasant cuisine. By the time of the Renaissance, Italian cooking was reaching its greatest period. Florence was the site of the world's first modern cooking school. The sophistication of its cuisine filtered down to the home kitchen. To this day, Tuscany is known for its simple yet sophisticated cooking methods and its use of the finest ingredients.

Italy brought the cooking and dining habits of the rest of Europe out of the Middle Ages. When Caterina de' Medici married King Henry II of France, she brought with her the kitchen staff of her home, forever changing the face of European cuisine. Her chefs taught the French how to cook, and she introduced the technique of using a fork to the French dinner table. Truffles were brought from Italy and the earthy, sensuous flavor captured the palate of her new home.

One of the most significant events in Italian culinary history was the introduction of New World produce in the sixteenth century. The first tomato was introduced to Europe in the 1500s and the first Italian reference to this fruit came in 1554. Called the *pomo d'oro* (golden apple), the first tomatoes were yellow "cherry" tomatoes. First used as a salad vegetable, it took 200 years for Italy to develop the large, red tomato that is so popular today and that is used in so many ways. The red pepper was also taken to heart in the Italian kitchen. Corn, another New World crop, was dried and ground and cooked as a mush and became polenta. (It is believed that the word polenta is derived from the wheat mush of early Rome, *pulmentum.*) The potato was also introduced, but it did not replace rice and pasta as the preferred starch in the diet. Finally, the kidney bean was to become quite popular across the country as a source of quality protein and augmented the fava bean, introduced by the Arabs.

Modern Italian cooking styles can be separated into three broad regions: north, central, and south. Each region can be further subdivided: northeast vs. northwest or the islands of Sicily and Sardinia from the southern peninsula. The northwest features the cooking of Lombardy, Piedmont, Liguria, and, to some extent, Valle d'Aosta. Lombardy, Piedmont, and Liguria feature rice as the staple, risotto originating in Lombardy. Butter is the fat of choice and cream and cheeses dominate the sauces. Liguria, located on the coast, showcases fish. Fine herbs grow in the surrounding hills, basil in particular. This is the home of pesto (the name comes from the verb "to pound," the method of preparing this sauce), originally a paste consisting of basil and other herbs, olive oil, pecorino cheese (ewe's milk cheese), parsley, and marjoram. Beef, veal, and game, especially in the Valle d'Aosta, are the preferred meats of the region.

In the northeast, the Veneto is the predominant region. Fresh produce from around the region makes its way to Venice, whose cuisine can be seen as a mix of local cuisines. Fish and shellfish are more important than meat, especially in Venice. Polenta is quite popular in the northeast, as are rice dishes. Other regions in the northeast have culinary traditions more in line with Austria and Hungary, having been part of the Austro-Hungarian Empire for many years. The northeast is known for one of the most delicious of all pork products, San Daniele prosciutto. It has been cherished throughout Europe for at least three hundred years.

The very heart of Italian cuisine can be found in the central region. This is the region of Tuscany, Emilia-Romagna, Latium (Rome), and Umbria. The finest olive oil comes from Tuscany, and it is the defining ingredient in Tuscan cuisine. Some of the best bread is baked here and the best wines are produced in Tuscany. The cuisine is not complicated. It is elegant in its simplicity, relying on the profound flavors of the earth. Neither pasta nor risotto is the first choice of the Tuscan diet. Overly fatty foods are not appreciated. Emilia-Romagna is distinguished by its buttery and creamy foods, which come from the rich farmlands. This is the land of the finest Parmesan cheese, outstanding prosciutto, and egg pasta. Roman cuisine is a metropolitan cuisine, yet Rome is famous for its vegetable dishes. Romans are not particularly fond of fish, but they do have a love affair with pasta (spaghetti made its appearance in Rome in 1800). Rice is not normally part of the staple diet; it is usually found in croquettes and as a stuffing for vegetables. Umbria produces fine pork products; sausages are its specialty. Its strong-flavored olive oils give a characteristic flavor to the region's dishes. Umbria is known for using the absolute finest ingredients in its dishes.

The cuisines of southern Italy (the Mezzogiorno) are vastly different from those of the north or central regions. This is a land redolent with Mediterranean influences. Eggplant, tomatoes, lamb, and seafood mark the cuisines of this region. Tomato-based meat sauces served with pasta are a must. Campagna encompasses Naples, known for its pizza, and Capri, the romantic seaside resort. The Abruzzi region is known for a limited number of expertly prepared dishes. Chiles are used more in the Mezzogiorno than anywhere else. Compared to the exotic (and expensive) spices brought by the spice trade, most of the rest of Italy considers chiles to be a "poor man's" spice. Apulia favors vegetable sauces for pasta dishes. The olive oil of Apulia is quite acidic and is much more strongly flavored than the delicate Tuscan oils. The islands of Sicily and Sardinia reflect North African and Arab influences. Cinnamon, cloves, and mint often appear in Sicilian cooking. Olives and cheese complement this simple diet. Since Sicily is an island, such fish as sardines, tuna, and swordfish are common in the diet. It is said that Sicilian cuisine, more than any other in Italy, is a mixture of the foods of the rich and poor. Sardinia is known for its careful attention to the details of cooking, and roasted piglet is a delicacy. Seafood, such as lobster, turtle, and sardines, are prepared ceremoniously. An excellent pecorino cheese is produced in the mountainous regions.

Pumpkin-Filled Tortellini with Rabbit Sauce

Tortellini di Zucca con Ragù alla Coniglio

serves 12

Bologna and Modena both claim the origin of tortellini and depending on the region, they may be called *cappellacci* (big hats) or *cappelletti* (little hats), which have slightly different shapes. The shape of the folded tortellini is said to represent the navel of Venus de Milo. Whether or not that is true, the shape serves the dual purpose of ensuring that the filled pasta gets cooked evenly and the individual tortellini are surrounded with flavorful sauce. The filling here is unusual in that it combines cooked pumpkin with sweet amaretti cookies and Parmesan cheese. The pairing of pumpkin with rabbit is typical of a dish of late fall, the time of both the pumpkin harvest and the hunting season for rabbit and hare. Tortellini is always eaten on Christmas Eve at traditional family gatherings.

CHEF NOTES

The pasta may also be cut into 2-inch [5-cm] squares, then filled and folded. The basic method for making the tortellini can be adapted to a variety of fillings, flavored pastas, and sauces. Canned pumpkin may substitute for fresh baked pumpkin.

RABBIT SAUCE: MAKES ABOUT 2 CUPS [480 mL]

3 tablespoons [45 mL] olive oil

1 large onion, diced

1 carrot, diced

One 3-pound [1.4-kg] rabbit, boned, and meat cut into ½-inch [1-cm] cubes

3 garlic cloves, minced

2 teaspoons [10 mL] rosemary leaves, chopped

3 large fresh sage leaves, chiffonade

1 tablespoon [15 mL] parsley, minced

1 tablespoon [15 mL] tomato paste

1 teaspoon [5 mL] black pepper

¼ teaspoon [1 mL] ground cloves

¼ teaspoon [1 mL] ground cinnamon

¼ cup [60 mL] balsamic vinegar

1 cup [240 mL] fruity, dry red wine

2 cups [480 mL] rich veal, beef, or game stock

Salt and black pepper to taste

FILLING: MAKES ENOUGH FILLING FOR 5 DOZEN TORTELLINI

1 small pumpkin or Hubbard-type squash

½ cup [120 mL] grated Parmesan cheese

10 amaretti, finely crumbled

Pinch of ground nutmeg

Salt and pepper to taste

PASTA: MAKES ENOUGH PASTA FOR 5 DOZEN TORTELLINI

3 cups [750 mL] all-purpose flour

5 eggs

5 quarts [5 L] hot water

1 tablespoon [15 mL] salt

Grated Parmesan and ground black pepper, for service

Sprigs of fresh sage leaves, for garnish

1. All advance preparation may be found in the ingredient list.

PREPARATION OF THE SAUCE

2. Heat the olive oil over medium heat in a 4-quart [4-L] heavy pot and sauté the onion and carrot until the onion is soft. Add the rabbit pieces and brown them, stirring, until the bottom of the pan has a deep brown (but not burned) glaze.

3. Add the garlic, rosemary, sage, and parsley and cook for 1 minute. Add the tomato paste, pepper, cloves, cinnamon, and vinegar and cook, stirring, for 3 minutes. Deglaze the bottom of the pan with ½ cup [120 mL] of the red wine.

4. Increase the heat to high and reduce the wine, stirring, until little liquid remains. Add the remaining wine and the stock and return to a boil.

5. Reduce the heat to a slow simmer, partially cover the pot, and simmer the sauce for 1½ hours, or until the rabbit is tender and the sauce has reduced to a medium-thick consistency. Season and adjust the flavors as necessary. (The sauce may be refrigerated for several days.)

PREPARATION OF THE FILLING

6. Cut the pumpkin into large pieces, remove the seeds, and bake at 350°F [175°C] until tender, about 45 minutes. Remove the skin and cut the flesh into small pieces.

7. Purée the pumpkin and combine 2 cups [480 mL] of the purée with the Parmesan, amaretti, nutmeg, and salt and pepper and mix well. Reserve, refrigerated, until ready to use.

PREPARATION OF THE PASTA

8. Mound the flour on a flat surface and form a well in the center. Break the eggs into the center of the well and using a fork, beat the eggs. Gradually bring in flour from the inside of the well into the liquid egg mixture to incorporate. Continue until all of the mixture is incorporated and the dough is smooth and free of lumps. Form the dough into a ball. If using a processor, add the flour to the workbowl. With the processor running, add the eggs one at a time, forming a smooth ball. Remove to a floured surface and knead 1 minute.

9. Lightly dust a work surface with flour. Flatten the ball of dough and using the heels of your hands, knead the dough for 5 minutes. The dough should be soft, elastic, and firm. If the dough is too moist, work in more flour, a little at a time.

10. Divide the dough into 4 equal parts and keep those not being worked covered at all times. Take 1 piece of the dough and pass it through a pasta machine, from widest to narrow setting in 5 increments, in strips approximately 2 inches [5 cm] wide. Using a 2-inch [5-cm] round cookie cutter, cut circles from the dough.

PREPARATION OF THE TORTELLINI

11. Place a heaping ¼ teaspoon [1 mL] of the pumpkin filling in the bottom half of each circle, moisten the edge of the circle with a finger dipped in water or egg white, then fold the circle in half, forming a half moon. Press the edges to seal.

12. Holding the semicircle with the curve toward you, bring the corners of the straight side toward each other. Overlap the corners, pressing 1 corner over another, and pinch to secure. Press the overlap down, forming the classic tortellini shape. Repeat until all the tortellini are formed.

COOKING METHOD

13. Heat 5 quarts [5 L] of water with the salt to a very low boil (cooking the tortellini too rapidly may cause them to break open). Have a buttered wide dish or shallow bowl handy to place the cooked tortellini in when removed from the water (a colander or a deep bowl might cause some of the tortellini to break).

14. Cook the tortellini, in batches, until they rise to the surface and the filling is hot. Remove with a slotted spoon to the buttered dish, allowing time to drain well. Continue cooking in batches until all of the tortellini are cooked. Keep the tortellini warm until service.

SERVICE

15. Place ¼ cup [60 mL] of the sauce in a small bowl or on a small, deep plate, and top with 5 tortellini. Top with grated Parmesan cheese and black pepper. Serve immediately, garnished with sprigs of sage leaves.

Tuna Carpaccio with Herb Sauce Carpaccio di Tonno alla Salsa Verde

serves 8

The rich taste of tuna, brought to port frequently in Sicily, matches perfectly with *salsa verde*, the classic zesty sauce from Tuscany. Countless variations on this sauce exist, so feel free to experiment. Some variations to consider when making the sauce include arugula, sorrel, and green olives. For an authentic texture use a mortar and pestle to grind the sauce components. This sauce is also used with the classic *bollito misto* (boiled dinner) and matches well with grilled or roasted meats and poultry as well as with seafood.

CHEF NOTES

Purchase only the highest grade tuna for this dish (sashimi-grade or "A" grade). Partially freezing the tuna will make it easier to slice very thin. Do not over-marinate the fish, as it will "cook" in the marinade.

When making the green sauce to serve with meat or poultry, you may add ½ cup [120 mL] grated Parmesan cheese.

HERB SAUCE (*SALSA VERDE*): MAKES ABOUT 2 CUPS [480 mL]

2 cups [480 mL] basil leaves

1 cup [240 mL] flat-leaf parsley leaves

½ cup [120 mL] mint leaves

1 tablespoon [15 mL] anchovy fillets, crushed (or paste)

4 garlic cloves, minced

2 tablespoons [30 mL] capers, drained

1 slice (1 inch [2.5 cm] thick) stale peasant-style bread, soaked in water, squeezed dry, and torn into pieces

½ cup [120 mL] fruity olive oil

2 tablespoons [30 mL] balsamic vinegar

Salt to taste

TUNA

¼ cup [60 mL] fruity olive oil

Juice of 2 lemons

Salt to taste

1 teaspoon [5 mL] black pepper

2 tablespoons [30 mL] fresh oregano, chopped

¼ cup [60 mL] fresh parsley, chopped

1¼ pounds [560 g] sashimi-grade tuna fillet, cut into 2 pieces

Green lettuce leaves, to line plates

Basil leaves, for garnish

Thin lemon slices, for garnish

ADVANCE PREPARATION

1. Combine the basil, parsley, mint, anchovy fillets, and garlic in the bowl of a food processor and process until coarsely chopped. Add the capers and bread and pulse to combine.

2. With the processor running, add the olive oil in a thin stream to emulsify. Add the vinegar and pulse briefly. Season to taste with salt. Cover tightly with plastic film and refrigerate. (The sauce may be made up to one week in advance. Allow to return to room temperature before serving.)

PREPARATION OF THE TUNA

3. Whisk the olive oil, lemon juice, salt and pepper, oregano, and parsley together to combine. Place the pieces of tuna in a large resealable plastic bag. Add the marinade and refrigerate for 1 to 2 hours, turning periodically. Remove the tuna, drain, and slice into very thin slices and reserve. (The tuna may be wrapped into portions for service.)

SERVICE

4. Line a plate with lettuce leaves. Arrange 2½ ounces [70 g] of tuna slices artfully on the plate. Dress with herb sauce and garnish with basil leaves and lemon slices.

Grilled Eggplant and Roasted Red Pepper Terrine with Prosciutto
Terrina di Melanzane con Peperoni e Prosciutto

serves 8

This beautiful terrine is a specialty of the village of Marina di Gioiosa Ionica in Calabria. It is formed into a rectangular terrine, but may also be prepared in a bowl in the style of a *timballo*. When grilling the eggplant, take care to leave uniform grill marks for presentation when the terrine is unmolded. A charcoal fire will yield the best flavor when roasting the eggplants and peppers. The prosciutto and eggs may be omitted for a vegetarian version of the terrine.

CHEF NOTES

Yellow, orange, or purple bell peppers may be used in place of the red. A layer of thin-sliced salami or soppressata may be added when forming the terrine.

1 large eggplant, cut lengthwise into slices ⅛ inch [3 mm] thick

½ cup [120 mL] extra virgin olive oil

4 large garlic cloves, roasted and peeled

4 large red bell peppers, roasted, peeled, seeded, and sliced into strips

4 ounces [110 g] prosciutto

3 large hard-boiled eggs, peeled and sliced into thin rounds

2 cups [480 mL] basil leaves, loosely packed

Salt and freshly ground black pepper to taste

8 ounces [225 g] pecorino cheese, such as Romano, grated

2 tablespoons [30 mL] flat-leaf parsley, chopped

Mixed field greens, for garnish

Grated Parmesan cheese, for garnish

Freshly ground black pepper, for garnish

8 red cherry tomatoes, halved, for garnish

8 yellow cherry tomatoes, halved, for garnish

ADVANCE PREPARATION

1. Brush the eggplant slices lightly with some of the olive oil and grill over a moderate charcoal fire, taking care to make the grill marks on one side uniform and attractive. The eggplant should be cooked to medium doneness and should still be firm when done. (The eggplant may be grilled one day in advance.)

2. Combine the remaining olive oil and the roasted garlic in a small processor or blender and purée. Reserve. (The purée may be made several days in advance.)

ASSEMBLY

3. Line the sides and bottom of an 8 × 4-inch [20 × 10-cm] loaf or terrine pan with eggplant slices, with the grill marks facing out, overlapping the side pieces and letting them hang

over the sides, to fold over and enclose the terrine later. Reserve some slices for the top.

4. Layer the peppers, prosciutto, eggs, and basil leaves to fill the terrine, seasoning each layer with salt and pepper, grated cheese, a drizzle of the garlic purée, and the parsley.

5. Top with the remaining eggplant slices. Fold over the ends of the overlapping eggplant slices to seal. Gently tap the loaf pan to compact the filling. Reserve. (The terrine may be assembled one day in advance.)

COOKING METHOD

6. Bake the terrine at 400°F [205°C] for 25 minutes, or until the cheese has melted, and the terrine is set. Allow to rest 30 minutes before inverting the terrine to unmold. Reserve any accumulated pan juices.

SERVICE

7. Slice the terrine with a thin-bladed, sharp knife dipped in hot water, cleaning the blade between slices. Line a plate with field greens and dress the greens with pan juices. Add a slice of the terrine and dust lightly with Parmesan cheese and black pepper. Garnish with red and yellow cherry tomatoes. The terrine may be served warm, at room temperature, or chilled.

Three-Cheese Tart with Soppressata Torta Rustica con Soppressata

serves 12 to 16

Many versions of ricotta cheese tart exist in Italy, both with and without the addition of ham or salami. This version offers a blend of three cheeses and includes soppressata, a spicy dry salami. The dish may be prepared as individual tartlets as well as a large *torta*.

 **CHEF NOTES**

Other dry, flavorful sausages or prosciutto may be substituted for the soppressata. The lattice top may be woven or the strips may be laid over one another for a similar effect.

FILLING

1 tablespoon [15 mL] olive oil

8 ounces [225 g] soppressata or other dry salami, cut into small dice

2 garlic cloves, minced

4 scallions, white parts only, minced

8 ounces [225 g] fresh mozzarella cheese, cut into ½-inch [1-cm] cubes

8 ounces [225 g] caciocavallo or provolone cheese, cut into ½-inch [1-cm] cubes

1 pound [450 g] ricotta cheese

2 eggs, beaten

Salt to taste

PASTRY DOUGH

4 cups [960 mL] all-purpose flour

¼ cup [60 mL] olive oil

⅔ cup [160 mL] dry white wine, or as needed to make a smooth dough

¼ teaspoon [1 mL] salt

1 teaspoon [5 mL] sugar

1 egg yolk mixed with 2 tablespoons [30 mL] cream, for egg wash

Freshly ground black pepper

Scallion greens, cut into thin curls, for garnish

ADVANCE PREPARATION

1. For the filling, heat the oil in a skillet over low heat and sauté the soppressata for 5 minutes, or until the fat is rendered and the soppressata is lightly cooked.

2. Stir in the garlic and scallions and cook until the scallions are soft. Allow to cool to room temperature. Once cooled, add the mozzarella, caciocavallo, and ricotta cheeses, the eggs, and the salt and mix very well. Reserve. (The filling may be made one day in advance and refrigerated.)

3. For the dough, make a mound of the flour with a well in the center. Add the oil, wine, salt, and sugar and gradually incorporate the flour into the liquid, forming a ball. Knead the dough for 5 minutes, or until smooth and elastic. If using a processor, add the flour to the workbowl. Mix the oil, wine, salt, and sugar together. Add this mixture gradually as the processor is running, forming a ball. Remove the dough to a floured surface and knead for 2 minutes.

4. Line a 10-inch [25-cm] springform pan with parchment and set aside.

5. Divide the dough into 2 equal portions. Roll 1 piece of dough into a 16-inch [40-cm] circle, and line the springform pan with the rolled pastry, pressing the dough into place against the sides and bottom. Add the filling mixture and smooth the top.

6. Roll the remaining piece of dough into a 12-inch [30-cm] circle, and cut into strips ¾ inch [2 cm] wide. Weave a lattice topping with the dough strips. Brush the top with egg wash.

COOKING METHOD

7. Bake the pie at 375°F [190°C] for 1½ hours, or until the crust is golden brown and the filling is set. Remove the sides of the springform pan and allow to cool.

SERVICE

8. Serve a slice of the tart, topped with a twist of black pepper and garnished with green onion curls. This tart may be served hot, at room temperature, or cold.

Pizza Two Ways: Tomato, Basil, and Mozzarella and Onion, Olive, and Anchovy Pizza alla Margherita e Pizzadalina

serves 8

It is believed that the pizza was introduced into Italy from the Middle East in the first century A.D. by Jews fleeing the Roman conquest of Judea. Raffaele Esposito, of Pizzeria di Pietro in Naples, created *pizza Margherita* in the year 1889 to honor a visit by Queen Margherita. The toppings represent the three colors of the flag of the United Kingdom of Italy: tomatoes for red, mozzarella for white, and basil for green. The *pizzadalina* version predates the tomato version described above, and many would consider it pizza in its purest form. The bread is topped with a mixture of slow-cooked onions and garlic that are tossed with bay leaf and oregano, sprinkled with pecorino cheese, and topped with black olives and anchovy fillets.

DOUGH: MAKES ENOUGH FOR EIGHT 6-INCH [15-CM] PIZZAS

1 tablespoon [15 mL] active dry yeast

½ teaspoon [3 mL] sugar

2 cups [480 mL] warm water (105° to 110°F [40° to 45°C])

4 to 6 cups [960 mL to 1.4 L] bread flour, as needed

⅓ cup [80 mL] olive oil, or more as needed

2 teaspoons [10 mL] salt

MARGHERITA TOPPING:
MAKES ENOUGH FOR FOUR 6-INCH [15-CM] PIZZAS

2 teaspoons [10 mL] minced garlic

4 plum tomatoes, sliced thin, or drained canned tomatoes, cut into ¼-inch [6-mm] pieces

6 to 8 ounces [180 to 225 g] buffalo mozzarella cheese, sliced or grated

¼ teaspoon [1 mL] salt

2 tablespoons [30 mL] olive oil, for drizzling

PIZZADALINA TOPPING:
MAKES ENOUGH FOR FOUR 6-INCH [15-CM] PIZZAS

3 tablespoons [45 mL] olive oil

3 large garlic cloves, halved

2 onions, sliced thin

1 bay leaf

1 tablespoon [15 mL] fresh oregano leaves

Salt

Black pepper

3 ounces [85 g] pecorino cheese, such as Romano, grated

½ cup [120 mL] Italian black olives, pitted, sliced

12 large anchovy fillets, whole or chopped

Cornmeal, as needed

8 large basil leaves, coarsely torn

Coarsely ground black pepper, for garnish (optional)

Crushed red pepper, for garnish (optional)

Grated Parmesan cheese, for garnish

A nice presentation of this recipe is to make each pizza "half *Margherita*, half *pizzadalina*." The pizzas may be made round or rectangular, large or small, and may be made with a variety of toppings. As a general rule, the more dense and moist the topping, the longer the pizza will need to cook. If necessary, lower the oven temperature by 25°F [15°C] to avoid burning the crust. If preparing a seafood pizza, remember that Italians traditionally do not combine seafood with cheese.

ADVANCE PREPARATION

1. Stir the yeast and sugar into the warm water in the bowl of a mixer fitted with the paddle. Allow to stand 5 minutes. Stir in 2 cups [480 mL] of the flour and allow to stand 5 minutes.

2. Add ⅓ cup [80 mL] of the oil and another 2 cups [480 mL] of flour and mix to form a smooth batter. Add the salt and continue to add flour until the dough starts to stick to the paddle and the sides of the bowl. The dough will form strands that tear as the paddle rotates in the bowl.

3. Remove the paddle, install the dough hook, and start the mixer at low speed. Add flour, a little at a time, until the dough cleans the sides of the bowl. Continue to knead for 5 minutes.

4. Place the ball of dough in a bowl lightly coated with olive oil. Brush the surface of the dough lightly with olive oil. Cover with plastic film and place in a warm, draft-free place for 1 to 1½ hours, or until the dough has doubled in volume. The dough may also be placed in an oiled resealable bag and allowed to rise, refrigerated, overnight.

5. Turn out the dough on a floured surface, punch the dough down, and knead for 1 minute. Divide the dough into 8 equal portions.

ASSEMBLY OF THE PIZZA *MARGHERITA*

6. Stretch a piece of dough to cover the bottom of a 6-inch [15-cm] pizza pan that has been brushed with olive oil. The dough may be patted, tossed in the air and spun, or rolled out with a rolling pin. Sprinkle with garlic and arrange slices of tomato and mozzarella in an interesting pattern on top. Sprinkle with salt and drizzle with olive oil. Allow to rest 10 minutes before baking.

ASSEMBLY OF THE *PIZZADALINA*

7. Heat the olive oil over medium heat in a skillet. Add the garlic halves and sauté for 2 minutes, or until golden. Add the onions, bay leaf, and oregano, and sauté the mixture until the onions are lightly browned, about 2 minutes. Remove and discard the garlic halves and bay leaf. Season with salt and pepper and allow the topping to cool. (The topping may be made one day in advance.)

8. Stretch a piece of dough to cover the bottom of a 6-inch [15-cm] pizza pan that has been brushed with olive oil. The dough may be patted, tossed in the air and spun, or rolled out with a rolling pin.

9. Spread the cooled onion topping evenly over the pizza dough. Add the pecorino cheese, olives, and anchovies. Brush the exposed edge of the pizza with olive oil. Allow to rest 5 minutes before baking.

COOKING METHOD

10. If using a pizza peel, dust it lightly with cornmeal before using. If baking on a pizza stone or in a stone-lined oven, dust the stone lightly with cornmeal before placing the pizza on to bake.

11. Bake the pizzas at 450°F [230°C] for 8 to 10 minutes, or until the cheese is melted and the edges are golden brown.

SERVICE

12. Top the *Margherita* pizza with fresh basil leaves. Cut each pizza into quarters with a pizza wheel or a knife. Serve either pizza accompanied with coarsely ground black pepper and/or crushed red pepper and grated Parmesan cheese. Serve hot.

Grilled Toasts with Cannellini Purée and Wilted Greens Capriata

APULIA

Grilled or toasted bread finished with a variety of toppings is quite popular throughout Italy. This combination is a southern Italian version, showing its simple, peasant roots. Any one of several fresh greens may be used—kale, chard, beet greens or radicchio—alone or in combination; the cannelini beans are essential to the authentic flavor of this dish.

CHEF NOTES

Canned cannellini beans can be used in a pinch, but they should be well rinsed, then flavored with some chicken stock. Add the garlic, sage, and olive oil prior to puréeing. Using a wood-fired grill to toast the bread adds a smoky flavor and complements the taste of the pancetta.

1½ cups [360 mL] dried cannellini beans, soaked overnight to soften

Chicken stock, to cover beans

3 large garlic cloves, minced

½ teaspoon [3 mL] rubbed sage leaves

¼ cup [60 mL] fruity olive oil

2 ounces [55 g] pancetta, chopped

1 small onion, diced

2 garlic cloves, minced

2 bunches greens, such as collard or kale, chard, or beet greens, thick stems removed and leaves coarsely chopped

½ cup [120 mL] chicken stock

1½ tablespoons [25 mL] balsamic vinegar

½ tablespoon [8 mL] sugar

½ teaspoon [3 mL] black pepper

8 thick slices peasant-style bread

Olive oil, for brushing on bread and for garnish

2 or 3 large garlic cloves, halved lengthwise

Parmesan or Asiago cheese, for garnish

Freshly ground black pepper, for garnish

ADVANCE PREPARATION

1. Drain the soaked beans and add just enough chicken stock to cover. Simmer 1 hour, or until very soft, adding more stock as required. Drain the beans if necessary.

2. Add the 3 minced garlic cloves, sage, and olive oil. Purée in a food processor. Reserve, refrigerated. (The purée may be made one day in advance.)

3. Sauté the pancetta in a large saucepan until lightly browned. Add the onion and garlic and sauté 2 minutes. Add the greens, stock, vinegar, sugar, and black pepper.

4. Cover and simmer 20 to 30 minutes, stirring occasionally, until the greens are thoroughly wilted. Drain and reserve. (The greens may be prepared one day in advance.)

499 | Italy

5. Brush the bread slices with olive oil and grill over a wood fire or toast on a charbroiler. Rub each slice with a garlic half. Top with warm bean purée, followed by the warm greens. Keep warm until service.

SERVICE

6. Lightly drizzle each toasted slice of bread with a few drops of fruity olive oil. Sprinkle with grated Parmesan or Asiago cheese. Finish with a twist of pepper.

Grilled Polenta with Wild Mushroom Sauté Crostini di Polenta con Peverada di Funghi

serves 8

This rich sauce of wild porcini mushrooms is traditionally served on toast points in the Veneto and Friuli, but the use of grilled polenta as a base adds another dimension. The original recipe calls for fresh porcini, which are available occasionally in specialty markets in the United States (or via the Internet). This recipe uses dried porcini (available year round) enhanced with crimini mushrooms and comes very close to duplicating the original recipe. The polenta may be served soft, pan-fried, or grilled, but grilling will give the best flavor.

 CHEF NOTES

Any blend of dried and fresh wild mushrooms may be used, but it should always be a combination of fresh and dried. Fresh porcini are preferable and should be used if available.

POLENTA

2½ cups [600 mL] water

2 cups [480 mL] chicken stock

½ tablespoon [8 mL] sea salt

1¾ cups [420 mL] stone-ground cornmeal

2 tablespoons [30 mL] unsalted butter, cut into pieces

Salt and white pepper to taste

Olive oil, for grilling

MUSHROOM SAUCE: MAKES ABOUT 2 CUPS [480 mL]

1 large shallot, minced

2 garlic cloves, minced

1 tablespoon [15 mL] unsalted butter

1 tablespoon [15 mL] brandy or Cognac

¼ cup [60 mL] chicken stock

¼ cup [60 mL] demi-glace

½ cup [120 mL] dried porcini, soaked 30 minutes in hot stock and strained through a fine sieve or paper coffee filter, reserving the liquid

12 ounces [340 g] crimini or wild mushrooms, cleaned and thinly sliced

¼ cup [60 mL] heavy cream

½ teaspoon [3 mL] grated lemon zest

2 tablespoons [30 mL] fresh parsley, minced

Salt and white pepper to taste

ADVANCE PREPARATION

1. Bring the water, the chicken stock, and the salt to a boil in a heavy-bottomed pot. Gradually whisk in the cornmeal in a steady stream, stirring constantly to avoid lumps.

2. Cook the polenta over medium-low heat, stirring occasionally, in a circular motion with a large wooden spoon, for about 1 hour. When the polenta begins to draw away from the sides of the pot as it is stirred, it is done.

3. Remove from the heat and add the butter, stirring to incorporate. Season with salt and white pepper. Turn out the polenta onto a baking pan lined with lightly greased parchment paper, spreading the polenta to about ½ inch [1 cm] thickness. An alternative method is to use a lined and greased loaf pan and cut ½-inch [1-cm] slices later.

4. Allow the polenta to cool to room temperature. Cover with plastic film and refrigerate. Allow to set, refrigerated, overnight. Cut into 2-inch [5-cm] squares.

COOKING METHOD

5. Sauté the shallot and garlic lightly in the butter. Deglaze with brandy or Cognac. Add the stock, demi-glace, and reserved soaking liquid. Bring to a boil and reduce by half. Add the porcini and crimini mushrooms and simmer 3 to 5 minutes.

6. Add the cream and lemon zest. Reduce the sauce until thickened. Add half of the parsley and adjust the seasoning with salt and white pepper.

7. Brush the polenta squares with olive oil and grill to warm and sear grill marks on the surface. Reserve warm until service.

SERVICE

8. Place a grilled portion of polenta on a serving plate and top with ¼ cup [60 mL] of mushroom sauce. Serve hot. Garnish with the remaining chopped parsley.

Spain and Portugal

Sausages with Sweet-and-Sour Figs
Salchichas con Higos Agridulce

Pork with Clams Alentejo Style
Lombo de Porco com Amêyoas à Alentejana

Béchamel-Coated Sea Bass Morsels in Orange Sauce
Pescado a la Naranja

Salt Cod–Stuffed Piquillo Peppers with Bayonne Ham and Chile Sauce
Pimientos del Piquillo Rellenos de Bacalao con Salsa Vizcaína

Garlic Shrimp with Sherry
Gambas al Ajillo

Chilled Langoustines with Two Sauces
Langostinos a la Plancha con Allioli y Romesco

Basque Cheese and Chile Tart
Idiazábal eta Biper Opila

IT IS HARD TO IMAGINE the influence Spain and Portugal has had on the cuisines of the entire world. These small countries, comprising the Iberian Peninsula were responsible for changing the way people cooked and dined, from Europe to Asia to North America. Can you imagine Italy without the tomato, Thailand without the chile, Switzerland without chocolate, California or Florida without the orange, or Japan without tempura? All of these foods, and more, were the result of Portuguese and Spanish exploration in the fifteenth and sixteenth centuries. The Portuguese Vasco da Gama rounded the Cape of Good Hope in 1497, discovered a water route to India, and established a colony at Goa. Indian spices, especially black pepper, could then be brought back to Europe by ship instead of overland, and a permanent connection with the East was formed. Other Portuguese explorers set up colonies in Macao in China, Timor near Bali, Angola and Mozambique in Africa, and Brazil in South America. Magellan, turned down by the Portuguese king for an idea to sail west to discover the Spice Islands, went to Spain for financial support. He found a passage around South America and eventually died in the Philippines after establishing a permanent Spanish presence there. Columbus, sailed west, in an attempt to find a route to India. He landed in the West Indies and established a presence in North America. Cortés and Pizarro helped to set up a presence in Mexico, Central America, and South America.

The cuisines of both Spain and Portugal have had influence beyond that of the explorations. The earliest settlers to the peninsula were the Phoenicians, bringing the Semitic language there. By 500 B.C. the Greeks colonized the Mediterranean coast, and Carthage conquered much of Spain by the time that the Celts had established a presence in northern Spain and Portugal. To this day the Celtic influence is quite strong in the north (as seen in the name of that region—Galicia), with Spaniards wearing kilts, playing bagpipes, and enjoying savory meat and fish pies commonly associated with the British Isles (and found no where else in Spain). Pigs were introduced by the Celts and pork products are favored throughout the region. A strong influence on the cooking of Spain came from the Romans, who brought garlic, grapes, wheat, and olives to the region. One of the most lasting influences must be from the Muslim Arabs, who invaded Europe through the Iberian Peninsula in 711. Known as the Moors, they brought with them such spices as cinnamon, saffron, nutmeg, and black pepper and introduced almonds (used as a thickener for sauces when ground and added to a sauce), lemons, oranges, quince, eggplant, and rice (the Spanish word for rice, *arroz*, is from the Arabic, *ar-rozz*). Muslims do not eat pork, but when the Moors were finally expelled from the peninsula, pork was reintroduced into the cuisines. The Spanish and Portuguese explorations of the fifteenth and sixteenth centuries brought the tomato, chile, sweet pepper, potato, corn, and a variety of legumes and squashes from the New World to the tables of Spain and Portugal.

Spain does not have a national cuisine. Rather, there are many regional cuisines, each with its own characteristic ingredients and cooking methods. These regional cuisines developed in part because of the geography of the peninsula (the Pyrenees kept most of Europe separate from Spain, and the rugged interior kept the north of Spain separate from the south). Galicia, at the northwestern corner of Spain, is known as "green" Spain. Every square inch of land is under cultivation or is used for grazing and Spain's finest veal is found there. Smoked pork fat is the cooking fat of choice, even for such fish as trout and salmon. Other seafood, such as scallops and squid (cooked in its ink), are delicacies that beg to go unadorned. The land is not suited for viniculture, so hard cider finds its way into dishes normally prepared with wine. The world-class blue-veined cheese Cabrales, which is ripened in limestone caves like French Roquefort, is found in the north central region of Cantabria.

The Basque Country, along with neighboring Navarre, may be home to Spain's most sophisticated cuisine. It is famous for its sauces and chocolate makes its way into some, providing a richness known to Mexican cooks for centuries. Parsley, the favorite green of the region, is combined with peas to make *salsa verde*. A dish prepared in the Basque style (*a la Vasca*) relies on red wine and green vegetables. La Rioja, one of the finest wine producing districts in all of Spain, lies partly in the Basque region. Biscayne style (*a la Vizcaína*) refers to a dish using a combination of hot chiles and sweet peppers. A popular cheese made from ewe's milk is Idiazabal; it can be found in desserts as well as in savory dishes. Game like boar and rabbit are enjoyed throughout this region.

Catalonia's culture is more aligned with France than with Spain. The Catalan language is closely related to old French, and its culture spawned the works of Miró and Dali and the unusual architecture of Gaudy. Dishes are a mixture of the foods of the forest and the sea, and Catalan cuisine is known for combining them in unusual ways. One popular combination is lobster and chicken; another is rabbit with squid. Wild mushrooms (*rovellons*) are a fall delicacy, and game, such as hare, quail, and partridge, is appreciated during this season. Sauces are important components of Basque dishes and one of the most prized sauces is *romesco*, a combination of almonds, peppers, and tomatoes, emulsified with oil. Catalan cuisine can be much spicier than that of the rest of Spain. Olives and sardines are of the highest quality as is the freshly caught monkfish. Catalonia has a historic connection to Italy, and stuffed pasta dishes such as *cannolini* can be found here.

In Aragon, high in the Pyrenees, and in the northeast territory of La Rioja, game is popular and accessible in the harsh land. As is typical of mountainous regions, goats, sheep, and pigs provide meat. The food is hearty but not refined. Sauces are often soaked up with *migas*, croutons that have been flavored with hot pepper. *Migas* are found throughout Spain and are eaten with almost anything including desserts, fruit, or chocolate.

The plateau of the Meseta is the land of La Mancha and Don Quixote. This is the land that produces over 70 percent of the world's saffron and is the granary of Spain. The famous windmills of that are associated with Don Quixote are still used to grind the wheat into flour. The sheep here produce Spain's most famous cheese, manchego. Madrid, the capital of Spain since the sixteenth century, is one of the few interior cities to enjoy fresh seafood, especially when served as the renowned *tapas*. The word *tapa* (from the verb *tapar*, "to cover") refers to any appetizer-size portion of food, usually served in a bar, and normally eaten by Spaniards late in the morning and again in late afternoon. The term originated in Andalusia, where tavern owners would serve complimentary slices of ham or sausage on a small plate covering the top of a sherry glasses. There is speculation as to whether *tapas* were to keep flies out (one legend states that bread was the first "cover" of the sherry) or simply to increase the thirst of the drinkers, but as the popularity of the custom grew, so did the variety of *tapas* available.

Andalusia, birthplace of the *tapa*, is what most foreigners picture all of Spain to be. Moorish influence is strongest here. Granada was the last Arab stronghold of Spain, and Moorish architecture is everywhere. The foods of this region reflect the influences of northern Africa much more than those of Europe. The climate is extremely hot and dry, and local dishes reflect this. Light foods, simply prepared, are in order. Andalusia is home to gazpacho, the chilled tomato-vegetable soup. Mediterranean crops of olives, almonds, citrus, and apricots are plentiful. Outdoor grilling and barbecue are common cooking methods, perfect for the warm climate. With such warm weather, nibbling *tapas* becomes the perfect way to eat. Seville is famous for its *tapas*, and bars serve the traditional drink to accompany them, sherry. Produced in Andalusia, this world-renowned drink derives its name from the town of Jerez; only fortified wines produced in Jerez are authentic and should be called sherry, much like Champagne and Cognac, which take their names from the places where they are made.

The Extremadura region is cut off by Portugal to the west and from the rest of Spain by the northern and southern high sierras. In this region such hardy animals as the pig are common. They feed on foraged chestnuts in the forests, and the meat is delicately flavored, a source of the famous air-dried hams of the region. Truffles are a regional specialty and are often combined with game, such as partridge, pheasant, hare, and deer.

Valencia is in the Levante, the land of rice, and is home to *paella*, the famous rice dish of the region. Normally associated with seafood, *paella* can be made with an assortment of meats, fowl, vegetables, and fish. The name of the dish is derived from the special two-handled pan in which it is cooked (*patella*). While most commonly prepared in the oven, the authentic dish is cooked over a wood fire, producing a crust on the bottom of the pan (*socarrat*) that is offered to the most honored guest. The Moors introduced the bitter orange to Andalusia and the Portuguese brought the sweet orange to the Levante from China.

The history of Portugal was inseparable from that of Spain until 1139, when Alphonso I was crowned king of Portugal. The cuisine of Portugal is more robust and bolder than that of Spain; it is family-style food. Spices are used in abundance and with a heavy hand. Potatoes accompany every meal and cooking on top of the stove is the most common cooking method, although stews and casseroles are cooked in the oven more frequently today. Lemons are combined with meats, especially beef. Copious amounts of olive oil are used along with peppers, chiles, and rice. There were strong links with the Moors and with the spice trade of the sixteenth century. Cloves, nutmeg, and cinnamon are frequently used, as is cilantro. Dishes that feature couscous can be found in Madeira, home to the famous fortified wine. (Oporto produces the other renowned fortified wine of Portugal, port.)

In the northernmost region of Portugal, Trás-os-Montes, the land is not fertile and the climate is harsh. Foods tend to be hearty and simple, with many stews and soups. Preservation is essential in harsh climates, and hams and sausages are practical and tasty ways to preserve pork, which is the staple of the diet here. The northern coastal region of Minho adds fish to the diet of the north, and some of the tastiest potatoes and finest cabbages are grown there. The central regions, the Beira provinces, produce the best cheeses of Portugal, which are mostly made from ewe's milk. Alentejo, to the south, is the breadbasket of Portugal, and bread is included in many of its dishes. Rice is grown, and the pigs have a unique flavor, being free to graze among the cork trees. Moorish influence was greatest in Algarve, which has the most Mediterranean flavor in its foods and crops. Almonds, citrus, figs, and pomegranates are all grown there, and the shellfish is of the highest quality. Grilling is the preferred method of preparing fish, especially sardines.

Sausages with Sweet-and-Sour Figs Salchichas con Higos Agridulce

EXTREMADURA, SPAIN

serves 8

This exceptional, modern-day *tapa* is based on spicing practices originating in the sixteenth century. During that period sweet-and-sour dishes were all the rage, but they gradually fell out of favor. Fresh figs are best, but bottled or dried figs may also be used. The figs should be prepared the day before to develop full flavor.

 **CHEF NOTES**

Sweet Italian or other coarsely ground pork sausages will work with this dish, but homemade sausages are preferred. If bottled figs are used, simmer 5 minutes. For dried figs, simmer 30 minutes.

FIGS

1 cup [240 mL] sugar

1 cup [240 mL] red wine vinegar

2 tablespoons [30 mL] port

½ teaspoon [3 mL] fresh lemon juice

1 cinnamon stick

2 cloves, whole

1 pound [450 g] fresh figs or 8 ounces [225 g] dried figs

SAUSAGES

1 tablespoon [15 mL] Spanish olive oil

1½ pounds [675 g] cooked sausages, such as Asturian or any coarse pork sausage, sliced ½ inch [1 cm] thick

¼ cup [60 mL] white wine

¼ cup [60 mL] chicken or pork stock

1 tablespoon [15 mL] tomato sauce

Salt and freshly ground black pepper to taste

ADVANCE PREPARATION

1. Combine the sugar, vinegar, port, lemon juice, cinnamon, and cloves in a nonreactive saucepan and simmer for 5 minutes. Quarter the figs and add them, covering the pan. Simmer slowly for 15 minutes. Remove from the heat and cool the figs in the poaching liquid. Allow to stand overnight. Drain, discarding the liquid prior to use.

COOKING METHOD

2. Heat the olive oil in a large, nonstick skillet over medium heat and sauté the sausages until browned. Remove the sausages to paper towels to drain.

3. Pour off most of the fat and deglaze the pan with the white wine. Add the stock, tomato sauce, and salt and pepper and bring to a boil. Lower the heat, add the reserved sausages and figs, and simmer 5 minutes to heat through.

SERVICE

4. Arrange 3 ounces [85 g] of sausages on a plate and top with figs and their juices.

Pork with Clams Alentejo Style Lombo de Porco com Amêyoas à Alentejana

serves 8

Despite the unusual sounding combination of pork with clams, this is a very famous Portuguese dish. It requires an overnight marination of the pork in white wine, bay, garlic, and a pepper paste called *massa de pimentão*. The pepper paste itself requires a day of resting to combine flavors, so plan accordingly. This dish is best eaten with crusty peasant bread to soak up all of the delicious sauce.

CHEF NOTES

To purge clams, scrub them under cold running water. Place in a bowl and cover with cold water. Sprinkle 1 tablespoon [15 mL] of cornmeal over the surface and allow to stand for 30 minutes. Drain well and proceed with the recipe.

MASSA DE PIMENTÃO: MAKES 1¾ CUPS [420 mL]

3 large red bell peppers, fire roasted, seeded, peeled, and cut into 2-inch [5-cm] strips

1 tablespoon [15 mL] sea salt or kosher salt

2 large garlic cloves, chopped

¼ cup [60 mL] olive oil

MARINATED PORK

1½ pounds [675 g] boneless pork loin or shoulder, cut into ½-inch [1-cm] cubes

Salt and pepper to taste

3 garlic cloves, minced

¼ cup [60 mL] *massa de pimentão* (see above)

1 cup [240 mL] fruity, dry white wine

1 bay leaf

1 tablespoon [15 mL] cilantro stems, chopped

½ teaspoon [3 mL] black pepper

CLAMS

3 tablespoons [45 mL] bacon fat, lard, or olive oil

1 large onion, diced

2 garlic cloves, minced

1½ tablespoons [25 mL] tomato paste

24 small or 16 medium littleneck clams, scrubbed and purged (see Chef Notes)

Salt and pepper to taste

Sprigs of cilantro, for garnish

Crusty country bread, for service

ADVANCE PREPARATION

1. Mix the pepper strips with the salt, place in a resealable plastic bag, and allow to stand for 24 hours at room temperature.

2. Place the peppers and garlic in the workbowl of a food processor and while the processor is running, slowly drizzle in the olive oil. (The *massa* will keep, refrigerated, for up to 2 weeks.)

3. Season the pork cubes with salt and pepper.

4. Combine the garlic, *massa de pimentão*, wine, bay leaf, cilantro stems, and black pepper and mix well to form a marinade. Place the pork in a resealable plastic bag, pour the marinade over the pork, and toss to coat the pork. Marinate overnight, refrigerated, turning occasionally.

COOKING METHOD

5. Drain the pork, reserving the marinade. Heat the fat in a heavy, nonreactive skillet over high heat and sauté the pork cubes until evenly browned. Transfer to a platter and reserve.

6. Add the onion to the pan and sauté for 3 to 4 minutes, or until soft. Reduce the heat to low and add the garlic and tomato paste. Add some water to prevent burning, stir well to incorporate, cover the pot, and sweat the onion mixture for 20 minutes.

7. Add the reserved marinade and the browned pork and simmer, covered, for 1 hour, or until the pork is very tender. (The pork can be cooked one day in advance.)

8. Add the clams, cover, and cook until the clams open, about 8 minutes. Season to taste with salt and pepper.

SERVICE

9. Serve about ½ cup [120 mL] of the stew and top with 2 or 3 clams, depending on size. Garnish with sprigs of cilantro and serve with slices of crusty bread.

Béchamel-Coated Sea Bass Morsels in Orange Sauce Pescado a la Naranja

serves 8

Béchamel coating before frying is a very popular technique all over Spain. Seville is justly famous for its citrus, especially its Seville oranges, a type of sour orange popular throughout Spain, Central America, and southern Europe, and in Britain for marmalade. If bitter or Seville oranges are unavailable, substitute a mixture of the juice of 1 orange with the juice of 1 lime or lemon.

 CHEF NOTES

Chicken tenderloins or pork loin strips are excellent when cooked by this method. Any type of firm, white-fleshed fish or shellfish may be substituted.

BÉCHAMEL SAUCE

2 tablespoons [30 mL] unsalted butter

2 tablespoons [30 mL] all-purpose flour

¾ cup [180 mL] milk

Salt and white pepper to taste

Pinch of grated nutmeg

ORANGE SAUCE: MAKES 2 CUPS [480 mL]

2 tablespoons [30 mL] butter

2 tablespoons [30 mL] leeks, minced

Zest of 2 sour (Seville) oranges, julienne, reserving the orange sections (without the pith)

¼ cup [60 mL] orange liqueur, such as Cointreau or curaçao

1 cup [240 mL] sour orange juice (see preface for substitute)

½ cup [120 mL] veal or chicken broth

3 tablespoons [45 mL] orange marmalade

2 ounces [55 g] cold butter, diced

2 tablespoons [30 mL] parsley, chopped

FISH

1 pound sea bass or other white firm-fleshed fish, cut into ½-inch [1-cm] cubes

Dry breadcrumbs, for coating

Olive or vegetable oil, for deep-frying

Orange zest curls, for garnish

ADVANCE PREPARATION

1. All advance preparation may be found in the ingredient list.

PREPARATION OF THE BÉCHAMEL SAUCE

2. Heat the butter in a skillet over low heat. Slowly whisk in the flour, forming a light roux. Slowly whisk in the milk. Simmer until thickened, then season with salt and pepper and nutmeg. Allow to cool to room temperature and reserve.

3. Heat the butter in a nonstick skillet over medium heat and sauté the leeks until soft. Add ¾ of the orange zest and orange segments and cook for 2 minutes. Add the orange liqueur off the heat, ignite to burn off the alcohol, and deglaze the pan.

4. Add the orange juice, broth, and marmalade. Stir to incorporate and bring to a boil. Reduce the volume by two-thirds. Remove the skillet from the heat and allow to cool slightly.

5. Swirl in the cold butter to emulsify. Stir in the chopped parsley and reserve.

COOKING METHOD

6. Dip the fish morsels into the cooled béchamel to coat, place on a sheet pan lined with parchment, and refrigerate for at least 1 hour.

7. Toss the coated fish morsels in breadcrumbs. Heat the oil to 360°F [180°C] and deep-fry, in batches, until the morsels float and are golden brown. Drain on paper towels and keep warm until service.

SERVICE

8. Arrange 4 to 5 pieces of fish on a plate. Top with orange sauce. Garnish with curls of orange zest.

Salt Cod-Stuffed Piquillo Peppers with Bayonne Ham and Chile Sauce
Pimientos del Piquillo Rellenos de Bacalao con Salsa Vizcaína

serves 8

Salt cod is used all over Spain and Portugal. Cod has been fished in the Grand Banks, off Newfoundland, for centuries by Basque fishermen. Piquillo chiles are produced primarily in the Basque region of Navarre and can be found bottled or canned at specialty food stores. Biscayne sauce or *salsa vizcaína* (*vizcaína* is Basque dialect for Biscayne) is one of the most renowned of the sauces of the Basque region. It features Bayonne ham, similar to Italian prosciutto or Spanish serrano ham, and choricero chiles. These chiles can be difficult to find, but dried red Anaheim or New Mexico chiles can be substituted. The salt cod needs to soak for 24 hours.

CHEF NOTES

Any combination of seafood or shellfish may be combined with the béchamel to stuff the peppers but salt cod will be the most authentic.

BISCAYNE SAUCE: MAKES ABOUT 1½ CUPS [360 mL]

4 choricero or 3 dried red Anaheim or New Mexico chiles, stemmed

About ¾ cup [180 mL] rich chicken stock

¼ cup [60 mL] olive oil

1 medium sweet onion, diced

½ medium red onion, diced

3 garlic cloves, minced

1½ tablespoons [25 mL] Bayonne ham or serrano ham or prosciutto, chopped

⅓ cup [80 mL] prepared tomato sauce

Salt and black pepper to taste

Pinch of sugar

CHILES WITH STUFFING

12 ounces [340 g] dried salt cod, reconstituted (see page 156 for advance preparation)

3 tablespoons [45 mL] olive oil

1½ tablespoons [25 mL] all-purpose flour

3 cups [720 mL] half-and-half, at room temperature

16 canned or bottled piquillo peppers, drained

About 2 cups [480 mL] Biscayne sauce

Choricero or dried red Anaheim chiles, seeded and very thinly sliced, for garnish

ADVANCE PREPARATION

1. To prepare the Biscayne sauce, place the dried chiles in a saucepan and add the chicken stock. Bring to a boil, reduce the heat to a simmer, and cook the chiles for 5 minutes. Allow the chiles to cool in the stock, then remove and drain them, reserving the stock. Slit the chiles open and discard the seeds.

2. Heat the olive oil in a nonreactive skillet over medium heat and sauté the onions until soft. Add the garlic and sauté for 30 seconds. Add the reserved chiles and ham and cook for 5 minutes more.

3. Reheat the reserved chile stock and add 1 cup [240 mL] of the stock and the tomato sauce and simmer for 30 minutes, stirring occasionally.

4. Pass the sauce through a food mill or pulse in a food processor, allowing a bit of texture to remain. Adjust the seasoning with salt and pepper and sugar. Store, covered, in the refrigerator until needed. (The sauce should be made one day in advance to develop flavor.)

PREPARATION OF THE STUFFED CHILES

5. Sauté the reconstituted flaked salt cod in the oil in a skillet over medium heat for 5 minutes, or until lightly browned. Add the flour and combine thoroughly to form a light roux.

6. Slowly add the half-and-half while stirring, to form a béchamel sauce with cod. Allow the sauce to cool and set.

7. Using a teaspoon or pastry bag, stuff each chile two-thirds full with the filling. Close the chiles with toothpicks. Arrange the stuffed chiles in a parchment-lined baking dish or casserole just large enough to hold them.

COOKING METHOD

8. Top each chile with some of Biscayne sauce and bake at 350°F [170°C] for 10 minutes, or until the stuffed chiles are thoroughly heated and the sauce is bubbling.

SERVICE

9. Serve each person 2 stuffed chiles, topped with additional warm Biscayne sauce. Garnish sparingly with sliced chiles.

Garlic Shrimp with Sherry Gambas al Ajillo

serves 8

This is, perhaps, one of the most famous and popular of all Spanish *tapas*. Garlicky sautéed shrimp are splashed with dry sherry, spiced with slices of dried red chile, and flavored with copious amounts of garlic. In Spain, the shrimps used for this dish are small and served unpeeled, with only the very top of the shrimps cut off, leaving most of the head. Serve the shrimps in the shell, if practical (the shells add greatly to the flavor of the dish).

CHEF NOTES

This method works well with scallops or small baby octopus. Thin slices of lobster tail or langoustines are an excellent substitute, as are chicken tenders trimmed of the tendons. For formal dining situations, remove all but the tail section of the shrimp shell.

¼ cup [60 mL] Spanish olive oil

2 tablespoons [30 mL] unsalted butter

1½ pounds [675 g] small to medium shrimp, shells split and deveined, shells left on

6 garlic cloves, minced

2 tablespoons [30 mL] fresh lemon juice

3 tablespoons [45 mL] dry sherry

1 teaspoon [5 mL] sweet paprika

1 dried red Anaheim or New Mexico chile, seeds and stem removed, sliced crosswise into very thin rings

Salt and black pepper to taste

3 tablespoons [45 mL] chopped parsley, for garnish

Thin slices of peasant bread for service

ADVANCE PREPARATION

1. All advance preparation may be found in the ingredient list.

COOKING METHOD

2. Heat the olive oil and butter in a nonstick skillet over high heat. Add the shrimp and sauté 2 minutes. Add the garlic and cook for 1 minute more.

3. Add the lemon juice, sherry, paprika, and chile rings. Toss to combine. Season with salt and pepper to taste and serve immediately.

SERVICE

4. Serve 3 ounces [85 g] of shrimp per person, with some of the sauce. Sprinkle with the chopped parsley and serve with thin slices of peasant-style bread.

Chilled Langoustines with Two Sauces Langostinos a la Plancha con Allioli y Romesco

serves 8

The langoustines in this recipe are grilled, then chilled, and served with two sauces for which Spain is justifiably famous: *allioli*, or garlic mayonnaise, and *romesco*, which is a blend of dried peppers, almonds, and garlic. Mayonnaise is said to have been invented in Mahón in the Balearic Islands off the coast of Spain and later adopted by the French. *Romesco* originated in the city of Tarragona almost one thousand years ago, and there are countless variations. The two sauces should be served side by side, to be eaten separately, or mixed together, as desired.

CHEF NOTES

Both sauces are excellent with all seafood, as is the marinade.

MARINADE FOR THE LANGOUSTINES

8 langoustines or 4 lobster tails or 16 prawns, shells split but left on, deveined

½ cup [120 mL] Spanish olive oil

1 tablespoon [15 mL] dry sherry

1 teaspoon [5 mL] lemon juice

6 garlic cloves, minced fine

½ teaspoon [3 mL] paprika

½ teaspoon [3 mL] salt

¼ teaspoon [1 mL] white pepper

ALLIOLI: MAKES ½ CUP [120 mL]

1 large egg yolk, at room temperature

1 tablespoon [15 mL] lemon juice or sherry vinegar

¼ teaspoon [1 mL] Dijon-style mustard

½ teaspoon [3 mL] salt

¼ teaspoon [1 mL] white pepper

5 fluid ounces [150 mL] Spanish olive oil

4 to 6 garlic cloves, minced, or to taste

ROMESCO SAUCE: MAKES 1½ CUPS [360 mL]

1 dried red Anaheim or New Mexico chile, stem and seeds removed

½ dried red Guajillo chile, seeds removed

1 cup [240 mL] chicken stock

½ cup [120 mL] red wine vinegar

¾ cup [180 mL] Spanish olive oil

2 slices French-style baguette bread, ¼ inch [6 mm] thick

1 large tomato, fire roasted, peeled, seeded, and chopped

½ cup [120 mL] sliced almonds, lightly toasted

½ red bell pepper, fire roasted, peeled, and seeded

6 garlic cloves, minced

¼ to ½ cup [60 to 120 mL] rich chicken stock

Salt to taste

3 tablespoons [45 mL] sliced almonds, chopped and toasted, for garnish

1. Place the langoustines in a resealable plastic bag. Combine the oil, sherry, lemon juice, garlic, paprika, salt, and pepper and mix well. Pour the marinade over the langoustines and toss to coat. Marinate at least 2 hours, or overnight, refrigerated.

PREPARATION OF THE *ALLIOLI*

2. Combine the egg yolk, lemon juice, mustard, salt, and white pepper in a blender or food processor and pulse to blend. With the motor running, pour in the olive oil very slowly to emulsify.

3. While processing, add garlic to taste. Adjust the seasoning and reserve the *allioli* in the refrigerator. (The *allioli* can be made 1 day in advance.)

PREPARATION OF THE ROMESCO SAUCE

4. Place the Anaheim and Guajillo chiles, stock, and vinegar in a saucepan and simmer for 5 minutes. Drain the chiles, reserving the liquid.

5. Heat ¼ cup [60 mL] of the olive oil in a nonstick skillet over medium heat and fry the bread on both sides until golden brown. Remove and reserve the bread.

6. Add the chopped tomato to the skillet. Sauté the tomato for 2 minutes and reserve with the oil.

7. Place the chiles, bread slices, tomato, oil, almonds, bell pepper, garlic, the remaining olive oil, 1½ tablespoons [25 mL] of the reserved chile liquid (in steps), enough stock to form a smooth sauce, and the salt in the workbowl of a food processor. Process until well mixed but slightly chunky with some texture remaining and reserve, refrigerated. (The *romesco* sauce can be made several days in advance. It will keep, refrigerated, for several weeks.) Allow the sauce to come to room temperature before service.

COOKING METHOD

8. Drain the langoustines of the marinade and skewer each one lengthwise with a wooden skewer to prevent curling while cooking. Grill slowly over an indirect charcoal fire until just

done. Do not overcook. Remove the skewers and chill the langoustines. Peel the langoustine meat from the shells, discarding the shells. Slice the tails into ½-inch [1-cm] slices and reserve.

SERVICE

9. Fan out slices of a langoustine tail on a plate. Serve portions of both sauces in ramekins or directly on the plate. Sprinkle the edge of the plate with chopped almonds for garnish. (Instruct the guests to feel free to experiment and mix the sauces together.)

Basque Cheese and Pepper Tart Idiazábal eta Biper Opila

serves 8

This tart, topped with strips of piquillo and other peppers, features. Idiazábal is the famous Basque ewe's milk cheese from the mountainous Guipúzcoa region. The cheese is made by the shepherds themselves as well as by cooperatives in the region. Piquillo peppers are smoky-flavored spicy red peppers from the Navarre region, the town of Lodosa producing some of the finest quality. They can be found bottled or canned, imported from Spain. Parsley is a favorite addition to many Basque dishes.

CHEF NOTES

Manchego cheese can be substituted for the Idiázabal, or a mixture of the two can be used. Do not salt the filling as the cheese itself can be quite salty.

DOUGH

2 cups [480 mL] all-purpose flour

½ teaspoon [3 mL] salt

½ teaspoon [3 mL] garlic powder

½ teaspoon [3 mL] *piment d'espelette* or New Mexico ground red chile

5 ounces [140 g] unsalted butter, chilled, cut into small cubes

¼ cup [60 mL] cold water, as needed

TOPPING

1 cup [240 mL] heavy cream or crème fraîche

3 large eggs, lightly beaten

White pepper to taste

Pinch of *piment d'espelette* or ground New Mexico red chile

¼ cup [60 mL] parsley, chopped coarsely

8 ounces [225 g] Idiazábal cheese, cut into very small dice

1 yellow bell pepper, fire roasted, peeled, seeded, and cut into thin strips

3 piquillo peppers, canned or bottled, cut into strips

1 green Anaheim or New Mexico chile, fire roasted, peeled, seeded, and cut into strips

ADVANCE PREPARATION

1. Sift the flour, salt, garlic powder, and *piment d'espelette* together. Using a pastry knife or a food processor, cut in the butter to form a texture of coarse meal. Add only enough water to form a stiff dough. Wrap the dough in plastic film and refrigerate for at least 30 minutes.

2. On a lightly floured surface roll the dough into a 13-inch [33-cm] circle, approximately ⅛ inch [3 mm] thick.

3. Butter the bottom and sides of a 9-inch [23-cm] tart pan with a removable bottom. Press the dough into the pan and trim the edges.

4. Bake the pastry shell blind at 375°F [190°C] for 20 minutes, or until the crust is set, and reserve. (Pie weights, rice, dry

beans, or foil may be used to hold the shape of the crust while baking blind.)

COOKING METHOD

5. Mix the cream, eggs, white pepper, and *piment d'espelette* together.

6. Scatter the parsley across the bottom of the baked crust. Add the diced cheese, then arrange the pepper and chile strips across the cheese in an interesting pattern.

7. Pour the custard mixture over and bake at 375°F [190°C] for 30 minutes, or until the crust is golden, the filling is set, and the top just begins to brown. Allow the tart to rest 15 minutes before slicing.

SERVICE

8. Cut the tart into 8 slices. Serve 1 slice per person, warm or at room temperature.

France

Grilled Kid Goat Ravioli in Red Wine Meat Sauce
Ravioli au Brocciu et Cabri avec a Stufata

Rabbit Cakes with Wild Mushroom Champagne Sauce
Gateaux de Lapin avec Sauce Champagne et Champignons

Lemon-Garlic Glazed Chicken Wing Drumettes
Ailerons de Poulet en Gigots au Citron et à l'Ail

**Sautéed Duck Breasts with Apples and Calvados
in Pastry Cases**
Vol-au-Vent de Canard avec Pommes et Calvados

Duck Liver and Green Peppercorn Pâté
Pâté de Foie de Canard avec Poivre en Grains Vert

**Scallop and Caviar Sandwich with Lemon-Mussel
Cream Sauce**
Sandwich de Coquilles Saint-Jacques au Caviar

Savory Cheese Puffs
Gougères

Roquefort Cheese and Onion Tart
Tourte au Roquefort

OF THE WORLD'S CUISINES, none takes cooking to the level of fine art as the French do. The goal is perfection. The rules are rigid and exacting. Procedures are specific and techniques are to be mastered. No other cuisine has the attention to detail of classic French cuisine, and elegance is a key ingredient to its dishes. French cooking has a language all its own; the name of a dish will tell a trained chef of the sauces, garnishes, and accompaniments that must be served along with the featured meat, poultry, or fish. Presentation is elaborate and a requirement of classic French cuisine. Many dishes have several elements that can be considered finished dishes in their own right (quenelles of pike as a garnish for a sole fillet, for example). Service must be as impeccable as the food itself, not for haughty reasons but to reinforce the absolute splendor of the food and the dining experience.

One of the surprising aspects to this cuisine is how recently it has come into being. For all of the traditions, France was not considered a unique territory until the seventeenth century, when the French language took its standard form. It was Italy that helped to bring the cooking and dining habits of France out of the Middle Ages (although it has been recently demonstrated that Italy did not have the profound influence on French cooking that many commentators have attributed to it). When Catherine de Médici married King Henri II of France, she brought along her kitchen staff and introduced the fork to the French dinner table. Truffles were brought from Italy, and the earthy, sensuous flavor captured the palate of her new home. It was not until well into the nineteenth century that France could boast a national economy.

Certainly the rise of this special cuisine can be attributed to two talented chefs, Carême and Escoffier, and the country itself has much to do with it. The land shows extreme diversity. Its climate ranges from alpine to semitropical. France borders the North Sea and the Mediterranean, as well as the Atlantic Ocean. With long coastlines, navigable rivers, and the absence of high mountains within its interior, the varied produce and goods found across the land were accessible to everyone within the country. Efficient delivery of these goods allowed for produce from the north to be delivered fresh and ripe to the southern regions. Vegetables were—and still are—grown for flavor rather than appearance. Unlike in American markets, it is perfect taste not perfect looks that are important to the consumer. The French take their food seriously and care more about food than most other people; they are an appreciative audience. Chefs are given the highest respect, a respect that goes back to the pre-Revolutionary era, when the nobility held their chefs in esteem and encouraged them to create new dishes.

In spite of its modest size, France boasts many regional cuisines and specialties. Variation in climate, soils, and natural features provides for this diversity. In the north, dishes are hearty, relying on the local produce and game. *Hochepots*, or hearty stews, are common, as are thick soups. Rabbit and hare are quite popular, finding their way into these hearty offerings. Fishing ports and rivers abound, and much fish is eaten here. Herring, eels, and mussels are particularly enjoyed. There is a strong Flemish influence in this region, which includes Artois and Flanders. Chicory (Belgian endive) is cultivated in the north.

Normandy produces the richest dairy products in the country, including the famous Camembert and Pont-l'Evêque cheeses. Crème fraîche, a cultured cream, is an essential ingredient in Normandy's cuisine. Common vegetables thrive in the salty air and soils enriched with seaweeds, and apples grow in abundance (the apple brandy Calvados is produced here). Seafood is fresh and sweet, tiny crabs and shrimp being most favored. Herring, mackerel, turbot, and whiting are all harvested. Sausages, including *boudin noir* (blood sausage) and *boudin blanc* (veal sausage), and other charcuterie are excellent.

The food of Brittany is simple and straightforward. The sea supplies numerous fish to be enjoyed, especially crustaceans. Belon oysters are sought after all across France. Brittany is home to the pancake; *galettes* formed from buckwheat and crêpes are Brittany's culinary symbols. Ham and pork products are of especially high quality, and charcuterie from Brittany is regarded with esteem throughout the country. Baby vegetables develop well in the iodinized soils, especially new potatoes, *petit pois* (tiny peas), baby carrots, and artichokes.

Central France, one of the less populated regions, includes Limousin and Auvergne. Its cuisine is robust and simple. Mushrooms find their way into many dishes, and the beef and veal are of prime quality. Smoked hams and dry sausages fill the markets. Blue-veined cheeses are produced locally as well. The green lentils of le Puy are grown in Auvergne and are the basis of many dishes, especially those containing sausages.

The southwest regions of France include Gascony and Guyenne, the bastions of French gastronomy. Bordeaux is the capital of Guyenne, and it is no surprise that wine is featured in most dishes. Sauce *Bordelaise*, a rich roux-based sauce of red wine, is used to nap fish, eggs, poultry, and meats. In the ancient city of Périgueux, truffles are served, along with foie gras. Cèpe mushrooms are also a specialty of this region. Other famous foods include *cassoulet*, the original "casserole" made with beans, duck confit, or duck preserved in its own fat, rich game pâtés and terrines, and the most noble of blue-veined cheeses, Roquefort. Agen produces fine plums, which as prunes are added to many of Bordeaux's dishes.

Farther south the Pyrenees mountains, land of the Basques, mark the border with Spain. Peppers, both mild and spicy, are featured in many flavorful Basque dishes. Bayonne ham is a specialty of the region, and olive oil replaces goose fat and butter as the cooking fat of choice. Wild herbs flavor freshly caught trout and succulent lamb.

The cooking style of Provence is more aligned with the Mediterranean than any other region in France. Here tomatoes, garlic, and olive oil are found incorporated with other flavors of the Mediterranean, including citrus, capers, and olives. Bouillabaisse, the famous fish stew of the region, epitomizes the use of Mediterranean ingredients. Herbs, including lavender and thyme, are mixed together with other herbs to produce the seasoning mix known as *herbes de Provence*. Lamb, the staple meat, is often grilled, and rabbit is richly prepared in wine or flavored with *tapenade*, a purée of olives, capers, and anchovies. Fish is usually grilled after marinating in olive oil, lemon juice, and herbs. Another specialty of the region and an accompaniment to many of its dishes is the garlicky mayonnaise *aïoli*.

Burgundy is most famous for its wine, and many dishes are based on it. The fragrant court bouillon, a white wine–based poaching liquid, is used to prepare delicate fish and the famous dish *escargots de Bourgogne*, snails poached in the broth and then filled with garlic butter. Red wine sauces abound, as in *boeuf Bourguignonne*. The city of Dijon lends its name to the famous mustard.

Alsatian food resembles the food of Germany, with foods reflecting the heartiness of German food touched with the elegance of French cuisine. *Choucroute* (sauerkraut) is popular, and one of the most popular dishes is *choucroute garnie*, sauerkraut topped with sausages and smoked meats. Rivaling the foie gras of Périgord is that produced in Strasbourg. Lorraine, Alsace's neighbor, is decidedly more French in its cuisine, and the famous quiche Lorraine, a rich tart of eggs, cream, and bacon, attests to this.

In 1768 the Mediterranean island of Corsica, situated just north of the island of Sardinia, was given to the French by the Genoese. The Corsicans are fiercely independent, which is reflected in their cuisine. It is a flavorful mixture of Italian, French, and Mediterranean influences. Cattle graze on lush pastures filled with aromatic herbs; pigs are fed on chestnuts and acorns; and the catch from the pristine waters is the envy of the Continent. Cornmeal, commonly prepared like polenta, is a staple as is chestnut flour, although the latter has become too expensive for daily consumption. Olive and citrus groves have been successfully transplanted to the island, as have avocados and kiwis. Piquant peppers make a lively appearance. Pastas, such as ravioli and *involuti*, are popular. The yearly slaughter of the pig produces some of the finest charcuterie in all of France. A ricotta-style sheep's milk cheese, *brocciu*, is Corsica's most famous cheese. Roast lamb and kid are the meats of choice, and they are often served with a fiery vinaigrette.

Grilled Kid Goat Ravioli in Red Wine Meat Sauce Ravioli au Brocciu et Cabri avec la Stufata

serves 8 (3 ravioli per serving)

The ground cover blanketing the hills of Corsica is known locally as the *maquis* (scrub). It has a spicy perfume that comes from such native herbs as Corsican mint, sweet marjoram, wormwood, various thymes and sages, myrtle, rosemary, and fennel. Cattle, pigs, sheep, and goats graze on this scrub, and it subtly flavors the meats. This recipe uses the classic Corsican preparation for roasting or grilling *cabri* (baby goat), a very popular meat. Once cooked, the meat is pulled from the bones and is used with the famous sheep's milk cheese of the island, known as *brocciu*, to fill pasta. The ravioli are topped with the red wine and meat sauce of the region known as *la stufata*.

SPIT-ROASTED BABY GOAT (*GIGOT DE CABIRI À LA BROCHE*)

¼ cup [60 mL] olive oil

2 tablespoons [30 mL] red wine vinegar

1 tablespoon [15 mL] rosemary leaves, minced

2 tablespoons [30 mL] parsley, chopped

1 tablespoon [15 mL] garlic, minced

Salt and black pepper to taste

1½ pounds [675 g] leg of kid goat

Slivered garlic as needed

Small sprigs of parsley

MEAT AND RED WINE SAUCE

2 tablespoons [30 mL] olive oil

8 ounces [225 g] roasted kid goat meat or leftover roasted beef, pork loin, or lamb, finely diced

2 sweet onions, very finely minced

4 garlic cloves, very finely minced

1 cup [240 mL] dry, fruity red wine

2 teaspoons [10 mL] tomato paste

½ cup [120 mL] demi-glace

1½ cups [360 mL] beef or chicken stock

1 bay leaf

Salt and ground black pepper to taste

PASTA DOUGH: MAKES 24 RAVIOLI

4 cups [960 mL] all-purpose flour

⅛ teaspoon [0.5 mL] salt

6 eggs

RAVIOLI FILLING: MAKES ENOUGH TO FILL 24 RAVIOLI

Garlic slivers and parsley from the roasted kid goat

8 ounces [225 g] roasted kid goat, shredded

6 fresh sage leaves, minced

12 ounces [340 g] *brocciu* or dry ricotta cheese, diced

Salt and ground black pepper to taste

Grated Parmesan cheese, for service

Ground black pepper, for service

ADVANCE PREPARATION

1. Combine the olive oil, vinegar, rosemary, parsley, garlic, and salt and pepper and mix well to form a basting marinade.

2. Make small slits over the surface of the leg of kid goat and insert slivers of garlic and sprigs of parsley into each slit. Roast slowly over an indirect fire, basting frequently, until the meat reaches an internal temperature of 155°F [68°C], about one hour.

3. Allow the meat to rest at least 20 minutes. Pull the meat from the bone and reserve the meat for the ravioli filling. (The kid goat can be roasted one day in advance. Consider roasting a whole kid goat and freezing the remainder for later use.)

PREPARATION OF THE SAUCE

4. Heat the olive oil over medium-high heat in a nonstick skillet and brown the pulled meat. Remove the meat with a slotted spoon and drain. Reserve.

5. Reduce the heat to medium, add the onions, and cook just until translucent. Add the garlic and cook for 30 seconds. Deglaze with the wine and stir in the tomato paste.

6. Return the meat to the pan and add the demi-glace and stock. Add the bay leaf and season with salt and pepper. Increase the heat to a boil, then reduce the heat to a low simmer. Cover and cook for 2 to 3 hours, adding water as needed, or until the meat is very tender and the onions have dissolved and thickened the sauce. Reserve warm for service. (The sauce can be made one day in advance and refrigerated or frozen for later use.)

PREPARATION OF THE PASTA

7. Sift the flour and salt together on a clean surface or in a large bowl. Form it into a mound with a well in the center.

8. Break the eggs into the well and using your fingertips, draw the flour into the eggs until the eggs are incorporated and a dough is formed. Using the heels of your hands, knead the dough on a floured surface for 5 minutes, or until a smooth, elastic dough is formed. The dough can be made in a processor by first adding the flour to the bowl. With the processor running add the eggs, one at a time, and process until incorporated. Pulse to form a smooth dough. Remove to a floured surface and knead by hand 1 minute.

9. Divide the dough into 4 parts. Roll the pasta into thin sheets using a pasta rolling machine.

ASSEMBLY OF THE RAVIOLI

10. Chop the garlic slivers and parsley from the roasted meat and mix with the shredded meat, sage, and cheese. Season with salt and pepper.

11. Starting near the end of 1 sheet of pasta, place 1 teaspoon [5 mL] of filling 2 inches [5 cm] apart along its length. With a pastry brush dipped in water or beaten egg, lightly moisten the area around the mounds of filling. Take a second sheet of pasta and carefully place it over the top of the sheet with the filling. Press firmly around each mound to seal, being careful to remove any air pockets.

12. Using a pastry wheel, cut 2-inch [5-cm] square ravioli. Place the ravioli on a sheet pan that has been dusted with flour or cornmeal. Do not allow the ravioli to touch. Repeat with the remaining sheets of dough.

COOKING METHOD

13. Bring 6 quarts [6 L] of lightly salted water to a slow boil and cook the ravioli in batches for 5 to 6 minutes, or until they rise to the surface and the edges are cooked. Remove the ravioli with a slotted spoon to a large bowl. Toss with some of the sauce to prevent sticking. (This also flavors the pasta.)

SERVICE

14. Serve each person 3 ravioli, topped with sauce and garnished liberally with the Parmesan and black pepper.

Rabbit Cakes with Wild Mushroom Champagne Sauce
Gateaux de Lapin avec Sauce Champagne et Champignons

serves 8

These cakes are similar to crab or fish cakes, but based on braised rabbit meat. When making the cakes use only enough bread to hold the mixture together. It should be mostly rabbit meat and seasonings.

CHEF NOTES

The rabbit cakes may be served with a number of sauces, such as a garlicky mayonnaise (aïoli) or mustard cream sauce; they may be baked or pan-fried instead of broiled. A small amount of shredded Gruyère cheese added to the rabbit mixture will give extra depth and creaminess. Poultry can be substituted for the rabbit in this recipe, with reduced braising time.

RABBIT

One 2½ to 3 pound [1.1 to 1.4 kg] rabbit, cut into 8 to 10 pieces

10 garlic cloves, peeled and left whole

½ teaspoon [3 mL] fresh thyme, minced

½ teaspoon [3 mL] salt

¼ teaspoon [1 mL] black pepper

1 tablespoon [15 mL] olive oil

1 cup [240 mL] flat Champagne

½ cup [120 mL] olive oil or lard

1 to 2 cups [240 to 480 mL] chicken or rabbit stock

RABBIT CAKES

Meat from 1 braised rabbit, shredded or diced

Garlic cloves from the braising liquid, mashed

4 shallots, diced

2 scallions, finely chopped

½ cup [120 mL] wild or crimini mushrooms, diced

1 tablespoon [15 mL] Dijon mustard

1 tablespoon [15 mL] mayonnaise

1½ tablespoons [25 mL] parsley, chopped

2 large eggs, beaten

1 to 1½ cups [240 to 360 mL] soft breadcrumbs, cubed (small)

About ½ cup [120 mL] unseasoned dry breadcrumbs

½ teaspoon [3 mL] salt

¼ teaspoon [1 mL] black pepper

Flour, for dusting

SAUCE

2 tablespoons [30 g] unsalted butter

4 shallots, diced

2 garlic cloves, minced

½ cup [120 mL] fresh wild mushrooms, sliced

1 cup [240 mL] Champagne

½ cup [120 mL] chicken stock

½ cup [120 mL] demi-glace

½ cup [120 mL] crème fraîche

½ teaspoon [3 mL] Dijon mustard

Flour, for dredging

ADVANCE PREPARATION

1. Place the rabbit pieces in a resealable plastic bag. Mix the garlic, thyme, salt, pepper, oil, and flat Champagne together to form a marinade. Pour the marinade into the bag and toss to coat. Refrigerate overnight.

PREPARATION OF THE RABBIT CAKES

2. Drain the rabbit pieces, reserving the marinade. Pat the rabbit pieces and garlic cloves dry.

3. Heat the olive oil in a nonstick skillet over medium heat and fry the rabbit pieces in batches until browned. Remove the rabbit to paper towels and drain.

4. Fry the garlic cloves until browned and drain on paper towels. Return the rabbit pieces, garlic, and marinade to the skillet and add the stock.

5. Bring to a boil, reduce the heat to a simmer, cover the pan, and simmer the rabbit, turning occasionally, for 1½ hours, or until tender. Allow to cool.

6. Remove the meat from the bones. Reserve. Reserve the garlic cloves.

7. Combine the rabbit cake ingredients in a bowl, mixing well. Form into 8 large cakes or 16 small cakes, cover with plastic film, and reserve refrigerated until ready to cook. The rabbit cakes can be made several hours in advance.

PREPARATION OF THE SAUCE

8. Heat the butter in a nonstick skillet over medium heat. Add the shallots and cook until translucent. Add the garlic and mushrooms and cook for 3 minutes more.

9. Deglaze with the Champagne. Reduce the Champagne by half, then add the stock and demi-glace. Reduce by half, then

add the crème fraîche and mustard. Reduce to the desired thickness and reserve warm for service.

COOKING METHOD

10. Dredge the rabbit cakes in flour and pat off the excess. Place them on a lightly greased baking sheet and place under the broiler. Cook 4 to 5 minutes on 1 side, turn the cakes, and cook for 3 to 4 minutes more. The cooking time will vary with size.

SERVICE

11. Place a portion of the reserved sauce on a small plate and top with 1 or 2 rabbit cakes, depending on size.

Lemon-Garlic Glazed Chicken Wing Drumettes _Ailerons de Poulet en Gigots au Citron et à l'Ail_

serves 8

Gigots, or small legs, are made from chicken wing drumettes by cutting around the bony base of the first wing section (the one nearest the breast) and using a towel for gripping, pushing the meat back over itself to make a package of meat on the end of the bone handle. In more formal dining settings, attach paper frills to the bone.

CHEF NOTES

One-half cup [120 mL] of diced fennel bulb or 3-tablespoons [45 mL] chopped mint is a nice addition to the sauce as it is cooking. The drumettes may be baked at 375°F [190°C] for 10 minutes, or until done. The strained vegetables may be puréed and used as an accompaniment.

32 chicken wing drumettes or wings with the end sections removed

2 tablespoons [30 mL] shallots, grated

2 tablespoons [30 mL] parsley, chopped

1 teaspoon [5 mL] fresh lemon juice

½ cup [120 mL] olive oil

1 teaspoon [5 mL] black pepper

1 cup [240 mL] celeriac, diced

1 cup [240 mL] carrot, diced

1 cup [240 mL] onion, diced

½ cup [120 mL] tomato, diced

½ teaspoon [3 mL] fresh rosemary leaves

2 tablespoons [30 mL] parsley leaves and stems, chopped

1 bay leaf

½ teaspoon [3 mL] cayenne

1 quart [1 L] chicken stock

2½ tablespoons [40 mL] garlic, minced

2½ tablespoons [40 mL] fresh lemon juice

Paper frills (optional)

2 tablespoons [30 mL] parsley, chopped

ADVANCE PREPARATION

1. Make an incision around the bone of the first wing section of the chicken (the section nearest the breast). Grip the detached bone end tightly with a towel and push the meat up over itself to form a package of boneless meat at the end of the bone. Reserve.

2. Combine the shallots, parsley, lemon juice, ¼ cup [60 mL] of the olive oil, and black pepper in a small food processor and purée. Place the prepared drumettes in a resealable plastic bag and toss with the puréed mixture. Refrigerate for at least 3 hours or, preferably, overnight.

3. Heat 2 tablespoons [30 mL] of the olive oil over medium heat in a large nonstick skillet. Add the celeriac, carrot, and onion and sauté for 5 minutes.

4. Add the tomato, rosemary, parsley, bay leaf, cayenne, and stock and bring to a boil. Reduce the heat to a simmer and cook until the liquid is reduced to 1½ cups [360 mL].

5. Strain the liquid, pressing firmly on the solids. Discard or save the solids (see Chef Notes). Reserve the vegetable broth.

COOKING METHOD

6. Heat the remaining 2 tablespoons [30 mL] of the olive oil in a large nonstick skillet over medium heat and sauté the *gigots*, turning occasionally, until evenly browned and cooked through.

7. Remove the *gigots* and drain on paper towels. Keep warm. Add the garlic to the pan and briefly sauté for 30 seconds.

8. Deglaze the pan with lemon juice. Add the reserved vegetable broth and bring to a boil. Reduce to a syrupy glaze.

9. Add the *gigots* and toss to coat evenly. Warm the *gigots* in the pan over low heat for several minutes.

SERVICE

10. If using paper frills, install just before serving. Serve each person 4 *gigots*, topped with any remaining sauce. Garnish with chopped parsley.

Sautéed Duck Breasts with Apples and Calvados in Pastry Cases Vol-au-Vent de Canard avec Pommes et Calvados

serves 8

Normandy and Brittany are re-nowned apple-growing regions of France. Calvados, the famous apple brandy of Normandy, is produced by distilling hard cider. In the old days nearly every farmer produced his own Calvados from the cider made from damaged and non-sellable apples, but today the prac-tice is rare. Ducks are both raised domestically and hunted with fer-vor by the regions' inhabitants.

CHEF NOTES

This sauce goes well with goose breast, pork tenderloin medal-lions, or pork loin. Puréed root vegetables make a nice accom-paniment to this dish.

8 puff pastry cases

4 boneless duck breasts

Salt and pepper

2 tablespoons [30 mL] unsalted butter

I onion, sliced

4 shallots, diced

I cup [240 mL] baking apples, peeled, cored, and diced

2 garlic cloves, minced

¼ cup [60 mL] Calvados

½ cup [120 mL] unfiltered organic apple juice

½ cup [120 mL] chicken or duck stock

½ cup [120 mL] demi-glace

I tablespoon [15 mL] Dijon mustard

4 ounces [110 g] cold unsalted butter, cut into small cubes

ADVANCE PREPARATION

1. Bake the pastry cases at 425°F [220°C] for 15 minutes, or until flaky and browned.

2. Cut shallow diagonal slits in the skin of the duck breasts with-out piercing the flesh and season with salt and pepper.

COOKING METHOD

3. Heat the butter in a nonstick skillet over medium-high heat and add the duck breasts, skin side down. Sauté until browned. Turn the breasts and brown the other side.

4. Remove the breasts to a small roasting pan and bake at 325°F [160°C] until cooked medium rare, about 10 minutes. Re-serve warm.

5. Add the onion and shallots to the skillet and cook over medium heat until the mixture begins to brown and cara-melize. Add the diced apples and sauté until the apples be-gin to color. Add the garlic and cook 30 seconds.

6. Remove the skillet from the heat and add the Calvados. Return the skillet to the heat and ignite the alcohol. When the flames subside, add the apple juice, stock, demi-glace, and mustard. Reduce the sauce by one-half to two-thirds. When the sauce has reduced sufficiently, remove the skillet from the heat and allow to cool slightly.

SERVICE

7. Thinly slice the duck breasts on the diagonal, adding any released juices to the sauce. Add the cubes of cold butter to the warm sauce and swirl to emulsify.

8. Place a pastry case on top of a small pool of sauce and arrange overlapping slices of the duck in the case. Top with some of the sauce.

Duck Liver and Green Peppercorn Pâté Pâté de Foie de Canard avec Poivre en Grains Vert

serves 8

This smooth pâté spread is very popular wherever it is served. Any combination of mild livers can be used—goose, rabbit, or chicken. When butchering meats, poultry, or game, freeze the livers until enough have been saved. This pâté is best served with Dijon mustard, *cornichon* pickles, diced red onion, and a sliced crusty baguette.

CHEF NOTES

Frozen duck livers are available from quality meat or poultry suppliers. Goose liver (*foie gras*) can be substituted, with reduced cooking time, for an elegant alternative. Rabbit and duck liver make a delicious combination for this recipe. Cream cheese or butter whipped with minced herbs may be sparingly piped as a decoration to accompany this pâté.

6 ounces [170 g] lean smoked bacon, chopped

1¼ pounds [560 g] duck livers or a combination of mild-flavored livers, trimmed

⅓ cup [80 mL] celeriac, diced

½ cup [120 mL] red onion, diced

1 tablespoon [15 mL] shallots, diced

1 teaspoon [5 mL] garlic, minced

¼ teaspoon [1 mL] cayenne

½ teaspoon [3 mL] paprika

½ tablespoon [8 mL] dry mustard

1 tablespoon [15 mL] Dijon mustard

¼ cup [60 mL] dry sherry

¼ cup [60 mL] Cognac or brandy

4 sprigs of parsley, coarsely chopped

2 green onions, coarsely chopped

2 tablespoons [30 mL] green peppercorns, rinsed

Salt and black pepper to taste

6 tablespoons [90 mL] unsalted butter, cubed, slightly softened

Dijon mustard, for service

Cornichons, for service

Diced red onion, for service

Sliced crusty baguette, for service

ADVANCE PREPARATION

1. All advanced preparation may be found in the ingredient list.

COOKING METHOD

2. Sauté the bacon in a large nonstick skillet over medium heat until lightly browned. Remove the bacon and pour off half of the bacon fat.

3. Add the livers and sauté until medium rare. Remove the livers and reserve.

4. Add the celeriac, red onion, shallots, and garlic to the pan. Sauté the vegetables until the onions are soft and translucent, about 3 minutes.

5. Add the cayenne, paprika, dry mustard, and Dijon mustard. Stir well to combine. Return the livers to the skillet and increase the heat.

6. Carefully add the sherry and Cognac and deglaze the pan by scraping the bottom to loosen any browned bits. Add the parsley and green onions and reduce the liquid until almost all has evaporated.

7. Remove from the heat and stir in the green peppercorns. Place the skillet on a wire rack to cool rapidly to room temperature.

8. Add the cooled contents of the skillet to the workbowl of a food processor and pulse to form a smooth paste. Season with salt and pepper, then add the butter. Pulse to incorporate.

9. The pâté can be portioned into 3-ounce [85-g] servings in individual ramekins (a pastry bag is helpful), then covered with plastic film and refrigerated, or it can be refrigerated in bulk. Thoroughly chill before service. (The pâté should be made one day in advance.)

SERVICE

10. Serve a 3-ounce [85-g] portion of the pâté accompanied with Dijon mustard, sliced and fanned cornichons, diced red onions, and sliced French bread. (A small knife for spreading the pâté should be included.)

Scallop and Caviar Sandwich with Lemon-Mussel Cream Sauce
Sandwich de Coquilles Saint-Jacques au Caviar

serves 8

The area around Paris has long been the culinary center for French haute cuisine. This combination of just-cooked slices of sea scallops separated by caviar, resting in a sauce of lemon cream flavored with diced mussels is a classic representation of the sea, as expressed by the elegant cookery of the masters. The dish features sea scallops and mussels, which France is known for, and caviar, a delicacy from the Russian czars that the French have adopted as their own.

CHEF NOTES

The mussels can be omitted from the sauce. Crayfish tails or shrimp may be substituted in their place. Medallions of lobster or large prawns can be substituted for the scallops.

SCALLOPS

8 large sea scallops, trimmed and sliced horizontally into thirds

1 tablespoon [15 mL] clarified butter

2 tablespoons [30 mL] white wine

1 teaspoon [5 mL] fresh lemon juice

2 garlic cloves, minced very fine

Salt and white pepper to taste

SAUCE

1 tablespoon [15 mL] unsalted butter

3 shallots, minced

2 garlic cloves, minced

½ cup [120 mL] dry white wine

1 cup [240 mL] chicken stock

1½ cups [360 mL] cream

Bouquet garni of 1 sprig of lemon thyme and 2 sprigs of parsley

½ teaspoon [3 mL] lemon zest, grated

1 teaspoon [5 mL] fresh lemon juice

4 fresh mussels, chopped fine

Salt and white pepper to taste

1 ounce [30 g] Sevruga caviar or Beluga or Osetra, if not cost prohibitive

Lemon zest curls for garnish

ADVANCE PREPARATION

1. Gently place the scallop slices in a resealable plastic bag.

2. Combine the clarified butter, wine, lemon juice, garlic, and salt and white pepper and mix to form a marinade. Pour the marinade over the scallop slices and marinate for 30 minutes.

COOKING METHOD

3. Heat the butter in a nonstick skillet over medium heat and sauté the shallots until translucent. Add the garlic and sauté for 30 seconds.

4. Deglaze the pan over medium-high heat with the wine, then add the stock, cream, bouquet garni, and lemon zest. Reduce the sauce by half, then add the lemon juice and salt and pepper to taste. Cook 2 minutes.

5. Stir in the mussels, cook 30 seconds, and season with salt and pepper. Reserve warm. (The mussels are added just before service and cooked briefly just to heat them through and to release their juices.)

6. Heat a grill and lightly brush it with olive oil. Quickly sear the scallop slices on one side only, forming attractive grill marks, to the point that they just begin to turn opaque (They will continue to cook slightly when removed from the heat.) Reserve.

ASSEMBLY

7. Build stacks of 3 slices of scallops, alternating with a scant ½ teaspoon [3 mL] of the caviar between each layer, with the top scallop slice showing the best grill marks.

SERVICE

8. Ladle a small pool of the sauce in the center of a small plate. Place a scallop sandwich on the sauce. Garnish with a lemon zest curl.

Savory Cheese Puffs Gougères

serves 8

These light-as-air cheese puffs are the perfect accompaniment for wine tastings or drinks. These puffs also make an excellent case for a variety of seafood or vegetable fillings. A Burgundian specialty is to fill the *gougères* with calf kidneys sautéed in red wine. *Gougères* are at their best when served right from the oven, but they may be cooked in advance, stored in an airtight container, and reheated as needed.

CHEF NOTES

The puffs should bake, undisturbed, for 30 to 35 minutes, depending on the oven. (Opening the oven will allow moisture to escape, toughening the puffs and preventing them from attaining a full rise.)

Any cheese similar to Gruyère can be substituted. You may also reduce the cheese quantity by ¼ cup [60 mL] and add 10 minced anchovy fillets to make *choux aux anchois*. While best freshly baked, the puffs may be reheated in a 325°F [160°C] oven.

CHOUX PASTE (*PÂTE À CHOUX*):
MAKES TWENTY-FOUR 2-INCH [5-CM] PUFFS

4 ounces [110 g] chilled unsalted butter, cut into small dice

Pinch of salt

1 cup [240 mL] water

1 cup [240 mL] all-purpose flour

4 large eggs, at room temperature

½ cup [120 mL] Gruyère cheese, grated

Pinch of grated nutmeg

¼ cup [60 mL] Gruyère cheese, cut into small dice

Pinch of garlic powder

ADVANCE PREPARATION

1. All advance preparation may be found in the ingredient list.

PREPARATION OF THE *CHOUX PASTE*

2. Bring the butter, salt, and water in a heavy saucepan to a boil. Remove from the heat, add the flour all at once, and vigorously beat the mixture with a wooden spoon.

3. Return the pan to the heat and beat until the mixture holds together and cleans the sides of the pan, about 2 minutes.

4. Transfer the dough to the bowl of a mixer with a paddle attachment and mix at low speed. Add the eggs, one at a time, allowing each egg to be completely absorbed into the dough before adding the next. Increase the mixer speed for a few seconds after each egg has been absorbed.

5. Add the grated cheese and the nutmeg, then carefully fold in the diced cheese and the garlic.

COOKING METHOD

6. Fill a pastry bag fitted with a ½-inch [1-cm] plain or star tip. Pipe the dough into 2-inch [5-cm] mounds about 3 inches [8 cm] apart on parchment-lined baking sheets (or carefully drop spoonfuls by hand, using moistened fingers).

7. Bake at 425°F [220°C] for 5 minutes. Reduce the heat to 375°F [190°C] and bake for 30 minutes without opening the oven. When done, the puffs will be golden brown, light and airy, with moist, but cooked (not doughy) centers that are hollow.

    SERVICE

8. Serve 3 *gougères* per person on a small plate.

Roquefort Cheese and Onion Tart Tourte au Roquefort

serves 8

Roquefort cheese has been described as "the king of cheeses, and the cheese of kings." It is produced in the limestone caves of Combalou, near Rouergue in the south-central part of France. Roquefort is made from ewe's milk and is considered the most refined of the blue cheeses. True Roquefort is assertive and creamy, and every effort should be made to secure authentic Roquefort for this recipe. Roquefort goes well with red wines and some believe a crisp white wine or Sauternes to be an excellent pairing.

CHEF NOTES

The tart can be baked on a sheet pan, in rectangular form. Fold up the edges of the pastry and flute them. Cut into rectangles. The tart should be cut while at room temperature or when chilled. Maytag blue cheese from Iowa makes a reasonable substitute for authentic Roquefort.

PASTRY

1 cup [240 mL] all-purpose flour

Pinch of salt

Pinch of white pepper

¼ teaspoon [1 mL] garlic powder

5 ounces [140 g] cold unsalted butter, diced

About ¼ cup [60 mL] ice water

FILLING

¼ cup [60 mL] olive oil

2 pounds [900 g] sweet onions, thinly sliced

2 garlic cloves, minced

8 ounces [225 g] Roquefort cheese, crumbled

Salt and black pepper to taste

ADVANCE PREPARATION

1. Sift the flour, salt, white pepper, and garlic powder into a bowl. Add the butter. Using a pastry knife, cut in the butter to form a mixture resembling coarse meal. (There should be visible pieces of butter in the dough.)

2. Add only enough ice water to form a dough that holds its shape; do not overwork the dough. Cover with plastic film and refrigerate at least 1 hour before rolling out. (The pastry can be made 1 day in advance.)

PREPARATION OF THE FILLING

3. Heat 2 tablespoons [30 mL] of the olive oil in a large nonstick skillet over low heat. Add the onions and cook over very low heat, covered, for about 1 hour, stirring occasionally. The onions should achieve the consistency of a purée without coloring them.

4. Add the garlic and cook, uncovered, until almost all of the moisture has evaporated. Reserve and allow to cool. Mix in the Roquefort cheese and season with salt and pepper. The Roquefort may be quite salty, so use caution when seasoning.

ASSEMBLY OF THE TART

5. Roll out the dough into a 12-inch [30-cm] circle, ⅛ inch [3 mm] thick. Press the dough into a 9-inch [23-cm] fluted tart pan with a removable bottom. Add the Roquefort filling, smoothing the surface with an offset spatula.

COOKING METHOD

6. Drizzle the remaining 2 tablespoons [30 mL] of olive oil over the surface of the tart and bake at 375°F [190°C] for 45 minutes, or until the surface of the tart is golden brown. (The tart can be made one day in advance.)

SERVICE

7. Cut the tart into 8 wedges. Serve 1 wedge per person at room temperature.

United Kingdom and Ireland

England, Scotland,

Wales, Northern

Ireland, and Ireland

Beef Short Riblets with Spicy Butter Glaze
Deviled Beef Bones

Venison Open-Face Sandwich on Scallion Soda Bread
Fiafheoil Rósta Arán Sóide

Lamb and Vegetable Pies
Tuppeny Struggles

Sweetbread, Bacon, and Mushroom Brochettes
Skuets

Pheasant and Leek Pies with Port Cream Sauce
Phesand Pye

Individual Chilled Salmon Soufflés

Parsnip Cakes with Crispy Bacon and Cheese Sauce
Cisti Meacan Bán Anlann Cáise

THE UNITED KINGDOM consists of Great Britain and Northern Ireland. Great Britain is divided into England, the largest division, with Scotland to the north and Wales to the west. Northern Ireland is located in the northeastern section of the island of Ireland. The term British Isles refers to the island group including Great Britain, Ireland, and the smaller adjacent islands.

The climate is tempered by the Gulf Stream, and the weather is generally overcast and rainy, which gives a very green, lush appearance to much of the region. The islands have highly irregular coastlines, with many harbors. It is no surprise, then, that saltwater fishing is an important contributor to the region's economy. Cod, whiting, mackerel, and herring are the most important fish caught off shore. Shellfish such as lobster and crab are harvested along with freshwater fish such as salmon and trout. Aquaculture is responsible for the commercial harvesting of Atlantic salmon and trout (and shellfish such as shrimp and mussels), with the rivers and streams used for recreational fishing. Over 75 percent of the land is used for agriculture, most of it as grazing land.

The development of the cuisine of Britain begins in the Middle Ages. It was a hearty cuisine meant to sustain life in cold, damp climates. Meat, cheese, bread, and puddings formed the basis of the diet. The Normans brought a more sophisticated way of eating to the dinner table. In addition to table manners, the Normans introduced herbs and spices (such as cloves, cinnamon, and nutmeg), as well as the idea of separate courses. Pies became a favorite way of eating savories as well as sweets. To this day, encasing meat, fish, vegetables, and fruits in a pastry case is a popular way of snacking and dining. Today British cuisine is not known for subtleties or for fine sauces. Although things are changing, there is no local "haute cuisine." The food is uncomplicated and rarely embellished. At the foundation of the diet is meat, especially beef, with roasting the favored method of cooking it.

Puddings often accompany or follow the main dish. The term "pudding" can be confusing. It may refer to a sweet dish following a main course, or it may be the main dish itself, or it may be a side dish accompanying the main course. Usually steamed, puddings may also be baked, and the apple pie can be considered a pudding in the United Kingdom. Batter puddings seem to be traced to the Saxons. By the twelfth century roasts were being basted with a batter made from flour, eggs, and milk, which eventually became the famous Yorkshire pudding. It was not long after this that firm doughs were used to encase all sorts of meat and fish, becoming the pie, tart, and pasty of the region. A raised dough, known as a coffin, often encased a meat filling; the coffin was not intended to be eaten. In addition to the conventional meaning, the term "pie" may also describe a layered casserole, topped with fluffy potato rather than a pastry crust (shepherd's pie, for example.)

British cooking cannot be discussed without mentioning butter, cheese, and other dairy products. The Saxons brought the techniques of making butter and cheese to the region. Many foods are cooked in butter, and many local cheeses find their way into the dishes. World-famous cheeses include the cheddars, such as Cheshire, and blue cheeses, such as Stilton, a most aristocratic blue-veined cheese. Cream is often added to sauces to finish them, but few sauces benefit from the technique of reduction. Most are based on roux thickening, such as the béchamel.

The cuisine of Scotland is based on the healthy consumption of such grains as barley and oats. The seas provide an endless array of fish and seafood. Eating fish was forbidden by the Celts, but by the time Catholicism took hold, eating fish had become quite popular. Since fish run seasonally, preservation is critical, and cold and hot smoking are two common ways to do it. Preserved fish are enjoyed everywhere. It is believed that the Vikings introduced the techniques of fish preservation through smoking, pickling, and salting. Not particularly fond of meat, the Scots saw to it that the older, tougher animals found their way into the stew pot, and stewing became a traditional Scottish way of cooking meat.

As with the Scots, the staple grain for the Welsh is oats. Bacon is prized in Wales and is considered a staple there as well. Salted meats, garden vegetables, and dairy products form the basis of its simple and hearty cuisine. The best lamb is to be found in Wales.

Like Wales, Ireland clings to its traditions with regard to cooking, much more so than elsewhere, and local specialties abound. Fish and potatoes form the basis of the diet, and some of the finest shellfish and fish are found off the coast of Ireland. Lobster and salmon are particularly tasty as is the Dover sole caught many miles south of Dublin Bay. The Bay produces some of the most highly regarded shrimp (the famous Dublin Bay prawn) to be found anywhere. So popular are those prawns that most are exported to the Continent, with few finding their way to Irish tables. The Irish are fond of mackerel and prepare it in numerous ways. Irish cheeses are excellent as are Irish breads, particularly soda breads and scones.

Beef Short Riblets with Spicy Butter Glaze Deviled Beef Bones

serves 8

The most cherished British dish is the Sunday dinner of roast beef. Prior to the early 1700s the beef in Britain was of poor quality. Tainted or "high" meat was normally obscured with spicing, and this dish grew out of that tradition. The ribs used were usually left over from the standing rib roast that was served at Sunday dinner. British innovators such as Lord "Turnip" Townsend, named for his idea of feeding cattle turnips during the winter instead of slaughtering them, Lord Scudmore, who bred the Hereford strain of cattle, and Robert Bakewell, breeder of the first Angus cattle, rapidly raised the standard by which all other cattle was judged.

CHEF NOTES

This recipe works well with pork, lamb or mutton, buffalo, elk, or venison ribs. Adjust cooking time accordingly.

16 well marbled beef short ribs, cut in half lengthwise, then cut into individual riblets

SPICE RUB

2 tablespoons [30 mL] dry English mustard

2 tablespoons [30 mL] Madras curry powder

1 teaspoon [5 mL] cayenne

1 teaspoon [5 mL] Worcestershire powder or 1 tablespoon [15 mL] Worcestershire sauce

½ teaspoon [3 mL] garlic powder

2 teaspoons [10 mL] salt

1 teaspoon [5 mL] black pepper

BASTING SAUCE

½ cup [120 mL] unsalted butter, melted

¼ cup [60 mL] demi-glace

¼ cup [60 mL] rich chicken stock

3 scallions, minced very fine

2 tablespoons [30 mL] parsley, chopped

8 scallion brushes, for garnish

ADVANCE PREPARATION

1. Place the riblets in a stacking Chinese-style steamer and steam for 20 to 30 minutes, or until about ½ inch [1 cm] of bone protrudes from the ends of the ribs.

2. Allow to cool enough to handle, then make a series of ¼-inch [6-mm] crisscross cuts on the meaty surface of the riblets.

PREPARATION OF THE SPICE RUB

3. Combine the spice rub ingredients and mix well. Rub the riblets evenly with half of the spice rub, reserving the other half for the basting sauce. Place the seasoned riblets in a resealable plastic bag and allow to marinate overnight.

4. Combine the butter, demi-glace, stock, minced scallions, parsley, and the remaining spice rub and mix well. Place the riblets on a baking sheet lined with parchment and brush the riblets with the basting sauce.

5. Roast for 10 minutes at 450°F [230°C], reduce the heat to 400°F [205°C], and roast for an hour more, or until the meat is tender and easily pierced with a fork. Baste frequently, but lightly, with the basting sauce. Turn the riblets over about half way through the cooking process.

SERVICE

6. Serve 4 riblets per person with a side dish for the discarded bones. Garnish each serving with a scallion brush. Serve with extra napkins.

Venison Open-Face Sandwich on Scallion Soda Bread Fiafheoil Rósta Arán Sóide

serves 8

In ancient times the Irish aristocracy ate native red deer. When the Normans arrived they brought in fallow deer to replace the declining population of red stag, and eating venison became more accessible to all classes. Today, raising domestic deer is becoming commonplace in Ireland. Venison is very lean and should be larded and/or marinated to prevent the meat from becoming dry when cooked. Soda bread was traditionally baked fireside in a type of Dutch oven known as a *bastible*. The key to baking fine soda bread is to handle the dough as little as possible (as with biscuits), bake at a high temperature, and, for a lighter crust, cover the loaf with a dry cloth while cooling. Traditionally, a cross is cut into the top of the dough, some say to allow the fairies to escape, while others believe it is to allow the devil to escape.

CHEF NOTES

Originally in Ireland the term venison meant any sort of four-legged game, such as wild boar. This dish may be made using buffalo, elk, stag, beef, or pork. A leg or haunch of venison may be prepared in the same manner.

MARINADE

¼ cup [60 mL] oil

I small onion, sliced

2 garlic cloves, minced

I carrot, sliced

I celery stalk, sliced

¼ cup [60 mL] red wine vinegar

3 black peppercorns, crushed

¼ cup [60 mL] gin

Bouquet garni (parsley sprigs, thyme sprigs, and bay leaf)

¾ cup [180 mL] red wine

¾ cup [180 mL] game or beef stock

I ½ pounds [675 g] venison tenderloin or loin

SODA BREAD

2 cups [480 mL] all-purpose flour

½ teaspoon [3 mL] salt

½ teaspoon [3 mL] ground black pepper

½ teaspoon [3 mL] baking soda

¾ cup [180 mL] buttermilk

½ cup [120 mL] scallions, minced, green and white parts

ROAST

4 to 5 slices smoked bacon

2 tablespoons [30 mL] butter or bacon fat

SAUCE

½ cup [120 mL] reserved marinade

3 garlic cloves, finely minced

I cup [240 mL] rich game or beef stock

I teaspoon [5 mL] red wine vinegar

3 tablespoons [45 mL] red currant jelly

Salt and ground black pepper to taste

ADVANCE PREPARATION

1. Heat the oil in a nonreactive skillet over medium-high heat and sauté the onions, garlic, carrots, and celery until browned. Add all the remaining marinade ingredients and bring to a boil. Simmer for 30 minutes, then allow to cool completely.

2. Place the venison in a resealable plastic bag, pour the marinade over, and marinate for 1 to 3 days, refrigerated.

PREPARATION OF THE SODA BREAD

3. Sift the flour, salt, pepper, and baking soda together. Make a well in the center, pour in the buttermilk, and add the scallions.

4. Using a wooden spoon or spatula, gently mix the flour into the liquid, incorporating just enough of the flour to form a soft dough. (Some flour may be left over.) Turn out onto a lightly floured board and gently pat the dough into an 6-inch [15-cm] round, about 2 inches [5 cm] thick.

5. Place the dough in a heavy 9-inch [25-cm] baking pan and using a thin, sharp knife, cut a cross from edge to edge. Bake at 450°F [230°C] for 15 minutes.

6. Reduce the heat to 400°F [205°C] and bake for 10 minutes more, or until the top is browned and the bottom sounds hollow when tapped. Cover with a clean dishtowel to cool if a hearty crust is not desired.

PREPARATION OF THE ROAST

7. Drain the venison, straining and reserving the marinade. Dry the venison and wrap in the bacon slices, so that all bacon ends are tucked under the venison.

8. Melt the butter in a nonreactive roasting pan and add the venison, bacon ends on the bottom. Roast at 425°F [220°C] for 15 minutes, reduce the heat to 375°F [190°C], and roast for about 15 minutes more, depending on the degree of doneness desired.

9. Remove the venison to a platter. Unwrap the bacon and allow the venison to rest.

10. Dice the bacon and sauté over medium heat until crisp.

PREPARATION OF THE SAUCE

11. Pour off all but 2 tablespoons [30 mL] of the fat in the bottom of the roasting pan. Place the pan over medium heat and deglaze the pan with the reserved marinade. Add the garlic and sauté 30 seconds.

12. Add the stock and vinegar, and bring to a boil. Reduce by half, then stir in the jelly. Season with salt and pepper. Season to taste. Reserve warm until service.

ASSEMBLY AND SERVICE

13. Cut the soda bread into small wedges and place one slice off center on a plate. Slice the venison into thin slices, reserving any juices to add to the sauce.

14. Fan out 3 ounces [85 g] of venison over the wide edge of the soda bread. Sprinkle the crisped bacon over the top of the venison slices. Nap the fanned venison slices with sauce and serve immediately.

Lamb and Vegetable Pies Tuppeny Struggles

serves 12

The Scottish version of the famous Cornish pasty is made with lamb (it can also be made with the stronger tasting mutton). In the 1700s many Scots had to flee their homeland to preserve their freedom, and many immigrated to North America and Poland (the Polish surname Machlejd is from MacLeod).

CHEF NOTES

Ground beef can be used in the filling in place of the lamb. Diced vegetables may be added to the filling.

PASTRY

6 ounces [170 g] lard, roast beef fat drippings, or butter

¼ cup [60 mL] hot water

3 cups [720 mL] all-purpose flour

½ teaspoon [3 mL] salt

¼ teaspoon [1 mL] garlic powder

FILLING

1¼ pounds [560 g] coarse-ground or minced lamb

1 small sweet onion, grated or puréed

2 scallions, finely minced

2 garlic cloves, minced

½ tablespoon [8 mL] Worcestershire sauce

½ teaspoon [3 mL] salt

½ teaspoon [3 mL] ground black pepper

Pinch of freshly grated nutmeg

¼ cup [60 mL] rich beef or lamb stock

2 tablespoons [30 mL] parsley, minced

¼ teaspoon [1 mL] thyme leaves

2 tablespoons [30 mL] dry breadcrumbs

1 egg, lightly beaten with 1 tablespoon [15 mL] cream, for egg wash

Sprigs of parsley, for garnish

ADVANCE PREPARATION

1. For the pastry add the lard to the hot water and allow it to melt.

2. Sift the flour, salt, and garlic powder together and add to the workbowl of a food processor. Gradually pour the lard mixture through the feed tube while processing, pulsing occasionally for 15 seconds, or until a soft dough is formed.

3. Turn the dough out onto a floured board, knead briefly, and cover with plastic film. (The pastry can be made one day in advance and held refrigerated.)

4. Combine all of the filling ingredients and mix well, in one direction.

ASSEMBLY OF THE PIES

5. Butter twelve ½-cup [120-mL] ramekins or muffin tins and set aside. Divide the dough into 12 pieces, cutting each piece into 2 portions, 1 part twice as large as the other.

6. Roll out the larger dough portions and line each ramekin or muffin tin. Evenly distribute the filling into the pastry-lined ramekins, pressing firmly. Brush the tops of the filling with some of the egg wash and set aside.

7. Roll out the remaining smaller portions of dough to form the tops of the pies. Press the tops onto the filling and crimp to seal. Brush the tops of the pies with egg wash and cut two slits in the top of each pie.

COOKING METHOD

8. Bake at 400°F [205°C] for 40 minutes, or until the pastry is golden and the filling is bubbling.

SERVICE

9. Serve each guest one pie, garnished with parsley sprigs.

Sweetbread, Bacon, and Mushroom Brochettes _Skuets_

serves 8

The name _skuets_ derives from the mispronunciation of the word "skewers." This dish is a very popular old English preparation of sweetbreads. When Antonin Carême came to England from France to be the chef for the Prince Regent at the Royal Pavilion in Brighton in 1816, this is one of the few dishes that impressed him enough to include it in his cookbook, _L'Art de la cuisine française au dix-neuvième siècle._ Traditionally the skewers are served with bread sauce, a seasoned blend of cream and breadcrumbs, but the robust nature of the classic English caper sauce pairs well with this dish.

CHEF NOTES

Lamb sweetbreads make an excellent substitute for the veal sweetbreads. Lamb sweetbreads should simmer for 5 minutes before skewering.

SWEETBREADS

1 pound [450 g] veal sweetbreads, rinsed thoroughly

Lightly salted water for soaking

Veal or poultry stock to cover

1 tablespoon [15 mL] fresh lemon juice

CAPER SAUCE: MAKES 1½ CUPS [360 mL]

1½ tablespoons [25 mL] unsalted butter

2 shallots, minced

1½ tablespoons [25 mL] flour

1½ cups [360 mL] brown veal stock

3 tablespoons [45 mL] capers, rinsed

1½ tablespoons [25 mL] malt vinegar

Salt and black pepper to taste

SKEWERS

8 slices lean smoked bacon, precooked until partially done but still pliable, cut into squares

16 medium crimini or button mushroom caps

8 wooden skewers, soaked in warm water for 30 minutes

½ cup [120 mL] unsalted butter, melted

2 garlic cloves, very finely minced

Salt and pepper to taste

1½ tablespoons [25 mL] parsley, chopped

2 teaspoons [10 mL] fresh thyme, chopped

2 ounces [55 g] dry unseasoned breadcrumbs

ADVANCE PREPARATION

1. Soak the sweetbreads in lightly salted water for 2 hours. Drain, place in a saucepan, cover with veal stock, add the lemon juice, and bring to a boil. Reduce the heat and simmer for 15 to 20 minutes, or until the sweetbreads turn opaque and are firm.

2. Rinse the sweetbreads under cold running water until cool enough to handle. Remove any gristle and veins and as much membrane as possible.

3. Place the dressed sweetbreads under a weighted plate for several hours, refrigerated.

4. Cut the pressed sweetbreads into 1-inch [2.5-cm] squares and reserve.

PREPARATION OF THE CAPER SAUCE

5. Melt the butter in a skillet over medium heat and sauté the shallots until soft. Add the flour and stir well to form a light roux.

6. Slowly whisk in the stock and bring to a boil while stirring. Reduce the heat to a simmer, then stir in the capers and vinegar. Season with salt and pepper. Reserve warm for service.

COOKING THE SKEWERS

7. To assemble the skewers, alternate the sweetbread cubes, bacon squares and mushroom caps on 8 soaked wooden skewers and reserve.

8. Mix the butter, garlic, salt and pepper, parsley, and thyme together to form a basting mixture.

9. Brush the skewers with the basting mixture and broil or grill the skewers for 10 minutes, while basting and turning, using medium heat. Place on a platter and allow to rest 5 minutes.

10. Place the breadcrumbs in a nonstick skillet over medium heat. Add any remaining basting butter to the crumbs and sauté the crumbs to lightly brown.

SERVICE

11. For each serving, remove the wooden skewer and place the sweetbreads, mushrooms, and bacon on a small plate. Dust with browned breadcrumbs. Top with warm caper sauce.

Pheasant and Leek Pies with Port Cream Sauce Phesand Pye

serves 8

In the British Isles pheasant and grouse hunting is a favorite pastime for most hunters with shotguns, and the pheasant bagged is most often roasted, added to casseroles or soups, or made into game pies, such as this one. Pheasant are so plentiful in the Lothians that they are considered a driving hazard. The traditional method of cooking with pheasant requires that the birds be "well hung," meaning that they would be hung by the tail in cold weather for up to ten days to age (do not try this at home). When the carcass fell from the tail section on its own, the birds were ready to be used. Leeks are popular all across the British Isles since they have a high yield, require little care while growing, and are resistant to cold weather.

CHEF NOTES

Any type of poultry or game can be substituted for the pheasant. Scotch whisky with a splash of Drambuie liqueur can be substituted for the port in both the marinade and the sauce.

2 pheasant hen breasts

MARINADE

3 tablespoons [45 mL] ruby port

2 tablespoons [30 mL] olive or vegetable oil

2 garlic cloves, very finely minced

1 teaspoon [5 mL] juniper berries, lightly crushed

½ teaspoon [3 mL] ground black pepper

FILLINGS

¼ cup [60 mL] butter

1 pound [450 g] white part of leeks, well washed and sliced thin

¼ cup [60 mL] heavy cream

Salt and black pepper to taste

12 ounces [340 g] crimini or wild mushrooms, sliced

1½ tablespoon [25 mL] parsley, chopped

Salt and black pepper to taste

SAUCE

2 tablespoons [30 mL] butter

3 shallots, finely diced

½ cup [120 mL] ruby port

½ cup [120 mL] rich poultry or veal stock

½ cup [120 mL] heavy cream

Salt and black pepper to taste

12 ounces [340 g] puff pastry, commercially prepared or homemade

2 eggs, lightly beaten

ADVANCE PREPARATION

1. Place the pheasant breasts into a resealable plastic bag.

2. Combine the port, oil, garlic, juniper berries, and black pepper. Mix well to combine. Pour the marinade over the pheasant breasts, seal the bag, and toss to coat. Marinate a mini-

mum of 3 hours, preferably overnight. Remove the breasts and strain and reserve the marinade.

3. Heat the butter over medium heat in a skillet and sauté the pheasant breasts until they are nicely browned and the meat is still rare. Allow the pheasant breasts to rest 10 minutes. Thinly slice the breasts against the grain and reserve, saving any juices to add to the sauce later. (The pheasant breasts can be prepared one day in advance.)

PREPARATION OF THE FILLINGS

4. Heat half the butter over medium heat in a small skillet and sauté the leeks until soft. Add the cream and simmer until thickened. Season and reserve. (The leek filling can be made one day in advance.)

5. Heat the remaining butter in a small skillet and sauté the mushrooms until soft. Drain off any liquid, reserving it for the sauce. Add the chopped parsley, season with salt and pepper, and reserve. (The mushroom filling can be made one day in advance.)

PREPARATION OF THE SAUCE

6. Heat the butter in a nonstick skillet over medium heat and sauté the shallots until soft. Deglaze the pan with the port and cook off the alcohol.

7. Add the stock, cream, reserved marinade, reserved breast juices, and reserved mushroom liquid and bring to a boil. Lower the heat to a simmer and reduce the sauce until slightly thickened, season with salt and pepper. Reserve warm or reheat for service.

ASSEMBLY OF THE PIES

8. Roll out the puff pastry ¼ inch [6 mm] thick. Cut eight 3-inch [8-cm] circles and eight 5-inch [13-cm] circles.

9. Leaving a clean edge, place the leek filling on the smaller circles, then top with the mushroom filling. Arrange slices of pheasant breast over the mushroom layer.

10. Brush the edge of the pastry with beaten egg and cover with the larger circles, pressing around the edges. Crimp the edges with a fork to seal.

COOKING METHOD

11. Place the pies on a parchment-lined baking sheet. Brush with beaten egg. Make several slits in the top of the pastry to release steam.

12. Bake at 400°F [205°C] for 30 minutes, or until the pastry is golden brown and the filling is bubbling.

SERVICE

13. Ladle a small pool of warm sauce on a small plate and top with a warm pie.

Individual Chilled Salmon Soufflés

serves 8

Salmon is the fish of choice in Scotland, and it is caught primarily at sea. Sea-run salmon return to spawn in the rivers, but the inland catch is much lower than that of the ocean, partly because of restrictions based on fishing rights, limited access, and private ownership. The salmon used in this recipe is always precooked; it can be poached, broiled, or grilled. The soufflés should be made some time before service so that they have ample time to chill.

 CHEF NOTES

Any type of fish or seafood may be used instead of salmon as long as it is not oily or very strongly flavored. Only freshest seafood should be used when making this dish.

3 tablespoons [45 mL] unsalted butter

2 shallots, very finely minced

⅓ cup [80 mL] all-purpose flour

2 cups [480 mL] half-and-half, at room temperature

3 large eggs, separated

2 tablespoons [30 mL] (2 packages) unflavored gelatin

3 tablespoons [45 mL] fresh lemon juice

1¼ pounds [560 g] cooked salmon, flaked

1 ounce [30 g] Scottish smoked salmon or Nova-style lox or gravlox, finely diced

⅔ cup [160 mL] heavy cream

1 tablespoon [15 mL] Drambuie liqueur

Liberal pinch of cayenne

Liberal pinch of ground mace

Salt and white pepper to taste

Sliced cucumber, for garnish

Lemon slices, for garnish

ADVANCED PREPARATION

1. Prepare eight ½-cup [120-mL] miniature soufflé cups with a 2-inch [5-cm] parchment collar extending above the rims.

PREPARATION OF THE COLD SOUFFLÉS

2. Melt the butter in a skillet over medium heat and sauté the shallots until soft. Sprinkle the flour over the mixture, stirring well to incorporate. Slowly whisk in the half-and-half and bring to a simmer while stirring.

3. Temper the egg yolks in ½ cup [120 mL] of the hot sauce. Add the egg yolk mixture back into the sauce, whisking to incorporate. Allow the sauce to thicken (do not boil), remove from the heat, and allow to cool slightly.

4. Dissolve the gelatin in the lemon juice, allowing it to absorb the liquid, swell, and soften. Stir this into the sauce. Add the

flaked salmon, smoked salmon, cream, Drambuie, cayenne, and mace. Season to taste with salt and white pepper.

5. Whip the egg whites to form stiff peaks. Whisk a small portion of the beaten egg whites into the soufflé mixture to lighten it. Gently fold in the remainder of the egg whites. Pour ¾ cup [180 mL] of this mixture into each prepared soufflé cup. The filling should rise about 1 inch [2.5 cm] above the rim of the dish. Cover the top with plastic film and chill thoroughly.

SERVICE

6. Carefully remove the plastic film and the parchment collar from each soufflé dish. Place one slice of the cold soufflé on a chilled salad plate. Garnish with the cucumber and lemon slices. Serve chilled.

Parsnip Cakes with Crispy Bacon and Cheese Sauce Cisti Meacan Bán Anlann Cáise

serves 8

Parsnips have been popular in Ireland since early Christian times and were instrumental in helping many Irish survive the potato famine. They are often combined with carrots, and are eaten mashed, roasted, fried, and, as in this recipe, in cake or croquette form.

 CHEF NOTES

Cooked and mashed carrots can be substituted for some of the parsnips. The bacon may be omitted. Similar cakes can be made using a mixture of cooked and mashed potatoes and turnips.

PARSNIP CAKES

1 pound [450 g] parsnips, peeled, cored, cooked in water or stock until tender, and mashed

2 tablespoons [30 mL] flour

½ teaspoon [3 mL] baking powder

¼ teaspoon [1 mL] garlic powder

Salt and black pepper to taste

Pinch of ground mace

1 tablespoon [15 mL] unsalted butter, melted

CHEESE SAUCE

1½ cups [360 mL] half-and-half

1 slice onion

1 garlic clove, bruised

1 small carrot, sliced

3 peppercorns, cracked

2 sprigs of parsley

2 sprigs of thyme

Light roux of 2 tablespoons [30 mL] butter cooked with 2 tablespoons [30 mL] flour

½ cup [120 mL] grated Cheshire or cheddar cheese

¼ teaspoon [1 mL] dry mustard mixed with 1 tablespoon [15 mL] of sauce to form a slurry

BREADING

1 large egg, beaten

½ cup [120 mL] dry breadcrumbs

Butter or oil, for frying

4 strips smoked bacon, diced, fried until crisp, and drained on paper towels

Chopped watercress, for garnish

1. Combine all of the parsnip cake ingredients and mix well. Form into 8 cakes about ½ inch [1 cm] thick. Reserve, covered and refrigerated, until ready to cook. (The parsnip cakes can be made several hours in advance.)

PREPARATION OF THE CHEESE SAUCE

2. Combine the half-and-half, onion, garlic, carrot, peppercorns, parsley, and thyme in a saucepan and bring to a boil. Reduce the heat and simmer for 3 minutes. Turn off heat and allow to steep for 10 minutes.

3. Strain the milk mixture, discarding the solids, and reheat to a simmer. Stir in enough of the roux over medium heat to produce a smooth, slightly thickened sauce. Stir in the cheese and mustard slurry, mixing thoroughly. Keep warm (do not boil) until service.

COOKING METHOD

4. Heat the butter or oil in a wide, nonstick skillet. Dip the parsnip cakes in the beaten egg, then coat with breadcrumbs.

5. Sauté the cakes over medium heat until golden brown on both sides. Drain on paper towels and keep warm until service.

SERVICE

6. Place one parsnip cake on a small pool of sauce. Top with a half slice of crisp bacon. Garnish with chopped watercress.

Chef's Pantry

Adobo: A Latin American pickling sauce containing olive oil, vinegar, and spices used to flavor and preserve foods. The term also refers to a seasoning paste made from ground chiles, herbs, spices, and vinegar, which is used as a rub for meats, poultry, and seafood before grilling or as a seasoning agent in stews and some canned goods.

In the Philippines *adobo* is a term for pickling and preserving foods (usually pork, chicken, and, occasionally, seafood) by stewing in a mixture of vinegar, bay leaf, peppercorns, garlic, and soy sauce. The colonial Spaniards coined the term when they discovered a method similar to their own *adobo*. Considered the national dish of the Philippines, it refers both to the dish itself as well as the method of preparation.

African Bird Chile: A variety of *Capsicum frutescens* exported from the New World to the Old World by the Spanish and Portuguese. The Portuguese brought these small and searingly hot chiles to Africa, where they came to be known as *pili pili or piri piri* and were rapidly embraced. It is also a generic term for very hot powdered dried red chile used in Far Eastern cuisine.

Aguardiente: In Mexico the term refers to homemade brandy and translates literally to "fire water." In the region of Veracruz-Tabasco, *aguardiente* is made from the distilled sap of sugarcane that is macerated for weeks with fresh fruits. The brandy is then filtered and the fruits are eaten as dessert.

Ahi: A Hawaiian and Japanese term referring to the flesh of the yellow-fin tuna (*Thunnus albacares*). *Ahi* is prized by sushi chefs for its rich flavor, deep red color, and exquisite texture. *Ahi* tuna contains less total fat than any other source of animal protein. *Ahi* is caught worldwide in tropical and subtropical waters with the exception of the Mediterranean.

Amaretti Biscuit: An almond-flavored Italian cookie flavored with *Amaretto di Saronno* liqueur. These cookies are fine textured, crisp, and airy and often studded with sugar crystals. They are normally eaten alone, dunked into coffee or espresso drinks, or used as a seasoning agent.

Ancho Chile: The dried form of the poblano chile, named for the Puebla region of Mexico. Heat intensity can vary widely, from mild to medium hot. It is a common ingredient in chile powder mixes.

Annatto Oil: An infused oil colored and slightly flavored by the seeds of the achiote tree (*Bixa orellana*). To make the oil heat 1 cup [240 mL] of oil or lard over medium heat and add 2 ounces

[55 g] of annatto seeds. Cook 2 to 5 minutes, or until the oil turns a deep orange color. Strain and discard the seeds. Store the oil in a clean glass container. It is used primarily to color foods cooked with the oil in the Caribbean and in Latin America.

Annatto Seeds: These are the seeds of the tropical achiote tree *Bixa orellana*. They are used worldwide as a reddish-orange food coloring, primarily in cheeses and butter. Annatto seeds have a subtle musky flavor and are used extensively in Latin American and Caribbean cuisines. The seeds can be found bottled or in packets in the spice section of groceries; they should have a vibrant reddish-orange color.

Annatto Water: Annatto water is used to color dishes much as saffron or turmeric would. To make annatto water, simmer the seeds in water, covered, for 2 to 5 minutes, allow the seeds to cool, and then strain and discard them. Cracking the seeds prior to simmering will produce a more intense color.

Arborio Rice: A medium-grain pearly rice that is grown primarily in the Po River valley of the Piedmont region of northeastern Italy. It is the preferred rice for all Italian cooking, especially risotto. Slightly smaller-grained Italian rice, such as *vialone, nano, and carnaroli*, are acceptable substitutes.

Asafetida: A fetid-smelling resinous gum obtained from the taproots of a giant wild fennel grown in Iran and Afghanistan. It is used in curries, primarily by the vegetarian Jains and Kashmiri and Hindu Brahmans in India as a substitute for onions and garlic. It can be purchased in several forms (tan or reddish-brown powder is most common). When added to hot oil it produces a surprising onion aroma.

Asian Eggplant: Two types of Asian eggplant are commonly found in the United States. The first is known as Japanese eggplant, the most popular variety of which is *ichiban*. These are long, dark purple, and slender. The flesh is sweeter and the skin thinner than the common European eggplant. The second type, known as Thai eggplant, is used all across Southeast Asia. It grows from the size of grapes to golf balls and is generally green-and-white striped. Neither of the two types of Asian eggplant requires salting to extract bitter juices nor do they require peeling before use.

Asian Pear: Native wild pears from Asia of the species *Pyrus pyrifolia* (and *P. ussuriensis* from China) are known as Asian pears or apple-pears. These round pears are sweet, juicy, crisp and fine textured, usually with white or yellowish flesh. Popular varieties include *shinseki, twentieth century, shinko, tsu li, hosui,* and *nitaka.*

Asturian Sausage: Made in Asturias on the northwestern coast of Spain, these sausages are typically made of pork seasoned with spices, garlic, and paprika and smoke dried over oak fires. Linguiça is an acceptable substitute.

Balsamic Vinegar: An artisanal dark, syrupy, slightly sweet vinegar made from grape must and aged over a long period of time in wooden casks. Genuine *aceto balsamico* is produced only in Modena in northern Italy and must be approved in a blind tasting by members of the guild.

Barberry: The barberry is the dried fruit of the berberis shrub of the *Berberis* genus, primarily *B. vulgaris*. The berries are elongated, juiceless, and scarlet and hang in clusters. When the berries are dried, they have a tart, fruity taste. They are used primarily in the Near East (known as *zereshk* in Persia) and the Eastern Mediterranean in stews, pilafs, and stuffings. Dried cranberries are an acceptable substitute.

Basmati Rice: An aromatic long-grain, fine-textured rice from India and Pakistan, which is also grown in Texas and Louisiana. Imported rice requires less water when cooking since it is normally rinsed in water until the water is no longer milky and then soaked before cooking.

Bayonne Ham: A French ham called *jambon de Bayonne* in French, considered one of the world's finest. It is a smoked ham produced in the region of Orthez, east of Bayonne. Italian *prosciutto di Parma* or Spanish *jamón serrano* can be substituted.

Bean Curd: Also called tofu, bean curd is made from dried soybeans. After soaking and boiling in water the liquid (milk) is coagulated with a culture and formed into blocks. Firm bean curd has been pressed to remove some of the water content. Its firmness makes it less fragile in dishes that are stir-fried or vigorously mixed. It is interchangeable with soft or medium bean curd when cooking. Soft bean curd, or silken tofu, is a delicate form of tofu that is made like regular bean curd but the curds are not drained and it is gently formed, not pressed. The texture is soft and silky. Used primarily in soups, particularly in the summer months in Japan, it is available in Asian markets and health food stores.

Bean Curd Sheets: Bean curd sheets are formed from the skin that forms on the surface of soybean milk when tofu is made. It is sold as sheets (*fu pei*) if allowed to dry flat and as sticks (*fu chok*) when the skin is bundled up and draped to dry. Both need to be soaked before being used to become pliable. Sheets are normally used to wrap items before frying, while the sticks are used in stews and soups.

Bean Thread Noodles: Bean thread noodles, also called cellophane noodles, are very thin, vermicelli-like noodles made from the starch of ground mung beans. These noodles are used in all cuisines of the Far East, in soups or stews, in noodle bowls, in stir-fries, and as a coating for fried foods. They need to be soaked briefly in hot water to soften, then rinsed and drained before using.

Bean Thread Sheets: Similar to bean thread noodles, bean thread sheets are made from mung bean flour. In China the sheets are called *fenpi*, or "flour skin," and come in platter-size dried sheets and are generally used as wrappers.

Belgian Endive: Belgian endive is a form of *Cichorium intybus*, called Witloof chicory, developed in Belgium around 1850. The growing process involves planting chicory roots in dark cellars away from the sun, which can turn them green, so that they grow in tightly clustered clumps of white, blanched leaves. Belgian endive is used raw in salads and as a container or scoop for dips or is braised as a side vegetable.

Bird Pepper: Sometimes called bird's eye chile, bird pepper is an especially hot, tiny chile from Thailand, where it is known as *prikk kee nuu*, or "rat droppings," because of its small size and appearance. Bird peppers are available dried and packaged, either whole or ground. The *chiltepín* or *chilipiquín* chile of Mexico is an acceptable substitute.

Bitter Orange: *See* Sour Orange.

Black Sesame Seeds: Called *kuro gama* in Japan, black sesame seeds are used as a component in *furikake* (a spice-seaweed topping) and *goma shio* (sesame salt). They are also pressed to produce sesame oil and are used as a topping and garnish. Sesame seeds should be lightly toasted before use to release their nutty flavor and aroma.

Bok Choy: Also called *pak choi*, bok choy (literally, white vegetable) comes in many varieties. A loose-headed, open type of cabbage, it has a mild flavor and is used in stir-fries, stews, braises, hot pots, and soups. So-called "baby bok choy," a fully developed form that is about 6 to 9 inches [15 to 23 cm] long, has recently become a popular form of the vegetable.

Bonito Flakes: Bonito flakes (*katsuo-bushi*) come from dried slabs of bonito. The light rose-colored slabs are cut into thin slivers resembling wood shavings known as *hana-katsuo* (flower bonito) or *kezuri-bushi* (shaved fillets) in Japanese. They are the primary ingredient in *dashi*, or Japanese stock.

Bouquet Garni: A French term referring to a bundle of herbs either tied together with string or twine or wrapped in cheesecloth to aid in removal after infusing stocks or sauces. The herbs and spices, fresh or dried, can vary with the dish.

Brocciu: A traditional Corsican fresh cheese made from the whey of ewe or goat's milk. The cheese is used in local specialties, both sweet and savory.

Brown Bean Paste or Sauce: A Chinese bottled sauce made from fermented yellow soybeans. It should always be cooked before using. *Min sze jeung* (or "regular" bean sauce) contains some whole beans, and is preferred. It is a thick, salty, aromatic paste used to flavor and color dishes. A blend of equal parts of light and dark miso makes an acceptable substitute.

Buckwheat Groats: *See Kasha*.

Buffalo Mozzarella: A fresh, soft Italian cheese, *mozzarella di bufala*, traditionally made from the milk of water buffalo. It is sold packed in water or whey. Buffalo mozzarella is eaten fresh, with tomatoes and basil, for example, or used as a melting cheese.

Bulgur: Bulgur is whole-wheat kernels that have been steamed, dried, and crushed. It can be purchased in three size-related grades. Fine bulgur is usually not cooked—it is soaked to soften and is used in salads. Fine bulgur can also be used for some *kibbeh* recipes.

Cane Vinegar: A white vinegar made from sugarcane juice, with a slight taste of molasses. This type of vinegar is popular in the Caribbean and in India. A substitute may be made by adding a bit of molasses or brown sugar to distilled white vinegar.

Cannellini Bean: A bean of the genus *Phaseolus vulgaris* used extensively in Italian cuisine. The cannellini bean is medium to large in size and white, with a subtle, nutty taste and a smooth texture when properly prepared. Cannellinis can be purchased canned or dried. A reasonable substitute, though slightly smaller, is the Great Northern bean.

Cardamom Pods: These green (or white, if bleached) pods containing sticky brownish black seeds are the third most expensive spice (after saffron and vanilla). The seeds within the pod should be lightly toasted before use to provide best flavor. The pods are the dry fruit of *Elettaria cardamomium*, a member of the ginger family. India is the world's largest producer of cardamom.

Caul Fat: Caul, caul fat, or net fat is the lacy, fatty membrane that surrounds the intestines of pigs and cattle. It is normally sold refrigerated or frozen in specialty butcher shops or in Chinese markets. It should be soaked in salted, room temperature water for 15 minutes before unfolding and stretching. It is primarily used as a lining for pâtés and terrines, as a wrapper for sausages, to hold the shape of stuffed meats, or as a larding agent for lean meats that are to be roasted or grilled.

Celeriac: The enlarged, tuberous stem base of *Apium graveolens* var. *rapaceum*. Also called celery root, celeriac, while similar in taste to celery, has a more subtle, refined flavor, which is greatly favored in Europe. The turnip-like body is peeled before use and can be used like other roots in stocks and stews. It is excellent grated into salads and fried as chips.

Cellophane Noodles: *See* Bean Thread Noodles.

Cèpe: Cèpe, in French, or porcini in Italian, this bolete mushroom is highly prized and can be purchased fresh, in season, sometimes frozen, or dried. Cèpes have a rich, meaty flavor, which improves greatly with cooking, and a pleasing texture. They occur primarily in the Northern Hemisphere and often grow symbiotically near the roots of chestnut trees.

Chapati Flour: A finely milled whole-wheat flour known in India as *atta*. It is used in making *chapati*, unleavened, circular flat breads. *Chapati* flour is available in Indian and Pakistani markets, but a one-to-one mixture of whole-wheat flour and cake flour can be substituted.

Chayote: A pear-shaped green squash with one soft seed. The chayote called *mirliton* in New Orleans and *christophine* in France and the French Caribbean. It is produced by the perennial *Sechium edule* and has a mild, delicate flavor and crisp, firm flesh. Chayote is often stuffed and baked, but it can be cooked like any other squash or eaten raw. The shoots, leaves, and tuberous roots are edible as well.

Chicharrón: Pieces of pork skin that have been fried twice to make them crisp and puffy. They are eaten out of hand as a snack and used in fillings for tacos, tamales, and burritos in many Latin American countries.

Chile de Árbol: Literally named "of the tree" or "tree-like" from its lush growth and woody stems, this dried chile is small, pointed, and medium red in color. With searing heat similar to cayenne, this chile is most often used ground for making sauces.

Chile Oil: This piquant, red oil is made by infusing vegetable, peanut, or sesame oil or a combination with red chiles. The spiciness of the oil will fade with time. It can be made fresh. To 1 cup [240 mL] of hot oil (not smoking) add about 30 small, crushed, dry red chiles, and 3 or 4 tablespoons [45 or 60 mL] of red chile flakes or 1 tablespoon, of cayenne. Stir well, cover, and allow to steep until cool before straining.

Chinese Black Mushroom: Cultivated in China for at least two thousand years, the *Lentinus edodes* mushroom is used extensively in China and Korea. It is called *shiitake* in Japanese and as such is available, fresh and dried, in the United States. There are two grades: the better grade, known as flower mushroom, has thick caps and a velvety texture; the other grade, called fragrant mushroom, is thin, flat, and dark in color. The tough stems are removed before using. Dried mushrooms are reconstituted in warm stock or water.

Chinese Leek: *See* Garlic Chive.

Chinese Sausage: A sausage usually about 6 inches [15 cm] long, preserved by drying. The flavor should be sweet and full bodied, with no chemical aftertaste, the texture dense. Generally sold in pairs attached by a string, these sausages are usually made of pork (the type called for in most recipes) but beef or duck liver sausages are also available.

Chipotle Chile: A mature red jalapeño that has been smoked and dried over a wood fire, with additional smoke provided by the leaves and stalks of the pepper plant. This chile is quite spicy and smoky in flavor. It is used primarily in stews, soups, and salsas. Chipotles are available dried or canned (packed in adobo sauce).

Choricero Pepper: A dried sweet red pepper grown only in the Basque region of Spain, used locally to make the famous *vizcaína* sauce, and in the Bordeaux region of France. The pepper is also used in flavoring and coloring *chorizo* sausages of that region.

Chorizo Sausage: The Spanish sausage *chorizo* (*chouriço* in Portuguese) is a hard, cured sausage made from chopped or minced pork, blended with some fat, seasonings, and sweet and/or hot paprika or red pepper pulp. It has a reddish color and can be eaten cold or cooked. Spanish *chorizo* is available at fine sausage suppliers and European-style delis. Mexican *chorizo* sausage has a much finer grind of meat, is more heavily spiced with chiles and cumin, and is uncooked. The casings are often discarded and only the filling is used. South American recipes generally call for the Spanish or Portuguese style of *chorizo*.

Chusip: A traditional Tibetan cheese made from yak's milk, yogurt, and sugar. After separating the curds from the whey, the curds are formed into balls and then air dried. Sheep's milk feta cheese is a good a substitute.

Cilantro: The green foliage, stems, and roots of the coriander plant. Cilantro is also known as Chinese or Arab parsley and is sold fresh in bunches. Cilantro grows best in cooler weather, although it is used primarily in the tropics and subtropics. It has a distinctive strong taste and smell.

Coconut Milk: The juice extracted from the flesh of the fruit of the coconut palm (*Cocos nucifera*). The first extraction produces a thicker "coconut cream," while the second produces "coconut water." When the two are combined, the mixture is called "coconut milk." It is used across Southern Asia, Africa, and Brazil. It is most often purchased canned but can easily be made fresh.

Comino: The dried seeds of *Cuminum cyminum*, or the Spanish name for ground cumin seeds, widely used as a spice and flavoring in Latin America, Portugal, and Spain.

Corn husk: The dried outer husk of ears of corn, used in Latin American cuisines as a wrapper for tamales or other foods. The dried husks are soaked in warm water to rehydrate before using. Fresh green corn husks can be substituted but are somewhat more difficult to work with. Sheets of aluminum foil or banana leaves are also acceptable substitutes.

Cornichon: A small, tart gherkin pickle, available bottled (often combined with pearl onions and tarragon sprigs), canned, and in bulk at some delis and markets.

Court Bouillon: A broth, often containing wine or other acidic components, spices, and aromatics used almost exclusively in poaching fish and seafood.

Couscous: A pelletized form of semolina-flour pasta commonly served in North Africa and the Middle East as a side dish. The grains are rinsed and placed in the upper portion of a cooking dish called a *couscousière*. The lower portion of the dish contains a stew or flavoring broth, allowing the aromatic vapors of the stew or broth to pass through and flavor the couscous. The cooked couscous is often eaten with the stew that flavored it while cooking. Instant forms of couscous are available.

Cream of Rice: Granulated, partially cooked rice. It can be cooked as a breakfast cereal, used in doughs and batters, or used as a coating for frying.

Crème Fraîche: An essential ingredient in the French kitchen, crème fraîche is a lightly fermented, thickened cream with a butterfat content of roughly 30 percent. It enriches and thickens sauces to which it is added. It does not curdle when heated.

Crimini Mushroom: A dark brown version of the cultivated *Agaricus bisporus* (button) mushroom. Its flavor is more intense than the common button mushroom. When allowed to mature, it becomes a portobello mushroom, strictly a marketing name.

Cubanelle Chile: A form of *Capsicum annuum* having a bright yellow-green chile with a rather thin skin and thick, sweet flesh and very little spiciness. The shape is long and almost cylindrical. This chile is used in Latin American, Caribbean, and Mediterranean dishes; it is popular as a frying chile since it does not require peeling.

Curry Leaf: A shiny green leaf from a small tropical tree, *Murraya koenigii* or orange rue, used to flavor curries in India and Southeast Asia. The leaves are 1½ to 2 inches [4 to 5 cm] long, glossy, and dark green, with an intense aroma. First bruised to release their flavor, curry leaves are added to frying oil or directly to curries and stews. While the leaves can be purchased fresh, frozen, or dried at Indian and Pakistani groceries, fresh leaves are essential for authentic flavor.

Daikon Radish: A white radish popular in Japan, China, Korea, and Southeast Asia. Daikons can vary widely in shape and form. The taste is sharp yet sweet, and texture can vary from crisp to meltingly tender. Daikon can be eaten raw, stewed, pickled, or fried. When soaked in salted water the radish becomes pliable and can be cut into a variety of shapes as garnish.

Dark Soy Sauce: A soy sauce that has been aged slightly longer than usual to intensify the flavor and saltiness. Normally a small amount of molasses is added to dark soy to balance the flavor and deepen the color.

Dashi Stock: The basic stock of Japanese cuisine (*katsuo dashi*). It is a clear broth flavored with dried bonito shavings and a type of seaweed known as *konbu*. *Dashi-no-moto* (instant dashi mix) and *hon-dashi* (instant dashi granules) are available for making the stock, although both often include MSG. To make the stock from scratch add 1 tablespoon [15 mL] of bonito shavings and a 1 × 2-inch [2.5 × 5-cm] piece of *konbu* to 1 cup [240 mL] of boiling water. Allow the mixture to steep for 5 minutes, then strain.

Daun Salam: *See* Salam Leaf.

Demi-Glace: A highly reduced brown stock made from roasted beef, veal, and/or pork bones. The roasting pan is deglazed with brandy, Marsala, or red wine, then water is added and the sauce is simmered with spices and aromatic vegetables. The stock is successively reduced in smaller and smaller pans until a highly concentrated, gelatinous product is obtained. It is used as an addition to classic, European-style brown sauces, soups, and stews. *Glace de viande* is a similar product made from veal bones and is interchangeable with demi-glace.

Dendê Oil: A bright orange oil, high in saturated fats, extracted from the kernels of the oil palm, (*Elais guineensis*) favored as a cooking and flavoring oil in West Africa and Brazil, particularly in the region of Bahia. It is available in African and Latin American markets.

Dijon Mustard: A French mustard from the region of Dijon, popularized by Maurice Grey (inventor of the steam-driven mustard press), founder of Grey Poupon. Dijon-style mustard is a strong, pale yellow mustard with a fine texture. It is made from mustard seeds with hulls left on, flavored with white wine and vinegar.

Dried Kelp: There are many types of dried kelp or seaweed (also called sea vegetable or laver). They are widely used in Asian cooking, especially in Japan and Korea. *Konbu* is the kelp used to make Japanese dashi stock. *Wakame* is used in miso soup and *nori* is the wrapper of sushi roll fame. Kelp is used for flavoring, texture and the nutrients it contains. Kelp can be purchased, packaged dried, in most Asian markets.

Dried Limes: Dried whole limes (*loomi*) are used in stews in Southwest Asia, the Near East, and the Middle East (especially in the Gulf States). Dried limes have a musty, sour flavor and can be broken into pieces and then removed before service, or ground to a powder and left in the dish. Darker ones have been dried for longer periods and are used in dark-colored stews. Dried limes are commonly available in Middle Eastern and Asian markets.

Dried Shrimp: Used worldwide as a flavoring and textural element, dried shrimp can be simmered or soaked with stock (or sherry) to extract the flavor, or ground (usually after briefly toasting in a dry skillet) before adding to a dish. They are sold in small packets in Latin American, African, and Asian markets. A pale color indicates that the shrimp are old and undesirable.

Dried Shrimp Paste: Also known as *blacan* in Malaysia, *trassi* in Indonesia, and *kapi* in Thailand, this cake-like round of molded, dried puréed tiny shrimp, mixed with salt as a preservative. The shrimp go through varying degrees of fermentation while drying in the sun, and the final product can be quite strong smelling and salty. When used in moderation dried shrimp paste adds richness and body to a dish.

Dried Sour Cherry: The pitted and dried sour cherry is (and has been for centuries) a popular ingredient in the cuisines of the Eastern Mediterranean, Southwestern Asia, Eastern Europe, and the Near East. The cherries are commonly added to savory stews, combined with meats, and used in the preparation of sweets, liqueurs, and vinegars.

Emma: The name used in Tibet for Sichuan peppercorns (*sansho* in Japanese). They are the seeds of *Xanthoxylum piperitum*, a member of the prickly ash family, and have a peppery, numbing effect on the mouth. They were the source of spicy heat in Tibetan cuisine prior to the arrival of the chile pepper.

Emmentaler: A cheese originally produced in the Emme Valley of Switzerland, near Bern. It is the stereotypical Swiss cheese, slightly salty, with a nutty flavor and a firm texture. The holes (called "eyes") are olive shaped and can be as large as a walnut, but cherry-size holes are most common. Many copies are made worldwide, generically called "Swiss cheese." Jarlsberg cheese from Norway is an acceptable substitute.

Enoki Mushroom: A Japanese mushroom (*Flammulina velutipes*) named after its habit of growing in symbiosis with the stumps of the enoki tree (Chinese hackberry). The mushroom grows in clumps of slender 5-inch-tall stems topped with tiny caps. Both stem and cap are almost pure white when cultivated. They have a crisp texture and a mild aroma and flavor.

Epazote: An herb (*Chenopodium ambrosioides*) used in Mexico (particularly southern Mexico and the Yucatán), the Caribbean, and Central America in stews, soups, and especially beans; considered to be a carminative. The taste for epazote is said to be an acquired one among nonnatives. It is available dried year-round in Latin American markets and occasionally fresh.

Fariñha de Mandioca: Obtained from the processed tubers of the bitter cassava or manioc, this flour or manioc meal is made by first grinding and heating the manioc with water to extract the poisonous prussic acid before the meal is dried and ground into flour. Further processed into pellets manioc becomes tapioca. When toasted, the flour is called *farofa* and is used in Brazil as a table condiment to sprinkle over foods or like dry breadcrumbs in cooking.

Fermented Black Beans: The Chinese fermented black bean is a small soybean. The beans are cooked, salted, and fermented. They come in plastic bags in a semidried state and should always be rinsed thoroughly in water before use in braises or stir-fries. Black bean paste, often with garlic, is available canned or bottled; it can be used as is.

Fiddlehead Fern: The tightly wound shoot of new leaves of many fern species around the world, named for its resemblance to the scroll head of a violin. Fiddlehead ferns are usually blanched to remove bitterness before cooking. The flavor is reminiscent of a blend of broccoli, asparagus, and artichoke. They are available in specialty markets when in season.

Filo Pastry: *See* Phyllo Pastry.

Fish Sauce: A clear brown liquid, it is quite salty and strong by itself but gives a subtle richness and depth and greatly enhanced flavor when added to a dish. Vietnamese fish sauce (*nuoc mam*) takes the place of salt or soy sauce on the table. With Vietnamese brands look for the words *nhi* (signifying the highest quality) and *cá com* (meaning that only anchovies were used in its manufacture). It is also used when making *nuoc cham*, a dipping sauce or dressing for the Vietnamese table. Thai fish sauce (*nam pla*) tends to be slightly milder than the fish sauce of Vietnam or South Asia. Before fish sauce was introduced to Thailand, fermented fish were used for the same purpose. Thai and Vietnamese fish sauces can be purchased in Asian markets. See *patis* for Filipino fish sauce.

Five-Spice Powder: A highly aromatic Chinese seasoning blend made from grinding star anise, fennel seeds, Sichuan peppercorns, cloves, and cinnamon into a powder. It is used sparingly in the cooking of China as well as in many of the surrounding regions.

Foie Gras: Literally translated from the French as "fat liver," foie gras is the liver of a duck or goose that has been methodically force-fed. This overfeeding causes the liver to greatly expand and become very fatty, with a mild flavor. The finest foie gras is produced in Strasbourg, Alsace, and in southwestern France. (New York State produces an excellent foie gras.) Highest quality foie gras will hold its shape when seared. The best canned product is designated "Foie Gras Naturel en Bloc."

Furikake: A Japanese seasoning blend, sold in shaker bottles, containing small particles of nori seaweed, black and white sesame seeds, bonito flakes, and occasionally sansho powder. It adds an "ocean-like" accent to dishes when used as a garnish.

Galangal: Tuberous roots of the *Alpina galangal* plant, a member of the ginger, family. The flavor of galangal is a pungent combination of ginger and pepper with medicinal overtones. Slices of the smooth-skinned root are sold fresh or frozen as well as dried and in powdered form (called *laos*). Fresh is best, followed by frozen. Galangal is used in Southeast and Southwest Asian cooking, primarily to flavor soups, stews, and curries.

Garam Masala: An Indian spice mixture. There are as many different versions as there are cooks, as the combination of spices used depends on the type of dish, the region it is being cooked in, and the personal preferences of the cook. *Garam masala* is the best known of all of the *masalas* and is prominent in the cuisine of northern India. Typical ingredients might include cinnamon, cloves, cumin, coriander, pepper, fennel, and occasionally rose petals, and the proportions of spices can vary as well. *Garam masala* is usually toasted first (the whole spices), then ground and added to the dish at the end of the cooking process.

Garlic Chive: Also known as Chinese leek and Chinese chive, the leaf blades and flower stalks of this plant are wider and flatter than a conventional chive and have a strong taste reminiscent of garlic and leeks. Garlic chives are used raw and are usually cooked in stir-fries, in pancakes, and in dumpling fillings. Garlic chives are sold in fresh bunches in Asian markets.

Ghee: Clarified butter used in India, Southwestern Asia, and in some provinces of Burma as a cooking oil and flavoring agent. (Since it has been simmered for a period of time, it acquires a nutty flavor.) *Ghee* can be heated to a much higher temperature than whole butter when sautéing and can be stored at room temperature. It can be purchased or easily made at home.

Ginko Nut: The pit from the center of the fruit of the ginkgo tree, *Ginkgo biloba*, used primarily in Japan and China. Once peeled and blanched, the pits are pale green in color, with a meaty texture and nutty flavor. They are added to soups and custards and are skewered on pine needles and fried (or simply fried and eaten out of hand). They are available fresh in the autumn in Asia and can be found canned worldwide.

Gjetöst Cheese: A cheese from Norway made by cooking the whey from cow or goat's milk with caramelized sugar to color it dark golden brown and give it a slightly sweet taste.

Glace de Viande: A very reduced, gelatinous brown stock product made from veal bones. *See also* Demi-Glace.

Glutinous Rice: A short-grain rice with a very high starch content and sticky consistency when cooked, also called "sweet rice" or "sticky rice." It is often used for dessert rice dishes. Generally it is rinsed, soaked for long periods of time, and then rinsed again before steaming.

Glutinous Rice Flour: Glutinous rice that has been ground very fine to make a flour. It is used primarily for dough wrappers, pastries, and desserts in Asian cooking. Glutinous rice flour is also excellent for use in Western-style desserts that will be frozen, since it will not separate when thawed as cornstarch-thickened products often do.

Gorgonzola Dolce: A young Gorgonzola cheese from Lombardy, Italy, with a flavor that is sublime and mild. Also called sweet gorgonzola.

Green Curry Paste: A very spicy Thai seasoning paste (*krung gaeng kiao wan, kaeng keow wann*) made from fresh green chiles, Thai lime leaves or pepper leaves, cilantro, lemongrass, galangal, shallots, garlic, shrimp paste, and spices, used in making curries, soups, and stews. It can be purchased in cans but is superior when made fresh.

Green Lip Mussel: Bivalve shellfish named for the shell, which graduates from tan at one end to bright green at the tip. These mussels, imported from New Zealand, are quite large compared to common mussels. Green lip mussels can be purchased fresh or frozen in the shell.

Green Mango: The unripe fruit of a mango tree (*Mangifera indica*) native to India. Green mangoes are used extensively for making savory chutneys, pickles, and relishes in India and in parts of Southeast Asia. In the Philippines they are a favorite between-meal snack, eaten with salt or soy sauce. They are interchangeable with green papaya in Southeast Asian salads.

Green Papaya: The unripe fruit of a papaya tree (*Carica papaya*) native to eastern Central America. The fruit used as green papaya are the larger "Mexican" papayas rather than the smaller, sweeter Hawaiian papayas. They are grated or thinly sliced in salads and soups in Thailand and Southeast Asia. The flesh and the seeds of green papaya, rich in the enzyme papain, are also used as a meat tenderizer.

Green Peppercorn: The unripe and undried fruit of the pepper tree (*Piper nigrum*) of India. Green peppercorns are usually sold pickled in brine or vinegar or freeze dried. The flavor is milder and fruitier than black peppercorns, with less spiciness. Pickled green peppercorns should always be rinsed before use and discarded if they turn dark, as they have oxidized. Freeze-dried versions can be added directly to dishes without reconstitution.

Green Tomatoes: The unripe fruit of the common tomato (*Lycopersicon lycopersicum*), native to South America. Green tomatoes are made into pickles and relishes (piccalilli and chow chow), used in curries in Southeast Asia, made into pies and stews in the American West, and turned into fried green tomatoes, a favorite in the American South. Many uses for green tomatoes were developed as a means for using unripe fruit forced to be harvested before a freeze.

Gruyère Cheese: The best known of the Swiss cheeses, having smaller holes, a sharper flavor, and more butterfat than Emmentaler. It is one of the finest cooking cheeses of Europe.

Guajillo Chile: Also known as *chile travieso*, the Guajillo is a dried Mexican chile used primarily for salsas, cooked chile sauces, soups, and stews. It is especially popular combined with rabbit. The chile is dark brownish-red with a glossy, tough skin. Guajillos are usually 4 to 6 inches [10 to 15 cm] long, with a tapering point. Since the skin is tougher than those of other chiles, the Guajillo requires more soaking.

Güero Chile: Güero is Spanish for blonde or light-skinned and the term refers to any fresh yellow chile in Mexico. The heat can range from very mild to very hot. Güero chiles are used primarily in making yellow mole sauces but are also used in other sauces and in salads and are pickled.

Gyoza Dumpling Wrapper: Depending on the market or the shipper involved, these dumpling skins may be labeled as "gyoza wrappers" (Japanese) or "potsticker wrappers" (Chinese). The thicker wrappers will yield about 30 sheets per package, while the thinner ones up to 50. Wonton wrappers may be substituted, but they are thicker and less pliable.

Habanero Chile: Habanero means "from Havana" in Spanish and this fiery hot chile (possibly the world's hottest) is popular in the Caribbean and, increasingly, much of Latin America and the United States for use in salsas, marinades, chutneys, and stews. Roughly lantern shaped, a habanero chile can be yellow, orange, or red when ripe. The Scotch bonnet chile and Jamaican red chile are considered identical to the habanero, with a taste that is searing hot and a surprisingly fruity overtone.

Harissa: A fiery hot sauce, seasoning paste, and table condiment used throughout North Africa. *Harissa* is made from red chiles that are soaked and pounded with coriander, caraway, garlic, and salt, then moistened with olive oil. Moroccan versions tend to omit the caraway. Other spices such as cumin, chiles, and lemon may be added. Indonesian *sambal oelek* sauce makes a reasonable substitute.

Harusame Noodles: *See* Bean Thread Noodles.

Heart of Palm: The tender interior of the cabbage palm, pure white in color, with a silky texture and a taste suggestive of artichokes. Available fresh only in the tropics, and available canned worldwide.

Hijiki: A Japanese seaweed, or sea vegetable, sold in its dried form. Dried *hijiki* comes in small, thin, black, brittle strands, about ½ inch [1 cm] long. It needs to be rinsed, then soaked in warm water or *dashi* stock for 20 minutes to soften. After a final rinse it is often used in salads and as a textural and colorful foil to tofu. The flavor is faintly suggestive of anise and the sea.

Hoisin Sauce: Hoisin (the name in Chinese means sea freshness sauce) is a dark reddish-brown, thick Chinese sauce made from soybeans, red rice, flour, chile, garlic, sugar, and vinegar. The flavor is sweet, faintly garlicky, and pungent. It comes in bottles or cans and is used in marinades and sauces, as well as a table sauce. It is often thinned with rice wine or sesame oil for a dipping sauce.

Holy Basil: The leaves, stems, and seeds of *Ocimum sanctum*, a variety of basil used all across Southeast Asia and India. Native to India, it is considered sacred through its association with the Hindu god Vishnu. Holy basil has a subtle, clove-like scent. In Thailand (known there as *gapao*) it is used mostly with seafood. It is available fresh in Asian markets and some organic produce markets.

Horseradish Root: The cylindrical, tuberous root of the plant *Armoracia rusticana*, with a creamy white flesh. For the best flavor grate the root and add just before serving. Piquancy fades with cooking; therefore it is used in cold sauces for best flavor. Bottled horseradish is available but cannot compare to freshly grated.

Hubbard-Type Squash: The species *Cucurbita maxima* are considered winter squashes, suitable for long storage. Hubbards can be very large or relatively small and most have a bluish-gray skin and sweet orange flesh. Pumpkin makes an acceptable substitute.

Idiazábal Cheese: A Basque ewe's milk cheese that is lightly smoked. Idiazábal has a light, buttery, and nutty flavor with a hard, dark brown rind. As it ages it becomes quite sharp and dry. A young Spanish manchego cheese makes an acceptable substitute.

Injera: The staple bread of Ethiopia, which can be made from many different grains, t'eff being the most authentic. the batter is leavened with yeast or buttermilk, spread on a large flat surface, and baked. Being spongy and flexible, *injera* becomes the plate and eating utensil for the dishes that it accompanies.

Jalapeño Chile: Named after the Mexican town of Jalapa in the state of Veracruz, the jalapeño is one of the most recognizable of chiles, with a dark green skin and thick flesh. The characteristic shape is roughly 2 to 3 [5 to 8 cm] inches long by 1 inch [2.5 cm] in diameter. It is very hot (although piquancy varies with growing conditions). It is used fresh in salsas, pickled, roasted, and smoke-dried (called chipotle when prepared in this manner).

Jasmine Rice: High-quality long-grain rice with a decidedly floral aroma when cooked. It is the preferred rice of Thailand. Cooked grains are tender, fluffy, and moist. Basmati rice makes an acceptable substitute.

Jicama: A tuber of the Latin American vine (*Pachyrizus erosus*) with light brown skin and a pure white to ivory interior. The flesh is crisp and mildly sweet, with a neutral flavor. It is eaten fresh or cooked and can be used as a substitute for freshwater chestnuts.

Juniper Berry: The seed of the juniper bush (*Juniperous communis*) used in cooking, especially in Europe. Juniper berries are aromatic and green, ripening to dark purple. The berries are used fresh and can be purchased dried. Juniper berries are used to flavor meats (especially game), pâtés, and marinades.

Kabocha Squash: Kabocha is a generic name for a group of Japanese squashes that have a flattened drum-like or turban-like shape. The hard, inedible skin is often striped. The flesh is light orange and very sweet. Hubbard squash or pumpkin makes a good substitute.

Kasha: *Kasha* is the Russian name for a porridge made with buckwheat groats (whole-grain buckwheat). Buckwheat groats are the seeds of an Eastern European member of the rhubarb family *Fagopyrum esculentum*.

Kasseri Cheese: A firm ewe's milk cheese (occasionally made with goat's milk) from Greece. Kasseri has a golden color, sharp buttery flavor, and semifirm texture. Aged provolone makes a reasonable substitute.

Kecap Manis: A sweet, syrupy, very dark Indonesian soy sauce flavored with palm sugar, star anise, coriander, and other spices. It comes bottled and is sold in Asian groceries. An acceptable substitute can be made with 1 cup [240 mL] regular soy sauce, ⅓ cup [80 mL] molasses, 3 tablespoons [45 mL] dark brown sugar, 1¼ teaspoon [6 mm] coriander, ¼ teaspoon [1 mL] cayenne, and a pinch of toasted, ground star anise. Heat the mixture until the sugars dissolve.

Kerisik: A Sumatran component of thick stews that is usually added at the last minute for texture and extra flavor. To make *kerisik*, fresh coconut meat is slow-roasted until browned, then stir-fried in a dry wok while constantly being stirred. After cooling, the roasted pulp is finely ground.

Kimchee: *Kimchee* is a Korean specialty, served with every meal, of pickled and fermented cabbage, with other vegetables (and occasionally seafood). The mixture is added to very spicy brine with herbs and spices, then placed into large crocks or barrels and buried or stored throughout the winter to ferment. *Kimchee* is available in jars in various markets, but homemade is superior.

Kochu Chang: A Korean flavoring paste is made from fermented soybeans and ground chiles with salt, rice or jujube flour, dried beef, and soy sauce. It is available at Korean groceries.

Kua Curry Paste: A spicy Thai curry paste made with a large quantity of makroot leaves and a combination of chiles and white peppercorns. If made for seafood dishes, it often has fermented shrimp paste or grilled fish added, and if used with meats or vegetables, peanuts often replace the seafood. Kua curry paste is sold in cans in Asian markets.

Lemongrass: A perennial grass (*Cymbpogon citrates*) used primarily as a flavoring for curries, stews, and soups, and even as a skewer for grilled foods, especially in Asia. The lower portion of the thick stalks is used while the leaves are discarded or used for flavoring stocks. The stalks are tough and are usually sliced very thin, then pounded or ground before being added to curries. In soups lemongrass is usually added as thick slices that have been bruised to release flavor. Dried lemongrass is available but is a poor substitute for fresh stalks.

Limu Ogo: *Limu* means "edible seaweed" in Hawaiian and *Ogo* refers to the species *Graciliaria verrusca*, relatively small purple-brown seaweed that is used primarily in Hawaii in the fresh state. The young tender plants are popular all across Oceania and in Japan they are often used in salads.

Lingonberry: A small wild berry, similar to the cranberry, that is grown in Scandinavia, Russia, Canada, and Maine. Fresh berries are very difficult to locate outside these areas. Cranberries or lingonberry preserves are acceptable substitutes, depending on the application.

Linguiça Sausage: This Portuguese sausage is semidry and heavily flavored with garlic. It is almost always made with pork, with a fairly coarse texture. It is very popular in Portugal, Brazil, and Hawaii and is used in soups, stews, and casseroles and is often grilled.

"Lite" Soy Sauce: The term "lite" soy sauce refers to a type of soy sauce that is distilled to concentrate the flavor and reduce the salt content. It is a relatively modern term as the process is fairly new. The term "lite" has been adopted by Asian manufacturers.

Long Bean: The fruit of *Vigna unguiculata* ssp. *sesquipedalis* is also known as a yard-long bean or an asparagus bean and can grow up to 30 inches in length. The beans are more dense and chewier than typical green beans; the flavor is that of a nutty green bean with a mild asparagus aftertaste. Long beans are found fresh in Asian and Caribbean markets.

Mahi Mahi: A type of dolphin fish (*Coryphaena hippurus*), mahi mahi is found in tropical and semitropical waters worldwide. It should not be confused with the marine mammal dolphin or porpoise. Normally it is sold as frozen fillets. A dark vein and line of bones running down the center of the fillet should be removed before cooking, and the fillets are normally skinned.

Makroot: This thick, glossy, and dark green citrus leaf (*Citrus hystrix*) is used all across Southeast Asia and Indonesia as a flavoring ingredient in curries, soups, and stews. The flavor of the leaf is earthy, with a heady citrus perfume. The rind and juice of the fruit can be used interchangeably with the leaf, but the juice is extremely bitter. Makroot is available dried and powdered, but fresh and frozen leaves have the best flavor. Although sometimes called *kaffir* lime leaves, note that in South Africa the word *kaffir* is a racial slur and is considered an unacceptable term by some. The term Thai lime leaf should be used instead. Bay leaves are *not* a good substitute.

Malagueta Chile: The malagueta chile was brought to Africa from the New World by the Portuguese, then reintroduced to Brazil by the African slaves brought to work the sugarcane fields. The chile is small and medium green (ripening to red) with an aromatic and searingly hot flavor. Malagueta chiles are most often found bottled and packed in vinegar or, occasionally, in cane sugar rum, *cachaça*. They are indispensable in the cuisine of the Bahian region of Brazil.

Malt Vinegar: A type of golden vinegar popular in Britain, made from un-hopped beer. It is slightly bitter in taste and is normally used in pickling and on fish and chips. Bottles are widely available.

Manchego Cheese: A Spanish cheese made from ewe's milk, named for the dry plains of La Mancha. The color is a creamy whitish-yellow, with a full, buttery flavor. It is sold fresh (*fresco*), aged up to three months (*curado*), or aged longer (*viejo*)—the flavor intensifies with age. It is used grated in dishes or eaten sliced.

Mandarin Pancake: An English term for a very thin wheat flour pancake, similar to a crêpe used in several northern Chinese dishes and as wrappers for salads. *Mu shu* dishes use the pancake as the wrapper for fillings. The pancakes are sold in packages in the freezer section of Asian markets. Filipino *lumpia* wrappers or Vietnamese rice paper skins can be used in an emergency.

Masa Harina: Special corn flour that is used for making corn tortillas and tamales and as a thickener for stews and soups. It can be purchased in most supermarkets and in Latin American markets.

Mastic: The resinous sap exuded from wounds on the stems of plants of the *Pistacia* genus, particularly *P. lentiscus*. It is fruity and aromatic resin used in the Middle East, North Africa, and the Near East as chewing gum and in stews, soups, breads, drinks, and desserts. Mastic resembles clear or amber-colored crystals. It should be pulverized before use. There is no substitute.

Matsutake Mushroom: Matsutake (*Tricholoma matsukake*) literally translates as "pine mushroom" in Japanese, in reference to its habit of growing in red pine forests. The mushrooms are dark brown in color, with a meaty texture and stem, and a musky, pine scent. They are sliced thick and briefly cooked. Canned matsutake mushrooms are available (but inferior to fresh). Fresh matsutake mushrooms are generally found in autumn.

Medjool Date: The fruit of the *Phoenix dactylifera* palm tree. The medjool date is popular all over the world, especially in the Middle East, North Africa, and the Near East. Medjool dates are unusually large, deep red in color, and nonfibrous with thick flesh and an astounding, sweet flavor. They are considered the king of dates and are available in Middle Eastern and health food markets.

Mexican Chocolate: A rich, sweetened cooking chocolate flavored with cinnamon, vanilla, and sometimes almonds. The texture is grainy and extremely dense. It comes in flat cakes or cylinders from suppliers in Mexico, principally the brand name Ibarra. It is not an eating chocolate. It is used in mole poblano sauce, as well as in desserts and sweetened drinks.

Mirasol Chile: Mirasol literally means "look at the sun," and this chile is so named because the yellowish fruits point upward from the plant. It is the fresh form of the dried Guajillo chile. The mirasol is mistakenly called cascabel, which means "rattle" in Spanish, because the seeds rattle when dried like those of the real cascabel chile. The aji mirasol is a much hotter Peruvian dried chile with the same erect fruiting habit. Both mirasol and aji mirasol are used extensively in yellow mole sauces and salsas.

Mirin: A sweetened Japanese rice wine–based spirit used for cooking, especially in glazes and marinades. It is available in Asian food markets. Substitute equal parts of sake and sugar, heated together.

Miso: Miso is a soy bean paste that has been salted and allowed to ferment over an extended period of time. Brown or red miso (*akamiso* in Japanese, *misu* in Vietnamese) is made with the addition of barley and can be quite strong and salty. Sendai, Japan, is the region where the best red miso, referred to as Sendai miso, is made. It is used sparingly in soups, stews, pickles, and for basting or glazing when grilling. It needs to be tempered by whisking in warm stock or dashi until smooth. Brown or red miso is used primarily in Japan, Korea, China, Vietnam, and Indonesia.

Morel Mushroom: The highly prized fruiting bodies of eight species of the *Morchella* genus of fungi, having a distinctive upright honeycomb cap. Color ranges from whitish to yellowish-orange to dark brown. Because morels contain small amounts of (toxic) helvellic acid, they should never be eaten raw. Morels appear fresh in the spring or can be purchased dried year-round.

Mulato Chile: A dried Mexican chile similar in size, shape, and appearance to the ancho but decidedly brownish, with a smoother and tougher skin. The taste is fruitier and sweeter than the ancho and is used in making mole sauce and sauces for enchiladas.

Mung Bean: The seed of the legume *Vigna radiata*, popular in China as a source for bean sprouts and starch, which is made into bean thread or cellophane noodles. Mung beans are also used in India as a *pulse*. They are commonly available dried at health food markets.

Mushroom Soy Sauce: A Chinese dark soy sauce flavored with mushrooms during the final stages of processing. The flavor is rich and smooth. Mushroom soy sauce can be used interchangeably with other dark soy sauces and can be used in recipes calling for dark soy sauce.

Musk Lime: The fruit of *Citrofortunella mitis*, a hybrid of the Mandarin orange and kumquat, popular in the Philippines, where the bitter juice is used extensively in cooking. Musk limes are occasionally available at specialty markets; the juice can sometimes be found frozen. The preserved peel is found bottled in Asian groceries that cater to Filipinos.

Mustard Oil: An extract of the black seeds of *Brassica juncea* and *B. rapa*, producing an oil with a high smoking point and a slight nutty, mustard flavor. The color is slightly yellowish. It is used in India as cooking oil and as an ingredient in pickling. It can be found bottled in Indian and Pakistani markets. It should be stored refrigerated, as it turns rancid easily.

Naan Bread: A flat bread found across Southwestern Asia and the Indian Subcontinent. *Nan* is Persian for bread. The bread may be topped with sesame or nigella seeds and flavored with different spices and/or onions. *Naan* is available fresh and frozen in packages at Indian and Pakistani markets.

Nam Pla: *See* Fish Sauce.

Nigella Seeds: Also called black cumin (although not a true cumin), *kalongi, kalonji,* or *habba sauda,* these are the seeds of *Nigella sativa* used in the Middle East, India, and Southwestern Asia for flavoring bread, vinegar, and cooking oil and in making pickles. Nigella seeds are small, black, and pungent, with a slight onion fragrance. They can be purchased at Middle Eastern and Indian markets in packages.

Nori: A type of seaweed from the *Porphyra* genus used extensively in Japan and to a lesser degree in the British Isles. In Japan it is used in sushi making as wrappers for *nori*-wrapped sushi rolls (*norimaki*). The sheets are often briefly toasted before use to release the flavor and to darken the green color. *Nori* is sold in Japanese and Asian markets.

Nuoc Leo Sauce: This Vietnamese sauce is made from peanut butter and peanuts, pork liver and pork, garlic, tomatoes, Vietnamese soy sauce, sugar, sesame seeds, and chiles. It is used primarily with barbecued meats and is available bottled in Vietnamese and Asian markets.

Nuoc Mam: *See* Fish Sauce.

Orange Flower Water: A by-product of the distillation of the flowers of the bitter orange to obtain an essential oil (*neroli*) used in perfumes. After the oil is drawn off, the remaining solution is bottled as orange flower water. It has been used across the world for centuries. It can be purchased in many supermarkets or Middle Eastern markets.

Oyster Sauce: A rich, thick flavoring sauce from China (originating in Canton) made from oyster extract, cornstarch, salt, sugar, wheat flour, and caramel. It is sold in bottles in Asian markets and is used as a condiment and a flavoring for stir-fries, especially vegetables.

Palm Sugar: Also called jaggery, palm sugar is an unrefined, dark sugar produced from the sap of several palm trees, especially *Arenga pinnata* and *Borassus flabellifer*. It has a subtle wine-like taste and is used primarily in Southeast Asia and Indonesia. It can be purchased in Asian markets.

Panko Breadcrumbs: Very coarse Japanese breadcrumbs that look like very thin slivers of white bread. They are used for breading fried foods and are available packaged in Japanese and Asian markets.

Pappadam: A dried Indian flat bread that comes in different sizes and is made from *dal* (pea or seed) flour. *Pappadam* can be flavored with chiles, garlic, pepper, and spice mixes. It is usually heated over a flame or fried to puff and become crisp; there are even microwave versions. Packages of *pappadam* are available in Indian and Pakistani markets.

Parsnip: The tapered root of *Pastinaca sativa*, resembling a white carrot with broad top, thrives in very cold climates. Parsnips are enjoyed primarily in Northern Europe (and are under-appreciated in the United States and elsewhere). They provide a subtly sweet and earthy taste to stocks and braises, and are eaten as a side vegetable and made into cakes. Since much of the flavor lies just under the skin, parsnips are normally not peeled, but the tough central core is often discarded.

Pasilla Chile: In Spanish *pasilla* translates as "little raisins." The dried form of the chilaca chile from central Mexico. The pasilla is 5 to 6 inches [13 to 15 cm] long, with a thin raisin-brown skin and a wrinkled surface. The flavor hints of berries and anise, with a smoky quality. It is one of the three chiles used in mole poblano sauce (along with ancho and mulatto) and is excellent in other sauces. It is sold dried in Latin American markets.

Patis: A fish sauce that is a by-product of making *bagoong*, a Filipino fish paste. Unlike Thai or Vietnamese fish sauces, the clear liquid is skimmed from the top.

Pecorino Cheese: Pecorino is the generic name for certain types of cheese made in Italy from ewe's milk. Although they vary in maturity and firmness, the term generally refers to a hard salted sheep's milk cheese from central Italy or Sardinia that is used mostly for grating. Pecorino Romano is the most commonly available example of this style. *Pecorino dolce, pecorino toscano,* and *pecorino siciliano incanestrato* are examples of younger, milder pecorino cheeses that are eaten fresh.

Phyllo Pastry: Phyllo, also spelled filo, is a dough made into extremely thin sheets of pastry. Originating in Turkey, it has been adopted as the most common pastry dough of Greece. It is almost always purchased frozen; care must be taken to ensure that the delicate layers don't dry out while being used (normally they are covered with a damp towel or plastic film when not in use). Phyllo makes an excellent pastry for savory and sweet dishes alike.

Pickled Garlic: Used in Southeast Asia as a condiment and a flavoring agent. Whole heads of garlic are pickled in vinegar with seasonings. The cloves are eaten whole, sliced, or minced. The flavor is sweet and sour, not strongly garlic flavored, and the texture is crunchy. The pickling juice is added to soups and salad dressings. It is available in jars in Asian markets.

Pickled Ginger: A condiment used as garnish for sushi and in other Japanese dishes. Also called *beni-shoga, amazu-shoga,* and *gari,* thin slices of the ginger rhizome (*Zingiber officinale*) are pickled in a sweet and sour rice vinegar solution (often with a small amount of red dye). *Hajikami shoga* (or "blushing ginger") are the pickled shoots (not the rhizomes) of a different type of ginger (*Zingiber mioga*). This form is used primarily with grilled foods. Both types can be purchased bottled in Japanese and Asian markets.

Piment d'Espelette: This type of ground red pepper, similar to paprika, is produced in the town of Espelette in the Basque region of Spain. Small red peppers are allowed to air dry, after which they undergo a secondary drying in wood-fired ovens. They are then finely ground. The flavor is sweet and fruity, with a slightly smoky aroma and mildly spicy taste. Sweet paprika with a pinch of New Mexico red chile can be substituted.

Pine Nut: Also known as *piñon* (in Spain) and *pignolia* (in Italy), the seed of the *piñon* and stone pines (and *Araucaria* pines in the Southern Hemisphere) are the third most expensive nut in the world, as it must be hand harvested. Pine nuts are used extensively in the Middle East, the Mediterranean, and, to a lesser extent, the American Southwest in sauces, soups, and desserts and are also eaten out of hand. They are available at fine markets and health food stores.

Piquillo Pepper: A sweet red pepper produced in the Navarra district (especially near Lodosa) of the Basque region of Spain. The peppers are roasted over beech fires and hand peeled before packing in their own juice. *Piquillo* is the Spanish diminutive form of *pico* (peak) and is an apt description of the broad, 3-inch [8-cm] pointed pepper. The flavor is sweet with a hint of smokiness. Piquillos are available in cans and jars and should be labeled as authentic from the region.

Plantain: A type of starchy banana that is longer and thicker than a regular banana. Plantain is not sweet, and it is always cooked before being eaten. Plantains are used extensively in Africa, southern India, the Caribbean, Latin America, and, to a lesser extent, Southeast Asia.

Poblano Chile: Named for the town of Pueblo in central Mexico, the poblano is the most popular fresh green chile in Mexico, growing 4 to 5 inches [10 to 13 cm] long and 3 inches [8 cm] across, with thick flesh and a dark green skin. Spiciness varies with growing conditions. This chile is always cooked, often roasted, peeled, and stuffed for *chiles rellenos* or cut into strips (*rajas*) for garnishing or adding to dishes. Poblanos are also a frequent ingredient in mole and pipian sauces.

Pomegranate Molasses: Pomegranate molasses is pomegranate juice that is boiled and reduced without added sugar to form a thick syrup, called *dibs rumman* or *rubb al-rumman* in Arabic. In countries where it is used, it is generally homemade, but an excellent bottled product is made in Lebanon. The molasses adds tartness to meat, poultry, pork, game, dressings, and marinades and is diluted with water as a base for a refreshing drink. Pomegranate molasses is used extensively in the Caucasus, the Middle East, and the Eastern Mediterranean.

Pomegranate Seeds: The seed clusters of the sweet pomegranate (*Punica granatum*) used for decoration and garnish. The flavor is found in the juice sac that surrounds the seeds (after extracting the juice the seeds are discarded by the diners). Care must be taken not to puncture the sacs taken from the fruit.

Ponzu Sauce: A Japanese sauce used as a condiment and an accompaniment for some dishes. It is made from bitter citrus (*sudachi* citron in Japan), soy sauce, rice vinegar, mirin, bonito flakes, and konbu kelp. It is sold bottled in Japanese and Asian markets.

Porcini: *See* Cèpe.

Pot Cheese: Pot cheese is a term that applies to several different types of cheese. In the United States pot cheese is generally a very small-curd, dry cottage cheese. In England the term refers to a form of cottage cheese that is molded into small balls to be served fresh. The Greek whey cheese known as *mitzithra* is sometimes referred to as a pot cheese. In the United States pot cheese is often interchangeable with farmer's cheese, which is generally a grainy, dry cottage-cheese-like cheese.

Preserved Lemon: The preserved lemon, essential to the cuisine of North Africa and parts of the Middle East, is made by splitting open whole lemons and layering them with salt in sterilized jars and leaving them to ferment for 30 days in a warm place. A white film forming on the surface need only be rinsed off before use. Preserved lemons can be purchased in Middle Eastern markets.

Prosciutto: An Italian ham cured by salting and aged without smoking. *Prosciutto di Parma* is one of the best known. It is sliced very thin and often eaten as an appetizer, but it is also used in cooking. Import bans have been lifted in the United States and it is generally available.

Queso Blanco: A moist Mexican fresh white cheese made from partly skimmed milk, also called *queso fresco*. The texture can range from soft to firm and crumbly (depending on the amount of aging and the shaping process). The flavor is mild, fresh, and salty. It is commonly available in Latin American markets and in supermarkets near Latino communities.

Quince: An ancient fruit (*Cydonia oblanga*) that is enjoyed in Europe, North Africa, the Eastern Mediterranean, Southwestern Asia, and in Latin America. Quince has a perfume-like aroma. It is not eaten raw as the pulp is dense and bitter. The fruit is usually cooked with sugar or honey and contains substantial amounts of pectin, used as a thickener. Quince is also combined with meats.

Quinoa: Quinoa (*Chenopodium quinoa*), a cereal-like grain (technically a seed) from tough plants that can withstand cold and drought in high altitude, was the staple of the Incas before the introduction of wheat by the Europeans. The leaves of the plant are also eaten. These days quinoa is eaten elsewhere in South America, in North America, Australia, and northern Russia. It can be purchased in health food markets.

Ras el Hanout: A complex spice mixture used in North Africa that can have as many as twenty-seven ingredients, including cumin, coriander, cardamom, nutmeg, cinnamon, cayenne, rose petals, and oregano. It can be purchased in Middle Eastern markets, but most cooks make their own. It should be lightly toasted before using to enhance fragrance.

Red Curry Paste: A Thai curry paste used in stir-fries, curries, soups, and stews. It can be purchased in cans or bottles at Asian markets.

Rice Flour: Flour ground from long-grain rice, used in China for making dumpling dough and rice sticks. In Japan there are three types of rice flour—one made from ground short-grain rice (*joshinko*) and two made from ground glutinous rice (*mochiko* and *shiratamako*). The Chinese long-grain version is the best overall and makes an excellent breading for fried foods. It is can be found in Asian groceries.

Rice Paper: A thin Vietnamese wrapper (*bahn tráng*) made from ground rice, salt, and water that is brushed onto bamboo mats to dry, leaving a pattern on the surface. They are brittle and must be soaked briefly in water to soften before using. Rice papers make a crispy wrapper for fried foods and a pliable, translucent wrapper for fresh spring rolls. They are sold in packages in Asian markets.

Rice Vermicelli: Rice vermicelli (*bahn hoi*) is a thinner version of rice sticks (*bun*), and *bahn pho* is slightly larger still (¼ inch [6 mm] wide). All are from Vietnam and made of rice flour. *Sen mee* is the Chinese equivalent, while *wun sen* and *mee* (extra thin) are Thai versions. Preparation depends on use. For soups they are added directly; for stir-fries or for a noodle bowl they are either soaked in hot water or briefly boiled to soften. After softening, the noodles should be separated to prevent sticking.

Rice Vinegar: The two categories of rice vinegars are both milder than common European vinegars. Japanese rice vinegar, used primarily for dressings and sushi, is called *su* and can be seasoned with salt and sugar (primarily for dressings and sushi) or unseasoned. Chinese rice vinegar comes in three varieties: white (*bok cho*), used for dressings); black (*jit cho*), used as a dip or table condiment; and red (*hak mi cho*), used as a dip for fried snacks. When used generically rice vinegar usually refers to unseasoned Japanese rice vinegar.

Rice Wine: Chinese rice wine is brewed from rice and water and is called yellow wine (*hwang-jyo*); it has an alcohol content of about 17 percent. Japanese sake has a similar alcoholic content. For cooking purposes Chinese rice wine is preferable. A dry, golden sherry may be substituted.

Roasted Rice Powder: Rice, preferably jasmine, that has been dry-roasted in a skillet until golden tan, then finely ground. Although easily made in the kitchen (be careful that there are no large grains left after grinding), it is available at Asian markets.

Rose Buds and Rose Petals: Obtained from fragrant rose bushes, the dried buds and petals of roses have been used for thousands of years in Persia, the Near East, and India to flavor jams and sweet and savory dishes. They are a component of the Persian spice mix, *advieh*. The darker red petals and buds are said to have the best flavor and aroma.

Rose Water: A distillation of rose petals, primarily of the damask variety, used in Asia, Southwestern Asia, Eastern Europe, the Eastern Mediterranean, the Middle East, and North Africa. Rose essence is a highly concentrated form of rose water; a few drops of rose essence are equal to 1 tablespoon [15 mL] of rose water.

Saké: Although sometimes called rice wine, Japanese saké is actually fermented differently, so the term "wine" is a bit of a misnomer. It is used to tenderize meats, as a pickling medium, to reduce the smell of strong ingredients, to reduce saltiness, and for flavor preservation. Traditionally it is drunk warm, although not necessarily so. For cooking, it is first heated to remove the alcohol.

Salam Leaves: The leaves of *Eugenia polyantha*, used in Indonesian cooking for flavoring. They have an acidic quality and are highly aromatic. Some sources suggest, wrongfully, that bay leaves may be substituted for salam leaves (curry leaves would be a better substitute). Salam leaves can be purchased at Indonesian markets fresh or dried.

Salt Cod: Codfish preserved by salting and drying. Salt cod is popular across the northern shores of the Mediterranean, in Africa, Brazil, Scandinavia, and Portugal. The color should be as white as possible (yellowing indicates age) and belly cuts are preferred. Salt cod must always be soaked in repeated changes of fresh water to extract the salt; it loses half of its weight during the soaking process.

Saltpeter: Another name for potassium nitrate, saltpeter is used in brines for hams and bacon and as an addition to sausages and deli meats for color preservation. The Chinese often use it in red cooking meats. It is available at pharmacies in powdered form.

Sambal Oelek: A spicy, red chile condiment used throughout Southeast and Southern Asia. The word *sambal* is a Malay-Indonesian term for hot and spicy condiments and dishes. This fresh sauce is made from chiles and salt, with tamarind, vinegar, or citrus juice to acidify the mixture. Occasionally garlic is added as well. *Sambal oelek* is available in small bottles at Asian markets.

Sansho Powder: The Japanese term for ground Sichuan peppercorns. It is available in small shaker bottles in Japanese or Asian markets.

Scotch Bonnet Chile: A close Caribbean relative to the habanero chile. The Scotch bonnet is slightly smaller than the habanero but otherwise identical.

Sea Salt: Salt that has been evaporated from seawater, usually in the form of crystals or flakes. *Fleur de sel* is the French term for hand-harvested sea salt. Famous sea salts are harvested in Brittany, Sicily, Tunisia, Majorca, and Maldon, England. Large crystals, called *gros sel* in French, are normally ground in mills for table service.

Seasoned Rice Vinegar: This is a type of Japanese rice vinegar primarily used for dressings and flavoring rice to be used in making sushi. *See also* Rice Vinegar.

Serrano Chile: *Serrano* means "highland" in Spanish. Smaller than the jalapeño, the serrano is hotter. It is a chile with thick flesh and a searing, clean finish. It is commonly used fresh in salsas, pickled, or roasted for sauces.

Sesame Paste: An Asian (usually Chinese and Japanese) paste made with toasted sesame seeds spent from the process for extracting sesame oil. Sesame paste has a thick texture and has a darkish golden-brown color. It is similar in look and taste to peanut butter and is often used in making salad dressings. Peanut butter that has been thinned with a bit of warm water and seasoned with a small amount of sesame oil is a good substitute.

Seville Orange: *See* Sour Orange.

Sevruga Caviar: Sevruga, the lowest of the three grades of caviar (Beluga is the highest grade, followed by Osetra), is best in sauces. This caviar is the salted eggs of *Acipenser stellatus*, a sturgeon species native to the Caspian Sea, and is purchased in small amounts in tins that are available in specialty markets and delis. The eggs should be chilled in the tin, opened just before service, and served from the tin (or a porcelain bowl) with a nonmetallic spoon.

Shallot: A member of *Allium cepa,* the shallot is a small, mild, delicate form of onion that is used worldwide, especially in Europe and Southeast Asia. The skin can be golden, grayish-brown, pink, or red. Shallots are usually sold fresh, as clumping bulbs.

Shiitake Mushroom: *See* Chinese Black Mushroom.

Shiro Miso: A Japanese paste made from crushed, boiled soybeans and rice. It is light in color, fine textured, and slightly sweet. It is used as a flavoring for soups and dressings. The paste can be purchased in refrigerated tubs at Asian markets and health food stores.

Shisho Leaf: A member of the mint family, *Perilla frutescens,* shiso is used in Japan (especially), China, Burma, and regions of the foothills of the Himalayas. There are two varieties of *shisho,* green and red. Green is used primarily as a garnish, a sushi ingredient, and fried for tempura. Red is used to color pickled plums and in confections. Spearmint or basil is often substituted for green shisho, while dark opal basil is used for red.

Shoyu Soy Sauce: A type of Japanese soy sauce that is clearer and thinner than Chinese soy sauce but saltier. It is used when preparing foods that are light colored and has the advantage of seasoning foods without having to add much liquid. It is available in Japanese and Asian markets.

Shrimp Chip: The shrimp chip (*bahn phong* or *krupek*) has a delicate, subtle seafood taste. The chips are made from dried shrimp, egg whites, and tapioca powder and are used all across Southern and Southeast Asia. Sold dyed in garish colors, the chips can also be found without food coloring added. They are prepared by deep-frying and used for scooping foods when eating out of hand.

Shrimp Paste: A flavoring product used all across Southeast Asia (called *baboong alamang, kapee,* or *mam ruoc*) to add richness and a subtle seafood flavor to cooked dishes. Shrimp paste is available in two forms, as a semiliquid paste in a bottle or as a dried cake. Both have an unappealing odor that all but disappears once cooked. As a rule, twice as much paste is used as dried shrimp called for in a recipe. The dried form is always dry-toasted (in a sealed foil packet), then crumbled before use.

Sichuan Hot Bean Paste: Also called hot bean sauce, this paste is made from fermented soybeans, salt, flour, red chiles, and occasionally garlic. The beans can be ground or left whole. The flavor is rich and quite spicy. It is an addition to many Sichuan dishes and can be purchased in bottles or cans in Asian markets.

Sichuan Peppercorns: These are the fruit of *Zanthoxylum simulans* used as a flavoring spice in China and elsewhere with a peppery numbing effect on the mouth. *See also Emma.*

Silken Tofu: *See* Bean Curd.

Soppressata: Also known as *capocchia* and *coppa di testa,* soppressata is an Italian pressed sausage made from pork (and by-products) that is often flavored with clove, coriander, pepper, nutmeg, and a hint of cinnamon. The best soppressata is found in Siena and it can also be found at fine delis and Italian markets.

Sorrel: True French sorrel, *Rumex scutatus*, has a delightful sour flavor produced by oxalic acid. It has round leaves instead of the elongated leaves of common sorrel and should be searched for, as there is little comparison to its common cousin. It is used in sauces (especially with fish), soups, and salads. The American landscaping plant wood sorrel (*Oxalis spp*) has a similar flavor and can be substituted.

Sour Orange: Also known as the Seville orange or bitter orange, the sour orange is known botanically as *Citrus aurantium*. It is used in areas of Latin America, the Caribbean, the Mediterranean, and in England (for making marmalade). The juice is fruity and sour. If sour oranges are unavailable, a common substitute is 3 parts each of orange juice and grapefruit juice, 2 parts lemon juice, and 1 part grated grapefruit zest.

Sour Plum: *See* Umeboshi.

Sour Salt: Chemically known as citric acid, this is the sour component of many tart fruits (such as lemons); it is used in their place in dishes, especially from Eastern Europe. Citric acid can be found in the canning section of supermarkets and in pharmacies.

Spätzle: Small German egg dumplings formed by dropping (or flicking) the dough into simmering, salted water or stock to cook. Dried spätzle and dry mixes are available but are inferior to freshly made. Occasionally they can be found at supermarkets frozen and precooked, having only to be briefly blanched to reheat.

Sriracha Sauce: A bottled chile sauce made from chile, sugar, garlic, and salt that comes in a squeeze bottle and is a standard table condiment in Vietnamese and Thai restaurants. The name of this sauce is derived from a seaside town in Thailand called Siracha, known for its spicy chile condiment.

Sticky Rice: *See* Glutinous Rice.

Sumac Powder: A powder made from the dried fruit of the elm-leaf sumac (*Rhus coriaria*) used to impart a sour, fruity flavor to food. The berries are dark purple-red when ripe and the powder is brick red. Widely used in the Middle East and Southwestern Asia, sumac powder is almost always sprinkled over cooked foods at the last minute to add tartness. It can be purchased at Middle Eastern markets.

Sushi Rice: A plump short-grain rice used extensively in Japan. Although not as sticky as glutinous or sticky rice, sushi rice tends to be rather sticky when cooked; it is easily picked up with chopsticks. It can be purchased in Asian markets.

Sweet Black Soy Sauce: A bottled Thai sauce made from dark soy blended with molasses and palm sugar, similar to *kecap manis* from Indonesia. Sweet black soy sauce (*see-eu-wan*) is used for flavoring savory stir-fries, especially pork dishes. It can be purchased in Asian markets.

Tabil Spice Mix: A Tunisian spice mixture of dried seasonings or a paste made of fresh ingredients. Tabil contains equal proportions of coriander, caraway, garlic, and red chiles and is used primarily to flavor meats. It is available from specialty seasoning houses or Middle Eastern or North African markets.

Tahini: An oily paste made from soaked and ground, raw, hulled sesame seeds. The flavor is rich and sesame-like and the texture very smooth. It is used primarily in Middle Eastern dips and sauces.

Tamari Soy Sauce: An unrefined, thick, very dark soy sauce with a strong soy aroma and assertive flavor that is used primarily for making uncooked sauces and glazes and as a table condiment. It is available in health food stores and Asian markets.

Tamarind Liquid: A concentrate made from the pith surrounding the tamarind seed of *Tamarindus indica*. It is sold in bottles or jars from Asian markets and eliminates the soaking procedure involved with using tamarind pulp. The flavor is acidic and fruity, and it is grown and used throughout the tropics, especially Southeast Asia and Indonesia. It can be diluted with water or stock or added directly to stews, soups, and curries.

Tamarind Pulp: A cake of pulp surrounding tamarind seeds, extracted and compressed. It must first be soaked in warm water or stock to dissolve, then strained to obtain the flavoring liquid. It is available in Asian or Latin American markets.

Tapenade: A French olive paste made from ripe black olives, anchovies, capers, vinegar, olive oil, and occasionally garlic, used as a dip for crudités or a spread for toasted bread or sandwiches. It is available in jars or tubs at many fine delis and supermarkets and is easily made at home.

Tapioca Starch: A floury starch made from the processed roots of the cassava plant used primarily in the Far East for making pastries and wrappers or doughs, thickening soups and stews, and occasionally in batters for fried foods. Cornstarch is often substituted, but tapioca starch is more refined and makes a more delicate product. It can be purchased in Asian markets.

Tempura-Ko: Low-gluten Japanese wheat flour made specifically for tempura batters. A 50-50 mixture of sifted all-purpose flour and cake flour can substitute.

Thai Basil: A type of basil used in Southeast Asia, especially Thailand, in salads, stir-fries, and curries. The flavor of Thai basil (*bai horpha*) is slightly musty and pungent, with an anise-like, mint finish. It is available in Thai and Asian markets.

Thai Chile: Thai chiles can be purchased green (*prikk sodd*) or red and dried (*prikk haeng*). The chiles are thin and elongated. The flavor is extremely hot and lingering. They are available in both forms at Thai, Vietnamese, and Asian markets and are being grown in the United States. Serrano chiles can be substituted at a ratio of three to one.

Thai Eggplants: There are two types of eggplants used in Thailand and Southeast Asia. *Mahkheua pruang* is made up of clusters that resemble light green peas in grape-like form. These eggplants are dense and bitter and are generally added to a dish 15 minutes before completion of cooking. The other eggplant, *mah-kheua proh,* is golf ball size and white with green stripes, pure white, or occasionally purplish.

Thai Fish Sauce: *See* Fish Sauce.

Tofu: *See* Bean Curd.

Tofu Pouch: A hollowed-out fried cube or rectangle of tofu sold, refrigerated or frozen, in Asian markets. The pouches are usually stuffed with cooked savory fillings and then steamed or braised.

Tomatillo: The fruit of *Physalis ixocarpa,* also called *miltomates.* The tomatillo is used extensively in Mexico and Central America and, to a lesser extent, in Australia, South Africa, and India. The yellow-green, acidic fruit is enclosed in a papery husk. Tomatillos are used in Mexican and Southwestern green sauces and salsas. They are almost always cooked to bring out the full flavor; they can be boiled, roasted, broiled, or grilled. Tomatillos are available at most fine supermarkets.

Tonkatsu Sauce: A Western-inspired Japanese sauce used to accompany fried foods. It contains ketchup, Worcestershire sauce, sake, soy sauce, and mustard, with such spices as allspice and cloves. The flavor is similar to an American steak sauce; the texture can be thick or thin depending on the style purchased. It is available at Japanese and Asian markets.

Tostados: Corn tortillas (usually made with white corn) that are cut into wedges or rounds and then fried until crisp. Tostados are used as scoops for Latin American dips or salads, as garnishes for soups, and occasionally scrambled with eggs or used in casseroles in Mexican and Latin American cooking.

Trefoil: Trefoil sprigs are used almost exclusively in Japanese cuisine as a flavoring accent. It is used raw as a garnish or very briefly cooked. The taste is similar to a blend of celery and sorrel. The color can range from pale to bright green. Trefoil can be purchased in Japanese and specialty produce markets.

True Yam: Tuberous roots of many species of the genus *Dioscorea,* used worldwide in the tropics as a starchy vegetable are called the true yam (as opposed to the sweet potato of the United States). The flesh is white or light-colored and can be prepared by steaming, boiling, roasting, grilling, or frying. True yams have long-keeping qualities and are an important food staple in many places around the world.

Truffles: The underground fruiting body of the fungi *Tuber melanosporum* and *T. magnatum,* the black truffle and the white truffle of Europe grow only in symbiosis within the drip lines of certain trees and shrubs, principally white oak and filbert, in certain regions of France and Italy. They are available fresh at certain times of the year and can be purchased canned. Truffles are very expensive and quite strong in flavor. They are used in small amounts to perfume foods with their earthy aroma and taste.

Umeboshi: Umeboshi is a salted and dried Japanese fruit, usually referred to as a plum. The plums contain toxic compounds in small amounts and are never eaten raw. Red shisho leaves turn umeboshi purplish-red during processing. It is available in bottles or packages. Umeboshi is used in dishes requiring tartness. A puréed version is found in bottles. Both versions are available in Asian markets.

Vietnamese Bean Sauce: Not to be confused with Chinese or Sichuan bean paste, Vietnamese bean sauce (*tuong*) is a bottled sauce made from ground soybeans, roasted rice powder, and salt. It is used in making dipping sauces or as a substitute for Vietnamese fish sauce.

Wasabi: A very pungent Japanese condiment often used to accompany sushi and sashimi. Wasabi (*Eutrema wasabi*) is a tuberous root that comes grated or dried and powdered. Once the powdered form is mixed with mirin, stock, water, or a combination of the three, it should be used immediately because the sharp, pungent flavor fades quickly. It is commonly available in specialty or Asian markets.

Wood Ear Mushroom: The dried fruiting bodies of members of the *Auricula* genus of fungi is frequently used in Asian cuisines. Rarely available fresh, dried wood ear fungus is reconstituted in warm water or stock to soften. The texture is gelatinous and chewy, having no dominant flavor. Wood ears are used in soups, stir-fries, and fillings for textural interest and color contrast. They can be purchased in Asian markets. Also called cloud ear mushroom.

Yuca: Not to be confused with Yucca (the succulent members of the *Agavaceae* family), this is a Central American and Cuban term for cassava (*Manihot ultissima*), a tuberous root often cooked and used like potatoes. It is found in Latin American markets.

Yuzu Orange: A hybrid of two wild citrus fruits (*Citrus ichangensis* and *C. reticulata*), this unique, cold-hardy fruit is grown in Japan (where it is especially appreciated), Tibet, and China. A Yuzu orange is the size of a nectarine, with a thick yellow skin and seedy pale yellow flesh. The taste is bitter and cannot be compared to any common citrus flavors. Yuzu are occasionally available fresh in Japanese and specialty produce markets. The juice can also be purchased frozen and canned.

Bibliography

North America

CANADA

Canadian Home Economics Association. *The Laura Secord Canadian Cookbook*. Toronto: McClelland and Stewart, 1984.

Leighton, Myriam, and Chip Oliver. *A Taste of the Canadian Rockies Cookbook*. Canmore, Alberta: Altitude Canada Publishing, Ltd., 1994.

Stewart, Anita. *The Flavours of Canada*. Vancouver: Raincoast Books, 2000.

Wattle, Helen, and Elinor Donaldson. *Nellie Lyle Pattinson's Canadian Cook Book*. Toronto: The Ryerson Press, 1969.

AMERICAN REGIONAL, GENERAL

Clayton, Jr., Bernard. *Bernard Clayton's Cooking Across America:* Cooking with more than 100 of North America's Best Cooks and more than 250 of their Favorite Recipes. New York: Simon & Schuster, 1993.

Danforth, Randi, Peter Feerabend, and Gary Chassman. *Culinaria: The United States: A Culinary Discovery*. Cologne, Germany: Könemann, 1998.

Hewitt, Jean. *The New York Times Heritage Cook Book*. New York: G. P. Putnam's Sons, 1972.

Reichl, Ruth. *MMMM: A Feastiary*. New York: Holt, Rinehart and Winston, 1972.

Richards, Mary Anne, et al. *Americana Cookery: Favorite Recipes of Home Economics Teachers*. Birmingham, Ala.: Favorite Recipes Press, 1971.

Saveur Cooks Authentic American. Compiled and edited by the editors of *Saveur Magazine*. San Francisco: Chronicle Books, 1998.

Schulz, Phillip Stephen. *As American As Apple Pie*. New York: Simon & Schuster, 1990.

Stern, Jane, and Michael Stern. *A Taste of America*. Kansas City, Mo.: Andrews and McMeell, 1988.

NEW ENGLAND

Leonard, Jonathan Norton. *American Cooking: New England*. Alexandria, Va.: Time-Life Books, 1970.

MID-ATLANTIC STATES

Wilson, José, and the editors of Time-Life books. *American Cooking: The Eastern Heartland*. Alexandria, Va.: Time-Life Books, 1971.

THE SOUTH

Ferguson, Sheila. *Soul Food: Classic Cuisine from the Deep South*. New York: Weidenfield & Nicholson, 1989.

Glenn, Camille. *The Heritage of Southern Cooking*. New York: Workman Publishing, 1986.

Neal, Bill. *Bill Neal's Southern Cooking*. Chapel Hill, N.C.: University of North Carolina Press, 1989.

Payne, Susan Carlisle, ed. *The Southern Living Cookbook*. Birmingham, Ala.: Oxmoor House, 1987.

LOUISIANA

Bailey, Frank, ed. *Great Chefs of New Orleans*. New Orleans: Tele-record Productions, 1983.

Burton, Nathaniel, and Rudy Lombard. *Creole Feast: 15 Master Chefs of New Orleans Reveal Their Secrets*. New York: Random House, 1978.

Chef's Secrets from Great Restaurants in Louisiana. Compiled by the Louisiana Restaurant Association. Atlanta: Marmac Publishing Co., 1984.

China United Methodist Church: Cajun & Country Cooking. Compiled by the members of the China United Methodist Church. Sour Lake, Tex.: Harden-Jefferson VOE, 1975.

Collin, Rima, and Richard Collin. *The New Orleans Cookbook: Creole, Cajun, and Louisiana French Recipes Past and Present*. New York: Alfred A. Knopf, 1980.

Feibleman, Peter S., and the editors of Time-Life Books. *American Cooking: Creole and Acadian*. New York: Time-Life Books, 1971.

Guste, Jr., Roy F. *Antoine's Restaurant, Since 1840, Cookbook: A Collection of the Original Recipes from New Orleans' Oldest and Most Famous Restaurant*. New York: W. W. Norton & Co., 1980.

The Junior League of Baton Rouge, ed. *River Road Recipes*. Baton Rouge, La.: The Junior League of Baton Rouge, Inc., 1959.

Vidrine, Mercedes. *Louisiana Lagniappe*. Baton Rouge, La.: Claitor's Publishing Division, 1973.

THE MIDWEST

Good, Phyllis Pellman. *The Best of Amish Cooking: Traditional and Contemporary Recipes Adapted from the Kitchens and Pantries of Old Order Amish Cooks*. Intercourse, Pa.: Good Books, 1988.

Martin, Janet Letnes, and Allen Todnem. *The Lutheran Church Basement Women:* Hastings, Minn: Redbird Productions, 1992.

Puckett, Susan. *A Cook's Tour of Iowa*. Iowa City, Iowa: University of Iowa Press, 1988.

THE WESTERN STATES

Leonard, Jonathan Norton, and the editors of Time-Life Books. *American Cooking: The Great West*. Alexandria, Va.: Time-Life Books, 1971.

Steinhauer, Louise, ed. *Colorado Cache*. Denver: Junior League of Denver, Inc., 1978.

THE WEST COAST

Balsley, Betsy, and the L. A. Times Food Staff, eds. *The L.A. Times California Cookbook*. New York: Harry N. Abrams, 1981.

Brown, Dale, and the editors of Time-Life Books. *American Cooking: The Northwest*. Alexandria, Va.: Time-Life Books, 1970.

Brown, Helen Evans. *The West Coast Cook Book*. Boston: Little, Brown and Co., 1952.

Ferrary, Jeannette, and Louise Fiszer. *The California-American Cookbook: Innovations on American Regional Dishes*. New York: Simon & Schuster, 1985.

Milliken, Mary Sue, Susan Feniger, and Helene Siegel. *City Cuisine*. New York: W. W. Norton & Co., 1980.

THE SOUTHWEST

Beinhorn, Courtenay. *Beinhorn's Mesquite Cookery*. Austin, Tex.: Texas Monthly Press, 1986.

Brown, Ellen. *Southwest Tastes: From the PBS Television Series Great Chefs of the West*. Tucson, Ariz.: HP Books, 1987.

Bush, T. L. *A Cowboy's Cookbook*. Houston, Tex.: Gulf Publishing Co., 1992.

Fearing, Dean, and edited by Dotty Griffith. *The Mansion on Turtle Creek Cookbook*. New York: Weidenfield & Nicholson, 1987.

Fearing, Dean, and edited by Judith Choate. *Dean Fearing's Southwest Cuisine*. New York: Grove Weidenfield, 1990.

Hueske, Virginia. *The Home Place Cookbook: Driftwood, Texas*. Driftwood, Tex.: Driftwood Community Improvement Club, 1990.

Leona Cooking Through the Years. Compiled by the Leona Extension Homemakers Club, Leona, Tex.

Mexico

Bond, Richard, and Alice Mace, eds. *California Culinary Academy: Mexican Cooking*. San Francisco: Ortho Books, 1985.

Esquivel, Laura. *Like Water for Chocolate*. New York: Anchor Books, 1994.

Kennedy, Diana. *The Cuisines of Mexico*. New York: Harper & Row, Publishers, 1972.

————. *Recipes from the Regional Cooks of Mexico*. New York: Harper & Row, Publishers, 1978.

————. *The Tortilla Book*. New York: Harper & Row, Publishers, 1975.

Martínez, Zarela. *The Food and Life of Oaxaca. Oaxaca: Traditional Recipes from Mexico's Heart*. New York: Macmillan, 1997.

Miller, Mark. *The Great Chile Book*. Berkeley: Ten Speed Press, 1991.

Ortiz, Elisabeth Lambert. *The Complete Book of Mexican Cooking*. New York: Random House, 1979.

————. Quintana, Patricia. *The Best of Quintana*. New York: Stewart, Tabori, and Chang, 1995.

Ramirez Williams, Ileana. *Cocina de Mexico #4*. Mexico: Editoría Armonía, 1989.

Sloan, Sarah. *A Treasury of Mexican Cuisine: Original Recipes from the Chefs of the Camino Real Hotels, Mexico*. Chicago: Contemporary Books, 1985.

Trilling, Susana. *Seasons of My Heart: A Culinary Journey Through Oaxaca, Mexico*. New York: Ballantine Books, 1999.

Urdaneta, Maria Luisa, and Daryl F. Kantner. *Deleites de la Cocina Mexicana*. Austin, Tex.: University of Texas Press, 1996.

Willkinson, Marilyn, and William A. Orme. *Taste of Mexico*. New York: Stewart, Tabori, and Chang, 1986.

Willkinson, Marilyn, and William A. Orme, and Jack Bishop. *Cuisine of the Water Gods*. New York: Simon & Schuster, 1994.

Caribbean

Davila, Vivian. *Puerto Rican Cooking*. Secaucus, N.J.: Castle Books, 1988.

de Bornia, Ligia. *La Cocina Dominicana*. Santo Domingo: Editorial Arte y Cine, 1965.

Dedeaux, Devra. *Sugar Reef Caribbean Cooking*. New York: McGraw-Hill, 1989.

De Mers, John. *Caribbean Cooking*. Los Angeles: HP Books, 1989.

———. *The Food of Jamaica: Authentic Recipes from the Jewel of the Caribbean*. Boston: Periplus, 1998.

de O'Higgins, María Josefa Lluriá. *A Taste of Old Cuba: More than 150 Recipes for Delicious, Authentic, and Traditional Dishes, Highlighted with Reflections and Reminiscences*. New York: Harper Collins Publishers, 1994.

Elbert, Virginia F., and George A. Elbert. *Down-Island Caribbean Cooking: A Lively Recipe Collection from One of the World's Freshest Cuisines*. New York: Simon & Schuster, 1991.

Fenzi, Jewell. *This is the Way We Cook! Asina nos ta cushiná: Recipes from Outstanding Cooks of the Netherlands Antilles*. Oranjestad, Aruba: Thayer-Sargent, 1978.

Hamelcourt, Juliette. *Caribbean Cooking*. New York: Culinary Arts Institute, 1980.

Harris, Dunstan. *Island Cooking: Recipes from the Caribbean*. Freedom, Calif.: The Crossing Press, 1988.

Harris, Jessica B. *Sky Juice and Flying Fish: Traditional Caribbean Cooking*. New York: Simon & Schuster, 1991.

Indar, Polly, Dorothy Ramesar, and Sylvia Bissessar, eds. *Naparima Girl's School: Trinidad & Tobago Recipes*. La Romain, Trinidad: RPL Ltd., 1988.

Ortiz, Elisabeth Lambert. *The Complete Book of Caribbean Cooking*. New York: Ballantine Books, 1986.

Valldejuli, Carmen Aboy. *Puerto Rican Cookery: A New Approach of a Revised and Enlarged Edition of the Art of Caribbean Cooking*. Gretna, La.: Pelican Press, 1980.

Van Aken, Norman, and Susan Porter. *Norman Van Aken's Feast of Sunlight*. New York: Ballantine Books, 1988.

Willinsky, Helen. *Jerk, Barbecue from Jamaica*. Freedom, Calif.: The Crossing Press, 1990.

Wolfe, Linda. *Cooking of the Caribbean Islands*. New York: Time-Life Books, 1970.

Young, Joyce La Fray. *Tropic Cooking*. Berkeley, Calif.: Ten Speed Press, 1987.

Central America

Barquero, Humberto. *Nicaragua: Maiz y Folklore*. Managua: Papelera Industrial de Nicaragua, 1981.

Burns, E. L. *My Favourite Collection of Recipes*. Guelph, Belize: Self-published, 1980.

Central American Cooking. Compiled by the Association in Solidarity with Guatemala (ASOGUA). Waseca, Minn.: Walter's Publishing Co., 1982.

De Davila, Dolores Prats. *Reviviendo la Cocina Hondureña*. San Pedro Sula, Honduras: Impresera del Norte, 1997.

De Trejos, Olga. *La Cocina Practica*. San Jose, Costa Rica: Imprenta Universal, 1987.

Kitchen Fiesta. Guatemala: Women's Auxiliary of the Union Church, 1965.

Marks, Copeland. *False Tongues & Sunday Bread: A Guatemalan and Mayan Cookbook*. New York: M. Evans and Co., 1985.

Recetario de Cocina. Compiled by the Asociación de Esposas de Contadores de Guatemala. Managua: Tipografia Nacional, 1970.

Sargent, Mary Thomas. *Rico: A Cook Book*. Tegucigalpa: Sargent and Skelton for the Women's Club of Tegucigalpa, Honduras, 1972.

Zarzalejos Nieto, Maria del Carmen. *El Libro de la Cocina Iberoamericana*. Madrid, Spain: Alianza Editorial, 1992.

Latin America, General

Leonard, Jonathan Norton. *Latin American Cooking*. New York: Time-Life Books, 1970.

Ortiz, Elisabeth Lambert. *The Book of Latin American Cooking*. New York: Random House, 1979.

South America

Brown, Cora, Rose Brown, and Bob Brown. *The South American Cookbook: Including Central America, Mexico, and the West Indies*. New York: Dover Publications, 1971.

Karoff, Barbara. *South American Cooking*. Berkeley: Addison-Wesley, 1989.

Rojas-Lombardi, Felipe. *The Art of South American Cooking*. New York: Harper Collins Publishers, 1991.

Umaña-Murray, Mirtha. *Three Generations of Chilean Cuisine*. Los Angeles: Lowell House, 1997.

Brazil

Ang, Eng Tie. *Delightful Brazilian Cooking*. Seattle, Wash.: Ambrosia Publications, 1993.

Botafogo, Dolores. *The Art of Brazilian Cookery*. New York: Hippocrene Books, 1993.

De Andrade, Margarette. *Brazilian Cookery: Traditional and Modern*. Rutland, Vt.: Charles E. Tuttle, 1965.

Harris, Jessica B. *Tasting Brazil: Regional Recipes and Reminiscences*. New York: Macmillan, 1992.

Idone, Christopher. *Brazil: A Cook's Tour*. New York: Clarkson N. Potter, 1995.

Moliterno, Irene Becker. *The Brazilian Cookbook*. New York: Charles Frank Publications, 1963.

Pinto, Carla Barboza. *Brazilian Cooking*. Edison, N.J.: Chartwell Books, 1998.

Oceania

Alexander, Stephanie, and Ashley Mackevicius. *The Food of Australia: Contemporary Recipes from Australia's Leading Chefs*. Boston: Periplus, 1999.

The Australian Gourmet Cookbook: Selected Recipes from the Australian Gourmet Magazine. Melbourne, Australia: Sun Books, 1970.

Bazore, Katherine. *Hawaiian and Pacific Foods: A Cookbook of Culinary Customs and Recipes Adapted for the American Hostess*. New York: Gramercy Publishing, 1947.

Bennet, Victor. *The South Pacific Cookbook*. Englewood Cliffs, N.J.: Prentice Hall.

Bluebird Foods Ltd., and Robin Martin and Associates, eds. *Edmonds Cookery Book*. Auckland, New Zealand: Bluebird Foods Ltd., 1992.

Brennan, Jennifer. *Tradewinds & Coconuts: A Reminiscence & Recipes from the Pacific Islands*. Boston: Periplus, 2000.

Choy, Sam, Uʻi. Goldsberry, and Steven Goldsberry. *Sam Choy's Island Flavors*. New York: Hyperion, 1999.

Flower, Tui. *New Zealand: The Beautiful Cookbook*. Sydney: Weldon Publishing, 1990.

Newman, Graeme, Betsy Newman, and Graeme R. Newman. *Good Food from Australia*. New York: Hippocrene Books, 1997.

Steinberg, Rafael, and the editors of Time-Life Books. *Foods of the World: Pacific and Southeast Asian Cooking*. Alexandria, Va.: Time-Life Books, 1979.

Asia, General

Chatterjee, Sandeep. *The Spice Trail*. Berkeley, Calif.: Ten Speed Press, 1995.

Greeley, Alexandra. *Asian Grills*. New York: Doubleday, 1993.

Grodnick, Susan. *Accents of the Orient: Eastern Influence on Western Cooking*. Los Angeles: HP Books, 1989.

Harlow, Jay. *Southeast Asian Cooking*. San Francisco: Chevron Chemical Company, 1987.

Haydock, Yukiko, and Robert Haydock. *Oriental Appetizers*. New York: Holt, Rinehart and Winston, 1984.

Jaffrey, Madhur. *Madhur Jaffrey's Far Eastern Cookery*. New York: Perennial Library, 1989.

Jue, Joyce. *Asian Appetizers*. Emeryville, Calif.: Harlow & Ratner, 1991.

———. *Far East Café: The Best of Casual Asian Cooking*. Menlo Park, Calif.: Sunset Books, 1996.

King, Rani, and Chandra Khang. *Tiger Lily Street Food*. London: Piatkus, 1997.

Simonds, Nina. *Asian Wraps*. New York: William Morrow & Co., 2000.

Solomon, Charmaine. *The Complete Asian Cookbook*. New York: McGraw-Hill, 1976.

The Third Annual Worlds of Flavor International Conference and Festival: The Flavors of India and Southeast Asia. Napa Valley: The Culinary Institute of America at Greystone, 2000.

Wong, Irene. *The Great Asian Steambook*. Brisbane, Calif.: Taylor & Ng, 1977.

Philippines

Alejandro, Reynaldo G. *The Food of the Philippines: Authentic Recipes from the Pearl of the Orient*. Boston: Periplus, 1998.

————. *The Philippine Cookbook*. New York: The Berkeley Publishing Group, 1985.

Gelle, Gerry. *Filipino Cuisine: Recipes from the Islands*. Santa Fe, N. Mex.: Red Crane Books, 1997.

Hutton, Wendy, ed. *The Food of the Philippines*. Singapore: Periplus, 1995.

Noriega, Violeta A. *Philippine Recipes Made Easy*. Kirkland, Wash.: Paperworks, 1993.

Robles-Florendo, Sony. *Signature Dishes of the Philippines: "—Because We Do Them Best."* Manila: Sony Robles-Florendo, 1988.

South Asia

Brissenden, Rosemary. *Asia's Undiscovered Cuisine*. New York: Pantheon Books, 1982.

Lie, Sek-Hiang. *Indonesian Cookery*. New York: Crown, 1963.

Marks, Copeland. *The Exotic Kitchens of Indonesia: Recipes from the Outer Islands*. New York: M. Evans and Co., 1989.

Marks, Copeland, and Miontari Soeharjo. *The Indonesian Kitchen*. New York: Atheneum, 1981.

Mowe, Rosalind, ed. *Culinaria: Southeastern Asian Specialties: A Culinary Journey Through Singapore, Malaysia, and Indonesia*. Cologne, Germany: Könemann, 1998.

Rajah, Carol Salva. *Makan Lah!: The True Taste of Malaysia*. Sydney: Harper Collins Publishers, 1996.

Von Holzen, Heinz, and Lother Arsana. *The Food of Bali*. Singapore: Periplus, 1995.

Von Holzen, Heinz, Lother Arsana, and Wendy Hutton. *The Food of Indonesia*. Singapore: Periplus, 1995.

Japan

Andoh, Elizabeth. *An American Taste of Japan*. New York: William Morrow & Co., 1985.

————. *At Home with Japanese Cooking*. New York: Alfred A. Knopf, 1980.

Condon, Camy, and Sumiko Ashizawa. *The Japanese Guide to Fish Cooking*. Tokyo: Shufonotomo Ltd., 1986.

Detrick, Mia. *Sushi*. San Francisco: Chronicle Books, 1981.

Haydock, Yukiko, and Robert Haydock. *Food in a Japanese Mood*. Tokyo: Kodansha International Ltd., 1984.

Kamekura, Junichi, Gideon Bosker, and Mamoru Watanabe. *Ekiben: The Art of the Japanese Box Lunch*. San Francisco: Chronicle Books, 1989.

Kosaki, Tayayuki, Walter Wagner, and Wendy Hutton. *The Food of Japan: Authentic Recipes from the Land of the Rising Sun*. Boston: Periplus, 1998.

Õmae, Kinjiro, and Yuzuru Tachibana. *The Book of Sushi*. Tokyo: Kodansha International Ltd., 1981.

Shimizu, Kay. *Sushi at Home*. Tokyo: Shufonotomo Ltd., 1985.

Shimizu, Shinko. *New Salads: Quick, Healthy Recipes from Japan*. Tokyo: Kodansha International Ltd., 1986.

Slack, Susan Fuller. *Japanese Cooking*. Tucson, Ariz.: HP Books, 1985.

Tsuji, Shizuo. *Japanese Cooking: A Simple Art*. Tokyo: Kodansha International Ltd., 1980.

Korea

Chin-Hwa, Noa. *Healthful Korean Cooking: Meats & Poultry*. Seoul: Hollym, 1985.

———. *Practical Korean Cooking*. Seoul: Hollym, 1985.

———. *Traditional Korean Cooking: Snacks and Basic Side Dishes*. Seoul: Hollym, 1985.

Chung-Hea, Han. *Traditional Korean Cooking*. Seoul: Chung Woo Publishing Co., 1986.

Lee, Florence C., and Helen C. Lee. *Kimchi: A Natural Health Food*. Seoul: Hollym, 1988.

Marks, Copeland. *The Korean Kitchen: Classic Recipes from the Land of the Morning Calm*. San Francisco: Chronicle Books, 1993.

Millon, Marc, and Kim Millon. *Flavours of Korea*. London: A. Deutsch, 1991.

Wade, Lee, with Joan Rutt, Sandra Mattielli, et al., eds. *Lee Wade's Korean Cookery*. Elizabeth, N.J.: Hollym, 1985.

China

Chao, Buwei Yang. *How to Cook and Eat in Chinese*. New York: Vintage Books, 1972.

Chen, Pearl Kong, Tien Chen, and Rose Tseng. *Everything You Want to Know About Chinese Cooking*. Woodbury, N.Y.: Barron's, 1983.

Chin, Leeann, and Katie Chin. *Everyday Chinese Cooking: Quick and Delicious Recipes from the Leeann Chin Restaurants*. New York: Clarkson N. Potter, 2000.

Chinese Cuisine from the Master Chefs of China. Compiled by the editors of *China Pictorial, Beijing*. Boston: Little, Brown and Co., 1983.

Chu, Lawrence. *Chef Chu's Distinct Cuisine of China*. New York: Harper & Row Publishers, Inc.

Chung, Henry, and Tony Hiss. *Henry Chung's Hunan-Style Chinese Cookbook*. New York: Harmony Books, 1978.

Delfs, Robert. *The Good Food of Szechuan*. San Francisco: Kodansha International Ltd., 1974.

Gin, Maggie, and Alfred Castle. *Regional Cooking of China*. San Francisco: 101 Productions, 1975.

Hom, Ken. *Fragrant Harbor Taste: The New Chinese Cooking of Hong Kong*. New York: Simon & Schuster, 1989.

———. *Ken Hom's East Meets West Cuisine*. New York: Simon & Schuster, 1987.

———. *Ken Hom's Chinese Cookery*. New York: Harper & Row, Publishers, 1986.

Hom, Ken, with Harvey Steiman. *Chinese Technique*. New York: Simon & Schuster, 1981.

Huei, Cheng. *Wei-Chuan's Cookbook: Chinese Cuisine II*. Taipei: Wei-Chuan Foods Corporation, 1980.

Leung, Mai. *Dim Sum and Other Chinese Street Food*. New York: Harper Colophon Books, 1982.

Lo, Kenneth. *Ken Lo's New Chinese Cooking School*. Tucson, Airz.: HP Books, 1985.

Lo, Yin-Fei Eileen. *The Dim Sum Book: Classic Recipes from the Chinese Teahouse*. New York: Crown, 1982.

———. *The Dim Sum Dumpling Book*. New York: Macmillan, 1995.

Long, Jiang Jin. *Cantonese Dishes*. Taipei: Haiziwang Tushu Co., 1998.

———. *Vegetarian Gourmet*. Taipei: Haiziwang Tushu Co., 1998.

Mark, William. *The Chinese Gourmet*. San Francisco: Goldstreet Press, 1994.

Miller, Gloria Bley. *The Thousand Recipe Chinese Cookbook*. New York: Grosset & Dunlap Publishers, 1976.

Mock, Lonnie. *Favorite Dim Sum*. Walnut Creek, Calif.: Alpha Gamma Arts, 1979.

Pei-Mei, Fu. *Pei Mei's Chinese Cookbook*, Vol 1. Taipei: T. and S. Industrial Co. Ltd., 1974.

———. *Pei Mei's Chinese Cookbook*, Vol 2. Taipei: T. and S. Industrial Co. Ltd., 1974.

Su-Huei, Huang. *Chinese Appetizers & Garnishes*. Monterey Park, Calif.: Wei-Chuan's Cooking, 1982.

———. *Chinese Seafood*. Monterey Park, Calif.: Wei-Chuan's Cooking, 1984.

———. *Chinese Snacks*. Monterey Park, Calif.: Wei-Chuan Publishing, 1985.

Tropp, Barbara. *The China Moon Cookbook*. New York: Workman Publishing, 1992.

———. *The Modern Art of Chinese Cooking*. New York: William Morrow & Co., 1982.

Wu, Sylvia. *Madame Wu's Art of Chinese Cooking*. New York: Bantam Books, 1975.

Yee, Rhoda. *Dim Sum: The Delicious Secrets of Home Cooked Chinese Tea Lunch*. San Francisco: Taylor & Ng, 1977.

———. *Szechuan and Northern Cooking: From Hot to Cold*. San Francisco: Taylor & Ng, 1983.

Young, Grace. *The Wisdom of the Chinese Kitchen: Classic Family Recipes for Celebration and Healing*. New York: Simon & Schuster, 1999.

Vietnam

Choi, Trieu Thi, and Marcel Isaak. *The Food of Vietnam: Authentic Recipes from the Heart of Indochina*. Singapore: Periplus, 1997.

Miller, Jill Nhu Huong. *Vietnamese Cookery*. Rutland, Vt.: Charles E. Tuttle, 1983.

Ngo, Bach, and Gloria Zimmerman. *The Classic Cuisine of Vietnam*. Woodbury, N.Y.: Barron's, 1979.

Nguyen, Cam Van, Dzõan. *Vietnamese Traditional Dishes*. Ha Noi: Nhà Xuát Ban Phu Nû, 2000.

Routhier, Nicole. *The Best of Nicole Routhier*. New York: Stewart, Tabori, and Chang, 1996.

———. *The Foods of Vietnam*. New York: Stewart, Tabori, and Chang, 1989.

Tran, Paula. *Living and Cooking Vietnamese*. San Antonio, Tex.: Corona Publishing Co., 1990.

Trang, Corrine. *Authentic Vietnamese Cooking: Food from a Family Table*. New York: Simon & Schuster, 1999.

Southeast Asia

Alford, Jeffrey, and Naomi Duguid. *Hot Sour Salty Sweet: A Culinary Journey Through Southeast Asia*. New York: Artisan, 2000.

Bhumichitr, Vatcharin. *Vatch's Southeast Asian Cookbook*. New York: St. Martin's Press, 1998.

Castoriana, Jan, and Dimitra Stais. *A Taste of Indochina*. Hauppauge, N.Y.: Barron's, 1996.

De Monteiro, Longteine, and Katherine Neustadt. *The Elephant Walk Cookbook: Cambodian Cuisine from the Nationally Acclaimed Restaurant*. New York: Houghton Mifflin, 1998.

Robert, Claudia Saw Lwin. *The Food of Burma*. Boston: Periplus, 1999.

Sing, Phia, Phouangphet Vannitone, Boon Song Klausner, et al. *Traditional Recipes of Laos*. Devon, England: Prospect Books, 1995.

Taik, Aung Aung. *The Best of Burmese Cooking: Under the Golden Pagoda*. San Francisco: Chronicle Books, 1993.

Xayavadong, Daovone. *Taste of Laos*. Berkeley, Calif.: SLG Books, 2000.

Thailand

Bhumichitr, Vatcharin. *The Taste of Thailand*. New York: Macmillan, 1988.

Brennan, Jennifer. *Thai Cooking*. London: MacDonald and Co., Ltd., 1984.

Buranasombati, Duangduen. *A Touch of Thailand*. Bangkok: Self-published, 1984.

Crawford, William, and Kamolmal Pootaraska. *Thai Home Cooking*. New York: Penguin Books, 1985.

Kahrs, Kurt. *Thai Cooking*. New York: Gallery Books, 1990.

Kittivech, Sukhum. *Thai Cooking Made Easy*. Monterey Park, Calif.: Wei-Chuan Publishing, 1999.

Kongpan, Sisamon, and Pinyo Srisawat. *The Elegant Taste of Thailand*. Berkeley, Calif.: SLG Books, 1989.

Pinsuvana, Malulee. *Cooking Thai Food in American Kitchens*. Bangkok: Thai Watana Panich Press, 1976.

Sananikone, Keo. *Keo's Thai Cuisine*. Berkeley, Calif.: Ten Speed Press, 1999.

Schmitz, Puangkram, and Michael Worman. *Practical Thai Cooking*. Tokyo: Kodansha International Ltd., 1985.

Sodsook, Victor, Theresa Laursen, and Byron Laursen. *True Thai: The Modern Art of Thai Cooking*. New York: William Morrow & Co., 1995.

Yu, Su-Mei. *Cracking the Coconut: Classic Thai Home Cooking*. New York: William Morrow & Co., 2000.

Indian Subcontinent

Balasuriya, Heather Jansz, and Karin Winegar. *Fire & Spice: The Cuisine of Sri Lanka*. New York: McGraw-Hill, 1989.

Ballentine, Martha. *Himalayan Mountain Cookery: A Vegetarian Cookbook*. Honesdale, Pa.: Himalayan International Institute of Yoga Science and Philosophy of the U.S.A., 1981.

Bhandar, Ratna. *Cooking in Nepal*. Kathmandu: Damlen Press, 1982.

Chapman, Pat. *Balti Curry Cookbook*. London: Piatkus, 1997.

Complete Indian Cooking. New York: Hamlyn/Octopus Publishing, 2000.

Husain, Shehzad, and Rafi Fernandez. *The Indian Recipe Book*. London: Anness Publishing, Ltd., 2000.

Jaffrey, Madhur. *Madhur Jaffrey's Indian Cooking*. Hauppage, N.Y.: Barron's, 1983.

Kaimal, Maya. *Savoring the Spice Coast of India: Fresh Flavors from Kerala*. New York: Harper Collins Publishers, 2000.

Khokar, Sabiha, Lali Nayar, and Geeta Samtani. *Favourite Balti & Indian Recipes*. London: Merehurst Ltd., 1997.

Marks, Copeland. *Indian & Chinese Cooking from the Himalayan Rim*. New York: M. Evans and Co., 1996.

———. *The Varied Kitchens of India: Cuisines of the Anglo-Indians of Calcutta, Bengalis, Jews of Calcutta, Kashmiris, Parsis and Tibetans of Darjeeling*. New York: M. Evans and Co., 1986.

Mohan, Rocky. *The Art of Indian Cuisine*. New Delhi: Roli Books, 1999.

Moore, Isabelle, and Jonnie Godfrey. *Foods of the Orient: India*. London: Marshall Cavendish Books Ltd., 1978.

Mridula Baljekar's Real Balti Cookbook. London: Ebury Press, 1996.

Panjabi, Camelia. *The Great Curries of India*. New York: Simon & Schuster, 1995.

Purewal, Jasjit, Karen Anand, et al. *The Food of India*. Boston: Periplus, 1998.

Sahni, Julie. *Classic Indian Vegetarian and Grain Cooking*. New York: William Morrow & Co., 1985.

Wangmo, Tsering, and Zara Houshmand. *The Lhasa Moon Tibetan Cookbook*. Ithaca, N.Y.: Snow Lion Publications, 1999.

Southwestern Asia

PAKISTAN

Currimbhoy, Zainab. *The Joy of Cooking in Pakistan*. Karachi: Pak Publishers Ltd., 1971.

AFGHANISTAN

Amini, Rahima. *A Pinch of Salt: Classic Afghan Cookery*. London: Quartet Books, 1991.

Parenti, Cathy. *A Taste of Afghanistan: The Cuisine of the Crossroads of the World*. Phoenix, Ariz.: Parenti Books, 1987.

Saberi, Helen, Najiba Zaka, and Shaima Breshna. *Noshe Djan: Afghani Food and Cookery*. Devon, England: Prospect Books, 1985.

PERSIA

Batmanglij, Najmieh. *Persian Cooking for a Healthy Kitchen*. Washington, D.C.: Mage Publishers, 1994.

———. *A Taste of Persia: An Introduction to Persian Cooking*. Washington, D.C.: Mage Publishers, 1999.

Ghanoonparvar, M.R. *Persian Cuisine, Book 1: Traditional Foods*. Lexington, Ky.: Mazdâ Publishers, 1982.

———. *Persian Cuisine, Book 2: Regional & Modern*. Costa Mesa, Ca.: Mazdâ Publishers, 1984.

Hekmat, Forough. *The Art of Persian Cooking*. New York: Doubleday, 1961.

Mazda, Maideh. *In a Persian Kitchen: Favorite Recipes from the Near East*. Rutland, Vt: Charles E. Tuttle, 1972.

Ramazani, Nesta. *Persian Cooking: A Table of Exotic Delights*. Bethesda, Md: Iranbooks, 1997.

Middle East, General

Atiyeh, Wadeeha. *Scheherazade Cooks!'* New York: Gramercy Publishing, 1960.

Mallos, Tess. *The Complete Middle East Cookbook*. Boston: Charles E. Tuttle Publishing, 1993.

Roden, Claudia. *A Book of Middle Eastern Food*. New York: Alfred A. Knopf, 1972.

Scott, David. *Recipes for an Arabian Night: Traditional Cooking from North Africa and the Middle East*. New York: Pantheon Books, 1983.

Weiss-Armush, Anne Marie. *The Arabian Delights Cookbook: Mediterranean Cuisine from Mecca to Marrakesh*. Los Angeles: Lowell House, 1994.

ISRAEL

Ansky, Sherry. *The Food of Israel: Authentic Recipes from the Land of Milk and Honey*. Boston: Periplus, 2000.

EGYPT

Abdennour, Samia. *Egyptian Cooking: A Practical Guide*. Cairo: American University in Cairo Press, 1985.

LEBANON

Helou, Anissa. *Lebanese Cooking*. New York: St. Martin's Press, 1998.

Rayess, George. *Rayess' Art of Lebanese Cooking*. Beirut: Librarie du Liban, 1991.

Ward, Susan. *Lebanese Cooking: An Introduction to this Special Middle Eastern Cuisine*. Secaucus, N.J.: Chartwell Books, 1992.

SAUDI ARABIA

Weiss-Armush, Anne Marie. *Arabian Cuisine*. Beirut: Dar an Nafaés, 1991.

SYRIA, LEBANON, AND JORDAN

Uvezian, Sonia. *Recipes and Remembrances: From an Eastern Mediterranean Kitchen*. Austin, Tex.: University of Texas Press, 1999.

Regional Africa

Hachten, Harva. *Kitchen Safari: A Gourmet's Tour of Africa*. New York: Atheneum, 1970.

Harris, Jessica B. *The Africa Cookbook: Tastes of a Continent*. New York: Simon & Schuster, 1998.

Hultman, Tami, ed. *The Africa News Cookbook: African Cooking for Western Kitchens*. New York: Penguin Books, 1986.

Sandler, Bea. *The African Cookbook*. New York: World Publishing Corp., 1970.

van Wyk, Magdaleen. *Taste of South Africa*. Capetown: Human and Rousseau, 1997.

Wilson, Ellen. *A West African Cookbook*. New York: M. Evans and Co., 1971.

ETHIOPIA

Mesfin, Daniel. *Exotic Ethiopian Cooking*. Falls Church, Va.: Ethiopian Cookbook Enterprises, 1993.

North Africa (The Maghreb)

Benkirane, Fettouma. *Moroccan Cooking: The Best Recipes*. Casablanca: Sochepress, 1997.

———. *Secrets of Moroccan Cookery*. Paris: Taillandier, 1980.

Day, Irene B. *The Moroccan Cookbook*. New York: Quick Fox, 1977.

Guinaudeau, Z. *Traditional Moroccan Cooking: Recipes from Fez*. London: Serif, 1994.

Marks, Copeland. *The Great Book of Couscous: Classic Cuisines of Morocco, Algeria, and Tunisia*. New York: Donald I. Fine, 1994.

Morse, Kitty. *Cooking at the Kasbah: Recipes from My Moroccan Kitchen*. San Francisco: Chronicle Books, 1998.

Walden, Hilaire. *North African Cooking: Exotic Delights from Morocco, Tunisia, Algeria, and Egypt*. Edison, N.J.: Chartwell Books, 1995.

Wolfert, Paula. *Couscous and Other Good Food from Morocco*. New York: Perennial, 1987.

Woodward, Sarah. *Tastes of North Africa: Recipes from Morocco to the Mediterranean*. New York: Hippocrene Books, 1999.

Ziani, Mehdi. *Mamounia Moroccan Cookbook*. San Francisco: Ziana Books, 1979.

Mediterranean, General

Galizia, Ann Caruana, and Helen Caruana Galizia. *The Food and Cookery of Malta*. Devon, England: Prospect Books, 1997.

Goldstein, Joyce. *Back to Square One: Old-World Food in a New-World Kitchen*. New York: William Morrow & Co., 1992.

————. *The Mediterranean Kitchen*. New York: William Morrow & Co., 1989.

————. *Taverna: The Best of Casual Mediterranean Cooking*. Menlo Park, Ca.: Sunset Books, 1996.

Mallos, Tess. *The Complete Mediterranean Cookbook*. Boston: Charles E. Tuttle, Inc., 1996.

Roden, Claudia. *Mediterranean Cookery*. New York: Alfred A. Knopf, 1992.

Wolfert, Paula. *Mediterranean Cooking*. New York: Perennial, 1994.

Eastern Mediterranean

GREECE

Chantiles, Vilma. *The Food of Greece*. New York: Simon & Schuster, 1992.

Condratos, Stelios. *Greek Cookery: Traditional Recipes*. Athens: Greco Edition Publications, Inc., 1998.

Howe, Robin. *Greek Cooking*. London: A. Deutsch, 1960.

Kochilas, Diane. *The Food and Wine of Greece*. New York: St. Martin's Press, 1990.

Kremezi, Aglaia. *The Foods of Greece*. New York: Stewart, Tabori, and Chang, 1999.

Maxwell, Sarah. *Greek Mezze Cooking: Tapas of the Aegean*. Edison, N.J.: Chartwell Books, 1995.

Morrissy, Lesley. *Australian Seafood: Greek Island Style*. Scarborough, Australia: Clare Dane Publishers, 1984.

The Recipe Club of St. Paul's Greek Orthodox Cathedral. *The Complete Book of Greek Cooking*. New York: Harper Perennial, 1991.

Souli, Sofia. *The Greek Cookery Book: 222 Recipes*. Athens: Michalis Toumbis Publications, 1989.

TURKEY

Algar, Ayla. *Classical Turkish Cooking: Traditional Turkish Food for the American Kitchen*. New York: Harper Collins Publishers, 1991.

Basan, Ghillie. *Classic Turkish Cooking*. New York: St. Martin's Press, 1997.

Gümüs, Dogan. *The Art of Turkish Cookery*. Istanbul: Do-Gü Yanilari, 1997.

Jackson, Bade. *Turkish Cooking: Authentic Culinary Traditions from Turkey*. Edison, N.J.: Chartwell Books, 1998.

Orga, Irfan. *Turkish Cooking*. London: A. Deutsch Ltd., 1975.

Ozan, Özcan. *The Sultan's Kitchen: A Turkish Cookbook*. Boston: Periplus, 1998.

Yayinlari, Minyatür. *The Famous Turkish Cookery*. Istanbul: Galeri Minyatür-Tunçay Yurtsever.

NORTHEASTERN MEDITERRANEAN

Mardikian, George M. *Dinner at Omar Khayyam's*. New York: Viking Press, 1944.

Uvezian, Sonia. *The Cuisine of Armenia*. New York: Hippocrene Books, 1996.

Eastern Europe

Ball, Caroline, ed. *East European Cookbook*. Edison, N.J.: Chartwell Books, 1996.

Brízová, Joza, and Adrienna Vahala. *Czechoslovak Cookbook*. New York: Crown, 1965.

Czerny, Zofia. *Polish Cookbook*. Warsaw: Panstwowe Wydawnictwo Ekonomiczne, 1976.

Klepper, Nicolae. *Taste of Romania: Its Cookery and Glimpses of Its History, Folklore, Art, Literature, and Poetry*. New York: Hippocrene Books, 1997.

Polvay, Marina. *All Along the Danube: Classic Cookery from the Great Cuisines of Eastern Europe*. Englewood Cliffs, N.J.: Prentice Hall, 1979.

Żerańska, Alina. *The Art of Polish Cooking*. Garden City, N.Y.: Doubleday, 1968.

HUNGARY

Derecskey, Susan. *The Hungarian Cookbook*. New York: Harper Perennial, 1987.

Gergely, Anikó, *Culinaria: Hungary*. Cologne, Germany: Könemann, 1999.

Kovi, Paul. *Paul Kovi's Transylvanian Cuisine*. New York: Crown, 1985.

Lang, George. *The Cuisine of Hungary*. New York: Atheneum, 1985.

————. *George Lang's Cuisines of Hungary*. New York: Wings Books, 1994.

RUSSIA

Goldstein, Darra. *The Georgian Feast: The Vibrant Culture and Savory Food of the Republic of Georgia*. Berkeley: University of California Press, 1999.

————. *A Taste of Russia: A Cookbook of Russian Hospitality*. New York: Harper Perennial, 1991.

Krasheninnikova, A. *Russian Cooking*. Moscow: MIR Publishers, 1978.

Papashvily, Helen, George Papashvily, and the editors of Time-Life Books. *Russian Cooking*. New York: Time-Life Books, 1969.

Volokh, Anne, and Mavis Manus. *The Art of Russian Cuisine*. New York: Macmillan, 1983.

von Bremzen, Anya, and John Welchman. *Please To the Table: The Russian Cookbook*. New York: Workman Publishing, 1990.

Ward, Susan. *Russian Regional Recipes*. Secaucus, N.J.: Chartwell Books, 1993.

Scandinavia and the Baltic States

Borgstrom, Greta, and Birgit Danfors. *The New Swedish Food*. Göteborg, Sweden: Wezäta, 1965.

Brown, Dale, and the editors of Time-Life Books. *The Cooking of Scandinavia*. New York: Time-Life Books, 1968.

Hardisty, Jytte. *Scandinavian Cooking for Pleasure: Denmark, Norway, Sweden*. London: Hamlyn Publishing Group Ltd., 1972.

Hazelton, Nika Standen. *The Art of Scandinavian Cooking*. New York: Macmillan, 1965.

Hovig, Ingrid. *The Best of Norwegian Traditional Cuisine*. Oslo: Glydendal Norsk Forlag, 1992.

Jensen, Ingeborg. *Wonderful, Wonderful Danish Cooking*. New York: Simon & Schuster, 1965.

Long, Cheryl, ed. *The Best of Scanfest*. Lake Oswego, Ore.: Culinary Arts, 1995.

Maxwell, Sonia. *Scandinavian Cooking: Classic Cooking from Sweden, Norway, Denmark, and Finland*. Edison, N.J.: Chartwell Books, 1995.

Ojakangas, Beatrice. *The Finnish Cookbook*. New York: Crown, 1989.

Wifstrand, Selma, and Emmie Berg, eds. *Favorite Swedish Recipes*. New York: Dover Publications, 1975.

Central Europe

Beer, Gretel. *Classic Austrian Cooking*. London: A. Deutsch Ltd., 1993.

Borer, Eva Maria. *Tante Heidi's Swiss Kitchen*. New York: Gramercy Publishing, 1965.

Elkon, Juliette. *A Belgian Cookbook*. New York: Hippocrene Books, 1996.

Halverhout, Heleen A. M. *Dutch Cooking*. Amsterdam: De Driehoek, 1972.

Hamelcourt, Juliette Elkon. *A Belgian Cookbook*. New York: Hippocrene Books, 1996.

Hazelton, Nika Standen. *The Swiss Cookbook*. New York: Atheneum, 1967.

Scheinpflug, Lotte. *Specialties of Austrian Cooking*. Innsbruck: Pinguin-Verlag, 1984.

Stirum, C. Countess van Limburg. *The Art of Dutch Cooking*. New York: Hippocrene Books, 1988.

Van Waerebeek, Ruth, and Maria Robbins. *Everybody Eats Well in Belgium*. New York: Workman Publishing, 1996.

Wechsberg, Joseph, and the editors of Time-Life Books. *Foods of the World: The Cooking of Vienna's Empire*. New York: Time-Life Books, 1968.

GERMANY

Anderson, Jean, and Hedy Würz. *The New German Cookbook*. New York: Harper Collins Publishers, 1993.

Erhardt, Tell, and Hermine Kranzdorf. *Chef Tell Tells All: A Gourmet Guide from the Market to the Table*. Exton, Pa.: Schiffer Publishers, Ltd., 1979.

Hazelton, Nika Standen and the editors of Time-Life Books. *Foods of the World: The Cooking of Germany*. New York: Time-Life Books, 1969.

Heberle, Marianna Olszewska. *German Cooking*. New York: HP Books, 1996.

Metzger, Christine. *Culinaria: Germany*. Cologne, Germany: Könemann, 2000.

Italy

Alberti, Miranda. *Cuisines of the World: Italy*. San Diego: Thunder Bay Press, 2000.

Bardi, Carla. *Antipasti: Appetizers the Italian Way*. New York: Time-Life Books, 1998.

Bianchi, Anne. *Italian Festival Food: Recipes and Traditions from Italy's Country Food Fairs*. New York: Macmillan, 1999.

Bruno, Pasquale. *Pasta Tecnica*. Chicago: Contemporary Books, 1981.

Bugialli, Giuliano. *Bugialli on Pasta*. New York: Simon & Schuster, 1988.

———. *The Foods of Tuscany*. New York: Stewart, Tabori, and Chang, 1996.

———. *Giuliano Bugialli's Classic Techniques of Italian Cooking*. New York: Simon & Schuster, 1982.

Carnacina, Luigi. *Luigi Carnacina Presents Italian Home Cooking*. Garden City, N.Y.: Doubleday, 1972.

della Croce, Julia. *Antipasti*. San Francisco: Chronicle Books, 1993.

———. *Pasta Classica: The Art of Italian Pasta Cooking*. San Francisco: Chronicle Books, 1989.

De Medici, Lorenza. *Tuscany: the Beautiful Cookbook: Authentic Recipes from the Provinces of Tuscany*. San Francisco: Collins Publishers, 1992.

Dettore, Mariapaola. *The Flavors of Italy: Sicily*. Florence: McRae Books (New York: Time-Life Books), 1999.

Garry, William J., ed. "The Italian Countryside," *Bon Appétit Magazine*. New York: Condé Nast Publications, May, 1997.

Grasso, Jean C. *The Best of Southern Italian Cooking*. Hauppauge, N.Y.: Barron's, 1984.

Hazan, Marcella. *The Classic Italian Cook Book: The Art of Italian Cooking and the Italian Art of Eating*. New York: Alfred A. Knopf, 1980.

———. *More Classic Italian Cooking*. New York: Alfred A. Knopf, 1978.

Kasper, Lynn Rosetto. *The Splendid Table: Recipes from Emilia-Romagna, the Heartland of Northern Italian Food*. New York: William Morrow & Co., Inc., 1992.

McNair, James. *Cold Pasta*. San Francisco: Chronicle Books, 1985.

Muffoletto, Anna. *The Art of Sicilian Cooking*. Garden City, New York: Doubleday, 1971.

Piras, Claudia, and Eugenio Medagliani. *Culinaria: Italy*. Cologne, Germany: Könemann, 2000.

Plotkin, Fred. *Recipes from Paradise: Life and Food on the Italian Riviera*. Boston: Little, Brown and Co., 1997.

Root, Waverley, and the editors of Time-Life Books. *Cooking of Italy*. New York: Time-Life Books, 1974.

Schwartz, Arthur. *Naples at Table: Cooking in Campania*. New York: Harper Collins Publishers, 1998.

Styler, Christopher. *Primi Piatti: Italian First Courses That Make a Meal*. New York: Harper & Row, Publishers, 1989.

The Good Cook: Pasta. Compiled by the editors of Time-Life Books. New York: Time-Life Books, 1980.

Wells, Patricia. *Patricia Wells' Trattoria: Healthy, Simple, Robust Fare Inspired by the Small Family Restaurants of Italy*. New York: William Morrow & Co., 1993.

Wright, Clifford. *Cucina Paradiso: The Heavenly Food of Sicily*. New York: Simon & Schuster, 1992.

Spain and Portugal, General

Feibleman, Peter S., and the editors of Time-Life Books. *The Cooking of Spain and Portugal*. New York: Time-Life Books, 1969.

Manjón, Maite. *The Gastronomy of Spain & Portugal*. New York: Prentice Hall Press, 1990.

Ortiz, Elisabeth Lambert. *The Food of Spain & Portugal: The Complete Iberian Cuisine*. New York: Atheneum, 1989.

SPAIN

Aris, Pepita. *Spanish Cooking: A Fiesta of Regional Recipes*. Secaucus, N.J.: Chartwell Books, 1993.

———. *The Spanishwoman's Kitchen*. London: Cassell, 1993.

Barrenechea, Teresa. *The Basque Table: Passionate Home Cooking from One of Europe's Great Regional Cuisines*. Boston: Harvard Common Press, 1998.

Boirac, Cathy, ed. *Spain Gourmetour Magazine*. Madrid: Spanish Institute for Foreign Trade (ICEX) of the State Secretariat for Trade and Tourism, Issue Nos. 39 through 53.

Casas, Penelope. *The Foods and Wines of Spain*. New York: Alfred A. Knopf, 1996.

———. *Tapas: The Little Dishes of Spain*. New York: Alfred A. Knopf, 1985.

de Molino, Cornelia Rosales. *Cuisines of the World: Spain*. San Diego: Thunder Bay Press, 1999.

Gilitz, David M., and Linda Kay Davidson. *A Drizzle of Honey: The Lives and Recipes of Spain's Secret Jews*. New York: St. Martin's Press, 1999.

Hirigoyen, Gerald, and Cameron Hirigoyen. *The Basque Kitchen: Tempting Food from the Pyrenees*. New York: Harper Collins Publishers, 1999.

Jessel, Camilla. *The Taste of Spain*. New York: St. Martin's Press, 1990.

Martinez, Efrain. *Classic Spanish Cooking with Chef Ef*. Chicago: Contemporary Books, 1993.

PORTUGAL

Anderson, Jean. *The Food of Portugal*. New York: Hearst Books, 1994.

Modesto, Maria de Lourdes. *Traditional Portuguese Cooking*. Lisbon: Editorial Verbo, 1989.

Walden, Hilaire. *Portuguese Cooking*. Edison, N.J.: Chartwell Books, 1994.

France

The Best of French Cooking. New York: Larousse and Co., Inc., 1978.

Child, Julia. *The French Chef Cookbook*. New York: Alfred A. Knopf, 1968.

Claiborne, Craig, and Pierre Franey. *Foods of the World: Classical French Cooking*. New York: Time-Life Books, 1978.

de Groot, Roy Andries. *Feasts for All Seasons*. New York: McGraw-Hill, 1976.

Escoffier, Auguste. *The Escoffier Cookbook: A Guide to the Fine Art of Cookery*. New York: Crown, 1941.

———. *Le Guide Culinaire: The Complete Guide to the Art of Modern Cookery*. New York: Mayflower Books, 1979.

Fisher, M. F. K. *Foods of the World: The Cooking of Provençal France*. New York: Time-Life Books, 1968.

Holuigue, Diane. *Master Class: Lessons with the World's Greatest Chefs*. New York: E. P. Dutton, 1988.

Marshall, Lydie. *Chez Nous: Home Cooking from the South of France*. New York: Harper Collins Publishers, 1995.

Olney, Richard. *Lulu's Provençal Table: The Exuberant Food and Wine from Domaine Tempier Vineyard*. New York: Harper Collins Publishers, 1994.

Pépin, Jacques. *Jacques Pépin's Art of Cooking*. New York: Alfred A. Knopf, 1987.

———. *La Methode: An Illustrated Guide to the French Techniques of Cooking*. New York: Times Books, 1979.

———. *La Technique: The Fundamental Techniques of Cooking: An Illustrated Guide*. New York: Pocket Books, 1978.

Saulnier, Louis. *Le Répertoire de la Cuisine*. Woodbury, N.Y.: Barron's, 1976.

Saveur Cooks Authentic French. Compiled by the editors of *Saveur Magazine*. San Francisco: Chronicle Books, 1999.

Tillery, Brigitte. *The Frenchwoman's Kitchen*. London: Cassell, 1992.

Verdon, René, and Rachel H. Norman. *The Enlightened Cuisine: A Master Chef's Step-by-Step Guide to Contemporary French Cooking*. New York: Macmillan, 1985.

Villegas, Maria, and Sarah Randell. *The Food of France*. Vancouver: Whitecap Books, 2000.

Voss, Roger. *The Food and Wine of France*. London: Mitchell Beazley, 1995.

Wells, Patricia. *Simply French: Patricia Wells Presents the Cuisine of Joël Robuchon*. New York: William Morrow & Co., 1991.

Willan, Anne. *The La Varenne Cooking Course*. New York: William Morrow & Co., 1982.

Wolfert, Paula. *The Cooking of South-West France: A Collection of Traditional and New Recipes from France's Magnificent Rustic Cuisine, and New Techniques to Lighten Hearty Dishes*. New York: Harper & Row, Publishers, 1988.

United Kingdom and Ireland

Allen, Darinda. *The Complete Book of Irish Country Cooking*. New York: Viking-Penguin, 1996.

Bailey, Adrian, and the editors of Time-Life Books. *The Cooking of the British Isles*. New York: Time-Life Books, 1969.

Cameron, Sheila MacNiven. *The Highlander's Cookbook: Recipes from Scotland*. New York: Gramercy Publishing, 1966.

Connery, Clare. *In an Irish Country Kitchen*. New York: Simon & Schuster, 1992.

Dutton, Joan Parry. *Good Fare and Cheer of Old England*. New York: Reynal, 1960.

Freeman, Bobby. *Traditional Food from Wales*. New York: Hippocrene Books, 1997.

Garmey, Jane. *Great British Cooking: A Well Kept Secret*. New York: Harper Perennial, 1992.

Grigson, Jane. *Jane Grigson's British Cookery*. New York: Atheneum, 1985.

Murray, Janet. *Traditional Scots Recipes: With a Fine Feeling for Food*. New York: Bramhall House, 1972.

Sheridan, Monica. *The Art of Irish Cooking*. Garden City, New York: Doubleday, 1965.

Step-by-Step Scottish Cooking. Compiled by the editors of Könemann. Ultimo, England: Murdock Books, 1994.

Walker, Sara. *The Highland Fling Cookbook*. New York: Atheneum, 1971.

Warren, Janey. *A Feast of Scotland*. London: Lomond Books, 1990.

General Information

Aidells, Bruce, and Denis Kelly. *Bruce Aidells' Complete Sausage Cookbook: Recipes from America's Premier Sausage Maker*. Berkeley: Ten Speed Press, 2000.

———. *The Complete Meat Cookbook*. New York: Houghton Mifflin, 1998.

————. *Hot Links & Country Flavors: Sausages in American Regional Cooking*. New York: Alfred A. Knopf, 1990.

————. *Real Beer and Good Eats: The Rebirth of America's Beer and Food Traditions*. New York: Alfred A. Knopf, 1992.

Alford, Jeffrey, and Naomi Duguid. *Flatbreads & Flavors: A Baker's Atlas*. New York: William Morrow & Co., 1995.

————. *Seductions of Rice*. New York: Artisan, 1998.

Appetizers. Compiled by the editorial staff of *Bon Appétit Magazine*. Los Angeles: The Knapp Press, 1982.

Bonar, Ann. *The Macmillan Treasury of Herbs: A Complete Guide to the Cultivation and Use of Wild and Domesticated Herbs*. New York: Macmillan, 1985.

Davidson, Alan. *The Oxford Companion to Food*. Oxford, England: Oxford University Press, 1999.

Duffy, Gillian. *Hors d'Oeuvres*. New York: William Morrow and Co., 1998.

————. *Poultry*. Los Angeles: The Knapp Press, 1984.

————. *Seafood*. Los Angeles: The Knapp Press, 1983.

Fresh Produce: A to Z. Compiled by the editors of *Sunset Magazine* and Sunset Books. Menlo Park, Calif.: Lane Publishing Co., 1987.

Hazen, Janet. *Rolled, Wrapped, and Stuffed: Great Appetizers from Around the World*. New York: Addison-Wesley, 1991.

Hensperger, Beth. *The Bread Bible: Beth Hensperger's 300 Favorite Recipes*. San Francisco: Chronicle Books, 1999.

————. *Bread for All Seasons: Delicious and Distinctive Recipes for Year-Round Baking*. San Francisco: Chronicle Books, 1995.

Hillman, Howard, Lisa Loring, and Kyle MacDonald. *Kitchen Science: A Guide to Knowing the Hows and Whys for Fun and Success in the Kitchen*. Boston: Houghton Mifflin, 1989.

King, Shirley. *Saucing the Fish*. New York: Simon & Schuster, 1986.

McClane, A. J. *McClane's North American Fish Cookery*. New York: Holt, Rinehart and Winston, 1981.

The Meat Buyer's Guide. McLean, Va: The National Association of Meat Purveyors, 1981.

Meyer, Arthur L. *Baking Across America*. Austin, Tex.: University of Texas Press, 1998.

Microsoft. *Encarta 98 Encyclopedia*. Microsoft, 1998.

Ortiz, Elisabeth Lambert. *The Encyclopedia of Herbs, Spices, and Flavorings*. New York: Dorling Kindersley Publishing Inc., 1992.

Paterson, Kent. *The Hot Empire of Chile*. Tempe, Ariz.: Bilingual Press, 2000.

Raichlen, Steven. *The Barbecue Bible*. New York: Workman Publishing, 1998.

————. *The Barbecue Bible: Sauces, Rubs, Marinades*. New York: Workman Publishing, 2000.

————. *How to Grill*. New York: Workman Publishing, 2001.

Rombauer, Irma, and Marion Rombauer Becker. *The Joy of Cooking*. Indianapolis: Bobbs-Merrill Co., 1975.

Rozin, Elisabeth. *Ethnic Cuisine: How to Create the Authentic Flavors of 30 International Cuisines*. New York: Penguin Books, 1992.

Schneider, Elizabeth. *Uncommon Fruits and Vegetables: A Commonsense Guide*. New York: Harper & Row, Publishers, 1986.

Schremp, Gerry. *Beef and Veal*. New York: Time-Life Books, 1979.

———. *Fish*. New York: Time-Life Books, 1979.

———. *Hors d'Oeuvres*. New York: Time-Life Books, 1982.

———. *Pork*. New York: Time-Life Books, 1980.

———. *Poultry*. New York: Time-Life Books, 1979.

———. *Shellfish*. New York: Time-Life Books, 1982.

———. *Variety Meats*. New York: Time-Life Books, 1982.

Sterling, Richard, ed. *The Adventure of Food: True Stories of Eating Everything*. San Francisco: Travelers' Tales, 1999.

The Essential Appetizers Cookbook. editors of Whitecap Books. North Vancouver: Whitecap Books, Ltd., 1999.

Von Welanetz, Diana, and Paul Von Welanetz. *The Von Welanetz Guide to Ethnic Ingredients*. Los Angeles: J. P. Tarcher, 1982.

Wolf, Donald D. *The Family Circle Encyclopedia of Cooking*. New York: Lexicon, 1990.

Zibart, Eve, and Muriel Stevens. *The Unofficial Guide to Ethnic Cuisine and Dining in America*. New York: Macmillan Travel, 1995.

Index

Goat
  in curry ragôut, 104–105
  kid goat ravioli, 525–527
Goat Cheese–Stuffed Grape Leaves, 59
Goose, breast of, pickled cooked,
    458–459
Gooseberries, 52, 53
  spiced, 52
Goose fattening, 18
Gorgonzola dolce, 572
Goulash, 429
Grains
  in African cuisines, 372
  quinoa croquettes, 142
Grape Leaves Stuffed with Lamb,
    Rice, and Herbs, 339–340
Grape Leaves Stuffed with Rice,
    Lemon, and Herbs, 422–423
Gratin, lobster, 154–155
Gravad lax, 175, 447, 461
Gravy
  country cream, 24
  meatball, 456
"Grazing," xii
Greek cuisine, 409, 410
Green bean rolls, 213, 214–215
Green Corn Chicken Tamales with
    Tomatillo Sauce, 66–68
Green curry paste, 572
Green lip mussels, 176, 572
Green mango, 572
Green papaya, 572–573
Green peppercorn, 573
Greens, wild, 333
Green tomatoes, 573
Griddle cakes
  plantain and banana, 387–388
  wild rice, 48–49
Grilled Bruschetta with Cannellini
    Purée and Wilted Greens,
    499–500
Grilled Eggplant and Roasted Red
    Pepper Terrine with Prosciutto,
    492–493
Grilled Fish and Eggplant Dip with
    Crudités, 288–289
Grilled Goat Cheese-Stuffed Grape
    Leaves, 59
Grilled Jalapeño-Stuffed Dove Breast
    Skewers with Bacon, 69–70
Grilled Kid Goat Ravioli in Red Wine
    Meat Sauce, 525–527
Grilled Polenta with Wild Mushroom
    Sauté, 501–502

Grilled Pork Tenderloin Cubes with
    Papaya Relish, 180–181
Grilled Shrimp on Sugarcane Skewers,
    160–161
Grilled Skewered Pork with Roasted
    Chile Sauce, 299–300
Grilled Swordfish Kebabs with
    Lemon-Herb Glaze, 418–419
Grilled Trout Fillet with Sour Cherry
    Vinegar with Rose Petals and
    Mayonnaise, 435–436
Grilled Tuna Kebabs with Herb-
    Lemon Marinade, 405
Grilled Veal Kebabs with Apricot-
    Curry Glaze, 377–378
Grilling, 276, 333
Grits, 5
Ground Beef and Lamb Kebabs,
    341–342
Ground spice mix, 343
Gruyère cheese, 573
Guajillo chile, 573
Güero chile, 573
Gulf State cuisine, Middle Eastern,
    354
Gumbo, 5
Gyoza dumpling wrapper, 573

Habanero chile, 75, 573
Ham
  Ardennes, 467
  potato dumplings stuffed with,
    454–455
  Smithfield, corn cakes with, 17
Hamburgers, mini, 42–43
Hare, 475
Harissa, 390, 392, 396, 573
Harusame noodles, 574
Hawaiian cuisine, 163
Hazelnuts, 60, 61
Heart of palm, 145, 184–186, 574
Herb dressing, spicy, 304
Herbsaint, 36
Herb sauce, 490
Herring, 446, 447, 448
Hijiki, 574
Hoisin sauce, 574
Hole-in-the-ground oven, 164
Holy basil, 574
Hominy, 2, 5
Horseradish root, 574
Horseradish sauce, 437, 438
Hospitality, in Persian life, 331
Hot-and-sour tamarind broth, 328, 329

Hot peanut sauce, 297
Hot pot, 467
Hot sauce, 369
Hubbard-type squash, 574
Hudson Valley Foie Gras with
    Caramelized Apples, 18
Hungarian cuisine, 429
"Hushpuppies," 5

Idiazábal cheese, 574
Incan agriculture, 130–131
Indian cuisine, 197, 312–329, 373
Individual Chilled Salmon Soufflés,
    558–559
Indonesian cuisine, 95, 195–196
Inihaw, 180–181
Injera, 373, 376, 574
Iranian cuisine, 331–332
Iraqi cuisine, 354
Irish cuisine, 543–561
Israeli cuisine, 354–355
Italian cuisine, 483–502
  modern, 485

Jalapeño chiles, 136, 140, 574
Jambalaya, 6
Japanese cuisine, 163, 210–229
Jasmine rice, 574
Javanese Fried Chicken Drumettes,
    203
Jerk-Marinated and Smoked Pork
    Spareribs, 100–101
Jerk rub, 100
Jicama, 575
Jonnycake, 2
"Journey cake," 2
Juniper berry, 575
Just-Seared Tuna Salad with *Ogo*
    Seaweed, 173

Kabocha squash, 575
Kasha, 575
Kasseri cheese, 575
Kebab basting mixture, 341
Kebabs, 333, 409, 411
  ground beef and lamb, 341–342
  lamb, 102–103, 396–397, 416–417
  swordfish, grilled, 418–419
  tuna, grilled, 405
Kecap manis, 575
Kerisik, 575
Kimchee, 232, 236, 575
Kochu chang, 575
Korean cuisine, 163, 211, 230–238